Scott Foresman

Science

See learning in a whole new light

PEARSON
Scott Foresman

Editorial Offices: Glenview, Illinois • Parsippany, New Jersey • New York, New York
Sales Offices: Boston, Massachusetts • Duluth, Georgia • Glenview, Illinois
Coppell, Texas • Sacramento, California • Mesa, Arizona

Series Authors

Dr. Timothy Cooney
Professor of Earth Science and Science Education
University of Northern Iowa (UNI)
Cedar Falls, Iowa

Dr. Jim Cummins
Professor
Department of Curriculum, Teaching, and Learning
The University of Toronto
Toronto, Canada

Barbara Kay Foots, M.Ed.
Science Education Consultant
Houston, Texas

Dr. James Flood
Distinguished Professor of Literacy and Language
School of Teacher Education
San Diego State University.
San Diego, California

Dr. M. Jenice Goldston
Associate Professor of Science Education
Department of Elementary Education Programs
University of Alabama
Tuscaloosa, Alabama

Dr. Shirley Gholston Key
Associate Professor of Science Education
Instruction and Curriculum Leadership Department
College of Education
University of Memphis
Memphis, Tennessee

Dr. Diane Lapp
Distinguished Professor of Reading and Language Arts in Teacher Education
San Diego State University
San Diego, California

Sheryl A. Mercier
Classroom Teacher
Dunlap Elementary School
Dunlap, California

Dr. Karen L. Ostlund
UTeach,
College of Natural Sciences
The University of Texas at Austin
Austin, Texas

Dr. Nancy Romance
Professor of Science Education & Principal Investigator
NSF/IERI Science IDEAS Project
Charles E. Schmidt College of Science
Florida Atlantic University
Boca Raton, Florida

Dr. William Tate
Chair and Professor of Education and Applied Statistics
Department of Education
Washington University
St Louis, Missouri

Dr. Kathryn C. Thornton
Professor
School of Engineering and Applied Science
University of Virginia
Charlottesville, Virginia

Dr. Leon Ukens
Professor of Science Education
Department of Physics, Astronomy, and Geosciences
Towson University
Towson, Maryland

Steve Weinberg
Consultant
Connecticut Center for Advanced Technology
East Hartford, Connecticut

ISBN: 0-328-10005-6 (SVE); ISBN: 0-328-15675-2 (A); ISBN: 0-328-15681-7 (B); ISBN: 0-328-15687-6 (C); ISBN: 0-328-15693-0 (D)

7 8 9 10 V063 12 11 10 09 08 07 06

Consulting Author

Dr. Michael P. Klentschy
Superintendent
El Centro Elementary School District
El Centro, California

Science Content Consultants

Dr. Frederick W. Taylor
Senior Research Scientist
Institute for Geophysics
Jackson School of Geosciences
The University of Texas at Austin
Austin, Texas

Dr. Ruth E. Buskirk
Senior Lecturer
School of Biological Sciences
The University of Texas at Austin
Austin, Texas

Dr. Cliff Frohlich
Senior Research Scientist
Institute for Geophysics
Jackson School of Geosciences
The University of Texas at Austin
Austin, Texas

Brad Armosky
McDonald Observatory
The University of Texas at Austin
Austin, Texas

NASA Content Consultants

Adena Williams Loston, Ph.D.
Chief Education Officer
Office of the Chief Education Officer

Clifford W. Houston, Ph.D.
Deputy Chief Education Officer for Education Programs
Office of the Chief Education Officer

Frank C. Owens
Senior Policy Advisor
Office of the Chief Education Officer

Deborah Brown Biggs
Manager, Education Flight Projects Office
Space Operations Mission Directorate, Education Lead

Erika G. Vick
NASA Liaison to Pearson Scott Foresman
Education Flight Projects Office

William E. Anderson
Partnership Manager for Education
Aeronautics Research Mission Directorate

Anita Krishnamurthi
Program Planning Specialist
Space Science Education and Outreach Program

Bonnie J. McClain
Chief of Education
Exploration Systems Mission Directorate

Diane Clayton, Ph.D.
Program Scientist
Earth Science Education

Deborah Rivera
Strategic Alliances Manager
Office of Public Affairs
NASA Headquarters

Douglas D. Peterson
Public Affairs Officer, Astronaut Office
Office of Public Affairs
NASA Johnson Space Center

Nicole Cloutier
Public Affairs Officer, Astronaut Office
Office of Public Affairs
NASA Johnson Space Center

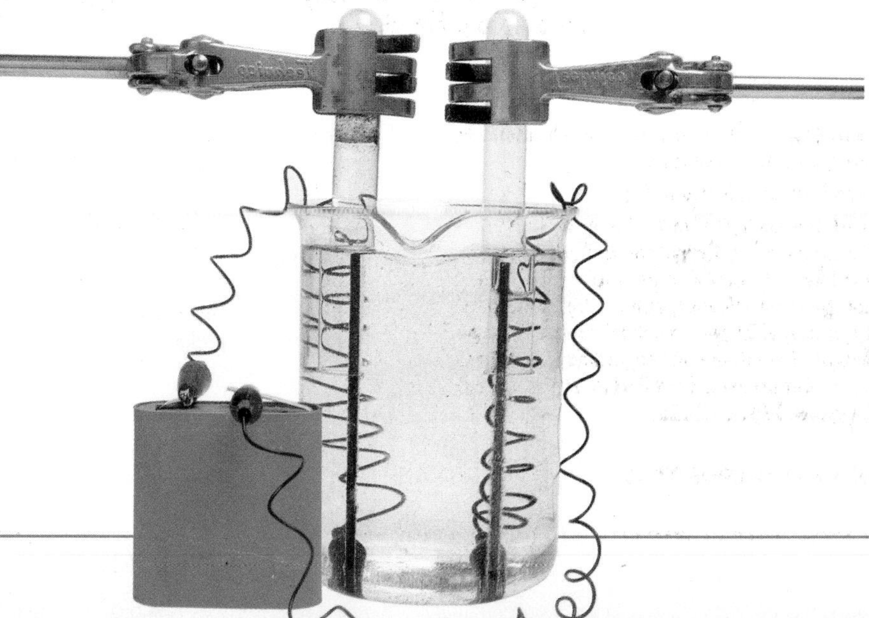

Reviewers

Dr. Maria Aida Alanis
Administrator
Austin ISD
Austin Texas

Melissa Barba
Teacher
Wesley Mathews Elementary
Miami, Florida

Dr. Marcelline Barron
Supervisor/K-12 Math and Science
Fairfield Public Schools
Fairfield, Connecticut

Jane Bates
Teacher
Hickory Flat Elementary
Canton, Georgia

Denise Bizjack
Teacher Dr. N. H. Jones Elementary
Ocala, Florida

Latanya D. Bragg
Teacher
Davis Magnet School
Jackson, Mississippi

Richard Burton
Teacher
George Buck Elementary School 94
Indianapolis, Indiana

Dawn Cabrera
Teacher E.W.F. Stirrup School
Miami, Florida

Barbara Calabro
Teacher
Compass Rose Foundation
Ft. Myers, Florida

Lucille Calvin
Teacher
Weddington Math & Science School
Greenville, Mississippi

Patricia Carmichael
Teacher
Teasley Middle School
Canton, Georgia

Martha Cohn
Teacher
An Wang Middle School
Lowell, Massachusetts

Stu Danzinger
Supervisor
Community Consolidated School District 59
Arlington Heights, Illinois

Esther Draper
Supervisor/Science Specialist
Belair Math Science Magnet School
Pine Bluff, Arkansas

Sue Esser
Teacher
Loretto Elementary
Jacksonville, Florida

Dr. Richard Fairman
Teacher
Antioch University
Yellow Springs, Ohio

Joan Goldfarb
Teacher
Indialantic Elementary
Indialantic, Florida

Deborah Gomes
Teacher A J Gomes Elementary
New Bedford, Massachusetts

Sandy Hobart
Teacher
Mims Elementary
Mims, Florida

Tom Hocker
Teacher/Science Coach
Boston Latin Academy
Dorchester, Massachusetts

Shelley Jaques
Science Supervisor
Moore Public Schools
Moore, Oklahoma

Marguerite W. Jones
Teacher Spearman Elementary
Piedmont, South Carolina

Kelly Kenney
Teacher
Kansas City Missouri School District
Kansas City, Missouri

Carol Kilbane
Teacher
Riverside Elementary School
Wichita, Kansas

Robert Kolenda
Teacher
Neshaminy School District
Langhorne, Pennsylvania

Karen Lynn Kruse
Teacher
St. Paul the Apostle
Yonkers, New York

Elizabeth Loures
Teacher
Point Fermin Elementary School
San Pedro, California

Susan MacDougall
Teacher
Brick Community Primary Learning Center
Brick, New Jersey

Jack Marine
Teacher
Raising Horizons Quest Charter School
Philadelphia, Pennsylvania

Nicola Micozzi Jr.
Science Coordinator
Plymouth Public Schools
Plymouth, Massachusetts

Paula Monteiro
Teacher
A J Gomes Elementary
New Bedford, Massachusetts

Tracy Newallis
Teacher
Taper Avenue Elementary
San Pedro, California

Dr. Eugene Nicolo
Supervisor, Science K-12
Moorestown School District
Moorestown, New Jersey

Jeffry Postrak
School District of Philadelphia
Philadelphia, Pennslyvania

Helen Pedigo
Teacher
Mt. Carmel Elementary
Huntsville Alabama

Becky Peltonen
Teacher
Patterson Elementary School
Panama City, Florida

Sherri Pensler
Teacher/ESOL
Claude Pepper Elementary
Miami, Florida

Virginia Rogliano
Teacher
Bridgeview Elementary
South Charleston, West Virginia

Debbie Sanders
Teacher
Thunderbolt Elementary
Orange Park, Florida

Grethel Santamarina
Teacher
E.W.F. Stirrup School
Miami, Florida

Migdalia Schneider
Teacher/Bilingual
Lindell School
Long Beach, New York

Susan Shelly
Teacher
Bonita Springs Elementary
Bonita Springs, Florida

Peggy Terry
Teacher
Madison District 151
South Holland, Illinois

Jane M. Thompson
Teacher
Emma Ward Elementary
Lawrenceburg, Kentucky

Martha Todd
Teacher
W. H. Rhodes Elementary
Milton, Florida

Renee Williams
Teacher
Central Elementary
Bloomfield, New Mexico

Myra Wood
Teacher
Madison Street Academy
Ocala, Florida

Marion Zampa
Teacher
Shawnee Mission School District
Overland Park, Kansas

Science

See learning in a whole new light

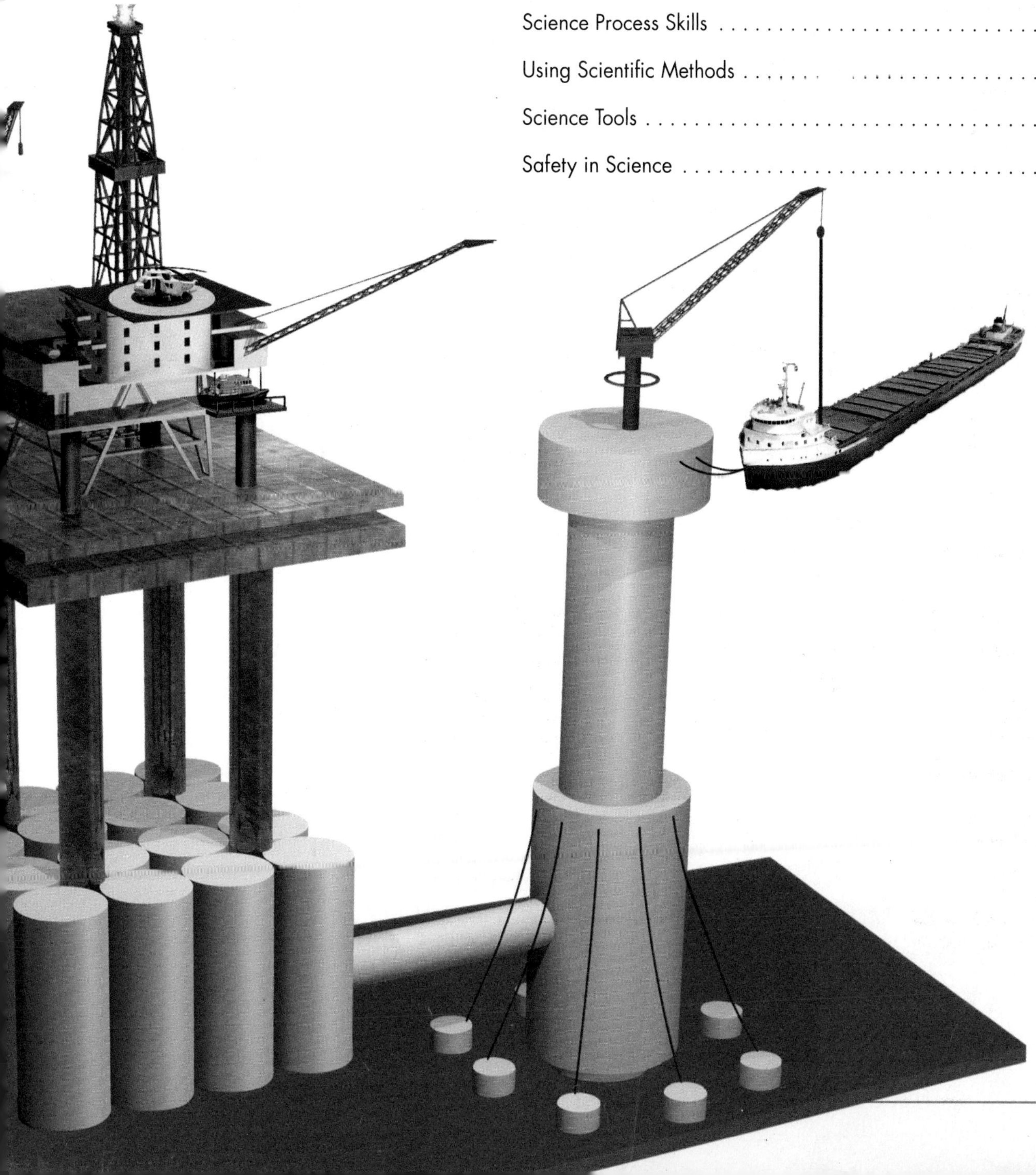

Unit A Life Science

Chapter 1 • Classifying Organisms

How are living things classified?

Chapter 2 • Cells to Systems

What do cells have to do with our lives?

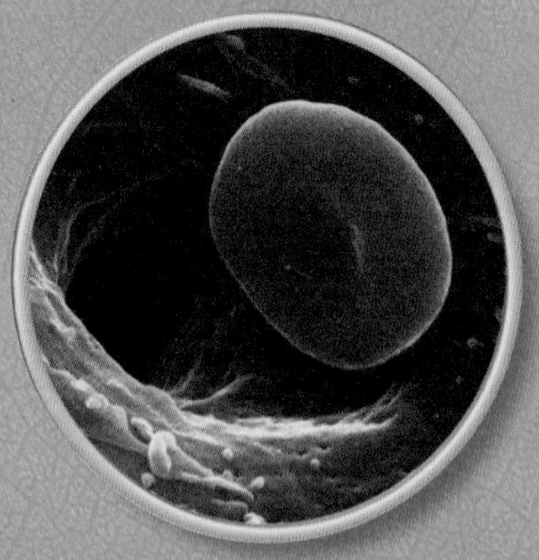

Chapter 3 • Human Body Systems

How do the systems in your body keep you alive?

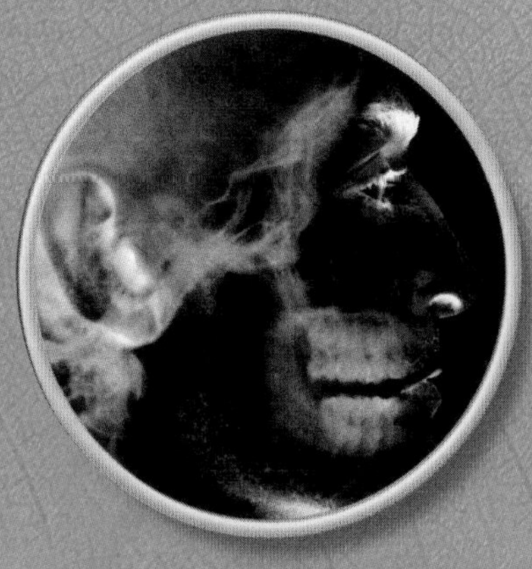

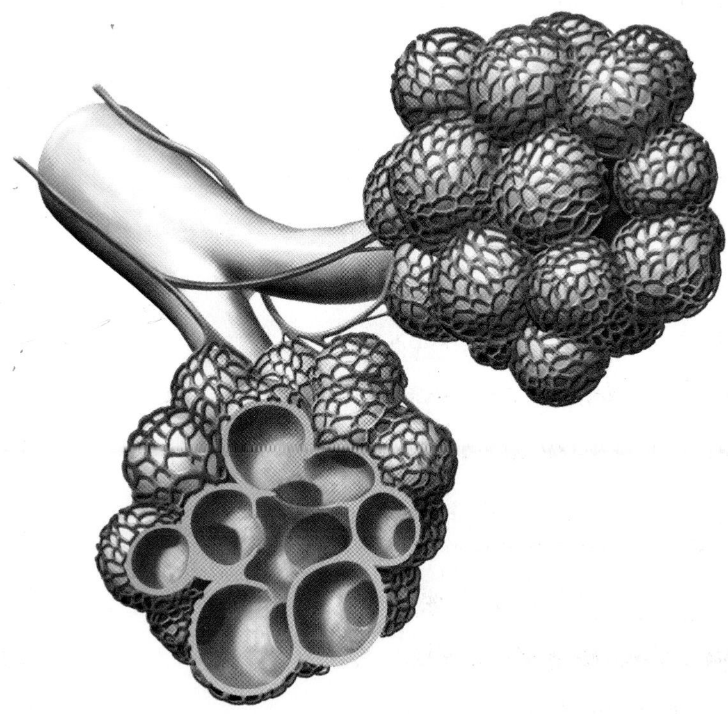

Unit A Life Science

How do plants stay alive and produce offspring?

Chapter 4 • Plants

How do the parts of an ecosystem interact?

Chapter 5 • Interactions in Ecosystems

Chapter 6 • Changes in Ecosystems

How do changes in habitats affect living things?

Unit B Earth Science

How does water move through the environment?

Chapter 7 • Water on Earth

Chapter 8 • Weather Patterns

Change
Rain
Fair
Stormy
Very Dry
BAROMETER
MILLIBARS
INCHES

Why does the weather change?

Unit B Earth Science

What kinds of processes change Earth's surfaces?

Chapter 9 • Earth's Changing Surface

Chapter 10 • Protecting Earth's Resources

Why is it important to conserve Earth's resources?

Unit C Physical Science

What makes up everything around us?

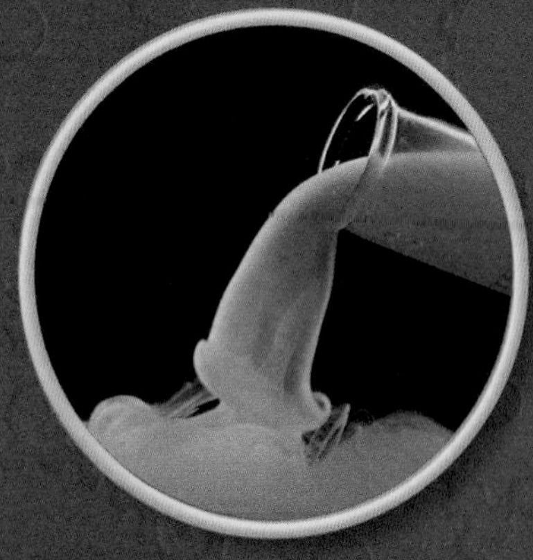

How do you use chemistry every day?

Chapter 11 • Matter and Its Properties

Chapter 12 • Changes in Matter

Chapter 13 • Forces in Motion

How are forces and motion part of your everyday life?

Unit C Physical Science

How many types of energy do you use every day?

Chapter 14 • Changing Forms of Energy

Chapter 15 • Electricity

What is electrical current and how does it work?

Unit D Space and Technology

How has the study of stars expanded our knowledge of the universe?

How does the motion of objects in space create cycles?

Chapter 16 • Stars and Galaxies

Chapter 17 • Earth in Space

Chapter 18 • Technology in Our Lives

How does technology affect our lives?

How to Read Science

A page like this one is toward the beginning of each chapter. It shows you how to use a reading skill that will help you understand what you read.

Before Reading

Before you read the chapter, read the Build Background page and think about how to answer the question. Recall what you already know as you answer the question. Work with a partner to make a list of what you already know. Then read the How To Read Science page.

Target Reading Skill
Each page has one target reading skill. The reading skill corresponds with a process skill in the Directed Inquiry activity on the facing page. The reading skill will be useful as you read science.

Real-World Connection
Each page has an example of something you might read. It also connects with the Directed Inquiry activity.

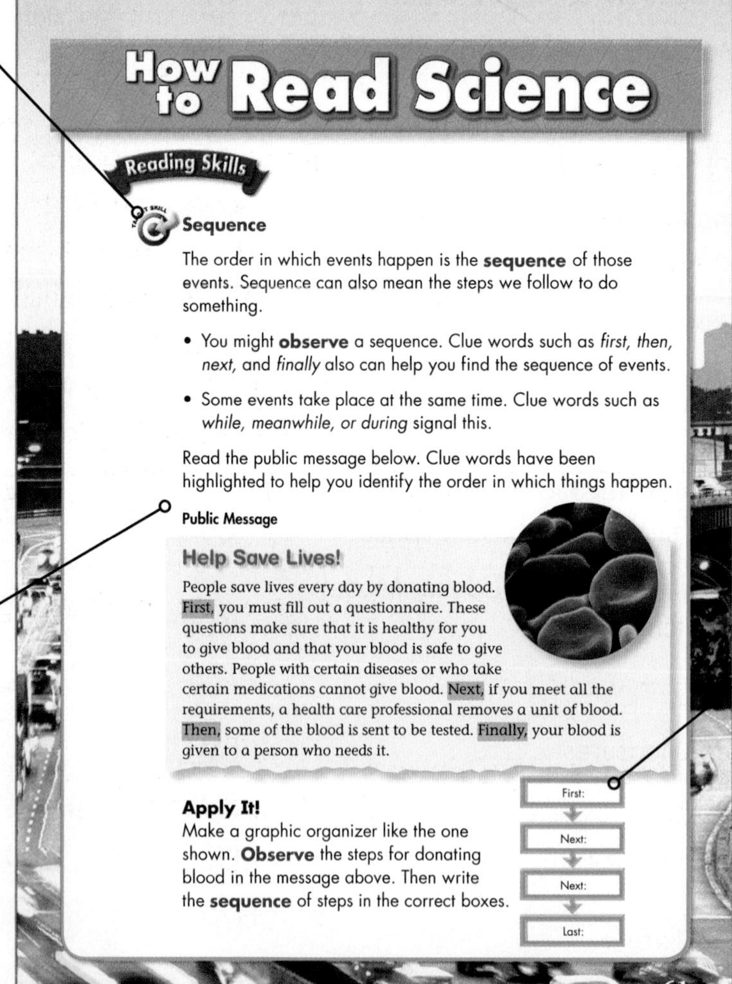

How to Read Science

Reading Skills

Target Skill

Sequence

The order in which events happen is the **sequence** of those events. Sequence can also mean the steps we follow to do something.

- You might **observe** a sequence. Clue words such as *first, then, next,* and *finally* also can help you find the sequence of events.
- Some events take place at the same time. Clue words such as *while, meanwhile, or during* signal this.

Read the public message below. Clue words have been highlighted to help you identify the order in which things happen.

Public Message

Help Save Lives!

People save lives every day by donating blood. First, you must fill out a questionnaire. These questions make sure that it is healthy for you to give blood and that your blood is safe to give others. People with certain diseases or who take certain medications cannot give blood. Next, if you meet all the requirements, a health care professional removes a unit of blood. Then, some of the blood is sent to be tested. Finally, your blood is given to a person who needs it.

Apply It!
Make a graphic organizer like the one shown. **Observe** the steps for donating blood in the message above. Then write the **sequence** of steps in the correct boxes.

First:
Next:
Next:
Last:

61

Graphic Organizer
A useful strategy for understanding anything you read is to create a graphic organizer. A graphic organizer can help you think about the information and relate parts of it to each other. Each reading skill has a certain graphic organizer.

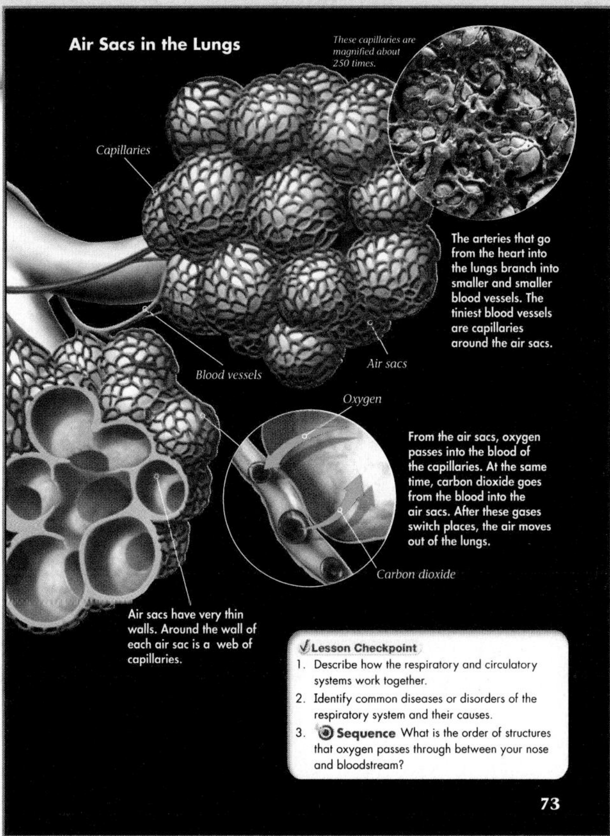

Air Sacs in the Lungs

These capillaries are magnified about 250 times.

Capillaries

The arteries that go from the heart into the lungs branch into smaller and smaller blood vessels. The tiniest blood vessels are capillaries around the air sacs.

Blood vessels

Air sacs

Oxygen

From the air sacs, oxygen passes into the blood of the capillaries. At the same time, carbon dioxide goes from the blood into the air sacs. After these gases switch places, the air moves out of the lungs.

Carbon dioxide

Air sacs have very thin walls. Around the wall of each air sac is a web of capillaries.

Lesson Checkpoint

1. Describe how the respiratory and circulatory systems work together.
2. Identify common diseases or disorders of the respiratory system and their causes.
3. Sequence What is the order of structures that oxygen passes through between your nose and bloodstream?

73

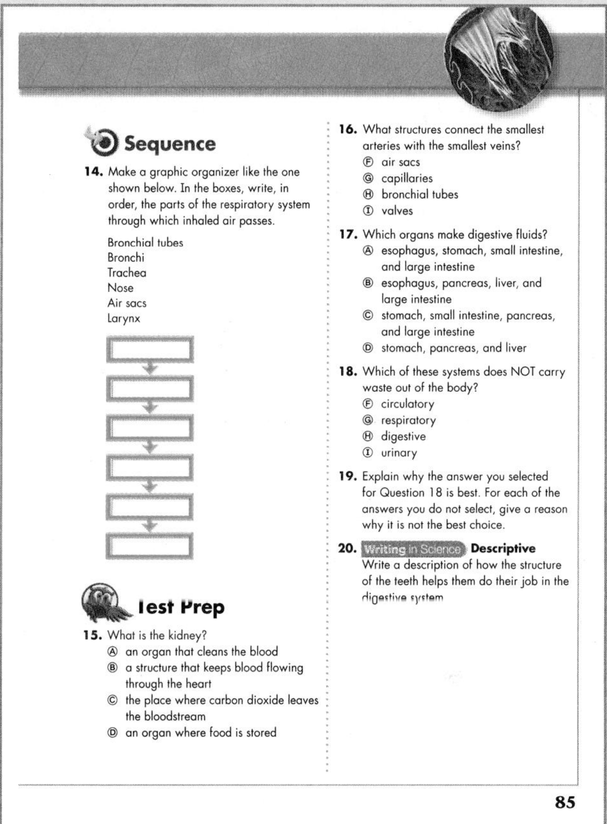

Sequence

14. Make a graphic organizer like the one shown below. In the boxes, write, in order, the parts of the respiratory system through which inhaled air passes.

Bronchial tubes
Bronchi
Trachea
Nose
Air sacs
Larynx

Test Prep

15. What is the kidney?
Ⓐ an organ that cleans the blood
Ⓑ a structure that keeps blood flowing through the heart
Ⓒ the place where carbon dioxide leaves the bloodstream
Ⓓ an organ where food is stored

16. What structures connect the smallest arteries with the smallest veins?
Ⓕ air sacs
Ⓖ capillaries
Ⓗ bronchial tubes
Ⓘ valves

17. Which organs make digestive fluids?
Ⓐ esophagus, stomach, small intestine, and large intestine
Ⓑ esophagus, pancreas, liver, and large intestine
Ⓒ stomach, small intestine, pancreas, and large intestine
Ⓓ stomach, pancreas, and liver

18. Which of these systems does NOT carry waste out of the body?
Ⓕ circulatory
Ⓖ respiratory
Ⓗ digestive
Ⓘ urinary

19. Explain why the answer you selected for Question 18 is best. For each of the answers you do not select, give a reason why it is not the best choice.

20. Writing in Science Descriptive
Write a description of how the structure of the teeth helps them do their job in the digestive system.

85

During Reading

As you read the lesson, use the checkpoint to check your understanding. Some checkpoints ask you to use the reading target skill.

After Reading

After you have read the chapter, think about what you found out. Exchange ideas with your partner. Compare the list you made before you read the chapter with what you learned by reading it. Answer the questions in the Chapter Review. One question uses the reading target skill.

Graphic Organizers

These are the target reading skills and graphic organizers that appear in this book.

- Cause and Effect
- Compare and Contrast
- Sequence
- Predict
- Draw Conclusions
- Summarize
- Main Idea and Details

Science Process Skills

Exploring Space

Scientists use process skills when they investigate places or events. You will use these skills when you do the activities in this book. Which process skills might scientists use when they explore space?

Observe

A scientist investigating space observes many things. You use your senses too to find out about other objects, events, or living things.

Classify

Scientists classify objects in space according to their properties. When you classify, you arrange or sort objects, events, or living things.

Estimate and Measure

As they build satellites and other machines, scientists first estimate the sizes of the various parts, and then they measure each part.

Infer

During an investigation, scientists infer what they think is happening, based on what they already know.

Predict

Before they do an experiment with a satellite, scientists tell what they think will happen.

Make and Use Models

Before scientists build a satellite to investigate space, they make and use models to help develop the best design.

Make Operational Definitions

When scientists make operational definitions, they describe objects or events based on their experiences.

Science Process Skills

If you were a scientist, you might explore the Moon. What questions might you have about the things you see? How would you use process skills in your investigation?

Form Questions and Hypotheses

Think of a statement that you can test to solve a problem or answer a question about the Moon or other objects in space.

Collect Data

Scientists collect data from their observations in space. They put the data into charts or tables.

Interpret Data

Scientists use the information they collected to solve problems or answer questions.

UNITED
STATES

Investigate and Experiment

As scientists explore space, they investigate and experiment to test a hypothesis.

Identify and Control Variables

As scientists perform an experiment, they identify and control the variables so that they test only one thing at a time.

Communicate

Scientists use words, pictures, charts, and graphs to share information about their investigation.

Lab zone

Using Scientific Methods for Science Inquiry

Scientists use scientific methods as they work. Scientific methods are organized ways to answer questions and solve problems. Scientific methods include the steps shown here. Scientists might not use all the steps. They might not use the steps in this order. You will use scientific methods when you do the **Full Inquiry** activity at the end of each unit. You also will use scientific methods when you do Science Fair Projects.

Ask a question.
You might have a question about something you observe.

What material is best for keeping heat in water?

State your hypothesis.
A hypothesis is a possible answer to your question.

If I wrap the jar in fake fur, then the water will stay warmer longer.

Identify and control variables.
Variables are things that can change. For a fair test, you choose just one variable to change. Keep all other variables the same.

Test other materials. Put the same amount of warm water in other jars that are the same size and shape.

Test your hypothesis.

Make a plan to test your hypothesis. Collect materials and tools. Then follow your plan.

Collect and record your data.

Keep good records of what you do and find out. Use tables and pictures to help.

Interpret your data.

Organize your notes and records to make them clear. Make diagrams, charts, or graphs to help.

State your conclusion.

Your conclusion is a decision you make based on your data. Communicate what you found out. Tell whether or not your data supported your hypothesis.

Fake fur did the best job of keeping the water warm.

Go further.

Use what you learn. Think of new questions to test or better ways to do a test.

Ask a Question

State Your Hypothesis

Identify and Control Variables

Test Your Hypothesis

Collect and Record Your Data

Interpret Your Data

State Your Conclusion

Go Further

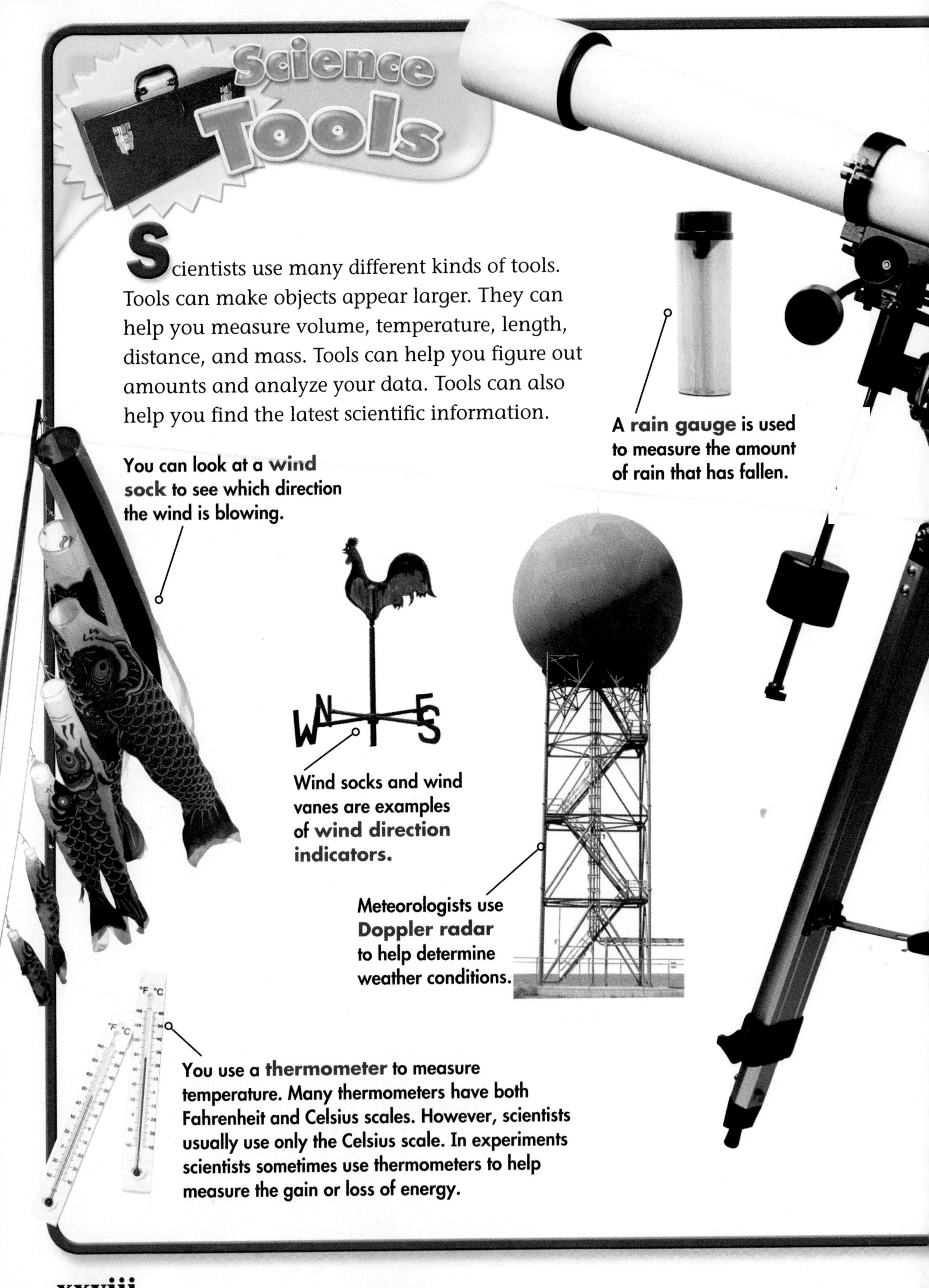

Science Tools

Scientists use many different kinds of tools. Tools can make objects appear larger. They can help you measure volume, temperature, length, distance, and mass. Tools can help you figure out amounts and analyze your data. Tools can also help you find the latest scientific information.

A **rain gauge** is used to measure the amount of rain that has fallen.

You can look at a **wind sock** to see which direction the wind is blowing.

Wind socks and wind vanes are examples of **wind direction indicators.**

Meteorologists use **Doppler radar** to help determine weather conditions.

You use a **thermometer** to measure temperature. Many thermometers have both Fahrenheit and Celsius scales. However, scientists usually use only the Celsius scale. In experiments scientists sometimes use thermometers to help measure the gain or loss of energy.

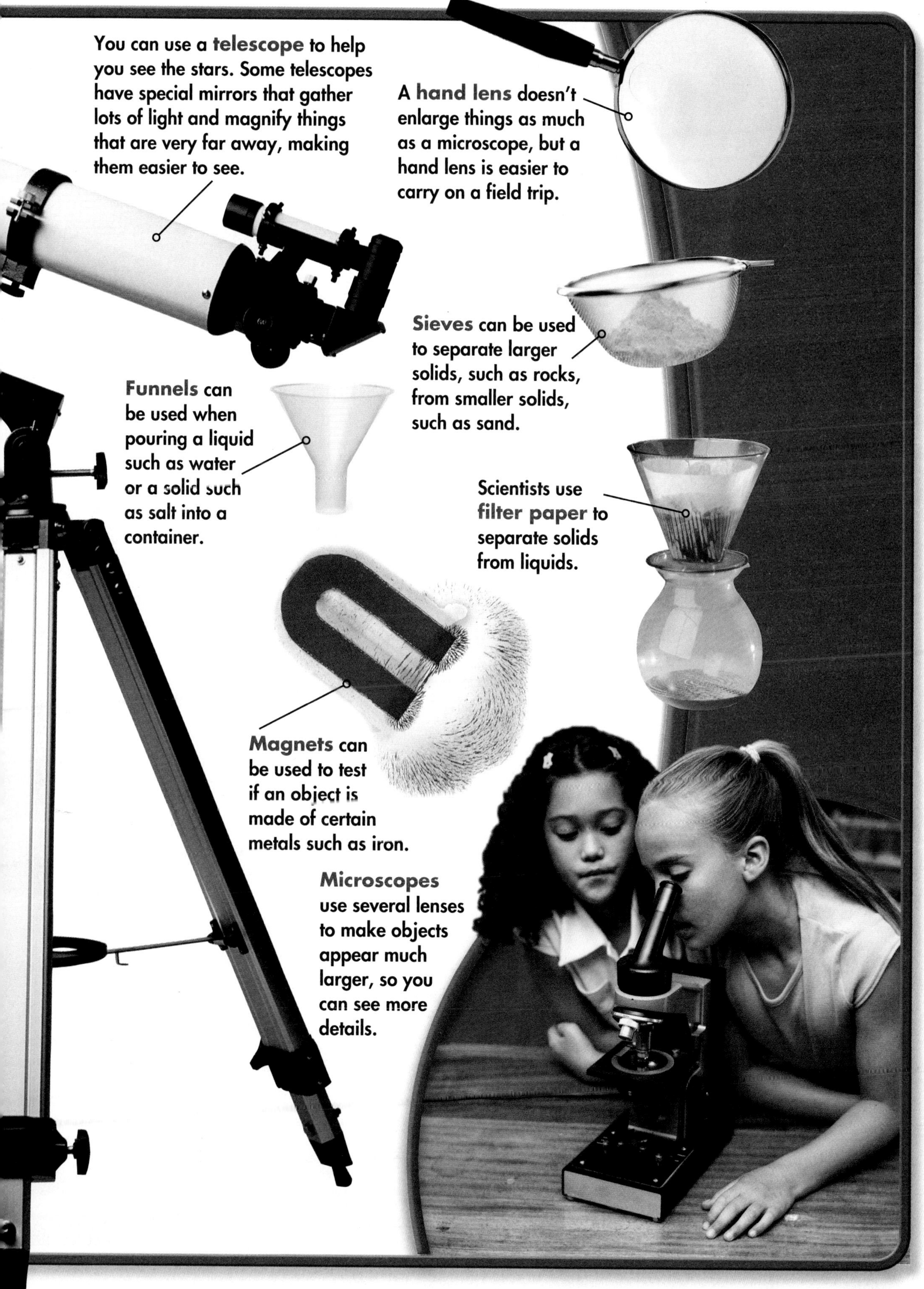
You can use a **telescope** to help you see the stars. Some telescopes have special mirrors that gather lots of light and magnify things that are very far away, making them easier to see.
A **hand lens** doesn't enlarge things as much as a microscope, but a hand lens is easier to carry on a field trip.
Sieves can be used to separate larger solids, such as rocks, from smaller solids, such as sand.
Funnels can be used when pouring a liquid such as water or a solid such as salt into a container.
Scientists use **filter paper** to separate solids from liquids.
Magnets can be used to test if an object is made of certain metals such as iron.
Microscopes use several lenses to make objects appear much larger, so you can see more details.

Science Tools

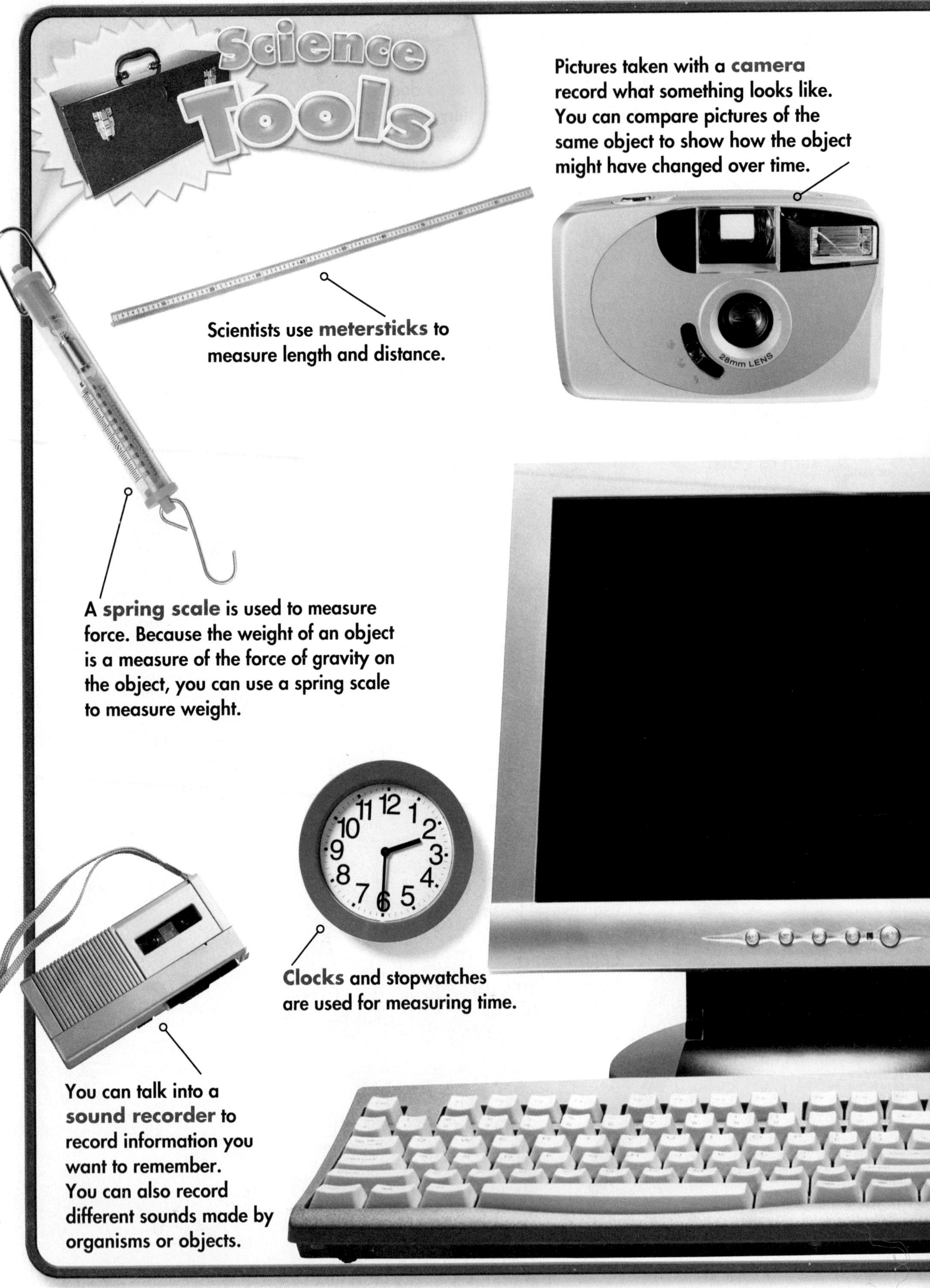

28mm LENS

Pictures taken with a **camera** record what something looks like. You can compare pictures of the same object to show how the object might have changed over time.

Scientists use **metersticks** to measure length and distance.

A **spring scale** is used to measure force. Because the weight of an object is a measure of the force of gravity on the object, you can use a spring scale to measure weight.

Clocks and stopwatches are used for measuring time.

You can talk into a **sound recorder** to record information you want to remember. You can also record different sounds made by organisms or objects.

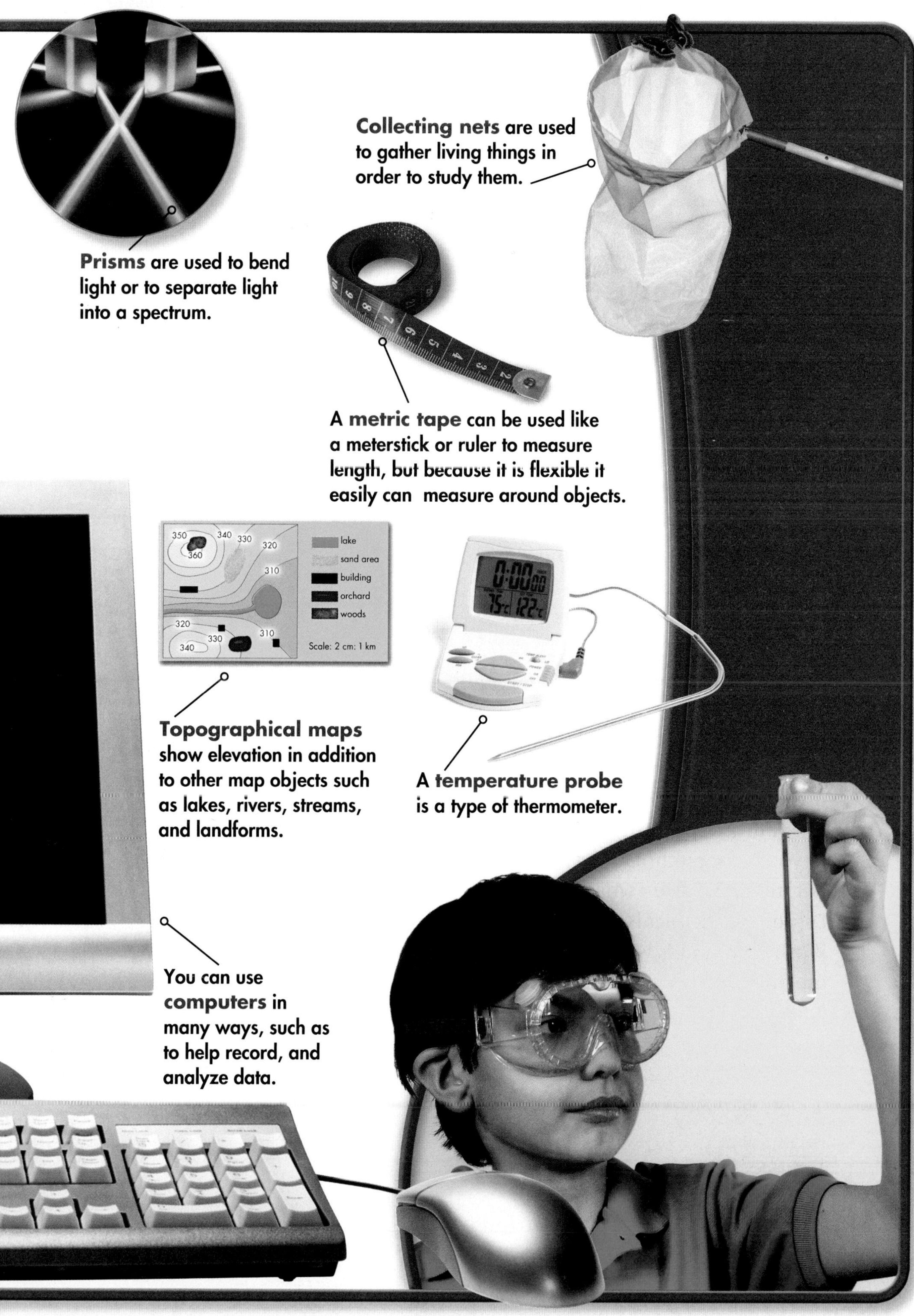
350
340
330
320
360
310
lake
sand area
building
orchard
woods
320
330
310
340
Scale: 2 cm: 1 km

Prisms are used to bend light or to separate light into a spectrum.

Collecting nets are used to gather living things in order to study them.

A **metric tape** can be used like a meterstick or ruler to measure length, but because it is flexible it easily can measure around objects.

Topographical maps show elevation in addition to other map objects such as lakes, rivers, streams, and landforms.

A **temperature probe** is a type of thermometer.

You can use **computers** in many ways, such as to help record, and analyze data.

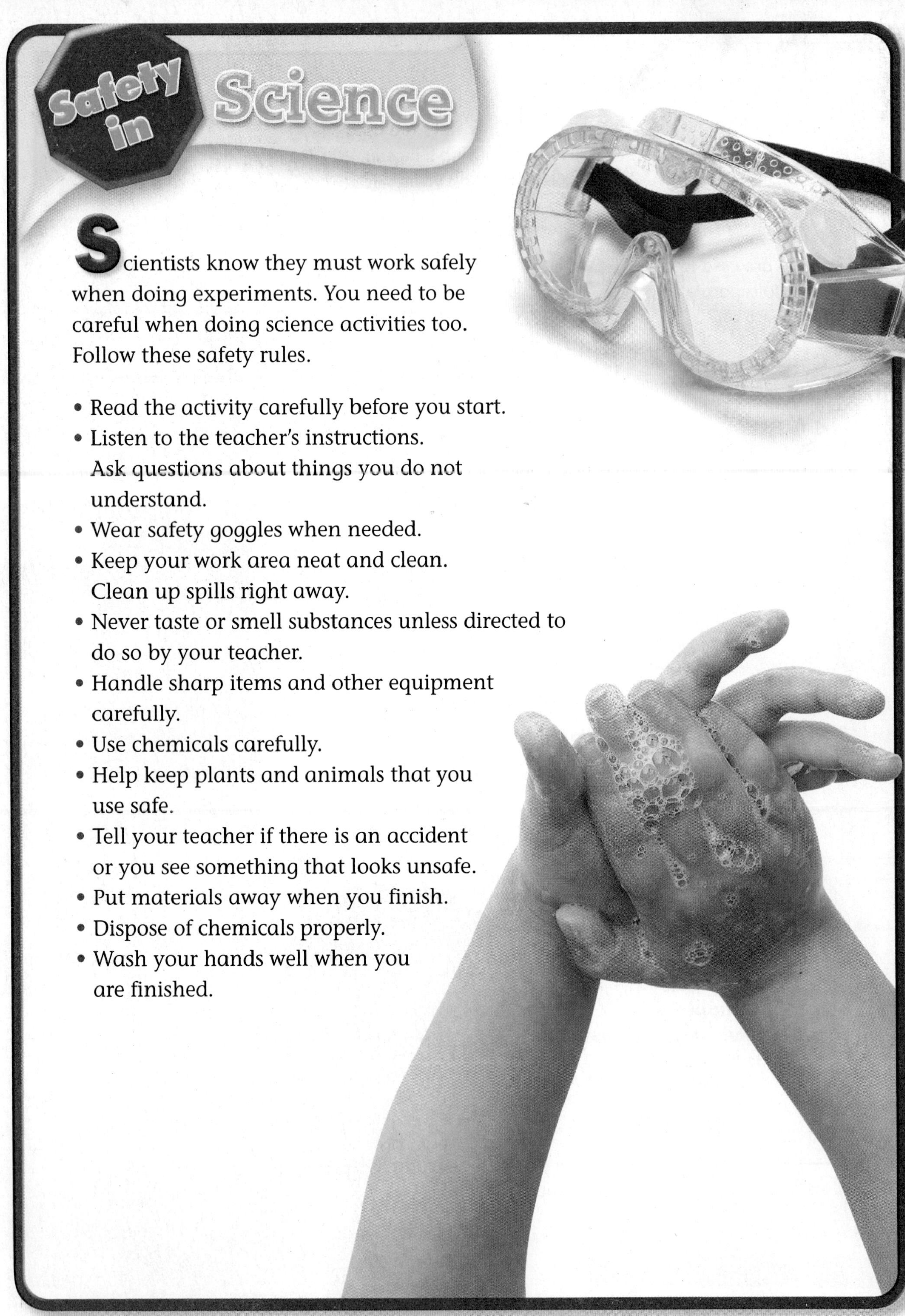

Safety in Science

Scientists know they must work safely when doing experiments. You need to be careful when doing science activities too. Follow these safety rules.

- Read the activity carefully before you start.
- Listen to the teacher's instructions. Ask questions about things you do not understand.
- Wear safety goggles when needed.
- Keep your work area neat and clean. Clean up spills right away.
- Never taste or smell substances unless directed to do so by your teacher.
- Handle sharp items and other equipment carefully.
- Use chemicals carefully.
- Help keep plants and animals that you use safe.
- Tell your teacher if there is an accident or you see something that looks unsafe.
- Put materials away when you finish.
- Dispose of chemicals properly.
- Wash your hands well when you are finished.

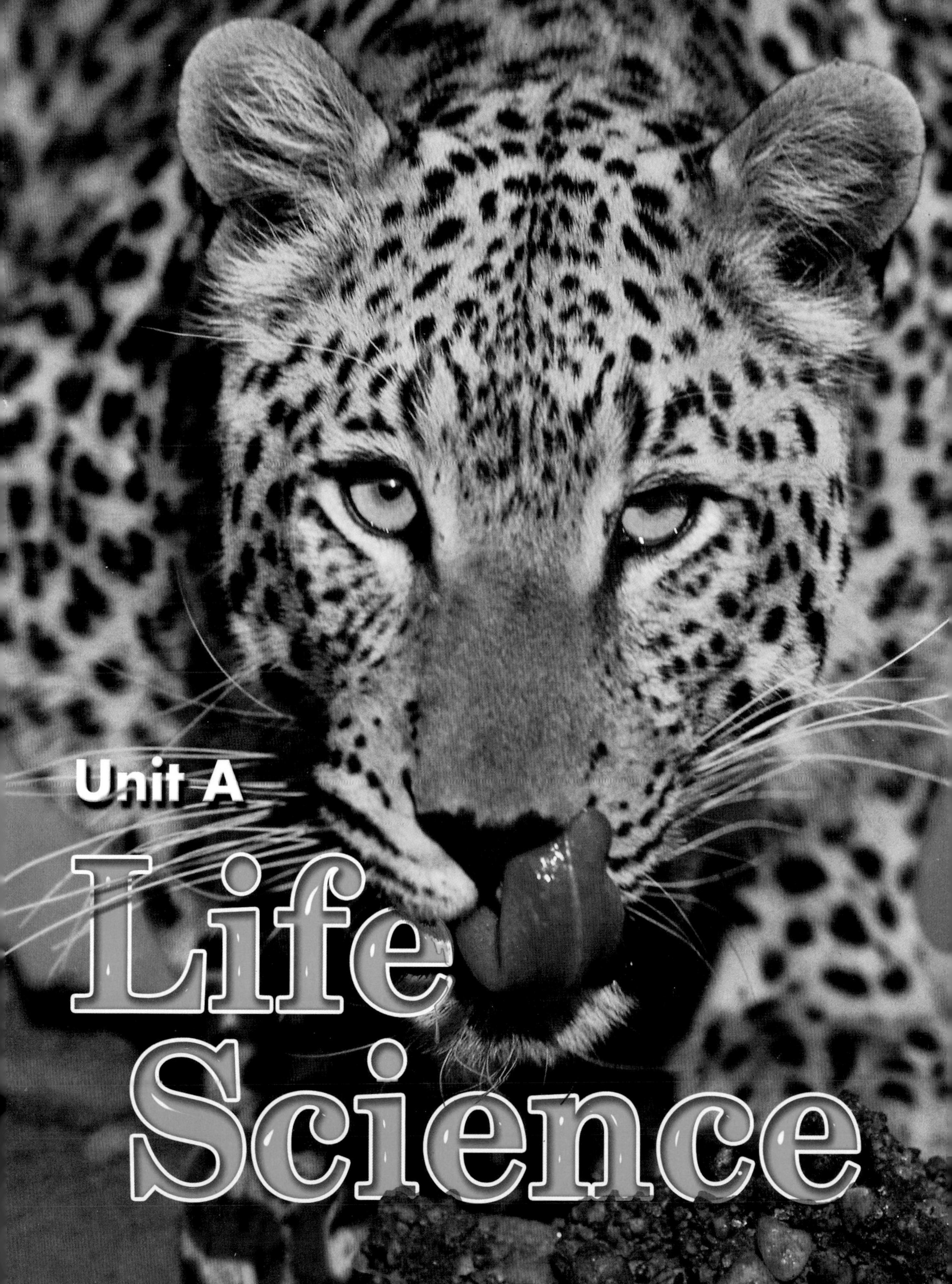

Unit A

Life Science

Chapter 1

Classifying Organisms

online Student Edition
sfsuccessnet.com

You Will Discover

- how living things are classified.
- characteristics that animals have.
- what vertebrates and invertebrates are.

Build Background

How are living things classified?

classify

kingdom

phylum

class

species

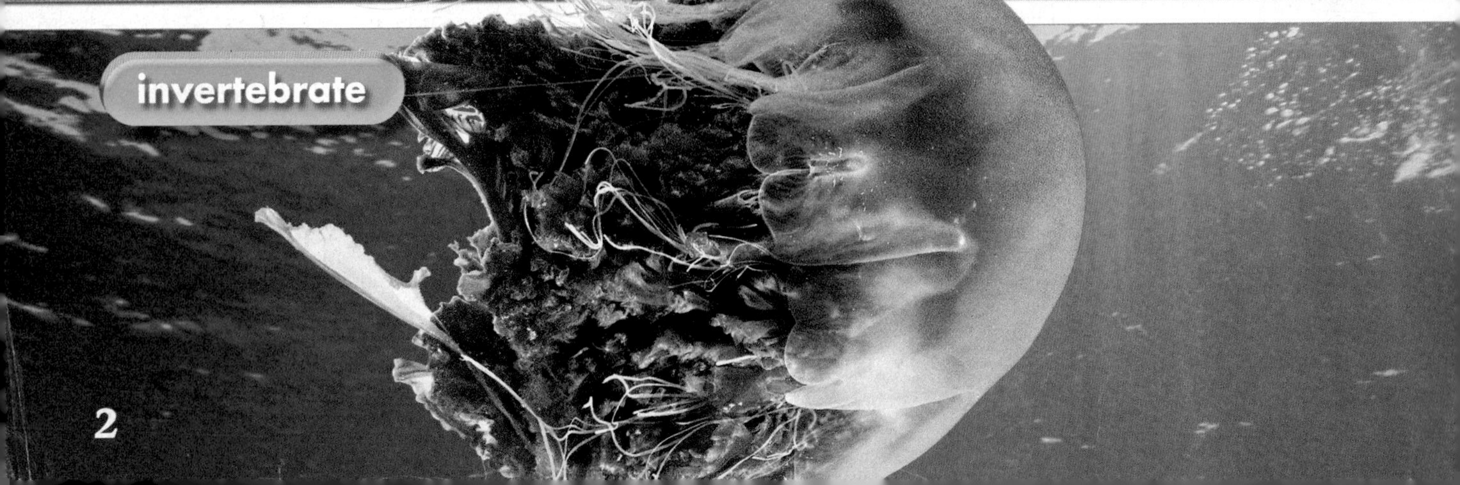

invertebrate

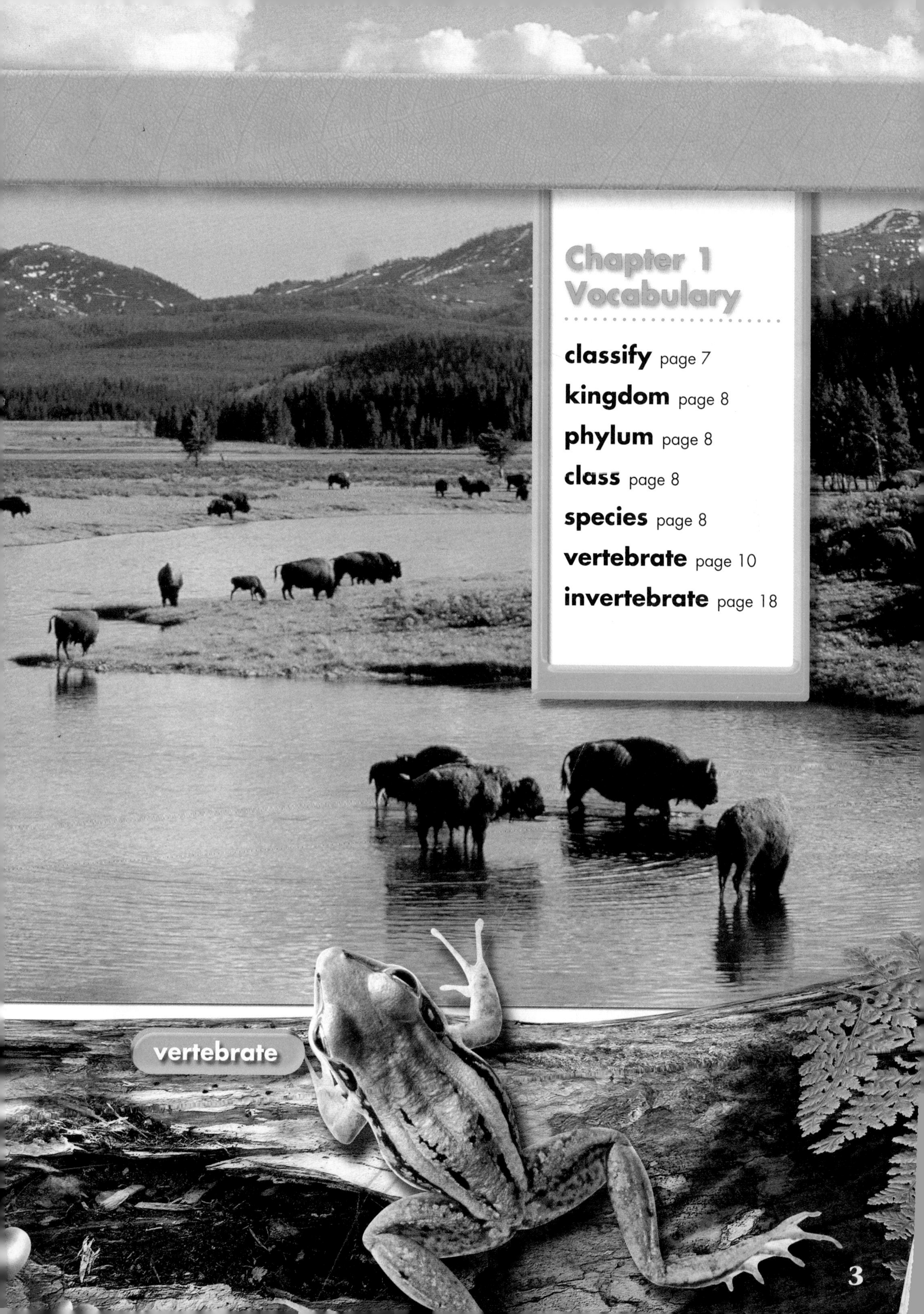
vertebrate

Chapter 1 Vocabulary

classify page 7

kingdom page 8

phylum page 8

class page 8

species page 8

vertebrate page 10

invertebrate page 18

Lab zone

Directed Inquiry

Explore How can you classify seeds?

Materials

Seed A

Seed B

Seed C

Seed D

Seed E

Seed F

What to Do

Classify your seeds. Sort the seeds into 2 groups at the first step using the property listed. Continue down the chart with the remaining seeds until each is identified.

This chart is one type of dichotomous key, a set of rules scientists use to help classify organisms.

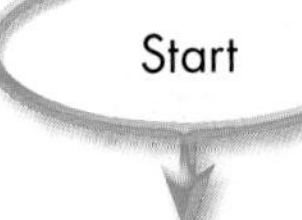
Start

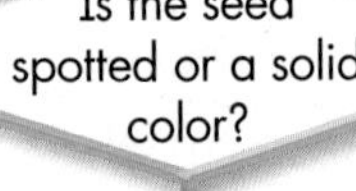
Is the seed spotted or a solid color?
spotted
pinto bean
solid color

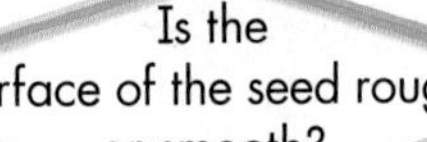
Is the surface of the seed rough or smooth?
rough
garbanzo bean
smooth

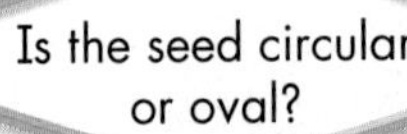
Is the seed circular or oval?
circular

pea
oval

Is the seed red or another color?
red

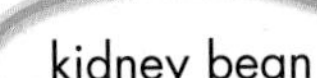
kidney bean

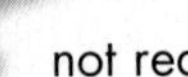
not red
Is the seed large or small?
large
lima bean
small

black bean

Process Skills

When you **classify** objects into groups, you compare and contrast their properties.

Explain Your Results

List the properties you used to **classify** your seeds into groups. Identify each seed.

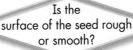

How to Read Science

Reading Skills

TARGET SKILL

Compare and Contrast

- To **compare,** writers may use clue words or phrases such as *both, like, as,* or *also.* To **contrast,** writers may use clue words such as *yet, but,* and *however* to signal differences.
- When there are no clue words, ask yourself "How are these events or things alike? How are they different?" Read the paragraph below. Comparisons and contrasts have been highlighted.
- You can use a graphic organizer to show how things are alike and different.

Science Article

With or Without Seeds

All plants are alike in one way. All plants use water, carbon dioxide, and energy from sunlight to make sugar. Then the plants use some of this sugar to grow. Some plants, such as sunflowers and pine trees, make seeds. But other plants, like ferns and mosses, do not make seeds.

Apply It!

When you **classify,** you show how things are alike and different. Use a graphic organizer like the one at the right to show **comparisons and contrasts** from the article above.

Sunflower **Fern**

Different
Alike
Different

You Are There!

It is the year 1805. For months you have been part of the Lewis and Clark exploration team. The team has explored places never before seen by biologists. One of your jobs is to help name and describe the new animals seen on the journey. The team stops for a rest. Far away, you see a great herd of animals. What are these? How should they be described?

Lesson 1

Why do we classify?

From 1804 to 1806, Meriwether Lewis, William Clark, and their team described hundreds of plants and animals so these could be classified. To classify organisms, the skills of observation and comparison are used.

Lewis and Clark's Mission of Discovery

Lewis and Clark led their team to find a route between the Atlantic and Pacific Oceans, and to investigate the organisms that lived in the West. The team described hundreds of animals and plants. They also collected many samples of plants and animals. Later, biologists used the samples and descriptions to classify the organisms. To **classify** means to put things into groups.

To classify an organism, these biologists used skills of observation and comparison that most scientists use in their work. First, they observed each organism carefully. Then they compared and contrasted their observations with known plants and animals. They tried to place similar organisms in one group. A plant or animal that was very different from others would be put in a new group.

Reasons to Classify

A classification system makes it easier to communicate clearly by having just one name for each organism. Without a classification system, scientists might call one organism by different names. Or they might use one name for more than one organism. That could be confusing!

A system can also help to organize information about organisms. By just knowing what category an organism is in, much can be known about it. For example, an organism classified as a plant most likely needs light to live.

1. ✓ **Checkpoint** How do scientists classify organisms?
2. **Art** in Science Research the animals that Lewis and Clark observed. Draw a picture of two of them and label ways they are different and ways they are the same.

Classification Systems

A classification system lists organisms in a series of groups. Today's classification system has been developed by many people over many years. In fact, it is still changing.

At one time, people believed that all living things were either plants or animals. So scientists divided all living things into two kingdoms—the plant and animal kingdoms. A **kingdom** was the highest or most general group of organisms. Today, a popular system uses six kingdoms, shown below.

Within each kingdom, scientists compared and contrasted the structures of the organisms and put similar organisms into groups. Each group was called a phylum. A **phylum** was the next level of classification below kingdom. Scientists then separated organisms of each phylum into smaller groups called classes. A **class** was the next level of classification below phylum. Scientists kept dividing each level into smaller and smaller levels—order, family, and genus—continuing to the lowest level, called the **species.**

Six Kingdoms of Living Things

Archaebacteria

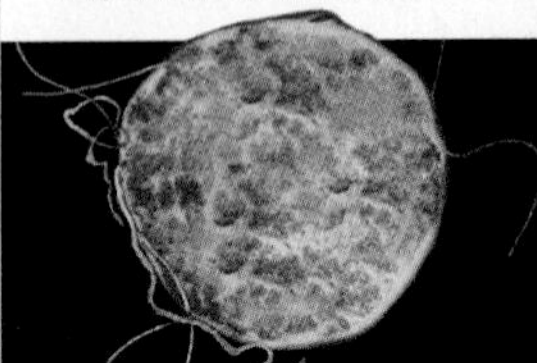

Archaebacteria live as single cells. Many do not need oxygen or sunlight to live.

Eubacteria

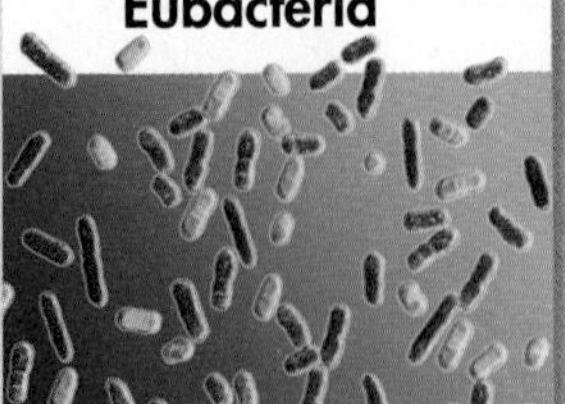

Eubacteria are single cells that have materials not found in archaebacteria.

Protists

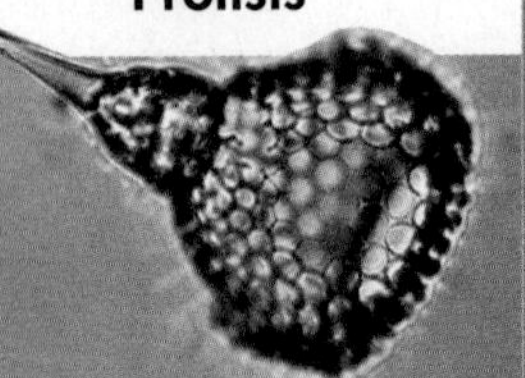

Most protists are single cells, but some have many cells. Algae are protists.

Fungi

Mushrooms and molds are fungi. Fungi can be made of one or many cells.

Here you see how the gray wolf is classified at different levels of the classification system. As you go down the levels, the groups get smaller and have less variety of animals.

Animal Kingdom
All these organisms are animals.

Phylum Chordata
All these animals have spinal cords.

Class Mammalia
All these animals give milk to their young.

Order Carnivora
All these animals eat meat.

Family Canidae
All these animals have dog-like features.

Genus *Canis*
This level includes all dogs, coyotes, and wolves.

Species *lupus*
This level names a particular kind of wolf, the gray wolf.

Plants

Plants have many cells and make their own sugar for food.

Animals

Animals have many cells and get their food by eating other organisms.

✓ Lesson Checkpoint

1. Describe one advantage of having a classification system.
2. What kinds of observations did scientists use at first to group organisms into a phylum or class?
3. **Math in Science** A museum wants to make one display for each of the 6 kingdoms. In each display, 17 organisms will be shown. How many organisms will be shown in all?

Lesson 2

How do we classify vertebrates?

The chordata is one phylum of animals. One subphylum of chordata is divided into five classes. Each class has its own unique features.

Class: Fish

Clownfish

Class: Amphibians

Golden-Lined Frog

Animals have many cells.

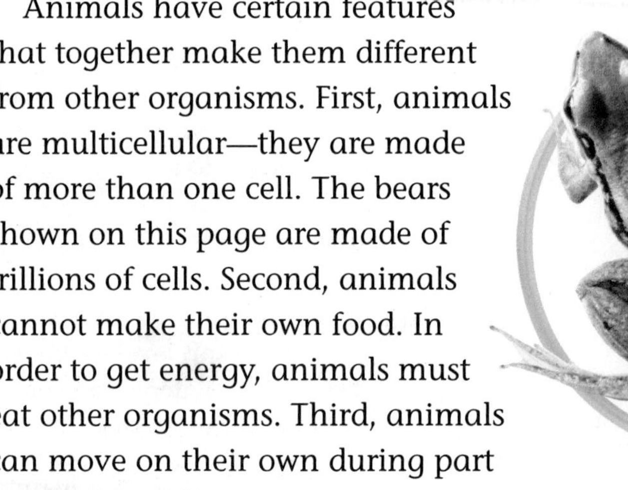

Characteristics of Animals

Animals have certain features that together make them different from other organisms. First, animals are multicellular—they are made of more than one cell. The bears shown on this page are made of trillions of cells. Second, animals cannot make their own food. In order to get energy, animals must eat other organisms. Third, animals can move on their own during part or all of their lives.

Vertebrate Animals

Today, the animal kingdom is divided into more than 30 phyla. Only one phylum, the chordata, contains organisms that have spinal cords. One subphylum of this group contains animals with backbones that surround the spinal cord. These animals are called **vertebrates.** Backbones protect a very important set of nerves that go to the brain. Bison and sheep are vertebrates. What other vertebrates do you know? This subphylum is divided into five classes. The classes are mammals, birds, reptiles, amphibians, and fish.

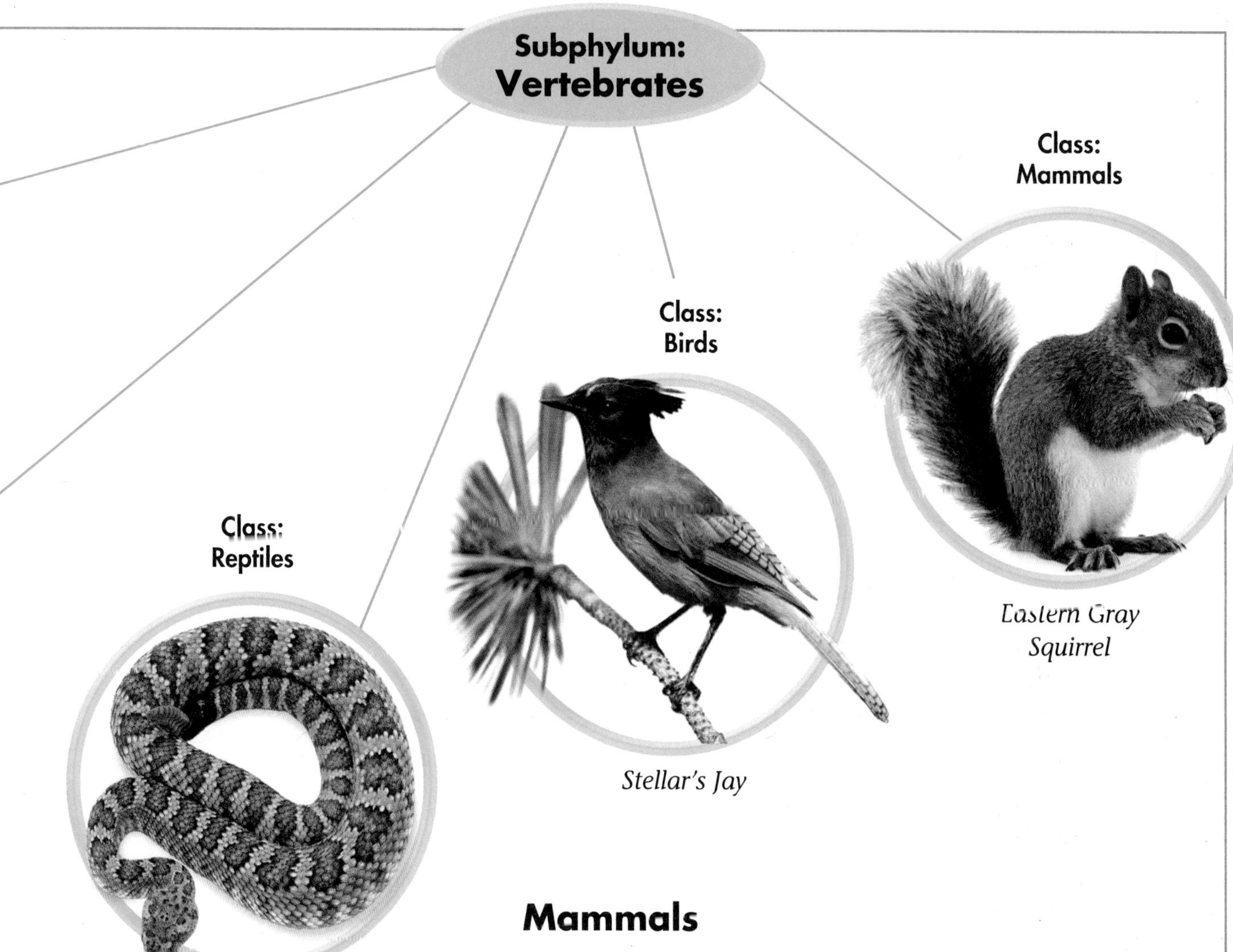
Subphylum:
Vertebrates
Class:
Reptiles
Class:
Birds
Class:
Mammals

Western Diamondback Rattlesnake

Stellar's Jay

Eastern Gray Squirrel

Mammals

One class of vertebrates is the mammals. All mammals share several characteristics. They breathe air with lungs and make milk for their young. Most mammals have hair or fur. Mammals are warm-blooded. That means they keep their body temperature nearly the same all the time. Young mammals are usually born looking very much like their parents.

All life continues through different life cycles. A life cycle is a pattern of birth, growth, reproduction, and death. As they grow, animals develop and then reproduce. At the end of their life cycle, animals die. Their offspring repeat the cycle.

Characteristics of Mammals	
Body covering	Hair or fur
Body temperature	Warm-blooded
Feed young	Mothers' milk

1. **Checkpoint** What are 3 of the features that make animals different from other organisms?
2. **Compare and Contrast** How would you compare and contrast a squirrel and a bear?

Reptiles

Reptiles do not look much like mammals. How would you compare and contrast the two classes—reptiles and mammals?

Reptiles are similar to mammals in many ways. Their lungs and stomachs are similar. Their heads have the same basic arrangement of eyes, nose, and mouth.

Reptiles are different from mammals because reptiles do not have any hair or fur covering their bodies. Instead, they have tough, dry skin with scales. Unlike mammals, reptiles are cold-blooded. The temperature of cold-blooded animals will change as the temperature of the air or water changes. Their temperature will be higher when the air or water is warm or when they are in sunlight.

Life Cycle of Reptiles

The life cycle of a reptile is usually similar to that of a mammal. Young reptiles look very much like their parents, just as young mammals do. Unlike mammals, most reptiles lay eggs. Also, when young reptiles hatch from eggs, they are ready to live on their own.

Lewis and Clark and their team described many species of reptiles. These include the bull snake, the prairie rattlesnake, and the soft-shelled turtle.

Birds

Birds make up another class of vertebrate animals. Like mammals, birds are warm-blooded. They also have many organs, such as eyes, tongues, and bones similar to those of mammals.

What makes birds different from all other animals? It is not the ability to fly, because many insects and bats can do that. Some birds do not fly at all. The special characteristic of birds is their feathers.

Feathered wings help many birds soar with ease. Some bird wings are shaped much like airplane wings. The front edge of their wing is thick. The top surface curves to a thin back edge. While not all birds can fly, they all have beaks and they all lay hard-shelled eggs.

Life Cycle of Birds

A bird's life cycle is very similar to a reptile's life cycle. One difference is that young birds need to be fed by their parents. Reptiles are born ready to find their own food.

Sea turtles hatch from eggs laid on beaches. Sea turtles spend the rest of their lives in the water, except to lay more eggs.

Characteristics of Reptiles	
Body coverings	Scales
Body temperature	Cold-blooded
Feed young	No

Baby robins are born needing to be fed and protected by an adult bird.

Characteristics of Birds	
Body coverings	Feathers
Body temperature	Warm-blooded
Feed young	Yes

1. **√Checkpoint** How are some bird wings like airplane wings?
2. **Writing in Science** **Narrative** In your **science journal,** write a short story using a bird and a reptile as the main characters. In the story, describe each main character using the information mentioned in the lesson.

Characteristics of Amphibians	
Body coverings	Soft Skin
Body temperature	Cold-blooded
Feed young	No

Amphibians

Frogs, toads, and salamanders are amphibians. Amphibians are like reptiles in many ways. For instance, the shape of a salamander is very similar to the shape of a lizard. Amphibians are also similar to reptiles because they are cold-blooded. However, the soft, moist skin of amphibians is very different from the reptiles' scales. Amphibians' skin can absorb water and oxygen.

Life Cycle of Amphibians

Amphibians have a very different life cycle than that of other vertebrates. You are probably familiar with the stages of the life cycle of a frog. They hatch from eggs as tadpoles. Slowly, the tadpoles grow legs and the tail gets shorter. Soon they develop lungs and stop getting oxygen through gills. Then they begin to live on land. As adults, frogs look nothing like they did when they were young. No other class of vertebrates changes so much during their lifetime. This kind of large change is known as metamorphosis.

Characteristics of Fish	
Body coverings	Usually scales
Body temperature	Cold-blooded
Feed young	No

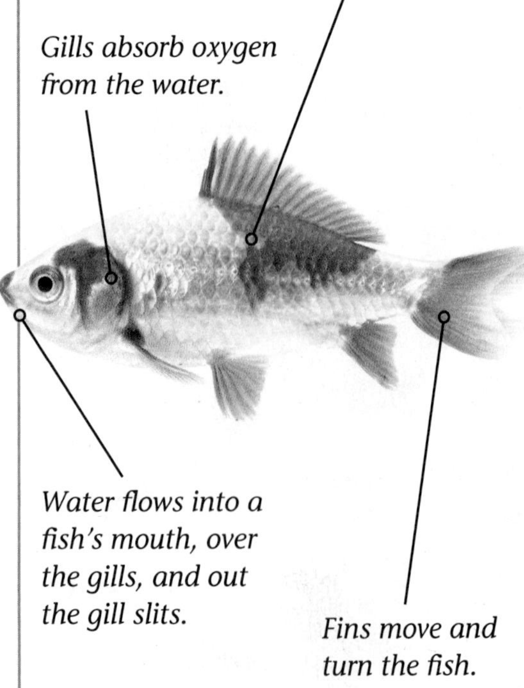

The streamlined shape of a fish helps it move through the water.

Gills absorb oxygen from the water.

Water flows into a fish's mouth, over the gills, and out the gill slits.

Fins move and turn the fish.

Fish

Some mammals live in the water. Some reptiles do too. But the only class of vertebrates made up only of water-living animals is the class of fish. Some fish live in fresh water, while others live in salt water. Fish get oxygen through gills located on each side of the head.

Most fish have scales, similar to a reptile. Fish also have a slimy coating that helps water flow past them. Many fish swim by bending their entire body. Others just move their fins. The life cycle of a fish is most like the life cycle of a reptile. Fish hatch from soft or jelly-coated eggs, and can feed themselves right away.

Amphibian Life Cycle

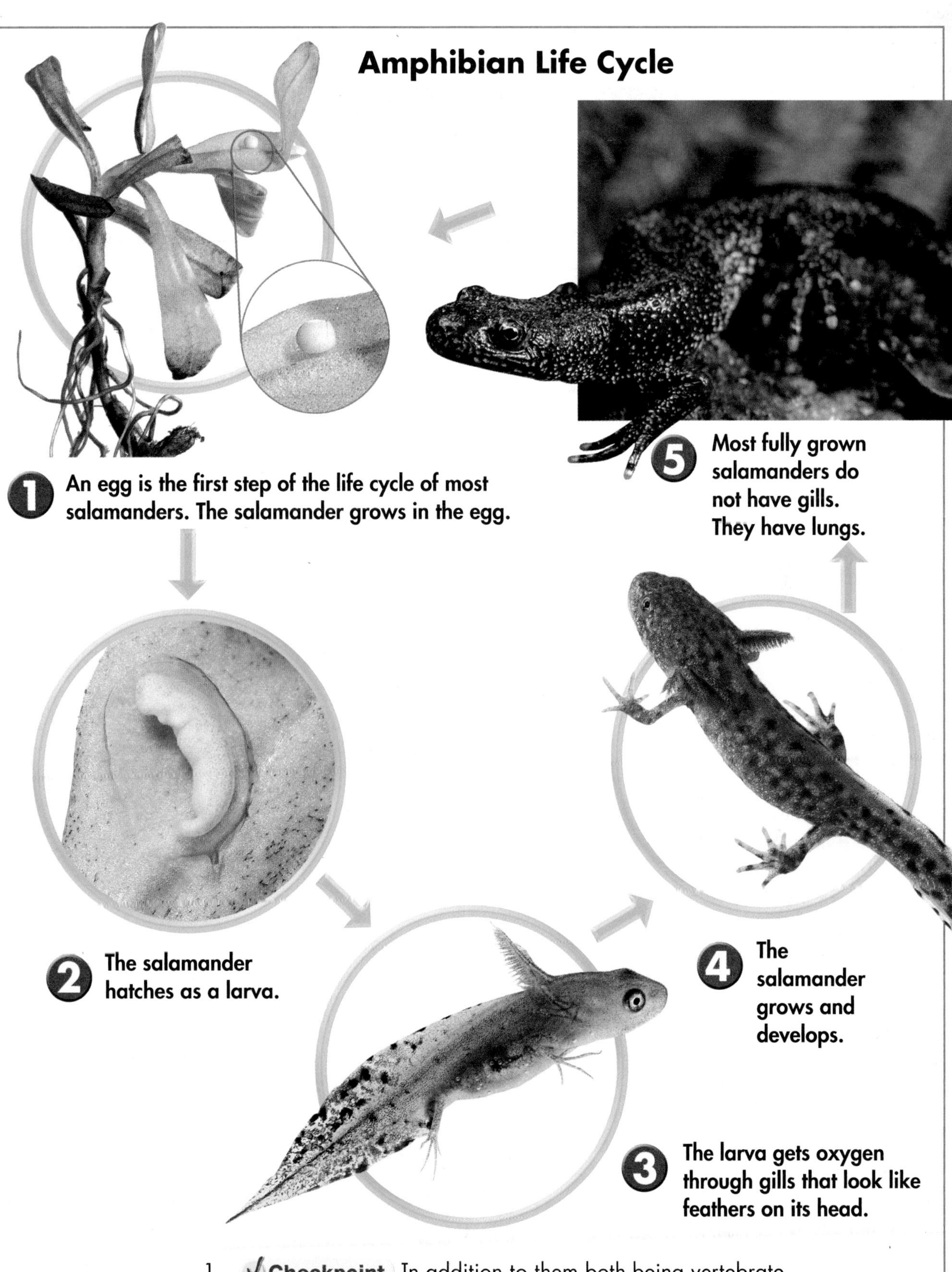

1 An egg is the first step of the life cycle of most salamanders. The salamander grows in the egg.
2 The salamander hatches as a larva.
3 The larva gets oxygen through gills that look like feathers on its head.
4 The salamander grows and develops.
5 Most fully grown salamanders do not have gills. They have lungs.

1. **✓Checkpoint** In addition to them both being vertebrate animals, how else are amphibians and fish similar?
2. **Writing in Science** **Narrative** In your **science journal,** compose a short poem about fish. Be sure to mention as many fish characteristics as possible in your poem.

Discovery of Dinosaur Fossils

During the early 1800s, scientists began classifying fossils of ancient animal bones. These bones were not those of any species alive at the time.

Scientists looked at the differences and similarities between these strange fossils and bones of living animals. They also compared complete fossils with fossils that were not complete. They concluded that these fossil bones were from animals like present-day lizards. Since these fossils were often huge, scientists called the ancient animals *dinosaurs*, which means "terrible lizards." Although the best-known dinosaurs were huge, many were much smaller, perhaps only 0.9 meters (3 feet) long.

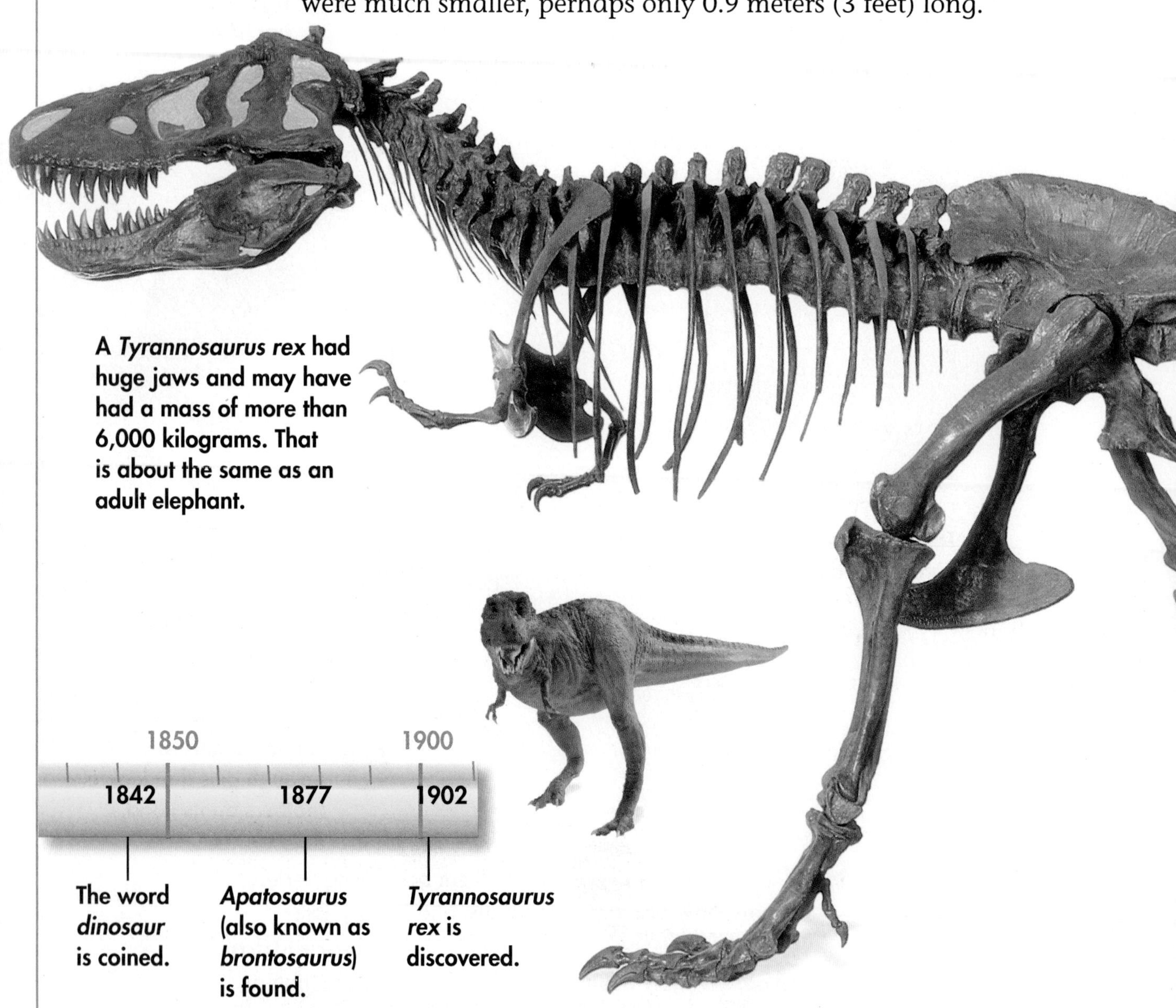
1850
1900
1842
1877
1902
The word *dinosaur* is coined.
Apatosaurus (also known as *brontosaurus*) is found.
Tyrannosaurus rex is discovered.

A *Tyrannosaurus rex* had huge jaws and may have had a mass of more than 6,000 kilograms. That is about the same as an adult elephant.

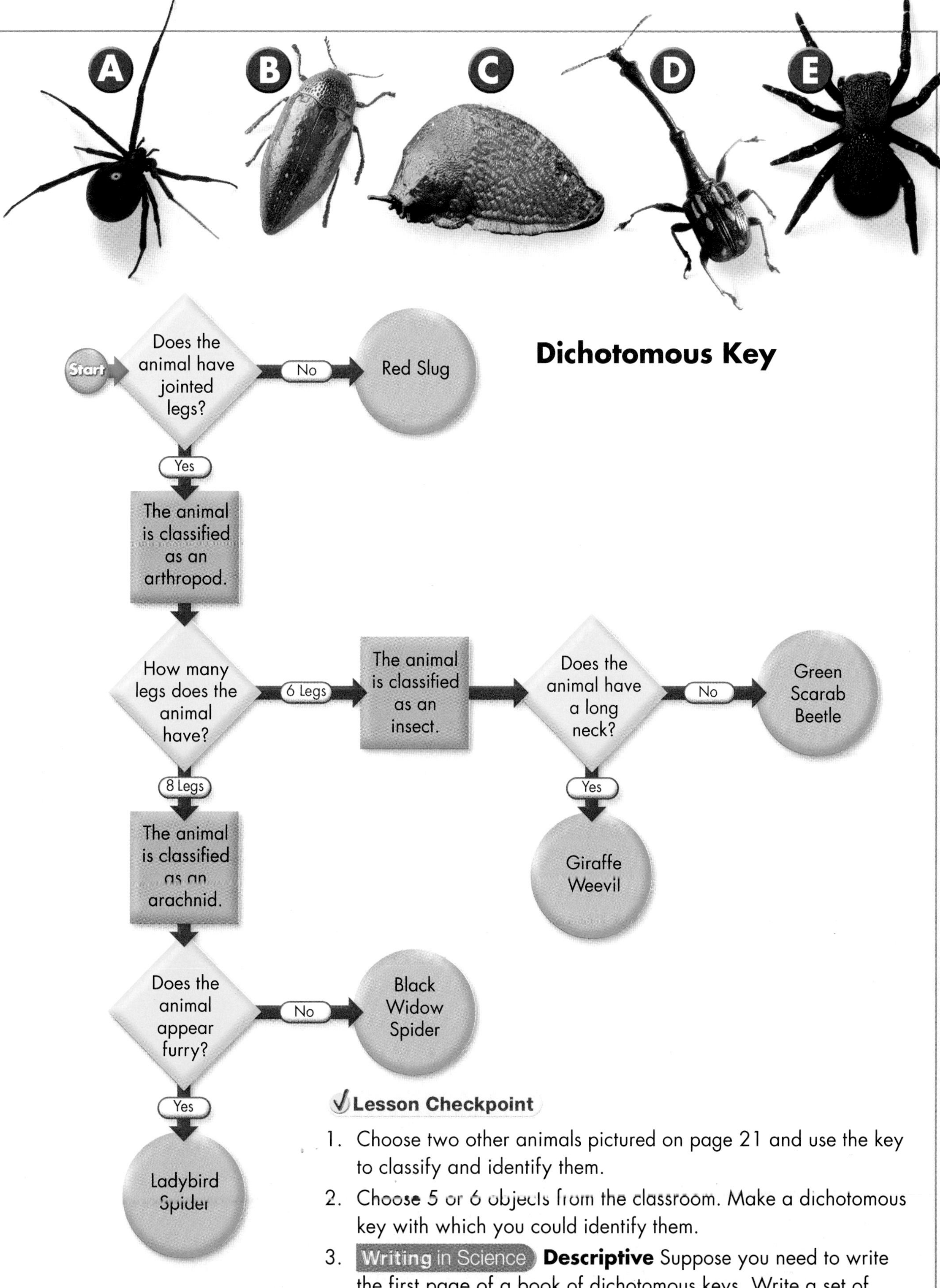
A
B
C
D
E
Dichotomous Key
Start
Does the animal have jointed legs?
No
Red Slug
Yes
The animal is classified as an arthropod.
How many legs does the animal have?
6 Legs
The animal is classified as an insect.
Does the animal have a long neck?
No
Green Scarab Beetle
Yes
Giraffe Weevil
8 Legs
The animal is classified as an arachnid.
Does the animal appear furry?
No
Black Widow Spider
Yes
Ladybird Spider

Lesson Checkpoint

1. Choose two other animals pictured on page 21 and use the key to classify and identify them.
2. Choose 5 or 6 objects from the classroom. Make a dichotomous key with which you could identify them.
3. Writing in Science **Descriptive** Suppose you need to write the first page of a book of dichotomous keys. Write a set of instructions to teach the reader how to use the dichotomous keys.

Lesson 4

How are other organisms classified?

Members of the animal kingdom are only a small fraction of all the living things on the planet. Other living things belong to other kingdoms—Plants, Fungi, Protists, Eubacteria, and Archaebacteria.

Qualities of Plants

Plants differ from animals in a special way—they use sunlight, water, and carbon dioxide to make their own sugar for food. They may have other distinctive features, such as stems, roots and leaves. Many plants are vascular. This means the plant has special tubes for carrying food and water to all its parts. Organisms in the plant kingdom are multicellular, just like animals. Four common plant phyla are shown on these pages.

Characteristics of Mosses	
vascular	no
seeds	no
flowers	no

Mosses

You have probably seen moss growing on trees or in shallow streams. A single moss plant is very small and has very tiny leaf-like structures. Mosses have no flowers or seeds.

Ferns

Most ferns have feather-like leaves. Look at the picture of the young, folded fern leaves at the right. At this stage, these leaves are called fiddleheads.

One way ferns are different from mosses is that ferns are vascular. Vascular plants can grow larger than nonvascular plants. This is because the vascular tubes can carry materials to parts of the plant high off the ground. Ferns and mosses are alike in that they both use spores to reproduce.

Characteristics of Ferns	
vascular	yes
seeds	no
flowers	no

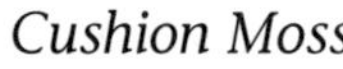

Cushion Moss

Conifers

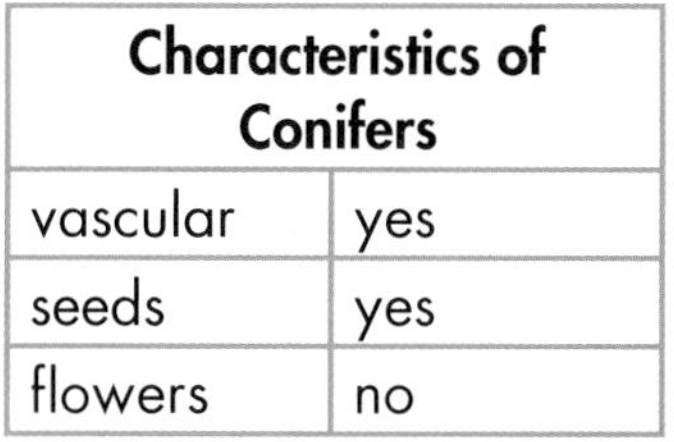

Characteristics of Conifers	
vascular	yes
seeds	yes
flowers	no

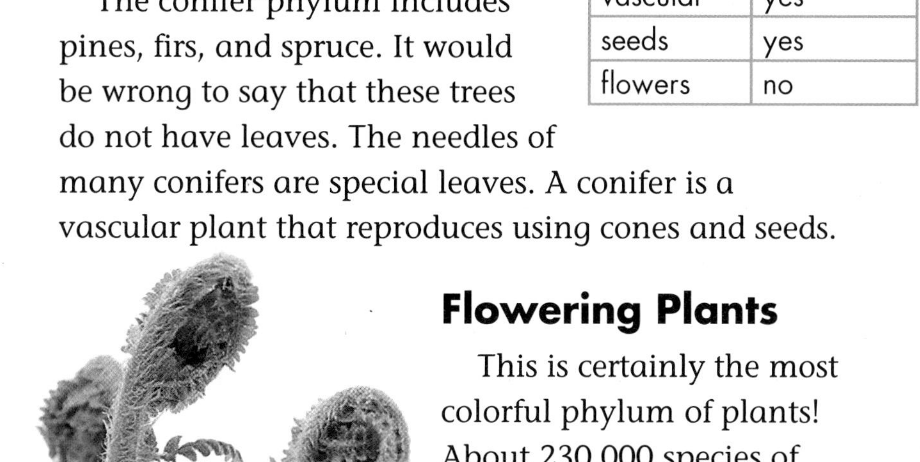

The conifer phylum includes pines, firs, and spruce. It would be wrong to say that these trees do not have leaves. The needles of many conifers are special leaves. A conifer is a vascular plant that reproduces using cones and seeds.

California Redwood

cone

Flowering Plants

This is certainly the most colorful phylum of plants! About 230,000 species of flowering plants have been identified. All flowering plants are vascular. These plants use their flowers to make seeds for reproduction. Mosses, ferns, and conifers don't produce flowers.

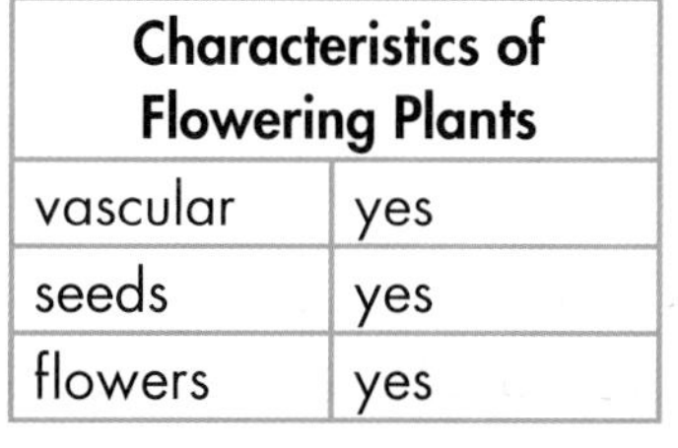

Characteristics of Flowering Plants	
vascular	yes
seeds	yes
flowers	yes

Fiddlehead

Tulip

1. **√Checkpoint** How would you classify a plant that has seeds, is vascular, and has needle-like leaves?
2. **Math in Science** If one fern produces an average of 500,000 spores, about how many spores could 10 ferns make?

Neither Plant Nor Animal

Over the years, many new organisms have been discovered. Some of these do not fit well in either the plant or animal kingdom. For example, some organisms can move on their own like animals, but they perform photosynthesis like plants. Many of these organisms are made of only one cell and can only be seen with a microscope. Some organisms are collections of single cells that could live alone but benefit by working together in colonies. Some of the microscopic organisms cause disease. Many, though, are harmless. Some are even helpful.

Organisms that are not classified as plants or animals can be classified as fungi, protists, eubacteria, or archaebacteria. These four kingdoms are described on the following page. Even though these organisms are not plants or animals, they have some similarities. They all need an environment for food, water, and waste removal. Many need carbon dioxide or oxygen, like plants or animals.

Single-celled organisms found in the hot springs of Yellowstone National Park were different from other cells. Discoveries like this can lead to debates between scientists and to new ways of classifying organisms.

Debates in Classifying

At various times biologists have changed the number of kingdoms to better fit the organisms they have found in places like the hot springs of Yellowstone National Park. Not all biologists agree on exactly how to make these changes.

Even when biologists agree on the number of kingdoms, there can be debates on how to classify a newly discovered organism. This is because a newly discovered organism may be very much like two groups of organisms. Biologists may disagree as to which group the new organism should be placed in.

These debates are sometimes confusing. One thing is for sure—as long as new information is found, the classification system will keep changing.

Shaggy Mane mushrooms

Fungi Kingdom
Fungi, such as mushrooms, are not plants because they are not able to make their own sugar for food. Mushrooms use hair-like structures to absorb and digest food from the material they grow on.
Yeast are single-celled fungi. Bakers use them in the baking of bread. Yeast take in sugar from bread dough and release carbon dioxide. This gas gets trapped in the dough, causing the dough to rise. A yeast cell reproduces by dividing into two cells.

Diatom protist

Protist Kingdom
Most protists are single cells. Some, such as some algae, live in colonies. Protists such as algae are food for many animals. Some protists even live inside the digestive systems of certain animals, such as termites and cows, and help them digest plants they eat. These animals would die without the protists.

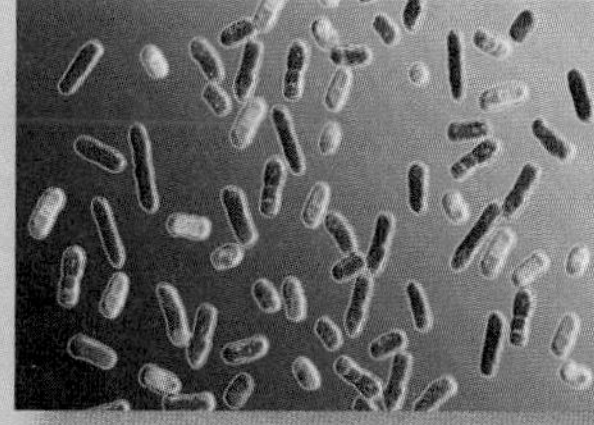
Eubacteria

Eubacteria Kingdom
Organisms in this kingdom are also single cells. These organisms may have many different shapes. Some are spheres. Others look like rods. Some are even spirals. Some have structures like tails that wiggle and move them through water. These cells do not have a true nucleus.

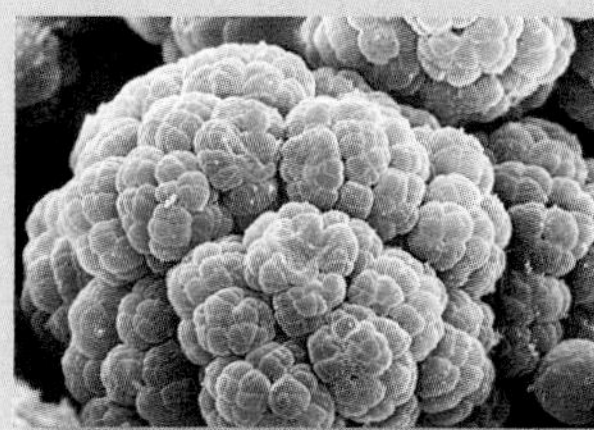
Archaebacteria

Archaebacteria Kingdom
Archaebacteria are single-celled organisms that can survive environments that are deadly to most other kinds of life. They live well in very hot, acid springs. Others can live in very salty water. These cells do not have a true nucleus.

√ Lesson Checkpoint

1. How do protists help some animals?
2. How are the needs of single-celled organisms similar to the needs of plants or animals?
3. Why has the classification system changed over the years?
4. **Compare and Contrast** Compare the fungi and protist kingdoms.

Lab zone **Guided Inquiry**

Investigate What are some characteristics of yeast?

Yeast are tiny organisms. Each is a single cell. In a warm place with sugar and water, yeast grow quickly. Bakers put yeast in bread dough to help the bread to rise.

Materials

watermelon slice

yeast

spoon

plastic bag

hand lens

microscope and microscope slide

What to Do

1. Shake $\frac{1}{2}$ spoonful of yeast on the watermelon slice.

2. Put the watermelon slice in the bag. Seal it and set it in a warm place. Use a hand lens to **observe** the yeast.

3. After 1 hour, observe the yeast. Describe any changes.

Process Skills

The yeast you observed are **classified** as fungi, based on their properties

 More Lab zone Activities Take It to the Net sfsuccessnet.com

4. Observe the yeast 2 more times. Describe any changes.

Time	Appearance of Yeast on Watermelon Slice
After 1 hour	
After 2 hours	
After 3 hours	

5. Observe a tiny amount of the yeast with a microscope. Notice that the cells are similar to each other. Draw your observations.

What tiny organisms did you see through the microscope?

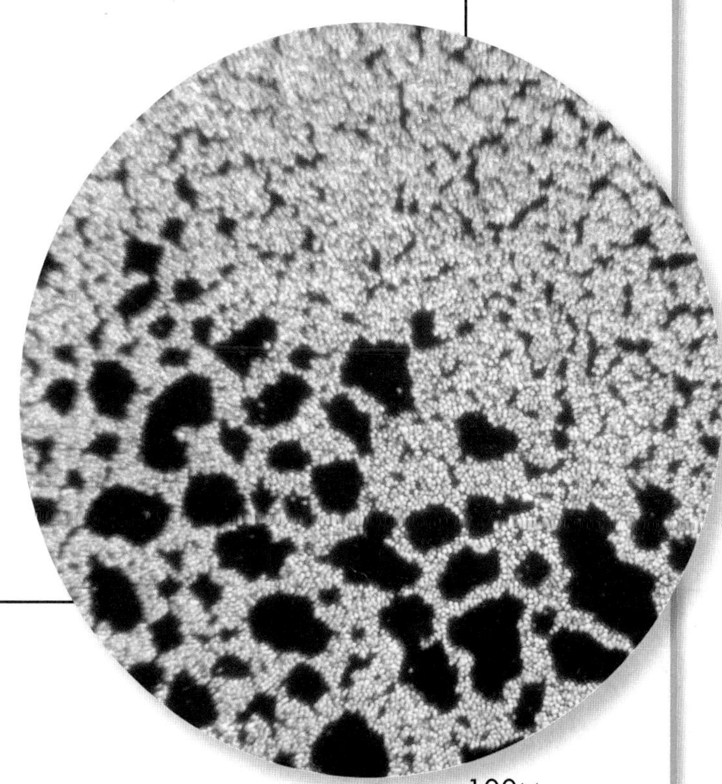

100×

Explain Your Results

1. Did the appearance of the yeast change? How?
2. Yeast are not **classified** in the plant kingdom or the animal kingdom. Why?
3. **Infer** Which kind of bread has yeast added to its dough, flat bread or loaf bread? Why do you think so?

Go Further

Does yeast need light to grow? Develop a plan to answer this or other questions you may have.

Math in Science

Classifying Figures

Living organisms are not the only things that are classified according to their characteristics. In math, you have learned about classifying geometric figures as plane figures or solid figures.

Plane figures can be classified as closed or not closed. Closed plane figures can be classified as symmetric or non-symmetric, polygons or not polygons. When polygons are classified by number of sides, the four-sided polygons are called quadrilaterals. The chart shows how quadrilaterals can be classified.

Quadrilaterals
trapezoid
Only one pair of parallel sides
parallelogram
Two pairs of opposite sides parallel and congruent
kite
No parallel sides Two pairs of congruent sides
rhombus
Parallelogram with all sides congruent
rectangle
Parallelogram with four right angles
square
Rectangle with all sides congruent

e Tools Take It to the Net sfsuccessnet.com

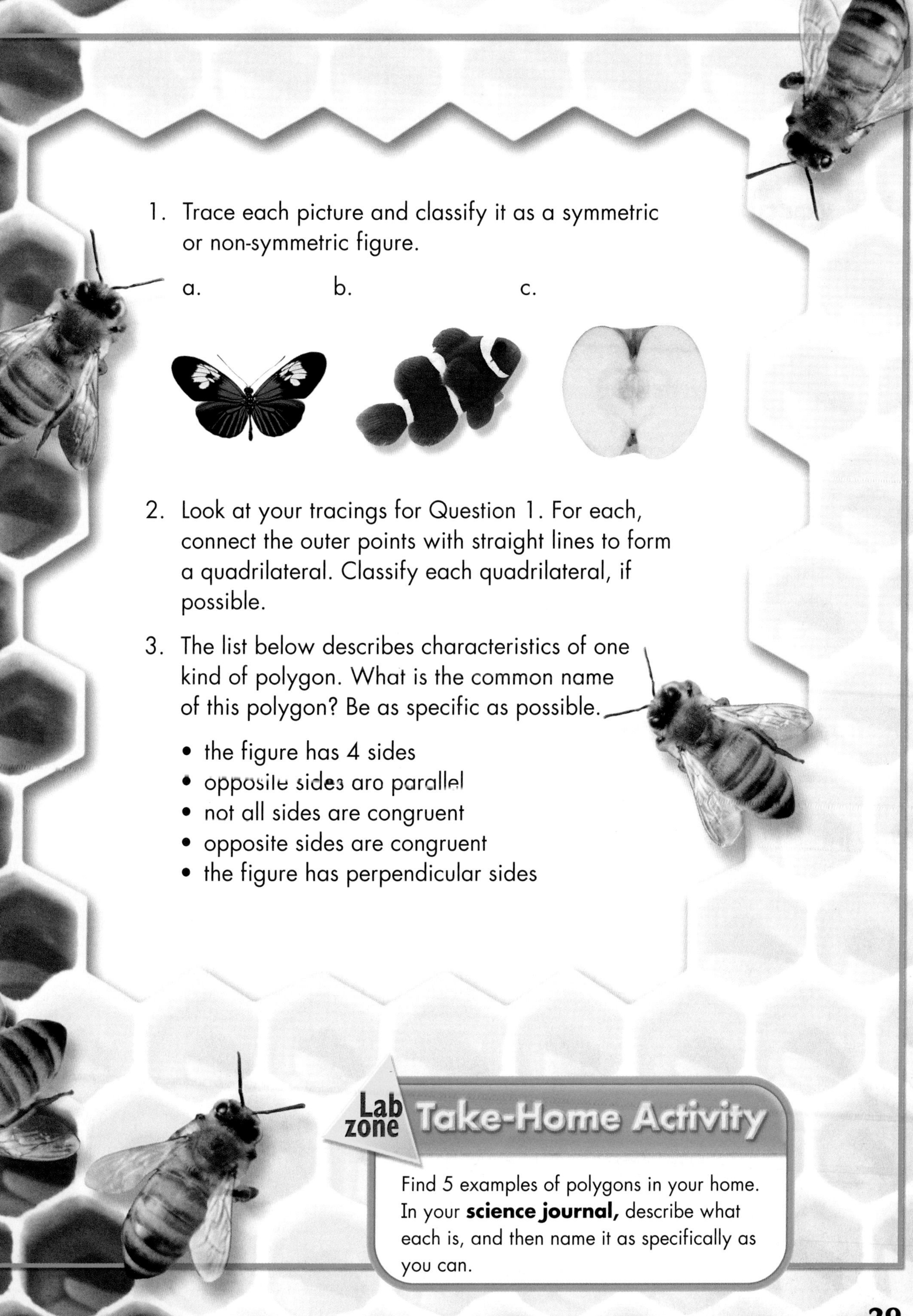

1. Trace each picture and classify it as a symmetric or non-symmetric figure.

   a. b. c.

2. Look at your tracings for Question 1. For each, connect the outer points with straight lines to form a quadrilateral. Classify each quadrilateral, if possible.

3. The list below describes characteristics of one kind of polygon. What is the common name of this polygon? Be as specific as possible.

   - the figure has 4 sides
   - opposite sides are parallel
   - not all sides are congruent
   - opposite sides are congruent
   - the figure has perpendicular sides

Lab zone Take-Home Activity

Find 5 examples of polygons in your home. In your **science journal,** describe what each is, and then name it as specifically as you can.

Chapter 1 Review and Test Prep

Use Vocabulary

class (p. 8)	**kingdom** (p. 8)
classify (p. 7)	**phylum** (p. 8)
invertebrate (p. 18)	**species** (p. 8)
	vertebrate (p. 10)

Choose the term from the list above that is described by each statement.

1. An animal without a backbone is a(n) _____.
2. The next level of classification below phylum is _____.
3. The highest level of the classification system is the _____ level.
4. A(n) _____ is the lowest level of classification.
5. A(n) _____ is the second highest level of classification.
6. An animal with a backbone is known as a(n) _____.
7. To _____ an organism means to put it into a group.

Explain Concepts

8. Explain three characteristics of all animals.
9. Explain why scientists use a classification system for organisms.
10. Suppose you had to combine the six kingdoms into just three groups. What would you name the three groups and what kingdoms would be in each?
11. Classify the following animals. Make a chart like the one below. Place each animal in its correct class in your chart.

    Clownfish
    Stellar's Jay
    Eastern Gray Squirrel
    Western Diamondback Rattlesnake
    Golden-Lined Frog

Class	**Animal**
Mammal	
Reptile	
Bird	
Amphibian	
Fish	

Process Skills

12. Infer What could you infer about the characteristics of an organism if you were given only the following information? It belongs to the kingdom of animals, phylum of vertebrates, and class of reptiles.

13. Classify A person tells you that he or she has discovered an organism that cannot be seen except through a powerful microscope. In which of these three kingdoms would such an organism most likely be classified: plants, animals, or protists? Explain.

Compare and Contrast

14. Make a graphic organizer like the one shown below. Tell how frogs and butterflies are different and how they are alike. In your answer, consider their body parts, their needs, and their life cycles.

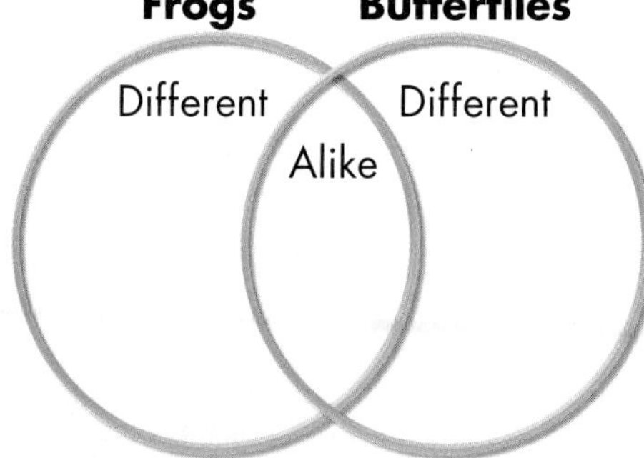
Frogs
Butterflies
Different
Different
Alike

Test Prep

Choose the letter that best answers the question.

15. Which of the following animals is an invertebrate?

Ⓐ rattlesnake Ⓑ woodpecker
Ⓒ worm Ⓓ bear

16. What are the levels of classification from largest to smallest?

Ⓕ phylum, kingdom, class, family, order, species, genus
Ⓖ kingdom, class, family, order, phylum, genus, species
Ⓗ family, order, phylum, class, species, genus, kingdom
Ⓘ kingdom, phylum, class, order, family, genus, species

17. Which type of plant is NOT vascular?

Ⓐ moss Ⓑ fern
Ⓒ conifer Ⓓ flowering plant

18. An animal has gills and jointed legs but no backbone. What is the most likely way to classify it?

Ⓕ reptile Ⓖ bird
Ⓗ arthropod Ⓘ fish

19. Explain why the answer you chose in Question 18 is best. For each answer you did not select, give a reason why it was not your choice.

20. Writing in Science **Descriptive**
Write a paragraph that names and describes six kingdoms of living things.

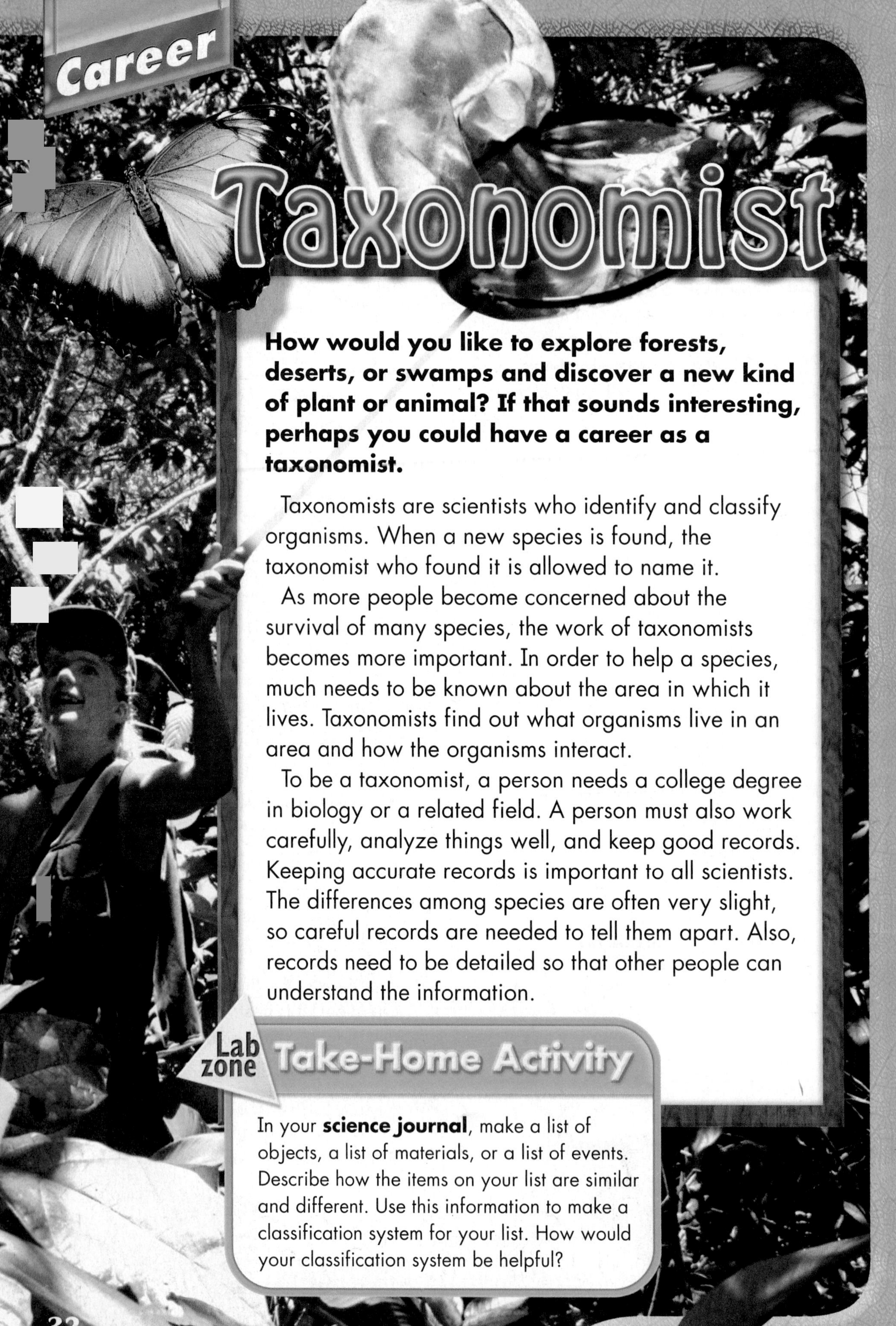
Career

Taxonomist

How would you like to explore forests, deserts, or swamps and discover a new kind of plant or animal? If that sounds interesting, perhaps you could have a career as a taxonomist.

Taxonomists are scientists who identify and classify organisms. When a new species is found, the taxonomist who found it is allowed to name it.

As more people become concerned about the survival of many species, the work of taxonomists becomes more important. In order to help a species, much needs to be known about the area in which it lives. Taxonomists find out what organisms live in an area and how the organisms interact.

To be a taxonomist, a person needs a college degree in biology or a related field. A person must also work carefully, analyze things well, and keep good records. Keeping accurate records is important to all scientists. The differences among species are often very slight, so careful records are needed to tell them apart. Also, records need to be detailed so that other people can understand the information.

Lab zone Take-Home Activity

In your **science journal**, make a list of objects, a list of materials, or a list of events. Describe how the items on your list are similar and different. Use this information to make a classification system for your list. How would your classification system be helpful?

EC NTL 10 9 8 7

Discovery Channel School
Student DVD
Discovery
SCHOOL

online
Student Edition
sfsuccessnet.com

You Will Discover

- the parts of cells.
- how cells form tissues and organs.
- how organs work together.

Chapter 2

Cells to Systems

Build Background

What do cells have to do with our lives?

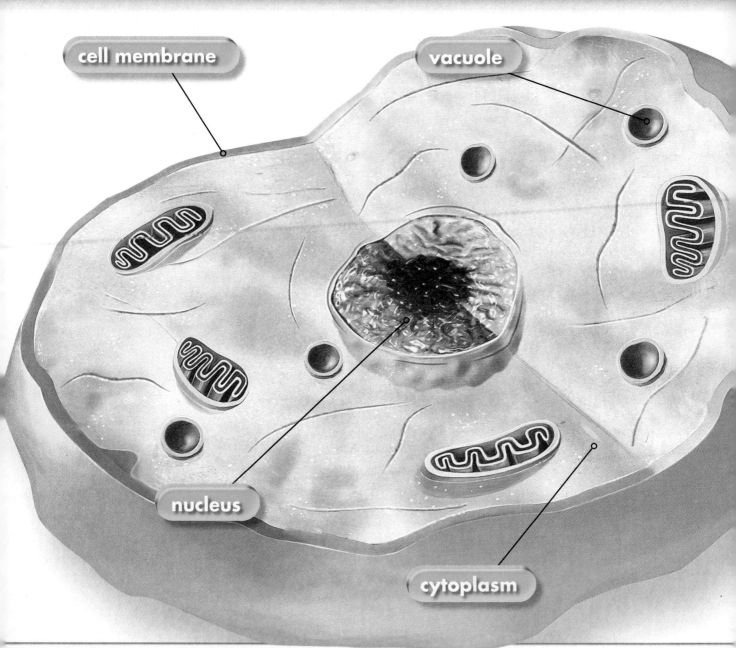

cell membrane

vacuole

nucleus

cytoplasm

tissue

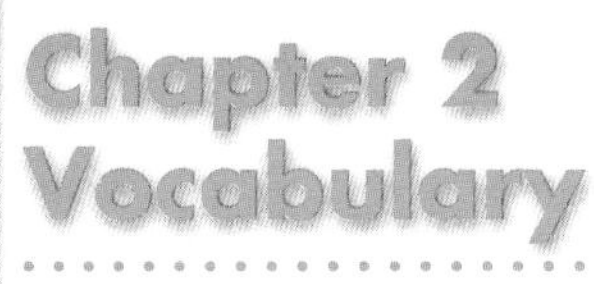
Chapter 2
Vocabulary

cell membrane page 40

nucleus page 40

cell wall page 40

chloroplast page 40

cytoplasm page 41

vacuole page 41

tissue page 44

organ page 44

organ system page 46

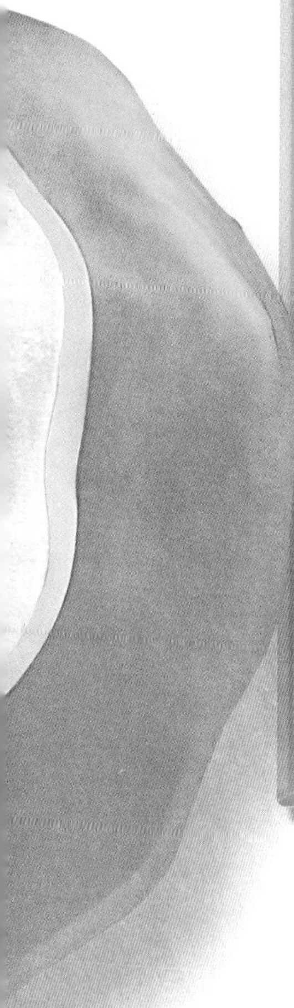

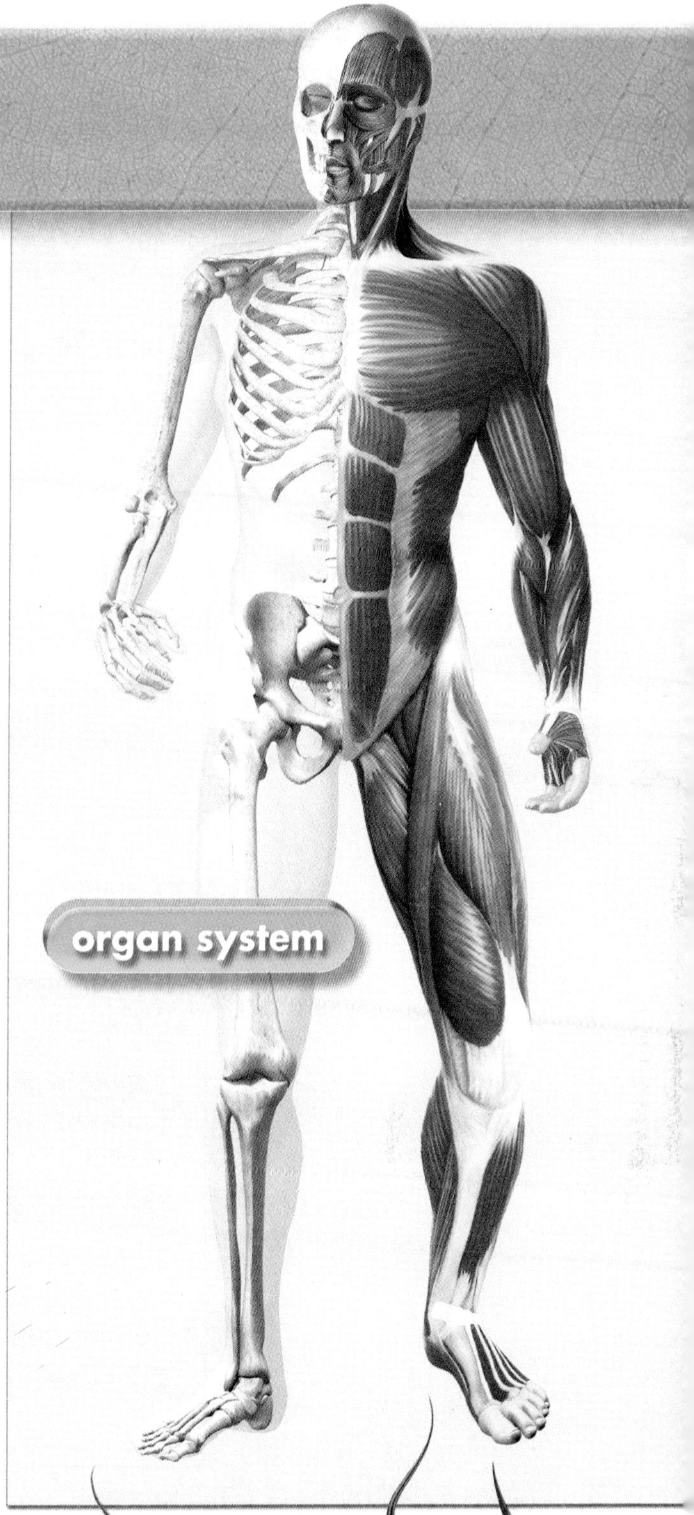

organ system

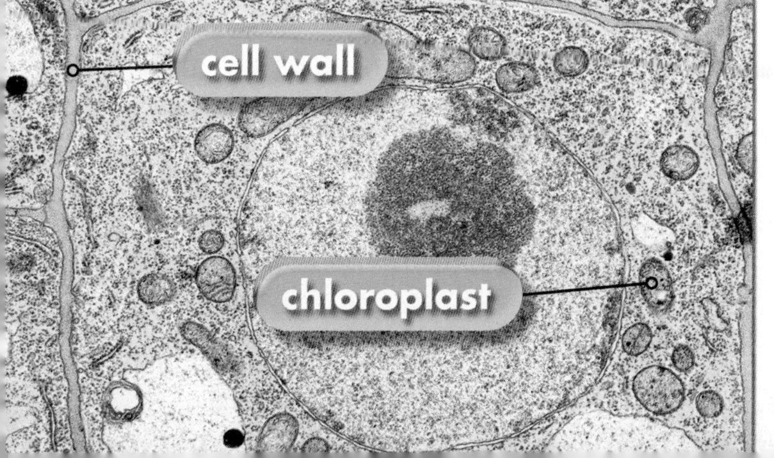
cell wall
chloroplast

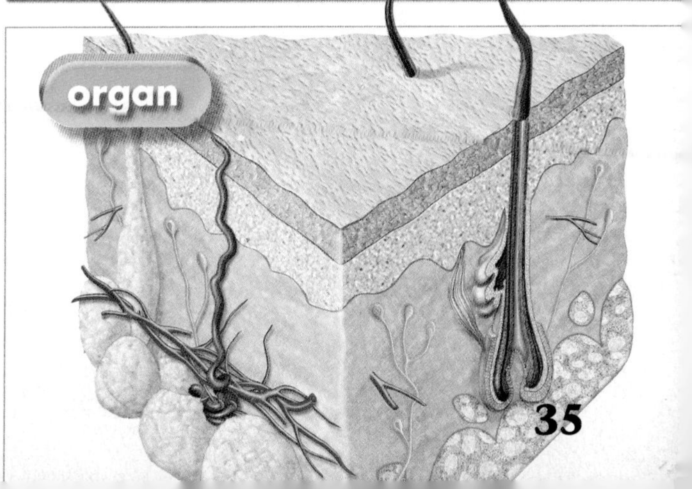

organ

Lab zone

Directed Inquiry

Explore What do yeast cells need to grow?

Materials

3 cups

sugar

yeast

warm water

spoon

masking tape

What to Do

1. Add the materials to the cups.

Label the contents of each cup.

cup 1
yeast, water, sugar

cup 2
yeast, sugar

cup 3
yeast, water

$\frac{1}{2}$ spoonful yeast
4 spoonfuls warm water
1 spoonful sugar

$\frac{1}{2}$ spoonful yeast
1 spoonful sugar

$\frac{1}{2}$ spoonful yeast
4 spoonfuls warm water

2. Set the cups in a warm place.
Observe every 15 minutes for 1 hour.

Process Skills

You used your **observations** of yeast in cups with different materials to **infer** what yeast cells need to grow.

Explain Your Results

1. **Observe** What happened to the contents of each cup?
2. **Infer** What materials are needed for yeast cells to grow?

More Lab zone Activities Take It to the Net sfsuccessnet.com

How to Read Science

Reading Skills

TARGET SKILL

Draw Conclusions

- A conclusion is a decision you reach after you think about facts and details.
- Sometimes writers present facts and details and then **draw conclusions** for the reader. Sometimes readers must **infer** or draw their own conclusions based on the facts.
- Read the science article. Some facts and details are highlighted in yellow. The conclusion is highlighted in blue.

Science Article

Types of Blood Cells

Blood contains both red and white blood cells. Both types are produced inside the long bones. Red blood cells carry oxygen from the lungs to all parts of the body. White blood cells protect the body by "eating" germs or by making chemicals that kill germs. Red and white blood cells are important parts of the circulatory system.

Apply It!

Make a graphic organizer like the one shown. Write the **observations** and facts and the conclusion from the article in the correct boxes. See what else you can **infer.** Add it to the graphic organizer.

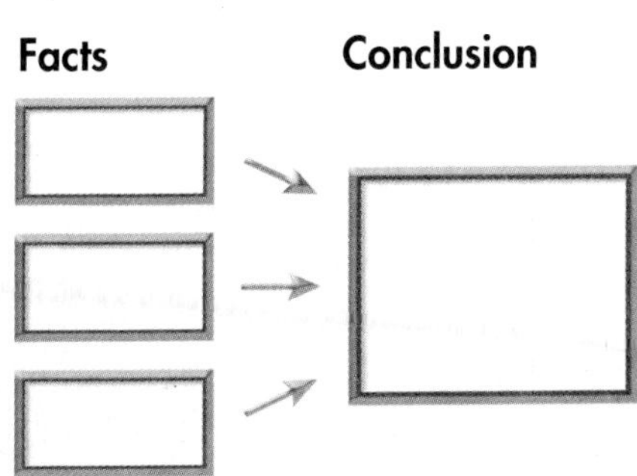
Facts
Conclusion

You Are There!

At this very moment, up to 100 trillion living things are forming, doing jobs, and dying off inside you. Hey, it's a busy place in there! What exactly are these things, and more importantly, what are they doing inside you?

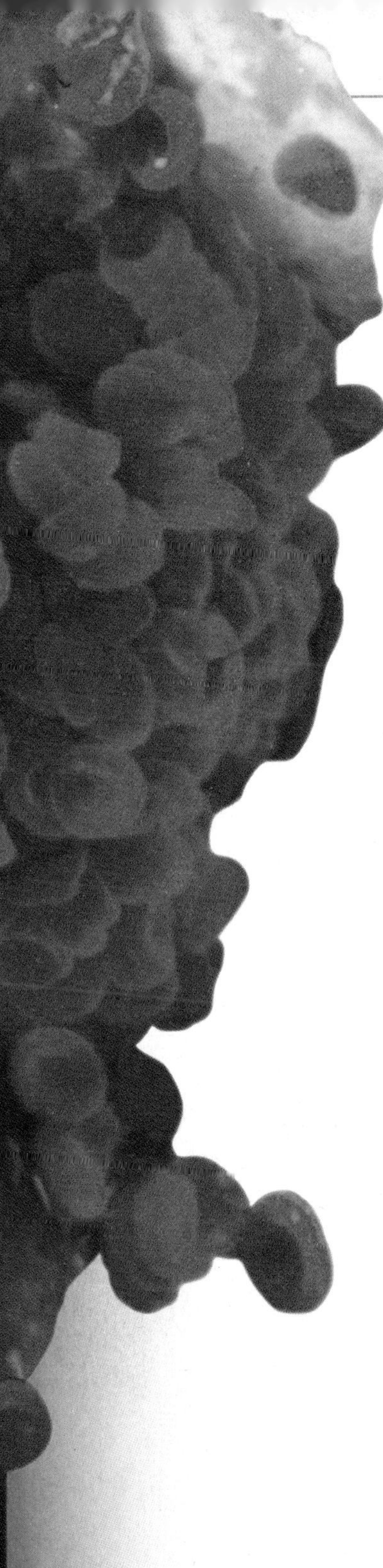

Lesson 1

What is inside a cell?

Cells are the smallest living parts of any living thing. Cells have the same needs as any organism and carry out many of the same activities. Cells contain smaller parts, each with a specialized job.

Cells and Their Functions

Of all your body parts, the smallest part that is considered alive is a cell. Cells are the basic building blocks that make up all living things. The tiniest organisms are only single cells. Multicellular organisms, on the other hand, have many cells, maybe trillions. Most cells are too tiny to be seen by the eye alone. A single drop of blood would hold millions of red blood cells like the ones pictured here. You definitely need a microscope to see them.

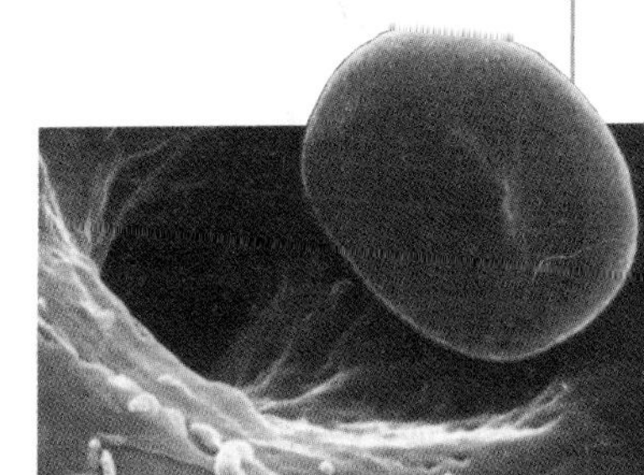

This red blood cell is magnified about 3,000 times.

Cells in most living things have the same needs for survival as you do. In other words, cells do many of the things you do each day to stay alive. Cells must take in food and get rid of wastes. Materials in food are used by the cell to grow and to repair wounds. While very few cells move around, all cells have parts that move inside them. Cells sense and respond to changes in their surroundings. They often communicate and cooperate with other cells.

All cells need to get energy. Most cells get energy through cellular respiration. Cellular respiration is the taking in of oxygen and food, such as sugar, in order to get energy. In this process, carbon dioxide and water are produced. Different cells need different amounts of energy for all the things that they do to survive, including growing, moving, and dividing to make new cells.

1. √ **Checkpoint** What is the most basic unit of living things?
2. **Draw Conclusions** Suppose you saw a small organism move across your desk. Would you infer that this organism was multicellular or a single cell?

The Parts of Cells

A cell is an amazing package made of a cell membrane, a nucleus, and many other structures. Most of the things your body does are really done inside cells. For example, you grow when your cells grow larger and divide. Your arm moves because small fibers are moving inside muscle cells.

All cells have some of the same parts, and many parts have similar jobs. Cells have the same needs as your whole body has. For example, your body needs an outside covering of skin, a control system of nerves, a support system of bones, and places to store food and wastes in the digestive system. Some cell parts can be compared to these larger structures in your body. Only a few of the parts of an animal cell are pictured here.

The **cell membrane** surrounds a cell, holding the parts of the cell together. It allows needed materials, such as sugar, water, and oxygen, to enter the cell. It allows certain other materials, such as carbon dioxide and other waste products, to exit.

The **nucleus** is the part of the cell that contains chromosomes. Chromosomes are made of materials including a chemical called DNA (deoxyribonucleic acid). DNA is a chemical shaped like a twisted ladder. Chromosomes carry the instructions for the cell to do its jobs. By telling every cell how to do its jobs, chromosomes control how the whole body grows and changes.

Every chromosome has small sections of DNA called genes. Genes are made of DNA. Each gene carries a single unit of information. Almost every cell in your body has the same set of thousands of genes. Heredity is the process of passing these genes from one generation to the next.

The cell membrane can be compared to your skin because both are outside surfaces.

Plant Cells

Plant cells have all the parts seen in the animal cell. Plant cells also have a few parts not found in animal cells.

A tough cell wall surrounds the cell membrane. The cell wall is stiff, unlike the thin cell membrane. Cell walls give plant cells extra support and protection.

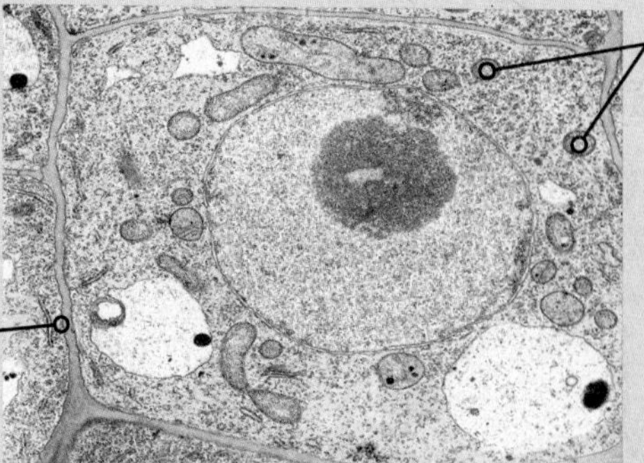

This plant cell is magnified about 6,000 times.

Chloroplasts use the energy in sunlight to turn water and carbon dioxide into oxygen and sugar. Plant cells use oxygen and sugar for respiration. Chloroplasts give plants their green color.

The Size of Cells

Like most things, cells have a limit as to how big or small they can be. They cannot be too small, or they will not have room for all their parts. They cannot be too big, or oxygen and other materials will not be able to reach the middle of the cell fast enough to keep the cell alive. Also, wastes must be able to leave.

Almost every cell nucleus in your body has 46 chromosomes. Each chromosome has hundreds of sections called genes.

Vacuoles can sometimes act like a stomach, storing and breaking down material. In plants, vacuoles may store water.

Mitochondria are the cell's power producers. Mitochondria combine oxygen and food to produce energy in the process of cellular respiration.

Cytoplasm is all the material of the cell between the cell membrane and the nucleus.

✓ Lesson Checkpoint

1. Describe why cells have limits as to how big or small they can be.
2. List five parts of all cells and their jobs.
3. 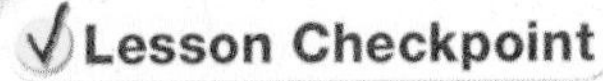 **Art in Science** Compare and contrast plant and animal cells by drawing pictures or a Venn diagram that shows what parts plant cells have and what parts animal cells have.

Lesson 2

How do cells work together?

Different types of cells are found throughout the body. Each cell's specialized shape and structures help it perform specialized jobs. Groups of similar cells make up tissues, and groupings of tissues make up organs.

Types of Cells and Their Work

Just as footballs, basketballs, and hockey pucks all have different shapes and different purposes, so do different cells. Your body has about 200 different kinds of cells. A cell's shape is often specialized to fit its job. Also, many cells often have special structures that help them in their work.

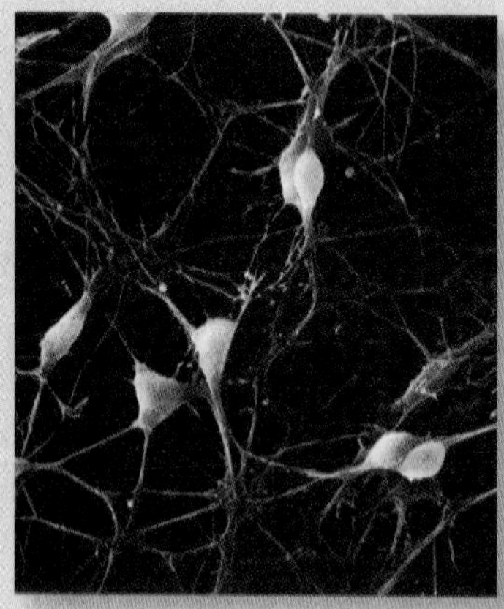

Branching Cells
The shape of nerve cells makes them great for communicating signals between the brain and the rest of the body. Their great length helps these signals reach the brain quickly. A nerve cell's branching structure can connect several parts of the body at once.

Flat Cells
Flat cells, such as skin cells, often join or overlap to cover a surface. They work something like the shingles on a building's roof. Your skin is built of many layers of flat cells, making it both strong and flexible. Flat cells are found lining many different parts of the body. For example, they line the surfaces of the mouth and the stomach.

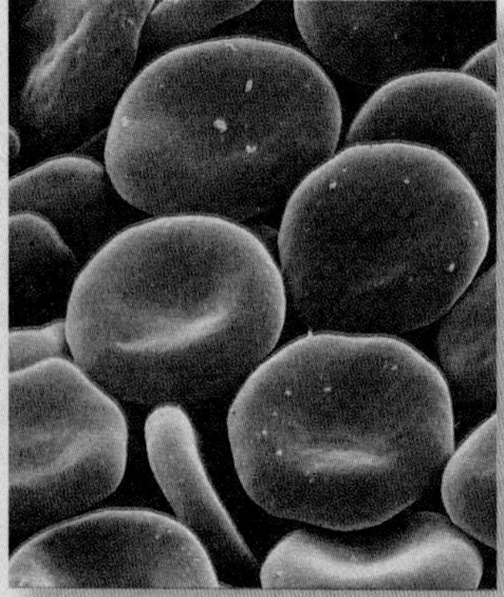

Round Cells
Red blood cells are rounded discs with two big dimples. Their job is to carry oxygen to all your cells. The smooth shape of red blood cells helps these cells move easily through blood vessels. This shape gives extra surface area for picking up and carrying oxygen.

The cells in the three pictures above are magnified many thousands of times.

Special Cell Structure

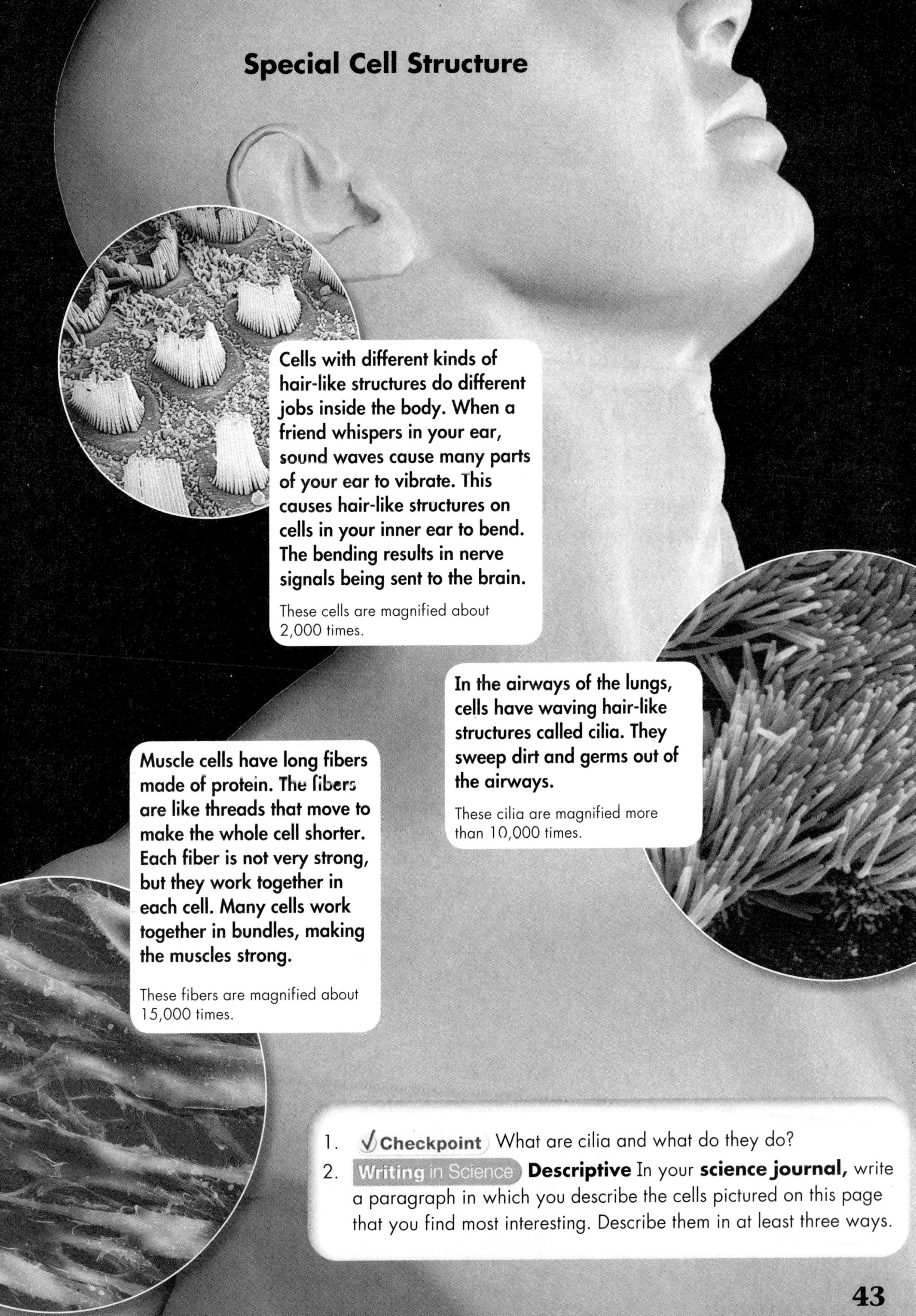

Cells with different kinds of hair-like structures do different jobs inside the body. When a friend whispers in your ear, sound waves cause many parts of your ear to vibrate. This causes hair-like structures on cells in your inner ear to bend. The bending results in nerve signals being sent to the brain.

These cells are magnified about 2,000 times.

In the airways of the lungs, cells have waving hair-like structures called cilia. They sweep dirt and germs out of the airways.

These cilia are magnified more than 10,000 times.

Muscle cells have long fibers made of protein. The fibers are like threads that move to make the whole cell shorter. Each fiber is not very strong, but they work together in each cell. Many cells work together in bundles, making the muscles strong.

These fibers are magnified about 15,000 times.

1. ✓ **Checkpoint** What are cilia and what do they do?
2. **Writing in Science** **Descriptive** In your **science journal,** write a paragraph in which you describe the cells pictured on this page that you find most interesting. Describe them in at least three ways.

Cells Form Tissues

You may have noticed that teamwork can be a great way to get work done. Cells rarely work by themselves and often work in tissues. A **tissue** is a group of the same kind of cells working together doing the same job. Muscle cells grouped in bundles make up muscle tissue. Bone cells grouped together make up bone tissue. Groups of nerve cells together make up nerve tissue.

Tissues Form Organs

Tissues join with other types of tissues to form organs. An **organ** is a grouping of different tissues combined together into one structure. These tissues work together to perform a main job in the body. Your heart, eyes, ears, and stomach are all examples of organs in your body. The largest organ you have is your skin. Many animals have tissues and organs similar to yours. Plants have tissues and organs too. Plant organs include stems, roots, leaves, and flowers.

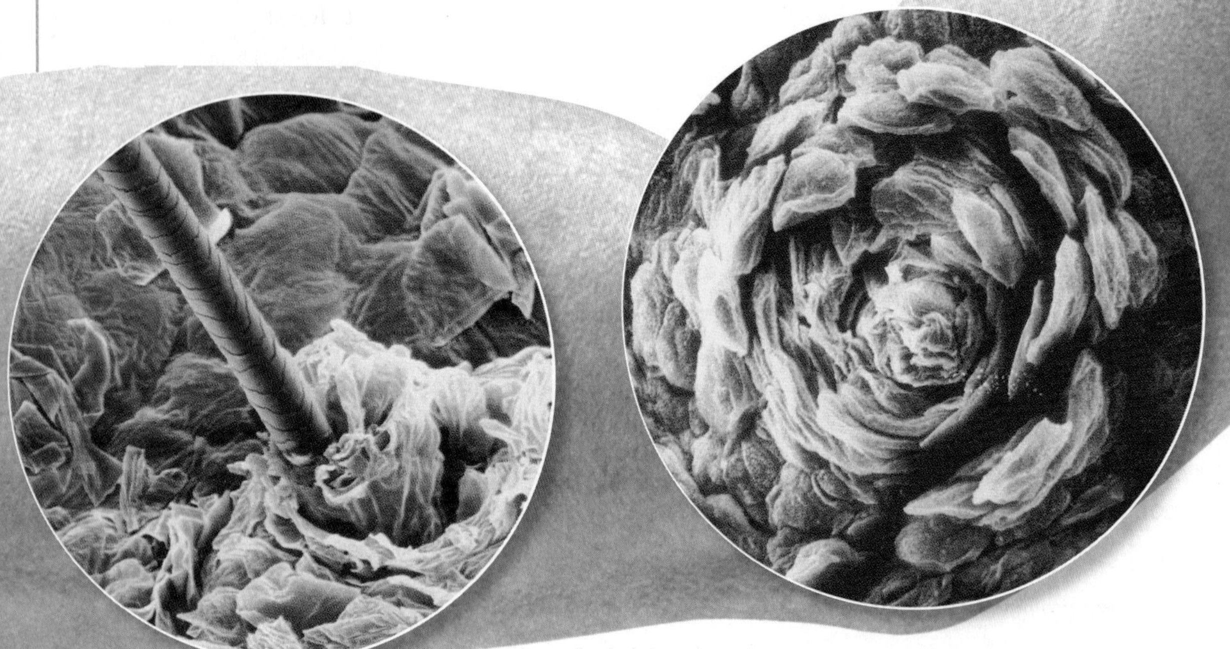

Hair follicle
Hair is a tissue in the organ called skin. Hair acts as a cushion to protect your skin. It also holds warm air next to your body. Hair forms in cells at the bottom of hair follicles. As new cells are forming, older ones are pushed outward. By the time you see a hair growing out of the skin, it is dead tissue.

Sweat gland pore
Sweat glands are tissues in your skin. Sweat leaves the gland through pores such as this one. When sweat evaporates from the skin, it carries heat away from the body. Sweat also can carry some waste products from cells.

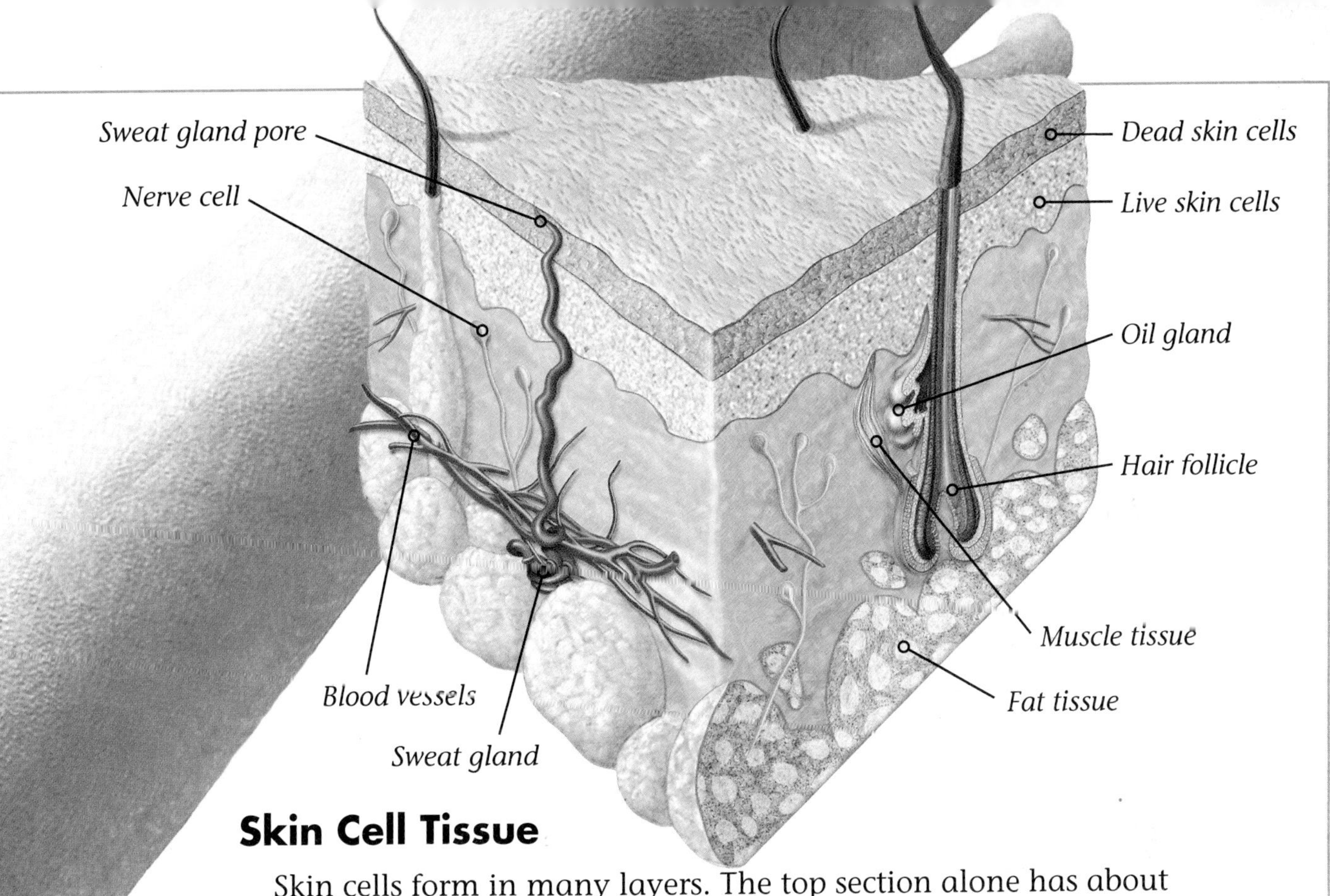
Sweat gland pore
Nerve cell
Dead skin cells
Live skin cells
Oil gland
Hair follicle
Muscle tissue
Fat tissue
Blood vessels
Sweat gland

Skin Cell Tissue

Skin cells form in many layers. The top section alone has about 25 layers of skin cells. When new cells form in the bottom layers, they push the other cells outward and away from any blood supply. By the time they are pushed to the outside surface, the cells are dead. It takes about one month for skin cells to get pushed to the surface. Dead cells at the outside surface simply fall off.

Other Tissues in the Skin

Your skin is more than just layers of flat skin cells. Skin has many tissues working together to do many jobs. Skin tissue protects the inside of your body, keeps out germs, and prevents too much water from leaving the body. Nerve tissue helps you sense touch, pressure, and temperature. Blood vessels carry food and oxygen to cells. Oil glands keep the skin soft. When you feel cold, muscle tissue pulls the hair upright, causing goosebumps. Upright hairs help you stay warmer by trapping warm air next to the skin.

√ Lesson Checkpoint

1. How does a nerve cell's shape and structure help it do its job?
2. How is a tissue like a team?
3. **Draw Conclusions** Why is it an advantage to have dead cells on the surface of the body?

Lesson 3

How do organs work together?

Organs work together in organ systems to carry out major life functions. Organ systems also interact with each other.

Organ Systems

In dogs, cats, fish, ferns, and you, many cells work together in tissues. Many tissues work together in organs. Organs work together in groups too. An **organ system** is a group of organs and tissues that work together to carry out a life process. For instance, the mouth, stomach, intestines, and other organs work together to digest food.

Bones Form a System

Each of your bones is an organ. Together, about 200 bones make up the skeletal system. This organ system has several important jobs. It provides the body with a strong support system. Imagine what life would be like if you did not have bones to help you stand or sit up. You would move like wiggling worms! Another job of the skeletal system is to protect internal organs. The skull is made of several bones that work together to protect the brain. The rib cage protects your lungs and heart. Bones have other jobs too.

Bones Work Together
This is a cut-away view of where the bone in your leg meets the bone in your hip.

Muscles Work as a System

Muscles are organs that work together to move your body. You have about 640 muscles that you control. When you run or dance, your brain tells dozens of these muscles how to work together. In other cases, muscles work by themselves without your thinking. Have you ever shivered in cold weather? Shivering can help you survive the cold. When you shiver, many muscles are working together to warm the body. You do not have to think about shivering for it to happen.

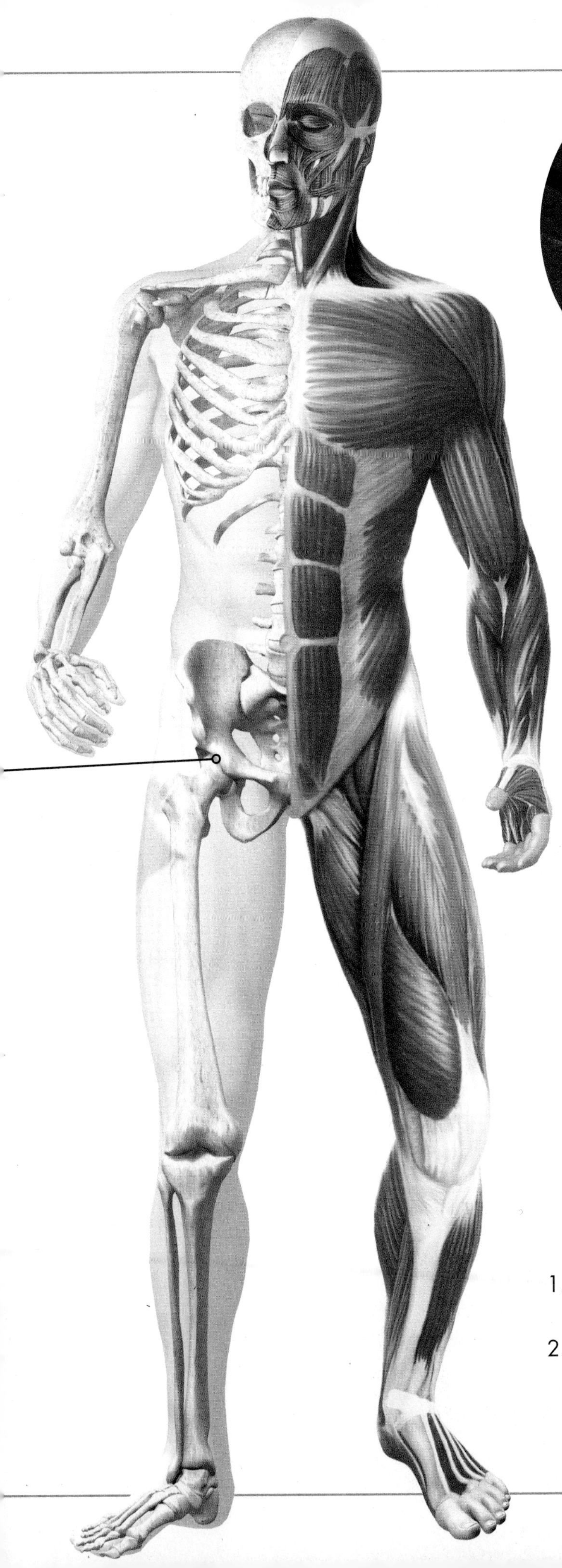

Muscles Work Together

Long, thin muscle cells work in bundles for increased strength. Squeeze your fist tight. Several muscles work together to make your fingers form a fist. Can you feel them get tight in your lower arm? It also takes several muscles to smile.

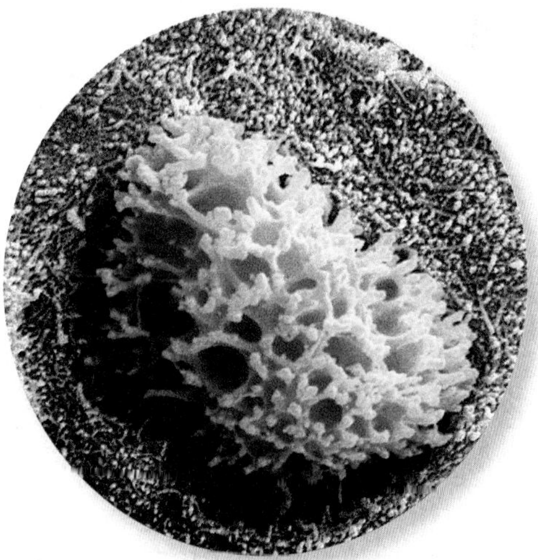

Bone Cells

Between the bone cells is a hard material that has lots of calcium. This material makes bones hard. Other parts of the body, like muscles, also use calcium from blood to do their work. Bones store calcium until the level of calcium in the blood is low.

1. **Checkpoint** How many bones make up the skeletal system?
2. **Math in Science** Muscles make up about four tenths of a man's body mass. What would be the muscle mass of a man whose body mass is 60 kg?

Organ Systems Work Together

One of the biggest jobs of your muscle and skeletal systems is to work together to move your body. Many muscles work in pairs to move bones.

Hold out your arm straight in front of you, and then bend your elbow. While you do this, the triceps muscle on the bottom of your arm relaxes and stretches. At the same time, the biceps muscle on top of your upper arm contracts or shortens. This makes the end of the muscle pull on the bone of your forearm to bend your elbow.

The opposite happens when you straighten your elbow. In this case, the triceps muscle on the back of your upper arm contracts. The biceps muscle on the top of the arm relaxes.

Muscles only pull on bones. They never push. That is why two or more muscles must work together to move each bone in opposite directions.

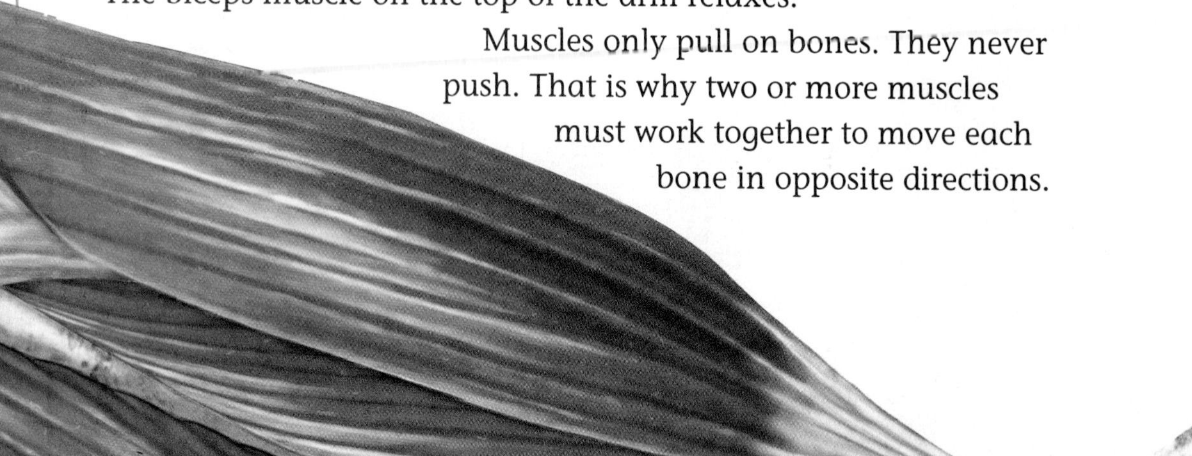

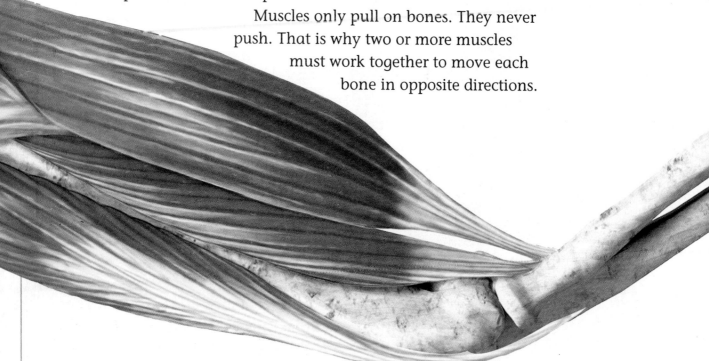

Muscles Flex and Extend

Your biceps muscles pull your arms toward your shoulders. Your triceps muscles pull in the other direction. They straighten your arm. Other muscles work in pairs to rotate your arm and to bend your wrists.

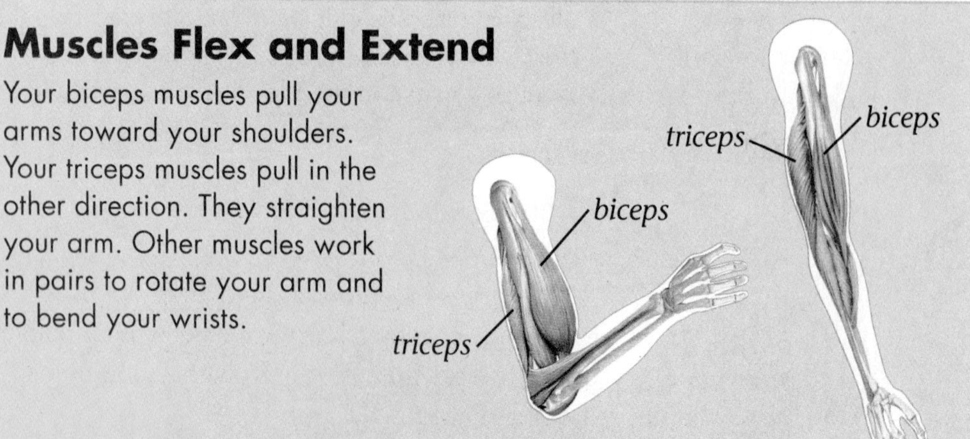
biceps
triceps
triceps
biceps

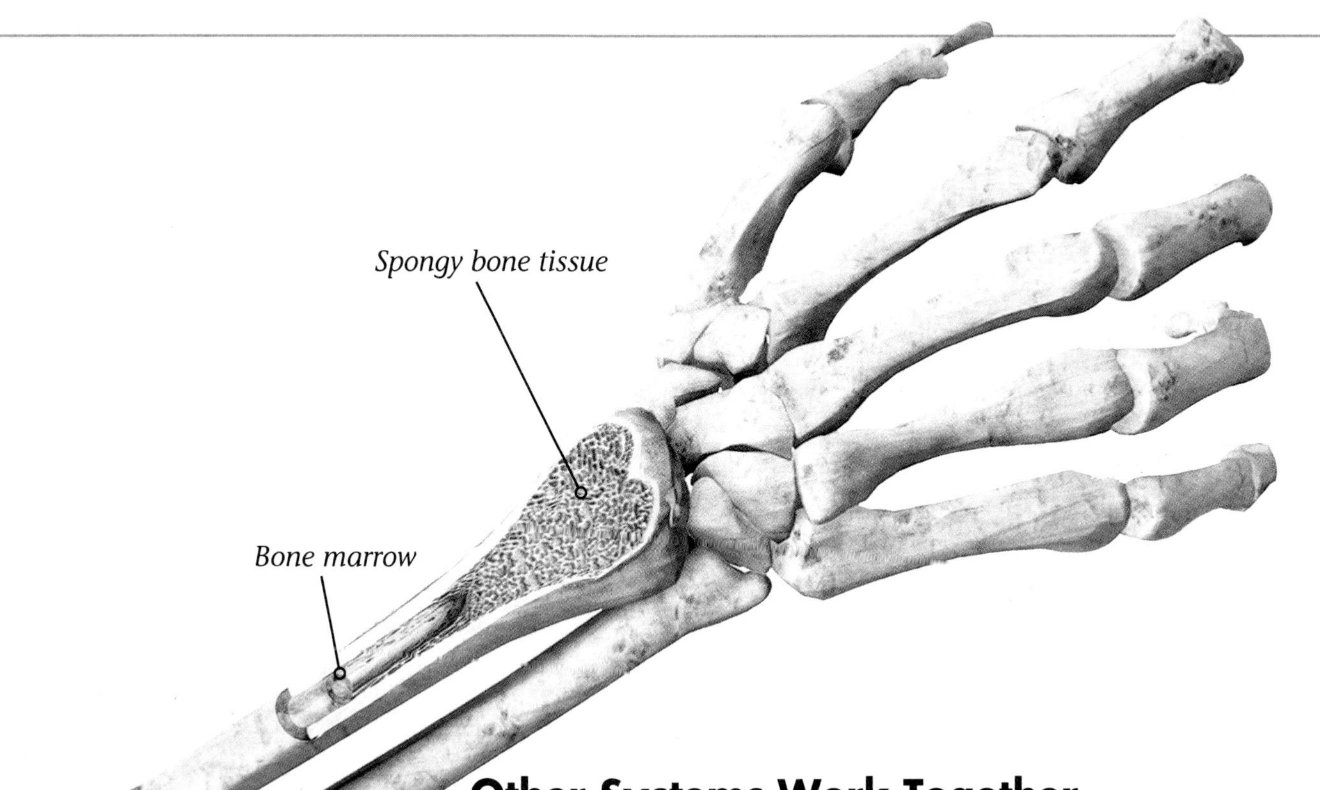
Spongy bone tissue
Bone marrow

Other Systems Work Together

Many organ systems work together in many ways to make a complex organism. For example, your nervous system controls how your muscles move your bones. Nerves carry electrical signals from your brain and spinal cord to your muscles. Without nerves you would never move a muscle.

Organ systems often work so closely together that some organs could be put into two organ systems. For example, muscles are not just connected to bones. Some of the strongest muscles in your body make up your heart. These muscles are working every minute of every day of your life to push blood through the system of blood vessels. Muscles also squeeze food through the digestive system.

Your skeletal system is very important to the circulatory system. The red and white blood cells in your body are made in bone marrow. Bone marrow is a soft material that fills cavities and spongy bone tissue inside some bones.

√ Lesson Checkpoint

1. List some organ systems and describe their jobs.
2. How do muscles work in pairs to move a bone?
3. Writing in Science **Descriptive** In your **science journal,** write a paragraph that describes how different structures in organ systems work together to help us walk.

Lab zone **Guided Inquiry**

Investigate How can you make a model arm?

Muscles help you move. Your biceps and triceps are a pair of muscles that help you bend your arm at the elbow. When you contract your biceps, your arm bends. To straighten your arm, you contract your triceps.

Materials

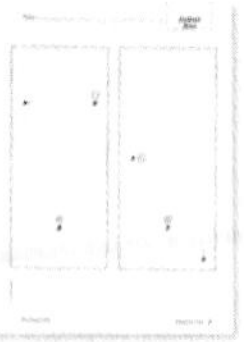

Model Arm Pattern

cardboard

hole punch (optional)

fastener

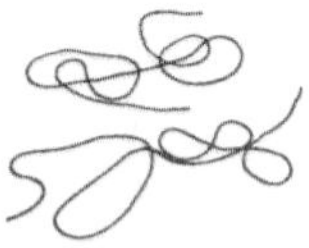

yarn

What to Do

1. Follow the diagram on the Model Arm Pattern to make a **model** arm. Make 6 holes in the cardboard. Use a fastener to hold the 2 pieces of cardboard together.

2. Thread yarn through the other holes. Tie 2 knots.

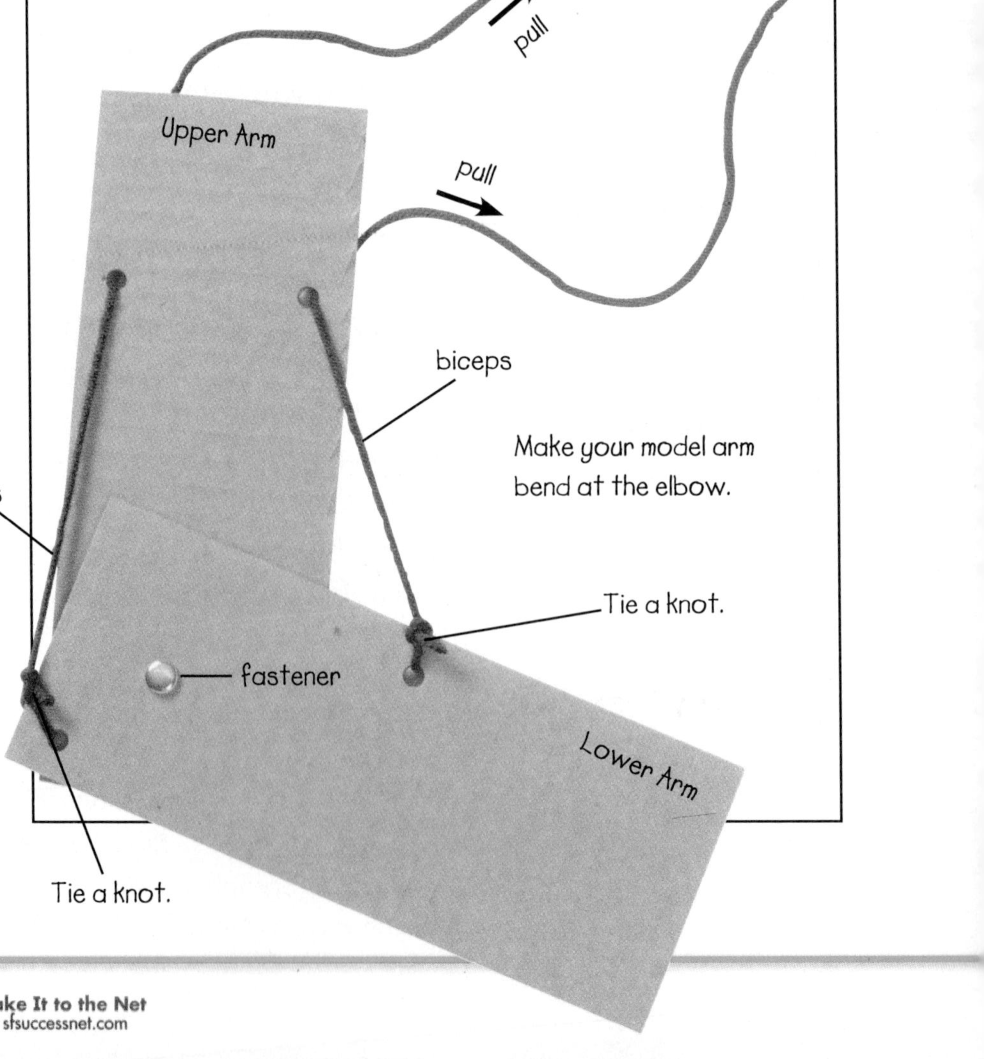

Upper Arm
pull
pull
biceps
Make your model arm bend at the elbow.
triceps
Tie a knot.
fastener
Lower Arm
Tie a knot.

Process Skills

When you use cardboard and yarn to show how an arm moves, you **make a model** of an arm.

More Lab zone Activities Take It to the Net sfsuccessnet.com

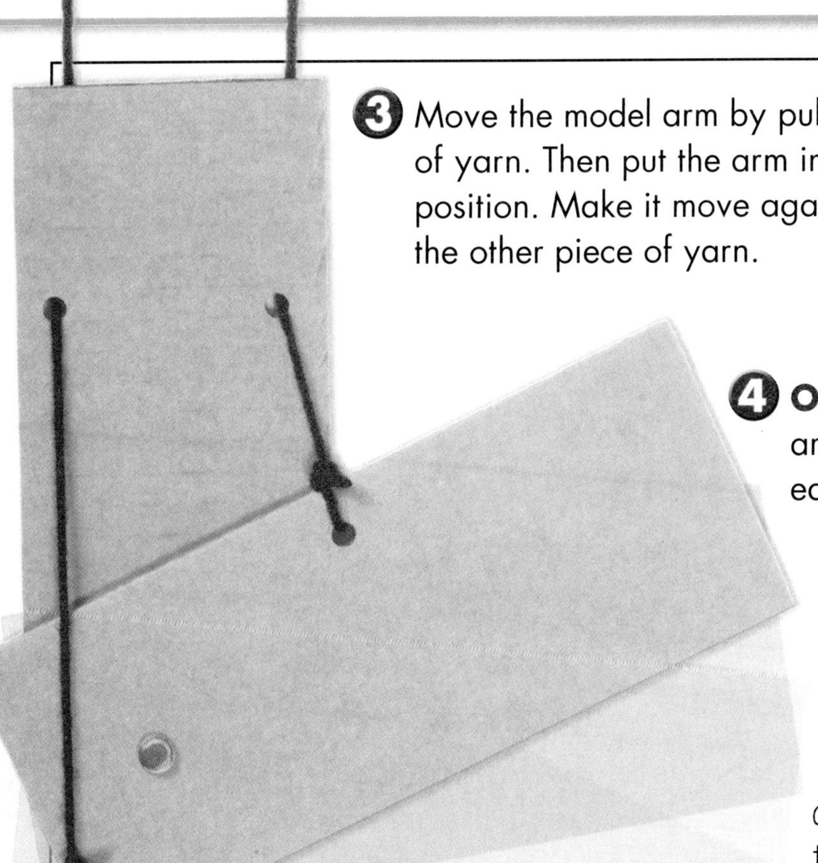

3. Move the model arm by pulling one piece of yarn. Then put the arm in its original bent position. Make it move again by pulling on the other piece of yarn.

4. **Observe** how the model arm moves when you pull each string.

Compare your model to your arm.

5. Record what you **observe**.

String Pulled	How the Model Arm Moved
Biceps string pulled	
Triceps string pulled	

Explain Your Results

1. What happens in your **model** when you pull each piece of yarn?
2. How are your model and a real arm alike and different?

Go Further

How can you make a model that shows how the muscular and skeletal systems work together in the leg? Make a plan to find out.

Math in Science

Large Numbers of Small Cells

The number of cells in the human body has been estimated to be in the trillions! It would take about 35,000 red blood cells to fill an area of 0.035 cm². That's about half the space inside a printed zero on this page.

You can think of one trillion as one thousand billion, or one million million. In standard form, one trillion is written as 1,000,000,000,000.

hundred trillions	ten trillions	trillions	hundred billions	ten billions	billions	hundred millions	ten millions	millions	hundred thousands	ten thousands	thousands	hundreds	tens	ones	tenths	hundredths	thousandths
		1	0	0	0	0	0	0	0	0	0	0	0	0.	0	0	0
										3	5	0	0	0.	0	0	0
														0.	0	3	5

eTools Take It to the Net sfsuccessnet.com

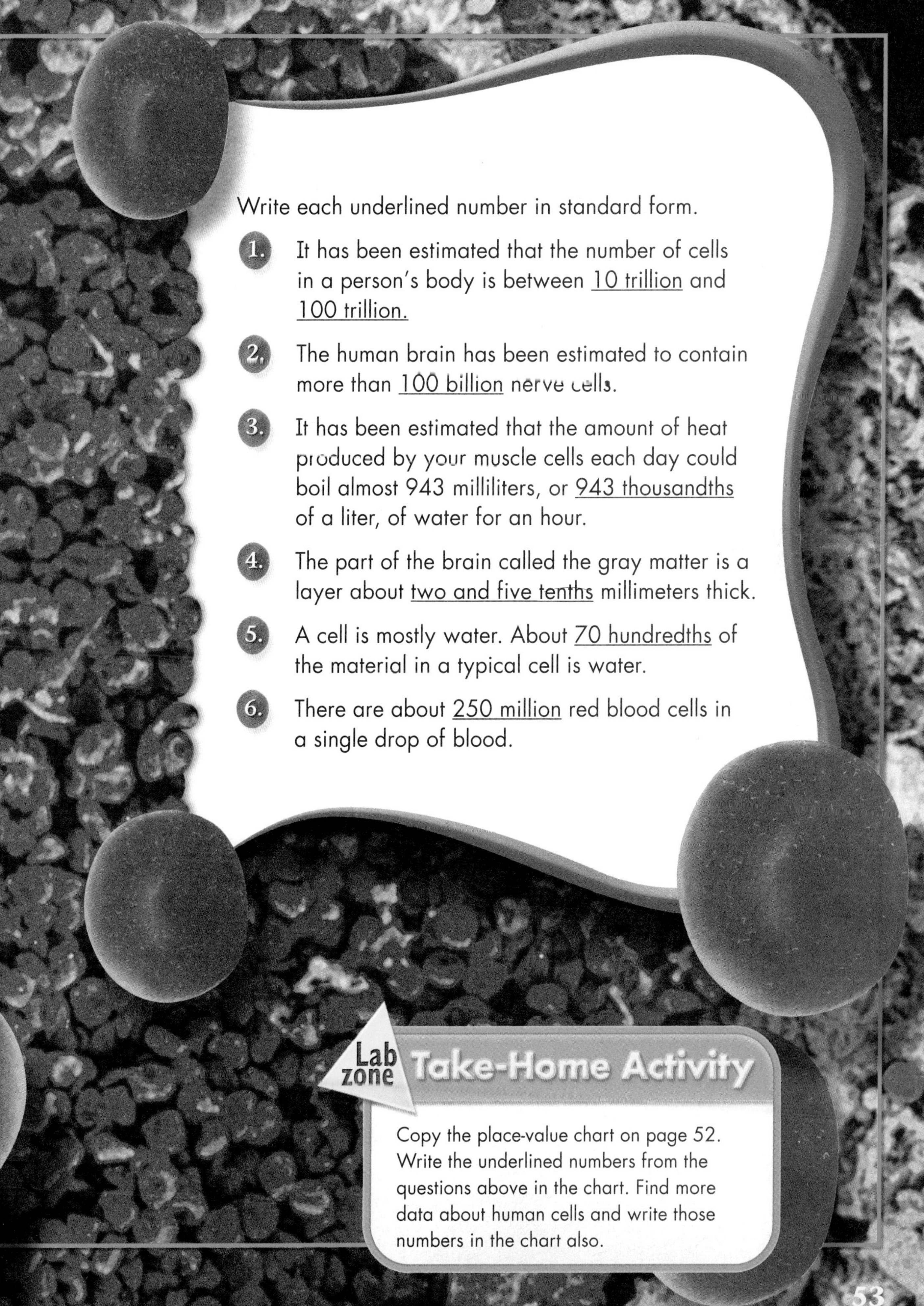

Write each underlined number in standard form.

1. It has been estimated that the number of cells in a person's body is between 10 trillion and 100 trillion.
2. The human brain has been estimated to contain more than 100 billion nerve cells.
3. It has been estimated that the amount of heat produced by your muscle cells each day could boil almost 943 milliliters, or 943 thousandths of a liter, of water for an hour.
4. The part of the brain called the gray matter is a layer about two and five tenths millimeters thick.
5. A cell is mostly water. About 70 hundredths of the material in a typical cell is water.
6. There are about 250 million red blood cells in a single drop of blood.

Lab zone Take-Home Activity

Copy the place-value chart on page 52. Write the underlined numbers from the questions above in the chart. Find more data about human cells and write those numbers in the chart also.

Chapter 2 Review and Test Prep

Use Vocabulary

cell membrane (p. 40)	**organ** (p. 44)
cell wall (p. 40)	**organ system** (p. 46)
chloroplast (p. 40)	**tissue** (p. 44)
cytoplasm (p. 41)	**vacuole** (p. 41)
nucleus (p. 40)	

Use the term from the list above that best completes each sentence.

1. Animal cells are surrounded by a(n) _____.
2. Organs work together in a(n) _____.
3. A(n) _____ stores food or water in a cell.
4. Tissues work together in a(n) _____.
5. A(n) _____ uses sunlight to produce oxygen and food in a plant cell.
6. Similar cells working together make up a(n) _____.
7. A cell's _____ stores DNA.
8. A cell's _____ is the material between the nucleus and the cell membrane.
9. The tough outer covering of a plant cell is its _____.

Explain Concepts

10. Explain what cellular respiration is and where it occurs in a cell.
11. Explain how the shapes of these cells are related to their job. Give more examples of cell shapes and describe the jobs of the cells.

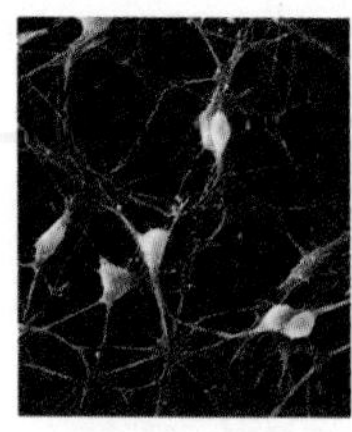
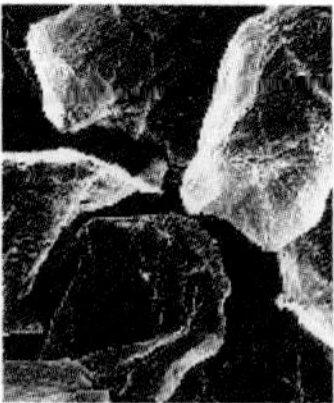
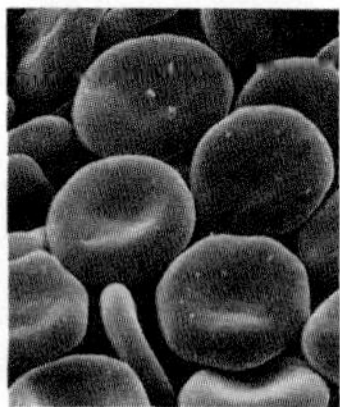

12. Explain how things that plants or animals do are done by the work of cells.

Process Skills

13. **Make a Model** of a cell that shows its different parts or structures.
14. **Infer** What would happen to a cell if you removed its nucleus? Explain your answer.

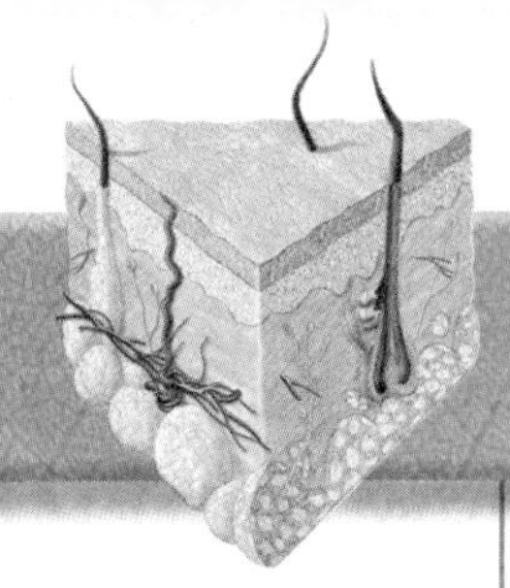

Draw Conclusions

15. A friend describes the cell he is looking at through a microscope. Your friend can see the nucleus of the cell. The cell is shaped like a box with a wall around it. There are small green shapes in the cell. Using the graphic organizer below, draw a conclusion about what kind of cell your friend is looking at.

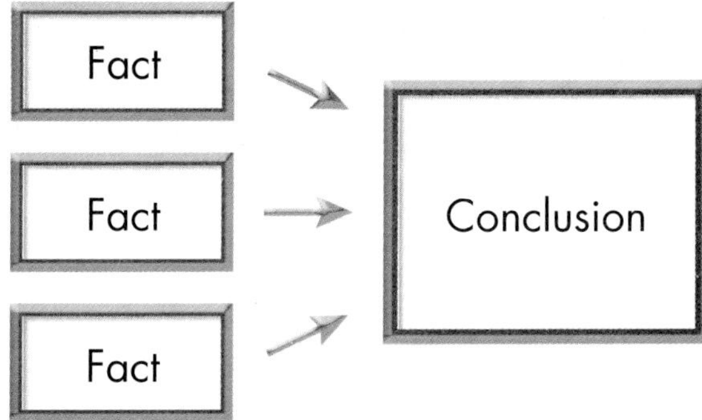

Fact
Fact
Fact
Conclusion

Test Prep

Choose the letter that best completes the statement or answers the question.

16. What type of tissue would most likely have flat cells?

Ⓐ nerve tissue
Ⓑ leg muscle tissue
Ⓒ bone tissue
Ⓓ stomach lining tissue

17. Jesse was looking at a cell through a microscope and saw mitochondria and cell membranes. What could Jesse say about the cell?

Ⓕ It can only be a plant cell.
Ⓖ It can only be an animal cell.
Ⓗ It is either a plant or an animal cell.
Ⓘ It is neither a plant nor an animal cell.

18. Which of the following is found in your skin?

Ⓐ bone cells
Ⓑ chloroplasts
Ⓒ oil glands
Ⓓ cell walls

19. Explain why the answer you selected for Question 18 is best. For each of the answers you did not select, give a reason why it is not the best answer.

20. Writing in Science **Expository** Write a paragraph that will teach others how cells, tissues, organs, and organ systems are related.

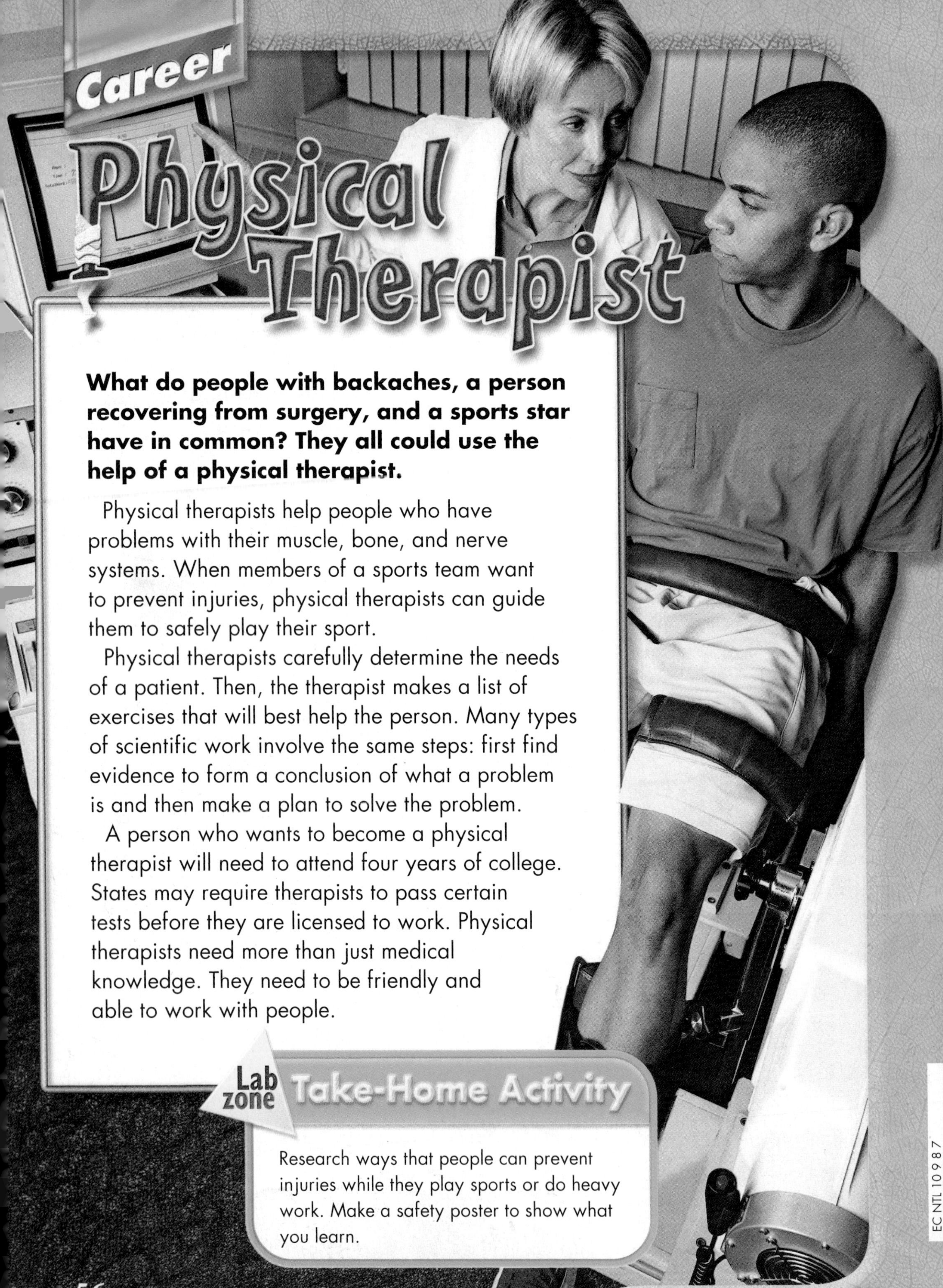

Career

Physical Therapist

What do people with backaches, a person recovering from surgery, and a sports star have in common? They all could use the help of a physical therapist.

Physical therapists help people who have problems with their muscle, bone, and nerve systems. When members of a sports team want to prevent injuries, physical therapists can guide them to safely play their sport.

Physical therapists carefully determine the needs of a patient. Then, the therapist makes a list of exercises that will best help the person. Many types of scientific work involve the same steps: first find evidence to form a conclusion of what a problem is and then make a plan to solve the problem.

A person who wants to become a physical therapist will need to attend four years of college. States may require therapists to pass certain tests before they are licensed to work. Physical therapists need more than just medical knowledge. They need to be friendly and able to work with people.

Lab zone Take-Home Activity

Research ways that people can prevent injuries while they play sports or do heavy work. Make a safety poster to show what you learn.

EC NTL 10987

Chapter 3

Human Body Systems

You Will Discover

- how blood flows through your body.
- how you breathe.
- how you digest food.

online Student Edition
sfsuccessnet.com

Build Background

How do the systems in your body keep you alive?

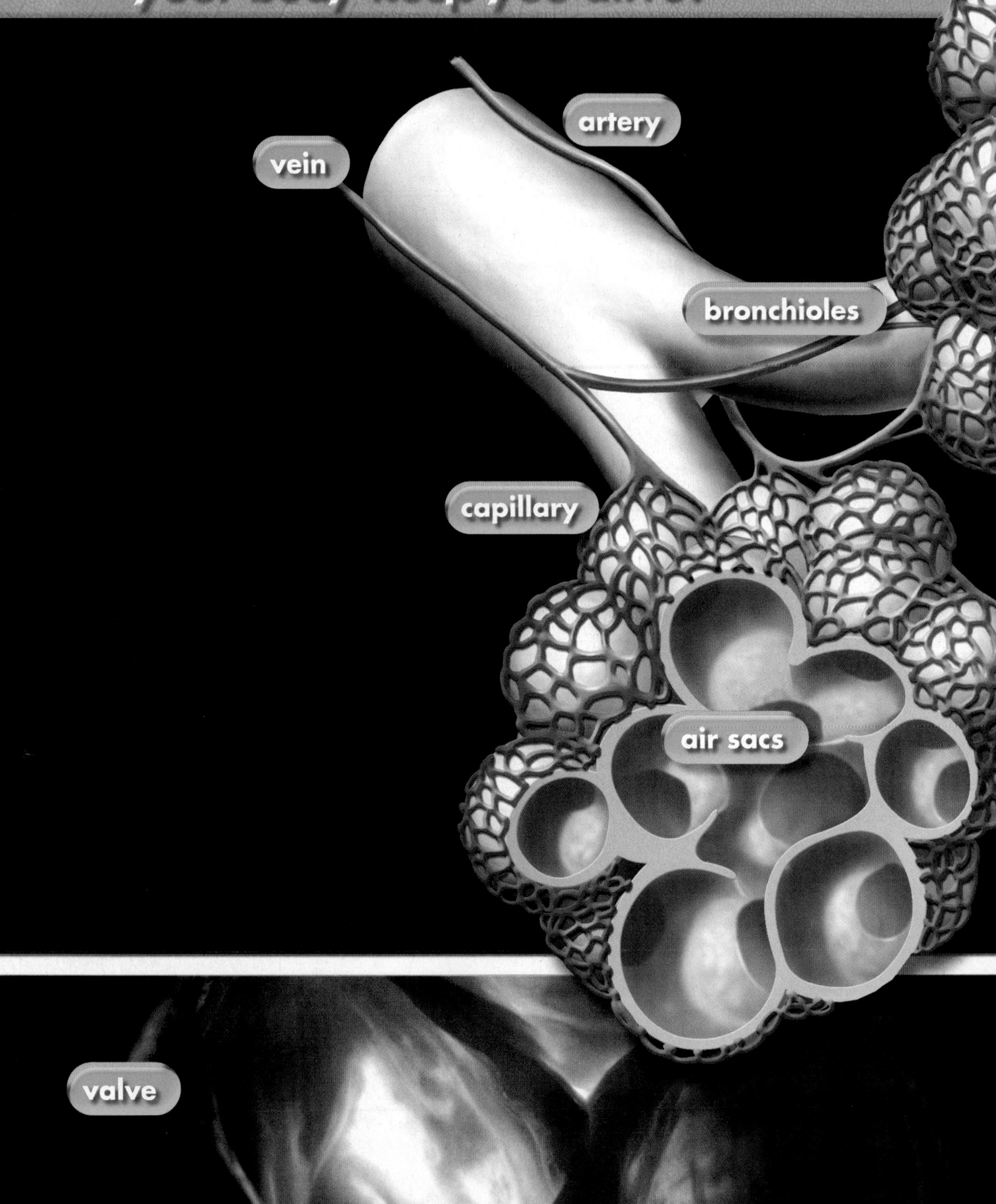
artery
vein
bronchioles
capillary
air sacs
valve

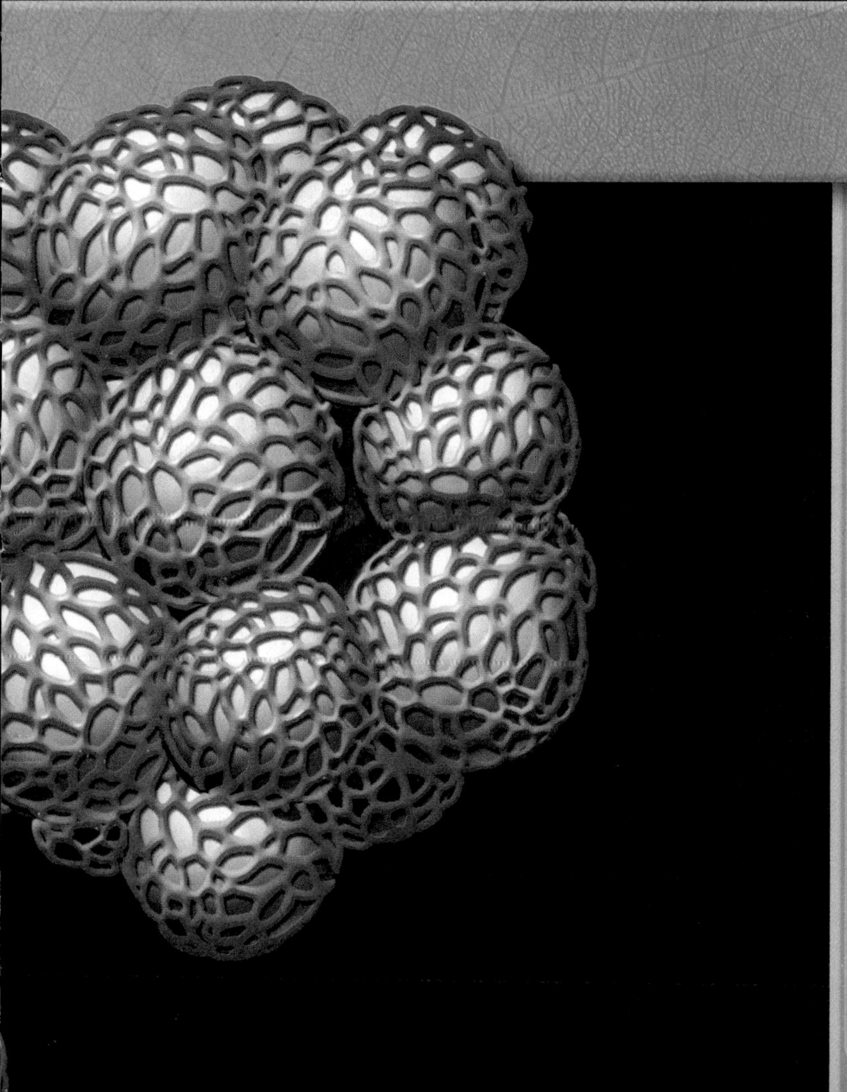

Chapter 3 Vocabulary

artery page 66

capillary page 66

vein page 66

valve page 66

mucus page 70

trachea page 70

bronchioles page 70

air sacs page 70

esophagus page 74

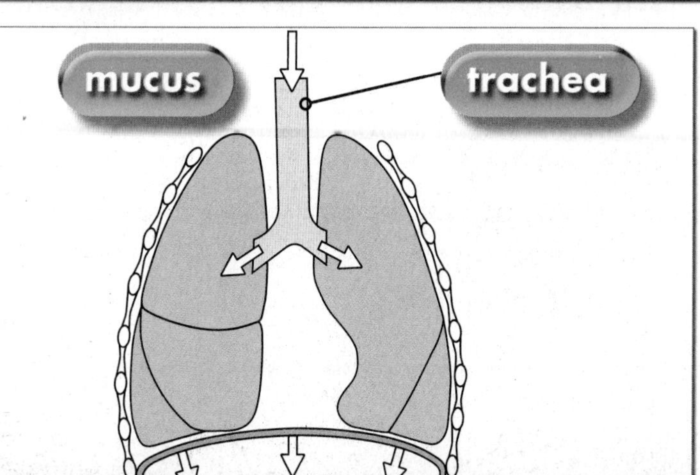
mucus
trachea

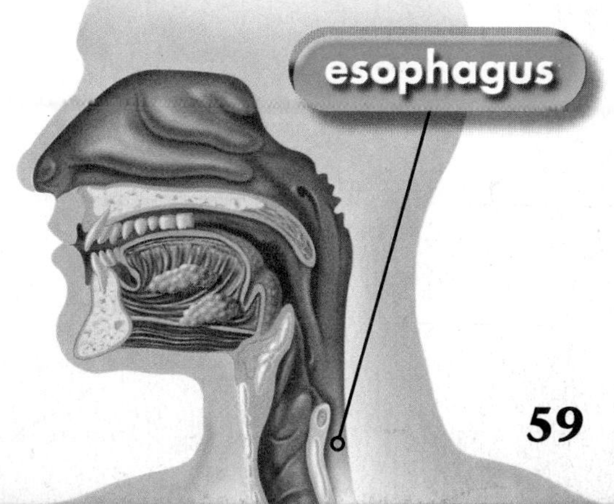
esophagus

Lab zone

Directed Inquiry

Explore How can you observe your pulse?

When your heart beats, it pumps blood into certain vessels.
The flexing of these vessels caused by your beating heart is your pulse.

Materials

short straw

clay

What to Do

1. Insert one end of the straw into a ball of clay.
2. Flatten the bottom of the clay.
3. Rest your hand on a flat surface with the palm side up.
4. Place the bottom of the clay on the thumb side of your wrist. Move the clay around until you **observe** the straw start to move.

Process Skills

Making detailed **observations** is an important part of science.

Explain Your Results

1. Describe the movements of the straw you **observed.**
2. **Infer** What caused the straw to move?

How to Read Science

Reading Skills

TARGET SKILL

Sequence

The order in which events happen is the **sequence** of those events. Sequence can also mean the steps we follow to do something.

- You might **observe** a sequence. Clue words such as *first, then, next,* and *finally* also can help you find the sequence of events.
- Some events take place at the same time. Clue words such as *while, meanwhile, or during* signal this.

Read the public message below. Clue words have been highlighted to help you identify the order in which things happen.

Public Message

Help Save Lives!

People save lives every day by donating blood. First, you must fill out a questionnaire. These questions make sure that it is healthy for you to give blood and that your blood is safe to give others. People with certain diseases or who take certain medications cannot give blood. Next, if you meet all the requirements, a health care professional removes a unit of blood. Then, some of the blood is sent to be tested. Finally, your blood is given to a person who needs it.

Apply It!

Make a graphic organizer like the one shown. **Observe** the steps for donating blood in the message above. Then write the **sequence** of steps in the correct boxes.

First:

Next:

Then:

Finally:

You Are There!

As you stand by a busy highway, you see cars, trucks, and buses moving from one part of town to another. A transportation system is important to a city. A city needs to move food, water, gasoline, garbage, and much more to meet the needs of its citizens. The same is true of your body. Your body needs to have food, water, oxygen, and wastes moved for it to stay healthy. How does your body do these jobs?

90

Lesson 1

What is the circulatory system?

Our bodies have structures and systems that serve special functions. The circulatory system moves material around the body. The parts of the circulatory system are the heart, the blood, and tubes called blood vessels.

The Body's Transportation System

A city depends on many systems for it to be healthy and grow. A system is a group of smaller parts working together to get a job done. No single part does everything by itself. The transportation system of a city has roads, buses, trucks, and cars to move people and supplies. The water system has pumps, pipes, and drains to move water through the city. The garbage system has trucks and garbage dumps to keep the city clean. The people in a city have their needs met by many different systems.

Think about the cells in your toes. Like the people in a city, these cells have needs that must be met. How do they get food and oxygen? How do wastes get carried away? Just as a city takes care of its people, your body has many systems to take care of its cells.

The body has a transportation system to move food and oxygen to each cell and then take away cells' wastes. This system is the circulatory system. It includes the heart, blood, and blood vessels. The blood vessels are the tubes that carry blood through the body. As with all systems, each part of the circulatory system has structures that help the system get the job done.

1. **√ Checkpoint** What is the job of the circulatory system?
2. **Math in Science** A person is born with about 0.25 liter of blood. An adult has about 20 times this amount. About how much blood does an adult have?

Functions of the Blood

Your blood has several different parts. Each part has a different job. The biggest part of your blood is a straw-colored liquid called plasma.

Just as people in a city depend on trucks and trains to carry food from the farms to the grocery stores, the cells in your body depend on the blood's plasma to carry food from the digestive system to your cells. Plasma also carries away the cells' wastes. Cells get their water from the plasma as well. Finally, plasma moves some chemicals from one part of the body to another. For example, adrenaline is a chemical made by glands in your lower back. Your blood carries adrenaline from these glands to your heart and muscle cells as a signal to be more active.

Blood Cells

Your cells need oxygen to get energy from food. The red blood cells carry oxygen to your body's cells. These cells are bright red when they are carrying oxygen. After they give the oxygen to the cells, their color turns a darker red.

White blood cells work hard to protect your body against germs and other harmful things. Some white blood cells wrap around and break down germs, pieces of waste matter, dead cells, or cells that are carrying germs. Others make chemicals that kill germs. The number of white blood cells is always changing. When the body needs to fight infection, it makes more white blood cells. Not all white blood cells are actually in the blood vessels. Some squirm their way between your body cells and attack germs there.

Platelets are pieces of cells that float in the blood. When a blood vessel is cut, platelets are there to stop the bleeding. They clump together and stick to the edges of the cut. They help form a clot, which is a plug made with long sticky threads. What would happen if clots did not form at a cut?

Plasma makes up a little more than half of the blood. Red blood cells make up a little less than half of the blood. Platelets and different kinds of white blood cells make up a very small fraction of the blood.

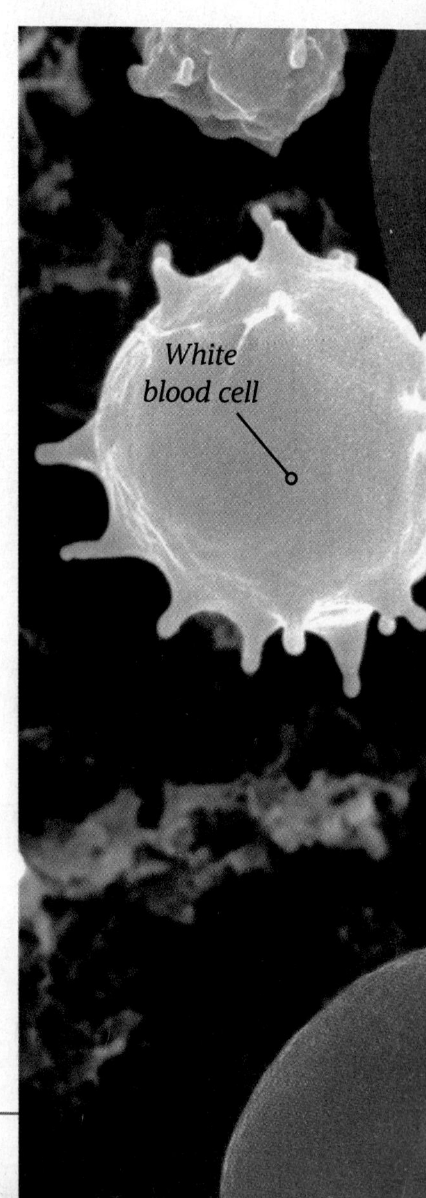
White blood cell

Types of Blood Cells

	Red Blood Cells	Platelets	White Blood Cells
Form	Red blood cells are shaped like discs with a dimple on each side.	Platelets are not complete cells.	White blood cells have different shapes and sizes. In fact, they may change size and shape as they work.
Function	These cells carry oxygen to the rest of the body.	Platelets form blood clots.	White blood cells protect your body from germs and other harmful things.
Disorder	Sickle-cell anemia is a disease in which the red blood cells have a shape like a crescent moon. Such cells do not carry oxygen as well as normal cells.	An embolism is a clot that floats freely in blood vessels and then blocks a vessel.	In a type of cancer known as leukemia, a person's white cells do not form correctly and their numbers increase too quickly.

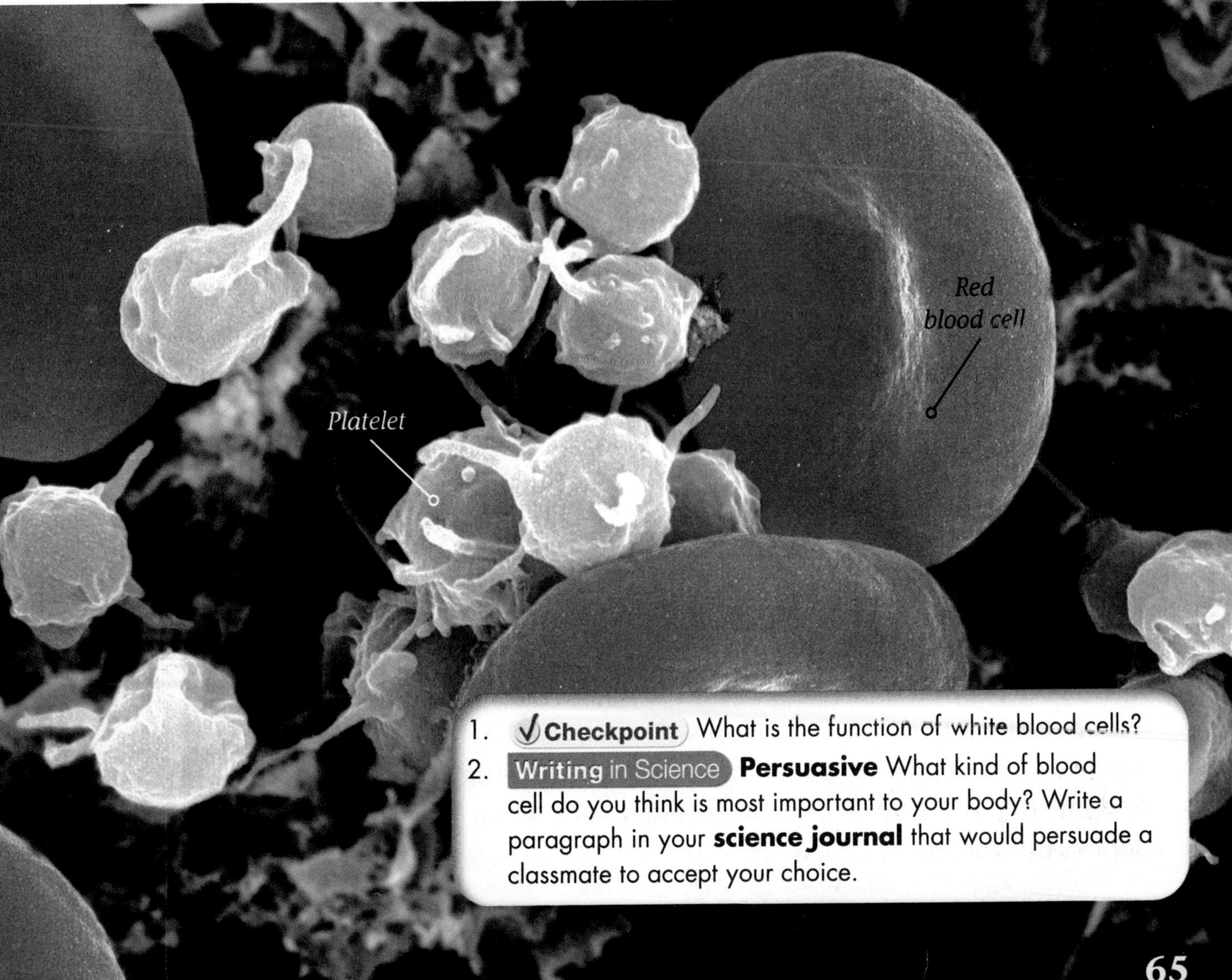

Red blood cell
Platelet

1. **√Checkpoint** What is the function of white blood cells?
2. **Writing in Science** **Persuasive** What kind of blood cell do you think is most important to your body? Write a paragraph in your **science journal** that would persuade a classmate to accept your choice.

Arteries, Capillaries, and Veins

The blood vessels can be thought of as highways your blood uses to move through your body. The three kinds of blood vessels are arteries, capillaries, and veins. Each kind has structures that help it do its job.

Arteries are blood vessels that carry blood away from your heart to other parts of your body. Arteries have thick, muscular walls that stretch when the heart pushes blood into it. Arteries branch many times into smaller and smaller tubes. Almost every artery carries blood with lots of oxygen.

Your smallest arteries branch to become your smallest blood vessels. The smallest kind of blood vessel is called a **capillary**. Side-by-side, ten of these tiny blood vessels would be barely as thick as one of your hairs. Some capillaries are so narrow that red blood cells must flow through them in a single-file line.

The walls of capillaries are only one cell thick. Gases can pass through these thin walls. Oxygen moves from the blood in your capillaries to your cells. Carbon dioxide and other wastes go in the other direction. They move from your cells to the blood in your capillaries.

Capillaries join together to form your tiniest veins. **Veins** are blood vessels that take blood from cells back to the heart. These tiny veins join many times to form larger and larger veins.

Veins have valves. **Valves** are flaps that act like doors to keep blood flowing in one direction. Valves open to allow blood to flow to the heart. Valves close if the blood begins to flow away from the heart. Arteries and capillaries do not have valves. The pumping of the heart keeps the blood flowing in the right direction through the arteries and capillaries.

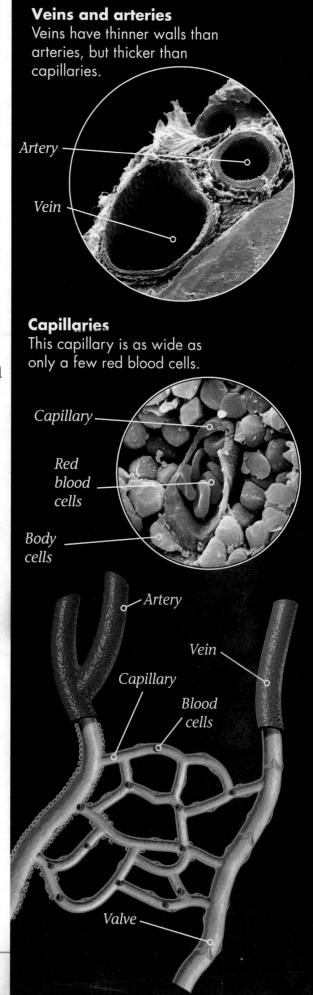

Veins and arteries
Veins have thinner walls than arteries, but thicker than capillaries.

Artery
Vein

Capillaries
This capillary is as wide as only a few red blood cells.

Capillary
Red blood cells
Body cells

Artery
Vein
Capillary
Blood cells
Valve

SciLinks Take It to the Net sfsuccessnet.com keyword: valves code: g5p66

The Circulatory System

Huge numbers of blood vessels form a network throughout your body. If all the blood vessels were laid end-to-end, they would stretch around Earth more than twice!

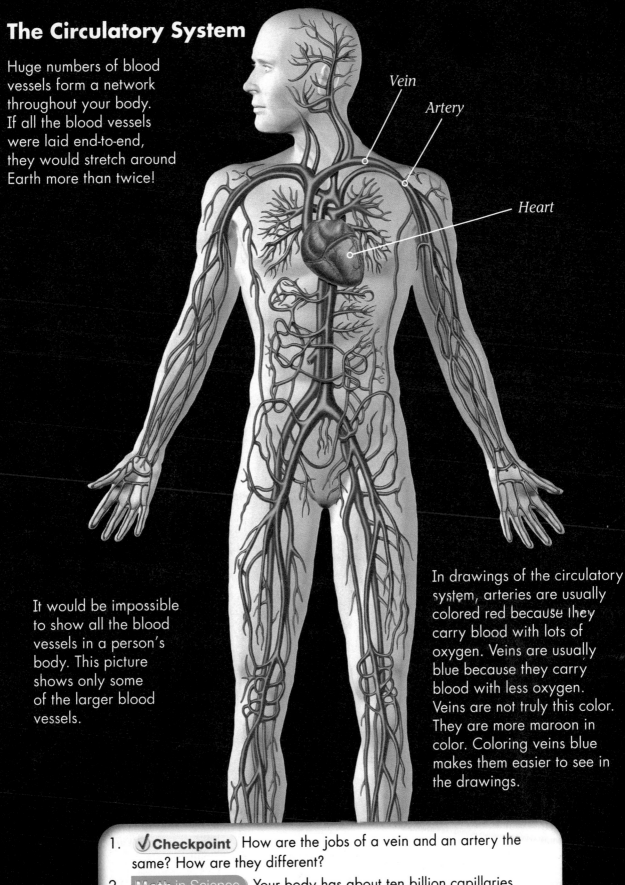

Vein

Artery

Heart

It would be impossible to show all the blood vessels in a person's body. This picture shows only some of the larger blood vessels.

In drawings of the circulatory system, arteries are usually colored red because they carry blood with lots of oxygen. Veins are usually blue because they carry blood with less oxygen. Veins are not truly this color. They are more maroon in color. Coloring veins blue makes them easier to see in the drawings.

1. **✓Checkpoint** How are the jobs of a vein and an artery the same? How are they different?
2. **Math in Science** Your body has about ten billion capillaries. Write this number in standard form.

Parts of the Heart

Your heart began pumping before you were born and will pump as long as you live. The heart is divided into two sides. Each side works as a separate pump and sends blood along different paths. The right side pumps blood to the lungs. In the lungs, the blood gets oxygen and gives up carbon dioxide. The blood then flows to the left side of the heart. The left side pumps the blood through arteries to the body.

Each side of the heart has two parts. The upper part of each side is called an atrium. The lower part is called a ventricle. Each ventricle is larger and more powerful than an atrium.

Many small blood vessels are in the muscles of your heart. The blood in these vessels gives the muscles in your heart oxygen, food, and water. In one form of heart disease these blood vessels get clogged and blood cannot reach the heart muscles.

The parts of your heart pump in a repeating pattern. The left atrium and right atrium pump first, then the two ventricles pump. After a brief rest, the pattern is repeated. As with most systems, the order in which things happen in the heart is very important. People can become very sick if the circulatory system does not follow this pattern.

During your life, your heart might beat almost 3 billion times. When you are running, your heart pumps faster to get extra oxygen to your muscles. It pumps more slowly when you are sleeping or sitting quietly.

Not all hearts are alike. The hearts of most reptiles only have three parts, or chambers. Fish hearts have two chambers.

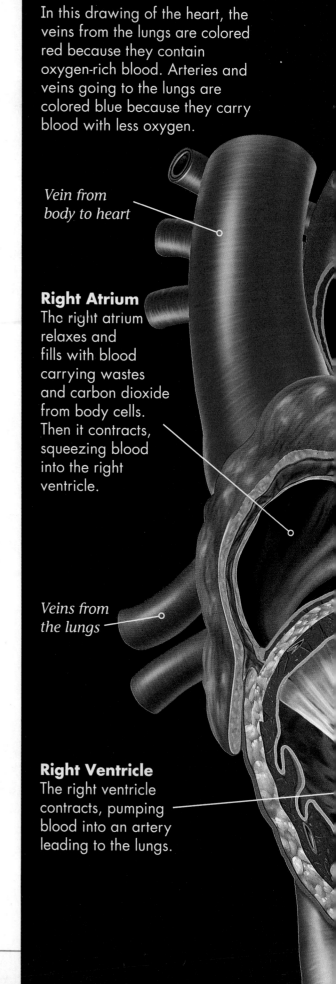

In this drawing of the heart, the veins from the lungs are colored red because they contain oxygen-rich blood. Arteries and veins going to the lungs are colored blue because they carry blood with less oxygen.

Vein from body to heart

Right Atrium
The right atrium relaxes and fills with blood carrying wastes and carbon dioxide from body cells. Then it contracts, squeezing blood into the right ventricle.

Veins from the lungs

Right Ventricle
The right ventricle contracts, pumping blood into an artery leading to the lungs.

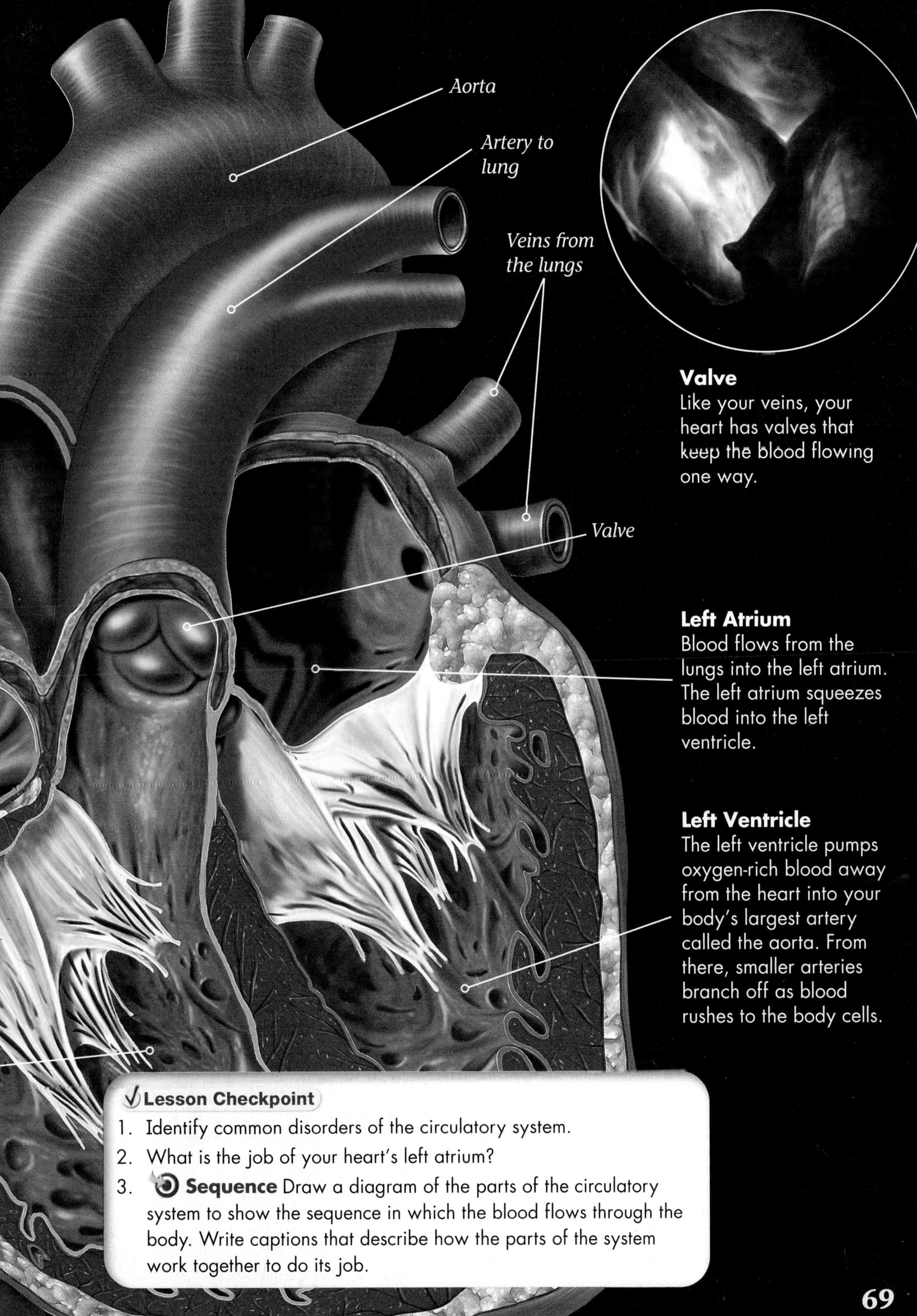
Aorta
Artery to lung
Veins from the lungs
Valve

Valve
Like your veins, your heart has valves that keep the blood flowing one way.

Left Atrium
Blood flows from the lungs into the left atrium. The left atrium squeezes blood into the left ventricle.

Left Ventricle
The left ventricle pumps oxygen-rich blood away from the heart into your body's largest artery called the aorta. From there, smaller arteries branch off as blood rushes to the body cells.

√ Lesson Checkpoint

1. Identify common disorders of the circulatory system.
2. What is the job of your heart's left atrium?
3. **Sequence** Draw a diagram of the parts of the circulatory system to show the sequence in which the blood flows through the body. Write captions that describe how the parts of the system work together to do its job.

Lesson 2

What is the respiratory system?

The job of your respiratory system is to carry gases between the outside air and your blood.

Parts of the Respiratory System

Your respiratory system is at work whenever you smell, sing, talk, laugh, or breathe. Many parts of the respiratory system are coated with **mucus.** Mucus is a sticky, thick fluid that traps dust, germs, and other things that may be in the air.

Air enters through the nose or mouth. Sinuses warm and moisten the air. With its hairs and layer of mucus, the nose traps dust and germs. Air passes from the sinus to the back of the throat and into the larynx. The larynx contains the vocal cords.

The **trachea** is a tube that carries air from the larynx to the lungs. The trachea leads to two branches called bronchi that go into the lungs. In the lungs, these tubes branch into smaller and smaller tubes called **bronchioles.** Asthma is a disease in which these tubes may become narrowed. This prevents air from easily traveling through the lungs.

The bronchioles end in clusters of tiny thin-walled pouches or air sacs in the lungs. **Air sacs** are where oxygen enters the blood and carbon dioxide leaves the blood. Air sacs are also called alveoli.

The diaphragm is a dome-shaped muscle that forms the bottom of the chest area. When this muscle contracts it moves down and gets flatter.

1. **Checkpoint** What is the job of the air sacs?
2. Art in Science Draw a diagram of the respiratory system. Label and describe the function of all the parts.

How You Breathe

Inhale (Breathing In)

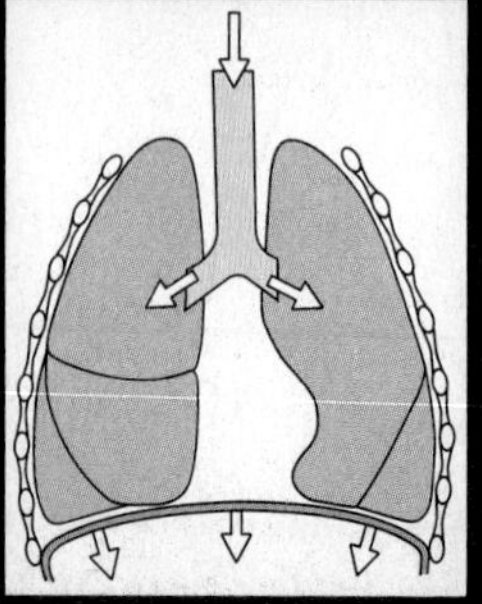

Exhale (Breathing Out)

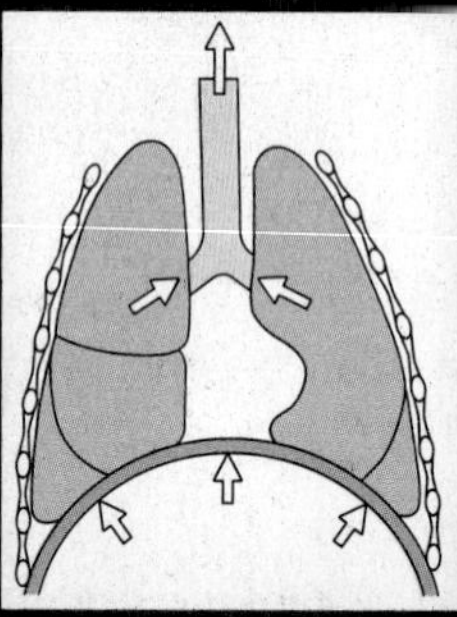

Several muscles work together when you breathe. When you inhale, your diaphragm contracts and moves down, making more space in your chest. Your rib muscles may also pull your rib cage up and out, making still more space. Air quickly rushes into the lungs and takes up these new spaces. When your diaphragm and rib muscles relax, they push air out of the lungs.

Vital lung capacity is the amount of air that a person can blow out after a deep breath. The vital lung capacity for an adult is often about 3 to 5 liters.

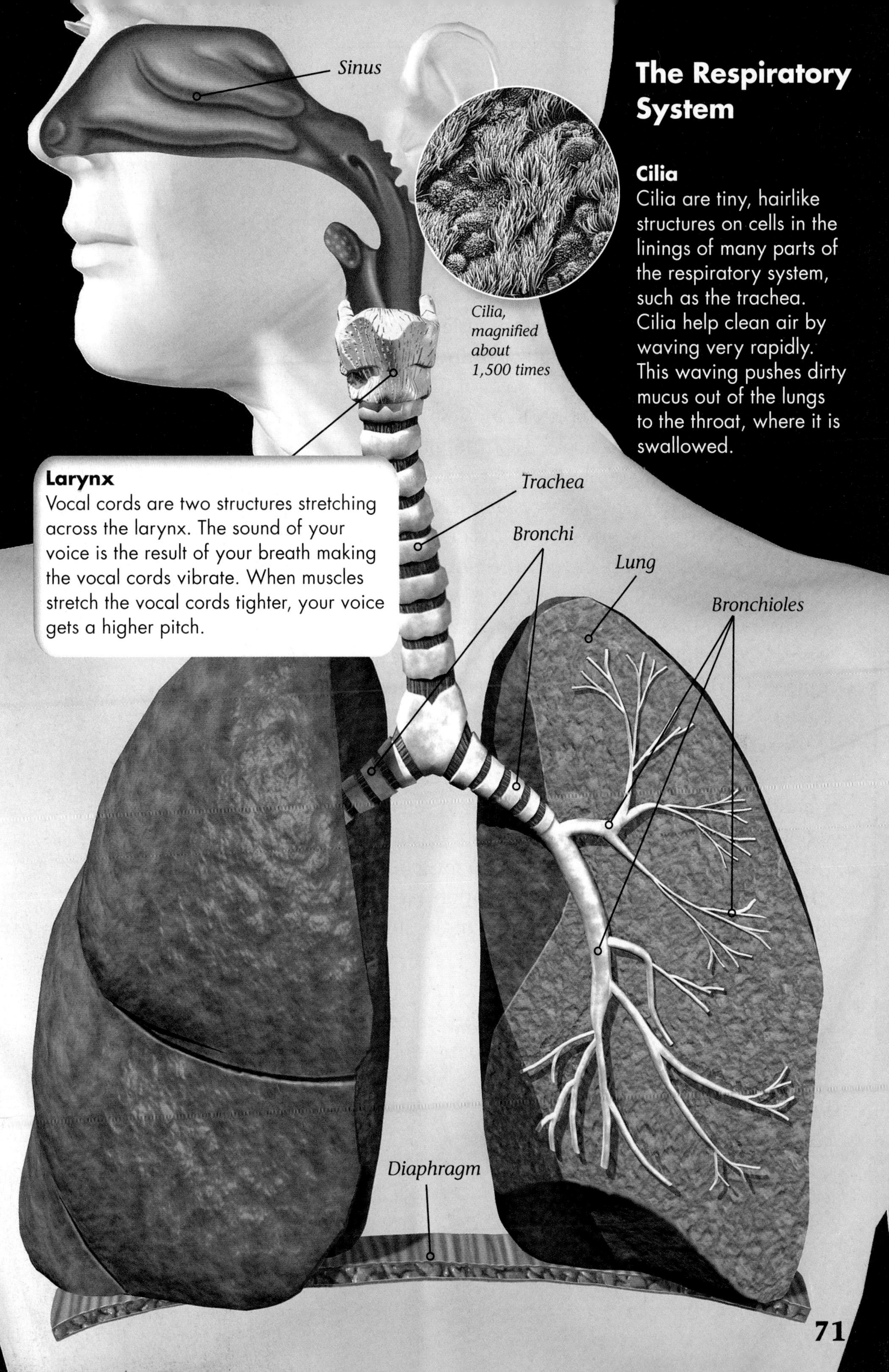
Sinus
Cilia, magnified about 1,500 times
Trachea
Bronchi
Lung
Bronchioles
Diaphragm

The Respiratory System

Cilia

Cilia are tiny, hairlike structures on cells in the linings of many parts of the respiratory system, such as the trachea. Cilia help clean air by waving very rapidly. This waving pushes dirty mucus out of the lungs to the throat, where it is swallowed.

Larynx

Vocal cords are two structures stretching across the larynx. The sound of your voice is the result of your breath making the vocal cords vibrate. When muscles stretch the vocal cords tighter, your voice gets a higher pitch.

Respiratory and Circulatory Systems Work Together

All multicellular organisms need oxygen for their cells to get the energy they need. Insects have a respiratory system to do this job. They have many tiny tubes that run through their body. These tubes open up at holes on their sides to let air in. Worms use their circulatory system to do this job. Their blood absorbs oxygen through their moist skin and carries it to all parts of the body.

Your body is more complex than these organisms. People have both respiratory and circulatory systems working together to get oxygen to their cells. The respiratory system gets the oxygen as far as the tiny air sacs inside your lungs. The blood picks up the oxygen there and carries it to all your cells—all the way down to your toes.

In the air sacs, two things happen at the same time. Oxygen leaves the lungs and enters the blood. Carbon dioxide goes the other way. It leaves the blood and enters the lungs. So, the output of one system is the input of the other system.

When you hold your breath, carbon dioxide builds up in your blood. Your brain can sense this. Without your making a decision, your brain sends a message to the diaphragm and rib muscles telling them to breathe. In this situation, we see several systems working together to make sure your cells get oxygen.

Bronchioles branch into smaller and smaller tubes. These end with a cluster of air sacs.

Some Diseases of the Respiratory System

Name	Cause	Effect
Cold	Virus	Runny nose, stuffy nose, sneezing
Influenza	Virus	Cough, sore throat, stuffy nose, fever
Pneumonia	Bacteria or virus	Cough, chest pain, shortness of breath, fever
Tuberculosis	Bacteria	Cough, fever, wheezing
Lung Cancer	Tobacco, chemicals	Lung cells grow incorrectly and very quickly

Air Sacs in the Lungs

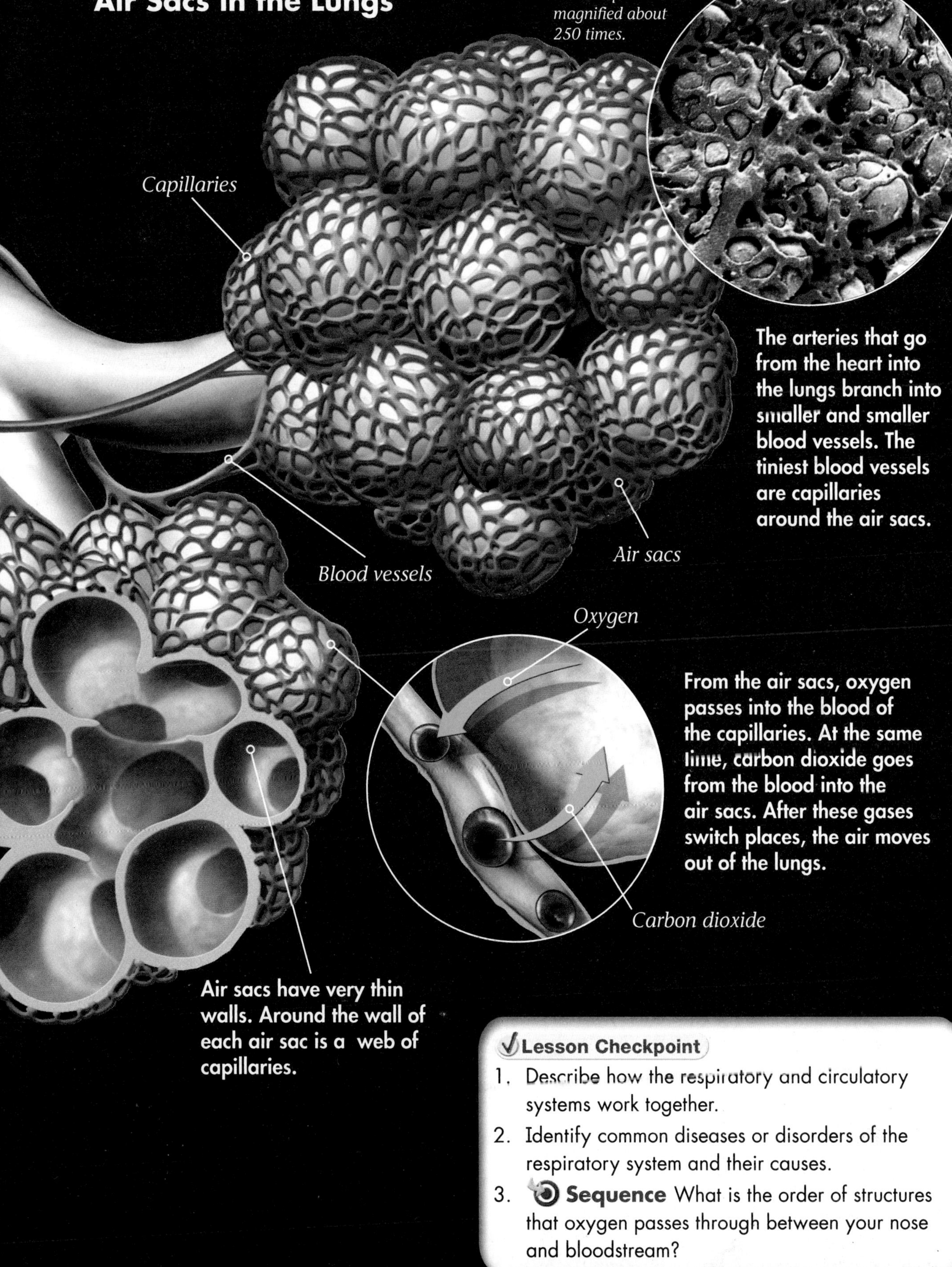

These capillaries are magnified about 250 times.
Capillaries
Blood vessels
Air sacs
Oxygen
Carbon dioxide

The arteries that go from the heart into the lungs branch into smaller and smaller blood vessels. The tiniest blood vessels are capillaries around the air sacs.

From the air sacs, oxygen passes into the blood of the capillaries. At the same time, carbon dioxide goes from the blood into the air sacs. After these gases switch places, the air moves out of the lungs.

Air sacs have very thin walls. Around the wall of each air sac is a web of capillaries.

✓ Lesson Checkpoint

1. Describe how the respiratory and circulatory systems work together.
2. Identify common diseases or disorders of the respiratory system and their causes.
3. **Sequence** What is the order of structures that oxygen passes through between your nose and bloodstream?

Lesson 3

What are the digestive and urinary systems?

When you eat, food passes through many organs. Each organ has structures to help it do its job in the digestive system.

Digestive System

Food has to be changed before your cells can use it. Your body first has to digest, or break down, food into very small materials. Then the food can enter the blood to get to your cells. Digestion is a hard job. It takes many organs working together. Each organ has structures that help it do its part of the job.

The Mouth and Esophagus

Chewing is the first step of digestion. Chewing makes food small enough to swallow, and it makes the job of the rest of the digestive system easier.

The **esophagus** is a tube that carries food to the stomach. Food does not move to the stomach because of gravity. The esophagus pushes food to the stomach by squeezing its rings of muscles in a pattern. As the lump of food passes each ring of muscle, the muscles behind the food contract. This pushes the food through the esophagus to the stomach in about two or three seconds.

Teeth
Most adults will have as many as 32 teeth. Front teeth have a thin shape to cut food when you bite. Flatter teeth in the back of the mouth crush food as you chew. Teeth are not simply rocklike structures. They contain live cells, blood vessels, and nerves.

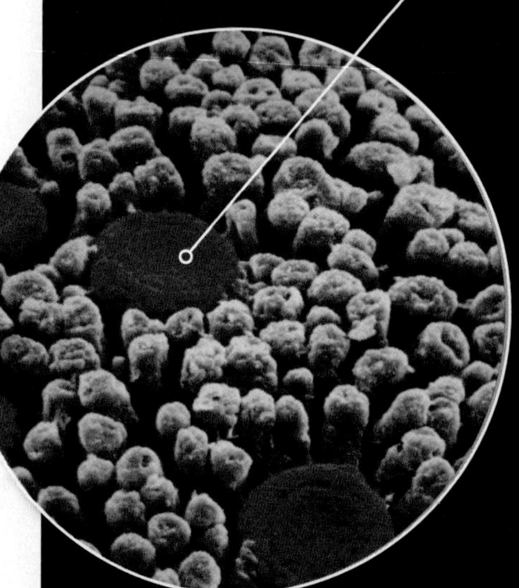

Taste buds

Surface of tongue magnified many hundreds of times

Tongue
The tongue does more than just help you taste food. The tongue moves food so it can be chewed. It also moves food to the back of the mouth where it is swallowed. Tiny taste buds on your tongue have special nerves in them. These nerves send signals of taste to your brain.

The Digestive System

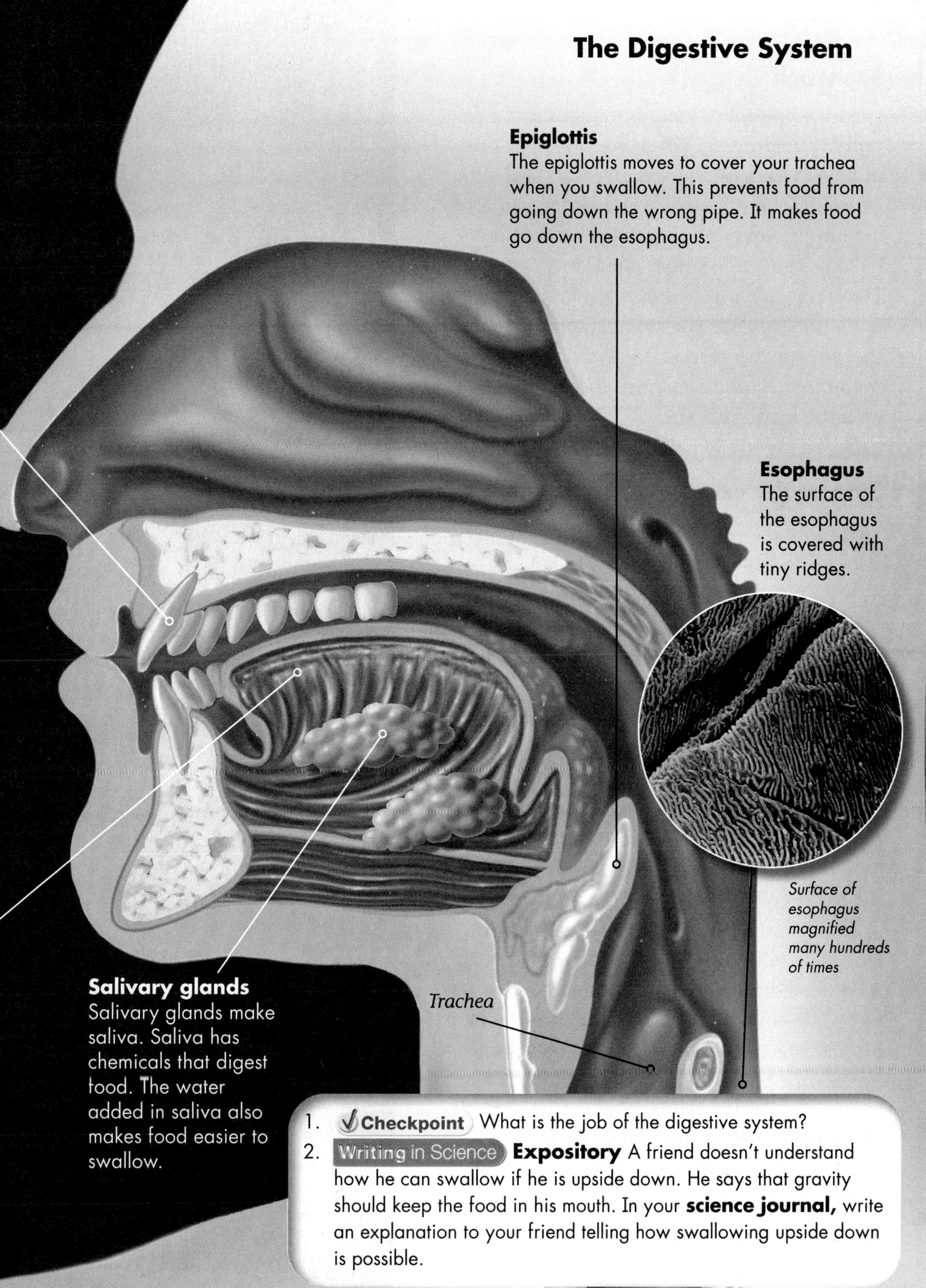

Epiglottis
The epiglottis moves to cover your trachea when you swallow. This prevents food from going down the wrong pipe. It makes food go down the esophagus.
Esophagus
The surface of the esophagus is covered with tiny ridges.
Salivary glands
Salivary glands make saliva. Saliva has chemicals that digest food. The water added in saliva also makes food easier to swallow.
Trachea

Surface of esophagus magnified many hundreds of times

1. **Checkpoint** What is the job of the digestive system?
2. Writing in Science **Expository** A friend doesn't understand how he can swallow if he is upside down. He says that gravity should keep the food in his mouth. In your **science journal,** write an explanation to your friend telling how swallowing upside down is possible.

Stomach

At the bottom of your esophagus is a tight round muscle. When you swallow, this muscle relaxes and opens to let food into your stomach. Then the muscle closes to keep the food from moving back into your esophagus.

Your stomach is under your lower left ribs. The stomach's walls can stretch to store all the food from a meal. The stomach produces fluids that help to digest foods. As strong muscles in the stomach's walls squeeze, these fluids mix with the food. After the food becomes a soupy paste, it is ready to leave your stomach.

Intestines

The stomach squeezes the partly digested food into a narrow, winding tube called the small intestine. Its muscles squeeze the food along in one direction. Your liver and pancreas are organs that send chemicals to your small intestine to help digest food. When digestion is finished, the particles of digested food can move into blood vessels that are in the walls of your intestine.

Tiny finger-shaped structures called villi are found all over the inside walls of the small intestine. Villi give the small intestine more surface area to absorb food.

At the end of the small intestine, some food that cannot be digested remains. This food waste moves to a wider tube called the large intestine. Most of the large intestine is also known as the colon. Helpful bacteria live here. Some bacteria make vitamins that your body uses. These bacteria also help keep out other bacteria that cause disease. The large intestine takes water and salts from the wastes making the waste more solid. Finally, muscles squeeze to push the waste out of the body.

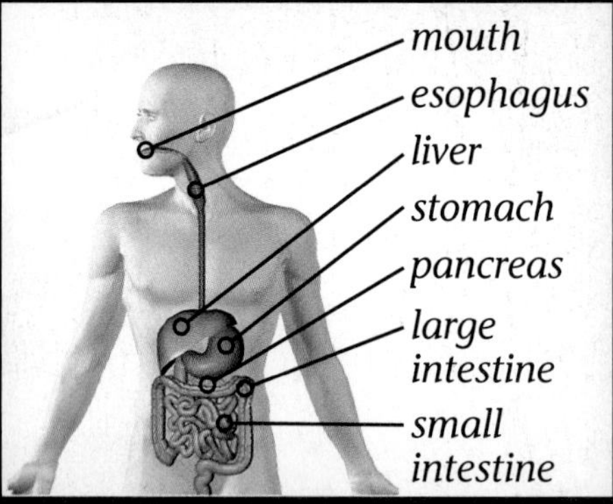

mouth
esophagus
liver
stomach
pancreas
large intestine
small intestine

Digestive System

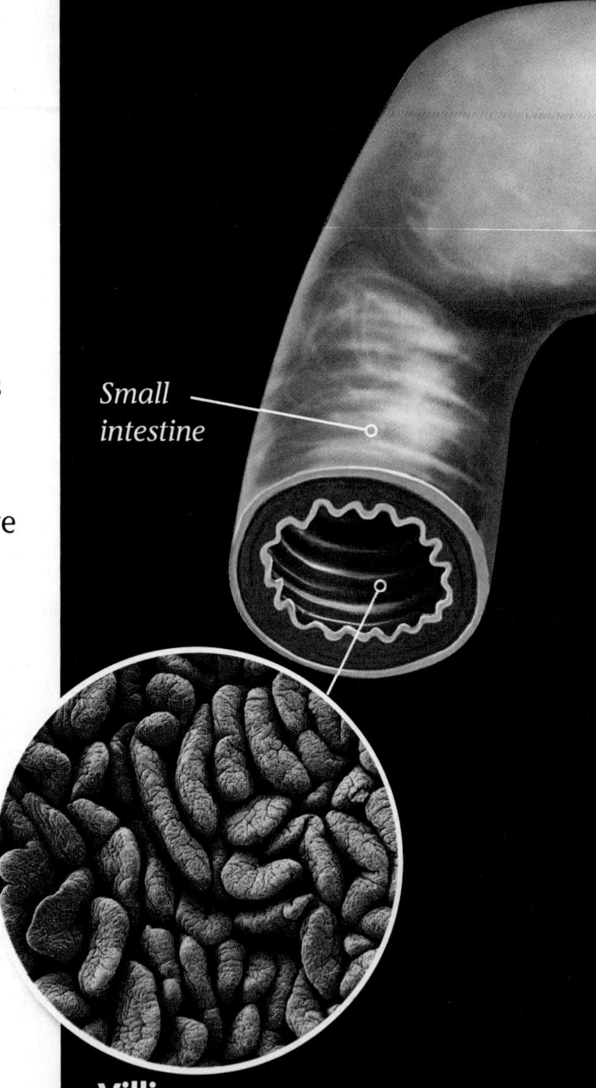

Small intestine

Villi

The villi seen in this magnified picture are actually about one millimeter tall. Beneath the villi's thin walls is a web of capillaries. Why is it helpful to have capillaries here?

The Stomach

Esophagus

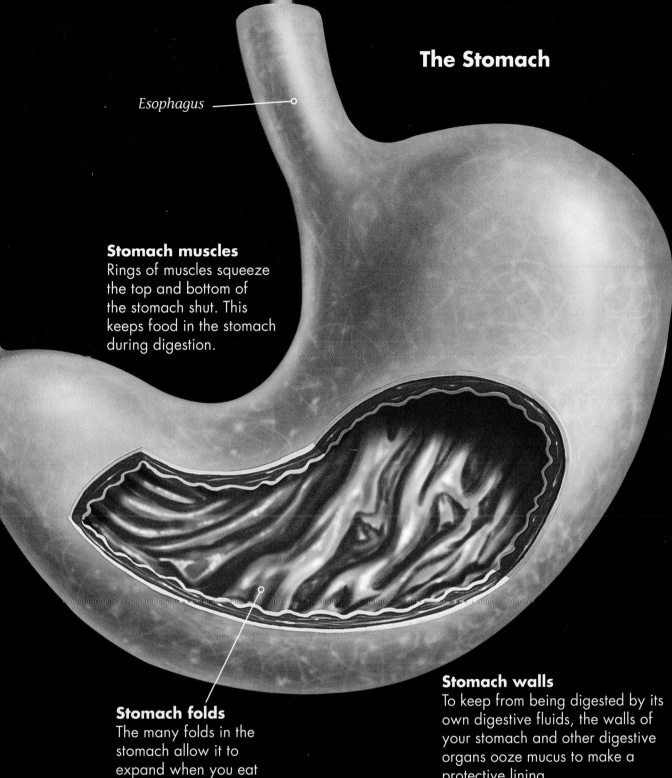

Stomach muscles
Rings of muscles squeeze the top and bottom of the stomach shut. This keeps food in the stomach during digestion.

Stomach folds
The many folds in the stomach allow it to expand when you eat a big meal.

Stomach walls
To keep from being digested by its own digestive fluids, the walls of your stomach and other digestive organs ooze mucus to make a protective lining.

1. **√ Checkpoint** What parts of the structure of the small intestine are specially shaped to help the intestine do its job?
2. **Writing in Science** **Narrative** In your **science journal,** write a story from the perspective of a berry that is being eaten. This berry is writing in order to tell other berries what to expect when they travel through the digestive system. Use all these words in the correct sequence: *colon, esophagus, large intestine, mouth, small intestine, stomach, teeth.*

The Urinary System

Your body cells make wastes and dump them into the blood. These wastes can poison your body. If your body did not have ways to rid itself of wastes, you could not live for long. People and other organisms have structures that work together to rid the body of wastes that are in the blood. In your body, this is done mostly by the urinary system.

Your kidneys are a pair of organs that remove wastes from your blood. Kidneys are shaped like kidney beans, and have the same dark red color. They are on either side of your backbone, just under your lowest ribs.

When wastes are filtered out of the blood, many other materials also leave the blood. These other materials include water, salt, calcium, nutrients, and other chemicals your body needs. The kidney has to put the right amount of these materials back into the blood to keep the body healthy. In this way, the kidneys help keep the amounts of these materials from getting too high or too low.

The kidney takes out some water with the wastes. This mix of wastes and water is urine. A tube carries urine away from the kidneys to the urinary bladder. This bladder stores urine until it leaves the body. At the bottom of the bladder is a tight round muscle that keeps urine inside until it is removed from the body.

The kidneys are not the only organs that get rid of cells' wastes. Remember that carbon dioxide is a waste product removed by the lungs. Sweat glands also release a small amount of cells' wastes in sweat.

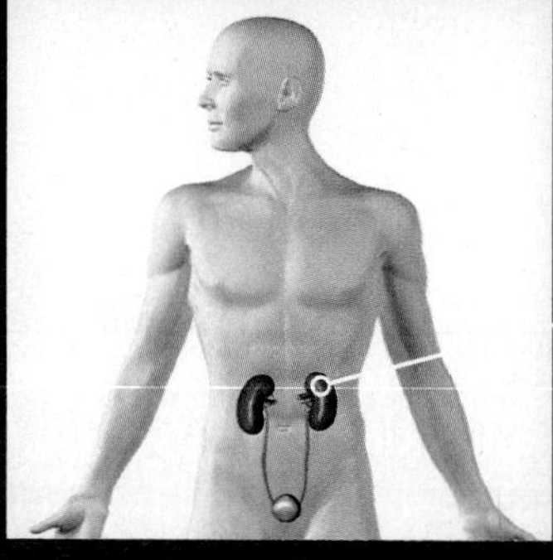

Urinary System

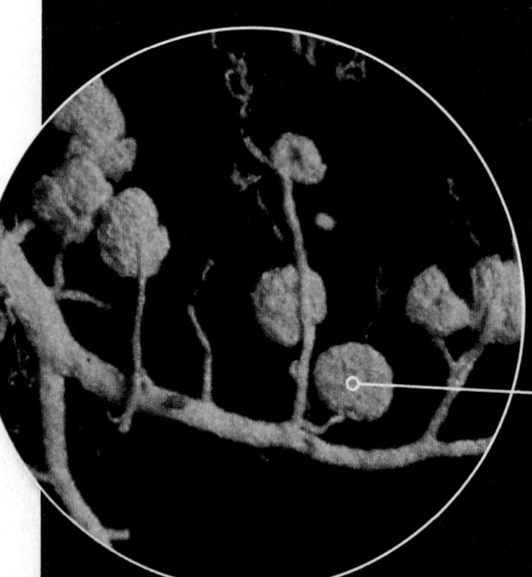

Blood Filters
Blood passes through this part of the kidney. These ball-shaped structures take wastes out of the blood into the tube. The tube puts some materials back into the blood. The wastes left in the tube then drain out of the kidney.

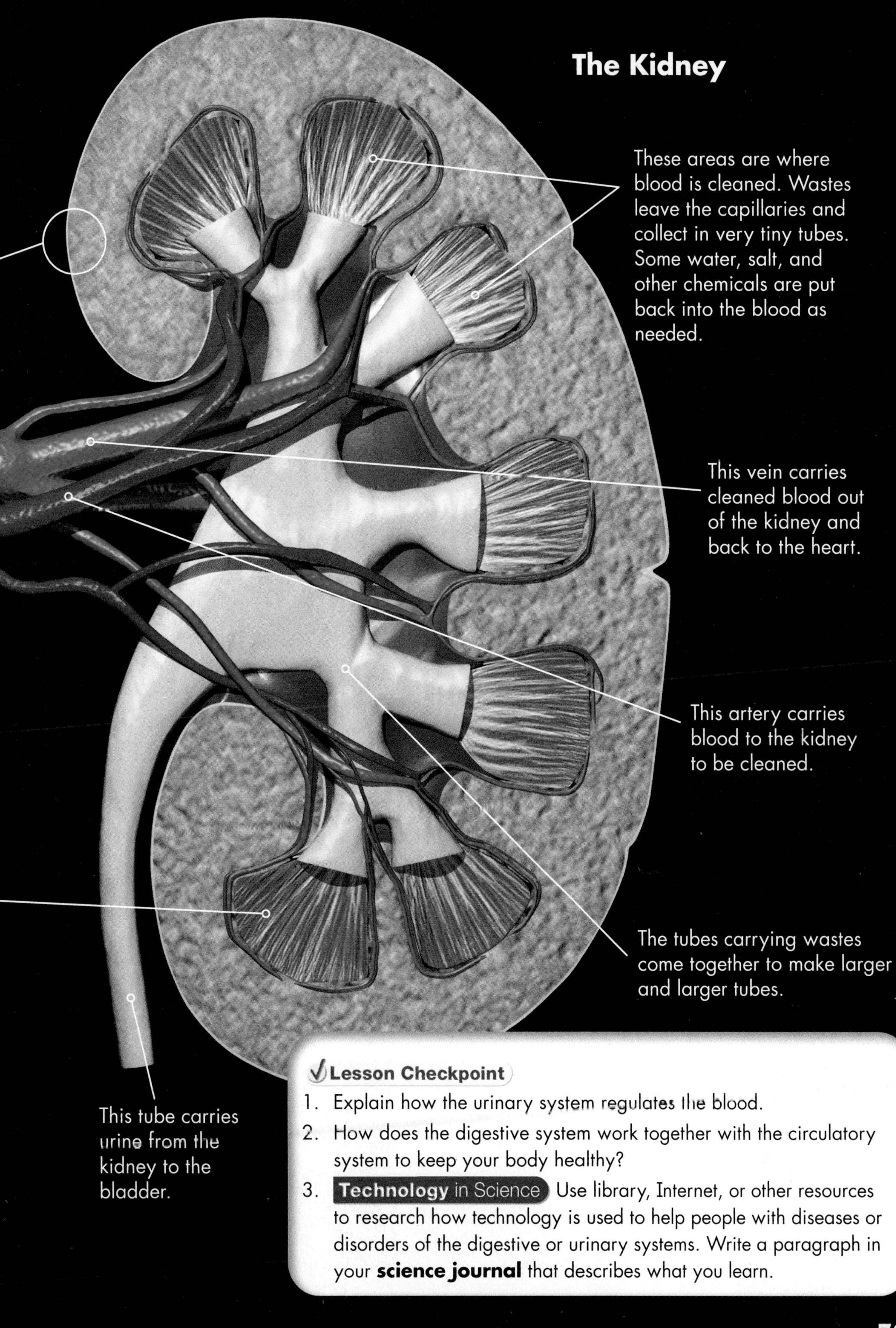
The Kidney
These areas are where blood is cleaned. Wastes leave the capillaries and collect in very tiny tubes. Some water, salt, and other chemicals are put back into the blood as needed.
This vein carries cleaned blood out of the kidney and back to the heart.
This artery carries blood to the kidney to be cleaned.
The tubes carrying wastes come together to make larger and larger tubes.
This tube carries urine from the kidney to the bladder.

√ Lesson Checkpoint

1. Explain how the urinary system regulates the blood.
2. How does the digestive system work together with the circulatory system to keep your body healthy?
3. **Technology** in Science Use library, Internet, or other resources to research how technology is used to help people with diseases or disorders of the digestive or urinary systems. Write a paragraph in your **science journal** that describes what you learn.

Lab zone

Guided Inquiry

Investigate What is your lung capacity?

How much can you breathe in or blow out? In this activity you can measure the amount in a simple way. The amount varies greatly by age, body size, and level of fitness.

Materials

trash bag

tape

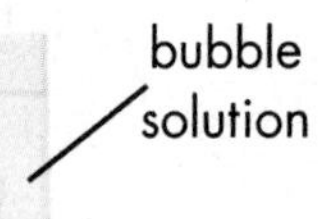

bubble solution

graduated cylinder (or measuring cup)

straws

metric ruler

What to Do

1. Tape the trash bag over the top of a desk. Pour about 50 mL of bubble solution onto the bag.

2. Spread the solution around on the bag with your hand. Dip a straw in the jar of bubble solution. Touch the straw to the solution on the bag. Take a deep breath and slowly blow as much breath as you can into the straw. **Observe** a bubble forming.

Do not inhale through the straw!

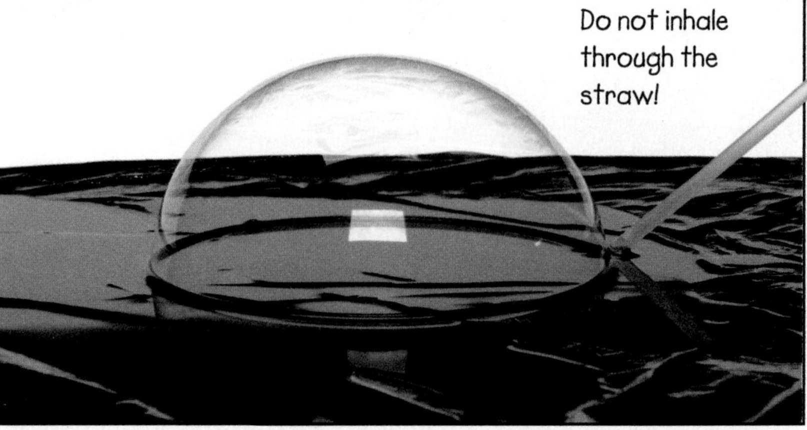

Process Skills

Measuring carefully can help you make more accurate **observations.**

3. Let the bubble burst. **Measure** the diameter of the ring left on the bag. Write the diameter in the chart like the one below. Use the chart on the right to estimate the amount of air you exhaled.

Diameter of Ring (centimeters)	**Lung Capacity** (liters)
14	0.7
15	0.9
16	1.1
17	1.3
18	1.5
19	1.8
20	2.1
21	2.4
22	2.8
23	3.2

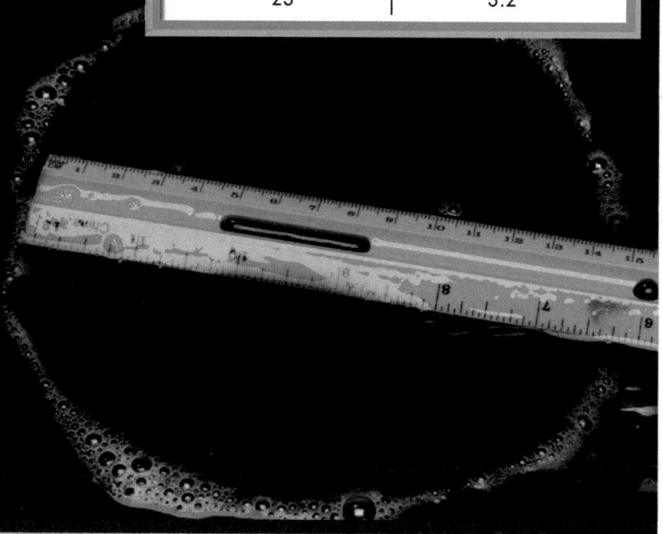

4. Have each student in your group use a new straw and repeat steps 2 and 3.

Name of Student	**Diameter of Ring** (centimeters)	**Lung Capacity** (liters)

Explain Your Results

1. When you blow into the straw, what happens to the air you breathed in?
2. **Infer** Why were there differences in the diameters of the rings for different students?

Go Further

Does posture affect how much air you can breathe in and out? With your teacher's permission, make and carry out a plan to investigate this or another question.

Math in Science

Average Heart Rates

Your heart muscles keep working your entire life without stopping, pumping blood to the entire body. With each heartbeat, your heart muscles push blood out of the heart and into the blood vessels. You can feel these pushes as a pulse at certain points in the body, such as your wrist or the side of your neck.

The bar graph shows how the heart rate of human adults compares to the heart rates of various animals.

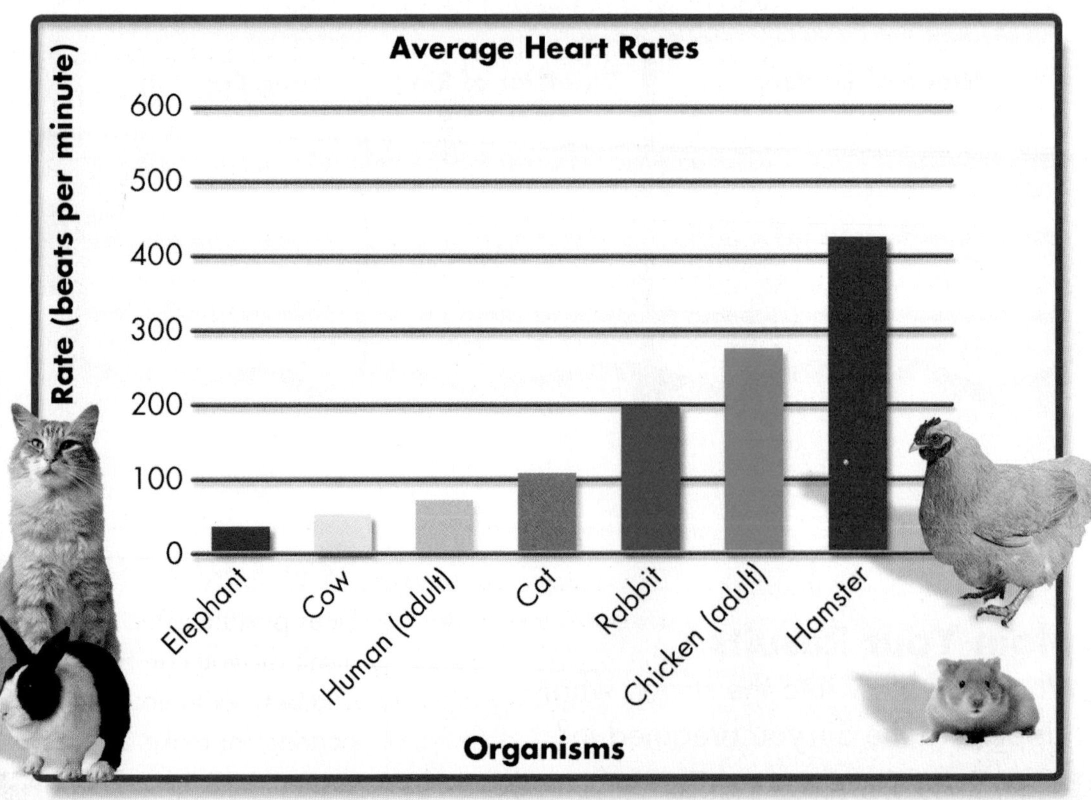
Average Heart Rates
Rate (beats per minute)
600
500
400
300
200
100
0
Elephant
Cow
Human (adult)
Cat
Rabbit
Chicken (adult)
Hamster
Organisms

e Tools Take It to the Net sfsuccessnet.com

Use the bar graph to answer the questions.

1. What is the best estimate of the heart rate of an elephant?
   A. 10 beats per minute
   B. 30 beats per minute
   C. 60 beats per minute
   D. 90 beats per minute

2. What general statement can be made from the information on this graph?
   F. The larger the animal, the faster the heart rate.
   G. The larger the animal, the slower the heart rate.
   H. Size and heart rate do not have any relationship.
   I. Small animals have a slightly slower heart rate than larger animals.

3. Using the trend in this graph, what would you predict would be the heart rate of a medium-sized dog?
   A. 30 beats per minute
   B. 60 beats per minute
   C. 100 beats per minute
   D. 180 beats per minute

4. Using the trend in this graph, what would you predict would be the heart rate of a horse?
   F. 50 beats per minute
   G. 100 beats per minute
   H. 150 beats per minute
   I. 200 beats per minute

Lab zone Take-Home Activity

Use a clock that has a second hand, and count your pulse for 20 seconds. Multiply this number times 3 to get your resting heart rate. Try different activities, such as walking, running, or bicycling for one minute each. Calculate your heart rate after each activity. Record your results in a bar graph.

Chapter 3 Review and Test Prep

Use Vocabulary

air sacs (p. 70)	**mucus** (p. 70)
artery (p. 66)	**trachea** (p. 70)
bronchioles (p. 70)	**valve** (p. 66)
capillary (p. 66)	**vein** (p. 66)
esophagus (p. 74)	

Use the term from the list above that best completes the sentence. You will use all of the terms.

1. The tube between the larynx and the bronchi is the ______.
2. The parts in the lungs where oxygen enters the bloodstream are ______.
3. The respiratory system cleans the air you breathe with a coating of sticky fluid called ______.
4. A(n) ______ keeps blood from flowing backward.
5. A(n) ______ carries blood from the heart to the smallest blood vessels, one of which is called a(n) ______.
6. Blood is carried by a(n) ______ toward the heart.
7. Ringed muscles of the ______ push food to the stomach.
8. Tubes that carry air inside the lungs are ______.

Explain Concepts

9. Explain how cells in your body benefit from different systems working together.
10. Explain the functions of the organs in the circulatory system.
11. Explain how systems in your body can be compared to mechanical systems or systems in a city's society.

Process Skills

12. **Infer** People with heart disease sometimes take drugs that prevent clots from forming in the blood vessels. Infer how and when these drugs might put a person's health and safety at risk.
13. **Make a model** of the digestive system by drawing a diagram like the one below. Label the job of each part.

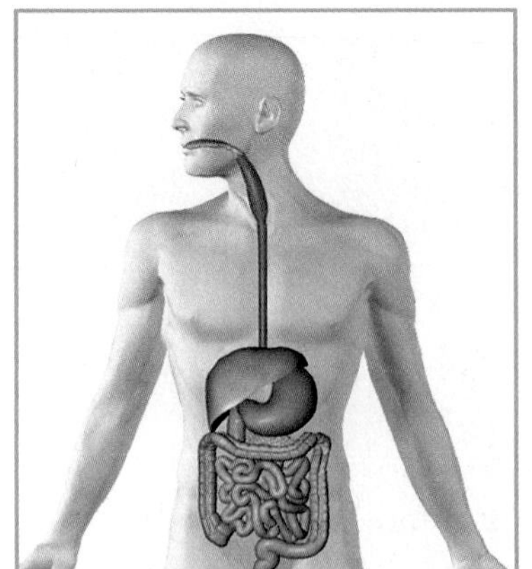

Sequence

14. Make a graphic organizer like the one shown below. In the boxes, write, in order, the parts of the respiratory system through which inhaled air passes.

Bronchial tubes
Bronchi
Trachea
Nose
Air sacs
Larynx

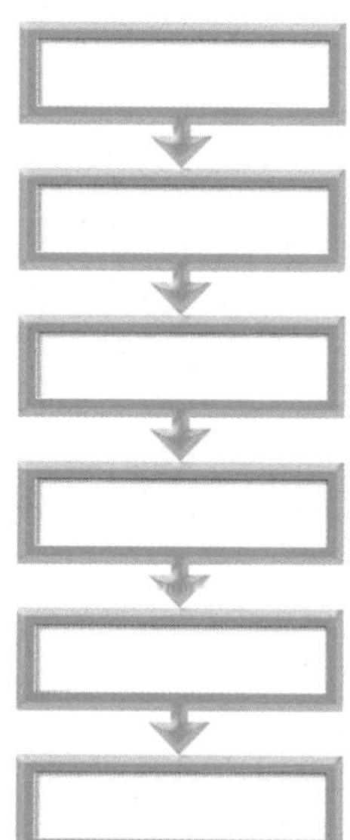

Test Prep

15. What is the kidney?

Ⓐ an organ that cleans the blood
Ⓑ a structure that keeps blood flowing through the heart
Ⓒ the place where carbon dioxide leaves the bloodstream
Ⓓ an organ where food is stored

16. What structures connect the smallest arteries with the smallest veins?

Ⓕ air sacs
Ⓖ capillaries
Ⓗ bronchial tubes
Ⓘ valves

17. Which organs make digestive fluids?

Ⓐ esophagus, stomach, small intestine, and large intestine
Ⓑ esophagus, pancreas, liver, and large intestine
Ⓒ stomach, small intestine, pancreas, and large intestine
Ⓓ stomach, pancreas, and liver

18. Which of these systems does NOT carry waste out of the body?

Ⓕ circulatory
Ⓖ respiratory
Ⓗ digestive
Ⓘ urinary

19. Explain why the answer you selected for Question 18 is best. For each of the answers you do not select, give a reason why it is not the best choice.

20. Writing in Science **Descriptive**
Write a description of how the structure of the teeth helps them do their job in the digestive system.

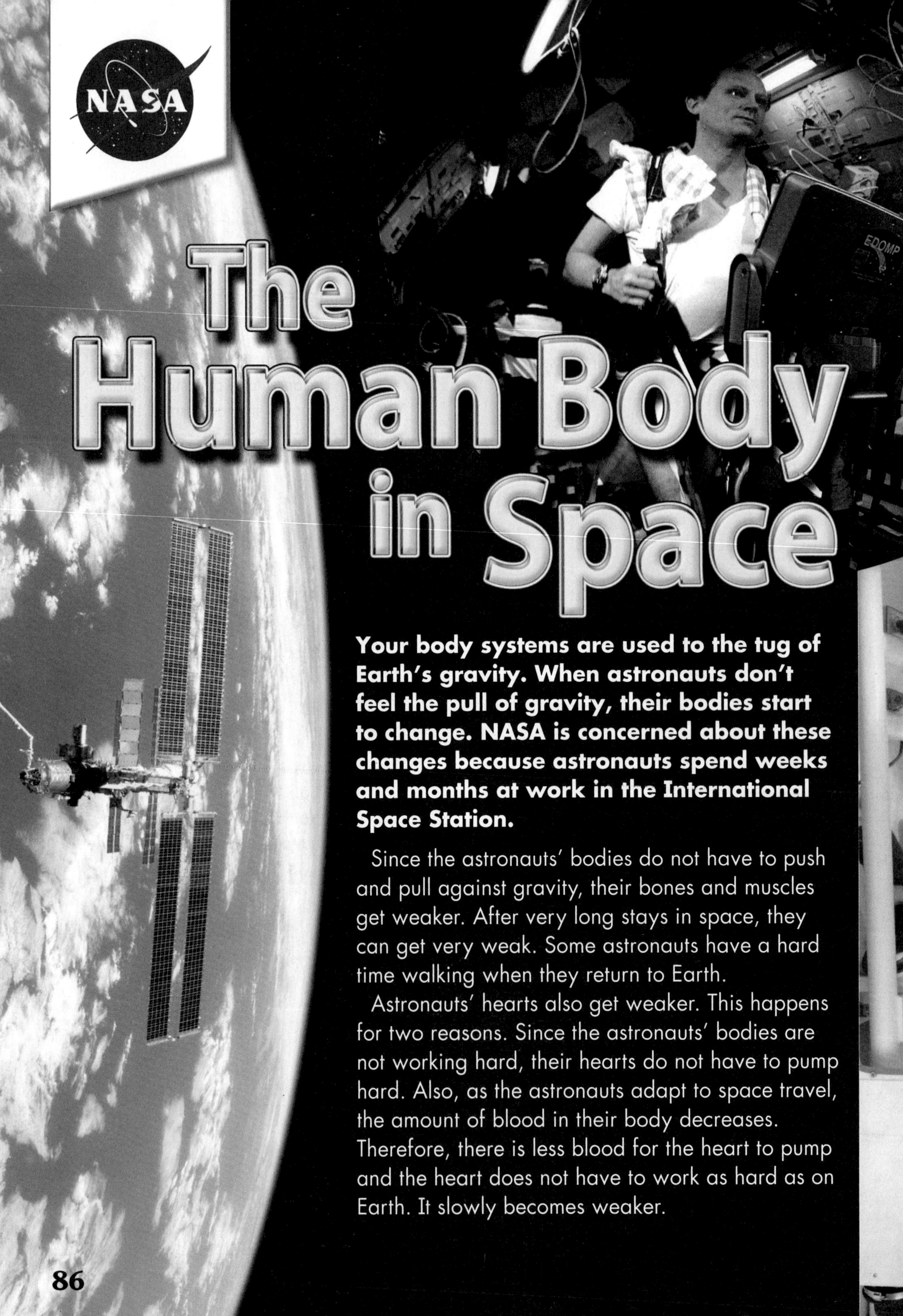
NASA
EDOMP

The Human Body in Space

Your body systems are used to the tug of Earth's gravity. When astronauts don't feel the pull of gravity, their bodies start to change. NASA is concerned about these changes because astronauts spend weeks and months at work in the International Space Station.

Since the astronauts' bodies do not have to push and pull against gravity, their bones and muscles get weaker. After very long stays in space, they can get very weak. Some astronauts have a hard time walking when they return to Earth.

Astronauts' hearts also get weaker. This happens for two reasons. Since the astronauts' bodies are not working hard, their hearts do not have to pump hard. Also, as the astronauts adapt to space travel, the amount of blood in their body decreases. Therefore, there is less blood for the heart to pump and the heart does not have to work as hard as on Earth. It slowly becomes weaker.

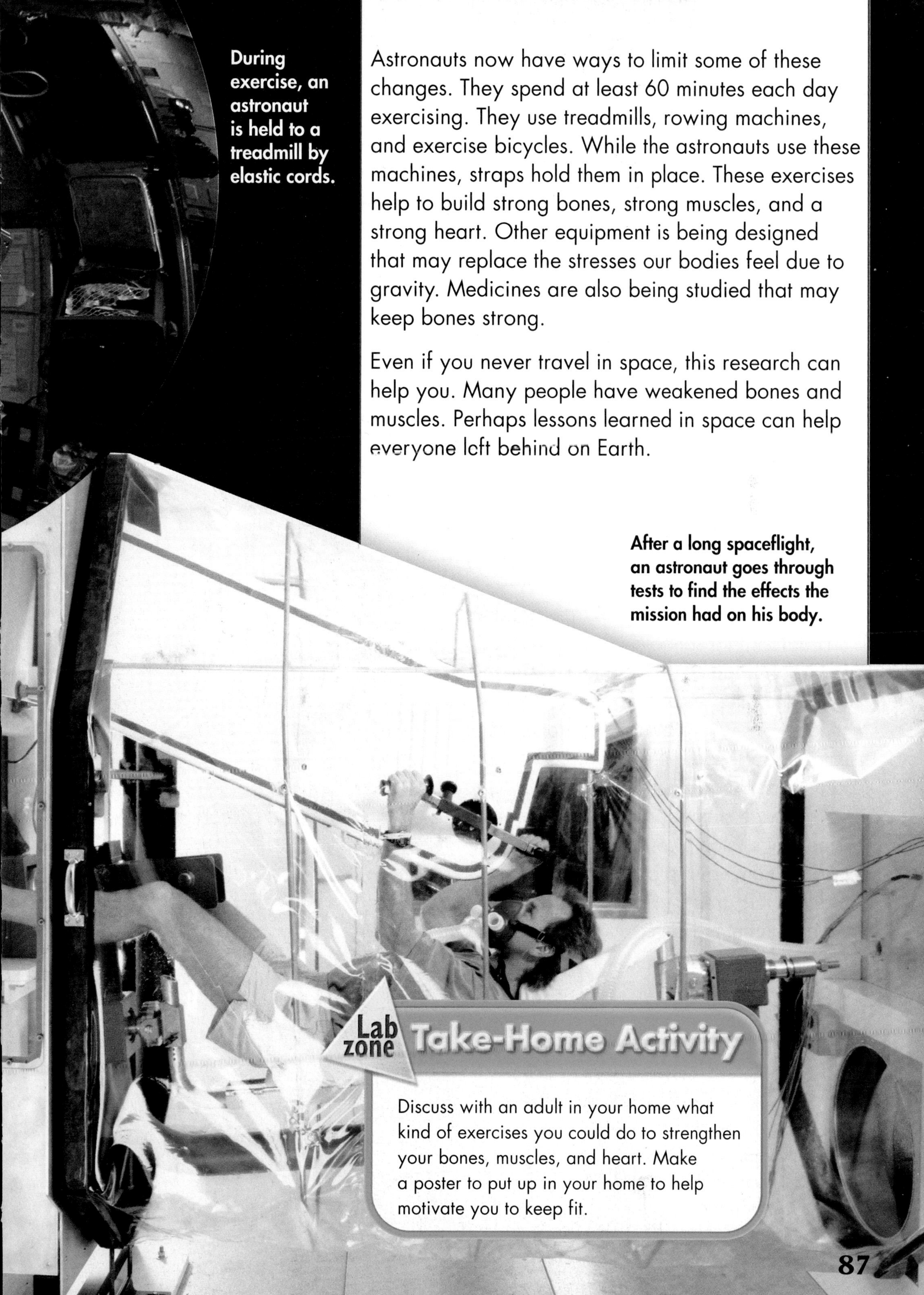

During exercise, an astronaut is held to a treadmill by elastic cords.

Astronauts now have ways to limit some of these changes. They spend at least 60 minutes each day exercising. They use treadmills, rowing machines, and exercise bicycles. While the astronauts use these machines, straps hold them in place. These exercises help to build strong bones, strong muscles, and a strong heart. Other equipment is being designed that may replace the stresses our bodies feel due to gravity. Medicines are also being studied that may keep bones strong.

Even if you never travel in space, this research can help you. Many people have weakened bones and muscles. Perhaps lessons learned in space can help everyone left behind on Earth.

After a long spaceflight, an astronaut goes through tests to find the effects the mission had on his body.

Lab zone Take-Home Activity

Discuss with an adult in your home what kind of exercises you could do to strengthen your bones, muscles, and heart. Make a poster to put up in your home to help motivate you to keep fit.

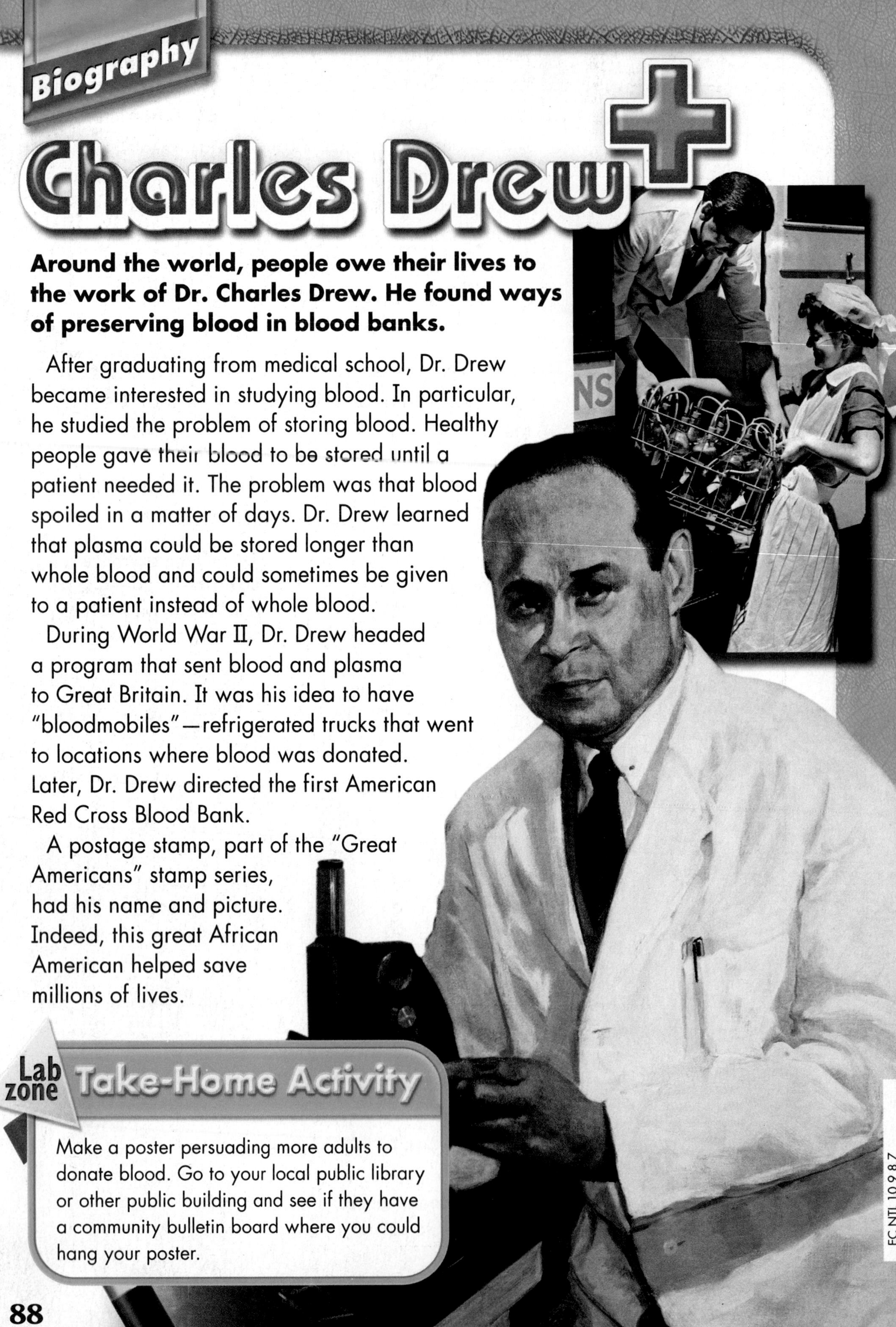
NS

Biography

Charles Drew

Around the world, people owe their lives to the work of Dr. Charles Drew. He found ways of preserving blood in blood banks.

After graduating from medical school, Dr. Drew became interested in studying blood. In particular, he studied the problem of storing blood. Healthy people gave their blood to be stored until a patient needed it. The problem was that blood spoiled in a matter of days. Dr. Drew learned that plasma could be stored longer than whole blood and could sometimes be given to a patient instead of whole blood.

During World War II, Dr. Drew headed a program that sent blood and plasma to Great Britain. It was his idea to have "bloodmobiles"—refrigerated trucks that went to locations where blood was donated. Later, Dr. Drew directed the first American Red Cross Blood Bank.

A postage stamp, part of the "Great Americans" stamp series, had his name and picture. Indeed, this great African American helped save millions of lives.

Lab zone Take-Home Activity

Make a poster persuading more adults to donate blood. Go to your local public library or other public building and see if they have a community bulletin board where you could hang your poster.

EC NTL 10987

Chapter 4

Plants

You Will Discover

- how plants make their own food.
- what stems and roots do.
- how plants reproduce.
- what affects plant growth.

online
Student Edition
sfsuccessnet.com

Build Background

How do plants stay alive and produce offspring?

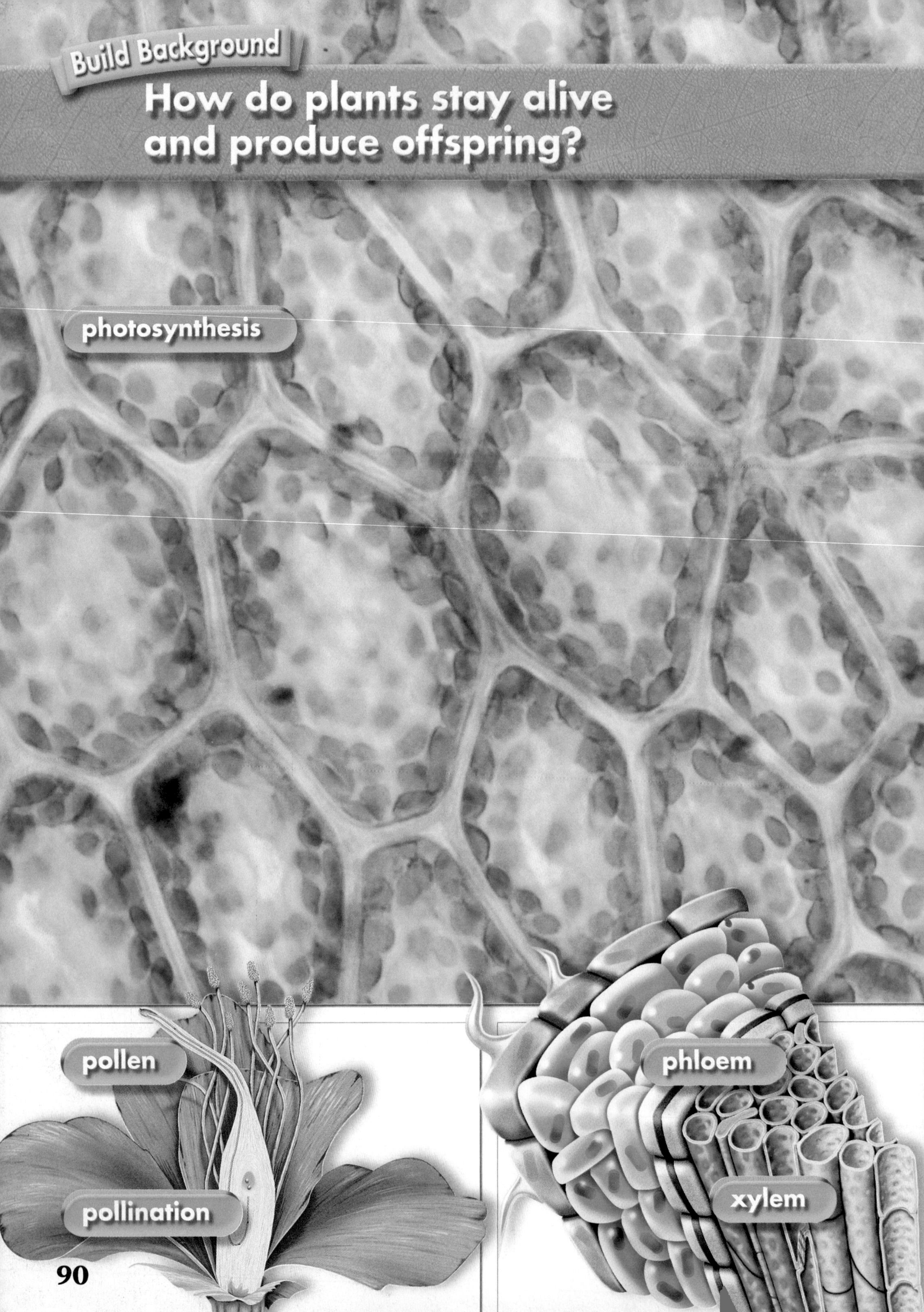
photosynthesis
pollen
pollination
phloem
xylem

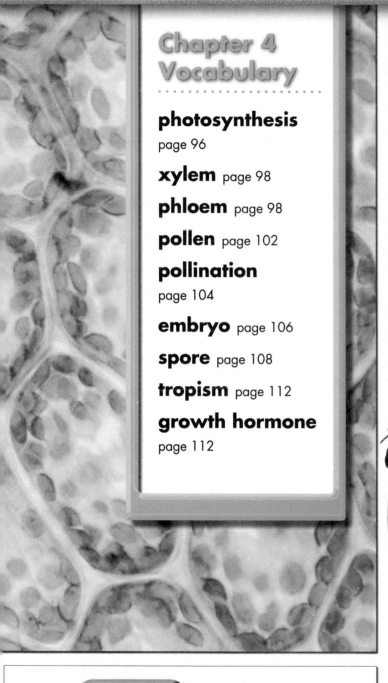

Chapter 4 Vocabulary

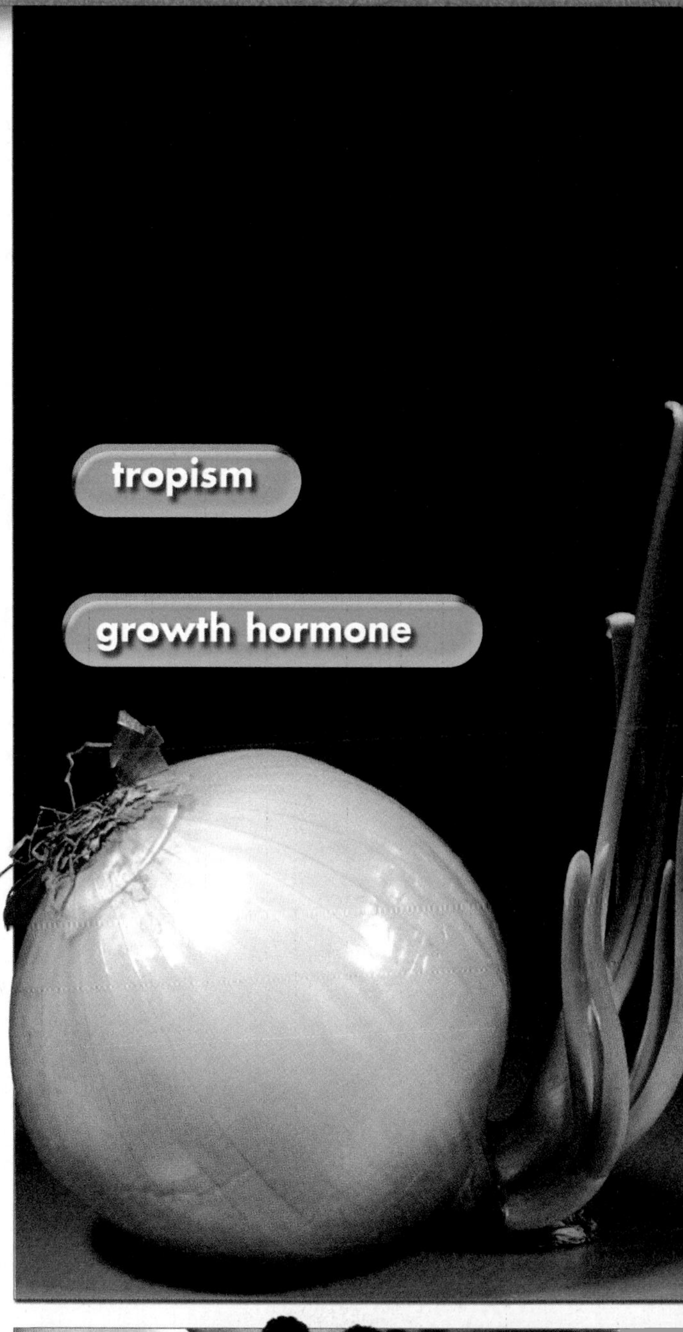

tropism
growth hormone

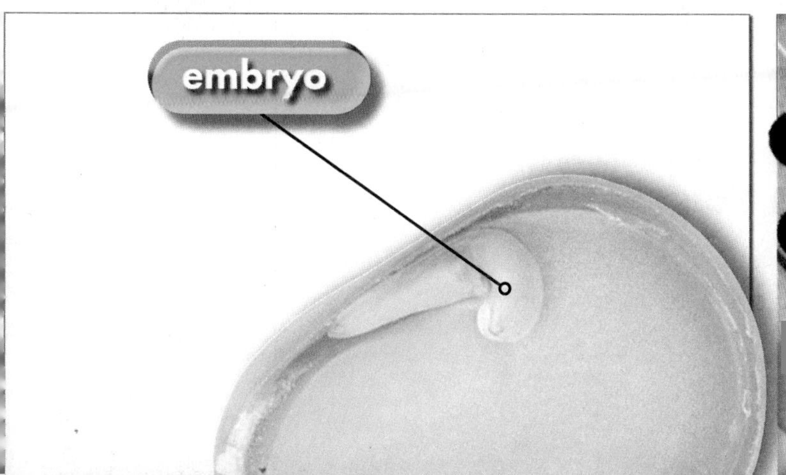

embryo

spore

Lab zone **Directed Inquiry**

Explore What color can come from leaves?

Materials

safety goggles

cup and spoon

5 leaves

scissors

rubbing alcohol

graduated cylinder (or measuring cup)

plastic wrap and paper towel

Process Skills

Before you **predict,** think about what you already know about the color of leaves.

What to Do

1. Cut the leaves into small pieces. Mash them in a cup with a spoon.

2. Add 50 mL of rubbing alcohol to the cup. Cover the cup with plastic wrap. Wait 15 minutes.

Be careful!

Wear safety goggles. Rubbing alcohol is poisonous. Do not taste.

3. Cut a strip of paper towel. Remove the plastic wrap from the cup. Drape the strip over the cup's edge. Put the plastic wrap back on.

4. **Predict** the color that will come from the leaves. **Observe** the strip after 15 minutes.

The strip must just touch the rubbing alcohol.

Explain Your Results

Explain the reasons for your **prediction.** Was your prediction accurate?

How to Read Science

Reading Skills

TARGET SKILL

Cause and Effect

A **cause** is why something happens. An **effect** is what happens.

When you read, sometimes clue words such as *because* and *since* signal a cause-and-effect relationship. Sometimes there are no clue words.

Sometimes the author does not give a cause, and you need to think about why something happened. Other times, you will **predict** the effects of an event the author describes.

Causes and effects are marked in the journal entry below.

Journal Entry

Plant Growth

The leaf I covered with foil a few days ago looks all shriveled. This is what I think happened. We were studying plant growth, so I did an experiment with a bean plant. I placed a bean plant on the window ledge. I covered one leaf of the plant with foil, because I wanted to see what effect it would have on plant growth. I left the plant on the ledge for several days. When I checked it today, the leaf looked dead.

Apply It!

Use a graphic organizer like the one at the right to show causes and effects from the journal entry above.

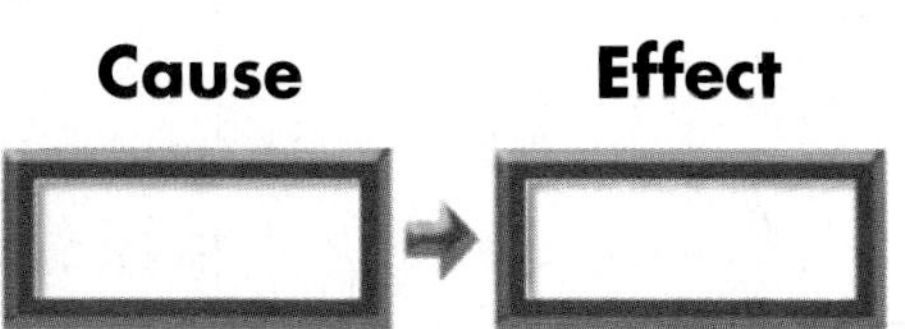
Cause
Effect

You Are There!

You are in a laboratory, using a microscope to study plant cells. As you peer through the lenses of the high-powered microscope, you see many different kinds of cells. Some are square. Some are long and narrow. You ask yourself, "How do these cells help the rest of the plant stay alive?"

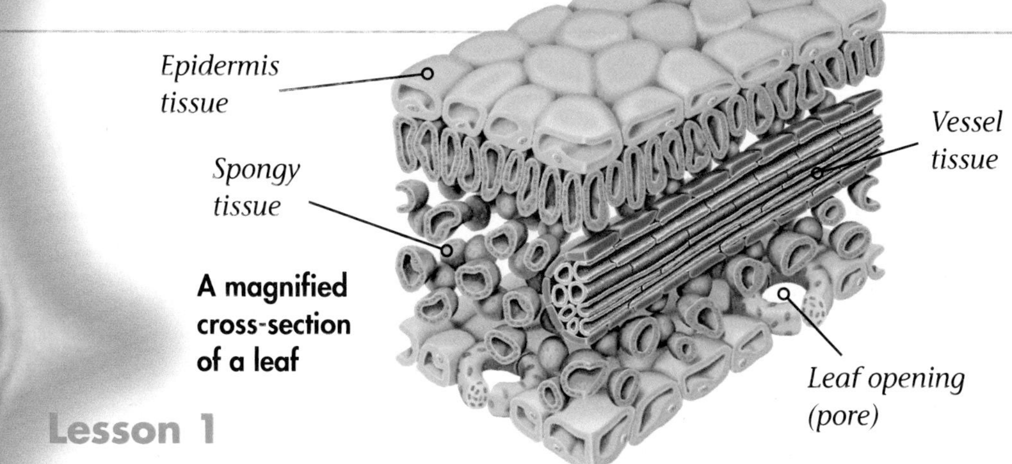
Epidermis tissue
Spongy tissue
Vessel tissue
Leaf opening (pore)

A magnified cross-section of a leaf

Lesson 1

How do leaves help a plant?

Leaves are made of cells and tissues. The process of photosynthesis takes place in the cells' chloroplasts.

Cells and Tissues in Leaves

What's your favorite green salad? You might like one made of spinach. Perhaps you choose iceberg lettuce or crispy romaine. When you munch on any of these, you're eating leaves. A leaf is a major plant part. Unlike animals, plants make their own food. Most of a plant's food is made in its leaves.

Leaves are organs made of cells and tissues. The diagram above shows the layers of a leaf. You can see layers of similar cells. These are the tissues that make up the leaf. The outside layer of flat cells is the epidermis. In some ways, this tissue is similar to the top layer of your skin. It helps protect the plant. The inner tissue looks like a sponge. It has spaces that air can pass through. Tiny openings at the bottom of the leaf can open to let air in and out of the inner tissue.

The vessel tissue is also made of cells. Look closely at the diagram. Do you see the tubes? In some ways these tubes are like our blood vessels. They carry food and water through the plant to all the other plant parts.

1. **√ Checkpoint** What part of the leaf can best be compared to your skin?
2. **Writing in Science** **Descriptive** Observe the diagram above. In your **science journal,** describe the similar cells that make up epidermis tissue in the leaf and how other tissues have different shapes of cells.

Photosynthesis

You have probably heard that in order for plants to live, their cells need energy from sunlight. That is true. But you may wonder how this happens. How does a plant use energy from sunlight? How can any of the cells do work at night without sunlight? How do the cells in the roots live without ever getting sunlight?

You can answer these questions if you know that plant cells use cellular respiration, just like our cells. That is, they use oxygen with food to get the energy they need for growth, repairs, and reproduction.

Photosynthesis is the process that plants and some other organisms use to make sugar for food. Photosynthesis happens in the chloroplasts of plant cells. Remember that chloroplasts are in plant cells but not in animal cells. In photosynthesis, carbon dioxide and water are used to make sugar and oxygen. Plants are a major source of oxygen in the atmosphere.

Sunlight supplies the energy needed for photosynthesis. This process is often written as:

carbon dioxide + water + sunlight energy → oxygen + sugar

The sugar is moved to all the cells of the plant, including the cells in the underground roots. The plant's cells do not always use the sugar immediately. The plant will store some of the sugar to use at night. For long-term storage, plants join many sugars to form a chemical called starch.

Plants are not the only organisms that get energy from sugar and starch. You do too! Whenever you eat foods from plants, you eat the plants' sugars and starches. Potatoes and grain are parts of plants that are made up mostly of stored starches. Your cells use these as sources of energy.

Sugar is not just a source of energy. Thousands of sugars combine in plants to form cellulose. This chemical makes up the strong cell walls of plants.

As the microscope zooms in to see individual plant cells, you can see that it is the chloroplasts that give a plant its green color.

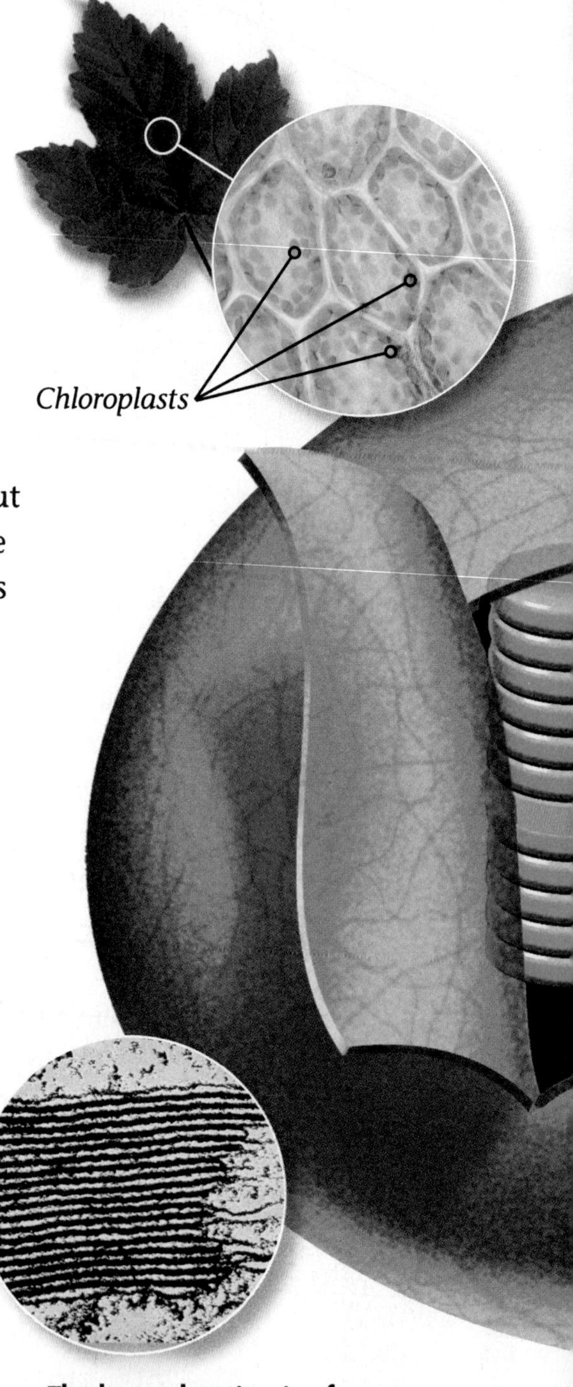
Chloroplasts

The large drawing is of a single chloroplast. Inside chloroplasts are structures that look like plates. Chlorophyll is in these plates. The small inset above is an image of these plates from a microscope.

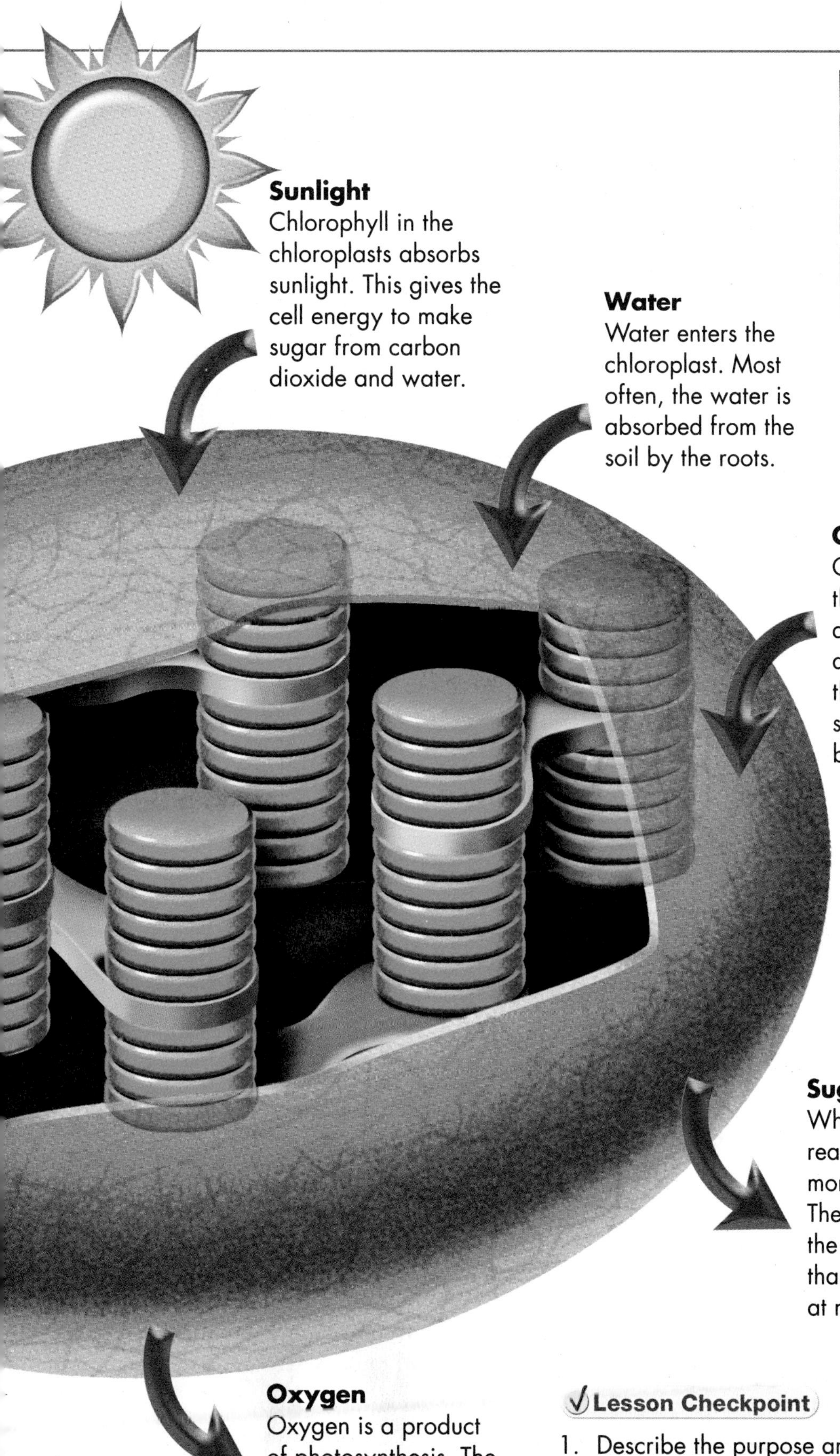

Tiny bubbles of oxygen on this water weed resulted from photosynthesis.

Sunlight
Chlorophyll in the chloroplasts absorbs sunlight. This gives the cell energy to make sugar from carbon dioxide and water.

Water
Water enters the chloroplast. Most often, the water is absorbed from the soil by the roots.

Carbon Dioxide
Carbon dioxide enters the chloroplast. Carbon dioxide comes from the atmosphere. It enters the plant through the small holes in the bottom of the leaves.

Sugar
When more sunlight reaches the chloroplast, more sugar is made. There is more sugar in the plant on sunny days than on cloudy days or at night.

Oxygen
Oxygen is a product of photosynthesis. The plant releases some of this oxygen through the holes in the bottom of the leaves.

√ Lesson Checkpoint

1. Describe the purpose and process of photosynthesis. How does the process change during a full day?
2. How does photosynthesis in plants benefit animals?
3. **Cause and Effect** What is one cause of oxygen being found in the atmosphere?

How do stems and roots help a plant?

Stems and roots are major plant organs. They have special structures and jobs to perform.

Stems

Stems, like leaves, are plant organs. Leaves are attached to stems. Many stems hold leaves high. Why do you think this is helpful? Plants need light to make food. The higher leaves are less likely to be shaded by their neighbors than lower leaves. Stems also hold fruit and flowers on plants.

Have you ever poked yourself on a plant's thorn? This sharp point may really be a protective stem. Some other pesky plant parts, such as cactus needles, are actually special leaves.

Xylem and Phloem

Material moves through two special tissues inside some plants. These tissues are called xylem and phloem. They are found in the roots, stems, and leaves. Not all plants have xylem and phloem, but those that do are called vascular plants.

Xylem tissues are tubes that carry materials from the roots to the leaves. The roots of plants soak up water from the soil. The water carries particles called minerals from the soil. Cells need minerals in some of their activities, including photosynthesis.

Phloem tissues are tubes that carry sugar away from the leaves. The sugar in plants is dissolved in water. This mixture of sugar water flows through the phloem from the leaves to the rest of the plant.

In trees, phloem is made just below the bark. When new phloem cells form and grow, they push old, dead phloem outward. This dead phloem makes up the bark. Bark protects the phloem behind it. You probably would not want to chew on a tree's stem, but you have probably eaten other plant stems. Did you know that asparagus spears are stems?

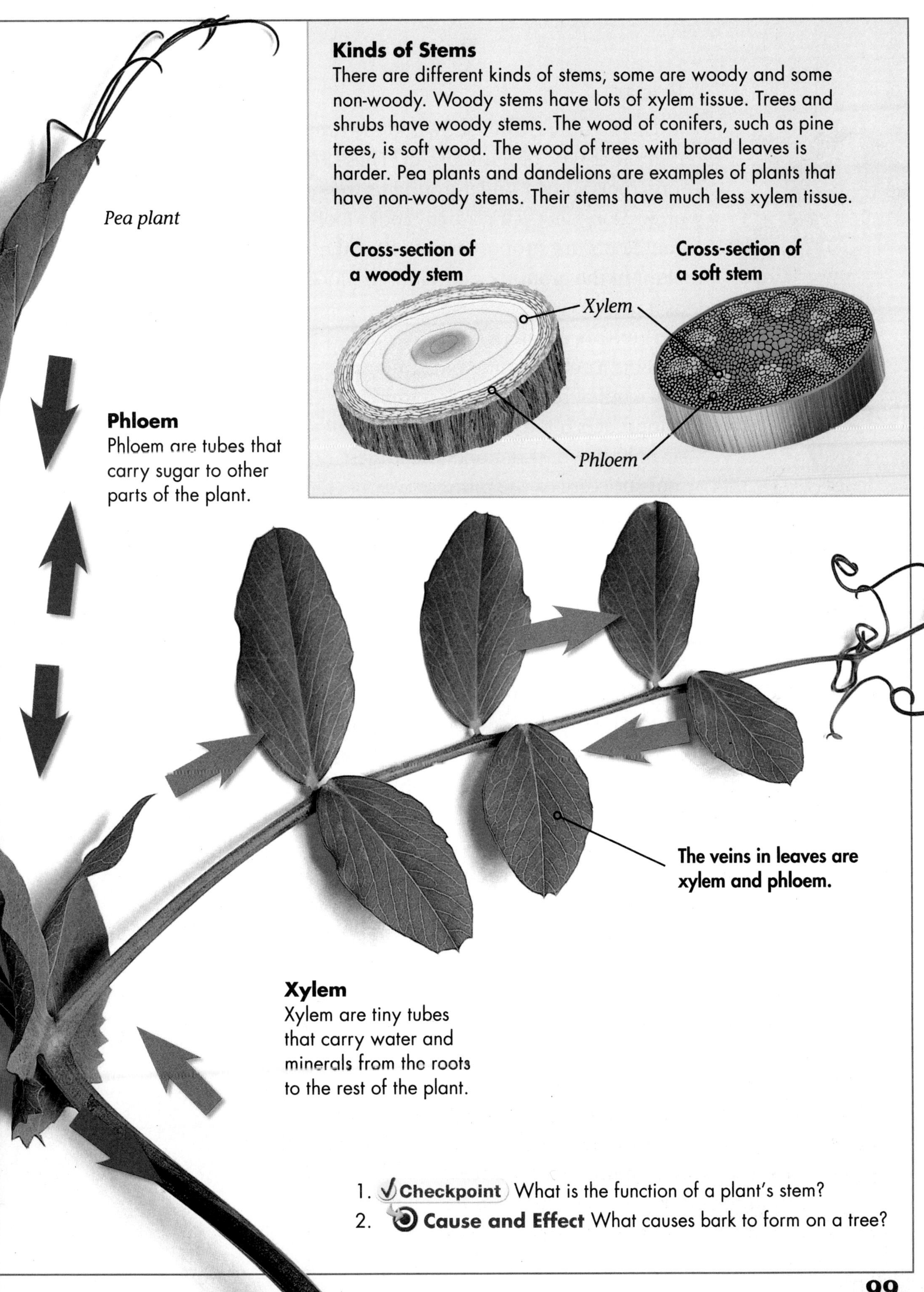
Pea plant
Phloem
Phloem are tubes that carry sugar to other parts of the plant.
Cross-section of a woody stem
Cross-section of a soft stem
Xylem
Phloem
The veins in leaves are xylem and phloem.
Xylem
Xylem are tiny tubes that carry water and minerals from the roots to the rest of the plant.

Kinds of Stems

There are different kinds of stems, some are woody and some non-woody. Woody stems have lots of xylem tissue. Trees and shrubs have woody stems. The wood of conifers, such as pine trees, is soft wood. The wood of trees with broad leaves is harder. Pea plants and dandelions are examples of plants that have non-woody stems. Their stems have much less xylem tissue.

1. **Checkpoint** What is the function of a plant's stem?
2. **Cause and Effect** What causes bark to form on a tree?

Roots

This spindly cluster shown to the right is another type of plant organ. These long roots spread underground as they grow. Don't let their scrawny looks fool you! Roots are strong. They anchor the plant in the ground and hold it in place as it grows.

There are different kinds of root systems. Each has different structures. One kind of root system is a taproot. A taproot is a large root that grows straight down. It remains the largest root structure as the plant grows. Taproots may store food for the plant. Small roots may grow sideways out of the main taproot.

Another root system is a fibrous root system. In this system, many roots grow out in all directions. The roots divide many times into smaller and smaller roots. The fibrous roots of a tree sometimes look like an upside-down version of the above-ground branches.

Roots grow longer because of special tissues near the root tips. Here, cells divide quickly to form new cells. As each of these new cells grows longer, together they push the root tip farther into the ground.

Edible Roots
Next time you chomp on a carrot, remember that you're eating a taproot. Beets, turnips, and radishes are also taproots.

This is a fibrous root system of a sweet pea.

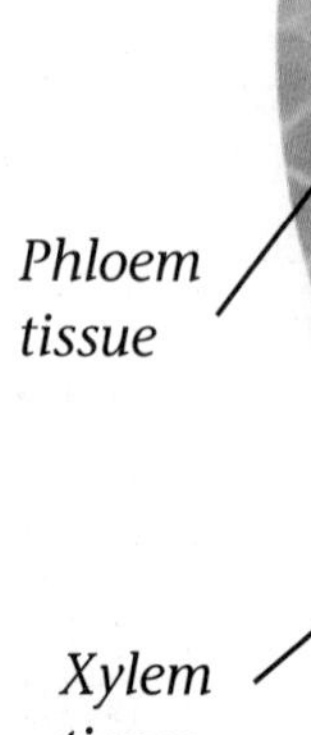

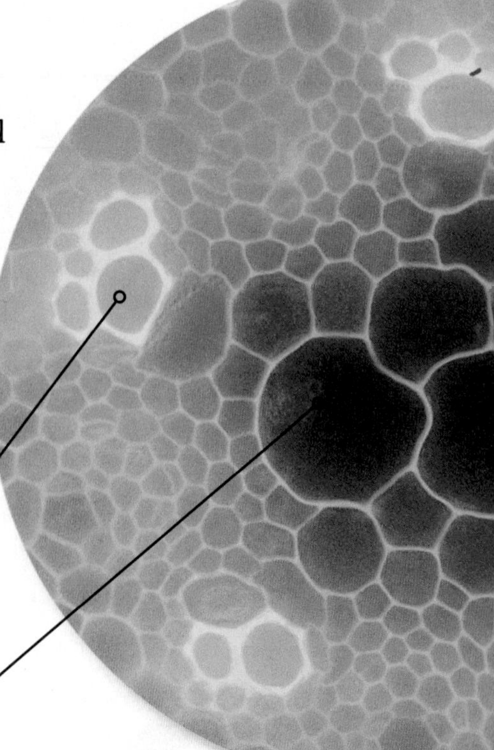
Phloem tissue
Xylem tissue

If you were to look at the center of a buttercup root through a microscope, you could see that the xylem are larger than the phloem.

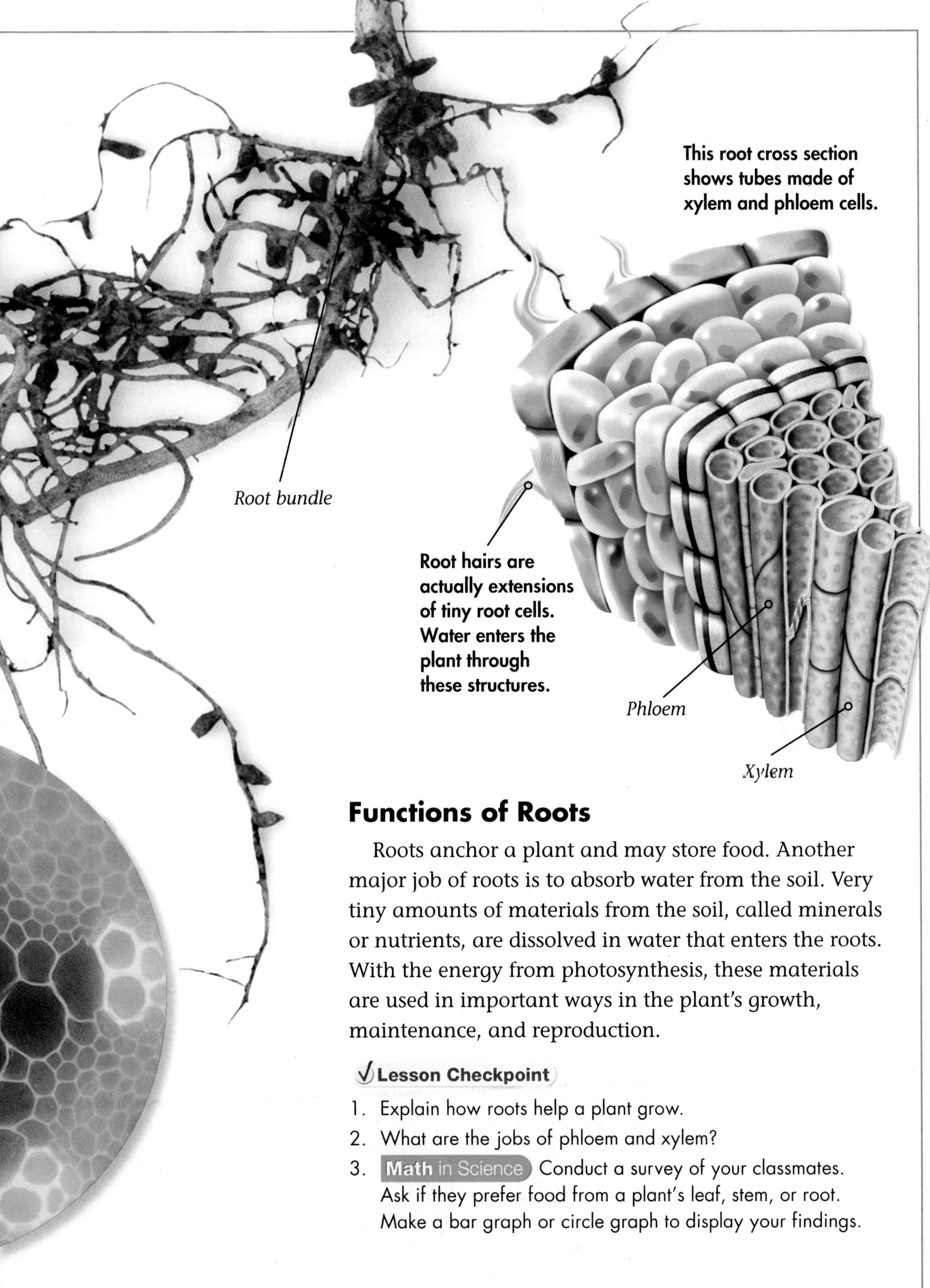
This root cross section shows tubes made of xylem and phloem cells.
Root bundle
Root hairs are actually extensions of tiny root cells. Water enters the plant through these structures.
Phloem
Xylem

Functions of Roots

Roots anchor a plant and may store food. Another major job of roots is to absorb water from the soil. Very tiny amounts of materials from the soil, called minerals or nutrients, are dissolved in water that enters the roots. With the energy from photosynthesis, these materials are used in important ways in the plant's growth, maintenance, and reproduction.

√ Lesson Checkpoint

1. Explain how roots help a plant grow.
2. What are the jobs of phloem and xylem?
3. **Math in Science** Conduct a survey of your classmates. Ask if they prefer food from a plant's leaf, stem, or root. Make a bar graph or circle graph to display your findings.

Lesson 3

How do plants reproduce?

Flowers are organs made of tissues of similar cells. Flowers are responsible for plants' reproduction. Some plants can reproduce without flowers.

Parts of the Flower

The petals are often the most colorful tissues of a flower. Animals may be attracted to a plant by the petals. Not every flower has showy petals. The tassels at the top of a corn plant and ears of corn are flowers.

The stamen is the male part of a flower. **Pollen,** a grainy, often yellow powder, is made in a tissue at the top of each stamen. A single flower may have many stamens.

The pistil is the female part of the flower. A pistil often has a bottle shape, with a wide bottom and a narrow neck. A flower may have more than one pistil.

Not all flowers have both stamens and pistils. Flowers with only one of these parts are called imperfect flowers. Some maple trees have imperfect flowers. Flowers with both parts are called perfect flowers. The passion flower shown here is a perfect flower.

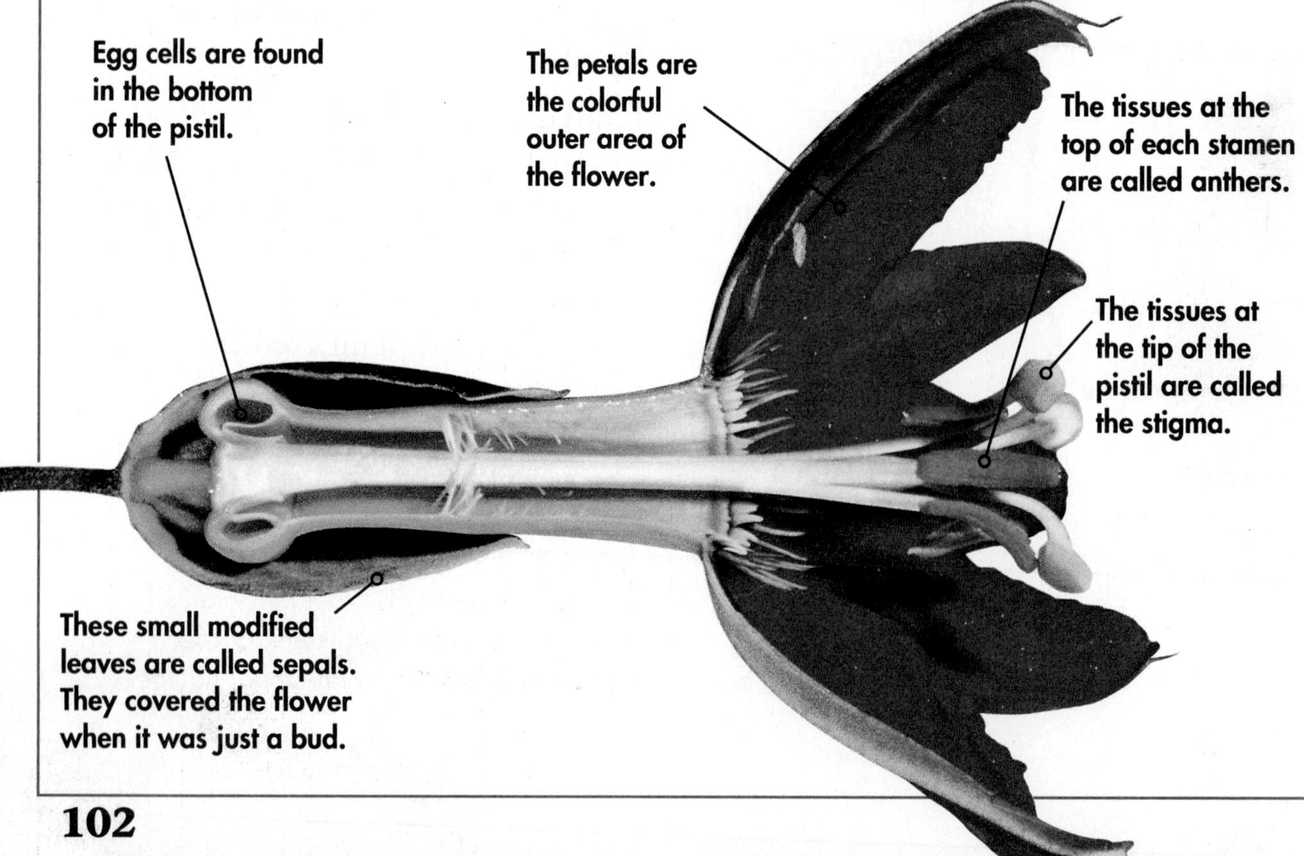
Egg cells are found in the bottom of the pistil.
The petals are the colorful outer area of the flower.
The tissues at the top of each stamen are called anthers.
The tissues at the tip of the pistil are called the stigma.
These small modified leaves are called sepals. They covered the flower when it was just a bud.

Composite Flowers

With those yellow petals fanning out, it's easy to see how the sunflower got its name, isn't it? Sunflowers are in the family of composite flowers. At first glance, this looks like one big flower. Take a closer look. The sunflower is actually made of hundreds of tiny flowers.

Passing Information

Plants must have a way to reproduce before they die. If a species did not reproduce, it would soon become extinct.

When plants reproduce, they make new plants that usually look like their parents. They have the same shapes of flowers and leaves. For this to happen, plants must have a reliable way to pass information from one generation to the next. This information is in DNA. DNA contains all the information for making flowers, leaves, and every part of the plant. Sexual reproduction is the passing of DNA from two parents to their offspring. In plants, flowers are the organs where sexual reproduction takes place.

1. **Checkpoint** How are plant offspring like their parents? Why does this happen?
2. **Writing in Science** **Descriptive** Use a magnifying glass to observe the parts of a flower. In your **science journal,** write a description of the different structures you see.

Parts of the Flower

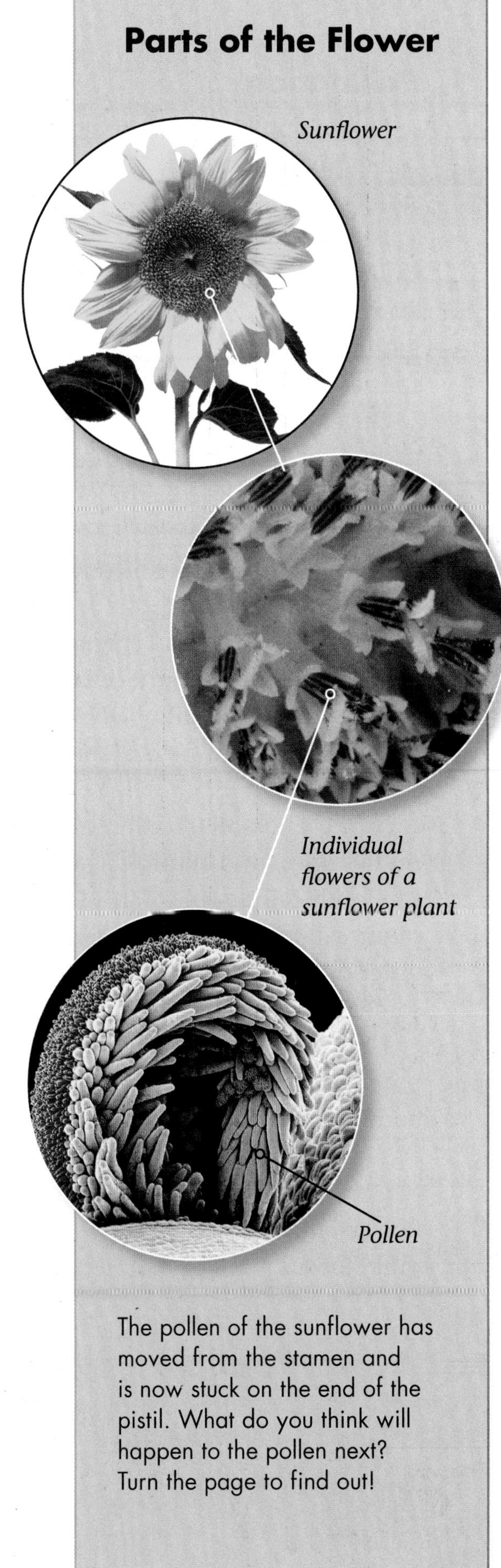
Sunflower
Individual flowers of a sunflower plant
Pollen

The pollen of the sunflower has moved from the stamen and is now stuck on the end of the pistil. What do you think will happen to the pollen next? Turn the page to find out!

Pollination

Moving pollen from the stamen to the pistil is called **pollination.** Pollination can involve the stamen and pistil of the same plant or of two plants.

Pollination takes place in different ways. Wind or water can move pollen. Insects, bats, and birds going from flower to flower can also move pollen. Some plant species are pollinated in only one way. Other species can be pollinated in many ways.

Once pollination takes place, a tube grows from the pollen down to the egg cells in the bottom of the pistil. Special cells called sperm cells travel down the tube and join the egg cells. This joining of cells is called fertilization. Fertilization is the first step in the life of a new plant.

The DNA of egg and sperm is a little unusual compared to other plant cells. Each egg or sperm has only half the amount of DNA found in other cells. When an egg and sperm join, they make one whole set of DNA.

As days pass, the fertilized egg will grow, divide many times, and change. The result is a seed with a tiny multicellular plant inside. Every cell of the new plant will have the same set of DNA. Sometimes the other parts of the flower grow around the seeds to be something tasty, such as an apple or an orange.

The young plant will grow to look much like the parents. There might be differences, though. That's because half of the young plant's DNA was from each parent plant. For example, when pollen from a plant with red flowers pollinates a plant with white flowers, the offspring may be a plant with pink flowers.

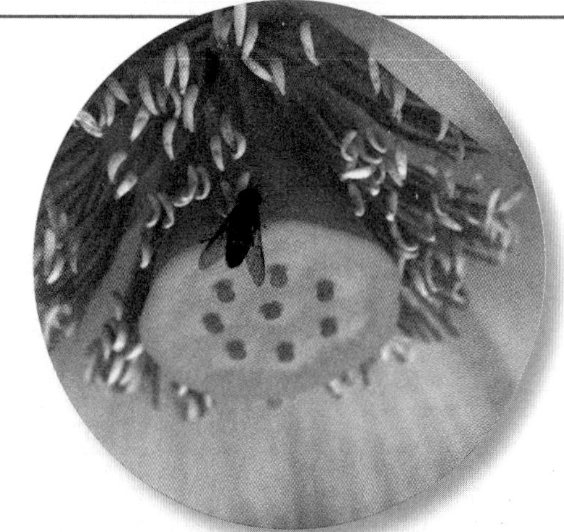

Insects find sweet nectar in flowers. When insects move around a flower to get nectar, they may move pollen from stamens to pistils.

Small differences in DNA lead to different flower colors in the same species of plant.

SciLinks Take It to the Net sfsuccessnet.com keyword: pollination Code: g5p104

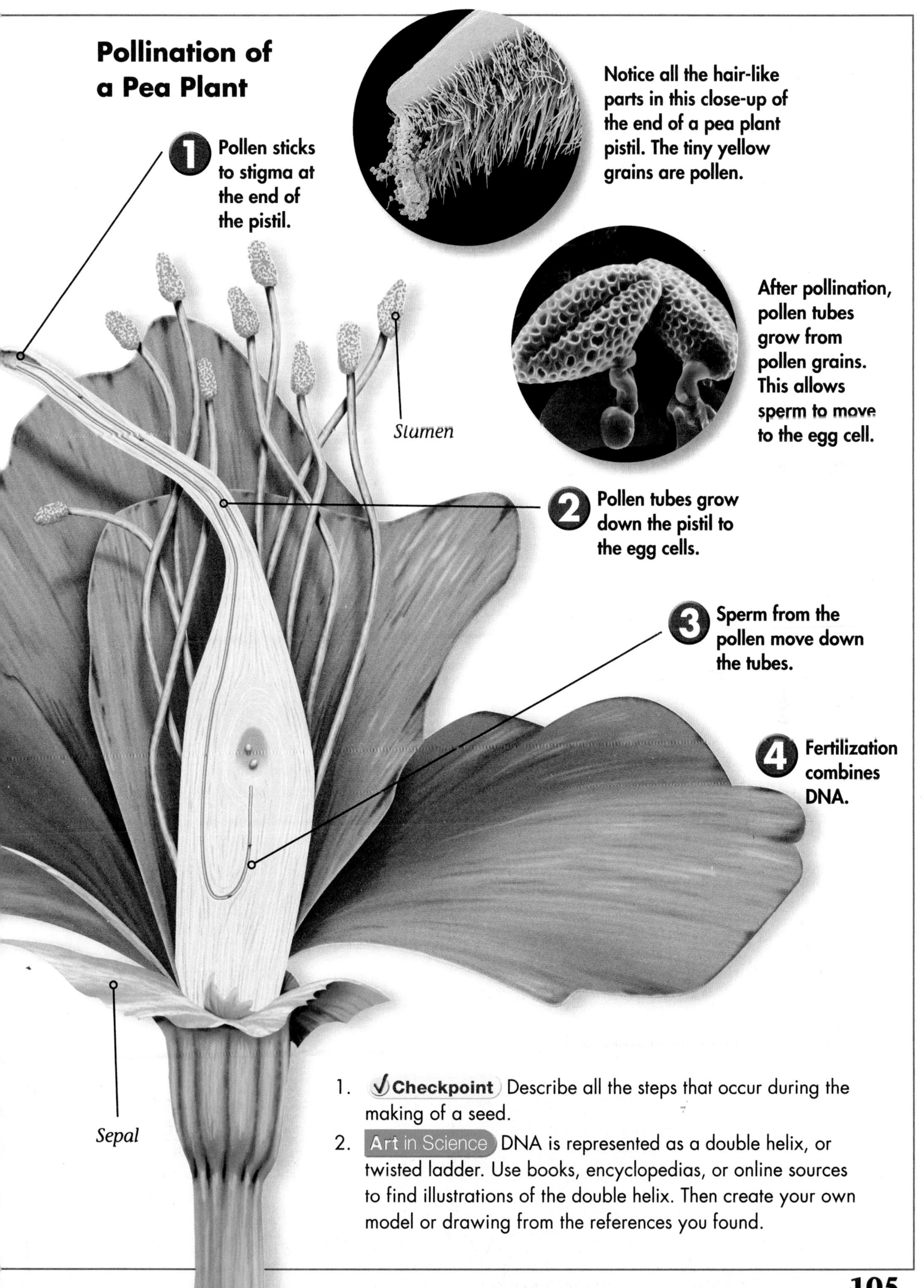
Pollination of a Pea Plant
1 Pollen sticks to stigma at the end of the pistil.
Notice all the hair-like parts in this close-up of the end of a pea plant pistil. The tiny yellow grains are pollen.
After pollination, pollen tubes grow from pollen grains. This allows sperm to move to the egg cell.
Stamen
2 Pollen tubes grow down the pistil to the egg cells.
3 Sperm from the pollen move down the tubes.
4 Fertilization combines DNA.
Sepal

1. ✓Checkpoint Describe all the steps that occur during the making of a seed.
2. Art in Science DNA is represented as a double helix, or twisted ladder. Use books, encyclopedias, or online sources to find illustrations of the double helix. Then create your own model or drawing from the references you found.

Going to Seed

A seed is made of three main parts, the seed coat, embryo, and endosperm. A seed coat is a covering that has two roles. It protects a new plant called an **embryo.** The seed coat also guards a stash of stored food called endosperm.

An embryo has structures called seed leaves or cotyledons. The seeds of some plants have one cotyledon. These plants are called monocots. Plants that have seeds with two cotyledons are called dicots.

Vessels in both kinds of plants are grouped in bundles. If you cut across a dicot stem, you will see a circle of bundles. In monocots, these bundles are scattered throughout the stem.

There are many differences between monocots and dicots. There is not a single difference that can be used to classify all flowering plants as one or the other.

	monocot	dicot
A monocot seed, like corn, has one area of stored food. A dicot, such as a bean, has two areas that are easily split apart.		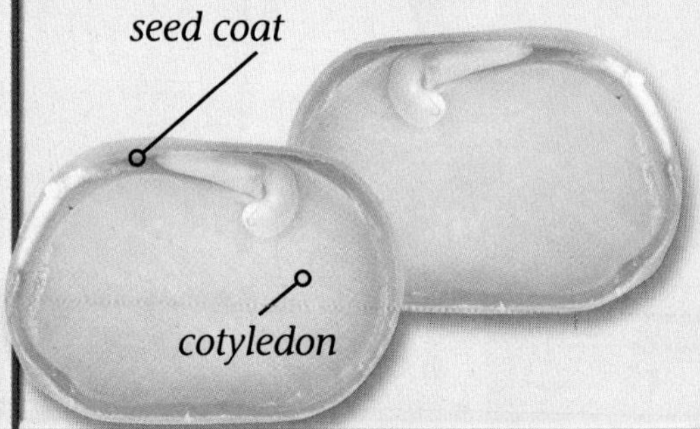 *seed coat* *cotyledon*
A monocot leaf has veins that are parallel, while a dicot's leaf has veins that branch out.		
Many monocots have fibrous root systems. Many dicots have taproot systems.		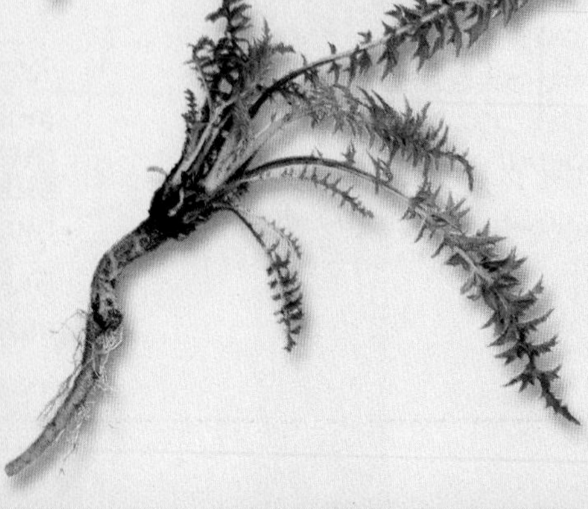

Some seeds such as this coconut can float on ocean currents and be carried for many miles.

Animals can spread seeds when they eat berries.

Spreading Seeds

In some plants, seeds just plop onto the ground and begin to sprout. Scattering seeds is not always that simple. Remember how some animals were helpful in pollination? They also help plants by scattering seeds.

When plants grow tasty fruit around their seeds, they are more likely to have their seeds spread by animals. When animals eat berries, sometimes the berry seeds pass through the digestive system of the animal. The seeds sprout far from the original plant. What other ways do you know that seeds can be spread?

Once the seed is moved from the parent plant, the embryo will stay in the seed until the outside conditions, such as temperature and moisture, are right. Then the seed will sprout. When the seed sprouts, the life cycle repeats. The sprout grows, develops into a mature plant that can reproduce, and it eventually dies. Most seeds cannot wait too long to sprout, though. Eventually, the embryo will die.

Burrs can get tangled on an animal's fur and may be carried far from the parent plant. When they drop to the ground the seeds inside may grow into a new plant.

1. **√Checkpoint** What is the life cycle of a plant that produces seeds?
2. **Math in Science** The double coconut tree produces the most massive seed, often more than 20 kilograms. Research the weights or masses of different types of seeds. Present your findings in a bar graph.

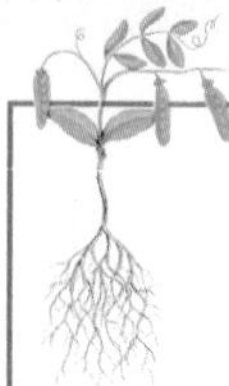

Spores

Mosses and ferns are plants that do not make flowers. The life cycles of these plants have two parts. During one part of the life cycle, the plants will have fertilization. During the other part of the life cycle, they use spores to reproduce. A plant **spore** is a single plant cell that can develop into a new plant, as you can see on page 109.

Spores are different from seeds in some ways. Plant spores do not have a multicellular embryo like seeds have. Also, spores are not made by fertilization like seeds are.

Spores are like seeds in many other ways. They both have stored food. Some spores are covered with a protective wall. Some spores can wait a long time for the right conditions before they start to grow.

Under the best conditions, duckweed reproduces every few days. At this rate, it can quickly cover a pond.

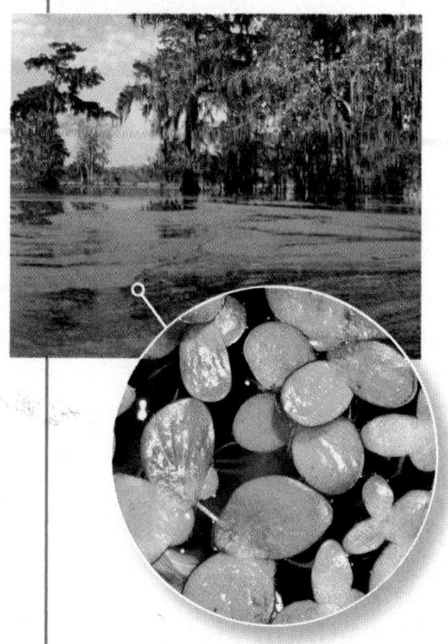

Reproducing Without Seeds

Many plants can reproduce without sperm cells and egg cells. This kind of reproduction is called asexual reproduction. In asexual reproduction, there is only one parent. Since all genetic information comes from one parent, the offspring will normally have the same genes as the parent.

Runners and Budding

Many plants can reproduce asexually by growing new plants from their stems or roots. Spider plants are common houseplants. They can reproduce by growing new plants on long stems called runners. Strawberries also can reproduce in this way. Many types of grass will spread by growing new plants from underground roots. All of these plants can also reproduce with seeds.

As its name hints, duckweed is a tiny plant that floats on ponds and is food for ducks and other birds. Duckweed is one of the smallest flowering plants, but it reproduces mostly by a kind of asexual reproduction called budding. Little buds form on the plant and drop off to grow as separate plants.

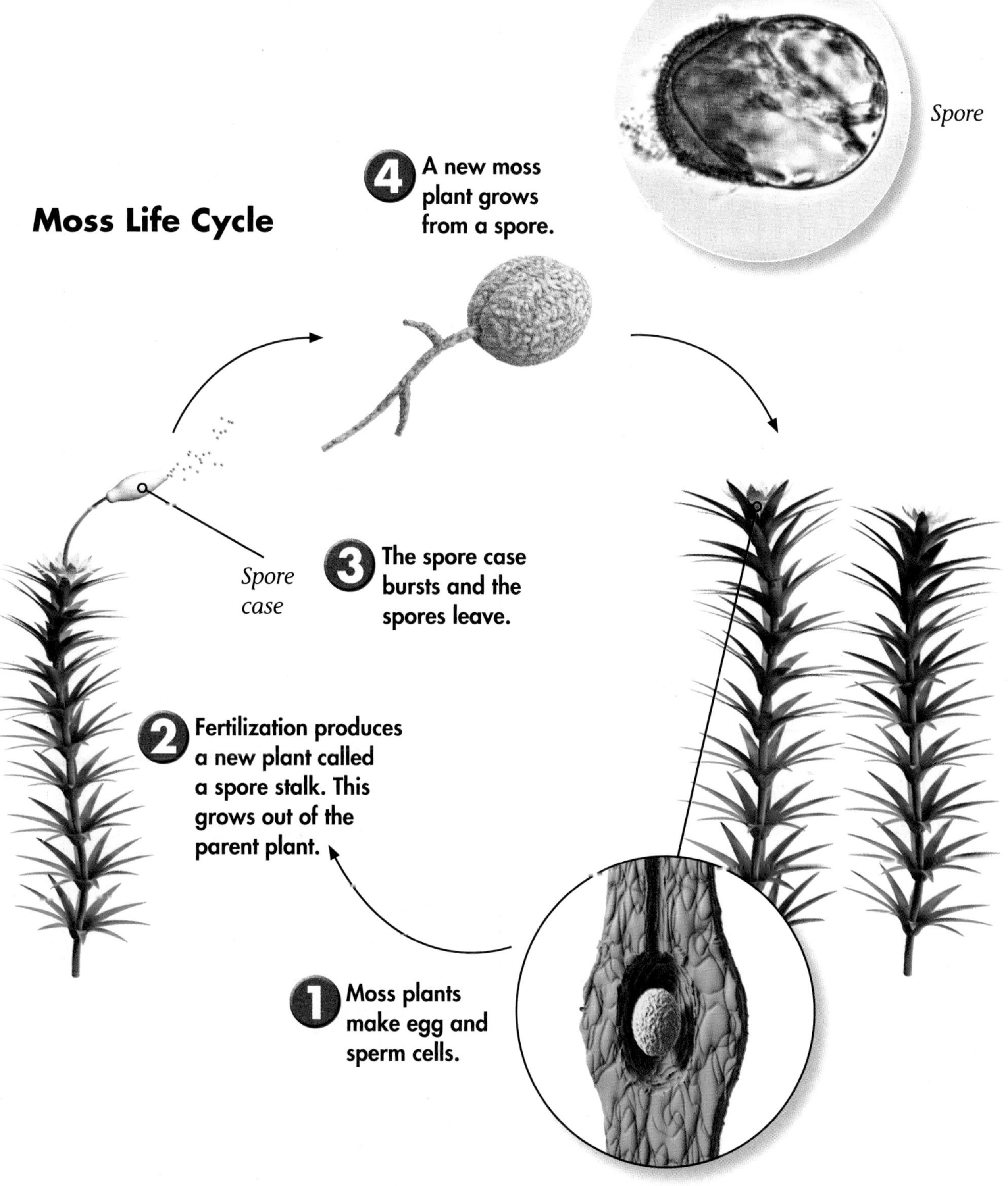
Moss Life Cycle
4 A new moss plant grows from a spore.
Spore
Spore case
3 The spore case bursts and the spores leave.
2 Fertilization produces a new plant called a spore stalk. This grows out of the parent plant.
1 Moss plants make egg and sperm cells.

✓ Lesson Checkpoint

1. Compare and contrast sexual and asexual reproduction.
2. Describe two methods of asexual reproduction.
3. **Writing in Science** **Descriptive** In your **science journal,** write an article that explains how animals help plants to reproduce and spread seeds. Write your article in the style of a television news broadcast or a newspaper article with the headline "Animals Help Plants in Need."

Lesson 4

How do plants grow?

Different plants grow in different ways. A plant's growth depends on its DNA and its environment.

DNA and Growth

When conditions are right a seed will sprout. Sprouting is sometimes called germination. Roots will grow out of the seed and grow downward. A tiny stem will grow out of the seed and grow upward. A plant embryo will not grow out of the seed if it is too cold or too dry for that kind of seed. The conditions a plant needs depend on its DNA. Different plants have different needs.

How many different shapes of plants can you describe? Some trees are tall and skinny. Some pines are cone-shaped. Bushes are often round like a ball. These shapes are the result of how the plant's DNA instructs the branches to grow.

How fast a plant grows is due partly to the environment and partly to its DNA. If the environment has the best conditions, the plant will grow more quickly than if the soil is too dry or if the air is too cold. But even if the conditions are perfect, plants will grow at different rates because of their different DNA. One of the fastest-growing plants was a yucca plant that grew about 4 meters (13 feet) in only two weeks!

A huge tree has different DNA than the small plants that cover it. This results in the very different shapes and growth patterns of the plants.

These Joshua trees have just a few branches that grow in many directions without a pattern. They are mostly found in dry areas where they grow very slowly. They might grow 2 or 3 centimeters each year.

As these conifer trees grow taller, small new branches form at the top. The branches on the bottom were the first to form. That is why they are the longest. This gives the trees their cone shape. Do you know of other conifers that are not shaped like a cone?

1. **Checkpoint** Kiesha plants a seed in moist, cold soil by her home. The seed does not sprout. What condition would you infer most likely needs to change for the seed to sprout?
2. **Cause and Effect** What is the effect of different species of plants having very different DNA?

Tropisms

Plants often change the direction they grow in order to better meet their needs. For example, they may turn their leaves to face the Sun or their roots may grow toward a source of water. When an onion sprouts, its stems grow upward and the roots grow downward. **Tropisms** are ways that plants change their direction of growth in response to the environment.

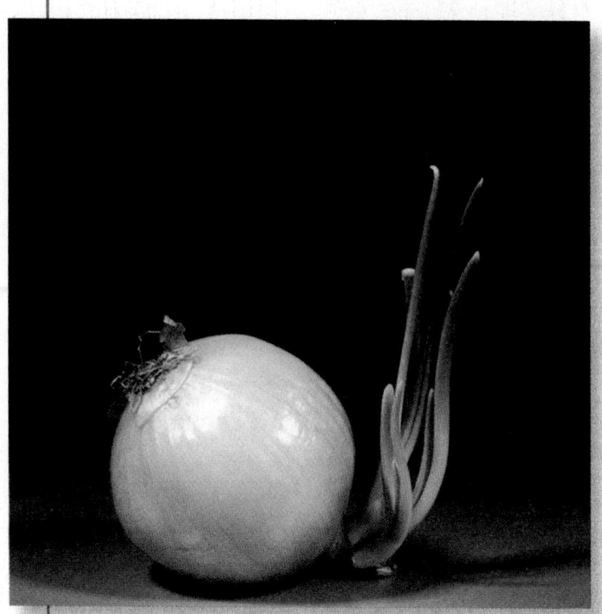

An onion's stem grows upward.

Tropisms often occur when the environment changes the amount that cells grow on different sides of a plant. If one side of a stem grows faster or larger than the other side, the stem will bend.

There are different reasons that cells will grow faster on one side of a plant than the other side. One reason is that different sides have different amounts of growth hormone. A **growth hormone** is a kind of chemical that affects plant growth. These chemicals cause more cells to grow in the plant. These chemicals can also make plant cells grow larger. Plants make their own growth hormones.

Cells may also grow to different sizes when the amount of water in them changes. Vacuoles are parts of plant cells that store water. Vacuoles can fill up with water and make the cell large. This increase can bend a plant just as if the cell itself grew larger.

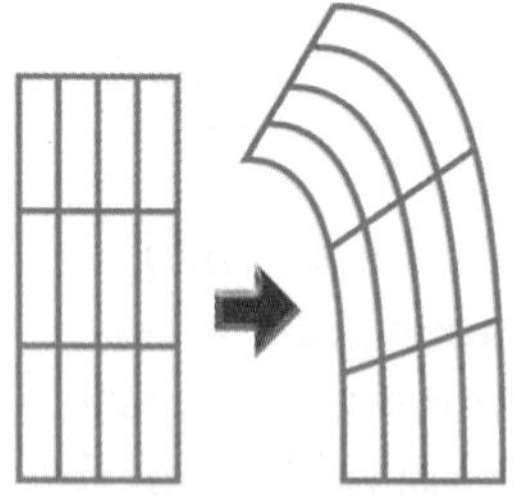

A plant will bend toward the left when the cells on the stem's right side grow more than cells on the left side.

✓ Lesson Checkpoint

1. What is a growth hormone?
2. Explain how plants or plant parts grow toward light or grow upward.
3. **Writing in Science** **Persuasive** Compare and contrast the effects of DNA and the environment on plant growth. Design a poster to convince your classmates which of the two has a greater effect.

Gravitropism

Gravitropism is the growth of a plant or plant part in relation to the pull of gravity. Gravitropism can occur in plant stems and roots. The roots tend to grow downward, in the direction that gravity pulls. The stems tend to grow upward, against the pull of gravity. How do you think this tropism helps a plant meet its needs?

Phototropism

Phototropism is a plant's reaction to a source of light. A plant's stem may grow toward a light. Sometimes just a plant's leaves turn toward light. Look at the picture of the plant. What do you think would happen if you turned the plant in the opposite direction?

Thigmotropism

Thigmotropism is a plant's growth in response to touching an object. Thigmotropism can happen in stems or in roots. Stems of vines will often grow around posts, fences, and trellises. This helps to support the vine so it can grow high and get sunlight. Roots may bend to grow away from rocks and hard soil.

Lab zone

Guided Inquiry

Investigate Does the direction seeds are planted affect the direction the roots grow?

Materials

3 paper towels

cup

water

4 pinto bean seeds

masking tape

What to Do

1. Fold a paper towel in half lengthwise.
Fold it in half again lengthwise.
Use it to line the inside of the cup.

2. Stuff wads of paper towels in the center of the cup. Pour water on the towels to moisten them.

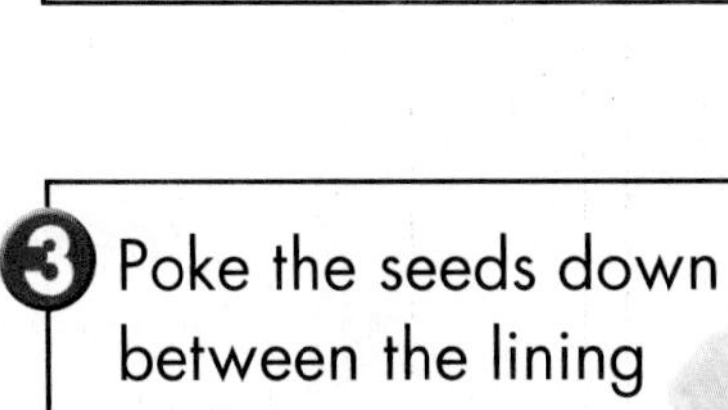

3. Poke the seeds down between the lining and the cup.

There are 4 seeds in the cup. Label the locations 1, 2, 3, and 4.

The seeds MUST be in these 4 positions in the cup.

1
2
3
4
front side
back side

Process Skills

You **interpret data** when you use information you collect in a chart to help draw a conclusion.

4 Place the cup in a warm place. **Observe** the seeds daily for a week. Keep towels moist. Water if needed.

5 Draw and describe how the roots grew.

Position of Bean	Direction of Root Growth
1	
2	
3	
4	

Explain Your Results

1. What direction did the roots grow?
2. **Interpret Data** What might you conclude about the effect of gravity on the growth of roots?

Go Further

What other factors affect how a plant grows? Develop a plan to find out what factors affect the growth, health, or reproduction of bean plants.

Math in Science

Comparing Plant Growth

The DNA in a seed provides the genetic information that determines what the plant will look like as it grows. The growing environment also affects the seed's development.

Suppose you plant two different kinds of bean seeds. You use two containers that are the same size and shape. You fill both with soil that is rich with minerals and nutrients. You add the same amount of water to each container and place them next to one another.

Soon the seeds sprout. You record their growth every 7 days and then use the data to make this double bar graph.

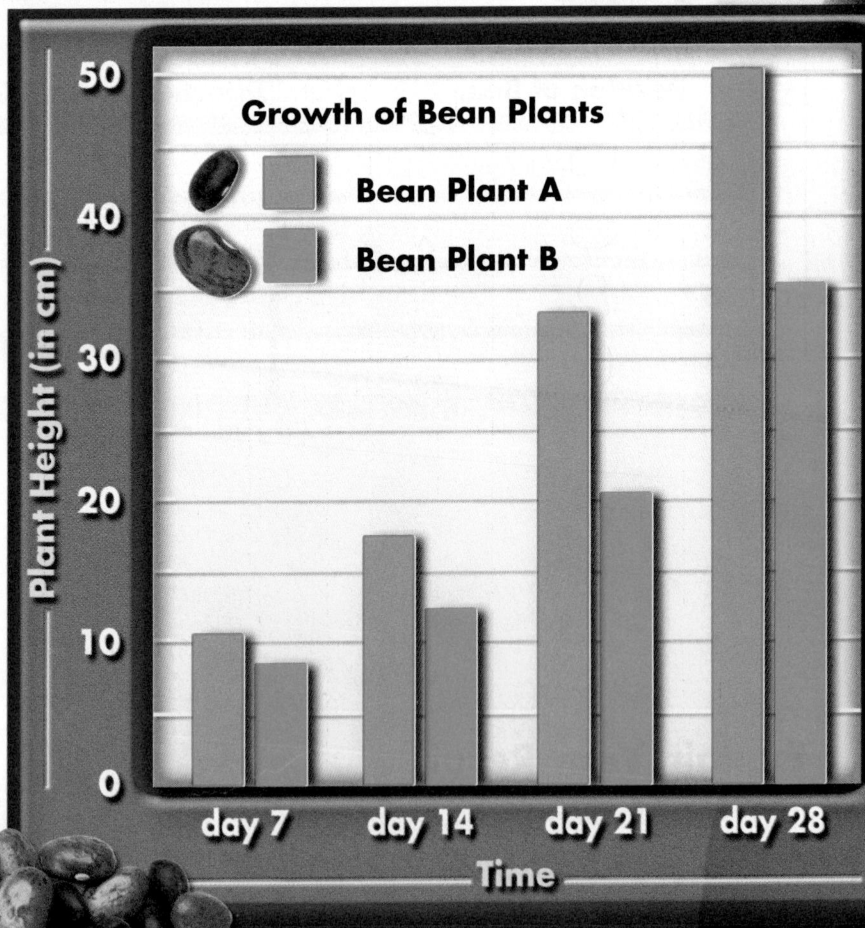

Growth of Bean Plants
Bean Plant A
Bean Plant B
Plant Height (in cm)
50
40
30
20
10
0
day 7
day 14
day 21
day 28
Time

e Tools Take It to the Net sfsuccessnet.com

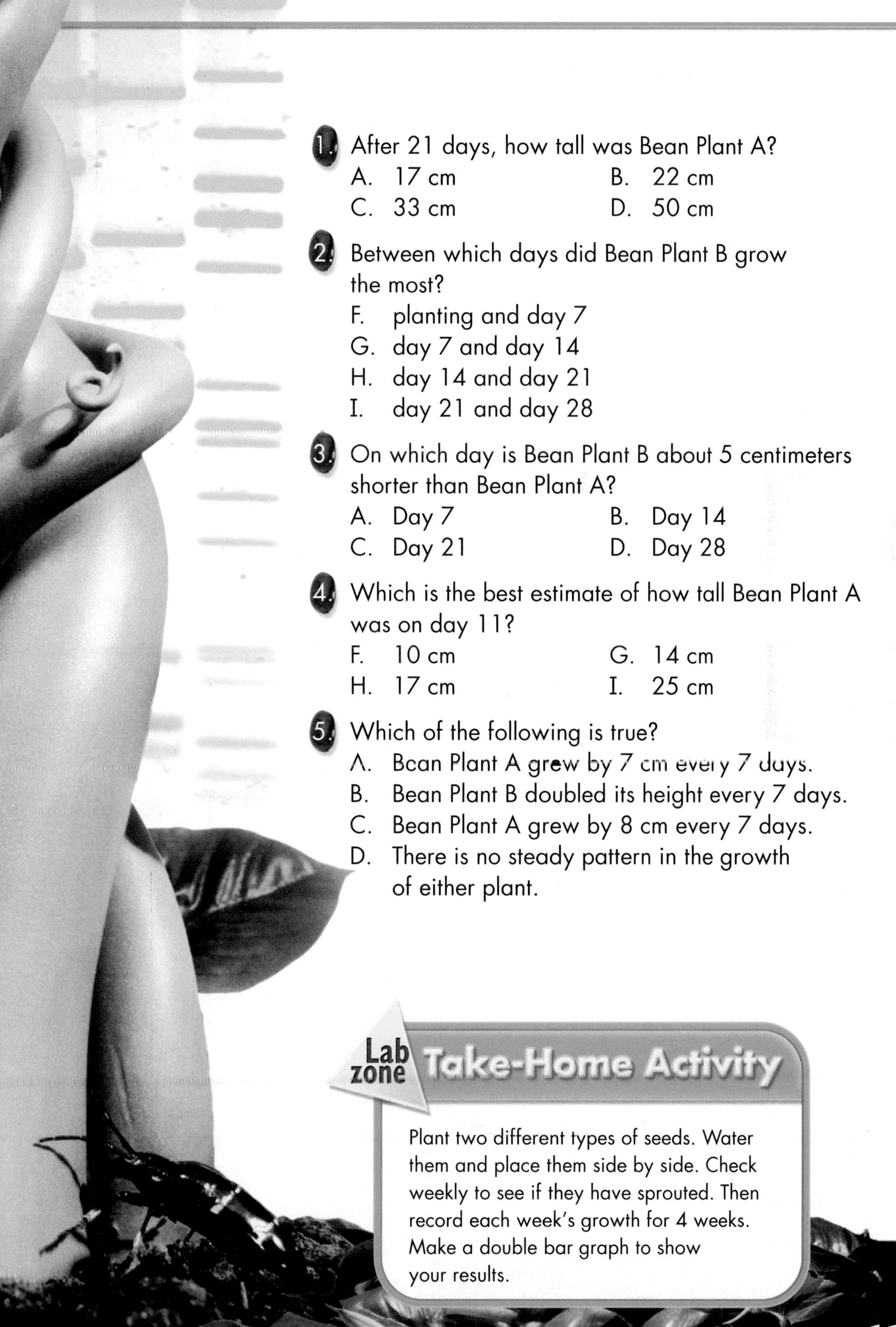

1. After 21 days, how tall was Bean Plant A?
   A. 17 cm B. 22 cm
   C. 33 cm D. 50 cm

2. Between which days did Bean Plant B grow the most?
   F. planting and day 7
   G. day 7 and day 14
   H. day 14 and day 21
   I. day 21 and day 28

3. On which day is Bean Plant B about 5 centimeters shorter than Bean Plant A?
   A. Day 7 B. Day 14
   C. Day 21 D. Day 28

4. Which is the best estimate of how tall Bean Plant A was on day 11?
   F. 10 cm G. 14 cm
   H. 17 cm I. 25 cm

5. Which of the following is true?
   A. Bean Plant A grew by 7 cm every 7 days.
   B. Bean Plant B doubled its height every 7 days.
   C. Bean Plant A grew by 8 cm every 7 days.
   D. There is no steady pattern in the growth of either plant.

Lab zone Take-Home Activity

Plant two different types of seeds. Water them and place them side by side. Check weekly to see if they have sprouted. Then record each week's growth for 4 weeks. Make a double bar graph to show your results.

Chapter 4 Review and Test Prep

Use Vocabulary

embryo (p. 106)	**pollen** (p. 102)
growth hormone (p. 112)	**pollination** (p. 104)
phloem (p. 98)	**spore** (p. 108)
photosynthesis (p. 96)	**tropism** (p. 112)
	xylem (p.98)

Use the term from the list above that best completes each sentence.

1. The process that plants use to make food is _____.
2. The process of moving _____ from a stamen to a pistil is _____.
3. A chemical that helps plant cells grow larger is a(n) _____.
4. In asexual reproduction, a(n) _____ is a cell that can grow into a plant.
5. A plant bending toward light is an example of a(n) _____.
6. _____ and _____ are tubes that carry materials through a plant.
7. A tiny plant inside a seed is called a(n) _____.

Explain Concepts

8. Explain how plants make sugar for food.
9. Explain how all plants are the same in some ways and different in other ways.
10. Explain what plants have in common with animals.
11. Explain how cells in a plant have different shapes and different jobs.

Process Skills

12. **Classify** the plant below as a monocot or dicot. Give two reasons for your classification.

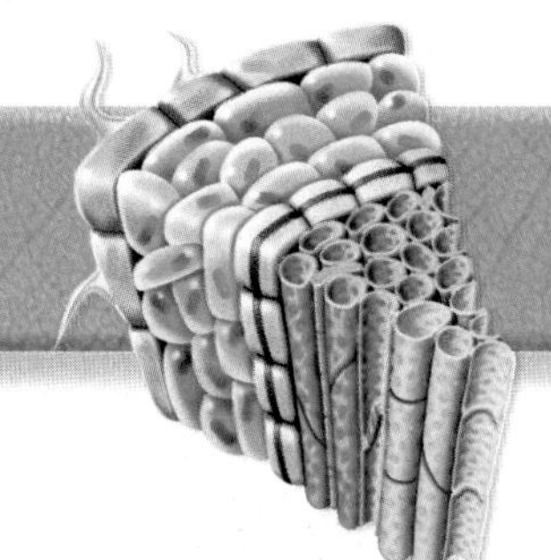

13. Interpret Data Make a conclusion about the effect of crowding on plants based on the data below. Ten seeds were planted in Cup A. Eighty seeds were planted in Cup B.

Number of Radish Plants Growing

Day	1	4	7	10	13	16	19
Cup A	0	1	10	10	10	9	9
Cup A	0	17	44	49	42	37	29

14. Communicate Make a double bar graph to communicate the data in Question 13.

Cause and Effect

15. Make a graphic organizer like the one shown below. Fill in the missing causes and effects.

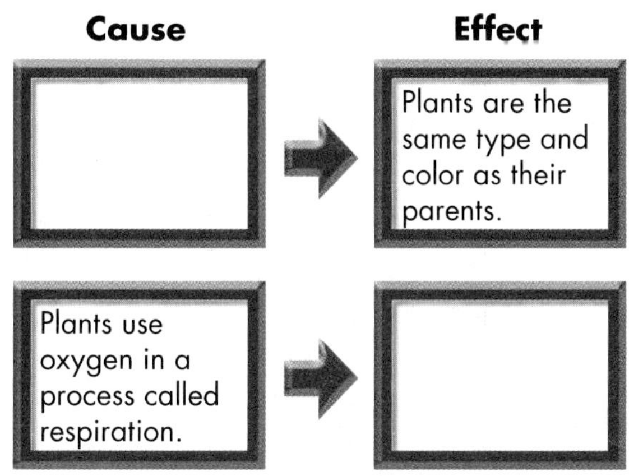

Cause
Effect
Plants are the same type and color as their parents.
Plants use oxygen in a process called respiration.

Test Prep

Choose the letter that best completes the statement or answers the question.

16. Two types of root systems are called taproot and ______ root systems.
Ⓐ mineral Ⓑ seed
Ⓒ DNA Ⓓ fibrous

17. Two types of plant reproduction are
Ⓕ respiration and photosynthesis.
Ⓖ chloroplasts and cell walls.
Ⓗ sexual and asexual.
Ⓘ DNA and environment.

18. How does chlorophyll help a plant?
Ⓐ It absorbs light energy in photosynthesis.
Ⓑ It moves water and minerals through the plant.
Ⓒ It moves sugar and water through the plant.
Ⓓ It absorbs water.

19. Explain why your answer for Question 18 is the best choice. For each of the others, tell why it is not the best choice.

20. Writing in Science **Descriptive** Describe the structures of a plant and how they give the plant food, water, support, growth, protection, or the ability to reproduce.

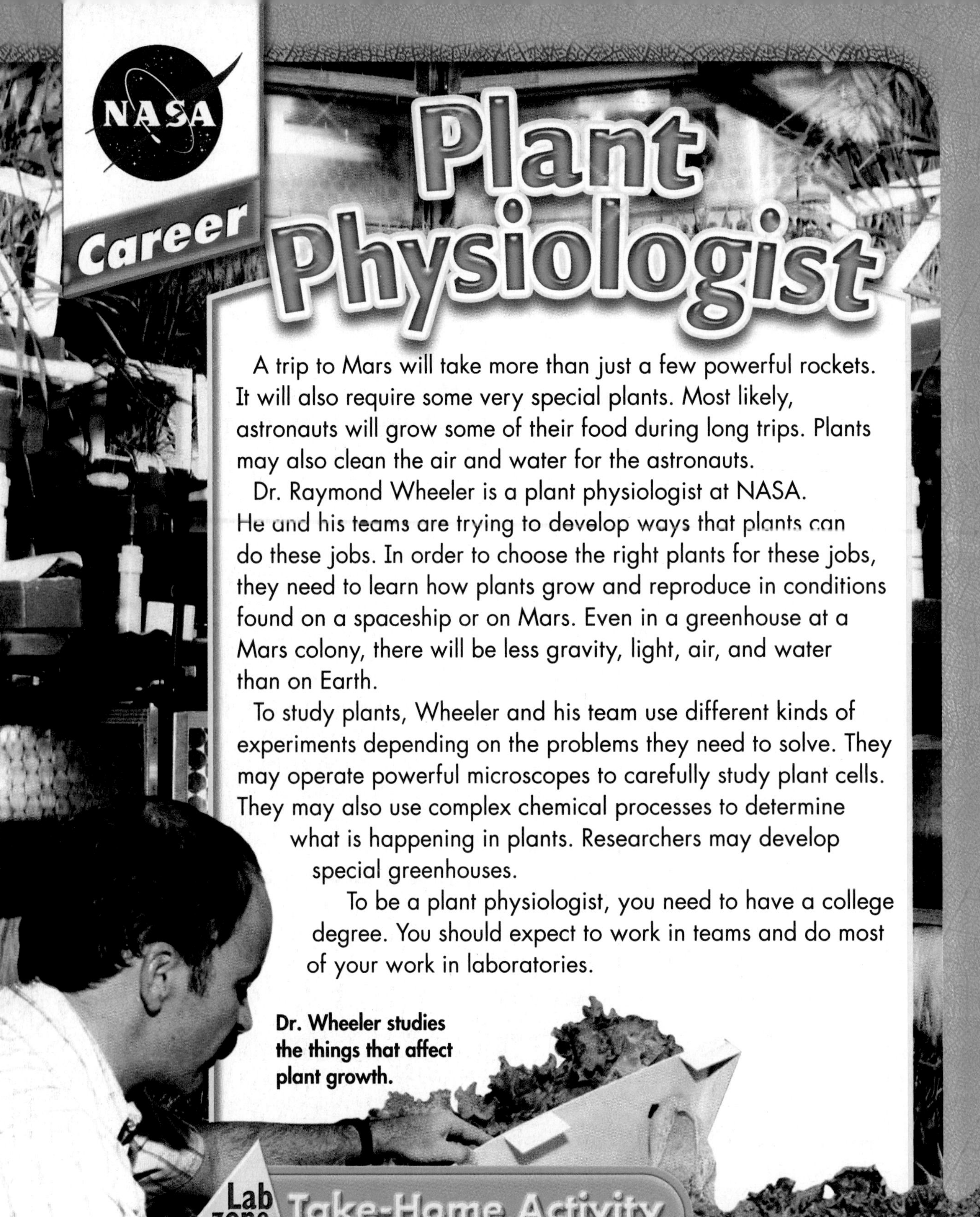
NASA
Career

Plant Physiologist

A trip to Mars will take more than just a few powerful rockets. It will also require some very special plants. Most likely, astronauts will grow some of their food during long trips. Plants may also clean the air and water for the astronauts.

Dr. Raymond Wheeler is a plant physiologist at NASA. He and his teams are trying to develop ways that plants can do these jobs. In order to choose the right plants for these jobs, they need to learn how plants grow and reproduce in conditions found on a spaceship or on Mars. Even in a greenhouse at a Mars colony, there will be less gravity, light, air, and water than on Earth.

To study plants, Wheeler and his team use different kinds of experiments depending on the problems they need to solve. They may operate powerful microscopes to carefully study plant cells. They may also use complex chemical processes to determine what is happening in plants. Researchers may develop special greenhouses.

To be a plant physiologist, you need to have a college degree. You should expect to work in teams and do most of your work in laboratories.

Dr. Wheeler studies the things that affect plant growth.

Lab zone Take-Home Activity

Observe the different plants that grow in your neighborhood. In your **science journal,** describe each plant and the environment in which you found it.

EC NTL 10987

Chapter 5

Interactions in Ecosystems

You Will Discover

- what an ecosystem is.
- what land biomes are like.
- what water ecosystems are like.
- how organisms interact in an ecosystem.
- how energy moves through an ecosystem.
- how materials move through an ecosystem.

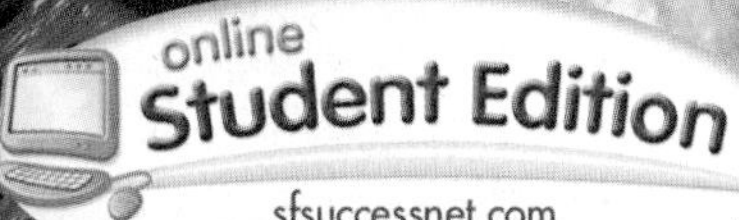
online
Student Edition
sfsuccessnet.com

Build Background

How do the parts of an ecosystem interact?

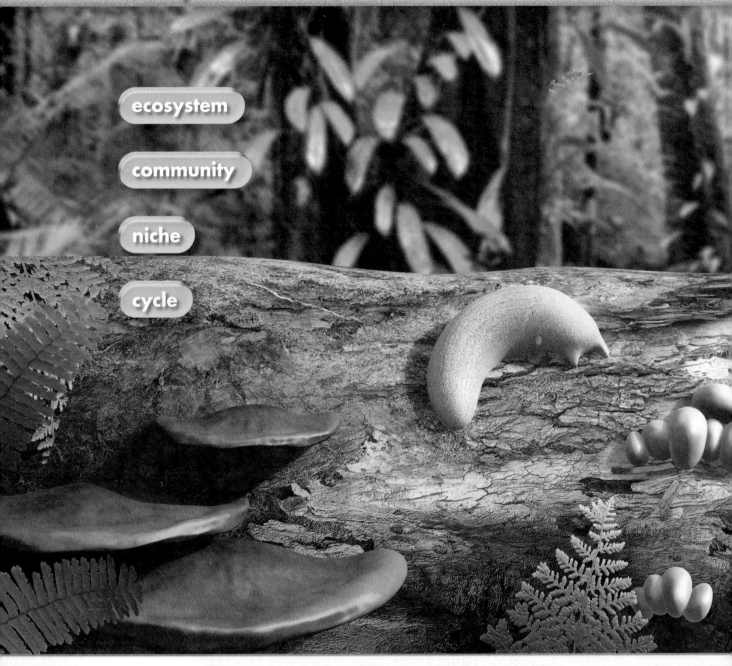

ecosystem

community

niche

cycle

habitat

population

Chapter 5 Vocabulary

ecosystem page 127

population page 127

community page 127

niche page 129

habitat page 129

energy pyramid page 146

cycle page 149

energy pyramid
Energy
Heat
Heat
Heat

Lab zone **Directed Inquiry**

Explore How can you find out how many animals live in an area?

Scientists can figure out how many animals live in a large area by counting how many animals there are in small parts of the area and then estimating. The more small parts they check, the better their estimate usually is.

Materials

checkerboard

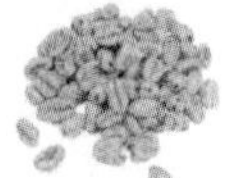

dry puffed cereal

calculator or computer (optional)

What to Do

1. Scatter 2 handfuls of cereal on a checkerboard. Guess how many pieces of cereal there are.
2. Count the number of pieces on 4 squares. Divide by 4. Multiply your answer by the total number of squares. The result is an **estimate** of the total number of pieces.

piece of cereal = animal

checkerboard = place where animals live

square = a small part of the place where animals live

3. Count all the pieces of cereal on the checkerboard.

Process Skills

Sometimes you can use mathematics to help you make a good **estimate.**

Explain Your Results

1. Which was easiest: guessing, estimating, or counting? Which was most accurate?
2. How do you think you could make your **estimate** more accurate?

How to Read Science

Reading Skills

Predict

When you **predict,** you make a statement about what you think might happen next. The statement you make is a **prediction.** An **estimate** is a kind of prediction.

- You can make predictions based on what you already know and what has already happened.
- After you predict something in a story or an article, continue reading to check your prediction. As you learn new information, you might need to change your prediction.

Science Article

Habitats

All plants and animals live in a habitat. The ocean is a habitat not only for fish, but for many types of plants, animals, and other organisms. Forests are habitats for foxes, squirrels, birds, and other animals. Sometimes habitats become polluted or destroyed, causing a serious effect on the plants and animals living there.

Apply It!

Make a graphic organizer like the one shown. Make a **prediction** to answer the question from the article.

Question		Prediction
If habitats are polluted or destroyed, what effect might this have on the animals living there?		

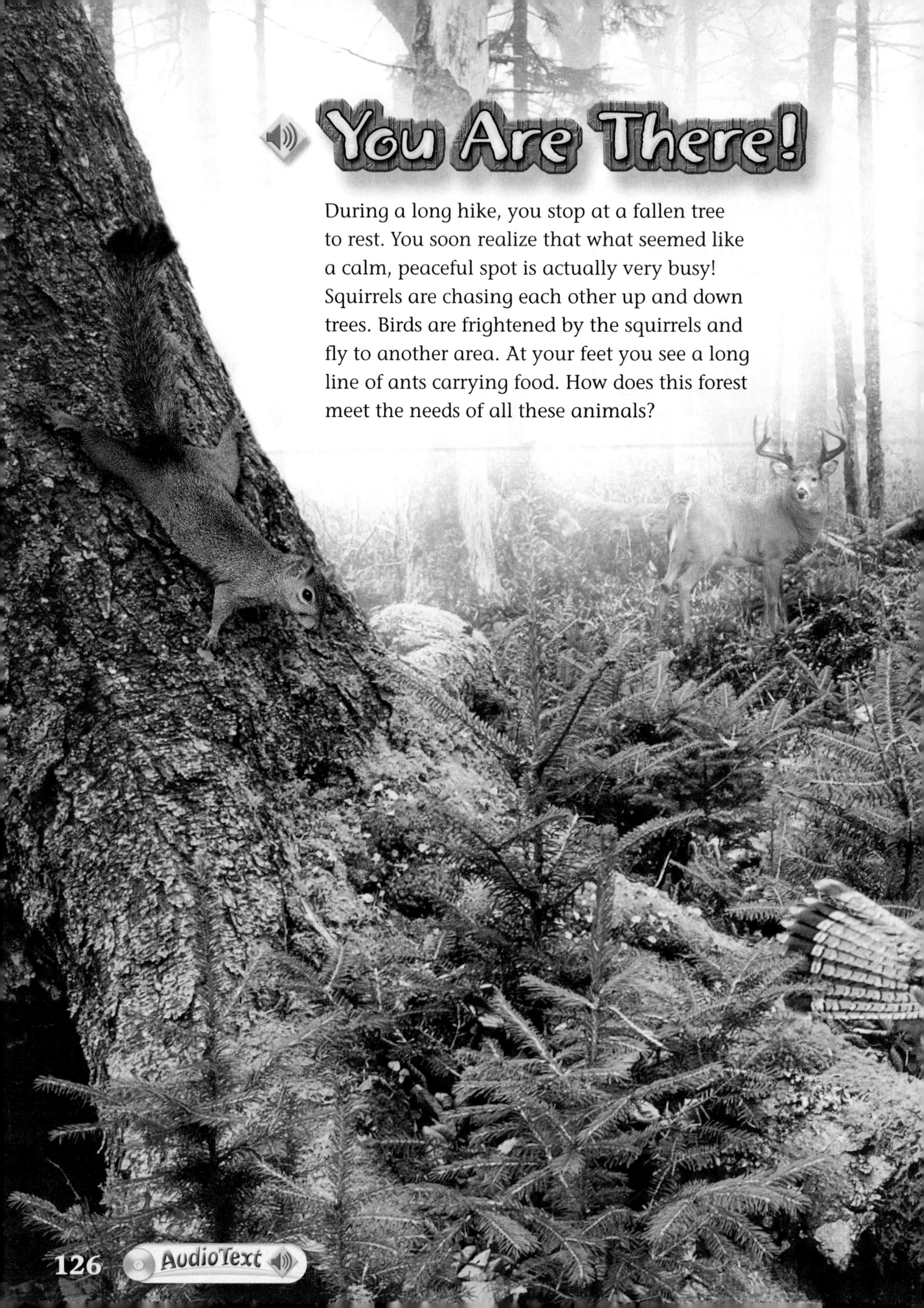

You Are There!

During a long hike, you stop at a fallen tree to rest. You soon realize that what seemed like a calm, peaceful spot is actually very busy! Squirrels are chasing each other up and down trees. Birds are frightened by the squirrels and fly to another area. At your feet you see a long line of ants carrying food. How does this forest meet the needs of all these animals?

AudioText

Lesson 1

What is an ecosystem?

Organisms live where they can have their needs met. These needs are met by the living and nonliving things around them.

Living and Nonliving Parts

What kind of ecosystem are you in right now? An **ecosystem** is all the living and nonliving things in an area. You might think that an ecosystem has to be something like the woods or the desert. Actually, an ecosystem is any place that living things are found. Your classroom is an ecosystem. What are the living and nonliving things in your classroom?

Many populations make up the living parts of an ecosystem. A **population** is a group of organisms of one species that live in an area at the same time. A population may be all the oak trees or all the red ants in an area. A **community** is made up of all the populations in an area. Members of a community depend on each other to fill needs, such as food, shelter, and reproduction.

The nonliving parts of an ecosystem include air, water, soil, temperature, and sunlight. They often determine what kinds of organisms and the number of organisms that can live there.

Like any system, an ecosystem is not just a collection of things. These living and nonliving parts interact in many ways. Each part has a role. In this way, the whole system works to meet the needs of all its parts.

In any ecosystem, some organisms survive; others do not. Populations can live and grow only where their needs are met. If a population's needs are not met, the population will get smaller. Some of its members might move away. Maybe none will survive.

1. **√Checkpoint** Describe the parts of an ecosystem that organisms need.
2. **Predict** What would happen to a community if half the water from an ecosystem were removed?

Biomes

Biologists have divided the world into regions called biomes. A biome is a large ecosystem with generally the same climate and organisms. A single biome may cover many countries. Together, all the biomes make up the biosphere.

When you hear the word "rainforest," do you think of a hot jungle on the other side of the world? A rainforest biome is any place that has large amounts of rain and thick plant growth. Did you know that there is a rainforest in the state of Washington? It is a temperate rainforest, which means that it receives a lot of rain during the year, but its temperature can be quite cool.

A temperate rainforest community has trees such as maple and spruce. These grow well in the wet, cool climate. Mosses often cover rocks. Elk, cougars, and bears are some of the animals in the area. Squirrels, raccoons, and owls also live in the temperate rainforest.

Look at the roles of the trees and squirrels in this ecosystem. Trees help squirrels by giving them food and shelter. Squirrels help trees by spreading seeds. These organisms help each other meet their needs.

The squirrels and trees are just two parts of this ecosystem. The whole system works because it has many parts and organisms that interact to meet each others' needs.

Raccoons can use their paws skillfully for climbing and hunting.

Elk use their antlers to defend themselves.

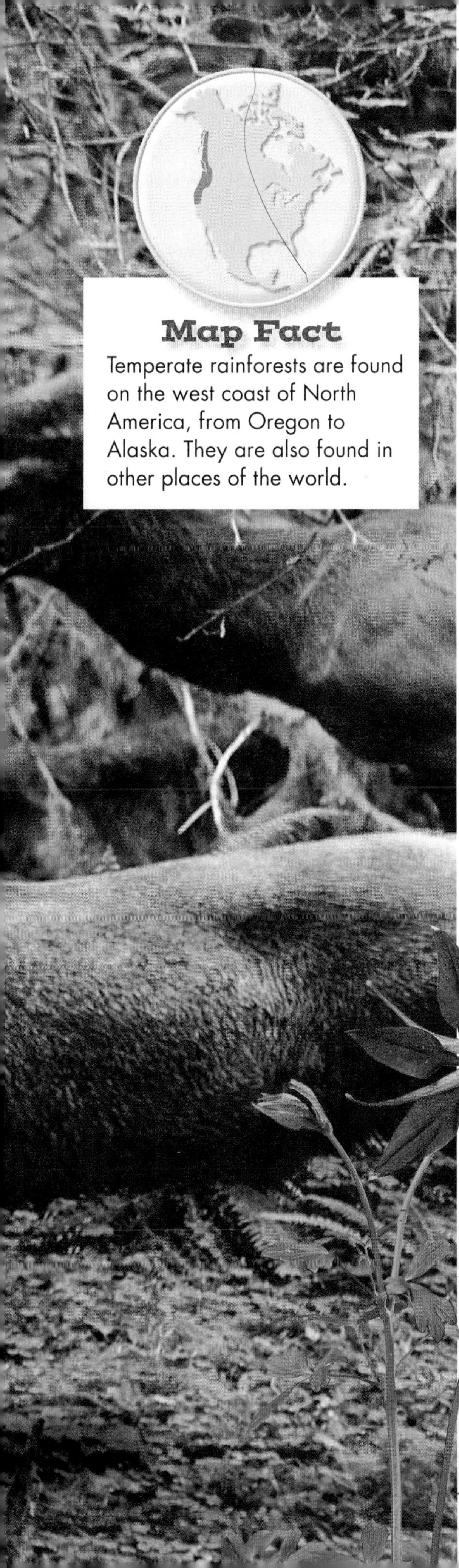

Spotted owls are hunters in temperate rainforests.

Map Fact

Temperate rainforests are found on the west coast of North America, from Oregon to Alaska. They are also found in other places of the world.

Every organism in an ecosystem has a niche and a habitat. A **niche** is the role that an organism has in an ecosystem. A **habitat** is the place in which it lives. A habitat is made up of the soil, air and water, as well as the plants of the area. The niche of a spotted owl in the temperate rainforest is that of a hunter. It eats small animals, such as mice and chipmunks. The habitats of spotted owls are the trees and the land on which they live.

All the relationships among organisms keep the ecosystem balanced. For instance, the population of spotted owls balances with the populations of small animals, such as mice, that are their food. If the number of small animals drops too low, the spotted owls will have less food. So, the number of owls will decrease as well. With fewer owls hunting for food, fewer mice will be eaten. As a result, the population of mice will grow. Then, when more mice are available for the owls, the number of owls will increase again. In this way, the populations of owls and small animals go up and down within a range and they balance.

Crimson Star

√ Lesson Checkpoint

1. What is a population? What determines the kind and size of populations in an area?
2. Describe the parts of an ecosystem and tell how they maintain the system's balance.
3. **Art in Science** Draw a picture of a habitat and label its parts.

Lesson 2

What are land biomes?

Organisms have structures or behaviors that help them live in the different land biomes.

Tropical Rainforest Biomes

Ecosystems near the equator are warm all year long. Some of these places get large amounts of rain. In some parts of Brazil, the average temperature is 26°C, and the average rainfall is more than 3 meters per year. In places like this, many plants can easily have their needs met. As a result, populations of these plants grow very large. A tropical rainforest results.

Tropical rainforests have more species than all other biomes. Dozens of different kinds of flowers and insects may be found on one tree.

Do you think that a rainforest would be the ideal place for any organism to live? In any environment, some organisms survive well, and some do not. Certain plants, such as orchids, survive well. Most kinds of cactus plants would not survive in the wet tropical rainforests.

Organisms have structures that help them survive in their ecosystems. For example, the kinkajou has a tail that can grab onto branches to help it move through the trees. Its long tongue can gather honey and insects to eat.

Map Fact

Tropical rainforests are found on all continents except Europe. The rainforest shown here is in Costa Rica, a country on the continent of North America.

Basilisk lizard

Kinkajou

Map Fact

Deciduous forests are the main biomes found in Europe and the eastern half of the United States of America.

Deciduous Forest Biomes

A deciduous forest may grow in cooler places that do not have huge amounts of rain. Deciduous forests cover large areas of the eastern part of the United States. These forests have trees such as oaks, elms, and maples. Deciduous trees lose their leaves in the colder fall and winter months. Losing leaves helps trees save food and water during the winter.

Besides trees, what organisms undergo some sort of change during cold months? With less food available, bears in the deciduous forest sleep through much of the winter. Snakes, frogs, and salamanders hibernate underground. The fur color of some rabbits changes to a snowy white. If it sees an enemy, the rabbit keeps itself very still and it blends in with the snow.

With the right conditions, such as plenty of food, few diseases, and few predators, a population will continue to increase. This has been seen in populations of deer in deciduous forests. The population of deer has increased so much that in some places, overcrowding is a problem. When overcrowding occurs, food supplies can run out. Then many deer may die of starvation.

1. √ **Checkpoint** Give examples of how an organism's behavior is related to changes in the deciduous forest biome.
2. **Math in Science** In a tree in a tropical rainforest, three dozen different flowers and forty-eight different insects were found. How many different species were found in all?

Populations of a deer's natural enemies, such as wolves, have decreased in recent years. This has led to large deer populations.

Grassland Biomes

Two hundred years ago, tall grasses covered huge areas of Midwest America. Some grasses grew to be over two meters tall. Pioneers called this area a sea of grass. Now, most of these grasslands have been turned into farms.

Grasslands are biomes that are covered with many types of grasses and have few trees. Decaying dead grasses form fertile soil. Trees do not grow well in this biome because of the small amount of rain it receives. Most trees in grasslands are near lakes or rivers. Animals such as bison, antelope, and prairie dogs eat the grass. They are hunted by wolves and coyotes.

Populations of animals often decrease when their habitat changes. The change can be in the climate, the number of enemies, or in their food or water supply.

The gray wolf is one species with a changing population. Gray wolves once lived over most of North America. When grasslands were changed into farms, animals such as prairie dogs decreased in number. Wolves then had less food and less space. At the same time, people were hunting wolves more. As a result, gray wolves now live only in lightly populated northern states.

In 1974, gray wolves in the U.S. were found in only three states. People worked for many years to increase their habitat. Most wolves in this species are gray, but some are black or brown.

Map Fact

One large grassland biome extends from Mexico to Canada.

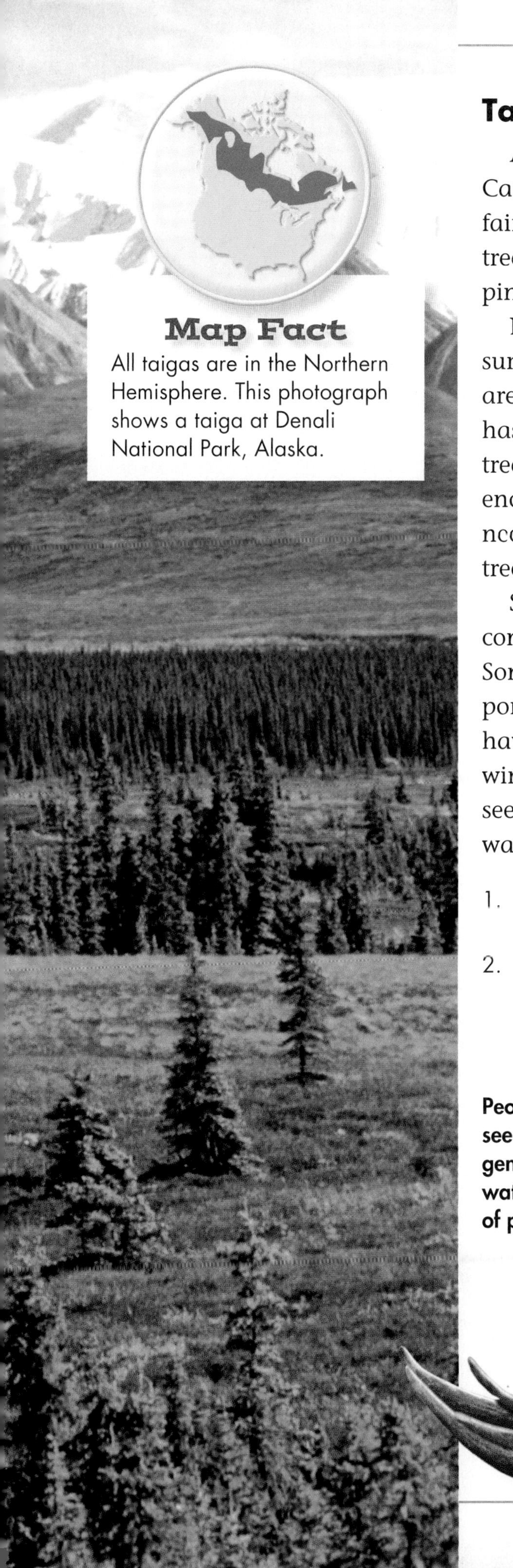
Map Fact

Map Fact

All taigas are in the Northern Hemisphere. This photograph shows a taiga at Denali National Park, Alaska.

Taiga Biomes

Another kind of forest biome covers much of Canada and Russia in places that are cold and fairly dry. In these places, called taigas, most trees are the kind that have needles, such as pines.

Needles have many qualities that help trees survive the cold conditions of the taiga. Needles are leaves that make food for the tree. The tree has needles throughout the year. This way, the tree is ready to make food as soon as it is warm enough for photosynthesis to happen. The needles have a waxy coating. This helps the tree hold water during the winter months.

Some of the animals that are found in taiga communities are bears, elk, moose, and wolves. Some smaller animals in the taiga are mice, porcupines, and wolverines. These animals have fur that helps keep them warm in the cold winters. Ducks, owls, and woodpeckers may be seen in the taigas. Their feathers help keep them warm.

1. **√Checkpoint** What changes in a habitat would cause a population to decrease?
2. **Technology in Science** Use Internet resources to investigate the taiga and grassland biomes. Compare and contrast the kinds of animals found in the two biomes and their needs.

People in a taiga will sometimes see a moose wading in a stream, gently dipping its head into the water to get a mouthful of plants.

Desert Biomes

What do you think makes a place a desert? Do all deserts have high temperatures and sand dunes? Although many deserts are very hot, they can be much cooler at night. Some can be quite cold most of the time. Not all deserts have sand dunes. Some are very rocky. A desert can also be covered by a very flat layer of salt. So what exactly is a desert? Deserts are often defined as areas that receive less than 25 centimeters of rain or snow each year.

Desert organisms have special structures and behaviors that help them survive in the dry conditions of many deserts. Some desert plants have large root systems close to the surface of the ground. These roots quickly take up any water from rain. To deal with high temperatures, many animals rest during the day. Some dig into the ground to get cool. They look for food in the cooler temperatures at night.

What desert organisms can you name? Communities of the desert may include rattlesnakes, lizards, jackrabbits, and beetles. Bushes, grasses, and cactuses may grow in deserts as well.

The largest deserts are found in northern Africa and southwest Asia. A large part of western Australia is a desert. What other places are deserts?

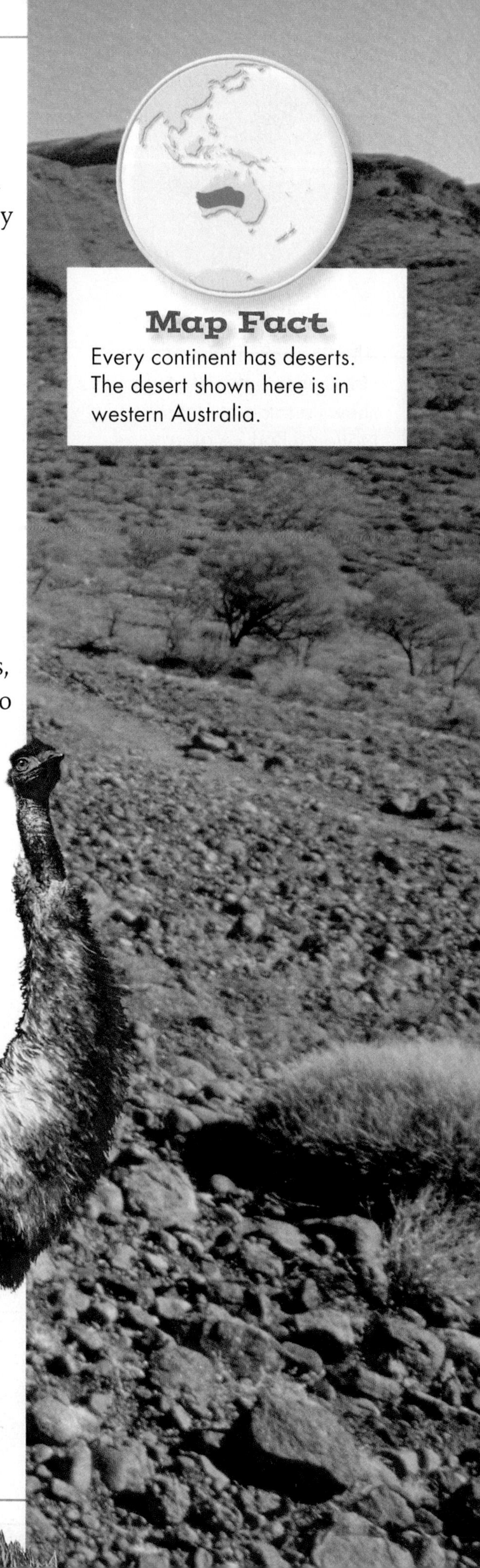

Map Fact

Every continent has deserts. The desert shown here is in western Australia.

Emus are found in many areas of Australia, including deserts. They may travel many kilometers each day to find food and water.

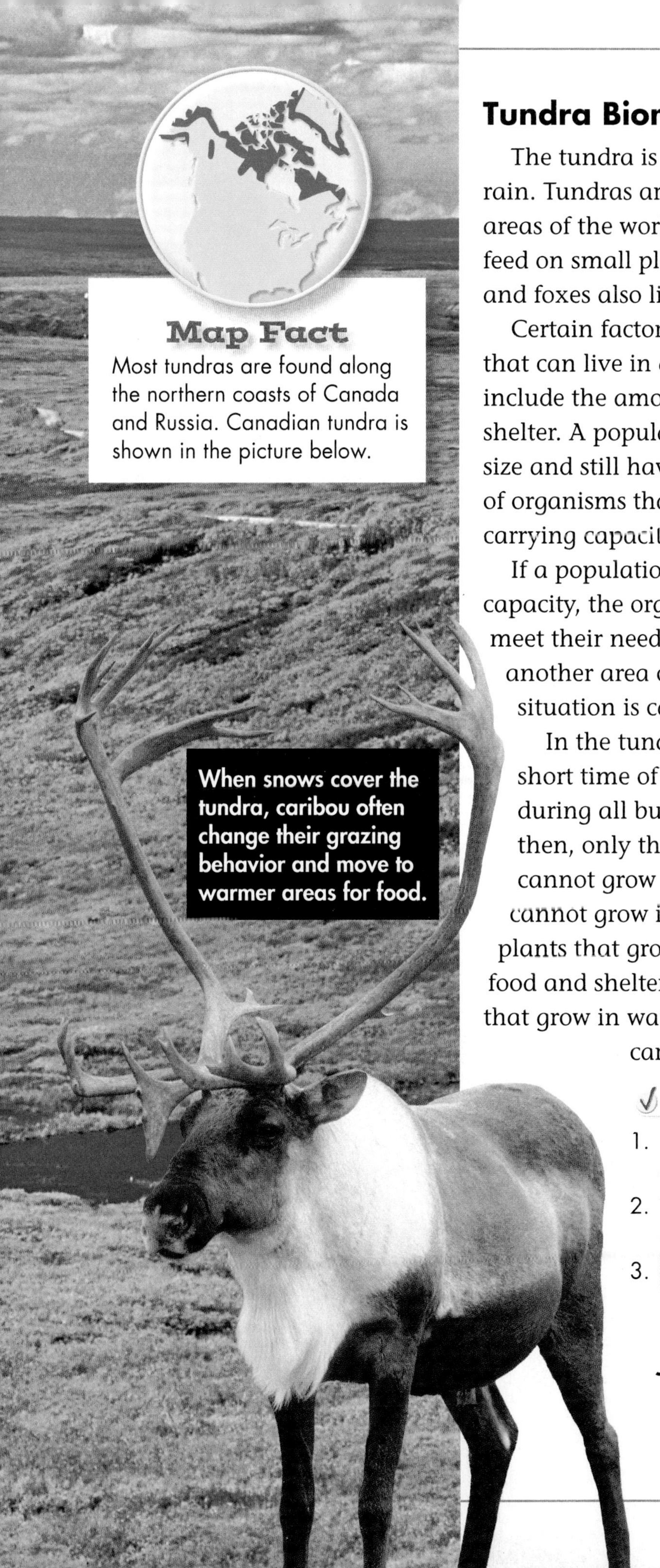

Map Fact

Most tundras are found along the northern coasts of Canada and Russia. Canadian tundra is shown in the picture below.

When snows cover the tundra, caribou often change their grazing behavior and move to warmer areas for food.

Tundra Biomes

The tundra is a very cold biome with little rain. Tundras are generally in the most northern areas of the world. Rodents, rabbits, and caribou feed on small plants and grasses. Weasels, owls, and foxes also live on the tundra.

Certain factors limit the number of organisms that can live in any ecosystem. Limiting factors include the amount of food, water, space, or shelter. A population may grow only to a certain size and still have all its needs met. The number of organisms that can live in a place is called the carrying capacity.

If a population grows larger than the carrying capacity, the organisms will not be able to meet their needs. They will need to move to another area or they will not survive well. This situation is called overcrowding.

In the tundra, a major limiting factor is the short time of warm weather. The soil is frozen during all but a few weeks each year. Even then, only the top layer of soil thaws. Plants cannot grow deep roots or tall stems. Trees cannot grow in these conditions. The small plants that grow in the tundra provide less food and shelter for animals than larger plants that grow in warmer forests. What biome has a carrying capacity like the tundra?

√ Lesson Checkpoint

1. Explain how characteristics of an organism help it survive in a desert.
2. What is the effect of a limiting factor on a population?
3. Writing in Science **Persuasive** What biome do you think is the best place to live? In your **science journal,** write an essay to persuade your classmates that your choice is the best.

Lesson 3

What are water ecosystems?

Water ecosystems differ in the kind of water they have, how fast it moves, and how deep it is.

Map Fact

The Mississippi River, shown here, is the largest river ecosystem in North America. The Amazon, Nile, and Yangtze Rivers are major rivers on other continents.

Rivers

What animals are found in a river ecosystem community? You may think of fish right away. Pike, bullhead, and bass are kinds of fish in rivers. Other animals, such as crayfish, otters, ducks, turtles, and insects, are also parts of many river ecosystems.

Different kinds of rivers have different kinds of organisms. Some animals live only in rivers that flow slowly. They are not strong enough to live in rivers that flow very fast. Few organisms of any kind can live in badly polluted waters.

Plants and animals that live in rivers usually do not also live in oceans. Their cells cannot handle the extra salt in ocean water. In the same way, plants and animals that live in the ocean usually cannot live in rivers and lakes.

Water ecosystems include animals that spend much of their time on land. Animals that live on land and in water need structures that allow them to do well in both environments. For example, the streamlined body of the river otter helps it to swim easily and catch fish. While it swims it can close its nose and ears. On land it can run and catch small mammals and frogs. Otters live in holes that they dig at the river's edge.

River otter

Map Fact

The Congaree Swamp is in South Carolina. Many kinds of wetlands are found all over the world.

Wetlands

A wetland is partly covered with water or is flooded at least part of each year. This means that many of the plants and animals of wetlands are found on land and in water.

There are many kinds of wetlands. The wetland of Florida's Everglades has vast areas of sawgrass over 3 meters tall. Alligators, fish, deer, snakes and other animals live there. A swamp is another kind of wetland with many trees and bushes. The Congaree Swamp community in South Carolina has deer, otters, turtles, snakes, and wild pigs.

Wetlands are helpful in many ways. The plants, soils, and microorganisms of wetlands often act as filters, cleaning water that flows through a wetland. This helps all organisms in the water.

Some important wetlands are parts of estuaries. Estuaries are places where rivers flow into oceans. An estuary's water is salty, but not as salty as the ocean. Salt marshes are grassy wetlands at the edges of estuaries. Salt marshes protect inland areas from stormy ocean waves. As the tides change, ocean water flows in and out of a salt marsh. This may change the water levels and the salinity of a salt marsh.

1. **√Checkpoint** Where are estuaries found?
2. **Technology in Science** Use Internet resources to investigate a river or wetland ecosystem. Write a paragraph that describes how organisms on land and in the water interact with each other and with the habitat.

Crayfish live in several water ecosystems, including swamps.

Jellyfish are not actually fish. They are in the same phylum as coral and sea anemones.

Coral Reefs

What ocean animals can you list? Many animals on your list probably live in warm, shallow waters around coral reefs. Because so many organisms live around them, coral reefs are like busy cities in the ocean. Around a reef, divers may see sharks, clams, crabs, clownfish, eels, and many other animals.

Corals are animals that have a special relationship with algae. Some algae carry on photosynthesis. They grow only in shallow, warm waters. If the water is too deep, sunlight will not reach them. These algae grow inside the coral. Others help the coral grow and build its skeleton. As corals grow and die, their hard skeletal parts pile up to make the reef. The nooks and crannies of the reef are homes for many kinds of plants and animals.

Coral reefs grow well in water that does not have many nutrients. Extra nutrients may actually harm a coral reef by helping the coral's enemies grow. Corals also need to be in water that is about 18°C or warmer. Reefs are found near the coasts of Florida, Australia, and many other places.

Coral reefs are important ecosystems. They often protect shore lines from ocean storms. The organisms found here have provided new kinds of medicines. Many kinds of food are found along reefs.

Brain coral colonies can grow to be as large as 2 meters across.

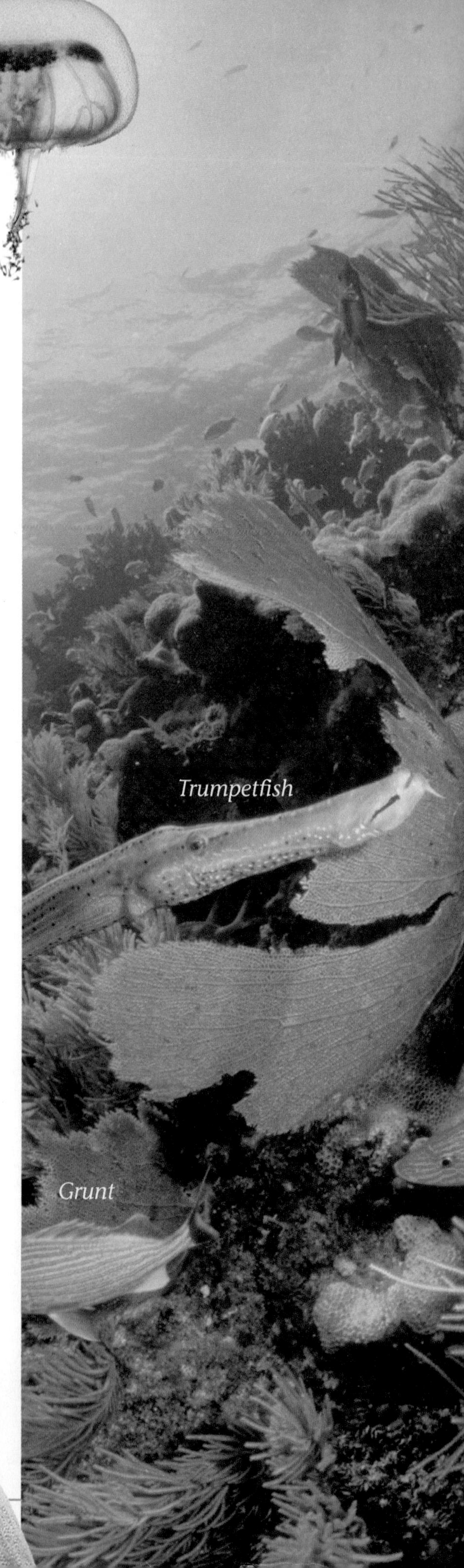
Trumpetfish
Grunt

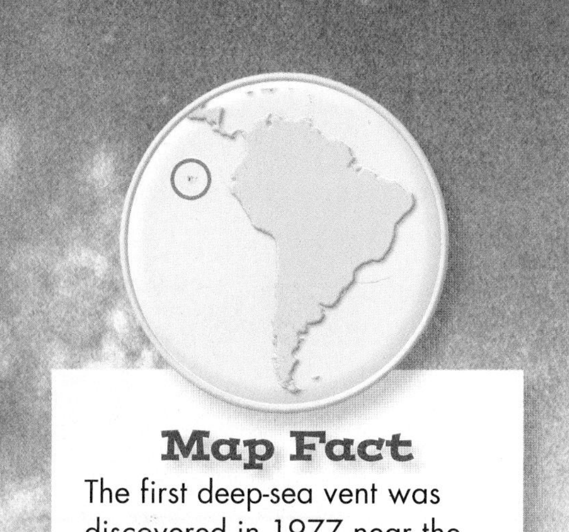

Map Fact

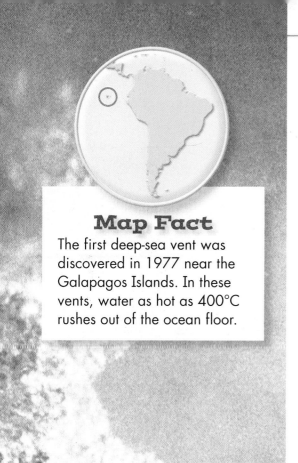

The first deep-sea vent was discovered in 1977 near the Galapagos Islands. In these vents, water as hot as 400°C rushes out of the ocean floor.

This fish lives about 1,000 meters below the surface. Special organs scattered over its body make the fish glow in the dark.

The Deep Sea

In the deeper areas of the ocean, you find some very strange creatures. These creatures have to deal with cold, darkness, and very high water pressure.

Sunlight cannot reach these cold depths, so no plants can grow. Many animals eat dead plants and animals that sink from higher levels. In other places, called deep-sea vents, bacteria make food from chemicals in the water. These bacteria are then eaten by bigger animals. Clams, crabs, and tubeworms also live around the vents.

Far below the ocean waves, the water pressure is very great. Amazingly, the animals' bodies are adapted for living under this crushing pressure. When the animals are lifted to the surface where the pressure is less, the animals die.

✓ Lesson Checkpoint

1. Why do coral live only in shallow water?
2. How does the type of water found in a water ecosystem affect the kind of organisms that live there?
3. **Art in Science** Research an estuary and another water ecosystem. Make a poster to show where the ecosystems are, the kind of water in them, and how the water flows.

Tubeworms don't have a mouth or stomach. Bacteria live inside the tubeworms and make food that they share.

Lesson 4

How do organisms interact?

Plants and animals interact with each other. Sometimes their interactions are helpful. Sometimes, they are not.

Competition

Have you ever competed in a sport? The prize for winning a sports event may be a trophy or just the pride of winning. The cost of losing is simply disappointment. In the world of animals, stakes of competition are much greater.

In all environments, organisms may compete for the things they need. They may compete over space, water, light, food, or mates. They do not compete for a trophy. They often compete for their lives. An organism that cannot compete may die or may be forced to move away to get its needs met.

Animals of the same species sometimes compete with one another. At other times, different species compete for resources. For example, rabbits, mice, and other animals of a desert community compete with each other when they search for plants to eat.

Animals such as cats, dogs, and bears may compete for territory. You may have heard cats screeching as they fight over territory in your neighborhood. Perhaps you have heard a dog's loud bark when it sees a person in its yard. This is the dog's way of warning, "Get out of my territory!" The dog may bite if its warning is ignored.

Have you heard of the plant that ate the South? This is what many people have jokingly said about kudzu, a vine that was brought to southern states in the mid-1880s. When it competes with other plants for sunlight, kudzu usually wins. The vine quickly grows and covers other plants, preventing them from getting sunlight. Since the covered plants cannot move away, they die.

Plants may also compete for water. Plants with larger root systems will absorb water more quickly than other plants. In what kind of biome do you think this competition is strongest?

Black bears will compete with each other for territory and mates.

These sheep are competing by hitting their horns together.

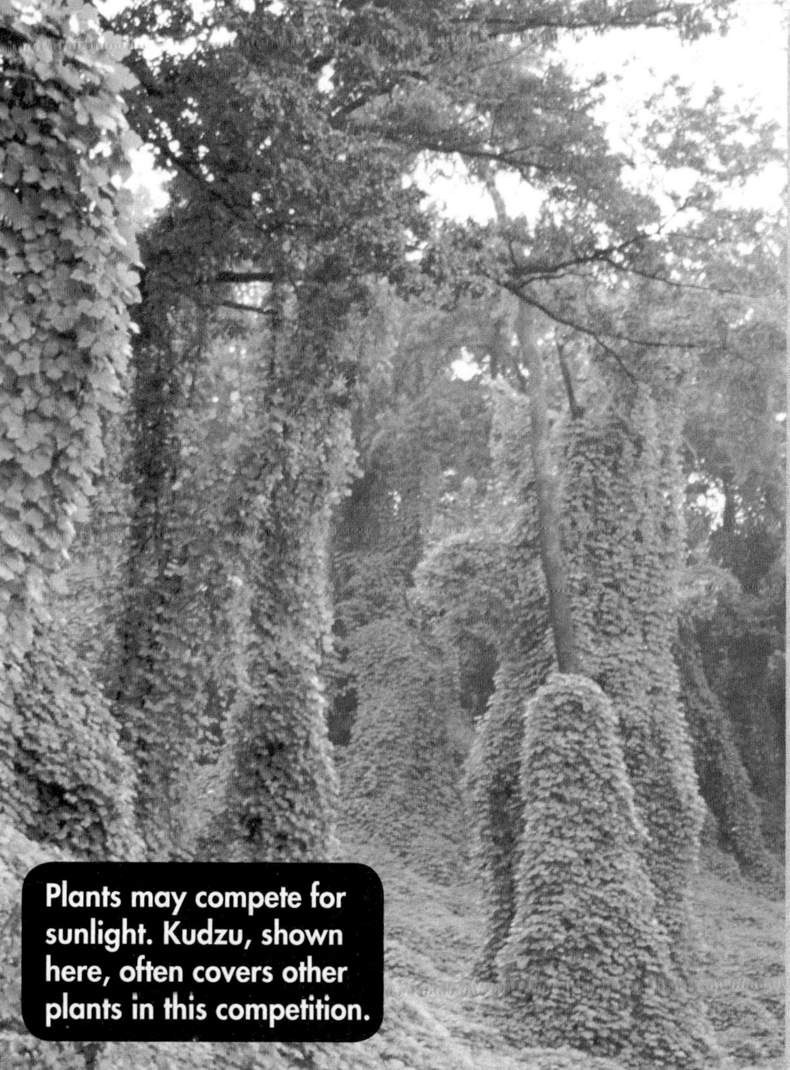
Plants may compete for sunlight. Kudzu, shown here, often covers other plants in this competition.

1. √ Checkpoint Describe why organisms compete and what the results of competition might be.
2. Math in Science How many years ago was kudzu brought to the southern states?

Symbiosis

Animals are not always in competition with each other. Just as there are many kinds of relationships between people, there are many kinds of relationships between species. Symbiosis is a long-term relationship between different species. One of the species is always helped. The other might be helped, harmed, or not affected at all.

The buffalo and the cattle egret show one kind of symbiosis. As the buffalo grazes, it causes insects hiding in the grass to fly or hop away. The bird can easily get a meal by feeding on these moving insects. In this kind of symbiosis, the bird is helped and the buffalo is not really affected. Egrets may eat insects off the back of buffalo, but whether or not this helps the buffalo is not certain.

A second kind of symbiosis does help the buffalo. Microorganisms inside its digestive system help the buffalo digest the food it eats. In this kind of symbiosis, both species are helped. The tiny creatures have a meal brought to them, and the buffalo can digest grass and leaves.

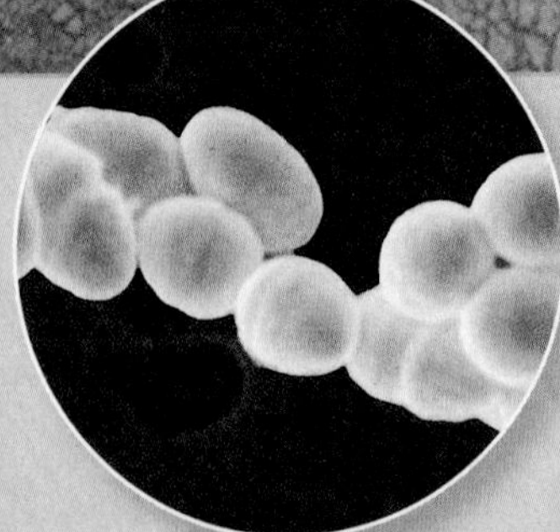

Bacteria and protists help buffalo, cows, sheep, elk, and other animals digest grass and other plants.

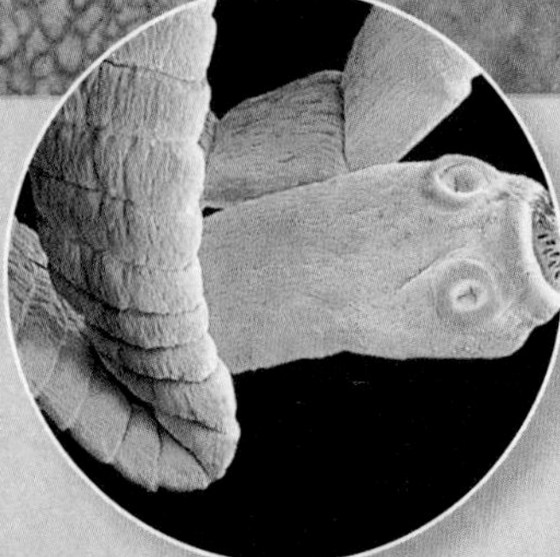

There are many kinds of tapeworms that live in the intestines of many kinds of animals.

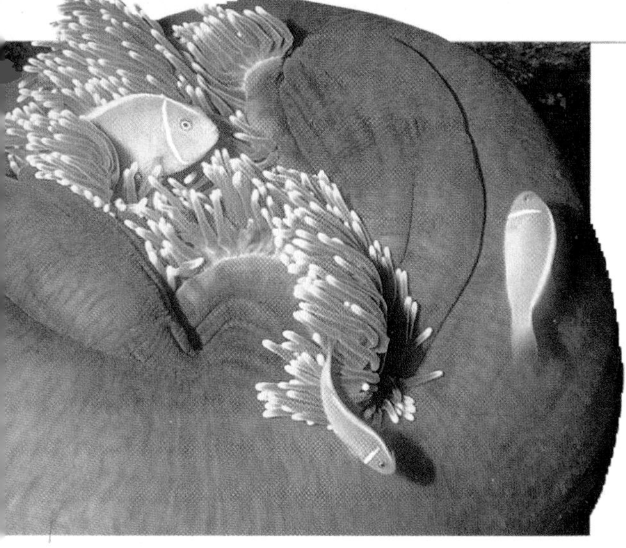

The relationship between the clownfish and sea anemone is an example of symbiosis. When the fish is among the anemone's tentacles, the anemone will sting any fish that attacks the clownfish. The anemone gets food from the clownfish by eating leftovers attached to the clownfish's body.

In a third kind of symbiosis, organisms might cause the buffalo great harm. These organisms are parasites. A parasite is an organism that feeds off another organism, called a host. Some parasites are worms that live in the buffalo's intestines or bloodstream. These parasites eat the buffalo's food before the food gets to the buffalo's cells. They also might take oxygen from the buffalo's blood. Parasites can make the buffalo weak and sick.

In another kind of symbiosis, one organism is not just helped by a partner, but rather it needs a partner in order to survive. Lichen is one example. It is made up of a fungus and a plant-like bacteria or algae. The bacteria or algae make food from sunlight. The fungus survives by getting some of this food. The fungus gives the bacteria or algae a safe home.

√ Lesson Checkpoint

1. Describe the symbiosis between a parasite and its host.
2. Give an example of a relationship where both organisms are helped.
3. **Predict** Suppose a veterinarian gave a buffalo some medicine that killed all organisms inside the buffalo. Predict what effects this would have on the buffalo.

Lesson 5

How does energy move in ecosystems?

Energy can pass through an ecosystem when food is eaten, but some energy is always changed to heat and not passed on.

Food Chains and Webs

Every organism needs energy in order to live. Energy moves to all organisms by processes known as food chains, energy chains, or food webs.

Plants, protists, and other microorganisms are producers. Producers are organisms that make their own food for energy. Producers get energy to make food from the energy of sunlight or chemicals in nature. This food can then be used by many other organisms.

Consumers are organisms that cannot make their own food. They usually eat other organisms to get energy to stay alive and grow. All animals are consumers. There are several kinds of consumers. Herbivores eat only plants. Carnivores, also called predators, eat only other animals, called prey. Omnivores eat both plants and animals. Decomposers eat waste or dead organisms.

When food is eaten, it is not only matter that moves into another animal. The energy in the food also moves. Arrows in the food chain at the right show how energy can flow through an ecosystem from a producer to an herbivore, a carnivore, and finally to a decomposer. You can see that the energy the spotted owl gets from eating the hare came from plants.

Sun → plants → snowshoe hare → spotted owl → bacteria

Northern Spotted Owl

Insects

On land, almost all kinds of animals' food can be traced back in some way to plants. In the ocean, food chains often start with plant-like microorganisms called plankton. Food chains at deep-sea vents start with bacteria.

Food chains can be very short, involving only a plant and a decomposer. Chains can also be longer, involving more than one carnivore. A food chain is not a complete way of describing energy flow in an ecosystem. This is because consumers usually eat many kinds of other organisms. To see an ecosystem more fully, you need to look at a food web like the one below. A food web combines many food chains into one picture.

1. **✓Checkpoint** What is the niche, or role, of a producer?
2. **Art in Science** Draw a diagram showing the sequence of organisms feeding in a food web. Your diagram may have organisms of your choosing. Describe how your diagram shows the flow of matter and energy.

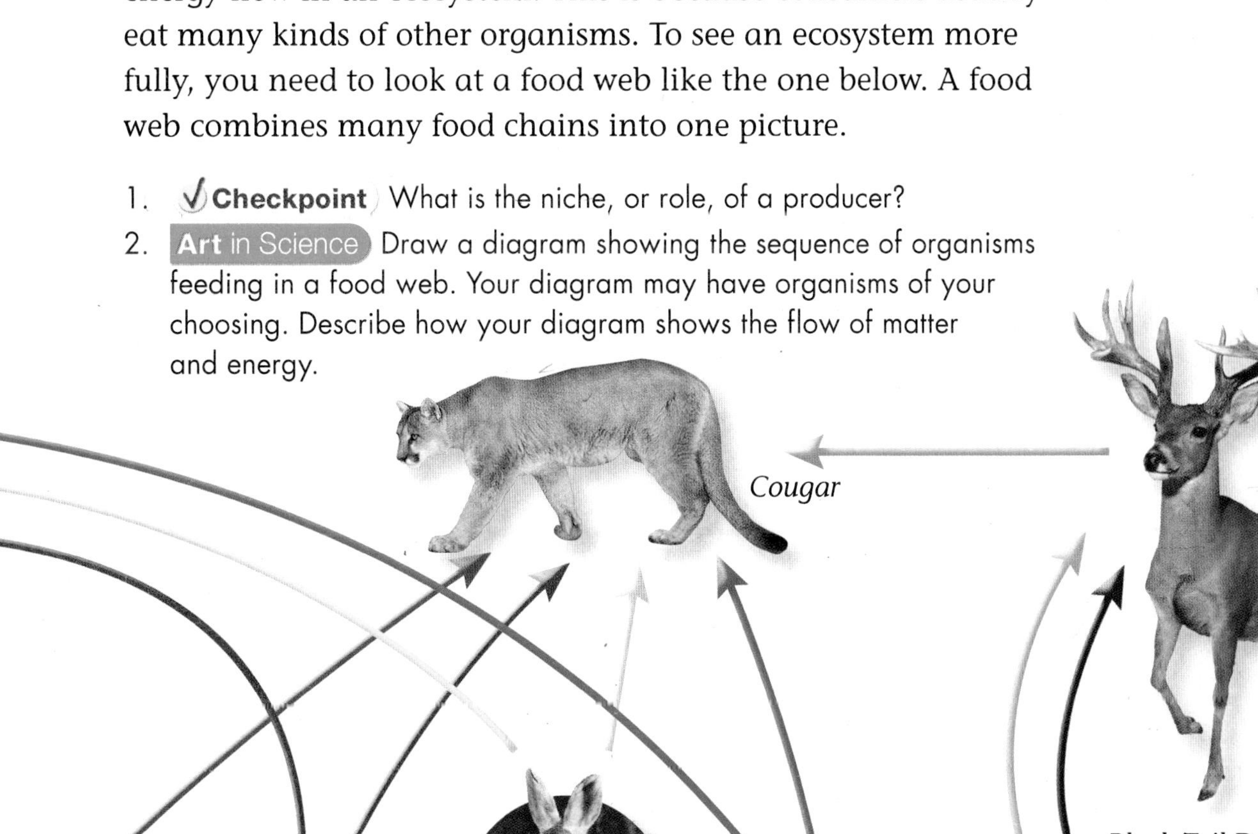

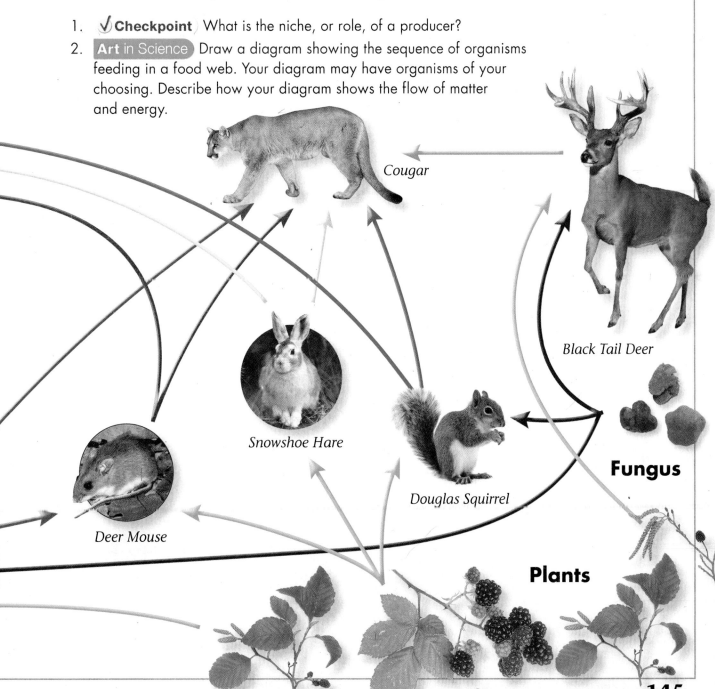

Cougar
Black Tail Deer
Snowshoe Hare
Douglas Squirrel
Deer Mouse
Fungus
Plants

Energy Pyramids

In an ecosystem, energy flows from the Sun to producers to herbivores and carnivores. Most of the energy of every organism, though, does not reach the next stage of the food chain.

An **energy pyramid** is a diagram that shows the amounts of energy that flow through each level of a food chain. The base of the energy pyramid is widest. This shows the energy in the producers. Producers have the greatest amount of energy in an ecosystem. As you look higher on the energy pyramid, from producers to consumers, the pyramid narrows. This shows that less energy flows through the higher levels. Decomposers are not shown in energy pyramids.

The reason that some energy does not reach the next level of the pyramid is that most of the energy is changed. The energy does not disappear. It is turned into other forms of energy that are not passed through the food chain. For example, a snowshoe hare gets energy by eating plants. The hare uses its food's energy to run, breathe, and do other life activities. These activities turn most energy from the rabbit's food into body heat. By the time an owl eats the hare, only a part of the plants' energy is still available.

Energy

√ Lesson Checkpoint

1. Explain how an energy pyramid shows the flow of energy in a food chain or food web.
2. Explain why an animal's food and energy can be traced back to plants and the Sun.
3. Why do animals eat?
4. Writing in Science **Expository** In your **science journal,** write directions to younger students explaining how to draw food chains and food webs. In your directions, use and define the words *producer, consumer, herbivore, carnivore, omnivore,* and *decomposer.*

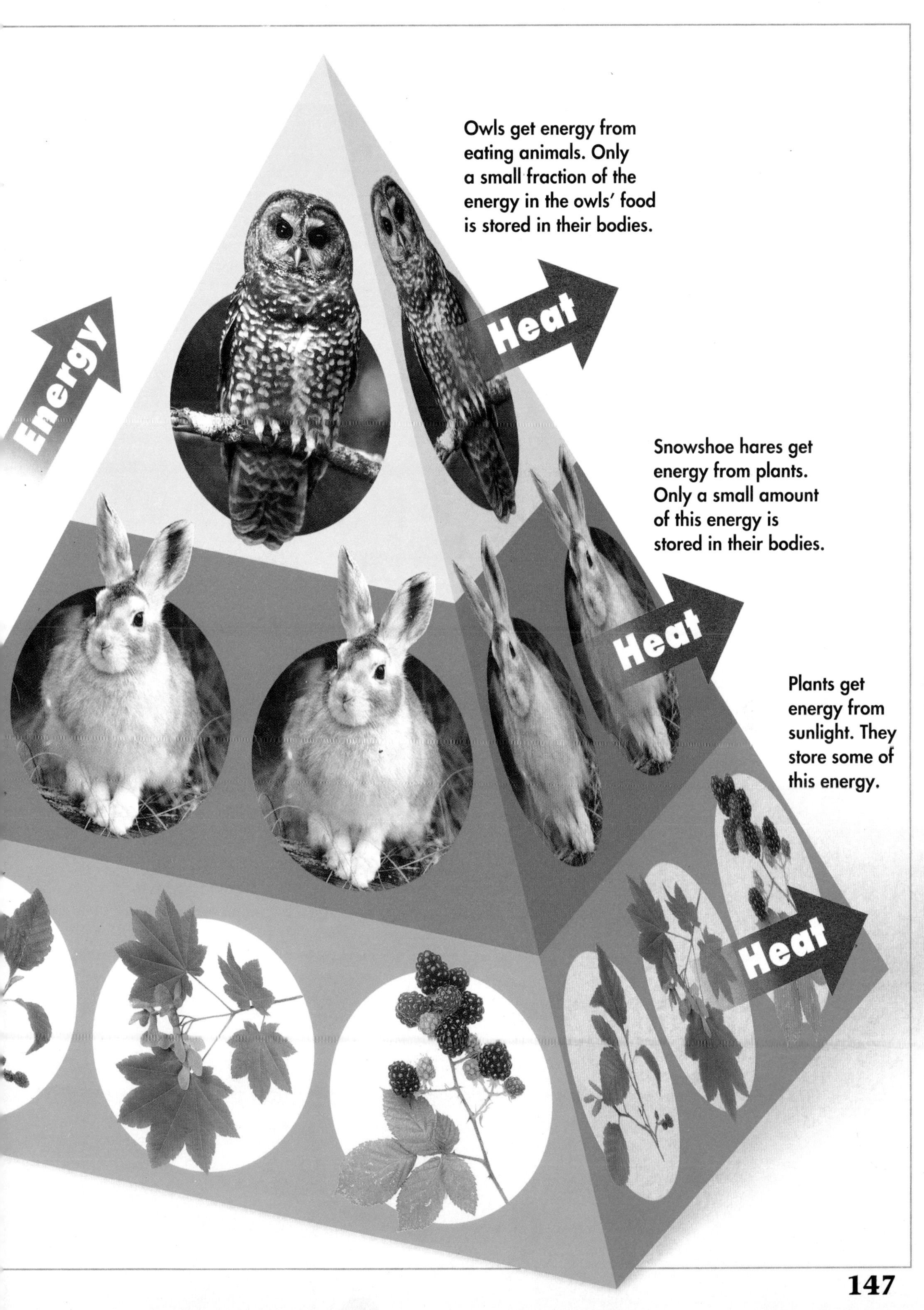
Owls get energy from eating animals. Only a small fraction of the energy in the owls' food is stored in their bodies.
Energy
Heat
Snowshoe hares get energy from plants. Only a small amount of this energy is stored in their bodies.
Heat
Plants get energy from sunlight. They store some of this energy.
Heat

Lesson 6

What cycles occur in ecosystems?

In an ecosystem, a substance may be passed from one organism to another. These substances go through an ecosystem again and again.

Recycling Matter

Every day in every ecosystem, animals produce waste products. Eventually plants, animals, and all other organisms will die. There must be a way to "clean up" the waste and dead matter.

With its yellow coloring and long body, it is not hard to see why this is called the banana slug. As it eats material on the forest floor, this decomposer can grow to be 25 centimeters long.

A fungus breaks down a log by releasing special chemicals. Materials from the log are then absorbed by the fungus and used as food.

Decomposers are organisms that eat wastes and dead matter. By doing this, they break material into smaller pieces and put it back into the soil. Most decomposers are microorganisms like bacteria and fungi. Earthworms, flies, and slugs are also decomposers. Whenever you see something decaying or rotting, decomposers have been at work.

Decomposers have the important niche, or role, of recycling wastes and dead material. They make minerals and nutrients that were in waste or dead materials available to living plants. These plants will then be food for other organisms. In this way, minerals and nutrients become part of a cycle. A **cycle** is a repeating process or a repeating flow of material through a system. There is a constant cycle of minerals and some nutrients moving from living things to the soil and back into living things.

Decomposers are not the only things that break down dead matter. Fire also does this. When plants burn, their ashes become part of the soil.

1. **Checkpoint** What is the niche of slime molds and other decomposers?
2. **Math in Science** A slug started moving across a log at 10:52 A.M. and got to the other end at 11:09 A.M. How many minutes did the slug take to cross the log?

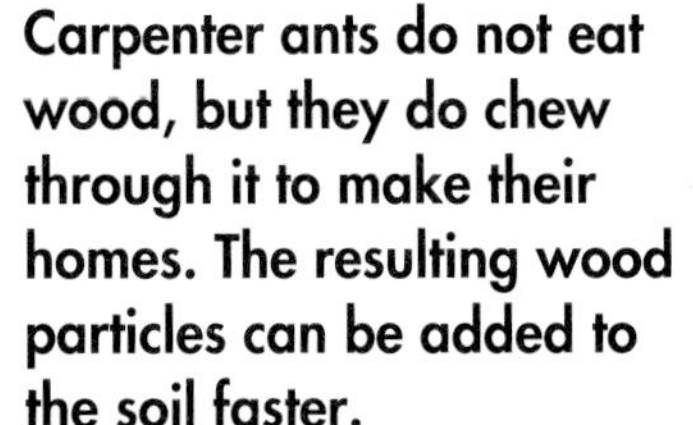
Carpenter ants do not eat wood, but they do chew through it to make their homes. The resulting wood particles can be added to the soil faster.

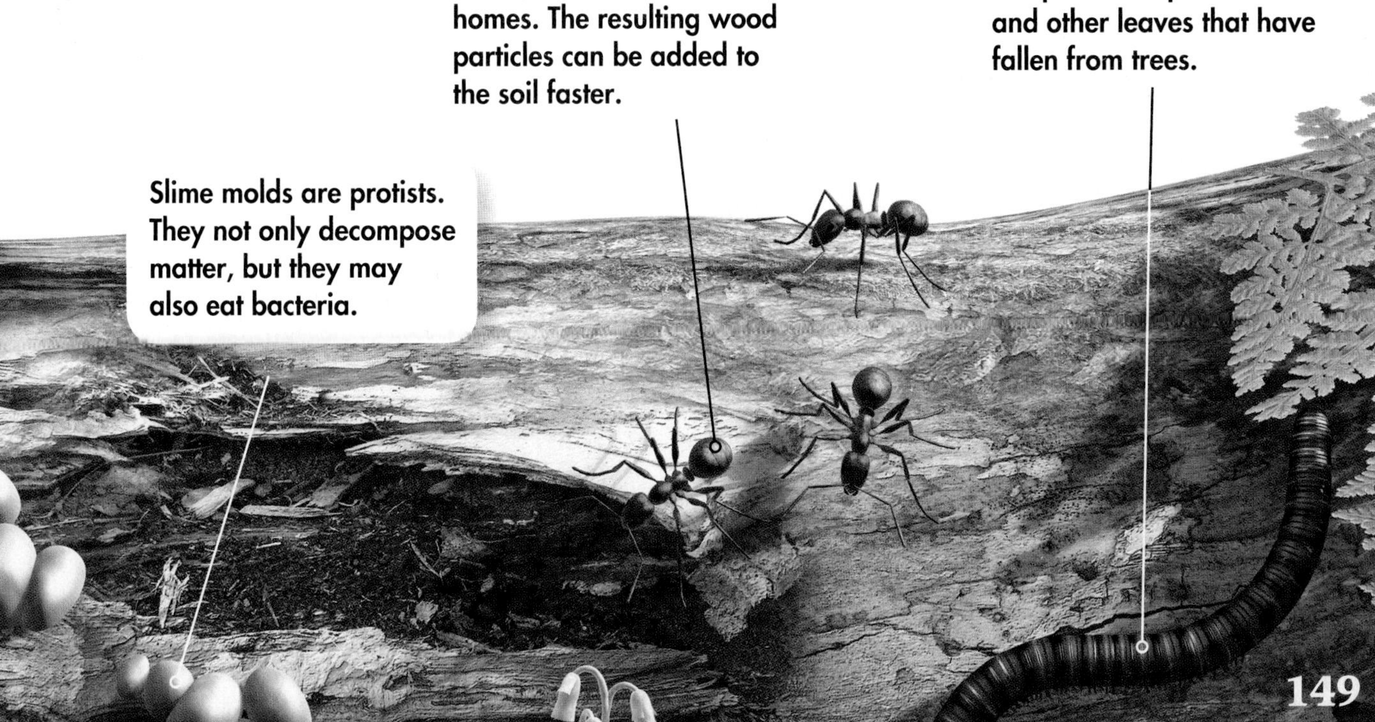
The almond-scented millipede eats pine needles and other leaves that have fallen from trees.

Slime molds are protists. They not only decompose matter, but they may also eat bacteria.

Nitrogen Cycle

Cells in plants and animals need nitrogen to do their work. Nitrogen cycles through ecosystems. It moves through the food chain and other processes.

Nitrogen is all around us. Almost $\frac{8}{10}$ of Earth's atmosphere is nitrogen gas. Most organisms cannot use nitrogen gas from the air. They must use nitrogen compounds. These are different kinds of chemicals that contain nitrogen. Nitrogen compounds are made in many ways in nature.

Nitrogen compounds can form in the atmosphere. The high temperatures of lightning can cause nitrogen to combine with other gases in the air and make nitrogen compounds. These compounds reach Earth's soil and water in rainfall.

Some kinds of bacteria make nitrogen compounds and put them into the soil. Plant roots absorb the compounds along with the water in the soil.

Some plants in tropical rainforests contain bacteria that make nitrogen compounds. These plants grow in the upper branches of the trees in the forest. Bacteria living in special roots are able to take in nitrogen directly from the air.

Herbivores get the nitrogen they need when they eat plants. Carnivores get nitrogen when they eat the herbivores.

Nitrogen returns to the soil or air when animals and plants die. It also returns in animals' waste products. Decomposers break down the remains of dead organisms and waste products. They change the animals' nitrogen compounds into kinds that plants can use. The compounds return to the soil or air and the cycle repeats.

People add nitrogen compounds to the soil. Many farmers use fertilizers that contain nitrogen. Fertilizers are materials that make soil better for growing crops. The discovery of how to make fertilizers with nitrogen was very important to society. Farmers can now grow more food in their fields.

A bromeliad is a plant that contains certain bacteria. These bacteria can make nitrogen compounds from nitrogen in the air.

Only a part of the nitrogen cycle is shown here.

3 Record how the color changes.

4 Put the elodea into the water. Put the cup in a bright place. **Observe** every 10 minutes. Record how the color changes.

	Color of Water with BTB
Before breathing out into the water	
After breathing out into the water	
After adding elodea to the water	

BTB indicates how much carbon dioxide is in the water.

greenish yellow = high level of carbon dioxide

blue = low level of carbon dioxide

Explain Your Results

1. What made the color of the water with BTB change when you breathed into it?
2. In your **investigation,** what made the color change after you added the elodea?

Go Further

What would happen if the elodea and water with BTB were put in a dark place? Write a procedure others could follow to answer this question.

Math in Science

Population Cycles

How do the populations of predators and their prey affect each other? Answering this question is very difficult. There are many things that can affect the size of a population.

Scientists use special computer programs called models to predict population changes. The models use data for just one population each of predators and prey living in a perfect habitat. The graph below shows one model's prediction of the cycle, or repeating pattern, of growth and decline during one month. The populations go up and down within a certain range.

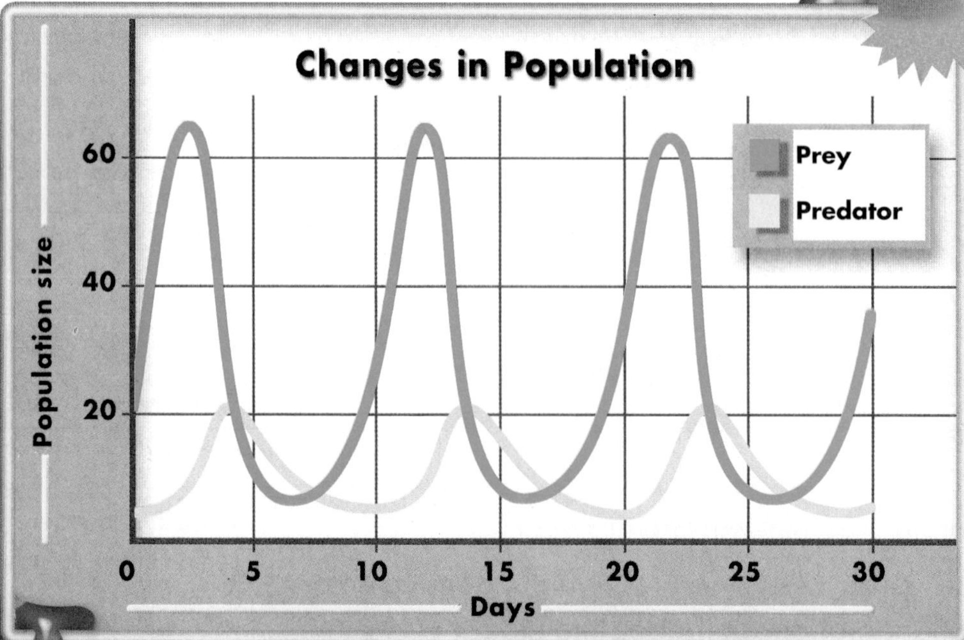

Changes in Population
Prey
Predator
Population size
60
40
20
0
5
10
15
20
25
30
Days

e Tools Take It to the Net sfsuccessnet.com

Use the graph of the population cycles to answer these questions.

1. When is the population of prey the greatest?
A. days 1, 13, and 25
B. days 7, 14, and 21
C. days 2, 12, and 22
D. days 2, 5, and 8

2. Which is a reasonable estimate for the difference between the greatest and the least number of predators?
F. 5 G. 10 H. 16 I. 22

3. Which compares the greatest population of prey to the greatest population of predators?
A. There are more than 3 times as many prey as predators.
B. There are about twice as many prey as predators.
C. There are about 10 more prey than predators.
D. The populations are the same.

4. What happens after the predator's population becomes greater than the prey's?
F. This never happens.
G The prey's population quickly decreases to zero.
H. Both populations decrease.
I. The prey's population immediately increases.

Lab zone Take-Home Activity

Keep a record of the amount of some type of food that is used each day in your home. Also, record the number of people who use this food each day. After one week of recording, graph your data.

Chapter 5 Review and Test Prep

Use Vocabulary

community (p. 127)	**energy pyramid** (p. 146)
cycle (p. 149)	**habitat** (p. 129)
ecosystem (p. 127)	**niche** (p. 129)
	population (p. 127)

Use the term from the list above that best completes each sentence.

1. A(n) _____ is one way of showing the amount of energy available at each stage of a food chain.
2. The place in an ecosystem where an organism normally lives is its _____.
3. A(n) _____ is the combination of living and non-living things and their interactions.
4. All of the populations of organisms in a(n) _____ belong to different species but live the same area.
5. The role each organism has in an ecosystem is its _____.
6. A group of organisms of the same species living in one area is a(n) _____.
7. Materials often repeat a pattern, or _____, as they move through different parts of an ecosystem.

Explain Concepts

8. Explain how energy and materials move through an ecosystem.
9. Explain ways that organisms interact in helpful and harmful ways.
10. Explain the flow of energy in an energy pyramid like the one below. Then tell how an energy pyramid and a food chain are the same and how they are different.

Energy
Heat
Energy
Heat
Heat

11. Explain how different structures or behaviors help organisms survive in their habitats.
12. Explain what a biome is. Describe four examples of biomes.

Process Skills

13. Estimate how many ants are on an entire sidewalk. Some students counted the number of ants on each of four sections of sidewalk. Their data is given in the table below. The sidewalk has a total of 20 sections. Explain how you estimated.

Section	Ants Counted
Section 1	6
Section 2	11
Section 3	10
Section 4	9

Predict

14. Predict A desert community has foxes, rabbits, and grasses. Predict what would happen to the population of grasses in this desert if the population of foxes increased.

Test Prep

Choose the letter that best completes the statement or answers the question.

15. Which of the following consists of parts working together?
- Ⓐ niche
- Ⓑ system
- Ⓒ population
- Ⓓ habitat

16. Which biome can be best described as an evergreen forest in a cold, dry location?
- Ⓕ taiga
- Ⓖ temperate rainforest
- Ⓗ tundra
- Ⓘ deciduous forest

17. Organisms can only live where
- Ⓐ there is sunlight.
- Ⓑ there is dry land.
- Ⓒ they can move around.
- Ⓓ their needs can be met.

18. What kind of organism helps clean a habitat of waste and dead remains?
- Ⓕ decomposer
- Ⓖ carnivore
- Ⓗ herbivore
- Ⓘ omnivore

19. Explain why the answer you select for Question 18 is best. For each of the answers you do not select, give a reason why it is not the best answer.

20. Writing in Science **Descriptive** Describe an ecosystem. List the living and nonliving parts and processes of the system. Discuss the niches of the organisms you list.

Career

Greenhouse Manager

As a greenhouse manager, your job would be to create a good ecosystem for the plants inside a greenhouse. The manager of a greenhouse makes sure that the temperature is just right for the plants and that the plants have the right amounts of soil, food, water, and, of course, sunshine.

Because greenhouses sell many different types of plants, the greenhouse manager must create a good ecosystem for each one. This means adjusting the moisture levels and amounts of sunlight or shade to those best suited for each type of plant.

Greenhouses are small businesses. The greenhouse manager may hire, train, and supervise workers to help.

If you like working with plants and people, a career as a greenhouse manager can begin by completing a two-year college program in horticulture.

Lab zone Take-Home Activity

Choose a kind of seed to grow in your home. Read about the seed you choose so that you can provide a good ecosystem for the plant. When the plant has grown, show it to your class.

EC NTL 10987

Chapter 6

Changes in Ecosystems

You Will Discover

- why some habitats change.
- how animals and plants change over time.
- what happens to plants and animals when their habitats change.

online
Student Edition
sfsuccessnet.com

Build Background

How do changes in habitats affect living things?

behavioral adaptation

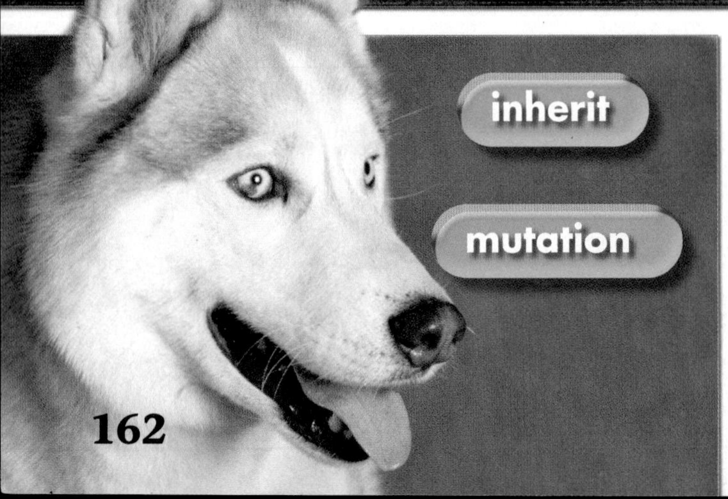

inherit

mutation

pesticide

STOP

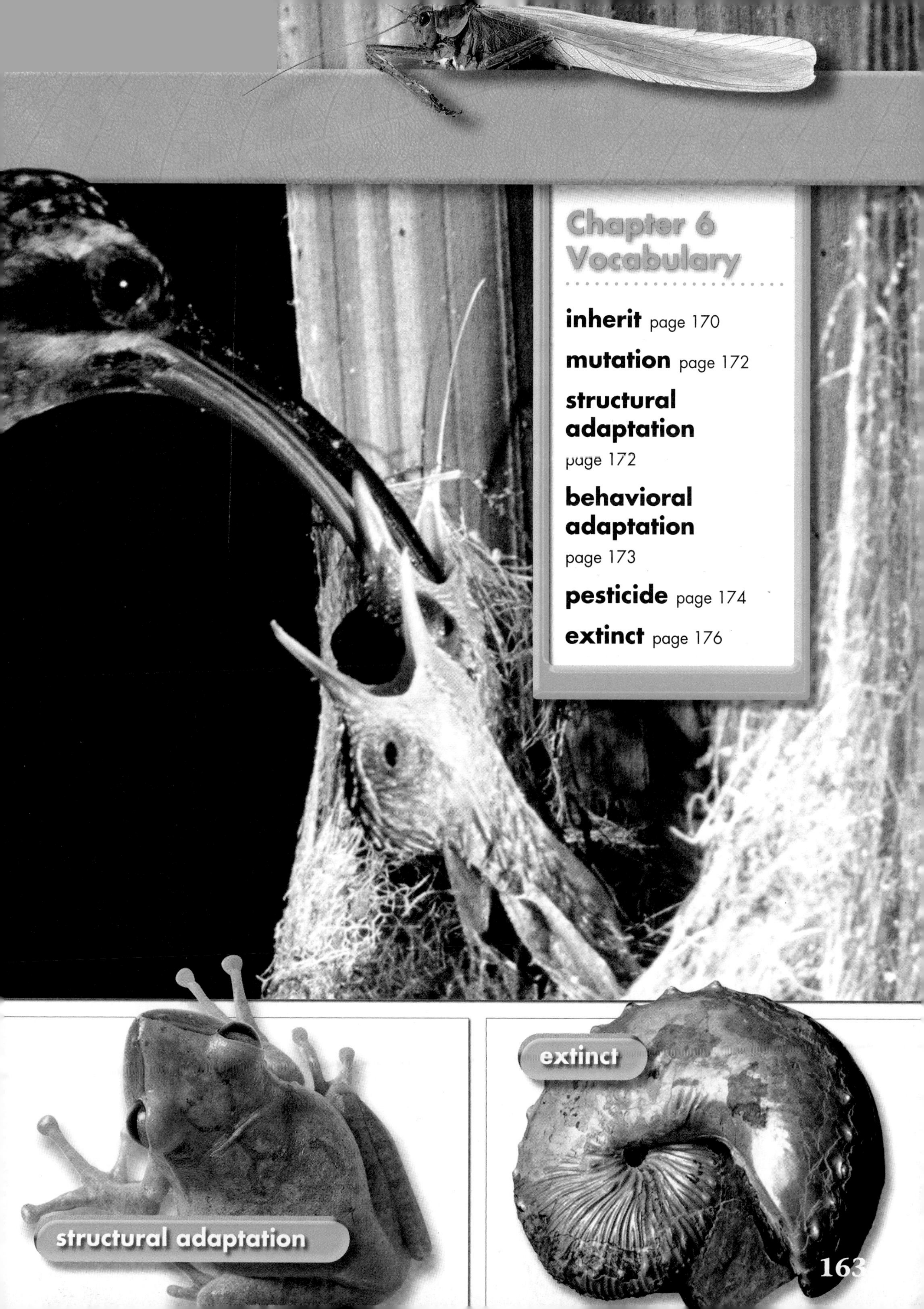
Chapter 6 Vocabulary
inherit page 170
mutation page 172
structural adaptation page 172
behavioral adaptation page 173
pesticide page 174
extinct page 176
structural adaptation
extinct

Lab zone **Directed Inquiry**

Explore How can pollution affect a habitat?

Materials

safety goggles

2 cups and graduated cylinder (or measuring cup)

vinegar and water

spoon and yeast

sugar

masking tape

Process Skills

You **infer** when you make an evaluation or judgment based on past experiences and **observations.**

What to Do

1. Label the cups. One cup represents polluted water.
2. **Measure** and add the materials to the cups as shown below. Stir gently.

Be careful!

Wear safety goggles. Do not breathe in vinegar fumes.

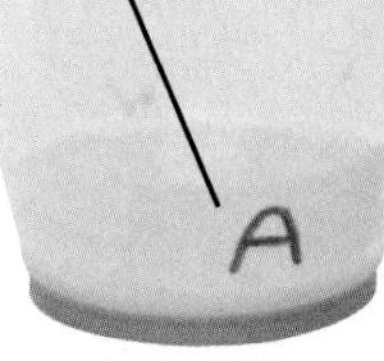
Label the cups.
A
B
30 mL water
$\frac{1}{2}$ spoonful yeast
1 spoonful sugar
30 mL vinegar
$\frac{1}{2}$ spoonful yeast
1 spoonful sugar

3. Put the cups in a warm place.
4. **Observe** what happens to the yeast in the cups after 5, 10, and 15 minutes. View the cups from the side.

Explain Your Results

1. What happened to the yeast in each cup?
2. **Infer** Pollution can harm or even kill living things. Which cup represents the polluted habitat? Explain your answer.

How to Read Science

Reading Skills

TARGET SKILL

Cause and Effect

A **cause** is why something happens. An **effect** is what happens. When you read, sometimes clue phrases such as *due to* and *as a result* signal a cause and effect relationship. Sometimes there are no clue words. You must **infer** which events are causes and which are effects.

Some causes and effects are marked in the newspaper article below. Learning to find causes and effects can help you understand what you read.

Newspaper Article

The Exxon Valdez

On March 24, 1989, beaches in southern Alaska became black. This was due to a shipping accident. A ship called the Exxon Valdez ran aground in Alaska and dumped more than 11 million gallons of oil into Prince William Sound. The oil spill covered more than 1,000 miles of coastline. Thousands of animals, including seabirds, sea otters, harbor seals, bald eagles, and whales were killed as a result of the spill. Thousands more were covered with the oil. Government agencies and many volunteers worked for years to clean up the area.

Apply It!

Make a graphic organizer like the one below. List each **cause** and **effect** from the science article in your graphic organizer.

Cause		Effect
	→	

You Are There!

The day is sunny, and the yellow wheat moves softly in the field beneath a blue sky. A strange black cloud seems to be moving toward you. Soon you see that it is not a rain cloud but a swarm of millions of locusts. As you run for your home, you feel locusts crunch under your feet. The desperately hungry insects are everywhere, nipping and chewing in search of food. What will be the effect of such a huge swarm?

Lesson 1

How do ecosystems change?

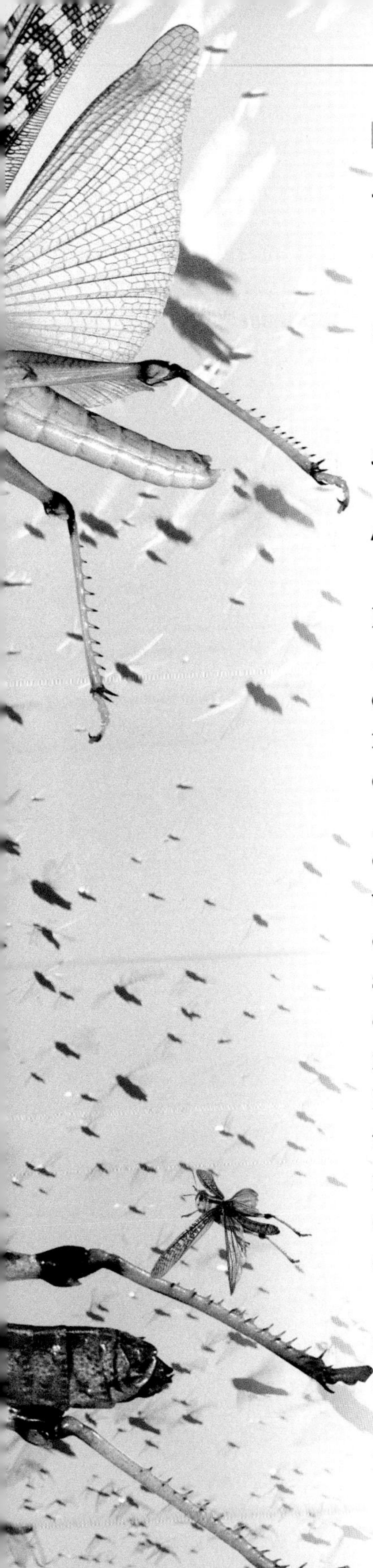

Ecosystems are always changing—sometimes quickly, sometimes slowly. People and animals may bring on these changes.

Animals Change Ecosystems

What kinds of changes could a huge swarm of locusts cause? In some parts of the world, locusts bring a great deal of trouble. As they move, they might feed on all the plants in the farm fields, causing food shortages for animals and people. Locusts have made paths 100 kilometers wide and 1,000 kilometers long.

Ecosystems are always being changed by organisms, wind, water, or other parts of the environment. By damming streams, beavers make new pond ecosystems where they are safe from wolves and other predators. For a few organisms, a new pond that floods their homes is bad news. But for many other organisms, a pond is a new home and is helpful.

Beaver dams change the environment.

Most changes in an ecosystem are not so dramatic, and not all changes are harmful. For example, earthworms slowly and quietly dig new holes through the soil, bringing oxygen to the plant roots. These worms improve the soil with digested materials they leave behind.

1. **✓Checkpoint** Explain how changes in an ecosystem can sometimes be helpful and sometimes harmful.
2. **Math in Science** A locust swarm in 1875 was about 177 kilometers wide. Its length was about 16 times its width. How long was the swarm?

People Change Ecosystems

People change ecosystems when they build houses, clear forests, or throw out garbage. People also change ecosystems by introducing new plants and animals. Plants and animals have been carried over deserts, mountains, and even oceans. When a species is introduced into an ecosystem, it causes changes. These changes often affect the survival of entire species.

Zebra mussels stick to hard surfaces like these shells.

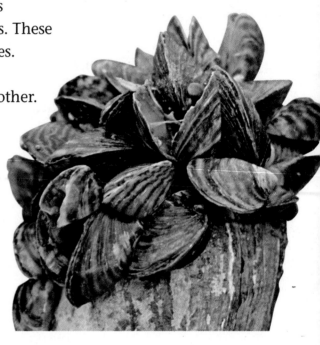

Zebra mussels are animals that people accidentally moved from one ecosystem to another. It seems that the zebra mussels stuck to ships that travelled from the other side of the world to the United States. Zebra mussels do not have predators in their new habitat, so their population has grown quickly. This species has changed the ecosystems of many rivers and lakes in many ways. For example, huge numbers of zebra mussels can take the food and space needed by other species. Those species may no longer be able to survive in the area.

The garlic mustard plant was carried to the United States on purpose. Early settlers used garlic mustard for food and medicine. Unfortunately, animals do not eat the plant, so it spread quickly. The plant can dominate forest floors, keeping other plants from getting water and sunlight. How do you think this affects plants and animals?

Zebra mussels can block water pipes.

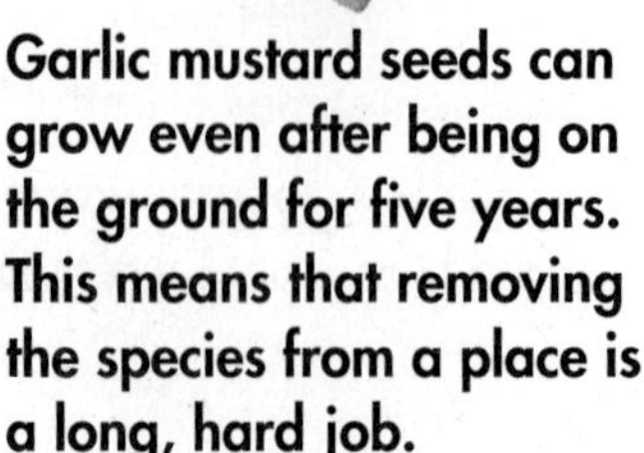

Garlic mustard seeds can grow even after being on the ground for five years. This means that removing the species from a place is a long, hard job.

A landfill may cover a few acres or a few thousand acres.

Each American produces about 1.8 kilograms of garbage each day—that adds up to about 200 million tons a year! Most garbage is put into a landfill. A landfill is a pile of garbage that is eventually covered with soil and grass. The local ecosystem is greatly changed while the landfill is being used. After the landfill is covered by grass, the ecosystem might return to being very similar to what it was like before the landfill. In the past, landfills unexpectedly leaked pollution into nearby bodies of water. Today, liners seal off the garbage to keep harmful chemicals from getting into the ground.

Acid rain is rain that has absorbed certain kinds of pollutants. Acid rain changes ecosystems because it pollutes soils and lakes. Plants and animals can die from this pollution. People can treat polluted lakes by dumping helpful chemicals into the water.

✓ Lesson Checkpoint

1. Why can populations of zebra mussels and garlic mustard grow so quickly in their new ecosystems?
2. How do beaver ponds help the beaver? How do they affect other organisms?
3. **Cause and Effect** What is the effect of people introducing new species to an area?

Fighting Acid Rain
Acid rain can hurt plants, animals, and other organisms in lakes. People can add material to a lake to control some of the effects of acid rain.

A Forest Damaged by Acid Rain
The pollutants in acid rain have damaged some of the trees and other plants in this forest.

Lesson 2

How do species change?

Parents in every species pass traits to their offspring. Traits of species may change and may help the species survive.

Inheriting DNA

Small changes occur in ecosystems over many years. Some of these changes happen because offspring are not exactly like their parents.

Remember, heredity is the process in which plants and animals receive, or **inherit,** half of the genes from each parent. The genes determine almost everything about how the organism grows. Since every animal inherits a new mix of genes from its parents, every animal is different. This kind of small change from parents to offspring usually is neither helpful nor harmful to the ecosystem.

Different combinations of DNA may cause offspring to be different from their parents in many ways. Some offspring may be taller than their parents. Some may have different-colored eyes. However, most things will be the same. The dog shown on this page has the same organ systems as its parents. It has the same number of legs and placement of eyes. The dog's body has thick fur like its parents, though the color may be different.

Different genes result in different colors of fur and eyes.

This dog inherited a set of genes that gave it blue eyes and brown fur.

Traits That Are Not Inherited

Differences among organisms of the same species are not all due to different DNA. The ecosystem can affect how plants and animals grow. Genes determine how big an organism can grow, but the environment also plays a role. Organisms may not grow well if there is not enough food and water or if the weather is very hot or very cold.

The ecosystem can also affect an organism's color. The American flamingo is not born with its bright colors. These flamingos are born with white feathers. The bird has pink or reddish feathers only after eating certain foods such as shrimp or other small crustaceans and algae.

A hydrangea is a plant that may have flowers of different colors depending on what is in the soil. The flowers can be red, pink, or blue. With many plants, too much sunlight can cause damage that results in leaves turning color from green to yellow or brown.

Without a diet of crustaceans and algae, a flamingo is white.

1. √ Checkpoint What are some characteristics that are determined by DNA? What are some characteristics that are influenced by the ecosystem?
2. Writing in Science **Descriptive** In your **science journal,** write a letter to a friend describing an animal species that you would like to have as a pet. In your letter, describe ways that all animals of the species are the same and how some are different from each other.

Hydrangea flowers

Adaptations

Sometimes a change, or **mutation,** happens in an organism's genes. The changed gene can pass from a parent to the offspring. Mutations may be harmful, helpful, or neutral. Mutations are often harmful. For example, a mutation may cause an animal to no longer have the correct genes to make white blood cells that fight germs. A helpful mutation can be the first step towards an adaptation. Adaptations make an organism fit an ecosystem better. Colors that help an animal hide are adaptations.

This frog can better avoid its enemies because of structural adaptations such as the suction cups on its toes and its green skin.

Adaptations are especially important when an ecosystem changes. At such times, competition for limited food, water, or other resources is the strongest. Organisms that have the best adaptations to compete for the limited resources may survive best, reproduce more, and pass their genes to their offspring.

Structural Adaptations

Helpful mutations or some new combinations of DNA may cause changes in body parts. **Structural adaptations** are changed body parts that help the organism survive in its ecosystem. For example, if a hummingbird was born with a longer beak than other hummingbirds, the bird might be better at getting food from some flowers in its ecosystem. The longer beak is a structural adaptation that is helpful when living around these flowers. During a drought, this bird may survive when many other birds cannot find enough food. The bird might pass the genes for this adaptation to its offspring. After many generations, a large part of the hummingbird population may have this kind of long beak and survive better than other hummingbirds.

Natural selection involves the process of a species developing adaptations. All species of living things may experience natural selection. Natural selection helps them survive in different niches and environments.

Rough play with their parents and other cubs helps these lion cubs learn to hunt.

Behavioral Adaptations

Were you born knowing how to build a house? That is impossible! Hummingbirds though, like other birds, are born knowing how to make the kind of home they need. They are also born knowing how to take care of their offspring. These behaviors are due to genes passed from parent to offspring.

Behavioral adaptations are inherited behaviors that help animals survive. Some behavioral adaptations are called instincts. They affect how an animal behaves around other animals of the same species or different species. Lemmings are small rodents that have an instinct to migrate if their population in an area gets too large. Some animals, like musk oxen, have an instinct to form a circle around their young when predators threaten them.

Not all behaviors of an animal are due to behavioral adaptations. Some behaviors are learned. For example, lion parents teach their offspring how to hunt. A lion cub stays with its mother for 2 or 3 years until it can hunt on its own.

The way that a hummingbird makes a nest is a behavioral adaptation.

Legs that can tuck close to the body make it easier for the hummingbird to fly. This is a structural adaptation.

√ Lesson Checkpoint

1. How are behavioral adaptations like structural adaptations? How are they different?
2. What are two reasons that an animal will not have the same DNA as its mother?
3. **Writing in Science** **Expository** During your life, you have learned some behaviors that have helped you survive. In your **science journal,** write a survival guide using information that you have learned about safety around the house.

Lesson 3

How do changes cause more changes?

Living things live together in a system where one change may affect many organisms. Other changes can happen as a result.

Pesticides are sprayed to kill mosquitoes.

Changes in Behavior

Ecosystems are systems of living and nonliving things. As in any system, changes in one part of an ecosystem can affect other parts.

Animals may change their behavior because there has been a change in the kinds or numbers of other animals in their ecosystem. For example, a pet cat might change its habits when a new puppy is brought into a home. The cat may spend more time on beds and chairs to keep away from the new animal.

Changes in Populations

Have you ever spent an evening outside and been bothered by mosquitoes? Mosquitoes are more than just annoying. They can spread diseases such as malaria and West Nile virus. To limit these problems, people put pesticides in the mosquitoes' ecosystem. **Pesticides** are poisons that kill insects.

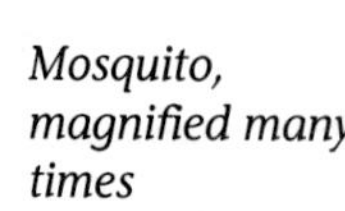

Mosquito, magnified many times

Some populations of mosquitoes have developed adaptations to this kind of change in their ecosystem. This happens when a few mosquitoes happen to have genes that make them able to live around the pesticide being used. While other mosquitoes die, the few mosquitoes with these genes survive and reproduce. Some of their offspring might have these genes too. They will survive and reproduce. This is an example of a species developing adaptations to a change in its ecosystem.

Antibiotics are medicines used to kill disease-causing bacteria. Just as some mosquitoes have developed adaptations to living with pesticides, some bacteria have developed adaptations to living around antibiotics. When many bacteria have developed adaptations to an antibiotic, the medicine no longer works well. The diseases the bacteria cause become harder to treat.

Many people were surprised when bacteria first developed adaptations to survive antibiotics. Today, doctors expect more adaptations to happen. Researchers look for new medicines that could be used when current medicines no longer work well.

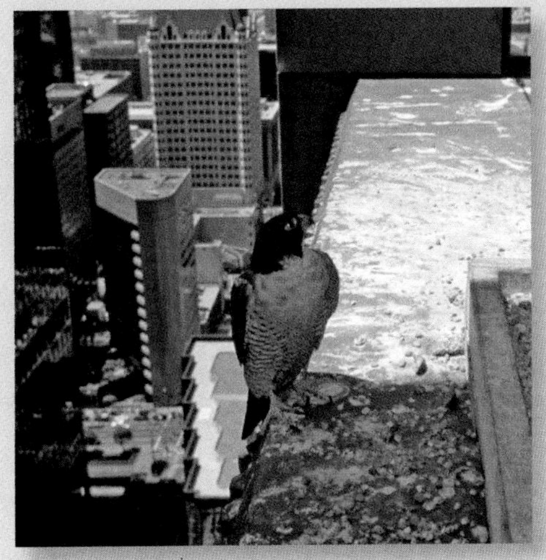

Moving into the City

Usually, the growth of cities is thought of as being bad for wild animals. However, some species of large birds such as hawks and falcons have unexpectedly begun to make cities their homes.

Why would these big birds choose a city as their new habitat? In cities, large birds can find pigeons and other small animals to eat and lots of water to drink. Also, the tall buildings are like the cliffs where the birds usually build nests.

1. **Checkpoint** Explain how a species of mosquitoes can become adapted to having pesticides in their ecosystem.
2. Writing in Science **Expository** Using available library and Internet resources, research how the antibiotic penicillin was discovered. In your **science journal,** write a paragraph about what you learned. In your writing, use the style of an encyclopedia article.

Extinction

When a plant or animal species cannot adapt to harmful changes in its ecosystem, it must migrate to another place or it cannot survive. This often happens when food and resources become limited during droughts or floods, in cold winters, or as cities grow.

The dodo became extinct when its ecosystem changed.

It is not always possible for a species to move to a new ecosystem. For example, plants cannot pull themselves up by the roots and walk to another place. Also, the changes may be so widespread that there is nowhere left to move. If a species does not move or adapt to harmful changes, its population size will decrease. The species may even become extinct. A species that is **extinct** has no members of its kind alive.

One extinct animal is the dodo. This flightless bird survived well on an island until sailors arrived and brought rats, pigs, and monkeys into the ecosystem. The birds could not defend themselves or fly to safety on other islands. They became extinct around 1680.

Fossils show that there have been a great variety of plants and animals that are now extinct. Species have become extinct as a result of many natural processes and human activities throughout history. What species do you know of that are extinct?

Scientists can learn about past extinctions by studying fossils. The kind and numbers of fossils found in different kinds of rocks give clues about past ecosystems. Fossils give evidence that, in any ecosystem, some plants and animals survive well, and some do not.

This is the fossil of an extinct animal that lived underwater.

Think about what happened to a symbol of the United States, the bald eagle. For many years, the pesticide DDT was put on farm fields to kill insects that ate the crops. Rains washed the pesticide into lakes and streams. Soon, fish had DDT in their bodies. Bald eagles ate the fish. When the eagles laid eggs, the DDT made the eggs' shells thin. Many eggs broke before the young bird was ready to hatch. Other eggs did not hatch at all.

The eagle did not adapt to the pesticide in its ecosystem. The eagle population kept getting smaller because fewer offspring hatched. It seemed that the eagles would disappear from most of the country. Their population started to grow again after using DDT was outlawed.

Lesson Checkpoint

1. What do fossils teach us about extinction?
2. Which is more likely to develop adaptations to a changing ecosystem: a population that has many mutations or a population that has few mutations?
3. **Cause and Effect** What was the cause of the bald eagle population getting smaller?

Whooping Cranes

When wetlands are drained for farms and cities, whooping cranes lose their nesting grounds. This beautiful bird came close to being extinct due to the loss of many wetlands and to hunting. In 1938, there were fewer than three dozen whooping cranes alive. Many people have worked together to save the whooping crane from becoming extinct.

This bald eagle is feeding its young.

Lab zone **Guided Inquiry**

Investigate What happens when a wetland ecosystem changes?

Wetland ecosystems can change due to natural causes. Sometimes people change wetlands.

Materials

bowl and cup

metric ruler and masking tape

soil

water

water plant and birdseed

What to Do

1. **Measure** 2 cm and 3 cm up from the bottom of the bowl. Mark the measurements on the container.

3cm
2 cm
water
soil

2. Add soil to the bowl up to the 2 cm mark. Pack down soil. Pour in water up to the 3 cm mark. Allow the contents to settle overnight.

Process Skills

When you **predict,** think about what you already know about evaporation.

3. Place a water plant in the bowl. Let the plant float. Set the container in a warm place with bright light.

Wash your hands after handling soil, the water plant, and birdseed.

water plant
3cm
2 cm

4. Every other day, add 4 seeds to the wetland.

5. **Predict** how the wetland will change from Day 3 to Day 13. Record your predictions every 2 days.

6. **Observe** the wetland and record how it changes.

	Predictions	Observations
Day 3		
Day 5		
Day 7		
Day 9		

Explain Your Results

1. What changes did you **observe** in the wetland?
2. How did the changes you observed compare to your **predictions?**

Go Further

How could you make a model to show how a wetland can help prevent floods and erosion? Make a plan to answer this or other questions you may have.

Recovery Plans for Species

Some plants and animals need extra protection because of the serious problems that threaten them. Various organizations develop recovery plans to preserve species that have trouble adapting to changes in their ecosystems.

The circle graph shows the various invertebrate species that had recovery plans in March 2004. You can use the graph to compare groups of species, to describe how one group compares to the total, or to estimate. For example, you can see that almost half of the 141 species that have recovery plans are clams. So, a good estimate may be that there are recovery plans for slightly fewer than 70 species of clams.

141 Invertebrate Species with Recovery Plans

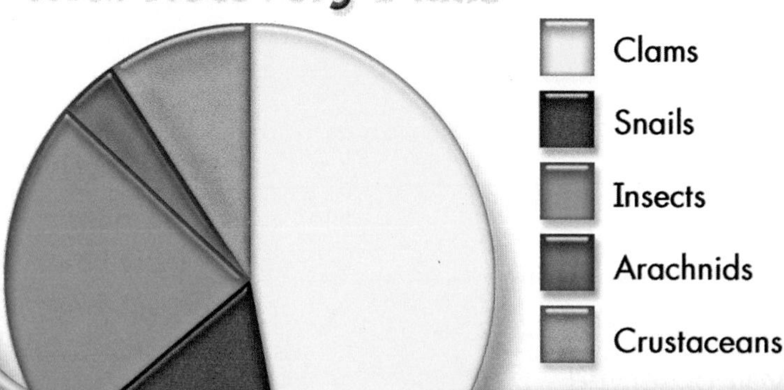
Clams
Snails
Insects
Arachnids
Crustaceans

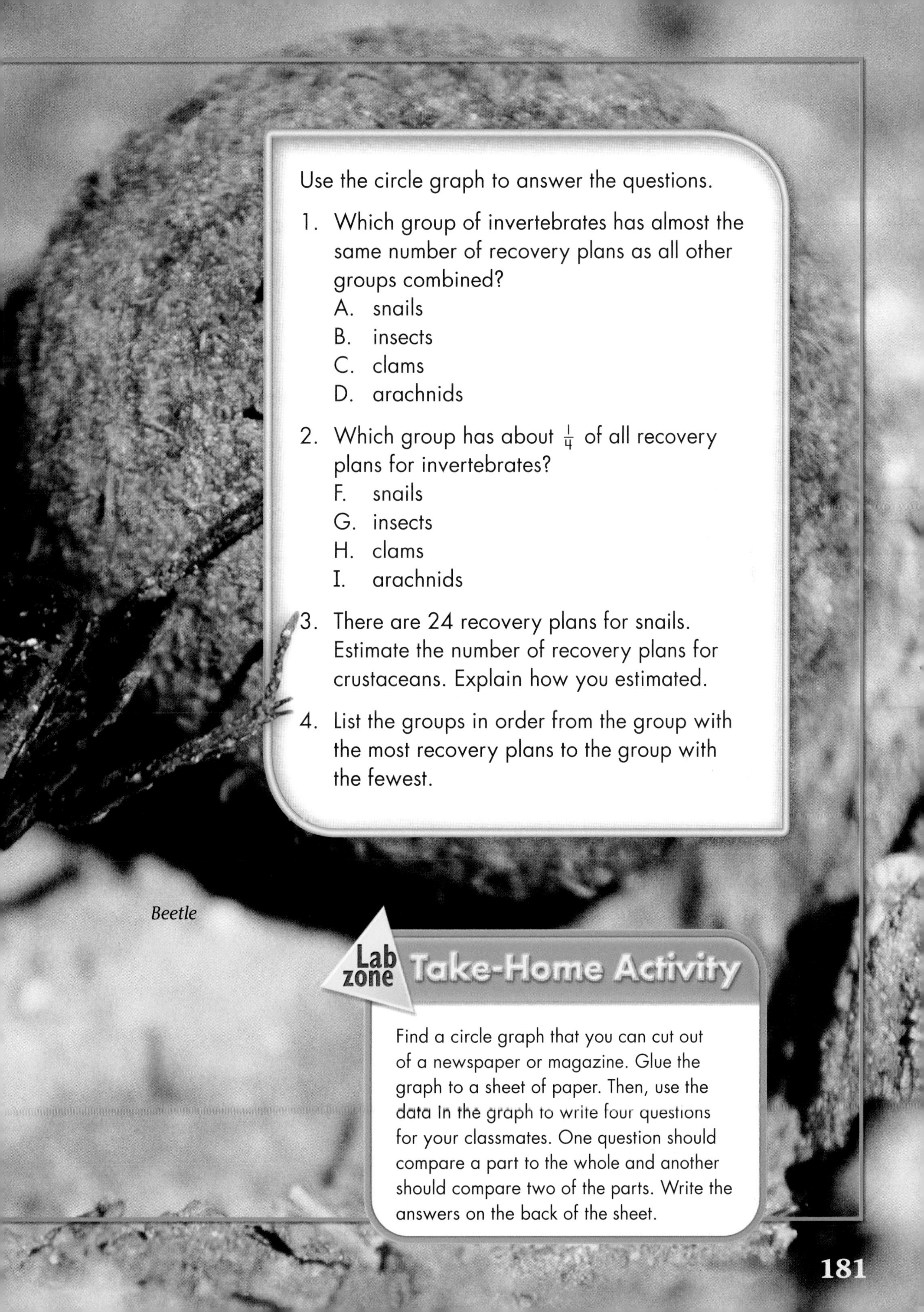

Use the circle graph to answer the questions.

1. Which group of invertebrates has almost the same number of recovery plans as all other groups combined?
   A. snails
   B. insects
   C. clams
   D. arachnids

2. Which group has about $\frac{1}{4}$ of all recovery plans for invertebrates?
   F. snails
   G. insects
   H. clams
   I. arachnids

3. There are 24 recovery plans for snails. Estimate the number of recovery plans for crustaceans. Explain how you estimated.

4. List the groups in order from the group with the most recovery plans to the group with the fewest.

Beetle

Lab zone Take-Home Activity

Find a circle graph that you can cut out of a newspaper or magazine. Glue the graph to a sheet of paper. Then, use the data in the graph to write four questions for your classmates. One question should compare a part to the whole and another should compare two of the parts. Write the answers on the back of the sheet.

Chapter 6 Review and Test Prep

Use Vocabulary

behavioral adaptation (p. 173)	**mutation** (p. 172)
extinct (p. 176)	**pesticide** (page 174)
inherit (p. 170)	**structural adaptation** (p. 172)

Use the term from the list above that best completes each sentence.

1. A(n) _____ is a chemical used to kill harmful insects.
2. When the last animal of a species dies, the species becomes _____.
3. Offspring _____ genes from their parents.
4. A(n) _____ is a changed part of the body that helps an organism survive.
5. A(n) _____ is a change in an organism's genes.
6. A(n) _____ is an inherited behavior that helps an organism survive.

Explain Concepts

7. Use examples from this chapter to explain how the solution to one problem can lead to new, unexpected problems.
8. Explain how a species can change over time.
9. Explain how ecosystems can change even if people are not involved.
10. The table below gives the number of whooping cranes observed in a national park over forty years. Make a line graph showing this data.

Year	Cranes
1955	28
1965	44
1975	57
1985	97
1995	158

Process Skills

11. Observe Describe the trend you observe in the line graph made in Question 10.

12. Infer Use the line graph you made in Question 10 to infer what the population of whooping cranes was in 1980.

13. Observe an animal in your yard or a family pet. What traits help this animal survive in its environment?

Cause and Effect

14. Draw a graphic organizer like the one shown below. Fill in the missing causes and effects.

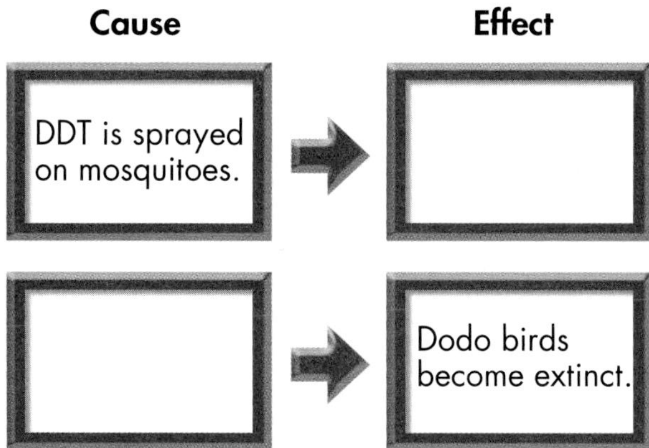
Cause
Effect
DDT is sprayed on mosquitoes.
Dodo birds become extinct.

Test Prep

Choose the letter that best completes the statement or answers the question.

15. Which of the following is a behavioral adaptation?
- Ⓐ a hummingbird's strong wings
- Ⓑ the way bees work together
- Ⓒ a frog's green, slimy skin
- Ⓓ the long beak of a hummingbird

16. How much of a dog's genes were inherited from its father?
- Ⓕ $\frac{1}{4}$ Ⓖ $\frac{1}{3}$
- Ⓗ $\frac{1}{2}$ Ⓘ $\frac{2}{3}$

17. What is an example of the environment affecting an organism's color?
- Ⓐ a dog's brown fur
- Ⓑ a flamingo's pink feathers
- Ⓒ a frog's green skin
- Ⓓ a dog's blue eyes

18. Which of the following is a chemical used to lower the population of insects?
- Ⓕ inheritance Ⓖ adaptation
- Ⓗ landfill Ⓘ pesticide

19. Explain why the answer you selected for Question 18 is best. For each of the answers you did not select, give a reason why it is not the best choice.

20. Writing in Science **Expository** Describe an animal's appearance and behavior. In your description, distinguish between traits that this animal inherited and those that the animal learned.

NASA

Biography

Patricia Larenas

How do organisms adapt to weightlessness in space? That is one of the questions that Patricia Larenas is helping to answer. Ms. Larenas is the head, or science lead, of a research team working on the Cell Culture Unit (CCU) for the Space Shuttle and the International Space Station. The CCU has a small artificial environment in which cells or single-celled organisms can be grown. The environment in the CCU can be changed and the effects on the cells can be observed.

Patricia Larenas

This career combines two of Ms. Larenas's life-long interests: biology and space. As a child, she liked to learn about space. Also, she often brought home animals, something her mother did not always like! After earning a two-year college degree, she had a job in animal medicine. After more time in college, she was a researcher studying how the human body fights disease.

Ms. Larenas, like many scientists, needs to communicate with others about the tests that are performed. Scientists need to do this carefully so that other scientists or the public can review their work. This way, other people may learn about research that is being done and they may suggest improvements to the tests or point out possible errors.

Lab zone Take-Home Activity

Choose an ecosystem that you can observe. It may be a fish tank, the playground, your yard, or other place. Describe the organisms you see in the ecosystem and how they interact.

Unit A Test Talk

Test-Taking Strategies

Find Important Words
Choose the Right Answer
Use Information from Text and Graphics
Write Your Answer

Find Important Words

You can organize information by underlining the important words as you read the passage. Some important words about living things are underlined in the following passage.

Scientists <u>classify</u> organisms by placing similar organisms in the same group. Knowing the group an organism is in can help tell you things about the organism. For example, <u>plants</u> have many cells and make their own sugar for food. <u>Vertebrates</u> are animals that have backbones.

<u>Cells</u> are the smallest living parts of a plant or animal. The parts of a cell work to carry out its functions. In organisms with many cells, groups of cells that are alike work together and make up a <u>tissue</u>. Different kinds of tissues are grouped to make up <u>organs</u>. Different organs work together in organ <u>systems</u>.

The organ systems in your body have important functions. Your <u>circulatory</u> system carries materials to and from cells. Parts of your <u>respiratory</u> system work together to let you breathe. Your <u>digestive system</u> breaks down food so your body can use it. Other systems have other tasks.

Plant cells use <u>photosynthesis</u> to make sugar for food for the plant. <u>Flowers</u> are the reproductive organs of plants.

Use What You Know

To help you answer the questions, find the important words in the passage. As you read each question, decide which word choice is being described.

1. To <u>classify</u> organisms, scientists
   Ⓐ group them by their appearance.
   Ⓑ put organisms that live in the same place in the same group.
   Ⓒ divide them into two kingdoms.
   Ⓓ put organisms with similar characteristics in the same group.

2. Which of the following statements about <u>organs</u> is not true?
   Ⓕ Different kinds of organs work together in an organ system.
   Ⓖ Each organ is made up of one kind of tissue.
   Ⓗ Both plants and animals have organs.
   Ⓘ Each bone and muscle in your body is an organ.

3. Which phrase best describes what your circulatory system does?
   Ⓐ changes materials so your body can use them
   Ⓑ moves materials through your body
   Ⓒ moves materials out of your body
   Ⓓ supports your body

4. What process do plants use to make sugar?
   Ⓕ photosynthesis
   Ⓖ xylem
   Ⓗ pollination
   Ⓘ tropism

Unit A Wrap-Up

Chapter 1

How are living things classified?

- Living things are classified by their structure.
- Vertebrates are animals that have backbones.
- Invertebrates are animals that have no backbones.
- Other groups of living things include plants, fungi, protists, eubacteria, and archaebacteria.

Chapter 2

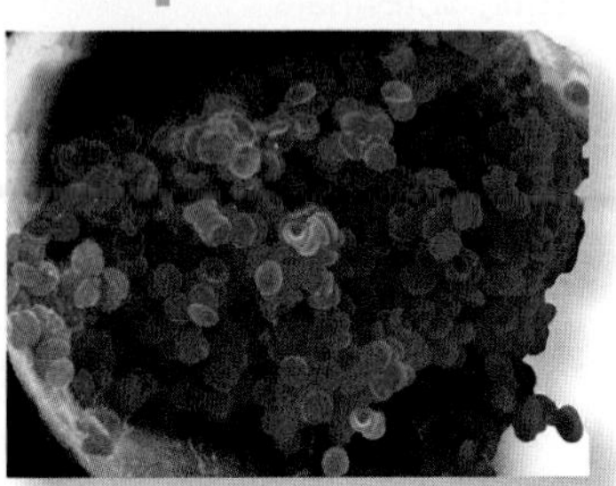

What do cells have to do with our lives?

- Cells are the basic units of living things.
- The body has different kinds of cells.
- Organs, which are made up of many cells, work together to carry out major life functions.

Chapter 3

How do the systems in your body keep you alive?

- The circulatory system, moves material around the body.
- The respiratory system carries gases between the outside air and the blood.
- The digestive system breaks down food into materials that cells can use.
- The urinary system filters wastes out of the blood and removes it from the body.

Chapter 4

How do plants stay alive and produce offspring?

- Photosynthesis takes place in chloroplasts in plant cells.
- Stems hold other plant parts in place and carry sugar, water, and minerals through the plant. Roots anchor a plant, absorb water from the soil, and may store food.
- Fertilization and seed formation take place in flowers.
- Different plants grow in different ways, depending on their DNA and on the environment.

Chapter 5

How do the parts of an ecosystem interact?

- Living things in an ecosystem can affect each other. Organisms can affect and be affected by nonliving parts of the ecosystem.
- Conditions in an ecosystem and relationships among its parts keep an ecosystem balanced.

Chapter 6

How do changes in habitats affect living things?

- If conditions change, organisms may or may not be able to survive in the new conditions.
- Some changes, such as adaptations, can help living things survive.

Performance Assessment

Stages in a Plant's Life

The stages in the life cycle of a plant include germination, seedlings, growth, and pollination. Choose a familiar plant. Using crayons or colored pencils, draw a picture illustrating each step in its life cycle. Add any other steps you think of. Cut out the pictures. Paste them on a large sheet of paper. Label each step. Be sure you put the steps in the right order.

Read More About Life Science

Look for books like these in the library.

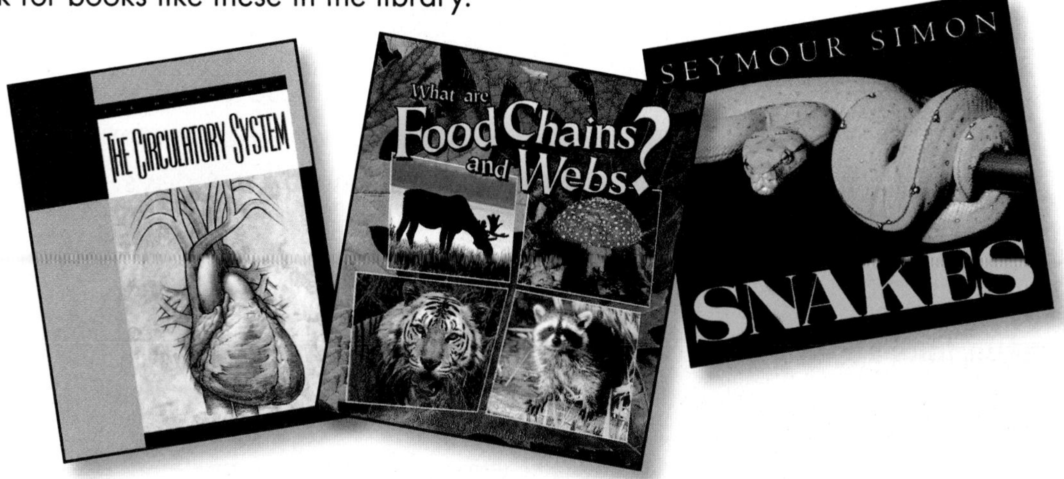
The Circulatory System
What are Food Chains and Webs?
SEYMOUR SIMON
SNAKES

Lab zone **Full Inquiry**

Experiment How does salt affect the hatching of brine shrimp?

Brine shrimp are tiny animals that live in salt water. They are in the same group of animals as crabs and lobsters.

Materials

5 cups and masking tape

water and graduated cylinder (or measuring cup)

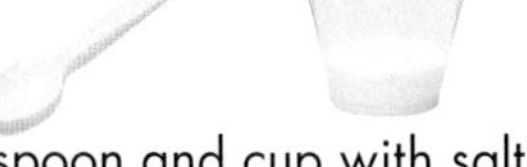

spoon and cup with salt

brine shrimp eggs and flat toothpick

hand lens

Process Skills

You **control variables** when you make sure conditions you are not testing are the same. Controlling variables helps make sure your **experiment** is a fair test.

Ask a question.

How does the amount of salt in the water affect how many brine shrimp eggs hatch?

State a hypothesis.

If brine shrimp eggs are put in water with no salt, a low salt level, a medium salt level, a high salt level, or a very high salt level, then in which will the most eggs hatch? Write your **hypothesis.**

Identify and control variables.

The amount of salt in the water is the **variable** that you will change. Set up 4 cups of water with different amounts of salt in them, and 1 cup with no salt.

It is hard to tell if a tiny egg has hatched. It is easier to see a moving brine shrimp after it has hatched. Because of this, the variable you will observe is how many brine shrimp are moving after 4 days.

All other conditions, such as temperature, light, amount of water, and amount of brine shrimp eggs are **controlled.** They must be the same for all the cups.

Test your hypothesis.

1. Put 150 mL of water in each cup.

2. Do not add salt to cup A. Put $\frac{1}{2}$ spoonful of salt in cup B, 1 spoonful in cup C, $1\frac{1}{2}$ spoonfuls in cup D and 3 spoonfuls in cup E.

Label the cups A, B, C, D, and E.

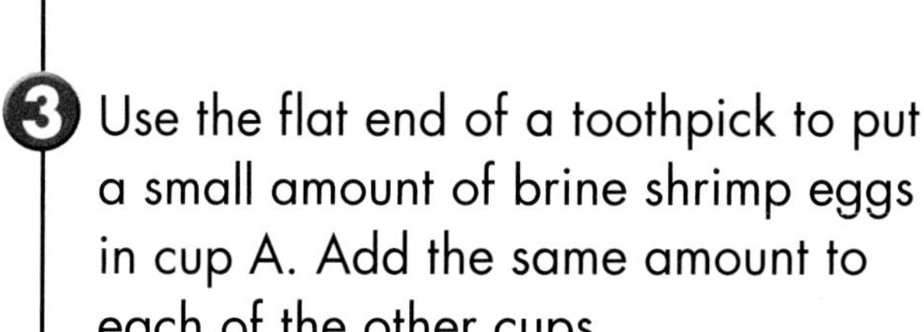

3. Use the flat end of a toothpick to put a small amount of brine shrimp eggs in cup A. Add the same amount to each of the other cups.

4 Use a hand lens to **observe** the cups every day. After a brine shrimp egg hatches, the brine shrimp begins to swim. Observe how many brine shrimp you see moving in each cup. Write *none, a few, some,* or *many* in your chart. This is a measure of how many eggs have hatched.

Collect and record your data.

Cup	How many brine shrimp are moving? (none, a few, some, or many)			
	After 1 day	After 2 days	After 3 days	After 4 days
Cup A (no salt)				
Cup B ($\frac{1}{2}$ spoonful salt)				
Cup C (1 spoonful salt)				
Cup D ($1\frac{1}{2}$ spoonfuls salt)				
Cup E (3 spoonfuls salt)				

Interpret your data.

Analyze your data. Think about the level of salt and how many brine shrimp were moving after 4 days. Make a chart like the one below. Use it to help you rank the levels of salt based on how many brine shrimp were moving after 4 days.

Levels of Salt
(spoonfuls)
most
Brine Shrimp Moving After 4 Days
least

When you make your chart, you may have ties. How could you change your chart to show a tie?

State your conclusion.

What conclusion can you draw from your data? Does it agree with your hypothesis? **Communicate** your conclusion.

Go Further

How can you continue to observe the brine shrimp? Design and carry out a plan to extend the investigation or to answer this and other questions you may have.

Discovery Channel School

Science Fair Projects

How Can You Estimate a Cell's Size?

You can estimate the size of a plant cell by comparing it to the width of your hair.

Idea: Prepare a microscope slide with a piece of your hair and a moss leaf. Using a microscope, locate the hair and moss cells. Find out how many moss cells can fit across the width of your hair. Hair is about 0.1 mm wide. Use this information to estimate the width of plant cells. Use a drawing or a graph to communicate what you find.

What Can Live in a Drop of Water?

A drop of water from an aquarium can have many organisms in it.

Idea: Using a hand lens or microscope, examine organisms found in a drop of water taken from a fresh water pond or aquarium or from the ocean or a salt water aquarium. Draw what you see.

Identifying Organisms Around You

Many different kinds of plants and animals live in your schoolyard or neighborhood.

Idea: Observe some of the organisms around you. Look in the library for a field guide to local plants or animals. Use the guide to help you identify what you saw.

Full Inquiry

Using Scientific Methods

1. Ask a question.
2. State a hypothesis.
3. Identify and control variables.
4. Test your hypothesis.
5. Collect and record your data.
6. Interpret your data.
7. State your conclusion.
8. Go further.

EC NTL 10987

Science Fair Central More science fair help sfsuccessnet.com

Unit B

Earth Science

Chapter 7

Water on Earth

You Will Discover

- what Earth's oceans are like.
- where to find Earth's fresh water.
- how water cycles through the environment.
- how clouds form and how they affect precipitation.

online
Student Edition
sfsuccessnet.com

Build Background

How does water move through the environment?

condensation

precipitation

evaporation

water table

aquifer

reservoir

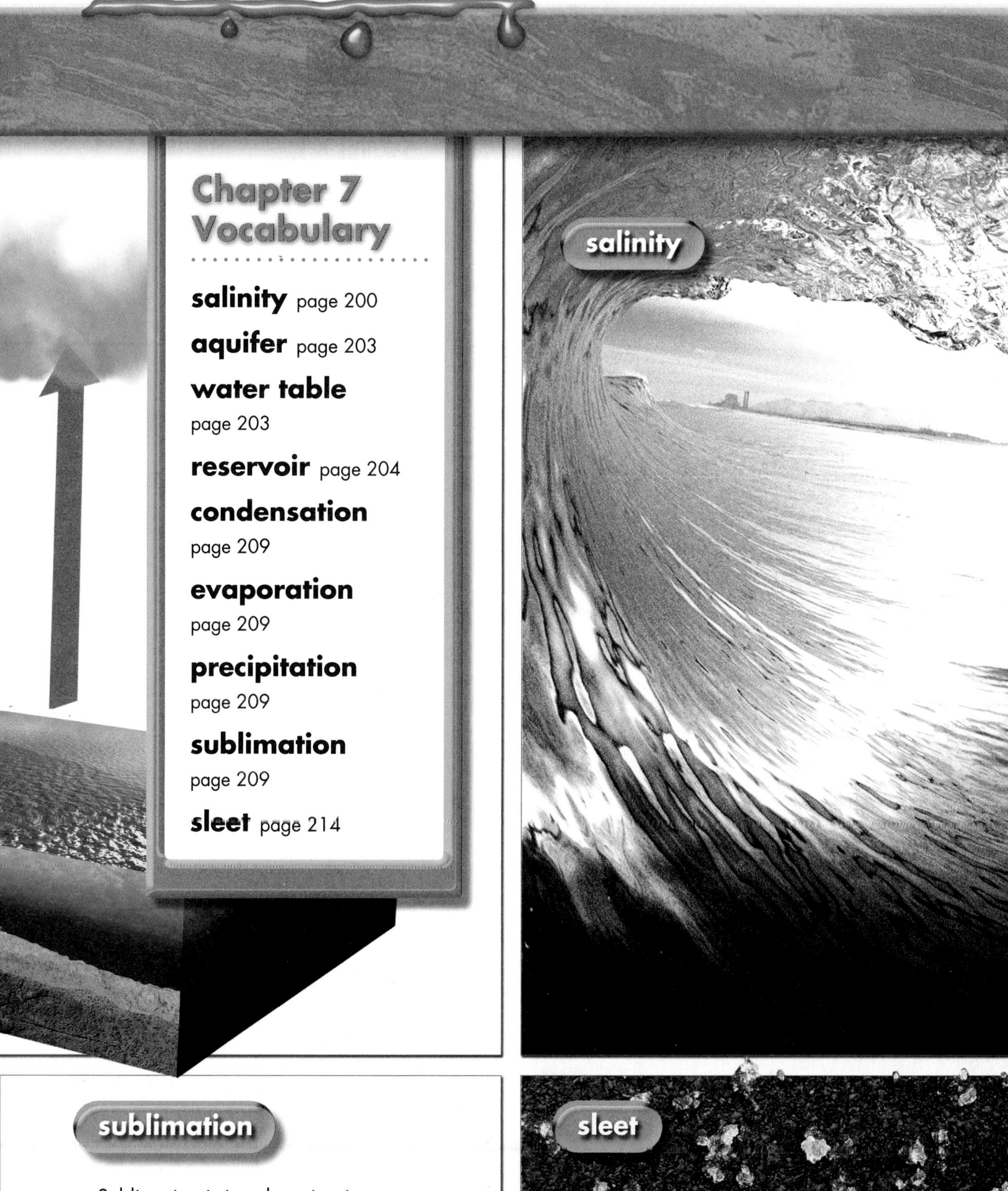
salinity
sleet

Chapter 7 Vocabulary

sublimation

Sublimation is ice changing into water vapor without first melting.

Lab zone **Directed Inquiry**

Explore How can you make layers of water float on each other?

Materials

graduated cylinder (or measuring cup)

very cold water, room-temperature water, very warm water

3 small cups

spoon and cup with salt

red and blue food coloring

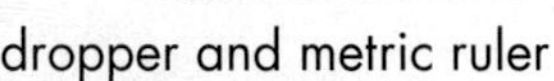
dropper and metric ruler

Process Skills

Based on what you observe, you can make an **inference** about the weights of equal volumes of the water from each layer.

What to Do

1. Add the materials to the cups. Stir.

The dropper should be very close to the water.

blue water

red water

blue layer

4 mm

uncolored water

30 mL room-temperature water, $\frac{1}{2}$ spoonful salt, blue food coloring

30 mL warm water, red food coloring

30 mL cold water, 2 spoonfuls salt

2. Use a dropper to gently add drops of the blue water to the cup with clear water. Stop when you have a blue layer about 4 mm tall. Then add red water to make a 4 mm layer.

Explain Your Results

1. **Infer** Suppose you weigh a spoonful of water from each layer. Which would be the heaviest? the lightest?
2. You observed the effect of salt and temperature together. How could you change the procedure to test only 1 variable, salt or temperature?

How to Read Science

Reading Skills

Sequence

Sequence is the order in which events happen.

- Sometimes writers use clue words such as *first, next, then,* and *finally* to show sequence.
- Sometimes you can **infer** what will happen next.

Science Article

Getting a Drink

You often walk only a few steps to get a cool drink of water. But how far did the water move before it reached the faucet? In many towns, water goes through many steps to get to your faucet. First, water falls as rain and may collect in a lake. Next, it is pumped to a treatment plant where it is made safe to drink. Then the treated water is pumped into a high water tower. Finally, water flows down from the tank and into pipes. You can turn on your faucet and get that drink.

Apply It!

Make a **graphic organizer** like this one. Find the clue words that tell the **sequence** in the science article.

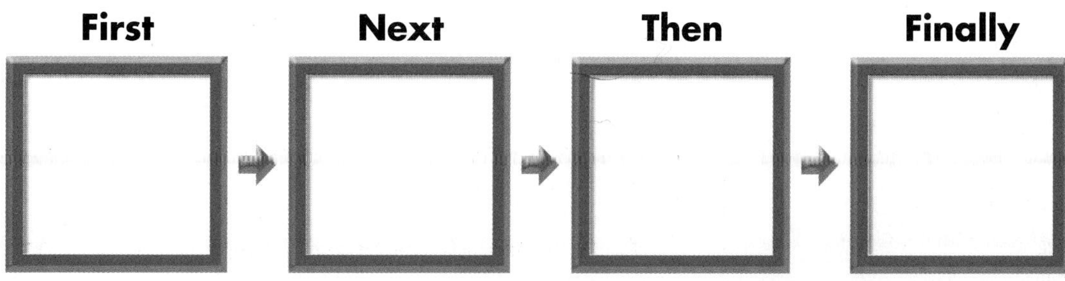
First
Next
Then
Finally

You Are There!

On a warm summer day, you lie on a surfboard, enjoying the waves. Each time a large wave curls over you, the sunlight shines through the spray. You take a deep breath before the water crashes over you. A moment later you start paddling your board back to shore. You're happy visiting the ocean and having fun at the shore even if you can't drink the water. But why does the water leave white grains on your skin?

Lesson 1

How can the oceans be described?

Unlike other planets, Earth has huge amounts of water. This water covers most of the surface of the planet. It is in different forms, but most of it is in the salty oceans.

The Hydrosphere

What body of water is closest to where you live? More than half the people in the United States live within about 80 kilometers of an ocean. Many people live near other bodies of water, such as rivers and lakes. Bodies of water play a huge role in our lives. They give us a way to travel, places to catch food, and beautiful sights to visit. What are some ways that oceans or lakes have affected your life?

All the waters of Earth make up the hydrosphere. Almost all of the hydrosphere is ocean water. Only $\frac{3}{100}$, or 3 percent, of the hydrosphere is in other places. The hydrosphere covers a little less than $\frac{3}{4}$ of the Earth's surface. The Pacific Ocean is the largest, followed by the Atlantic Ocean, the Indian Ocean, the Southern Ocean, and the Arctic Ocean. On a map or globe, you can see that the oceans are all connected.

The Pacific is not only the largest ocean, it is also the deepest. The average depth of the Pacific Ocean is about 4,000 meters. In its deepest place, it is more than 11,000 meters deep.

The oceans are all a bit different from one another. Some have more storms than others. Many properties of the water are different, such as how salty the water is or the average temperature. Even the levels of the oceans' surfaces, called sea level, are slightly different.

1. **√Checkpoint** How much of Earth is covered by water?
2. **Math in Science** The deepest part of the Arctic Ocean is about 5,500 meters. How many times as deep is the deepest part of the Pacific Ocean than the deepest part of the Arctic Ocean?

Salinity

Have you ever been swimming in the ocean and happened to get a mouthful of some seawater? If you have, you know it tastes salty. Ocean water tastes this way because it contains many kinds of salt. Ocean water not only tastes bad, it is bad for your health if you drink too much of it.

The oceans get salt from rivers. Rivers dissolve small amounts of salts from rocks and soil and carry the salts to the ocean. Most of this salt is sodium chloride—common table salt. When water evaporates from the ocean, the dissolved salts are left behind in the ocean water.

Salinity is a measure of how salty water is. Ocean water is more salty in some places than in other places. Places where rivers pour fresh water into the ocean have low salinity. In warm areas, ocean water evaporates fairly quickly. Salt is left behind, and the ocean water has higher salinity.

A liter of cold water with high salinity is heavier than a liter of water that is either warmer or has a lower salinity. Some currents in the ocean are caused by cold salty water sinking under warmer water. Most currents on the oceans' surfaces are caused by winds.

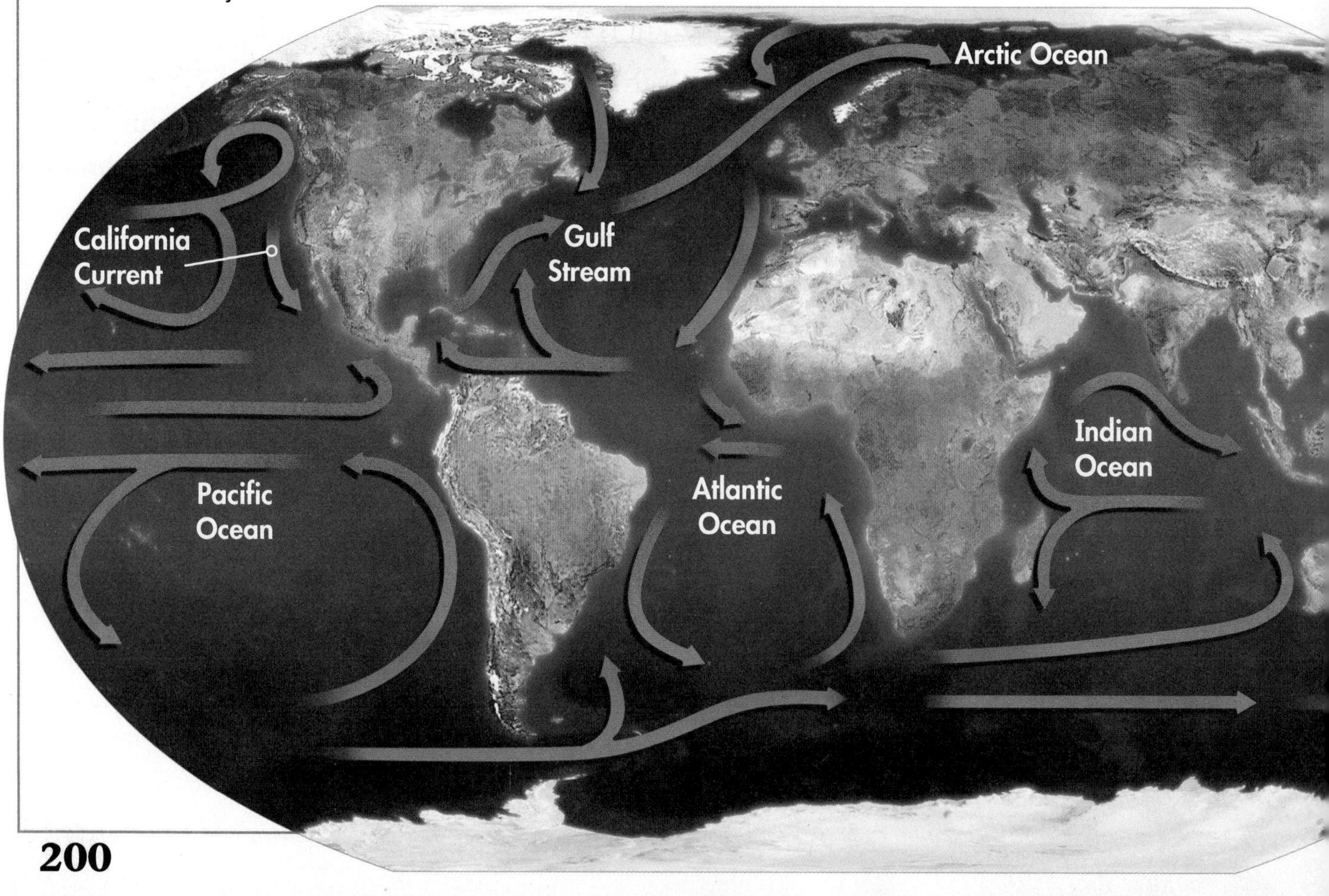

Arctic Ocean
California Current
Gulf Stream
Pacific Ocean
Atlantic Ocean
Indian Ocean

When ocean water in these shallow ponds evaporates, salt is left behind.

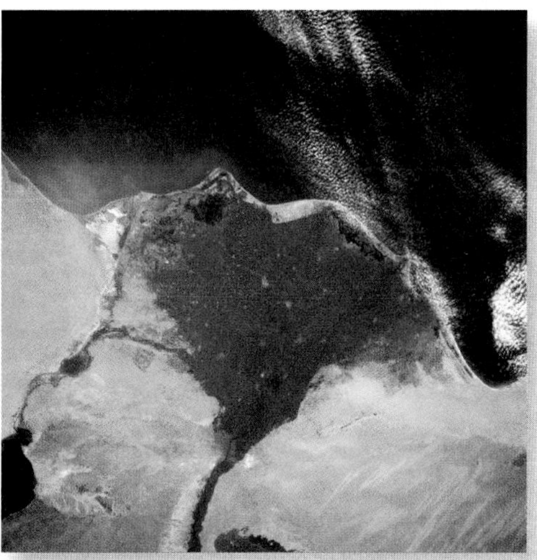

Ocean water near the mouth of the Nile River has less salinity than ocean water farther away.

Pacific Ocean

This map shows currents on the surface of the water. Currents below the surface flow in very different ways.

Map Legend
warm current
cold current

Ocean Temperatures

The temperature of ocean water varies from place to place. Ocean water near the equator is about 30°C. Near the poles, ocean water can be as cold as –2°C.

The water is not always colder just because it is farther north. Some currents carry warm water toward the poles. The Gulf Stream is such a current. It moves warm water from the Caribbean Sea to the North Atlantic Ocean. Other currents carry cold water toward the equator. The California Current carries cold water southward along the coast of the United States.

Ocean Resources

Much of the salt we add to our foods comes from the ocean. One way that we get salt is by evaporating ocean water. People who process the salt allow ocean water to flow into shallow ponds. The water evaporates and the salt is left.

Other materials, such as magnesium and drinking water, also come from ocean water. Ocean water can be made drinkable by removing the salt. This is expensive, so it is not done in many places.

The ocean is the source of many useful products. Do you like tuna fish? Tuna is just one of many foods that come from the ocean.

√ Lesson Checkpoint

1. Use the map to describe the shape, size, and connections of Earth's oceans.
2. What is salinity? What causes some ocean water to have a higher salinity than other ocean water?
3. Social Studies in Science Using the Internet or the library, find out about the history and importance of salt. Write about what you learn in your **science journal.**

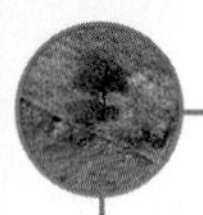

Lesson 2

Where is fresh water found?

Less than $\frac{3}{100}$ of Earth's water is fresh water. This is the water that we use for drinking, cooking, and cleaning. We also use this water to grow crops, make electricity, and make many products.

Fresh Water

Drinking water is also called fresh water. Fresh water has some dissolved salts, but much less than seawater has. After playing hard on a warm day, a cool glass of water can taste wonderful. Where does fresh water come from?

Almost all of Earth's fresh water starts as rain or snow. Some of this fresh water sinks into the ground. Some collects in rivers and lakes. Some is frozen in ice sheets and glaciers. Which of these do you think has the most fresh water? You will find the answer as you read this lesson.

Fresh water is not evenly spread over the world. Some places have much more fresh water than others. But no matter where you are, there is only a limited amount of fresh water. Water should be used wisely. The water supply can be extended by using less water whenever possible.

Scientists can help communities to use water wisely. They can give communities information about the location of underground water and about the water's quality. Scientists can also provide technology that reduces the amount of water a community needs.

Some water falling on the ground seeps into spaces in the soil and rocks.

The water table is rarely level. It usually follows the slope of the land. It is higher beneath hills and lower in valleys.

Groundwater

Rain or melted snow that soaks into the ground is called groundwater. This water fills spaces between particles of soil and rock. Groundwater keeps sinking until it reaches a layer of rock or clay that it cannot move through. Some layers of rock or clay act like a dam to keep the water from moving deeper. The water can slowly flow over the top of these layers.

The layer of rock and soil that groundwater occupies is an **aquifer.** The top level of groundwater in an aquifer is the **water table.** The level of a water table changes during the year. It will rise when water is added by rain or melting snow. It will become lower when there is a drought. Many people get their water from wells that go into an aquifer. The water table will become lower when people pump water out of the aquifer faster than it is replaced. If we do not use groundwater wisely, some aquifers may become dry.

If too much groundwater is pumped out of an aquifer, the water table in the area will drop. That can cause lakes like this one to dry up and wells to go dry.

1. ✓**Checkpoint** How is fresh water different from ocean water?
2. Writing in Science **Descriptive** In your **science journal,** write a description of how a lake or pond might change if the water table lowers.

Pollution from the surface can seep into the groundwater in the same way that rain does.

The water table is lower in places where people are using groundwater faster than it can be refilled.

A lake, pond, stream, or swamp forms where the water table meets the surface.

Rivers

Surface waters include rivers, streams, and lakes. Melting snow, rain water, and groundwater all help form Earth's surface waters. Water from rain and melting snow flows downhill in small streams. These small streams join to form larger streams and rivers. Most rivers eventually flow into the ocean. Groundwater also seeps into rivers. The area from which water drains into a river is called the river's watershed.

What happens on the land in a watershed can affect places far away. If chemicals are placed in the watershed, they may be carried by water to rivers. Rain water may erode soil from fields and construction sites. This soil could run into the rivers and cause changes to the ecosystems downstream. Many researchers are studying how these and other issues affect watersheds.

Lakes

Sometimes water flows into a place that is surrounded by higher land or blocked by a dam. Lakes form when the water collects in the low spot. A **reservoir** is an artificial lake that forms behind a dam.

Water that forms a lake is not really trapped. Water can leave a lake by flowing into a river, by seeping into the ground, or by evaporating into the air.

This reservoir stores water for a nearby community.

Map Fact

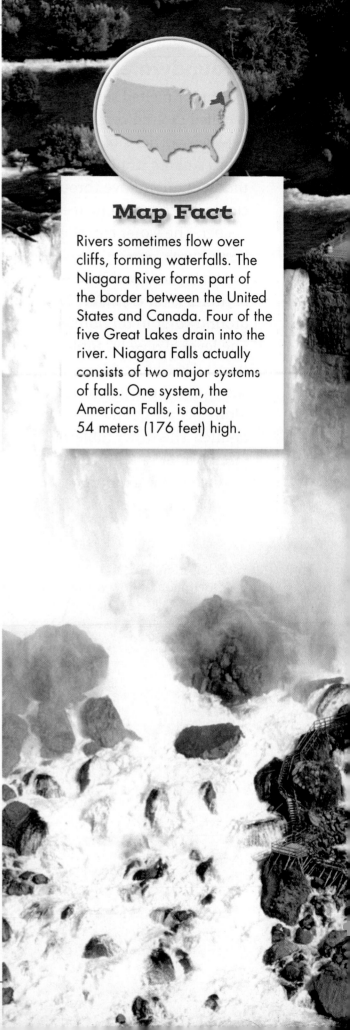

Rivers sometimes flow over cliffs, forming waterfalls. The Niagara River forms part of the border between the United States and Canada. Four of the five Great Lakes drain into the river. Niagara Falls actually consists of two major systems of falls. One system, the American Falls, is about 54 meters (176 feet) high.

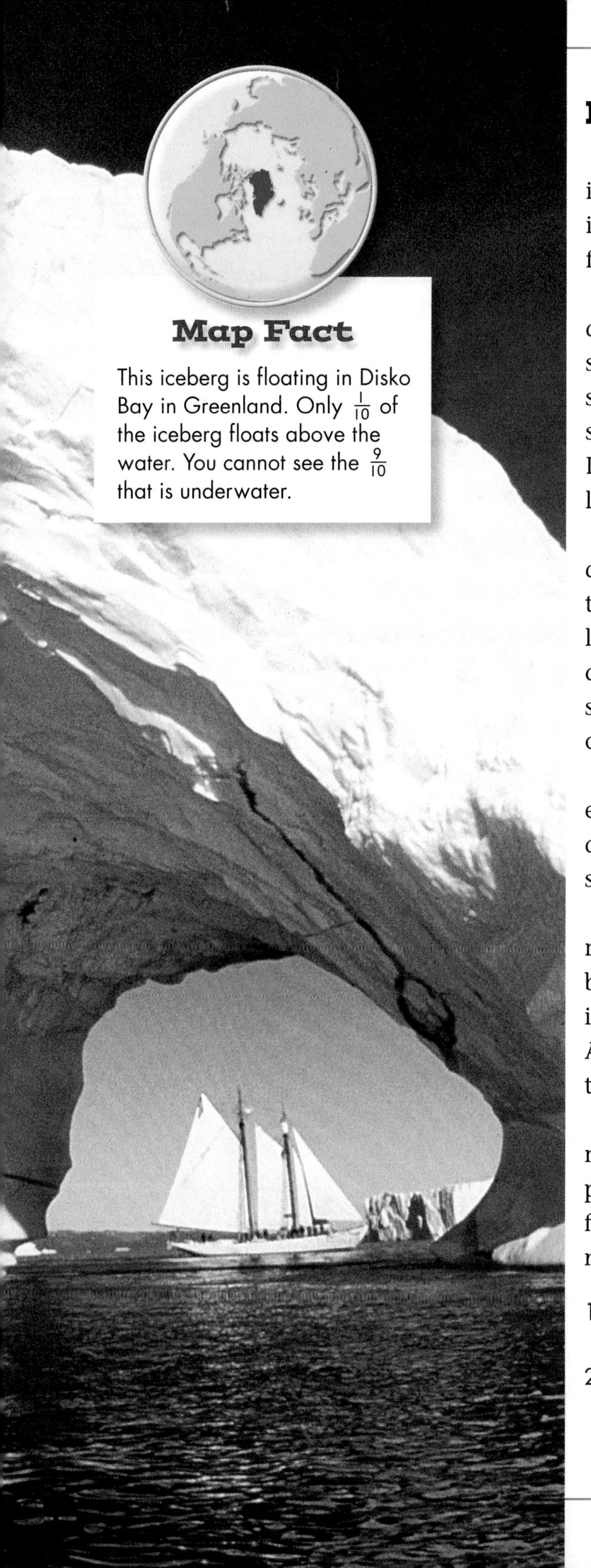

Map Fact

This iceberg is floating in Disko Bay in Greenland. Only $\frac{1}{10}$ of the iceberg floats above the water. You cannot see the $\frac{9}{10}$ that is underwater.

Ice

About $\frac{7}{10}$ of Earth's fresh water is frozen into ice. Since most of Earth's fresh water is frozen and far from cities, it is hard for people to use.

Much of Earth's ice is on Greenland and Antarctica. In these places, huge ice sheets cover most of the land. The ice sheets are several kilometers thick in some places. The icecap at the North Pole floats on the ocean. There is no land under it.

Glaciers and ice sheets are smaller areas of ice. Valley glaciers are found in the valleys of high mountains. They are long stretches of ice that flow slowly downhill. As valley glaciers and ice sheets flow, they crush and move rock, changing the shape of the land.

Glaciers and ice sheets form when each year's snowfall is greater than the amount that melts. The weight of new snow squeezes the snow into ice.

In places where glaciers and ice sheets reach the ocean, large pieces of ice can break off. The floating pieces of ice are icebergs. One iceberg that broke off the Antarctic ice sheet was twice the size of the state of Rhode Island.

When ocean water freezes, the resulting ice is not salty. The salt is pushed out of the ice crystals as they form. This causes the water around the new ice to become more salty.

1. ✓ **Checkpoint** How much of Earth's fresh water is in ice sheets and glaciers?
2. **Social Studies in Science** Research Robert E. Peary's expedition to the North Pole. Write about what you learn in your **science journal.**

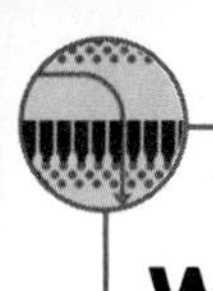

Water Treatment Plant

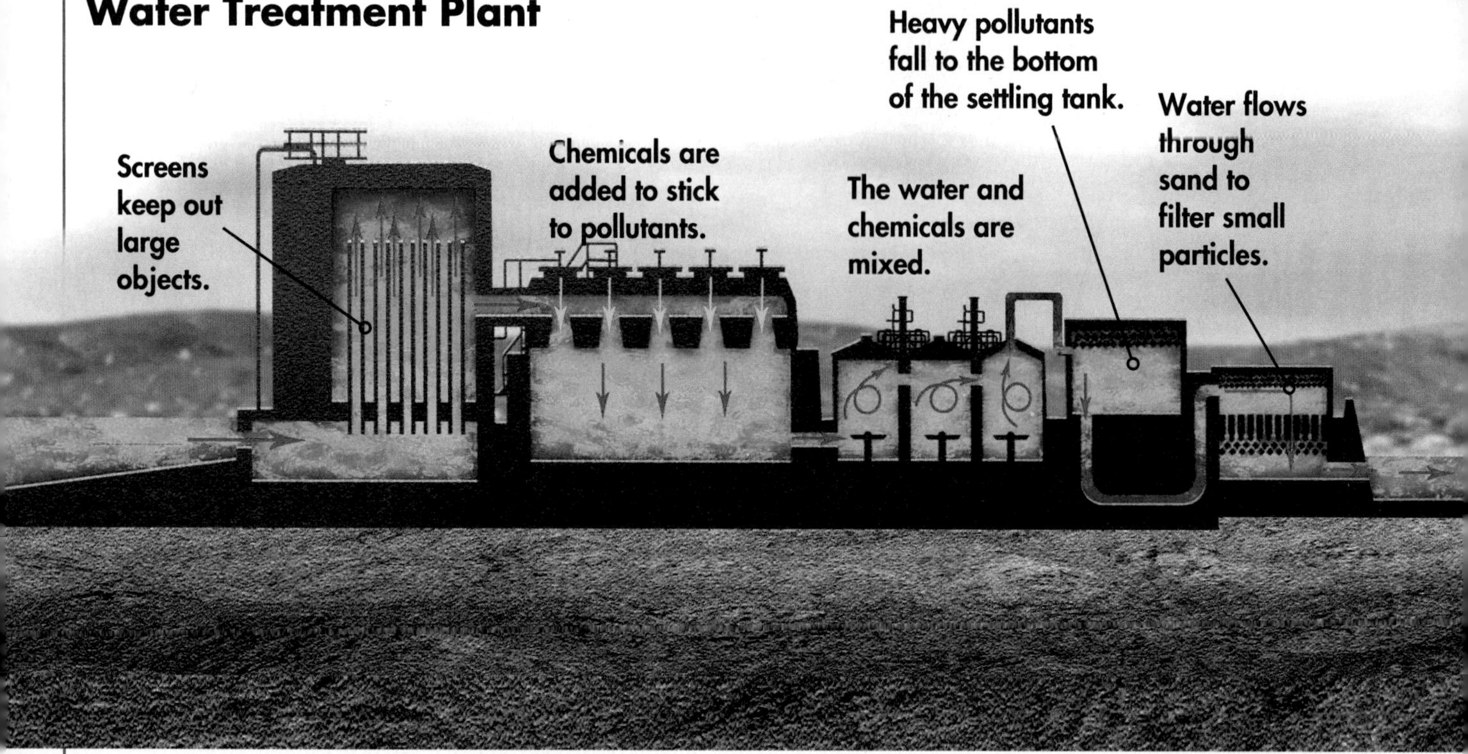

Screens keep out large objects.
Chemicals are added to stick to pollutants.
The water and chemicals are mixed.
Heavy pollutants fall to the bottom of the settling tank.
Water flows through sand to filter small particles.

Getting Water to Homes

Does your town have a water tower? Do you know how water gets into the tower? These towers are often the tallest structure of a small town. They are only part of the system that gets water to homes and businesses.

Some towns in the United States get their water from groundwater. Other towns use surface waters as an easy source of fresh water. But surface water might have harmful bacteria. Since water can easily dissolve many materials, it is easily polluted. Harmful chemicals that wash off farm fields, parking lots, and even lawns can end up in rivers and lakes. Even groundwater may have pollutants. Because of these problems, water must be treated before we use it.

The process of treating water is shown in the diagram. First, water is pumped to a treatment plant. This is done by pumps that are lowered into a well or to the bottom of a lake. Then, chemicals are added to the water. The chemicals form tiny sticky particles that attract dirt particles. The particles become heavy enough to sink to the bottom of a tank.

Pumping station
Chlorine, fluoride, or other chemicals may be added at the end of treatment.
The treated water is pumped to the top of a water tower.
Gravity pulls water down from the tank.
Water flows through pipes to homes and businesses in the community.

The water then passes through filters. Some filters are made of layers of sand and gravel. These filters remove smaller particles that did not settle earlier.

After the filters remove harmful materials from water, chemicals are added to the water. Many treatment plants add a small amount of chlorine to kill harmful bacteria. Other treatment plants use other ways to kill bacteria. Many towns add fluoride to the water. This chemical helps your teeth resist decay.

As you can see, getting water to your home is not an easy job. We should take care not to waste water. There are many easy ways to keep from wasting water. Do not run faucets or showers longer than needed. Water lawns in the evening, so less water will evaporate. Fix dripping faucets. A dripping faucet can lose many gallons of water each day.

Average Daily Water Use (Per Person)	
Toilet flush	71 L
Laundry	57 L
Shower/ bath	49 L
Other	38 L

Lesson Checkpoint

1. How do icebergs form?
2. **Health** in Science Why do cities and towns treat water before it is sent to homes?
3. **Sequence** the steps in treating water before it gets to a town's water tower.

Lesson 3

What is the water cycle?

Earth's water does not sit still. It changes form and moves from place to place.

Water in the Air

Look around the room you are in now. Can you see water around you? Even if you do not see it, water surrounds you all the time. This water is not in a liquid form as in rivers or a solid form as in glaciers. This water is an invisible gas called water vapor. Air always has some water vapor in it, even in the driest deserts. This water vapor was liquid water at some time in the past. It may have been water inside a plant, in a tropical river, or in the Arctic Ocean.

Water vapor makes up a very small fraction of the gases in the air. The particles of water vapor, like particles of other gases, are constantly moving. Air pressure is the pressure of these gas particles against another object. Air pressure pushes in all directions because the gas particles move in all directions. Air pressure decreases as you move higher in the atmosphere.

The Water Cycle

Water is always moving on, through, and above Earth as it changes from one form to another in the water cycle. The water cycle is the repeated movement of water through the environment in different forms. The steps of the water cycle include evaporation, condensation, precipitation, and runoff. These steps can be affected by temperature, pressure, wind, and the elevation of the land. A simple water cycle is shown here.

Evaporation

Evaporation is the changing of liquid water to water vapor. In **condensation,** the water vapor turns into liquid, such as water droplets in clouds. In **precipitation,** the water falls from clouds as rain, snow, sleet, or hail. The water cycle is not as simple as the picture below shows. The water cycle has many different paths that can be taken. For example, condensation does not happen only in the making of clouds. Condensation also forms dew.

Sublimation is another possible path in the water cycle. **Sublimation** is ice changing into water vapor without first melting. You can see this when ice cubes in a freezer shrink over a long period of time. Sublimation happens more slowly than evaporation. Lower temperatures slow the rate of sublimation.

Water vapor may freeze directly into ice without first becoming liquid water. The ice crystals that form on surfaces are called frost.

Condensation forms dew.

Frost forms when water vapor turns to ice crystals.

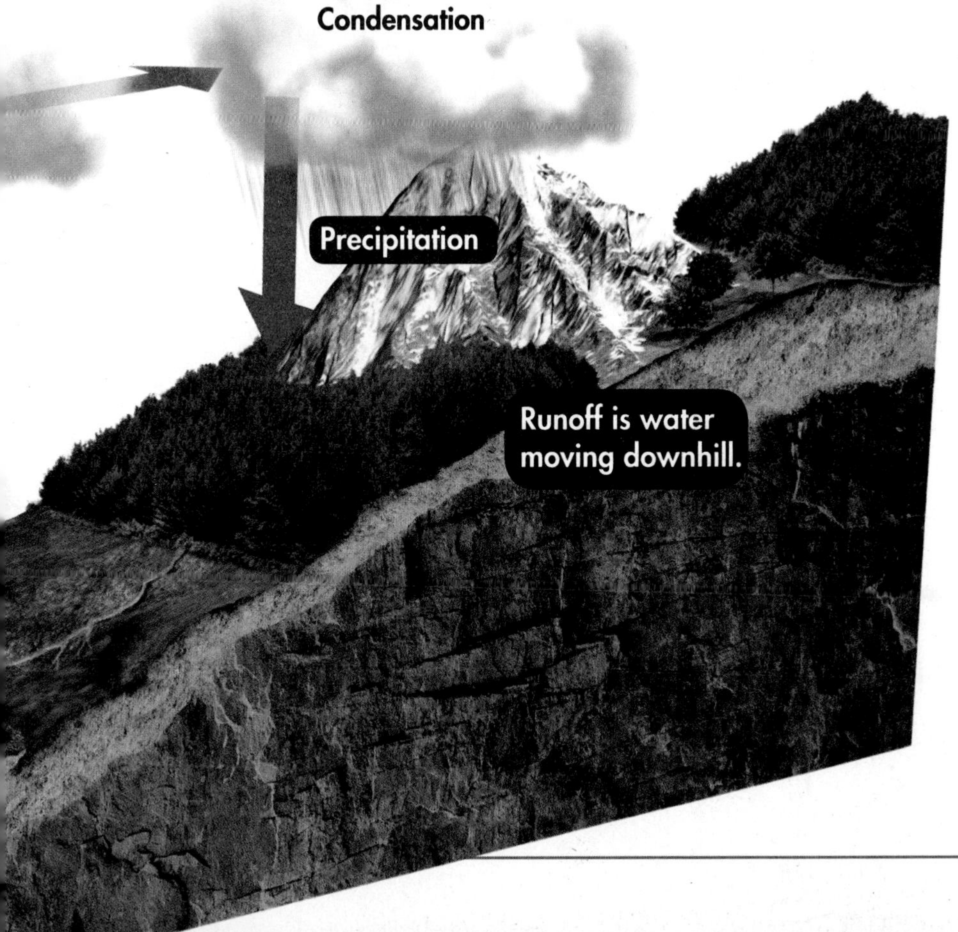
Condensation
Precipitation
Runoff is water moving downhill.

1. **Checkpoint** How are evaporation and condensation the same? How are they different?
2. **Writing in Science** **Descriptive** In your **science journal,** write a description of how water can be found as a solid, liquid, and gas.

Many Paths of the Water Cycle

A detailed picture of the water cycle is shown here. Water is not always in the water cycle. You know that water is used by and made in living things. Some water is broken down as plants make sugar during photosynthesis. Organisms produce water during respiration.

As water vapor rises, it may form a cloud.
Because salts are left behind when water evaporates, the oceans remain salty.
Water vapor turns into frost or dew. Frost and dew often form in the morning and evaporate soon after sunrise.
Water evaporates from oceans, lakes, and puddles faster with warm temperatures and winds.
Animals take in water. All animals also produce water in respiration. Animals that sweat give off water vapor.

Energy in the Water Cycle

The Sun has a major effect on the water cycle. The energy of sunlight causes most melting, evaporation, and sublimation. Energy is needed to raise water vapor to the clouds and move it by winds. This energy originally comes from the Sun.

When water vapor condenses into liquid water, it releases energy. This energy is heat. It warms the air or water in the immediate area.

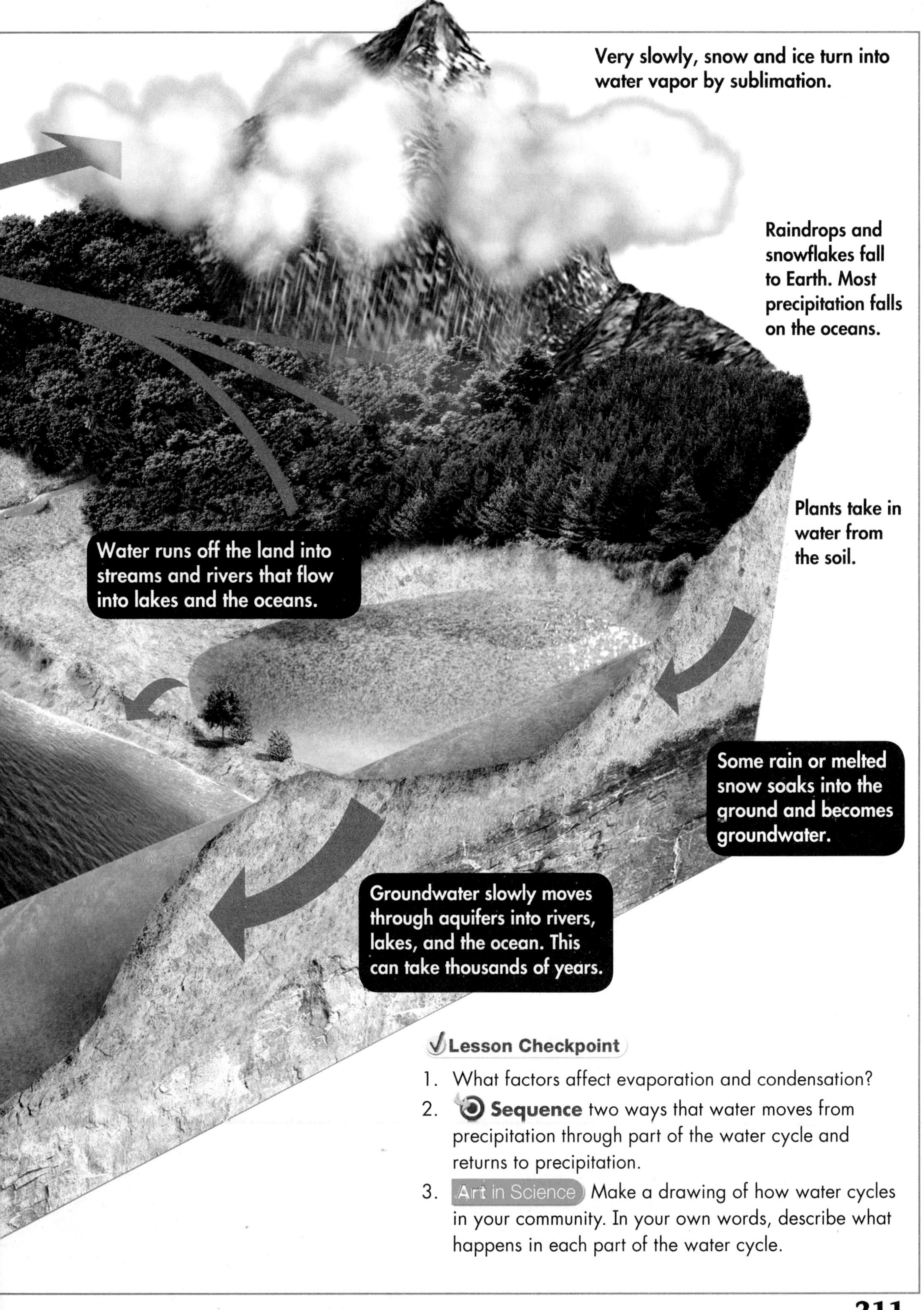
Very slowly, snow and ice turn into water vapor by sublimation.
Raindrops and snowflakes fall to Earth. Most precipitation falls on the oceans.
Plants take in water from the soil.
Water runs off the land into streams and rivers that flow into lakes and the oceans.
Some rain or melted snow soaks into the ground and becomes groundwater.
Groundwater slowly moves through aquifers into rivers, lakes, and the ocean. This can take thousands of years.

✓ Lesson Checkpoint

1. What factors affect evaporation and condensation?
2. **Sequence** two ways that water moves from precipitation through part of the water cycle and returns to precipitation.
3. **Art in Science** Make a drawing of how water cycles in your community. In your own words, describe what happens in each part of the water cycle.

Lesson 4

How do clouds form?

Clouds have an important part in the water cycle. Clouds bring rain and snow to all parts of the world. Without clouds, rivers and lakes would become dry.

Temperature and Pressure

Have you ever watched a cloud get larger and larger? Have you tried to see shapes in the clouds? Clouds come in many shapes and sizes.

Clouds form when water vapor changes into tiny water droplets or ice crystals. Most diagrams of the water cycle include this change. It is a major part of the water cycle.

Whether a cloud is made of water droplets or ice crystals depends partly on the air's temperature. The temperature of air high in the clouds is often much lower than the temperature of the air close to the ground. Even on summer days, many clouds are made of ice crystals.

Air pressure affects the forming of clouds. Clouds often form when air moves upward to areas of less air pressure. Saucer-shaped clouds like those shown in the picture on this page form when winds blow over a mountain. When air moves up, the air pressure is less. With less pressure, the air expands and cools. If the air cools enough at this new air pressure, water vapor will form droplets or ice crystals.

1. √ **Checkpoint** What are clouds made of?
2. Writing in Science **Descriptive** In your **science journal,** keep a cloud diary each day for one week. Write descriptive sentences or poems about the shape, color, and movement of the clouds you see.

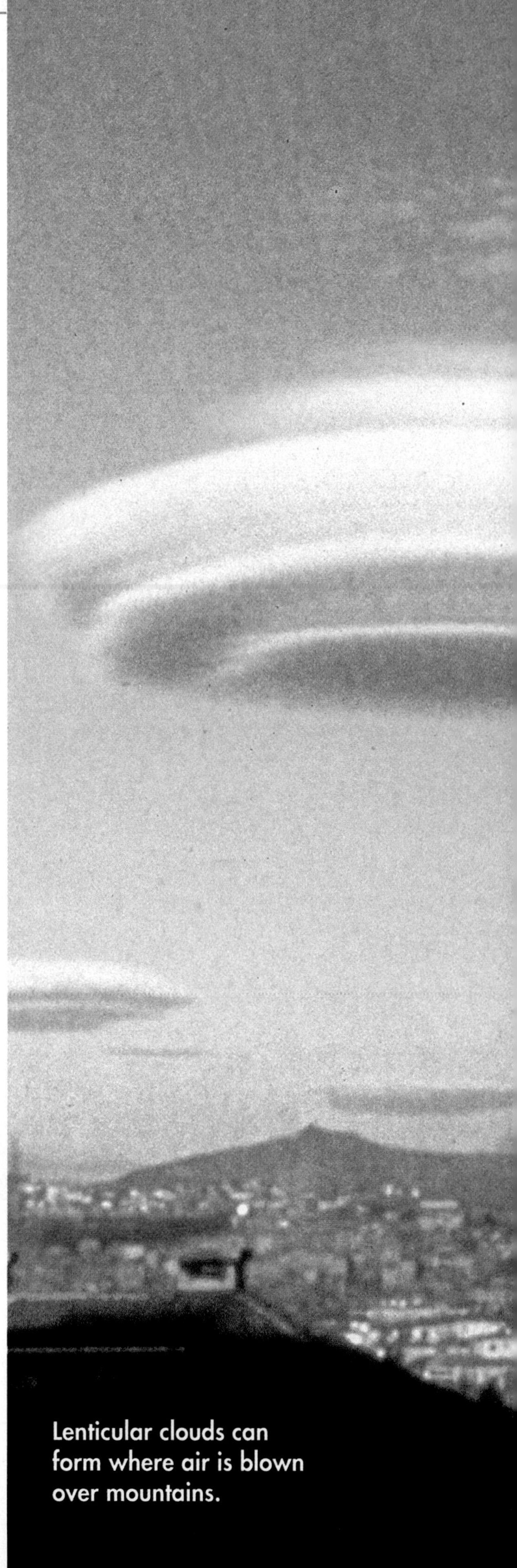

Lenticular clouds can form where air is blown over mountains.

Types of Clouds

High-altitude clouds form more than 6,000 m above the ground. This region overlaps the region for mid-altitude clouds. Cirrus clouds are high-altitude clouds that are thin, wispy, and white.

Clouds that grow vertically have rising air inside them. The bases of these clouds may be as low as 1,000 m above the ground. The rising air may push the tops of these clouds higher than 12,000 m up. Vertical clouds are sometimes called thunderheads because they often cause thunderstorms.

The bases of mid-altitude clouds are between 2,000 m and 7,000 m above the ground. Altocumulus clouds are mid-altitude clouds that look like small, puffy balls. The bottoms of the clouds can look dark because sunlight may not reach them. The sides of the clouds are white because sunlight is reflecting off them.

Low-altitude clouds are often seen less than 2,000 m above the ground. Stratus clouds are low-altitude clouds that cover the whole sky. They look dark because little sunlight gets through the layer of clouds.

Fog is a cloud at ground level. It can form in several ways. One kind of fog can form on clear, cool nights with no wind. Air near the ground cools. If the air cools enough, water vapor condenses into tiny droplets and forms a cloud at or near the ground. As more droplets form and get larger, the fog appears thicker.

Hailstones Form

Upward winds carry hail through a cloud many times.

Hail falls from a cloud when it is too big for the upward winds to lift it.

Precipitation

You may be surprised to learn that most rain in the United States starts as snow. The temperature of the air high above the ground is often below 0°C. Clouds of ice crystals form in the cold air. The ice crystals grow larger until they start to fall as snowflakes. As they fall, the crystals sometimes stick to other crystals and become larger snowflakes. If the temperature of all the air between the cloud and the ground is less than 0°C, the ice crystals will fall to the ground as snowflakes.

The ice crystals from a cloud may change as they fall through different layers of air. If the ice crystals fall into air that is warmer than 0°C, they will melt and fall as rain. If the air near the ground is very cold, the rain sometimes freezes before it hits the ground. The frozen raindrops are **sleet.** Sleet and hail are not the same. They form in different ways. Freezing rain, also called an ice storm, is rain that freezes as soon as it hits the cold ground or other cold objects.

Hail Formation

Hail forms when very strong winds blow upward into a cloud. These winds blow raindrops back up into the freezing air at the top of the cloud. This creates a small piece of ice. As the ice is blown through the cloud many times, many layers of water freeze on it. Finally, it gets too heavy for the winds to carry it back up. The hailstone falls to the ground. Most hailstones are about the size of a pea. Some can get bigger than a baseball.

✓Lesson Checkpoint

1. How does sleet form?
2. What happens to snow if it falls through a layer of warm air?
3. **Sequence** the steps taken from water vapor to sleet.

Types of Precipitation

Rain
Freezing Rain
Sleet
Snow
Most clouds over North America are made of ice crystals.
Ice crystals melt as they fall through warmer air. They fall to the ground as rain.
Ice crystals fall from clouds.
Ice crystals melt to form raindrops as they fall through warm air.
A layer of air close to the ground is colder than 0°C. This cold air makes the ground, trees, and other objects very cold. Rainwater freezes when it lands.
Ice crystals melt as they fall through a thin layer of warm air high above the ground.
If raindrops fall for a longer time through cold air, they freeze before they hit the ground. Frozen raindrops are called sleet.
Ice crystals will fall as snow if the air between the clouds and ground has a temperature below 0°C.

Lab zone **Guided Inquiry**

Investigate What is a cloud?

Tiny droplets of water (and sometimes tiny pieces of ice) make up a cloud. The water droplets form when moisture in the air collects on dust and other particles. In this activity, look for tiny droplets to form on the top and side of the bowls, not in the air. Inside the bowls, the moisture has no tiny particles on which to collect.

Materials

ice cubes

2 plastic bowls with lids

warm water

What to Do

1. Fill one bowl about $\frac{1}{3}$ full with warm water and close its lid.

warm water

2. Put nothing in the other bowl. Close its lid.

3. Put several ice cubes on top of each bowl.

Process Skills

Making and using a model can help you learn about a process, such as cloud formation.

4 **Observe** the bowls for 1 minute. Record what happens inside them.

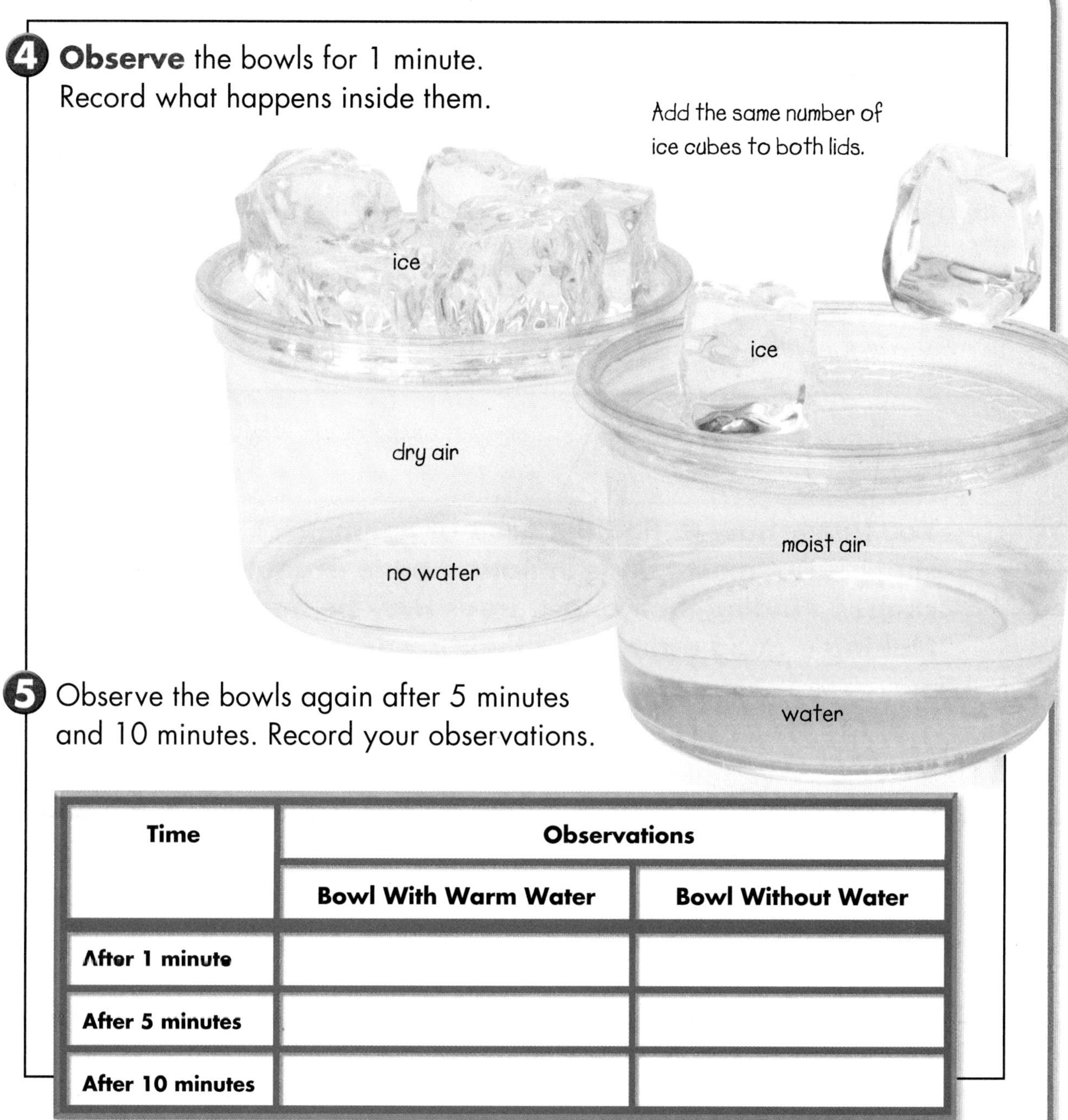
Add the same number of ice cubes to both lids.
ice
dry air
no water
ice
moist air
water

5 Observe the bowls again after 5 minutes and 10 minutes. Record your observations.

Time	Observations	
	Bowl With Warm Water	Bowl Without Water
After 1 minute		
After 5 minutes		
After 10 minutes		

Explain Your Results

1. Based on your **observations,** make an **inference.** Is there moisture in the air from which clouds form? Explain.
2. Use your **models** to describe some of the conditions necessary for clouds to form in the atmosphere.

Go Further

What effect does the ice have? Design and conduct a scientific investigation to answer this question or one of your own. Describe and demonstrate how to safely perform your investigation.

Math in Science

Estimating the size of a lake

You know how to find the area of geometric shapes. But most things in nature have irregular shapes. Finding their exact areas may be hard. Making a good estimate of their areas is easy!

Area is the number of square units that a figure covers. So, one way to find the area of an odd shape is to use a grid that divides the shape into square units. Then count the number of square units. To get a better estimate, you can combine half-squares and add them to your count.

Suppose you want to find the area of the lake shown on the map below. On this map, 1 unit represents a distance of 1 kilometer. This means that a square unit represents an area of 1 square kilometer.

Six squares are completely or almost completely covered. Eight squares are about half covered, making 4 more whole squares. A good estimate for the area of the lake is 10 square kilometers.

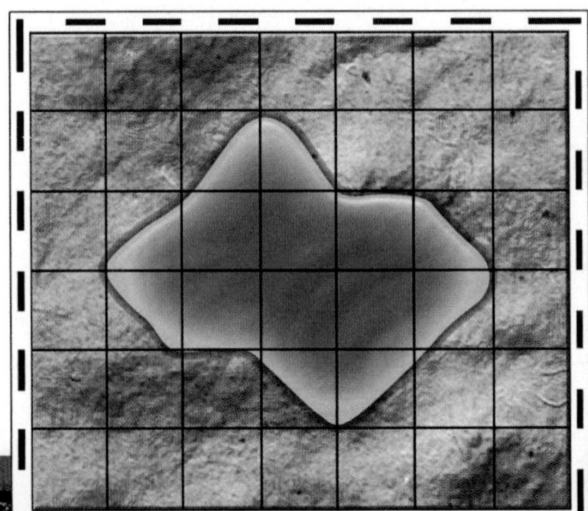

e Tools Take It to the Net sfsuccessnet.com

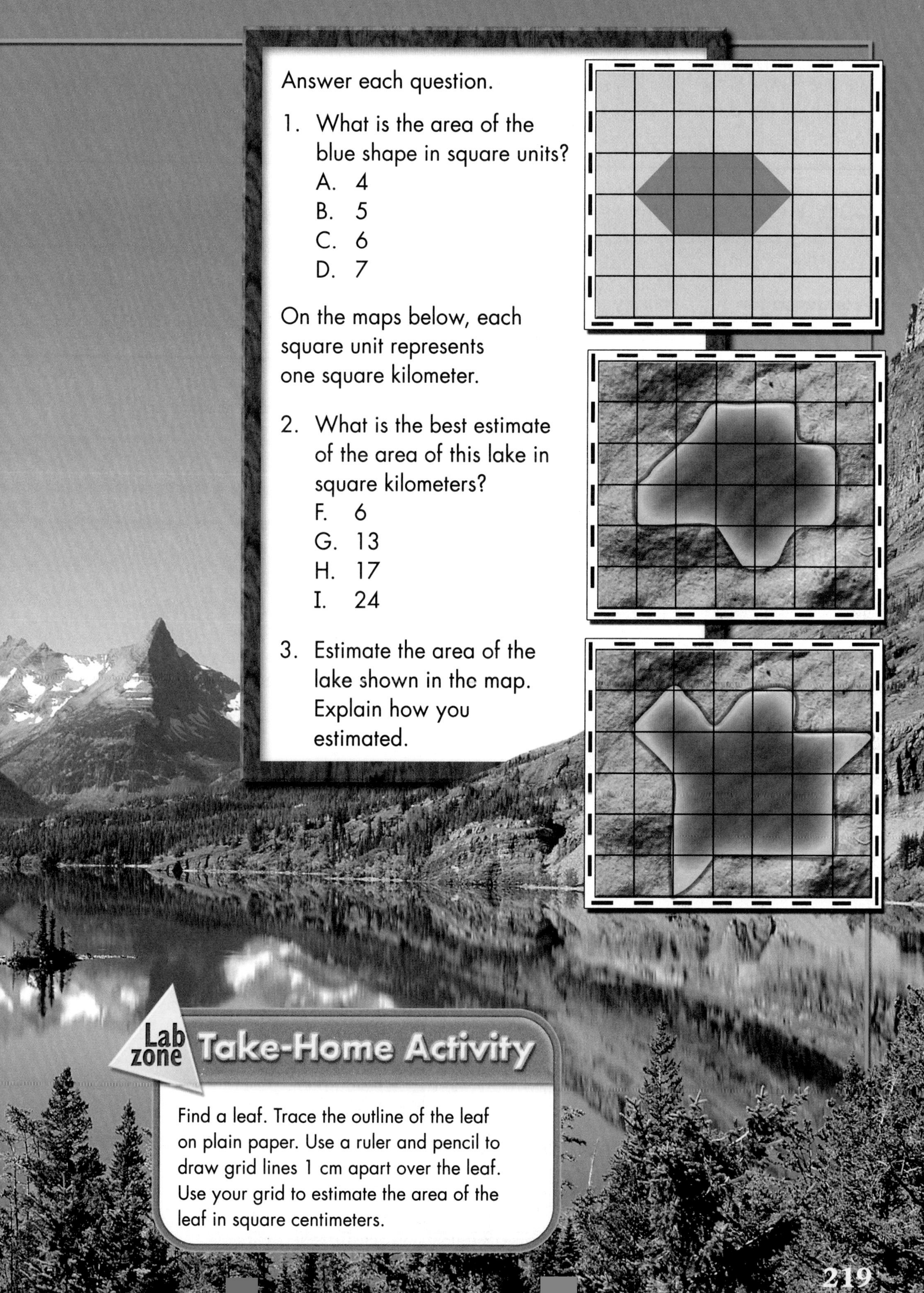

Answer each question.

1. What is the area of the blue shape in square units?
   A. 4
   B. 5
   C. 6
   D. 7

On the maps below, each square unit represents one square kilometer.

2. What is the best estimate of the area of this lake in square kilometers?
   F. 6
   G. 13
   H. 17
   I. 24

3. Estimate the area of the lake shown in the map. Explain how you estimated.

Lab zone Take-Home Activity

Find a leaf. Trace the outline of the leaf on plain paper. Use a ruler and pencil to draw grid lines 1 cm apart over the leaf. Use your grid to estimate the area of the leaf in square centimeters.

Chapter 7 Review and Test Prep

Use Vocabulary

aquifer (p. 203)	**reservoir** (p. 204)
condensation (p. 209)	**salinity** (p. 200)
evaporation (p. 209)	**sleet** (p. 214)
precipitation (p. 209)	**sublimation** (p. 209)
	water table (p. 203)

1. Rain, snow, sleet, and hail are types of _____.
2. The process of ice changing directly from a solid to gas is _____.
3. The layer of rock and soil that groundwater flows through is a(n) _____.
4. When raindrops freeze before they hit the ground, _____ forms.
5. The process of liquid water changing to water vapor is _____.
6. The top level of groundwater in an aquifer is the _____.
7. _____ is a measure of how salty water is.
8. A lake that forms behind a dam is a(n) _____.
9. The process of water vapor changing to liquid water is _____.

Explain Concepts

10. Describe how water may be treated before it is used by people.
11. Explain how clouds and rain usually form over the United States.
12. Describe the oceans and explain how the water cycle affects the salinity of the ocean.
13. Describe two sources of fresh water.

Process Skills

14. **Classify** the clouds shown below and describe their normal altitudes.

Sequence

15. Make a graphic organizer like the one shown below. Put the following steps in order to complete the sequence of one path water could follow in the water cycle.

Crystals fall from the cloud.
Water evaporates out of the plant leaves.
Crystals melt into rain.
Water vapor turns into ice crystals in a cloud.
Water moves into a plant.
Rain water sinks into the ground.

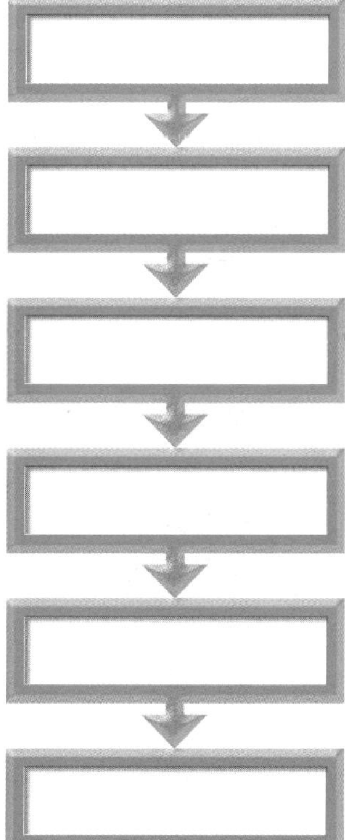

Test Prep

Choose the letter that best completes the statement or answers the question.

16. Which kind of cloud touches the ground?
- Ⓐ cirrus
- Ⓑ altocumulus
- Ⓒ fog
- Ⓓ stratus

17. Which kind of precipitation forms when strong winds toss ice crystals up and down in a cloud?
- Ⓕ sleet
- Ⓖ snow
- Ⓗ hail
- Ⓘ rain

18. Which is an example of evaporation?
- Ⓐ A river flows into the ocean.
- Ⓑ A drop of water on a car gets smaller.
- Ⓒ A lake gets a layer of ice.
- Ⓓ Water appears on plants in the morning.

19. Explain why the answer you selected for Question 18 is best. For each of the answers you did not select, give a reason why it is not the best choice.

20. Writing in Science **Descriptive** List and describe three different sources of water. Describe the role that each has in the water cycle.

NASA

Studying Earth's Water from Space

Earth is the only planet that we know has lots of liquid water. Its land, air, and oceans all interact. NASA has different ways of collecting data about Earth's water.

Tropical Rainfall Measuring Mission

The Tropical Rainfall Measuring Mission (TRMM) was launched in November 1997. Measurements from TRMM are used to find where rain is falling in the areas near Earth's equator. It also lets researchers know how hard it is raining in places without people nearby to measure the rain. It can even measure rain that falls from clouds but evaporates before it reaches the ground. This information helps researchers predict winds, ocean currents, and floods.

The winds in a hurricane circle around a center that has low air pressure.

Aqua Satellite

Aqua is the Latin word for water. The *Aqua* satellite was launched in May 2002. Its main goal is to gather information about water in the Earth's system. The information will help scientists understand more about Earth's water cycle, the oceans, and our environment. *Aqua* carries six instruments. One of the instruments can measure ocean temperature accurately, even though clouds might cover the ocean. Measuring ocean temperatures gives scientists important information about changes on Earth.

This *Aqua* satellite image shows waves near Indonesia.

ICESat

The *Ice, Cloud, and Land Elevation Satellite* was launched in January 2003. It uses lasers to measure ice sheets covering Antarctica and Greenland. It also uses the lasers to measure the altitudes of clouds, mountains, and forests. Scientists will use the measurements taken over several years to determine whether the ice sheets are melting or growing as Earth's climate changes.

Greenland's ice sheet melting.

Lab zone Take-Home Activity

Set up a rain gauge at your home. Measure the rainfall for one month and make a chart to show your data.

Career

Oceanographer

Can you imagine spending months at a time sailing the ocean? Would you like to protect our drinking water? Then maybe a career studying Earth's waters is for you.

Many careers involve studying the ocean. As a physical oceanographer, you would study the ocean tides, waves, currents, temperatures, and salinity. You might also study how the ocean affects Earth's weather and climate.

As a chemical oceanographer, you would study the chemicals in ocean water and on the sea floor. You might also study how pollution affects the ocean. Oceanographers must have a college degree. Many have advanced degrees.

Oceanographers work for governments, industries, and universities. Many of them spend a lot of time on ships. The work they do is important for understanding the role of the ocean in the Earth system.

Oceanographers can use submersibles to explore deep in the ocean.

Lab zone Take-Home Activity

Get two glasses of water. To one glass, add enough salt so that it no longer dissolves, no matter how much you stir. Float identical pencils in both glasses. Compare how well pencils float in fresh water and salty water.

Chapter 8

Weather Patterns

You Will Discover

- what causes air currents.
- what kinds of bodies of air make up weather.
- how severe weather forms.
- how weather forecasts are made.
- how climate is different from weather.

Discovery Channel School
Student DVD
Discovery Channel School

online
Student Edition
sfsuccessnet.com

Build Background

Why does the weather change?

climate

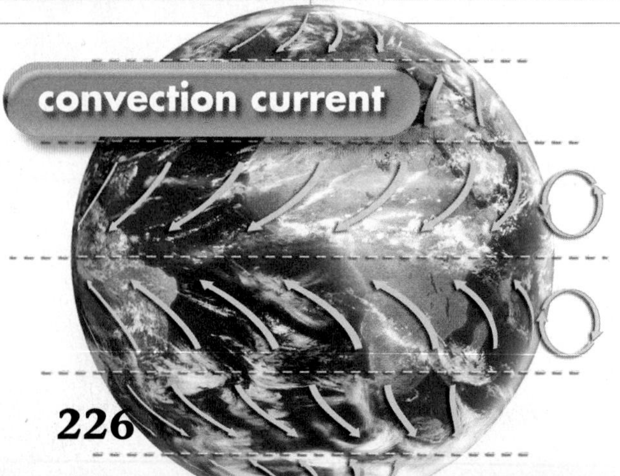
convection current

air mass

Chapter 8 Vocabulary
convection current page 232
air mass page 234
front page 236
anemometer page 242
barometer page 242
rain gauge page 243
climate page 246
anemometer
rain gauge
front
barometer
Change
Rain
Fair
Stormy
Very Dry
BAROMETER
MILLIBARS
INCHES

Lab zone

Directed Inquiry

Explore How does pressure affect an object?

Materials

marshmallow and marker

plastic jar

straw and clay

metric ruler

plastic mirror

What to Do

1. Draw a target on the marshmallow. Put the marshmallow in the jar.
2. Seal a straw in clay about 2 cm from one of its ends.
3. Put the short end of the straw into the jar. Seal the mouth of the jar with clay.
4. Use a mirror to **observe** the target on the marshmallow. Suck hard on the straw and then blow hard. Quickly repeat 5 times. Observe the target carefully for any small changes in size.

When you blow into the straw, you increase the pressure inside the jar. How can you decrease the pressure?

Process Skills

You used your **observations** of changes in the marshmallow to make an **inference.**

Explain Your Results

1. How did the marshmallow change when the pressure was increased and decreased?
2. **Infer** Why did the size of the marshmallow change when the pressure increased?

How to Read Science

Reading Skills

TARGET SKILL

Draw Conclusions

Learning to **draw conclusions** can help you evaluate what you read and **observe.**

- As you read, put together facts and then extend them to form a conclusion or to make an **inference.**
- Sometimes you may have more than one conclusion.
- You might change your conclusions when you get more facts.

Science Article

Rising to the Heights

Soon after people started flying in hot-air balloons, they began measuring air conditions above Earth's surface. Researchers who wanted to understand weather rose high into the air. But these flights were dangerous. At higher altitudes, air pressure can be dangerously low. In 1862, a pair of researchers rose so high they barely survived their flight. One passed out due to a lack of oxygen at the high altitude. The other could barely move for the same reason. He used his teeth to operate the balloon's controls and bring it down.

Apply It!

Make a graphic organizer like this one. List facts from the science article and **draw a conclusion.**

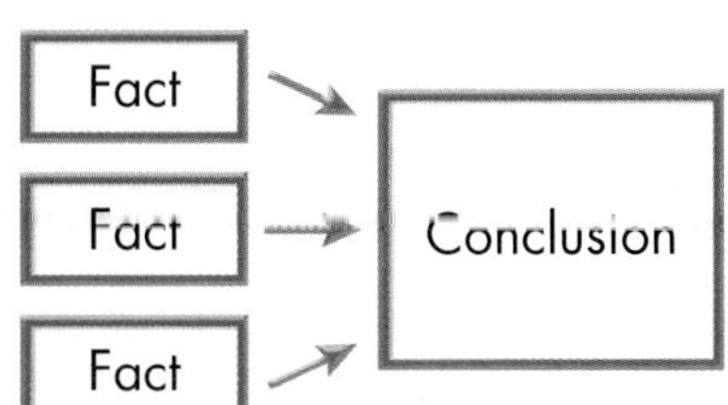
Fact
Fact
Fact
Conclusion

You Are There!

A cold wind blows around you as you climb higher up the ice-covered mountain. You spend a moment adjusting the tank on your back. At this altitude, you need a tank of oxygen to help you breathe. As you look at the clouds below, you think about all the planning that went into your climb. You are especially thankful that the weather forecasters could tell that this would be a good week for climbing. How were they able to predict this good weather?

Lesson 1

How does air move?

Air is a mixture of gases in constant motion. Differences in air temperatures create winds.

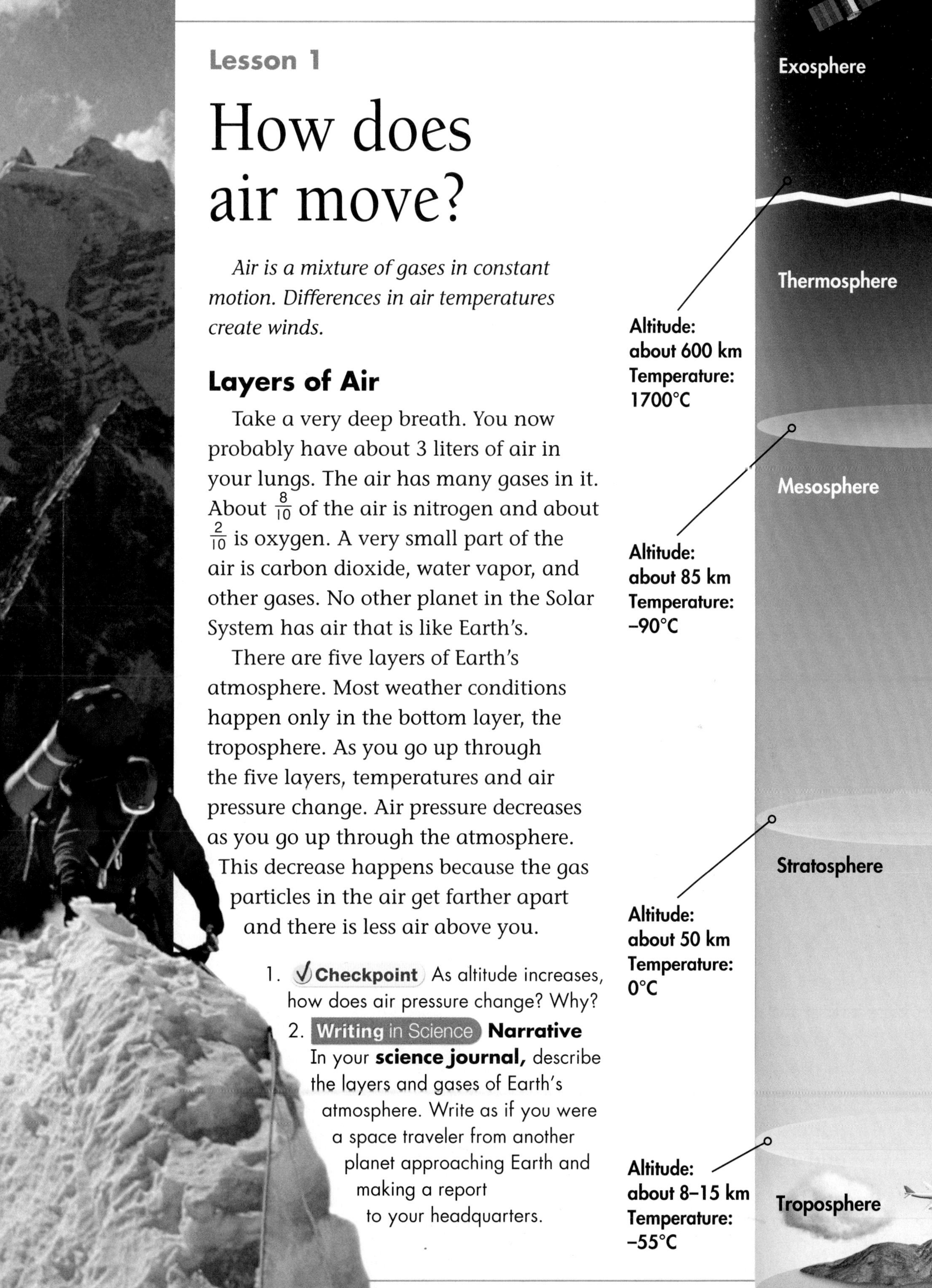
Exosphere
Thermosphere
Altitude: about 600 km Temperature: 1700°C
Mesosphere
Altitude: about 85 km Temperature: –90°C
Stratosphere
Altitude: about 50 km Temperature: 0°C
Troposphere
Altitude: about 8–15 km Temperature: –55°C

Layers of Air

Take a very deep breath. You now probably have about 3 liters of air in your lungs. The air has many gases in it. About $\frac{8}{10}$ of the air is nitrogen and about $\frac{2}{10}$ is oxygen. A very small part of the air is carbon dioxide, water vapor, and other gases. No other planet in the Solar System has air that is like Earth's.

There are five layers of Earth's atmosphere. Most weather conditions happen only in the bottom layer, the troposphere. As you go up through the five layers, temperatures and air pressure change. Air pressure decreases as you go up through the atmosphere. This decrease happens because the gas particles in the air get farther apart and there is less air above you.

1. √ **Checkpoint** As altitude increases, how does air pressure change? Why?
2. **Writing in Science** **Narrative** In your **science journal,** describe the layers and gases of Earth's atmosphere. Write as if you were a space traveler from another planet approaching Earth and making a report to your headquarters.

Convection Currents

Have you ever walked over hot sand to get to the cool water of a lake or ocean? Land gets warm more quickly in sunlight than does water. At night, land cools faster than water. This causes the air above the land and water to have different temperatures. Differences in the temperatures of air result in winds, storms, and all sorts of weather.

Different temperatures also cause convection currents to form. In a **convection current,** gases or liquids rise and sink in a circular path.

In cool air, gas particles are closer together than in warm air. This means that every liter of cool air is heavier than every liter of warm air. When the two kinds of air are next to each other, the cool air will sink and force the warm air to rise.

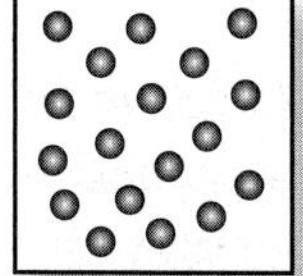
cool air

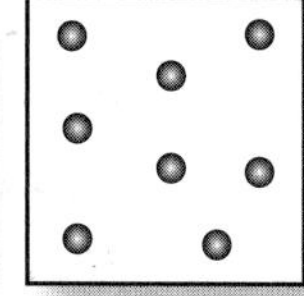
warm air

The kind of convection current shown here occurs near oceans and very large lakes during the daytime. Another convection current will flow in the opposite direction at night. These currents can form daily patterns of clouds, rain, wind, and air pressure.

Rising air will cool. It stops rising when it is the same temperature as surrounding air. This cooled air is pushed over the water by the rising air below it.

The cool water will not warm the air above it as much as the land warms the air above it. So, the cool air sinks below the warm air.

Cool, sinking air causes high air pressure at the surface.

As the cool air moves under the warm air, wind is created. Wind occurs as air moves from a place of high air pressure to a place of low air pressure.

Six huge convection currents form in the air above Earth. Part of the reason for these currents is that tropical regions get warmer than other parts of Earth. Warm air from tropical regions rises. After the air cools, it sinks farther north and south.

The combination of the movement of the huge convection currents and the spinning of Earth cause regional surface wind patterns. Winds generally blow from west to east over much of the United States.

Jet streams are found high above the ground between these huge convection currents. A jet stream is a band of very fast wind formed by the different temperatures between the convection currents. Even though it is very high, a jet stream can change temperature, winds, and precipitation by affecting the movement of air.

Six huge convection currents around Earth result in regional surface wind patterns.

The warm land makes air above it warm. This warm air is forced up by the cool air, causing sea breezes.

Warm, rising air causes a low air pressure at the surface

✓ Lesson Checkpoint

1. What causes convection currents?
2. In what direction do surface winds over the United States generally blow?
3. **Draw Conclusions** At night, land cools more than water. Air above land will be cooler than air above the water. What conclusion can you draw about convection currents near the ocean at night?

Lesson 2

What are air masses?

There are four basic bodies of air. These large bodies of air drift across the globe. When they are pushed together, the weather can change.

Kinds of Air Masses

Suppose your cousins just returned from a trip. You want to figure out where they went. When they show you the seashells they collected, you know that your cousins were at a beach. You can figure out where air has been too. The air's temperature and water vapor content can give you clues.

If air stays over an area for some time, it takes on properties of that area and becomes an air mass. An **air mass** is a large body of air with similar properties all through it. The most important properties are temperature and amount of water vapor. An air mass keeps its original properties for a while as it moves to a new area.

Four kinds of air masses are seen in the picture to the right. Generally, the kind of weather you have at any time is because of the air mass in your area. If you are having several warm, clear days, the weather will remain that way until a new air mass comes into your area. Some kinds of weather usually happen only at the edges of air masses.

Air masses move because of winds. These winds may be near the ground. Some air masses are guided by the jet stream high above the ground. If the jet stream guides an air mass from Canada to the middle of the United States, northerly winds will probably bring cold, dry air. At the edge of this air mass, storms may occur.

1. ✓ **Checkpoint** How do air masses form and move?
2. Writing in Science **Descriptive** In a letter, a friend wonders why the weather has been so hot and humid. In your **science journal,** write a reply to your friend explaining the role of air masses in making the weather hot and humid.

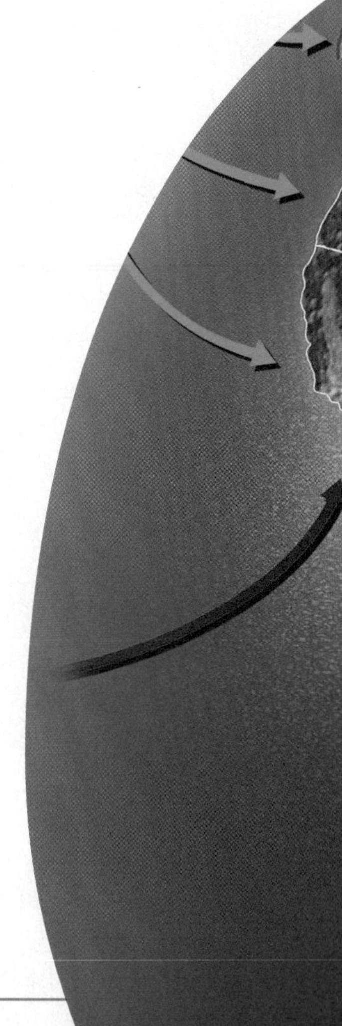

Maritime Polar Air
Even though the ocean near the poles is cold, water vapor evaporates into the air. An air mass forming over the poles is cold and moist.
Maritime Tropical Air
Humid air has lots of moisture. Over tropical oceans or rainforests, an air mass becomes warm and very humid because water can easily evaporate there.
Continental Polar Air
The land near the poles is not very moist. So, the air mass from this area is cold and fairly dry.
Continental Tropical Air
A large hot desert can cause the air above it to be warm and fairly dry.

When Air Masses Meet

Have you ever seen a line of clouds move from the horizon until it is overhead? What you have probably seen is the arrival of a front. A **front** is a boundary between two air masses. Most air masses move from west to east over the United States, so fronts have the same motion.

A front gets its name from the kind of air that moves into the area. A cold front brings colder air into an area. A warm front brings warmer air into an area. Sometimes a front does not move very much or it moves back and forth over the same area. This kind of front is called a stationary front.

Notice in the pictures shown that both fronts have rising warm air. Areas of rising air near the fronts have lower air pressure than areas in the middle of the air masses. Rising air at fronts often causes rain or snow.

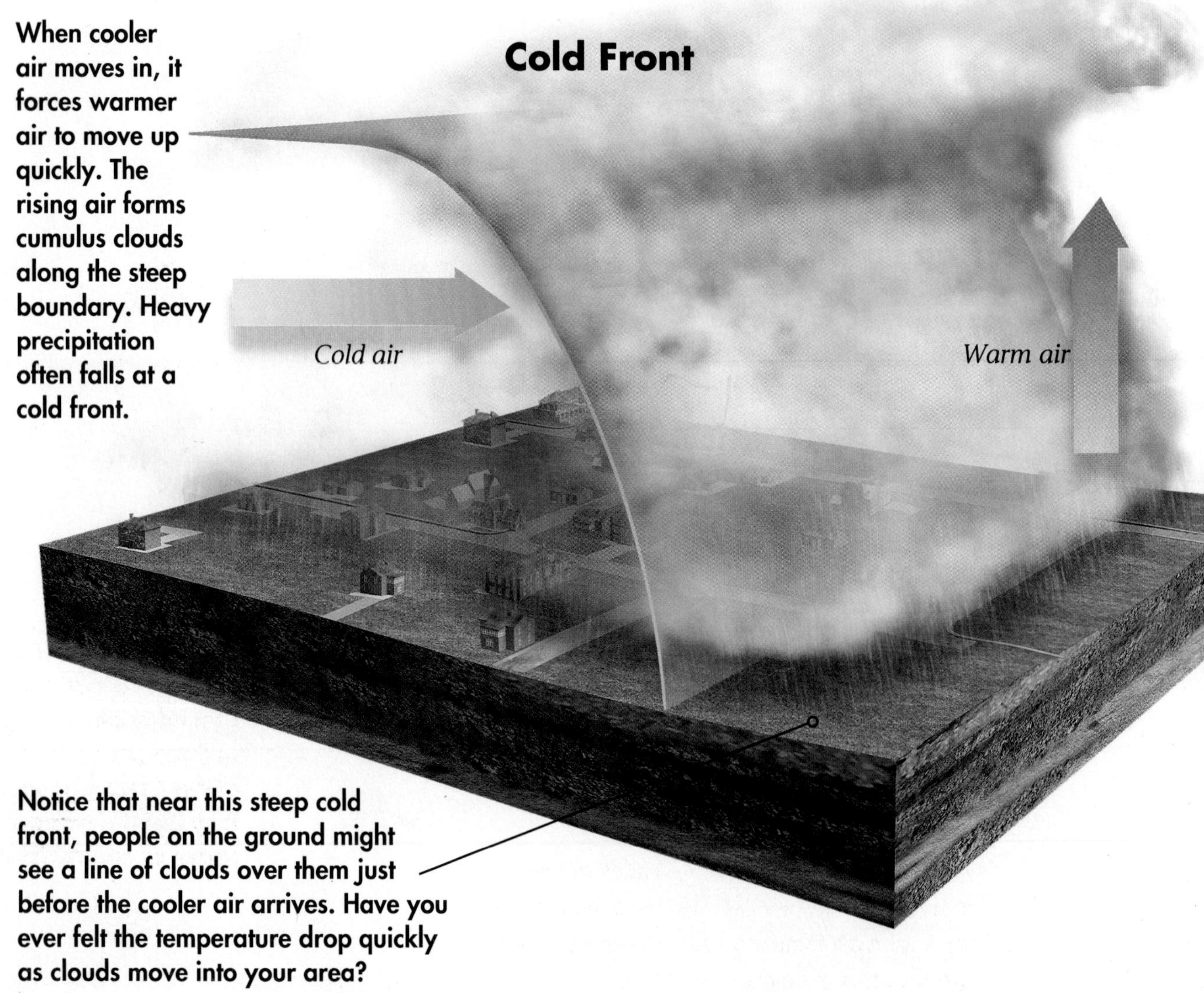
Cold Front
Cold air
Warm air

When cooler air moves in, it forces warmer air to move up quickly. The rising air forms cumulus clouds along the steep boundary. Heavy precipitation often falls at a cold front.

Notice that near this steep cold front, people on the ground might see a line of clouds over them just before the cooler air arrives. Have you ever felt the temperature drop quickly as clouds move into your area?

At warm fronts, warmer air moves against cooler air. The warmer air gradually rises above the cooler air. The clouds of a warm front often move more slowly and cause longer periods of precipitation than cold fronts.

Warm Front

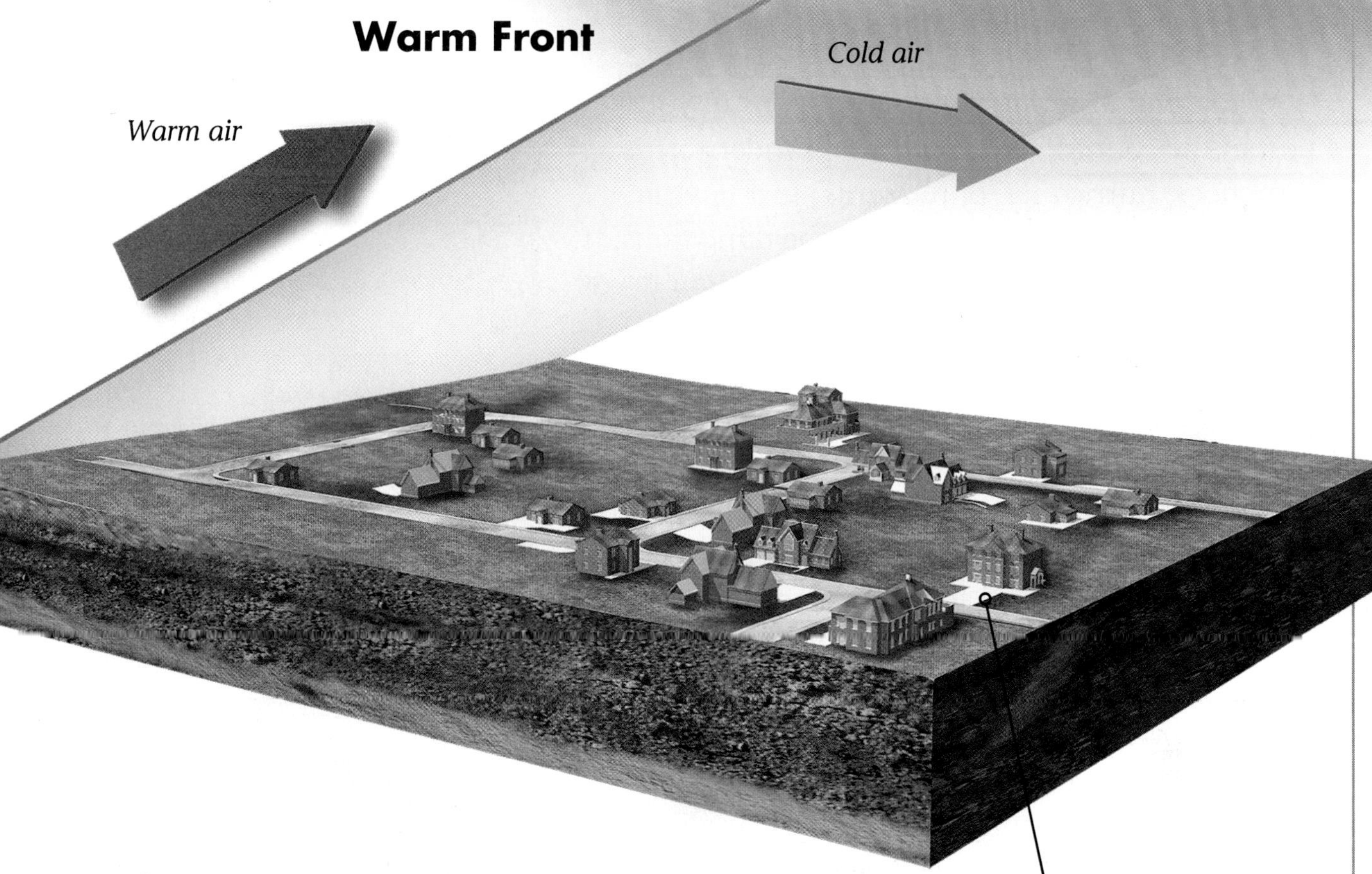
Cold air
Warm air

Notice that near a warm front, people on the ground might see high-altitude clouds form above them long before they feel the warmer air arrive at ground level.

✓ Lesson Checkpoint

1. Why does precipitation often happen at fronts?
2. Suppose one morning, you need a light coat to play outside. A thunderstorm forces you to go inside for several hours. That afternoon, you need a heavy coat to go outside. What kind of front has passed?
3. **Draw Conclusions** An air mass moves into the middle of the United States. It has low humidity and high temperatures. Where can you conclude that this air mass formed?

Lesson 3

What causes severe weather?

Sometimes the water cycle can lead to severe weather. Severe weather includes thunderstorms, tornadoes, and hurricanes.

Thunderstorms

What kind of severe weather happens in your part of the country? Do you have thunderstorms, tornadoes, hurricanes, or blizzards? Just having very high or low temperatures can be dangerous. If you know that severe weather is coming, you need to prepare for it.

Thunderstorms can form in different ways. Often, the first stage of a thunderstorm has strong, quickly rising currents of moist air. Clouds grow as moisture condenses in the rising air. The clouds have both ice crystals and water droplets.

In the storm's second stage, precipitation starts to fall, which pulls some air down with it. The storm now has both upward and downward moving currents.

In the storm's final stage, all the currents are moving downward, and the clouds get smaller as precipitation falls. Remember that the condensation and precipitation of thunderstorms are parts of the water cycle.

1. **Checkpoint** List four examples of severe weather.
2. **Draw Conclusions** Why do you think you should get inside as soon as possible when there is a severe storm warning?

First stage: All air currents move upward.

Second stage: Air currents are mixed.

Final stage: All air currents move downward.

+ + + +

— —

Different areas of a thunderstorm cloud have either positive or negative electrical charges. This may be caused by the precipitation colliding in the air currents of the cloud.

Lightning is a large electrical spark moving between areas of opposite charge. Lightning can warm air to 30,000°C in a fraction of a second. This high temperature causes the air to expand so rapidly that it makes vibrations in the air. We hear these vibrations as thunder.

What we see as one flash of lightning is often many flashes of both positive and negative charges going up and down.

Lightning often hits tall objects. If you cannot get inside a building during a thunderstorm, move away from trees or high towers. Stay low but do not lie on the ground.

The negative charges on the cloud cause positive charges to gather in the ground below.

Watches and Warnings

A **severe thunderstorm watch** means that severe thunderstorms with high winds and hail might form.

A **severe thunderstorm warning** means that severe thunderstorms have formed and you should prepare for them. Get inside as soon as possible.

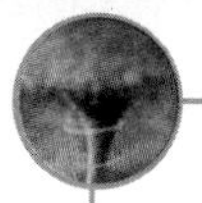

Tornadoes

Many things happen as a tornado forms. Layers of wind in a storm blow at different speeds or in different directions. Between these layers, a column of air starts spinning like a log rolling on its side. Then, upward winds lift one end of this spinning column. Downward winds push down on the other end. This spinning column of air is called a funnel cloud. It is called a tornado if it touches the ground.

Tornadoes usually last only a few minutes, but they can leave a path many kilometers long and hundreds of meters wide. Winds in a tornado move at hundreds of kilometers per hour. These winds can move cars and buildings around with ease.

If you hear or see a tornado warning, take shelter right away. It is best to go into a basement. If you cannot, go to a closet or windowless room in the center of the building. Why do you think it is important to stay away from windows?

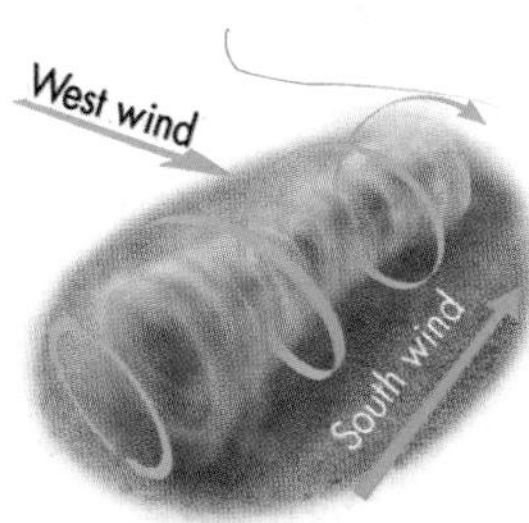
West wind
South wind

Air rolls between two layers of winds.

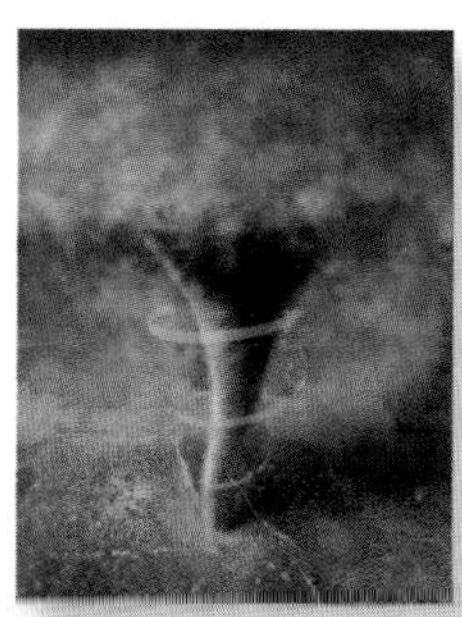

The rolling air is turned so it stands upright and becomes a funnel cloud. It is a tornado if it touches the ground.

Hurricanes

Hurricanes get their energy from warm ocean water. When water vapor from the ocean condenses, it releases energy. Under the right conditions, this energy builds and drives the winds of a hurricane. Once it is over land, the hurricane's energy is reduced.

Even though the swirling winds of a hurricane are not as fast as a tornado's winds, the winds of these ocean storms are more destructive. Why? First, hurricanes last for days, possibly hitting several locations. Second, a hurricane is hundreds of kilometers wide. Third, hurricanes can result in huge waves that cause severe damage and flood the shore. Heavy rains can also cause floods in areas farther inland.

Hurricane as seen from above.

Preparing for Hurricanes

To prepare for a hurricane, board up your windows. Store food and water. Have flashlights and battery-powered radios available. Put valuables in plastic containers high off the ground. Most importantly, stay inside. If authorities call for an evacuation, leave immediately. Why do you think these actions are helpful?

√ Lesson Checkpoint

1. What is the cause of a tornado?
2. What are the effects of a hurricane?
3. **Writing in Science** **Persuasive** Prepare a poster, play, or radio advertisement that would persuade people that severe weather is dangerous and tells what they can do to be safe.

Lesson 4

How are weather forecasts made?

People use many kinds of instruments to collect weather data. Weather forecasts are based on the data collected.

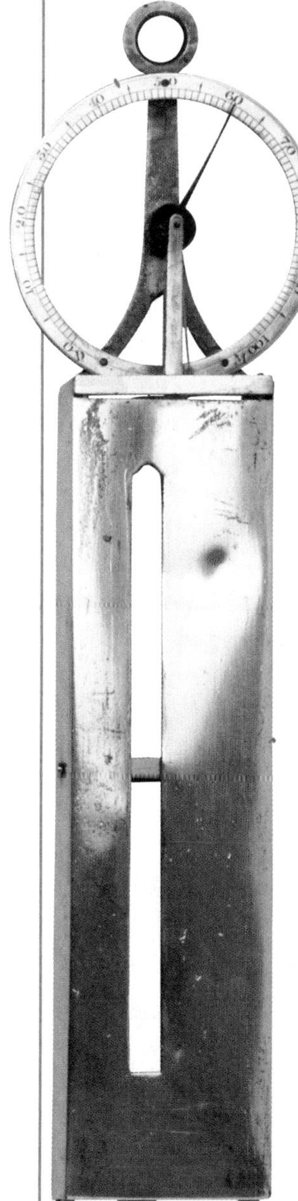

Horsehair hygrometer

Collecting Data

What exactly is weather? How would you define it? To completely describe a weather system at any particular place and time, you need to describe all its parts: the temperature, moisture, clouds, precipitation, wind speed, air pressure, and wind direction. All of these parts may interact with each other and change during the course of a day. They may change even more quickly than that!

Many kinds of tools measure all these parts of the weather. Some of these instruments might even be in your home. What weather-measuring tool have you used that is not shown here?

A **barometer** shows air pressure. In some barometers, air pressure pushes mercury up a tube. The barometer shown here has a small sealed container connected to the dial. When air pressure squeezes on the container, it causes the dial of the barometer to move

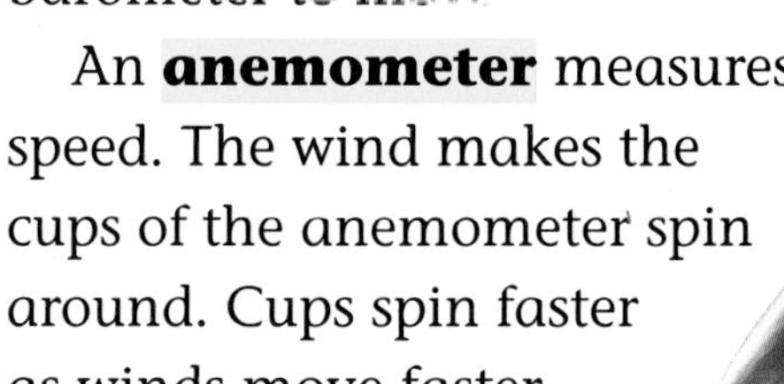

An **anemometer** measures wind speed. The wind makes the cups of the anemometer spin around. Cups spin faster as winds move faster.

A hygrometer measures the moisture in the air. Some hygrometers have a pointer attached to horsehair. The hair shortens in drier air, moving the pointer.

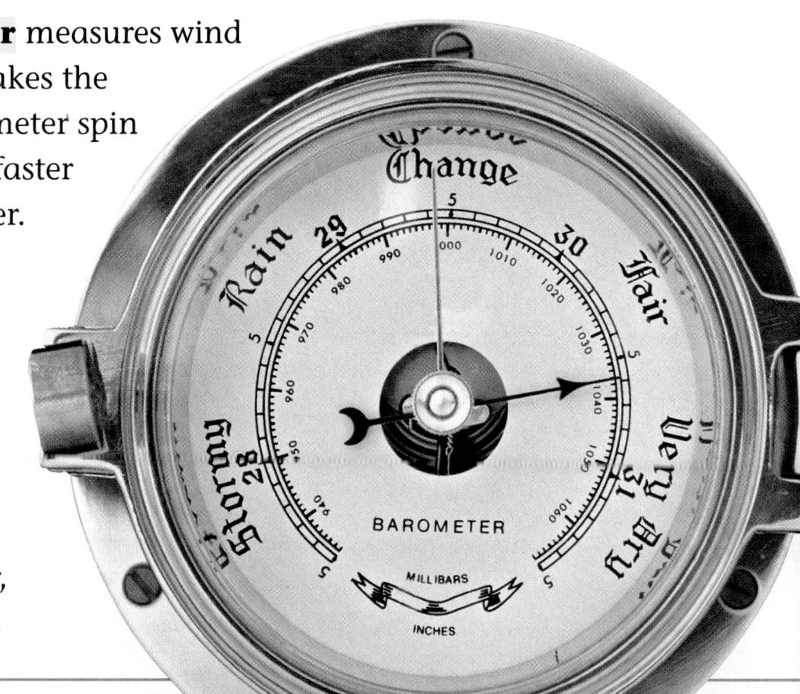
Change
Rain
Fair
Stormy
Very Dry
BAROMETER
MILLIBARS
INCHES

Weather Records				
	Lowest Average Yearly Rainfall	**Highest Average Yearly Rainfall**	**Highest Temperature**	**Lowest Temperature**
USA	4.00 cm	1,168 cm	57°C	–62°C
World	0.08 cm	1,168 cm	58°C	–89°C

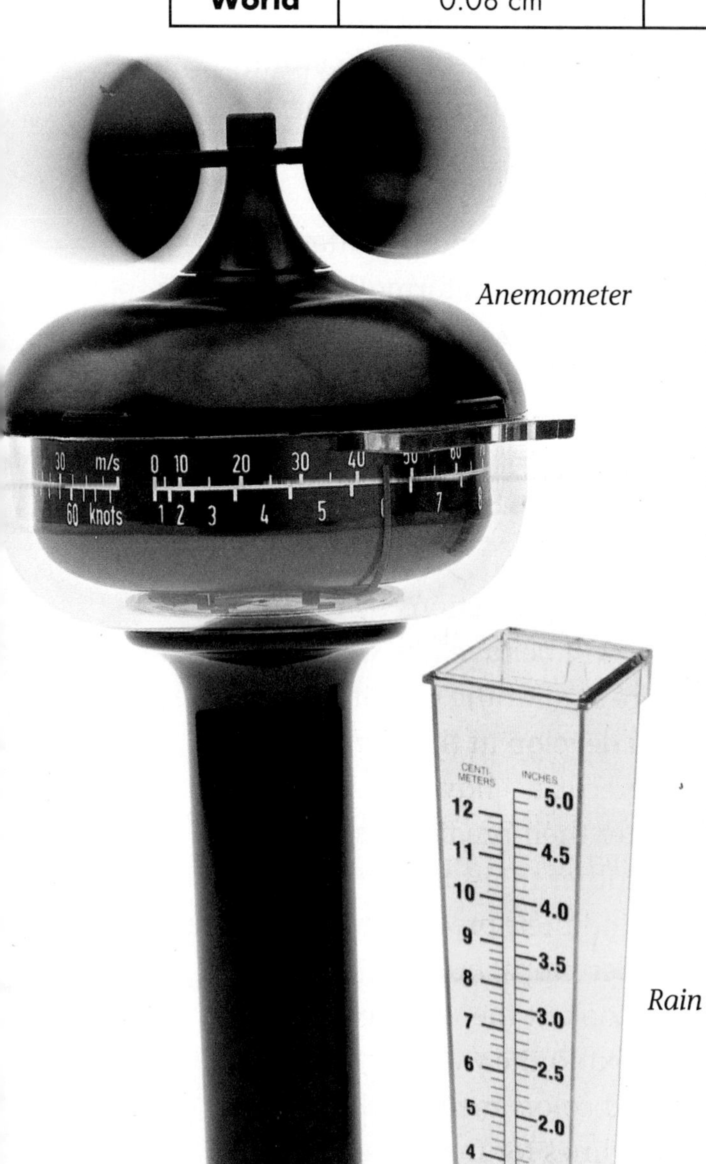

30 m/s 0 10 20 30 40
60 knots 1 2 3 4 5
CENTIMETERS
INCHES
12 11 10 9 8 7 6 5 4 3 2 1
5.0 4.5 4.0 3.5 3.0 2.5 2.0 1.5 1.0 0.5

Anemometer

Rain gauge

A **rain gauge** measures how much rain has fallen. The top of the rain gauge may be wider than the bottom. This allows the rain gauge to catch more rain when a small amount falls. It also makes measuring small amounts of rain easier.

Radar can measure the winds and precipitation inside a storm. The radar station sends out energy similar to signals from a radio station. Some of the energy bounces back from objects, including raindrops. Changes in the returning energy show the direction and speed of a rainstorm.

1. **Checkpoint** What are the parts of a weather system?
2. **Writing in Science** **Descriptive** Write in your **science journal** a description of daily and seasonal weather changes in your area.

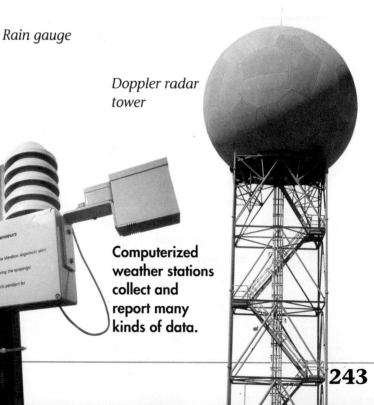

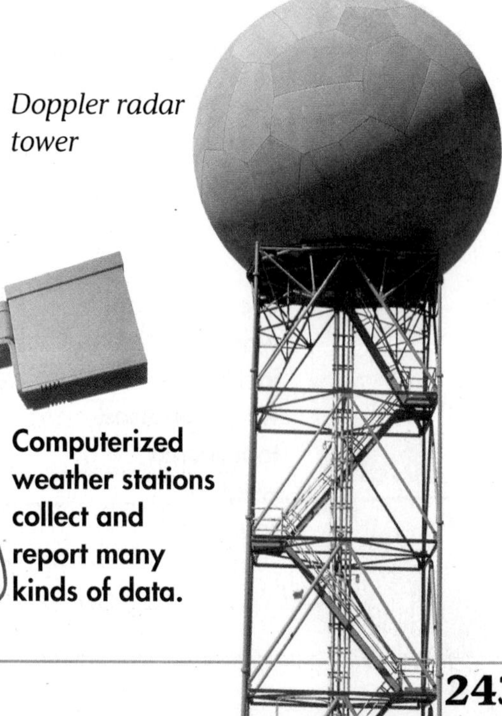

Sensors Box / Boîte à senseurs

Doppler radar tower

Computerized weather stations collect and report many kinds of data.

1970

The first weather satellite was launched in 1960.

1940

The first kind of weather balloon carried instruments in 1927.

1910

1900

1890

1880

1870

1860

The telegraph was invented in 1844. It was soon used to transmit weather reports.

1830

Weather Forecasts

Have you noticed any daily or seasonal patterns of change in the weather? For example, temperatures have a pattern of rising and falling during each day. Another pattern of temperature changes occurs throughout the seasons of the year. Temperatures rise and fall from January to December. There are also seasonal patterns of precipitation. Spring often has lots of precipitation.

Weather forecasters observe many patterns of weather change. They use the information from their observations to make inferences. These inferences are conclusions of how air, land, and the steps of the water cycle affect each other to make weather systems. With these inferences, forecasters make predictions, saying what the weather most likely will be in the future.

Forecasters make their predictions by assuming that current weather will behave like similar weather in the past. The more similar the conditions are, the more likely they will develop in the same way. The more information forecasters have when making this comparison, the better their predictions will be.

Forecasters use weather maps to display current weather conditions and their predictions. There are many kinds of weather maps, but most follow the same general rules. Look at the weather map on page 245. The key next to the weather map tells what the symbols and colors mean.

By themselves, the lines for fronts can tell you much about the current weather. First, the triangles or half-circles on the lines point in the direction the front is moving. Warm fronts bring warmer weather. Cold fronts bring cooler weather. Remember that fronts are always in places of low pressure. In most of the United States, fronts generally move from west to east. They often bring cloudy weather, but areas of high pressure that are away from fronts often have clear skies.

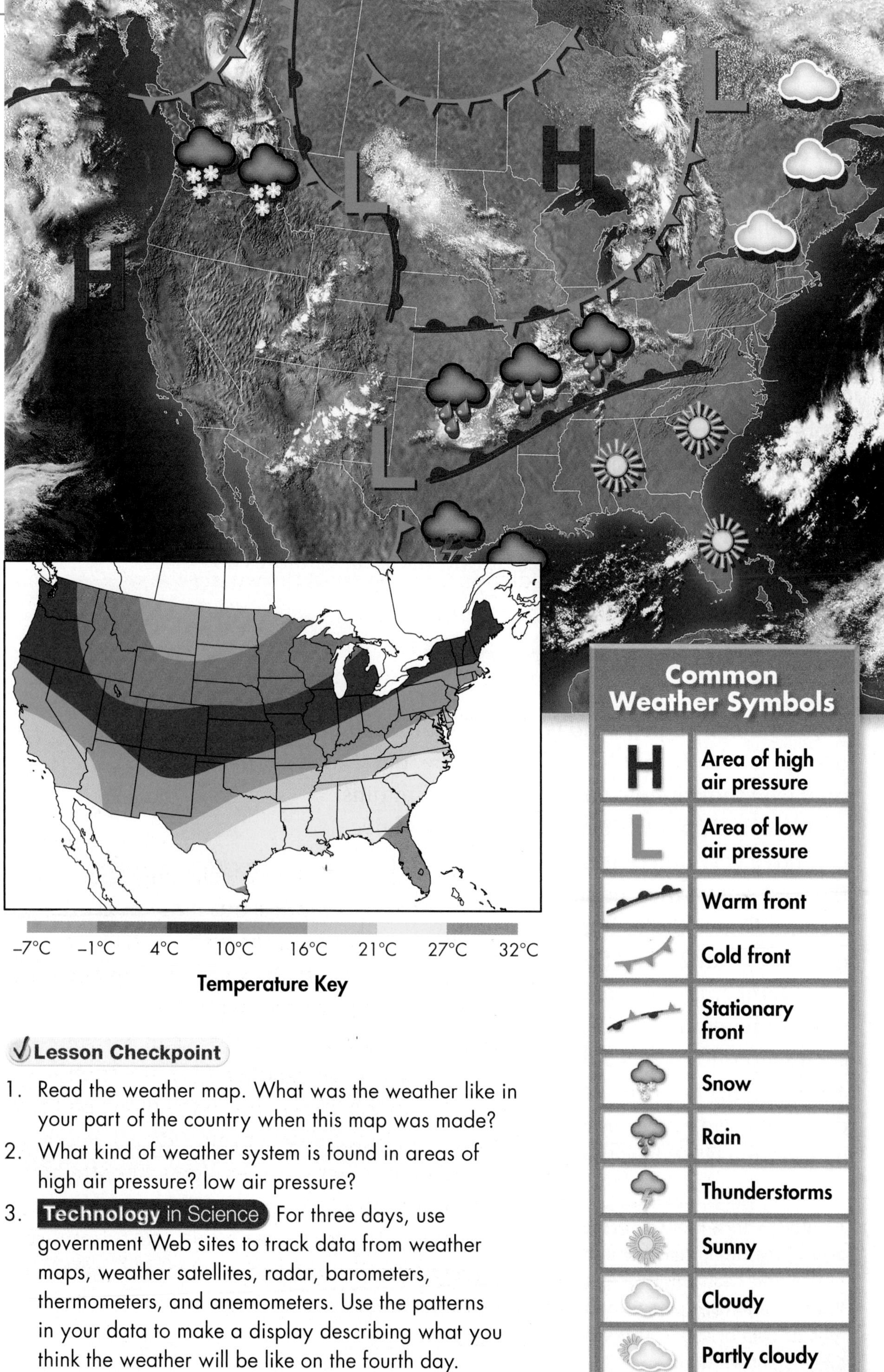

-7°C
-1°C
4°C
10°C
16°C
21°C
27°C
32°C
Temperature Key
Common Weather Symbols
Area of high air pressure
Area of low air pressure
Warm front
Cold front
Stationary front
Snow
Rain
Thunderstorms
Sunny
Cloudy
Partly cloudy

✓ Lesson Checkpoint

1. Read the weather map. What was the weather like in your part of the country when this map was made?
2. What kind of weather system is found in areas of high air pressure? low air pressure?
3. **Technology** in Science For three days, use government Web sites to track data from weather maps, weather satellites, radar, barometers, thermometers, and anemometers. Use the patterns in your data to make a display describing what you think the weather will be like on the fourth day.

Lesson 5

What is climate?

Weather and climate are not the same thing. The climate of an area does not change as often as the weather.

Weather and Climate

The words *weather* and *climate* do not have the same definitions. Weather is made up of all the conditions in one place at a single moment. Weather changes very often. **Climate** is the average of weather conditions over a long time, usually thirty years. Climate includes things like the average amount of precipitation, the average temperature, and how much the temperature changes during the year. Climates do not change as much as the daily weather does.

Landforms Affect Climate

Mountain ranges may have different climates than areas around them. Higher land is cooler because temperature decreases with height in the troposphere. But that is not the only way that climate varies around mountains.

Areas on opposite sides of a mountain range can have very different climates. For example, the west side of the Cascade Mountains in the western United States has a wet climate. It can get more than 2.5 m of precipitation each year. Temperate rain forests grow on this side of the mountains. But the area east of the mountains has a dry climate, like a desert. This happens because the air does not have much moisture in it by the time it reaches the east side.

As moist winds blow from the ocean, the mountains force the air to rise and cool. This makes clouds. Water condenses in the clouds and falls as rain or snow. This water cycle is shown here.

Oceans Affect Climate

Oceans can affect a climate by slowing the rise and fall of the air temperature. Remember that bodies of water become warm and cool more slowly than land. Because of this, the temperature of the air near an ocean does not change as quickly as air inland. In the winter, ocean beaches often do not get as cold as areas just a few miles inland. In the summer, the air over ocean beaches is often cooler than air over areas inland.

Ocean currents can make a climate warmer or cooler. The Gulf Stream and the North Atlantic Drift are large currents that carry warm water northward. The water warms the winds above it. These winds make northern Europe's climate much warmer than it would be otherwise. A change in these currents could change the climate of Europe. On the other hand, cold currents that flow from Alaska to California make that coastal climate cooler.

1. **✓Checkpoint** How are weather and climate different?
2. **Writing in Science** **Persuasive** Consider how the jet stream, oceans, mountains, and the water cycle affect climate. Write a paragraph in which you try to persuade the reader that one of them has the biggest effect on the climate in your area.

The air becomes drier after the rain or snow has fallen.
Air sinking down the side of a mountain does not make clouds or rain. This area is in a rain shadow.

Past Climates

Climates are determined by many years of weather, but that does not mean that climates do not change. In the 1600s, the climates of North America and Europe were much colder and wetter than they are now. This time is known as the Little Ice Age. Many written records of the weather during this time still exist.

Researchers can find clues about climate changes before written records. For example, during major ice ages huge glaciers moved across continents. They moved soil and rock of every size to form hills and lakes. Researchers can tell how the glaciers moved by making maps of these hills and lakes.

Climates have changed many times throughout history, sometimes quickly, but usually slowly. Looking at fossils is one way that scientists try to learn about climates in times before written records. Scientists assume that if an ancient plant looks very much like a modern plant, the two plants need the same kind of climate. For example, suppose a scientist working in a desert finds a fossil that looks like a fern. Since modern ferns do not survive in deserts, this fossil would be a clue that the area was once more wet than it is today. The same kind of comparison is done with fossils of animals and other organisms.

Fossils of ferns are found in areas that were likely warm and humid in the past.

The white areas on this map are places covered by glaciers during the last Major Ice Age.

Volcano eruptions may have changed climates in the past.

This crater was caused by an impact of a meteorite.

How Climates Change

There are many events that might cool a climate. The Little Ice Age may have occured because the Sun produced less energy. Volcanic eruptions and asteroid or meteorite impacts may have quickly caused cooler climates in the distant past. They could have done this by putting dust and other materials into the upper atmosphere. These materials can cool the climate by blocking sunlight or reflecting sunlight back into space.

Carbon dioxide, methane, and water vapor also can make climates warmer. They can be produced by human activities, such as burning coal and gasoline. These gases can also enter the atmosphere naturally, such as through decaying matter, forest fires, volcanoes, and the water cycle.

Many different events help to form a climate. Because of this, it is hard to determine why a climate has changed. Scientists have had debates on these changes and will probably have more in the future.

✓ Lesson Checkpoint

1. How are fossils used to study past climates?
2. What can cause a sudden climate change?
3. **Math in Science** During the last century, many places became warmer, but some became cooler. From 1901 to 1930, the average temperature for Waco, Texas, was 19.36°C. From 1971 to 2000, the average temperature was 18.57°C. How much did the temperature change?

Lab zone

Guided Inquiry

Investigate How does a thermometer work?

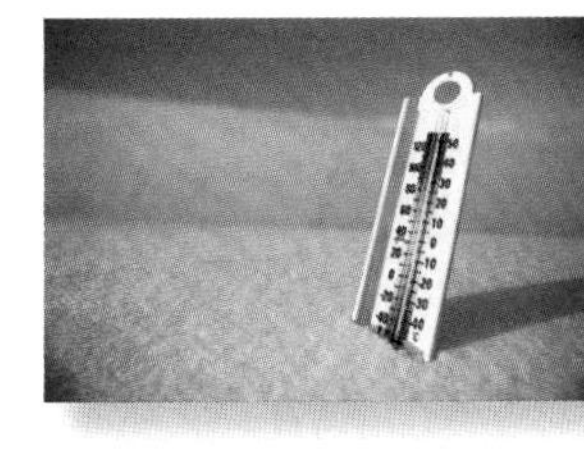

Materials

plastic jar and metric ruler

room-temperature water

red food coloring

plastic straw and clay

bowls of very warm water and very cold water

Process Skills

Before you **predict,** think about what you have already observed about the thermometer.

What to Do

1. Fill the jar 2 cm full with room-temperature water. Add red food coloring until the water turns red.

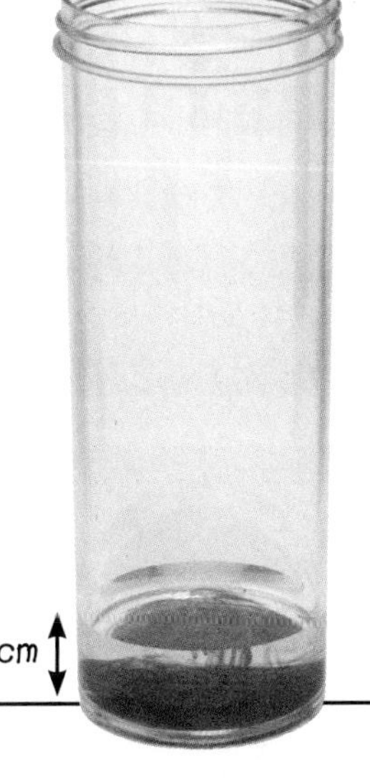
2 cm

2. Put the straw in the water. Do not let it touch the bottom of the jar.

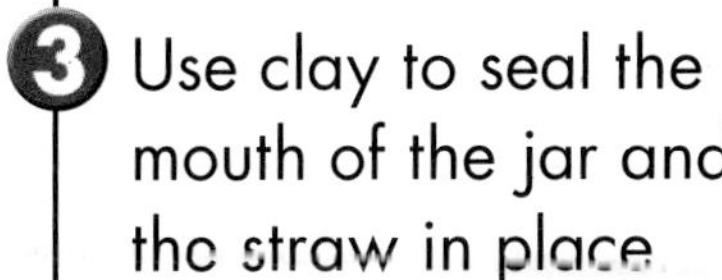

3. Use clay to seal the mouth of the jar and the straw in place.

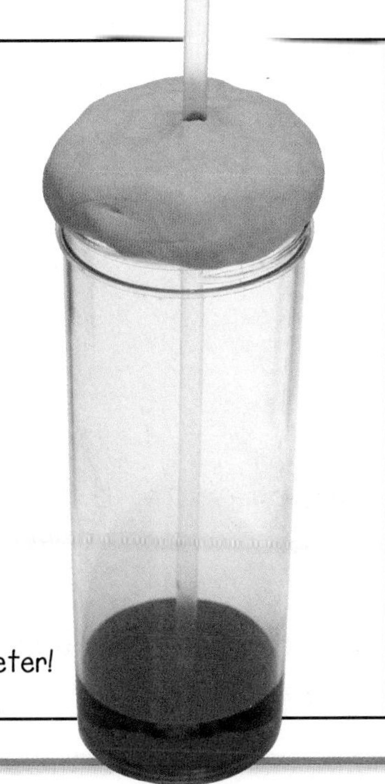

You have made a thermometer!

4. Place your thermometer in the very warm water. **Observe** whether the red liquid in the straw moves higher, moves lower, or does not change. Record your observation.

Be careful!

Do not use dangerously hot water!

5. **Predict** whether the red liquid in the straw will move higher or lower when you place the thermometer in cold water. Record your prediction. Test your prediction and record your observation.

Thermometer in Warm Water	Thermometer in Cold Water	
Observation	**Prediction**	**Observation**

Explain Your Results

1. What evidence did you use to make your **prediction?**
2. Explain how you think your thermometer works.

Go Further

How could you use weather instruments to describe weather patterns and how weather changes? Collect and analyze weather data.

Math in Science

Analyzing Tornado Data

Somewhere in the United States, thunderstorms may produce tornadoes this month. Tornadoes happen during all times of the year, and they happen in every state. The bar graph shows the average number of tornadoes that happen each month in the United States.

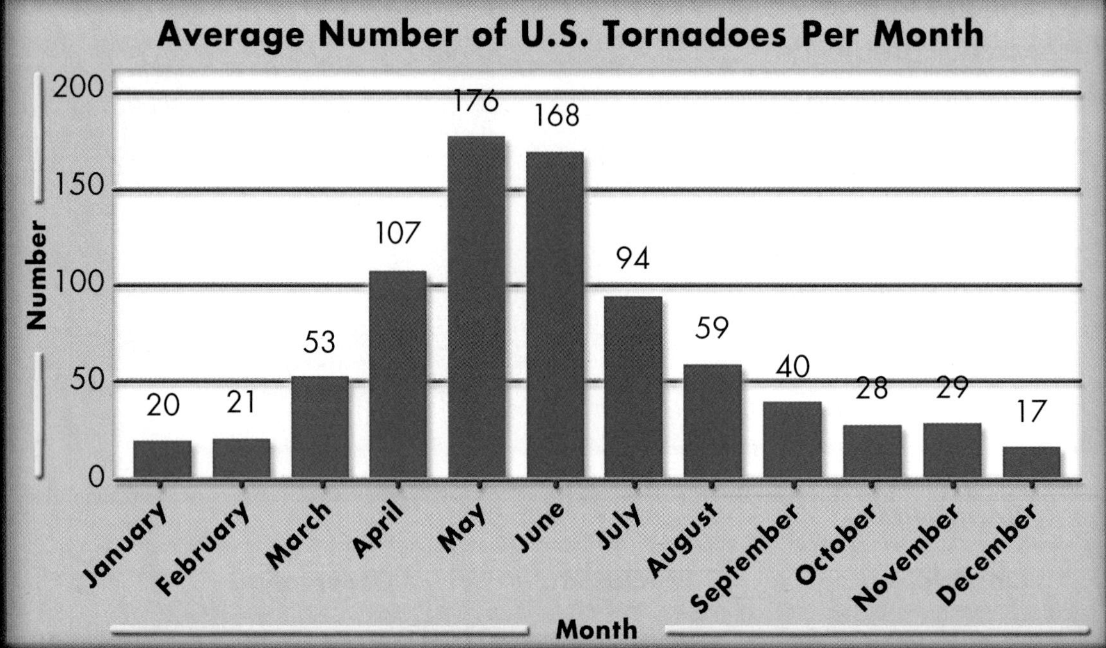

Average Number of U.S. Tornadoes Per Month
Number
200
150
100
50
0
20
21
53
107
176
168
94
59
40
28
29
17
January
February
March
April
May
June
July
August
September
October
November
December
Month

One way to describe a pattern in the data above is to use ranges. Ranges show how much the data changes. A lower range shows less change. A higher range shows more change. For example, the range in the three months of January, February, and March is 53 – 20, or 33. The range in the three months of March, April, and May is 176 – 53, or 123. So, the change in the number of tornadoes each month from March through May is almost four times the change from January through March!

Use the graph to answer the following questions.

1. What is the range from June through August?

   A. 146 C. 85

   B. 109 D. 74

2. What is the range in the number of tornadoes from September through February?

   F. 59 H. 23

   G. 40 I. 19

3. Between which two months does the number of tornadoes change the most?

   A. March–April

   B. April–May

   C. May–June

   D. June–July

4. Between which two months does the number of tornadoes change the least?

   F. January–February

   G. February–March

   H. March–April

   I. April–May

5. The number of tornadoes from January through May

   A. increases by 109.

   B. decreases by 109.

   C. increases by 156.

   D. decreases by 156.

Lab zone Take-Home Activity

Record the outside air temperature throughout one day in your **science journal.** At what time is the temperature at its highest point? lowest point? Is the greatest change in the morning, afternoon, evening, or overnight?

Chapter 8 Review and Test Prep

Use Vocabulary

air mass (p. 234)	**convection current** (p. 232)
anemometer (p. 242)	**front** (p. 236)
barometer (p. 242)	**rain gauge** (p. 243)
climate (p. 246)	

Use the terms from the list above that best completes each sentence.

1. A(n) _____ measures wind speed.

2. A(n) _____ measures air pressure.

3. A(n) _____ measures the amount of rain.

4. A(n) _____ is the average weather conditions over many years.

5. A(n) _____ is a circular current of air.

6. A(n) _____ is a large body of air with generally the same temperature and moisture.

7. A(n) _____is a boundary between two air masses.

Explain Concepts

8. Explain why the weather changes.

9. How are the water cycle in an area and the climate in the same area related?

10. How do weather forecasters make predictions about tomorrow's weather?

Process Skills

11. Interpret the Data The chart compares weather conditions in the same area at noon on two summer days. Interpret the data to conclude what type of front moved through the area.

Day	Noon Temperature
Monday	28°C
Tuesday	20°C

12. Predict St. Louis, Missouri, experiences large differences in temperature between summer and winter. Predict how the temperature difference would change if St. Louis were next to an ocean.

13. Predict what would happen if the amount of energy Earth gets from the Sun were to slowly decrease over time.

Draw Conclusions

14. Make a graphic organizer like the one shown below. Fill in your conclusion.

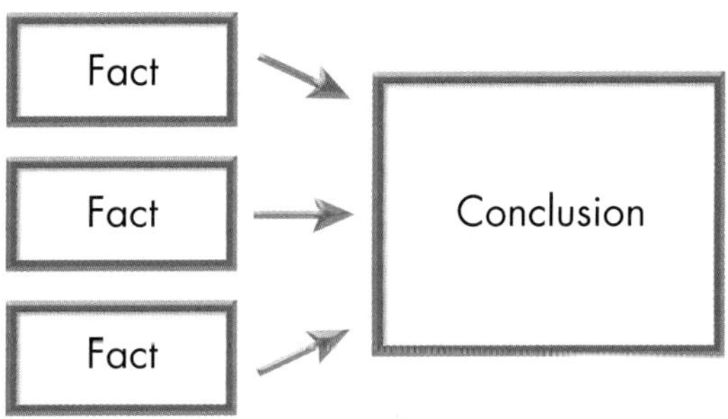
Fact
Fact
Fact
Conclusion

Fact: Gas particles become more spread out at higher altitudes.
Fact: At higher altitudes, there is less air above you pushing down so the air pressure is lower.
Fact: Mountain climbers need oxygen tanks to breathe well at high altitudes.

Test Prep

15. Where are clouds most likely to form?
Ⓐ in a rain shadow
Ⓑ in rising air
Ⓒ in sinking air
Ⓓ in high pressure

16. What causes air currents?
Ⓕ uneven heating of Earth's surface
Ⓖ boundaries between air masses
Ⓗ air heated by lightning
Ⓘ changes in wind direction

17. What does a capital letter H on a weather map show?
Ⓐ a hurricane
Ⓑ hot air
Ⓒ high pressure
Ⓓ heavy rain

18. What type of air mass comes from polar ocean areas?
Ⓕ cold and dry
Ⓖ cold and moist
Ⓗ warm and dry
Ⓘ warm and moist

19. Explain why the answer you selected for Question 18 is best. For each of the answer choices you did not select, give a reason why it is not the best choice.

20. Writing in Science **Descriptive**
Write a description of one type of severe weather and explain how it forms. Then describe what can be done to stay safe in that kind of severe weather.

NASA

Career

Atmospheric Scientist

Lin Chambers works with other scientists to understand how light energy flows through clouds.

When Lin Chambers was young, she and her family lived in Europe. Almost every year, they flew back to the United States for a visit. Those airplane rides inspired Chambers to study aeronautical engineering in college.

Chambers got her first full-time job at NASA. She studied how spacecraft heat up as they travel through the atmosphere. A few years later, she began to work on a project to study how light energy and heat energy move in and out of Earth's atmosphere. Chambers focuses on how light energy flows through clouds. She compares measurements from satellites with measurements taken from the ground. She runs computer models to understand how clouds can change the direction of light flow through the atmosphere.

Chambers works with many other scientists. Each scientist analyzes data in different ways. The scientists check each other's work and discuss different conclusions they can draw. Working as a team, each scientist is responsible for a different piece of the problem. The project goal is to produce accurate data about Earth's climate. Chambers says, "We rely on each other," stressing the importance of collaboration in her work.

Chambers loves studying clouds. It brings her back to the reason for her first career choice. Thinking about her experience on airplanes she admits, "The thing I enjoyed most about it was sitting at the window, looking down at the clouds."

Lab zone Take-Home Activity

Keep your own cloud journal in your **science journal,** identifying cloud types. Also find out about and look for the clouds known as contrails. Record information about the weather. Write down the date and time of your observations. Draw conclusions about cloud types and the weather, and compare your conclusions with those of a friend.

EC NTL 10 9 8 7

Chapter 9

Earth's Changing Surface

online
Student Edition
sfsuccessnet.com

You Will Discover

- what Earth's layers are.
- what causes earthquakes and volcanoes.
- how weathering and erosion change Earth's surface.
- how minerals and rocks are identified.

Web Games
Take It to the Net
sfsuccessnet.com

Build Background

What kinds of processes change Earth's surface?

crust

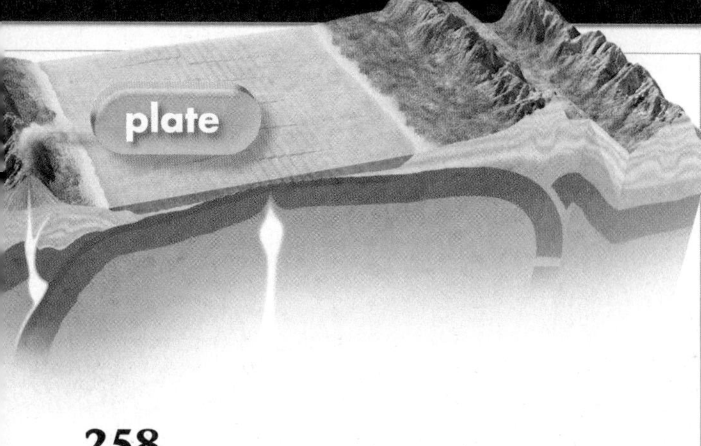
plate

mechanical weathering
chemical weathering

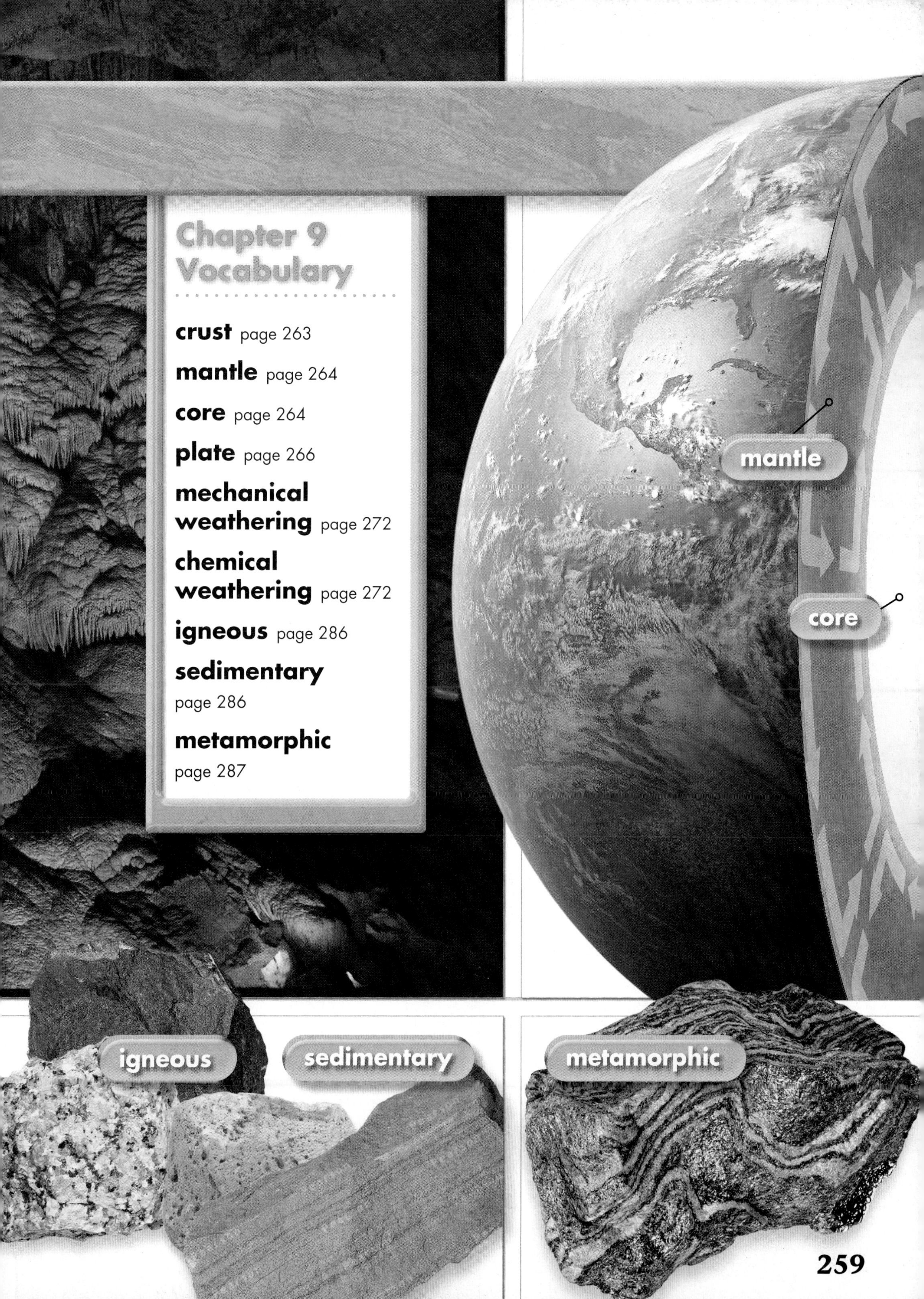

mantle
core
igneous
sedimentary
metamorphic

Chapter 9 Vocabulary

crust page 263

mantle page 264

core page 264

plate page 266

mechanical weathering page 272

chemical weathering page 272

igneous page 286

sedimentary page 286

metamorphic page 287

Lab zone

Directed Inquiry

Explore How can you make a model of material found in the Earth?

There is rock below Earth's surface that is melted or nearly melted. Under these conditions the rock loses it's strength, becomes soft, and can slowly flow like a liquid. Under some conditions a mixture of cornstarch and water also can show properties of a solid and a liquid.

Materials

newspaper

cornstarch and spoon

cup and water

What to Do

1. Put 5 spoonfuls of cornstarch in a cup. Add 3 spoonfuls of water. Stir.
2. Pour the mixture into your hand. Does it have the properties of a liquid or a solid?
3. Close your hand and squeeze. How do the mixture's properties seem to change?

Be neat. Put down newspaper before you begin.

Process Skills

When you explain your answer, you **communicate** your ideas.

Explain Your Results

Do you think the mixture acts like both a solid and a liquid? **Communicate** your reasons.

How to Read Science

Reading Skills

TARGET SKILL

Summarize

A summary is a short statement that **communicates** the main idea of a paragraph. A good summary should not include too many details.

The main idea might be the first sentence of the paragraph.

Newspaper Article

Drilling Stops Short of Goal

Dateline: 1966

Started in 1961, Project Mohole, a huge project drilling through the seafloor, has been cancelled. Its goal had been to drill through the earth's crust in order to get material from the mantle. The project had drilled about 200 meters into the ocean's crust. It was difficult for many reasons. First, it would be deeper than any other hole ever drilled. Second, it was drilled from a ship at sea. Third, rising costs caused officials to end Project Mohole.

Apply It!

Make a graphic organizer like the one shown. Then place the details in the smaller boxes and **communicate** a summary in the large box.

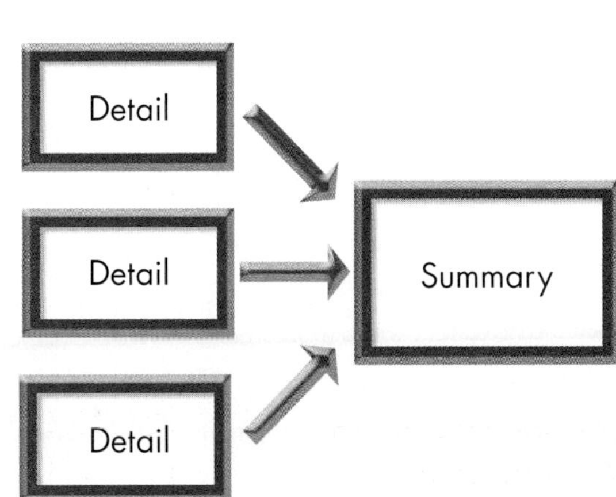
Detail
Detail
Detail
Summary

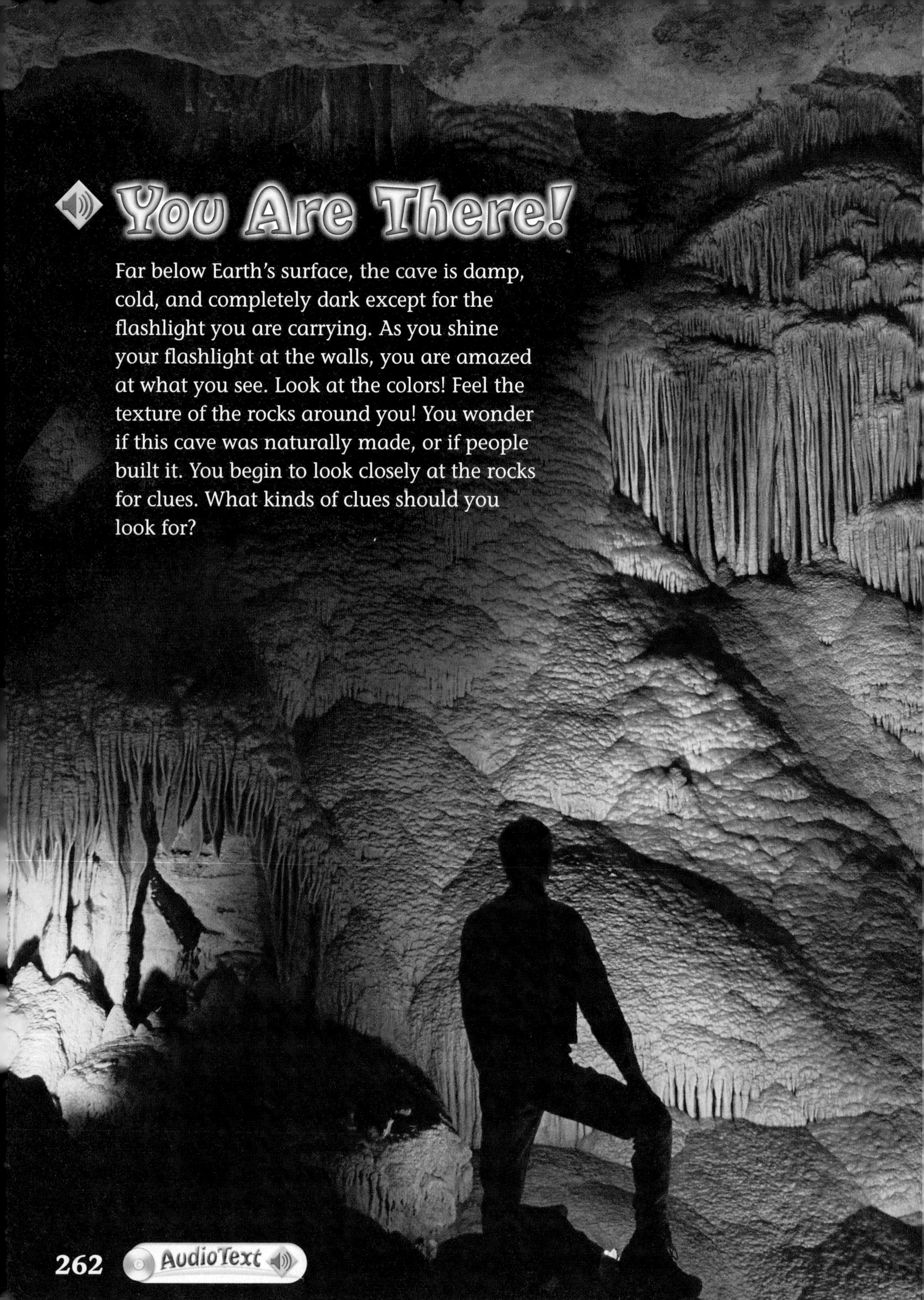

You Are There!

Far below Earth's surface, the cave is damp, cold, and completely dark except for the flashlight you are carrying. As you shine your flashlight at the walls, you are amazed at what you see. Look at the colors! Feel the texture of the rocks around you! You wonder if this cave was naturally made, or if people built it. You begin to look closely at the rocks for clues. What kinds of clues should you look for?

AudioText

Lesson 1

What is the structure of Earth?

Earth has layers called the crust, mantle, outer core, and inner core. Each layer has its own properties.

The Crust

When you are standing on the ground, you are standing on the **crust,** Earth's outermost and thinnest layer.

There are two general kinds of crust. Continental crust makes up all the lands of the continents. Continental crust is thickest in mountain areas. It can be about 75 kilometers thick and is mostly granite.

Oceanic crust lies beneath most of the ocean floor. It is made of different kinds of rock than the continental crust. Oceanic crust is made mostly of basalt, which is a dark green or black rock. This crust is about 6 to 11 kilometers thick.

The continental crust generally meets the oceanic crust underwater less than 100 kilometers from a coast. The continental crust dips underwater to form the continental shelf. The edge of the continental crust is seen at a steep drop-off called the continental slope. At the bottom of this slope is the continental rise. It is the beginning of oceanic crust.

1. **✓Checkpoint** What are Earth's layers?
2. **Math in Science** Is the continental crust more than 5 times as thick as oceanic crust?

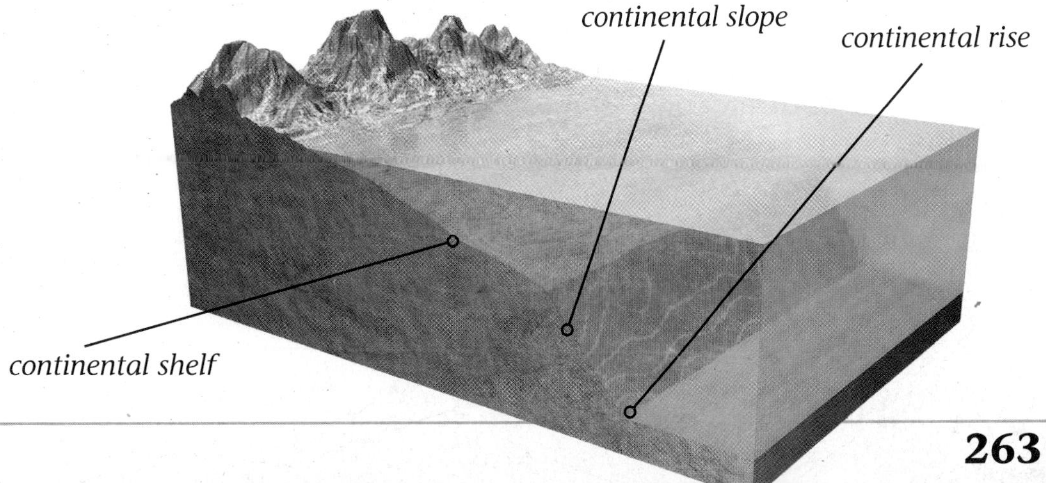
continental slope
continental rise
continental shelf

The Mantle and Core

Below the crust, Earth has other layers. The **mantle** is the layer that makes up most of Earth's material. The top part of the mantle is solid hot rock. This top part of the mantle and the crust above it form the lithosphere. Most of the lithosphere is under the oceans of the hydrosphere.

Layer	Average Thickness
crust	17 km
mantle	2,900 km
outer core	2,221 km
inner core	1,255 km radius

Deeper in the Earth, the mantle is under very high pressure. Its temperature ranges from about 360°C to 2,500°C. In conditions like this, the rock of the mantle is unusual. It is solid rock that shares the characteristics of liquids because it can flow very slowly when acted upon by forces in the Earth.

There are slow flows of convection currents in the mantle. In these currents, cooler rock flows down and hotter rock flows up. High temperatures inside Earth provide the energy needed for those currents to move. The lithosphere floats on the top of the convection currents in the mantle.

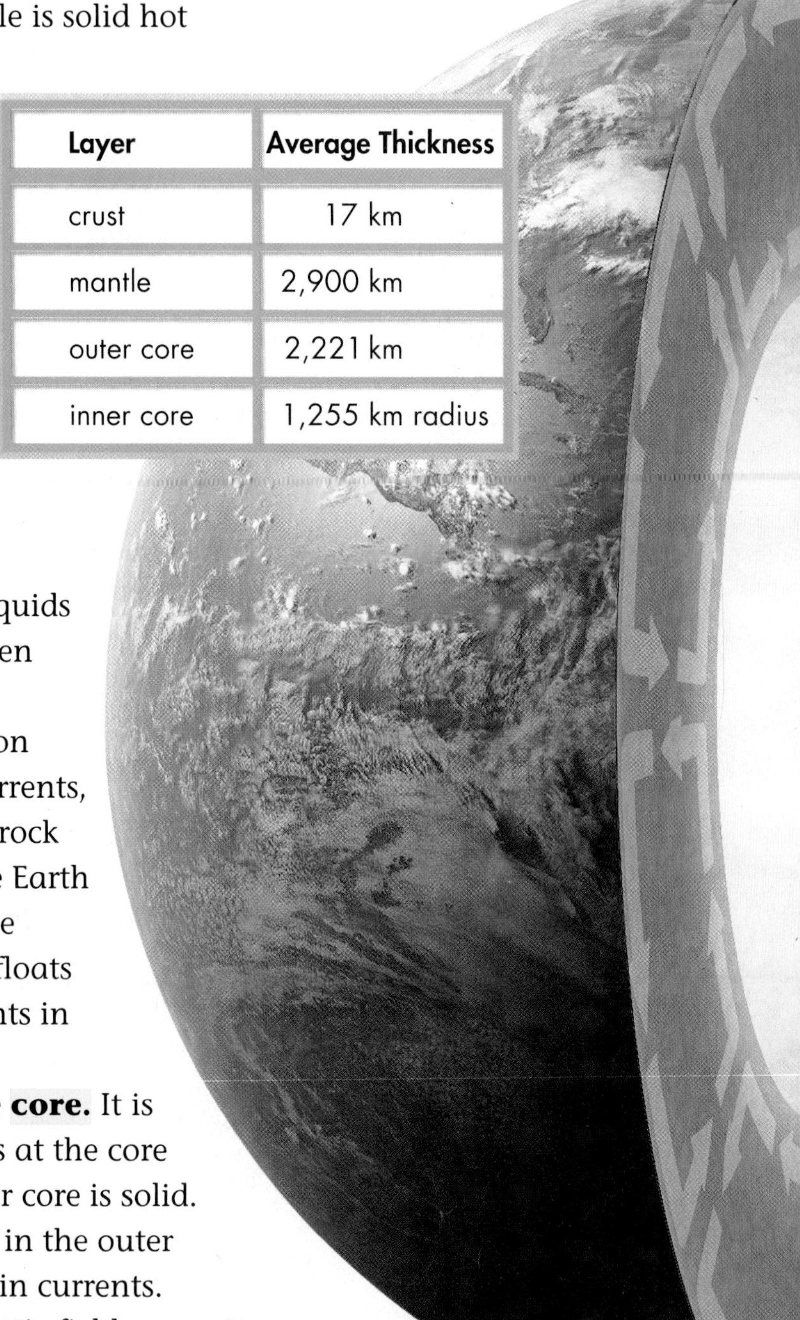

At the very center of Earth is the **core.** It is made mostly of iron. Temperatures at the core can be as hot as 7,000°C. The inner core is solid. The outer core is liquid. The liquid in the outer core is not stationary. It is flowing in currents. These currents make Earth's magnetic field.

Scientists cannot go to the mantle or core to study them. These layers are too deep for that. Scientists learn about Earth's layers in other ways. One way is by studying mantle material that is pushed up through cracks in the crust. This happens in some places in the deep ocean floor.

Material in the mantle flows in convection currents. There is some debate about the exact shape of these currents.

A second way scientists study Earth's layers is by measuring different kinds of vibrations from earthquakes. Some earthquake vibrations move all the way through Earth. These vibrations change speed and direction as they go into different layers. Some vibrations are stopped simply because the outer core is a liquid. By carefully studying the vibrations coming from earthquakes around the world, scientists can learn the depth of each layer and other properties of the layers.

An instrument called a seismograph records earthquake waves. These sensitive instruments can detect earthquakes from the other side of the world. A seismograph is firmly attached to the rock of the crust. Earthquake vibrations cause masses or weights in a seismograph to move. These movements are accurately recorded in a way similar to how a computer stores information.

A third way scientists learn about the mantle and core is by laboratory experiments. Materials that are thought to be inside Earth are tested to see how they respond to the kind of heat and pressure that would be found deep below Earth's surface.

Seismographs like this one were once used to detect vibrations from earthquakes.

√ Lesson Checkpoint

1. How does the mantle material get energy to move in convection currents?
2. Make a diagram of Earth's layers. On the diagram, label and describe the crust, mantle, inner core, outer core, and lithosphere.
3. How are earthquake vibrations used to study Earth's layers?
4. **Summarize** the main idea of this lesson. Include three details.

Lesson 2

What causes earthquakes and volcanoes?

You don't notice it, but Earth's crust is moving all the time. Parts of the crust slowly move into, under, or away from each other.

Earth's Plates

The lithosphere covers all of Earth like a thin shell, but it is not a solid sheet of material. It is broken up into several large sections and many smaller ones. A section of the lithosphere is called a **plate.** Several plates are larger than continents. A plate may include continents, parts of the ocean floor, or both. The edges of the plates are called plate boundaries. Plates meet each other at these boundaries.

Earth's plates are slowly moving. As the plates move, they might move into each other, pull apart from each other, or grind past each other. Their movement is small—sometimes slower than 1 centimeter per year, but sometimes as fast as 24 centimeters per year. Even so, these movements can cause big changes to Earth's surface. Some of these changes occur slowly over very long periods of time. These changes include mountains being built and valleys being formed. Some changes happen quickly during earthquakes.

Rift valleys between spreading plates can be seen in Iceland and at the bottom of the ocean. New crust is made as plates spread apart.

As an ocean plate moves below another plate, a deep-sea trench forms.

Patterns of where earthquakes strike, mountains form, and volcanoes erupt generally follow the patterns of where plates meet both on land and under the ocean.

Why do the plates move? In the diagram below you can see that much of the ocean plate is going down into the mantle. When gravity pulls down on this part of the plate, the rest of the plate is pulled along with it. Another reason plates move is that convection currents in the mantle push and pull on the plates.

There are three basic kinds of plate boundaries. At a converging boundary, two plates collide. Mountains are made when the crust folds, tilts, and lifts as a result of this meeting of plates.

A spreading plate boundary may form when plates move apart from each other. A spreading plate boundary is found in the Atlantic Ocean. The ocean floor appears like a mountain range at the edges of the plates. It is known as the mid-Atlantic ridge. The low area between the plates is a rift valley. As the plates continue to spread, the ocean is slowly becoming wider.

At a sliding plate boundary, two plates move past each other in opposite directions. An example of this is in California. Part of the coastline is on a plate moving southward. The other part is on a plate moving northward.

Mountains build where plates collide.

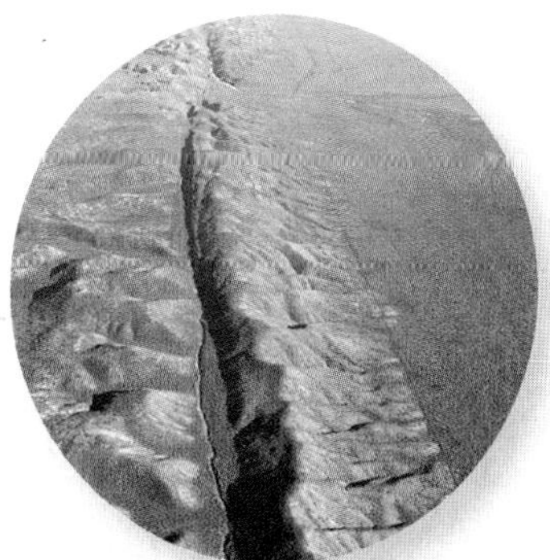

A sliding plate boundary can be easily seen in some places in California.

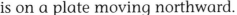

1. **Checkpoint** How do mountains form at plate boundaries?
2. **Art in Science** Create and label a model of the ocean floor. Include the continental shelf, slope, and rise. Also include ridges, rifts, and trenches.

Earthquakes

Many forces and processes change the surface of Earth. Constructive forces and processes build new features on Earth's surface. For example, new mountains form because of the bending and folding of colliding plates. Destructive forces and processes wear away or tear down features. One of the most dramatic destructive processes happens during an earthquake.

Most earthquakes happen at faults. Faults are cracks in Earth's crust where the surrounding rock has moved or shifted. Faults can form in many ways just about anywhere.

Earthquakes most often occur at faults that are along plate boundaries. Instead of moving smoothly, the plates get "hung up"—they lock in place. Eventually the plates jerk into a new position. This sudden movement and the vibrations it causes are what people feel as an earthquake. Plate movements usually happen far below ground. The place where the plates start to slip is called a focus. The place on Earth's surface above a focus is called an epicenter.

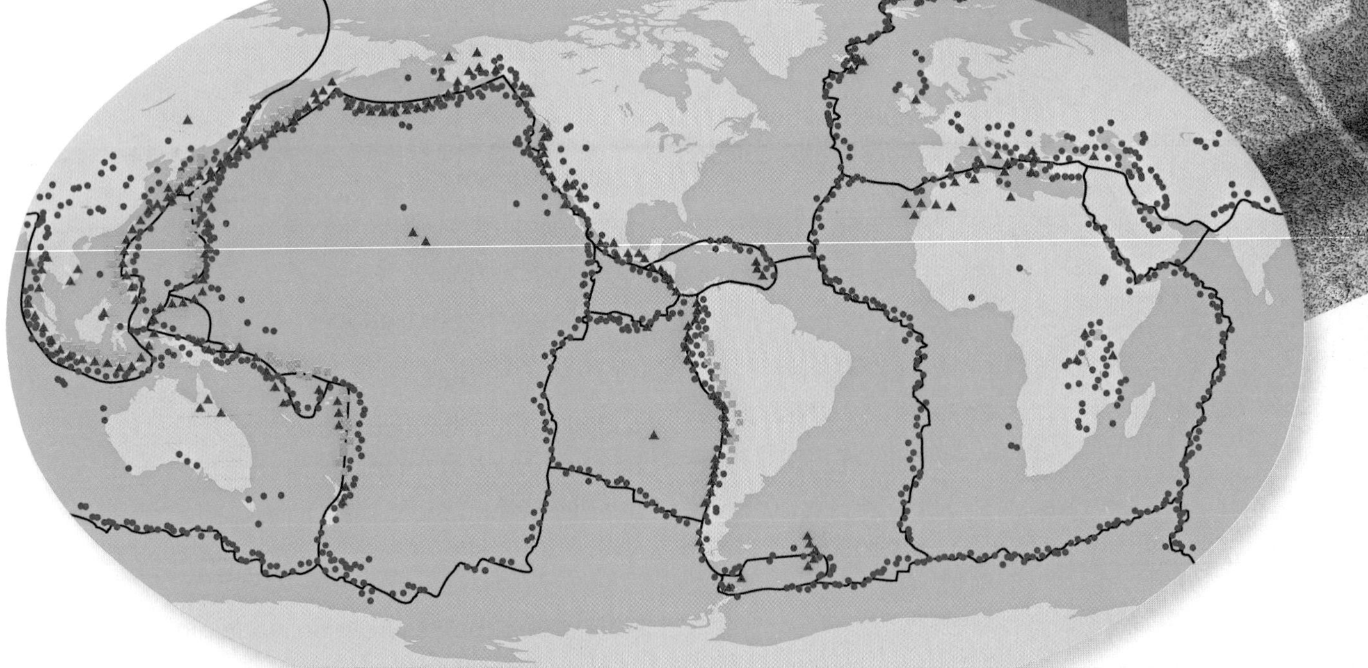

● Shallow Earthquake Areas
■ Deep Earthquake Areas
▲ Formed Volcanoes
— Plate Boundaries

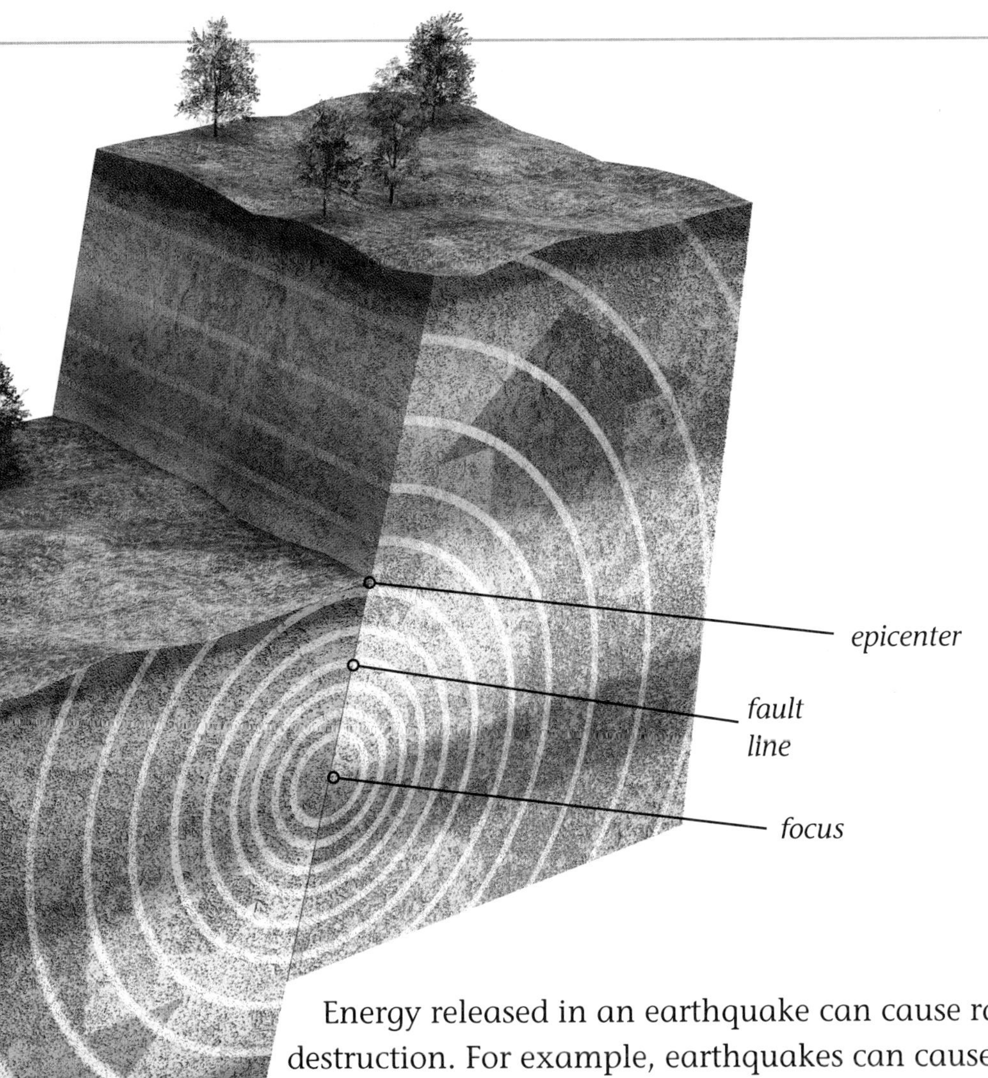
epicenter
fault line
focus

Earthquakes can cause landslides where soil and rock move down a hill. Landslides can happen for other reasons too.

An earthquake can cause sections of road to be cracked, twisted, or completely destroyed.

Energy released in an earthquake can cause rapid destruction. For example, earthquakes can cause landslides. A landslide is the downhill movement of large masses of rock and soil. Landslides can cover entire neighborhoods.

Most injuries in earthquakes occur because buildings become damaged. To prevent these injuries, buildings are being improved in many ways. Sometimes steel cables and bars are added to make a building stronger. Sometimes buildings are designed to be flexible. Flexible buildings move with the earthquake and stay standing.

Earthquakes under the ocean can lead to tsunamis. Tsunamis are waves that can be large enough to cause destruction when they crash into a coastline.

1. ✓ **Checkpoint** How are earthquakes, landslides, tsunamis, and plates all related?
2. **Social Studies in Science** Research two major earthquakes that have occurred in cities. Compare how each city and its people were affected by the events.

Volcanoes

Most volcanoes form near colliding plate boundaries. As one plate moves below another plate, rock partially melts to make magma. Sometimes the magma is forced to the surface through a weak spot in the crust. Have you seen pictures of lava erupting from a volcano at night? Such a sight can be more amazing than fireworks.

Volcanoes can do more than ooze fountains of lava. Gases such as water vapor and carbon dioxide are often mixed with the lava. Trapped gases can have enough pressure to blow apart the side of a volcano in a moment. These trapped gases can push lava high into the air. While it is still in the air, this lava may cool into ash or rocks.

Volcanoes can also build from the ocean floor. A volcanic island forms when a volcano reaches the surface of the water. The state of Hawaii is a string of islands formed in this way. This is an example of why volcanoes are sometimes considered a constructive process.

If a volcano produces only layers of lava, the volcano will have gently-sloped sides.

✓ Lesson Checkpoint

1. Name and describe the three types of plate boundaries.
2. How do volcanoes and volcanic islands form?
3. Use the Internet or library resources to write a report about how to be safe during an earthquake. Include in your report how technologies make buildings more safe to be in during an earthquake.
4. **Writing in Science** **Descriptive** In your **science journal,** write a news story about a famous earthquake or volcanic eruption. Include as many details as possible about the event, including some background about what causes earthquakes or volcanoes.

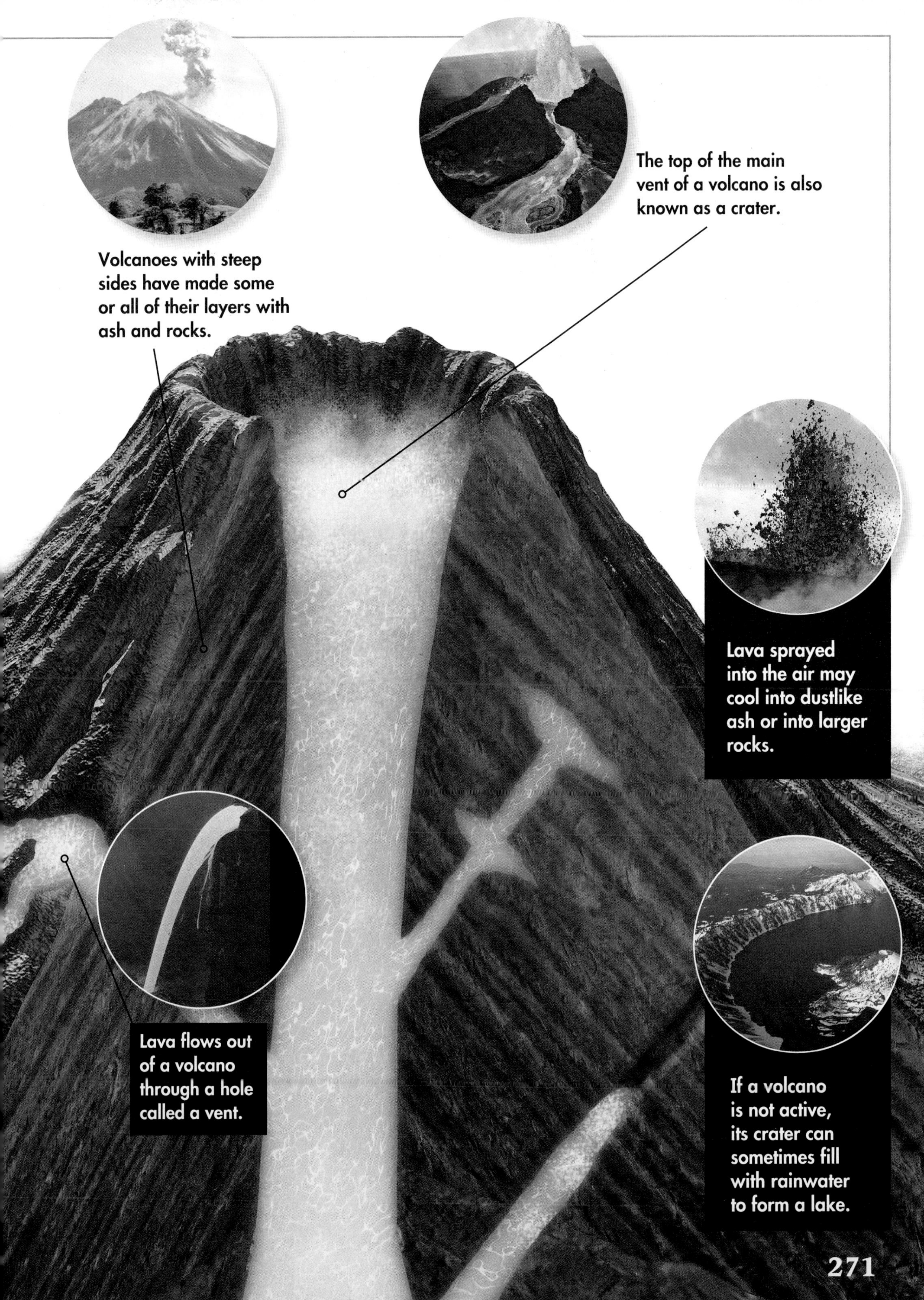
The top of the main vent of a volcano is also known as a crater.
Volcanoes with steep sides have made some or all of their layers with ash and rocks.
Lava sprayed into the air may cool into dustlike ash or into larger rocks.
Lava flows out of a volcano through a hole called a vent.
If a volcano is not active, its crater can sometimes fill with rainwater to form a lake.

Lesson 3

What is weathering?

From the tiniest insect to the most enormous glacier, many factors can cause changes in Earth's surface.

Weathering

Weathering is a slow, destructive process that breaks rocks into smaller pieces called sediments. What happens if you squeeze a piece of gravel in your hand as hard as you can? No matter how hard you squeeze your hand, the rock stays the same. But forces in nature are changing rock all the time. There are two types of weathering. **Mechanical weathering** is the breaking of rock into smaller pieces by forces due to gravity, ice, plant roots, or other forces. **Chemical weathering** is the changing of materials in a rock by chemical processes.

Mechanical Weathering

When water freezes, it expands. When water freezes in the cracks of rocks, it expands and forces the rock to split. This kind of mechanical weathering is called ice wedging. In what parts of the world do you think ice wedging is an important kind of weathering?

Changes in pressure can cause rocks to break. When wind or water remove large amounts of dirt from a mountainside, the rocks in the mountain are under less pressure. The rocks then slowly expand at different rates. This can cause cracks to form in the rock. Water can move into the cracks and freeze. As the cracks become larger, gravity pulls pieces of rock to the bottom of the slope.

Mechanical weathering of different rocks happens at different rates. The rate depends on the type of materials in the rock and the conditions around it. For example, plant roots can grow into cracks of a rock. As the roots grow, they push the rock apart. This kind of weathering will happen faster in warm, wet conditions in which plant roots grow very fast. Roots break soft rocks like sandstone more quickly than they break hard rocks like granite.

This rock is being split by ice wedging.

These cracks were formed by changes in pressure.

Tree roots can grow in cracks of rocks and break the rocks.

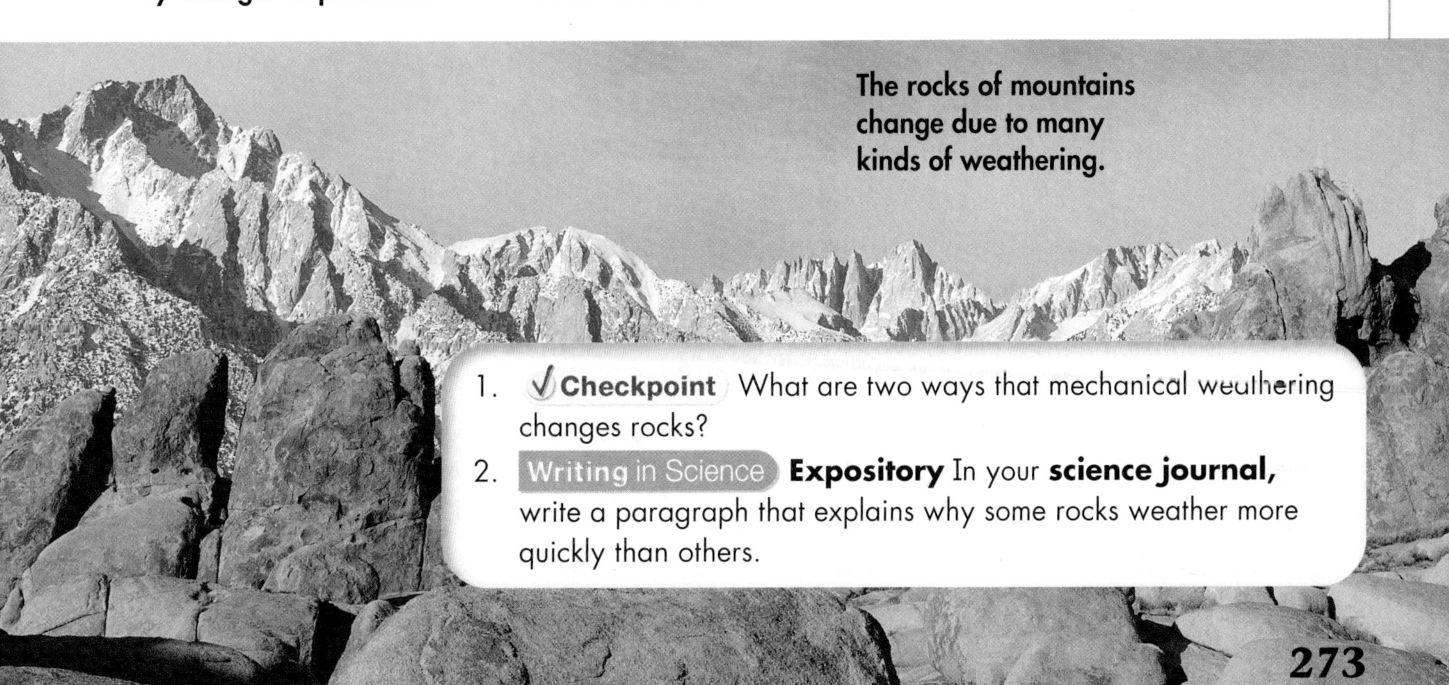
The rocks of mountains change due to many kinds of weathering.

1. **Checkpoint** What are two ways that mechanical weathering changes rocks?
2. Writing in Science **Expository** In your **science journal,** write a paragraph that explains why some rocks weather more quickly than others.

Chemical Weathering

Rocks are also broken down by the actions of chemicals during chemical weathering. Raindrops absorb carbon dioxide from the air. This makes a chemical called carbonic acid. This chemical can dissolve some types of rock. When the rain soaks down to the rock, the chemical in the water dissolves parts of the rocks. Caves can form. In other kinds of chemical weathering, fungi and other organisms give off chemicals that change some kinds of rocks.

Some rocks are affected by chemical weathering faster than others. Limestone weathers more quickly than granite. What kinds of climates would you think cause chemical weathering to happen the fastest? Since water is a large part of chemical weathering, areas with much rain will have more chemical weathering than deserts.

Parts of Soil
The exact make-up of soil greatly varies from place to place. The circle graph below shows a good soil make-up for growing plants.

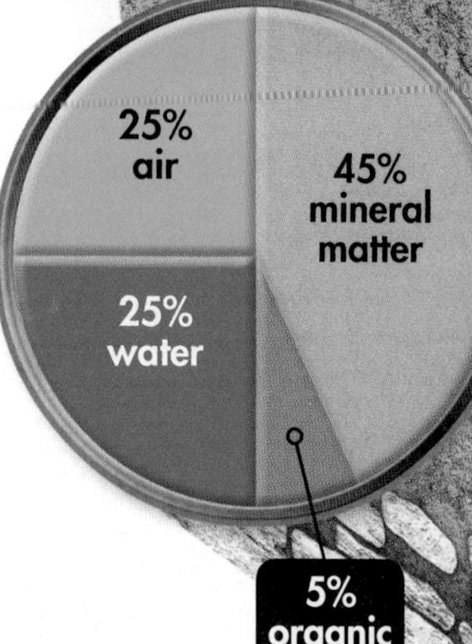
25% air
45% mineral matter
25% water
5% organic matter

Soil

Mechanical weathering and chemical weathering help make soil. Soil is usually a mixture of sediments from weathered rocks, decayed material from organisms, gases from air, and water.

There are many kinds of soil. The color of soil might be red, brown, black, or gray. The color depends on what kinds of materials are in the soil. The size of the sediments in the soil determines the soil's texture and its ability to hold water. Soils with very small sediments, such as clay, feel smooth and do not let water pass through easily. Sand particles are larger than clay particles. Sandy soils are gritty and let water pass easily. Most plants grow best in soils with large amounts of decayed matter.

Topsoil

Topsoil is the top layer of soil. It has a large amount of decayed material from plants, animals, bacteria, and other organisms. All these decayed materials make this soil very fertile.

Subsoil

The second layer of soil is called subsoil. It is often a different color than topsoil. Subsoil contains many minerals but less decayed matter than the topsoil. Why do you think there is less decayed matter in subsoil?

Bedrock

Bedrock is nearly solid rock that lies under the surface. It is deeper in some places than in others. Water may seep into cracks in bedrock and slowly weather it into smaller rocks. Eventually, bedrock may become sediments in soil.

This stone monument survived almost unchanged for centuries in the dry deserts of Egypt. When it was brought to the wetter climate of London, it quickly became weathered.

√ Lesson Checkpoint

1. How are mechanical and chemical weathering alike? How are they different?
2. Two identical statues are placed outside. One is made of limestone and one is made of granite. Which statue will weather more slowly?
3. Describe the layers of soil and how soil is made.
4. **Technology** in Science Use the Internet to research different kinds of soils. Compare their color, texture, ability to hold water, and ability to support the growth of plants.

Lesson 4

What is erosion?

Whenever water moves—in rivers, streams, oceans, even in rain—it transports particles from one place to another.

Erosion and Deposition

Erosion is the movement of materials away from one place. Erosion is a destructive process. Deposition is the placing of the materials in a new place. Deposition is a constructive process. Together, erosion and deposition result in sand dunes, valleys, and deltas.

Gravity is the main force causing erosion. A landslide is one kind of erosion. In a landslide, gravity quickly pulls rocks and dirt downhill. This happens during earthquakes, after heavy rains, or at other times. Landslides are more likely to happen on steep slopes with no trees. Tree roots help hold the soil in place.

Gravity also causes rivers to flow. As rivers flow downhill, they pick up and carry sediments. The sediments can wear away, or erode, the riverbeds. The faster a river flows, the more sediments it can carry and the heavier those sediments can be. Fast rivers may erode the land to form deep canyons.

Water does not have to be part of a river in order to erode. Ocean currents can erode deep valleys in the continental shelf, called submarine canyons. Rainwater flowing over bare farm fields can move tons of soil downhill. The steeper the field, the more soil can be lost. This is why farmers plow across fields. The furrows made by the plow catch rainwater, keeping the rain from carrying soil away.

Rivers can make deep canyons by erosion.

A satellite photo of the Mississippi delta

As a glacier moves down a hill, it moves sediment, eroding the hill.

When flowing water loses speed, it loses some of its ability to carry sediment. Some of the sediment is deposited. This happens when a river comes to the bottom of a hill or to an ocean or a lake. Deposits of sediment cause a problem when the lake is a reservoir behind a dam. These sediments need to be dug out from behind the dam.

A river flows much more slowly when it meets an ocean. As the river begins to slow down, the larger pieces of sediment are the first to be deposited. These deposits slowly create a delta. As the delta gets larger, the river forms branches, giving the delta its distinctive shape.

Water frozen in glaciers can cause erosion. Gravity pulls glaciers down along a valley. As this happens, glaciers grind rocks beneath them into sediments. Sediments are then moved downhill by the glacier. Over a long time, the action of glaciers can make the bottom of a valley more U-shaped.

1. **√Checkpoint** Suppose sand, gravel, and clay are being carried by a river. As the water enters a lake and slows down, in what order will these sediments settle out of the water? Explain why they settle out in this order.
2. **Writing in Science** **Narrative** In your **science journal,** write a story in which you are a scientist exploring a group of ancient stone buildings. In your story, describe how the buildings have been weathered and eroded.

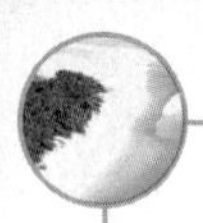

Wave Erosion

The constant action of waves is a major source of erosion and deposition along coastlines. As the waves from storms or the tides hit against rocks, the rocks can break. Sand and gravel in the waves act like sandpaper, wearing down the rocks even more. This is how some of the sand on beaches is made.

Not all parts of a shoreline are eroded at equal rates. Harbors and inlets may form as some areas erode more quickly than others. Harbors are areas that are protected from ocean waves. Waves make caves when parts of a cliff erode more quickly than other parts of the cliff.

Most waves hit a beach at an angle. This creates a current of water along the shore that constantly pushes sand to form many kinds of features. A sandy peninsula is called a spit. A baymouth bar is similar to a spit but forms all the way across a bay. The enclosed area is called a lagoon. Sandy islands called barrier islands can form along coastlines. Barrier islands can be slowly moved by erosion.

When people build cement barriers across beaches, they stop this movement of sand to nearby beaches. This causes those nearby beaches to get smaller. City and state governments will sometimes pay to have sand dug from the ocean floor just offshore and then put on beaches. This repairs erosion damage on the beaches due to storms, tides, and currents.

1. **√Checkpoint** Describe how waves, currents, tides, and storms affect the geological features of the ocean shore (beaches, barrier islands, inlets, and harbors).
2. **Technology** in Science Use the Internet to find a map or photograph of a coastline that shows spits, barrier islands, or other features discussed in this lesson. Print the map or photograph and label the features you see.

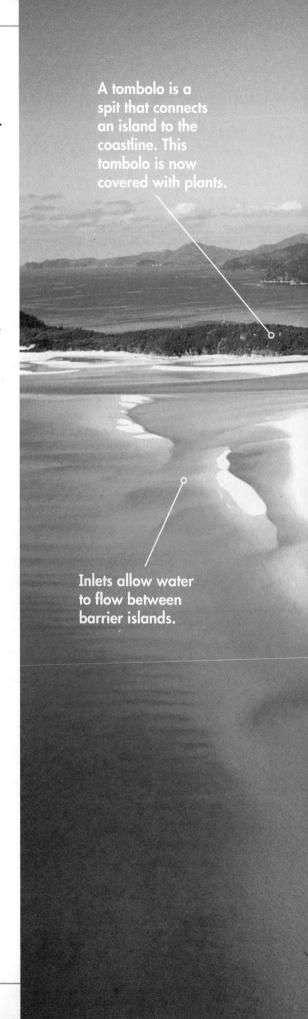

A tombolo is a spit that connects an island to the coastline. This tombolo is now covered with plants.

Inlets allow water to flow between barrier islands.

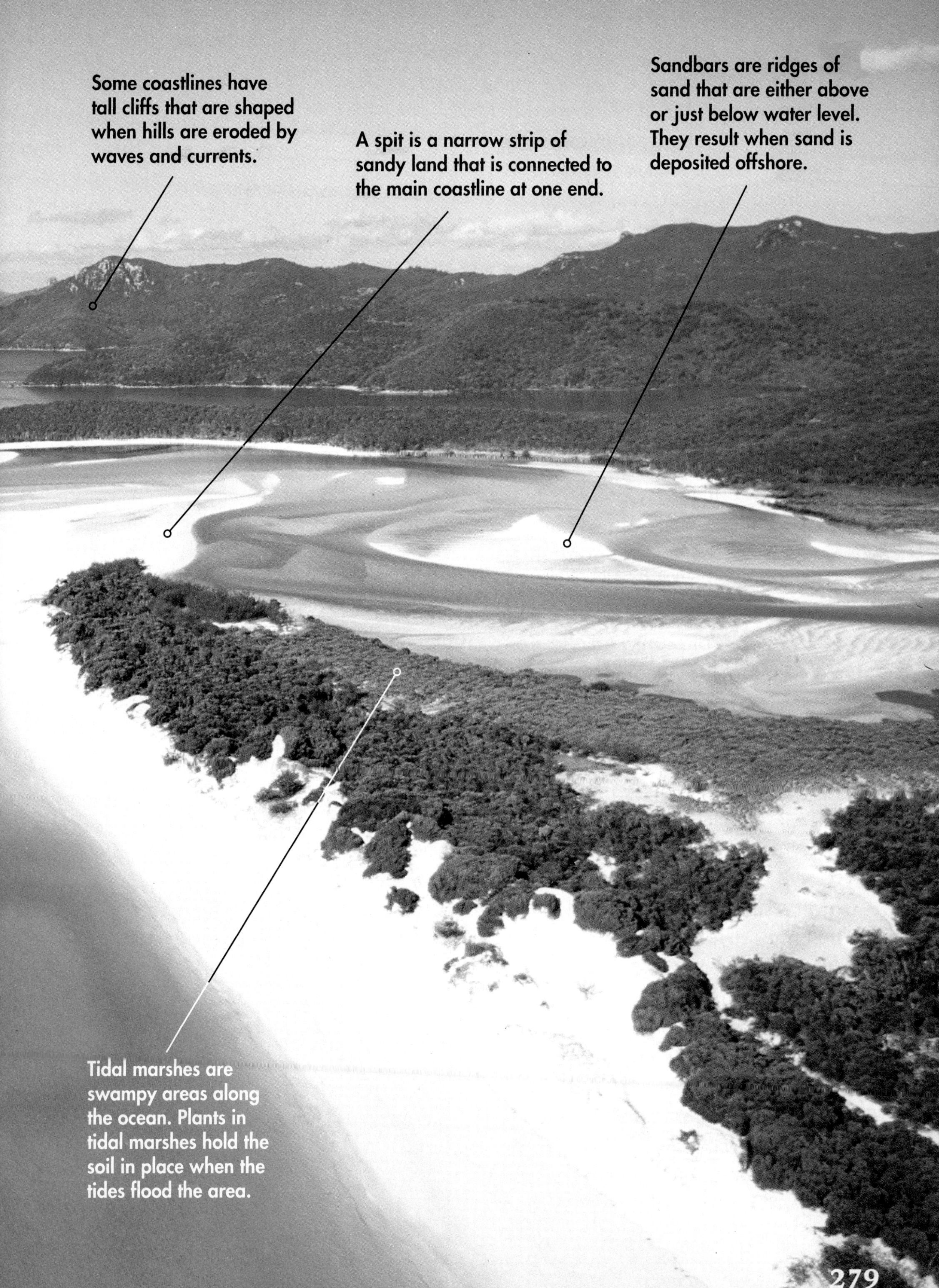
Some coastlines have tall cliffs that are shaped when hills are eroded by waves and currents.
A spit is a narrow strip of sandy land that is connected to the main coastline at one end.
Sandbars are ridges of sand that are either above or just below water level. They result when sand is deposited offshore.
Tidal marshes are swampy areas along the ocean. Plants in tidal marshes hold the soil in place when the tides flood the area.

Wind Erosion

Wind erosion is caused by wind blowing dust, soil, or sand from one place to another. When sand and dust blow against a rock, tiny bits of the rock might break off. These bits are immediately blown away. That is erosion. Sometimes, the wind can make fantastic rock formations such as arches and towers in this way.

Sand Dunes

Sand dunes are large, loose deposits of sand. Not all sand dunes look the same. The size and shape of a sand dune depends on the winds that are blowing, the amount of sand available, and the number of plants that grow in the area.

Winds that blow in a steady direction can move a dune. Such a wind will consistently pick up sand from one side and deposit it on the other side. This causes the entire dune to slowly move in the same direction the wind moves.

Notice that one side of a sand dune is steeper than the other side. Wind pushes sand up one side, making it bounce close to the ground. After the sand goes over the edge of the dune's top, the wind cannot reach it anymore. The sand piles up just over the top of the dune until gravity pulls it down. This creates a steeper slope than the slope that faces the wind.

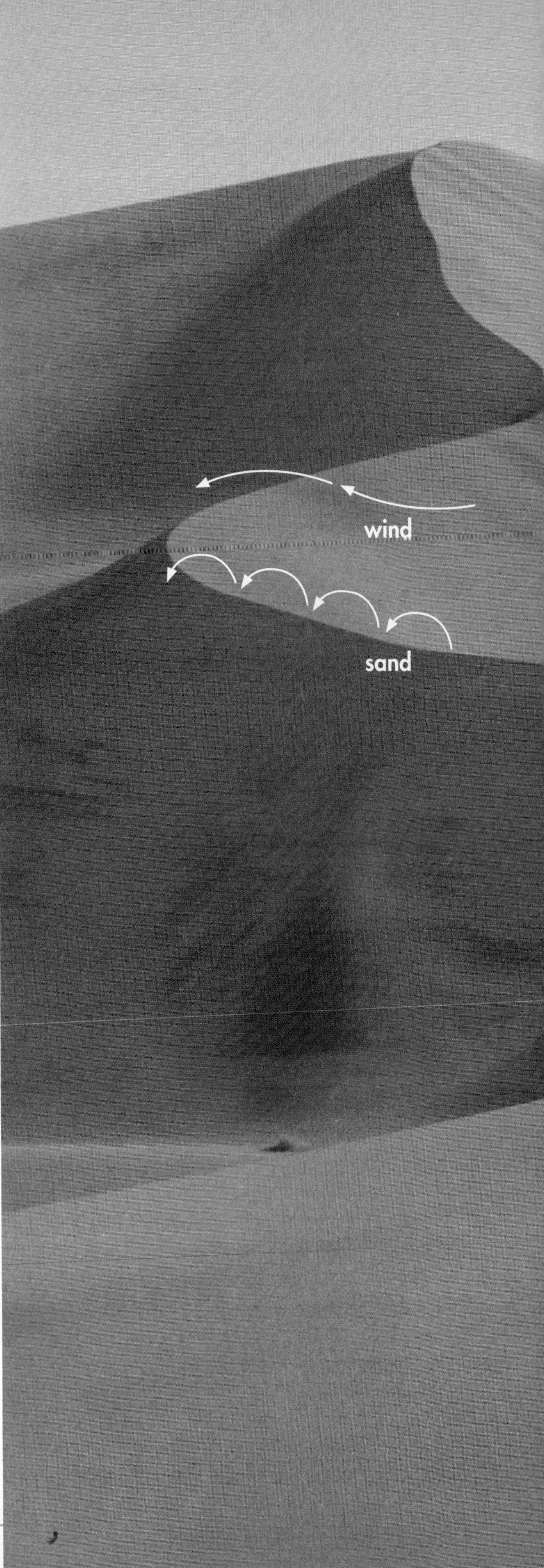
wind
sand

Field Erosion

Winds do not only cause erosion in deserts. Wind erosion can be a serious problem on farms as well. If bare, plowed fields become very dry, winds can blow topsoil off the fields. This topsoil is the best kind of soil for growing crops. It cannot be quickly replaced.

Farmers do many things to prevent wind erosion of topsoil. They often plant rows of tall trees along the edges of fields. This keeps some of the wind from blowing on the field. Some farmers are able to grow their crops with less plowing. In this way, the soil stays in larger clumps that do not get blown away.

Wind erosion made the edges of these rocks rounded.

Trees at the edge of fields reduce wind erosion by slowing the wind.

√ Lesson Checkpoint

1. Define erosion, and tell how gravity works with water, ice, and wind to cause erosion.
2. How does a delta form?
3. How do sand dunes form? Why is one side of a dune different than the other side?
4. **Writing in Science** **Expository** Staple several sheets of paper together to make a booklet. In this booklet, write an *Encyclopedia of Erosion.* Write encyclopedia entries for ideas you found in this lesson. Be sure to put your entries in alphabetical order.

Lesson 5

How are minerals identified?

If you hold a mineral in your hand, what can you tell about it? Is it smooth, shiny, rough, dull? Does it have a certain color or smell? You can identify a mineral by describing its characteristics.

Properties of Minerals

"Mineral" is a word that is used in different ways. There are minerals in your breakfast cereal that you need for good health. But to a scientist who studies Earth's layers, a mineral is defined as a naturally occurring solid that has a regular arrangement of particles in it. Minerals are found in soil and rocks. Although there are many different minerals, only a few dozen make up most of the rocks on Earth.

Properties of minerals are shown in the pictures on these pages. Many of these properties are used to identify a mineral. Some minerals can be identified by the way they smell. A mineral may give off a sour, sweet, earthy, or rotten egg smell. Some minerals make tiny bubbles when they touch chemicals called acids.

Hardness

Some minerals are harder than others. The Mohs scale is used to tell how hard a mineral is. The scale rates the hardness of minerals from 1 to 10. Talc has a hardness of 1. Diamonds are the hardest minerals. They have a hardness of 10. An uncut diamond is shown below.

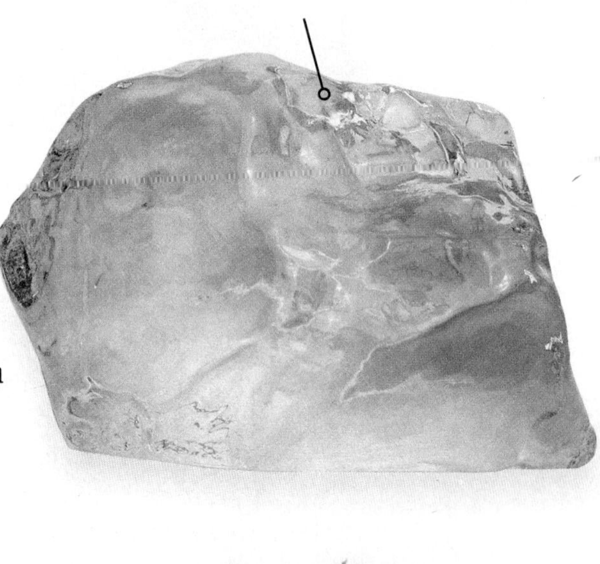

Magnetism

A few minerals have magnetic properties. Pyrrhotite and magnetite, pictured here with iron filings, are strongly magnetic.

Luster

Luster describes the way light is reflected by a mineral's surface. A glassy luster is shiny like glass. An earthy luster is chalky and dull. A metallic luster can look like polished metal. A soft shine can be described as a waxy, silky, or pearly luster. This hematite has a metallic luster.

Shape

The shape of a mineral is not always easy to see. But some minerals have a definite shape that is helpful for identification. This pyrite is shaped like cubes.

Streak

Streak is the color of a mineral in its powdered form. To see a mineral's streak, you rub it on a hard, rough, white surface. This produces a line of fine powder that is often a different color than the mineral's outside appearance. This streak is the streak of hematite.

Texture

The texture of a mineral describes the way it feels. Gritty minerals feel sandy. Waxy minerals have a smooth, sticky feel. Earthy minerals have a powdery texture. This opal has a smooth texture.

1. √ **Checkpoint** What properties are used to identify minerals?
2. **Health** in Science Find out which minerals are included in a healthy diet. Give examples of foods that have high amounts of each mineral.

Using Properties to Identify Minerals

In order to identify an unknown mineral, scientists will record many different observations. Then, they compare the observations with charts of known minerals. This often takes a large amount of training and patience. The chart on this page gives the names and properties of several minerals. Use this chart to identify the minerals shown on the opposite page.

Mineral	color	texture	smell	luster	hardness	shape	streak
Muscovite	colorless, light-colored	smooth	no	pearly	$2\frac{1}{2}$		white
Fluorite	colorless, pink, purple, green	smooth	no	glassy	4		white
Halite	colorless	smooth	no	glassy	$2\frac{1}{2}$		white
Calcite	white, colorless, pale colors	smooth	no	glassy	3		white
Quartz	clear-white	smooth	no	glassy	7		white
Pyrite	gold	smooth	no	metallic	6–7 (for crystals)		greenish black
Sulfur	pale to bright yellow	gritty	no	dull to glassy	$1\frac{1}{2}$ to $2\frac{1}{2}$		white to pale yellow
Talc	white, apple-green, gray	greasy	no	pearly	1		white
Arsenopyrite	brassy white or gray	gritty	garlic	metallic	$5\frac{1}{2}$ to 6		black

✓ Lesson Checkpoint

1. What is a mineral?
2. How is a mineral's streak determined?
3. **Technology in Science** Use the Internet to research the properties of a mineral. Make a poster that displays the information you find.

This mineral has a smooth texture, no smell, and a glassy luster. Its hardness is 4, and its streak is white.

This mineral has a smooth texture and a pearly luster. Its hardness is 2.5, and it forms sheets.

This mineral has a smooth texture, a hardness of 2.5, and leaves a white streak. Its luster is glassy.

This mineral has a smooth texture, a glassy luster, and a hardness of 3. Its streak is white.

This mineral has a smooth texture and a metallic luster. Its hardness is 6 to 7, and its streak is greenish black.

This mineral has a greasy texture and a pearly luster. Its hardness is 1, and it has a white streak.

This mineral has a gritty texture and dull to glassy luster. It has a white streak.

This mineral has a gritty texture and a metallic luster. It smells like garlic, has a hardness of 5.5 to 6, and it has a black streak.

This mineral has a smooth texture and a glassy luster. Its hardness is 7, and it has a white streak.

Lesson 6

How are rocks classified?

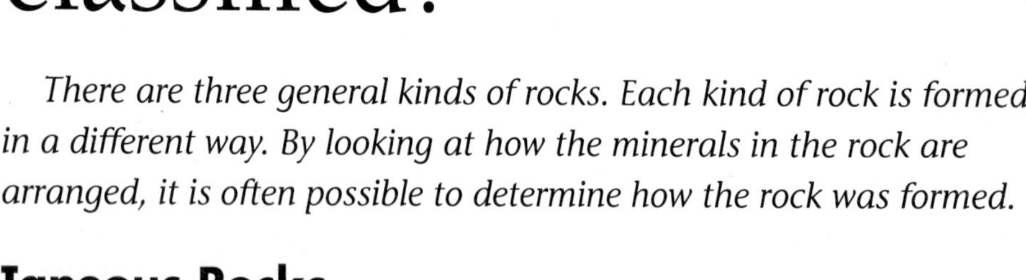

There are three general kinds of rocks. Each kind of rock is formed in a different way. By looking at how the minerals in the rock are arranged, it is often possible to determine how the rock was formed.

Basalt

Granite

Igneous Rocks

Igneous rocks are formed when melted rock cools and hardens. As hot, liquid rock cools, crystals of minerals form. Melted rock that cools slowly results in igneous rocks with large crystals of minerals. Melted rock that cools quickly results in igneous rocks with small crystals. Granite has large crystals. It forms when magma slowly cools underground.

Basalt is a commonly found dark green or black rock in the ocean crust. Basalt forms when lava is quickly cooled. Many islands are made of basalt. Would you expect basalt to have large or small crystals?

Pumice is a rock formed when lava is quickly cooled by air at the surface. It often has many tiny holes where gases were trapped in the lava as it cooled.

Sedimentary Rocks

Most **sedimentary** rocks form when layers of materials and rock particles settle on top of each other and then harden. Minerals may precipitate from water, acting like cement and holding the particles together. Gravel quarries and areas near beaches are good places to find sedimentary rocks.

Sandstone and conglomerate are examples of sedimentary rock. In the conglomerate shown here, you can see how particles have been pressed together. Some minerals have become like cement, holding the rock together. In the sandstone, individual layers of sand are clearly visible. Sandstone can form when layers of sand are buried and put under pressure.

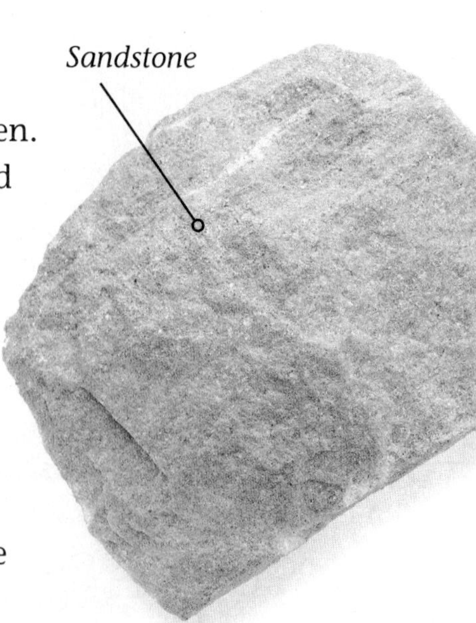

Sandstone

Plant and animal fossils are most often found in layers of sedimentary rock. When this happens, scientists try to identify the characteristics of the rock surrounding the fossil. They look at the size and shape of the sand grains. They also try to tell what minerals make up the sand grains. Such information can provide clues about the environment that was around when the organism was living.

Pumice

Metamorphic Rocks

When solid rock is squeezed and heated to very high temperatures, the particles inside the rock can take on different arrangements, changing the properties of the rock. New minerals may also be formed. When this happens, **metamorphic** rock is formed. Under very high pressure and high temperature, solid rock particles form rough layers, as seen in gneiss. At lower pressure, fine, thin layers are formed, as seen in slate.

Conglomerate

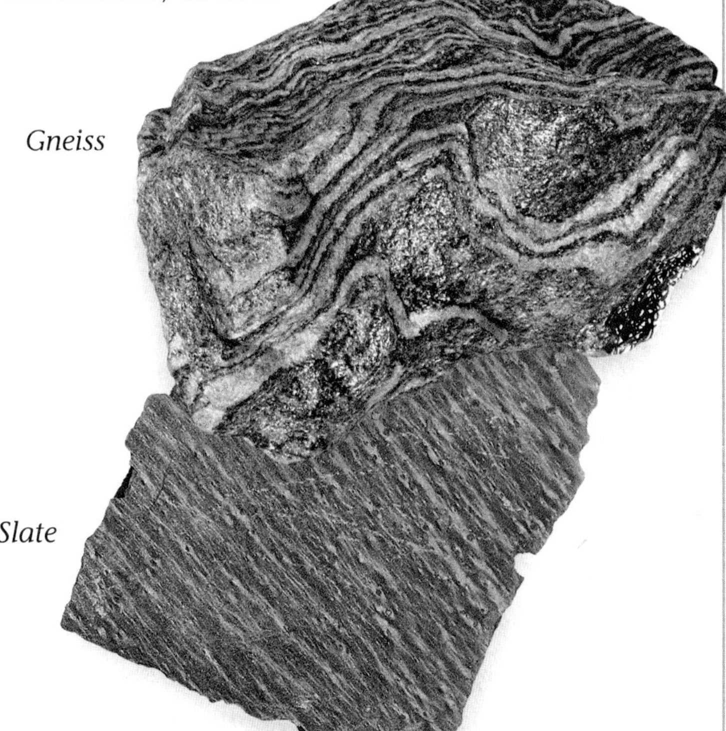

Gneiss

Slate

1. **✓Checkpoint** Why do some igneous rocks have larger crystals than others?
2. **Music in Science** Write a "rock" song that describes the differences between igneous, sedimentary, and metamorphic rocks. Be sure to include what rocks are made of and examples of each kind of rock.

The Rock Cycle

Rocks are constantly being formed and destroyed. An igneous rock that you hold in your hand today might become a metamorphic rock thousands of years in the future.

The rock cycle is not a one-way chain of events like the life cycle of a plant or animal. Rocks can change from one kind to another in any order, or stay the same for millions of years. The diagram on the next page shows the different ways that one type of rock can become another type of rock.

Relative Ages of Rocks

Rock layers are put down in the order in which they are formed. Therefore, the layers of rock at Earth's surface are younger than the rock layers below them. Over time, events may cause those layers to bend or even turn over. These processes include mountain building, earthquakes, and volcanic eruptions

Sediments usually form flat layers of rock. If a scientist sees bent, tilted, or broken layers of rock, it is assumed that something happened to move the layers after they were made.

Scientists who study fossils use the location of different fossils to determine their relative ages. Fossils found in upper rock layers are considered to be younger than fossils found in lower layers.

√ Lesson Checkpoint

1. Draw a diagram of the rock cycle. Label and describe each class of rock and the processes that form each.
2. What conditions are necessary in order for metamorphic rock to form?
3. How are sedimentary rock layers used by scientists to learn about the past?
4. **Summarize** List the four most important ideas you learned in this lesson.

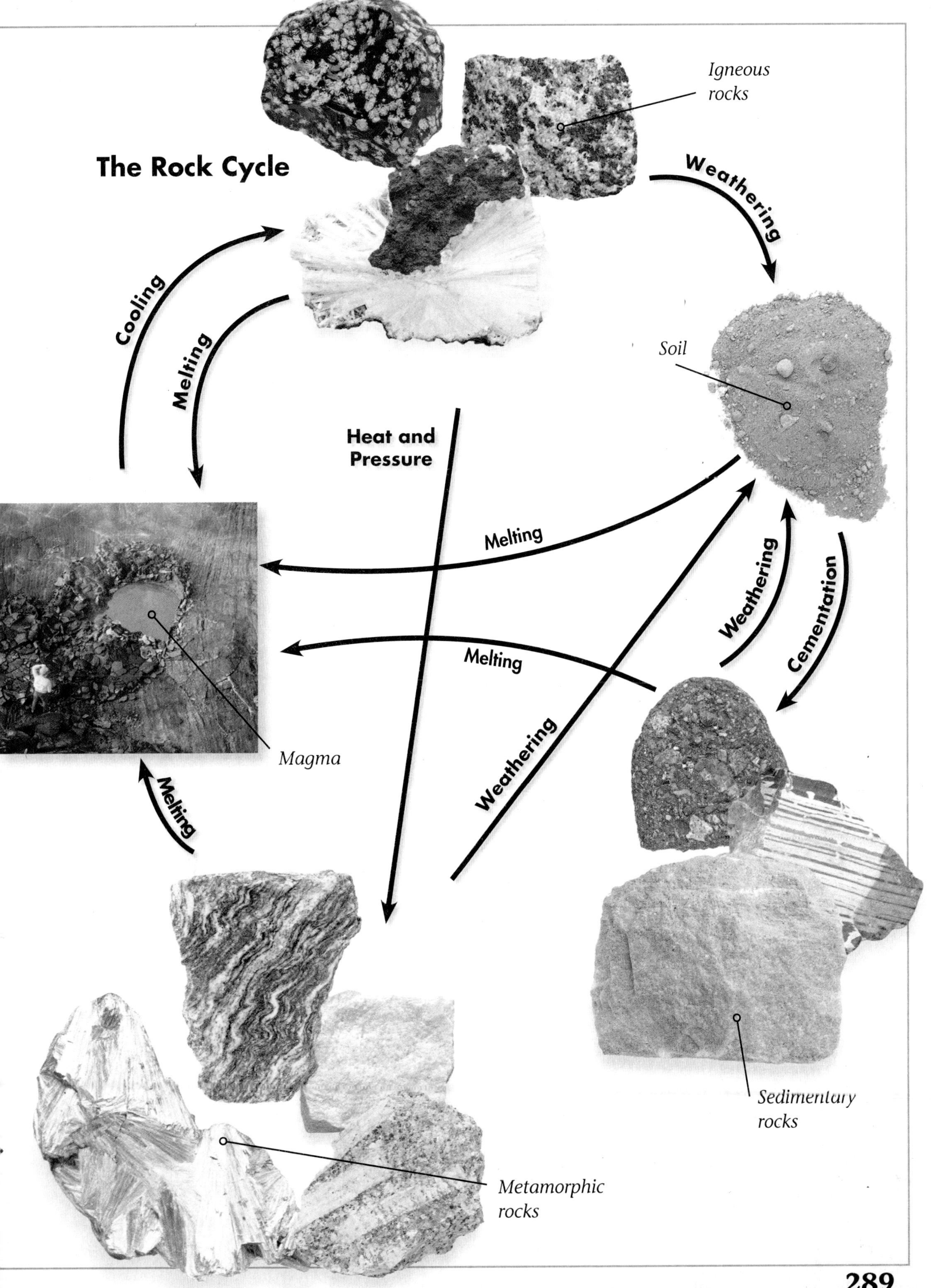
The Rock Cycle
Igneous rocks
Weathering
Soil
Cooling
Melting
Heat and Pressure
Melting
Weathering
Cementation
Melting
Magma
Weathering
Melting
Sedimentary rocks
Metamorphic rocks

Lab zone **Guided Inquiry**

Investigate What buildings are less damaged by an earthquake?

Some buildings survive sudden movement better than others. Scientists use **models** to help find good designs. Plan, design, and construct buildings to survive an earthquake. Test the prototypes you make. Your only building materials are sugar cubes.

Materials

40 to 50 sugar cubes

box (optional)

metric ruler (optional)

What to Do

1. Ask questions about what helps a building survive an earthquake.

Think of the models you build as prototypes for actual buildings.

upside-down box

2. Use 40 to 50 sugar cubes to design and build 4 different buildings.

Design a device to model an earthquake or use a device like this. If you use this idea, decide where and how hard to tap the box.

3. Test your buildings. Record your results. Repeat your test 2 more times.

Repeating a test can help make your results more reliable.

Process Skills

Asking questions can help you figure out what designs to build and test. **Making and using models** can help you answer those questions.

Describe or Draw Building	Results (toppled 1st, toppled 2nd, toppled 3rd, or toppled 4th)			Overall Results (best, 2nd best, 3rd best, worst)
	Trial 1	Trial 2	Trial 3	
Building A				
Building B				
Building C				
Building D				

Should the buildings be the same distance from the tapping spot? Why?

Are shorter buildings better? Are wider buildings better? Discuss your ideas with others.

Explain Your Results

1. Describe the device and procedure you used to test your buildings. Why did you repeat your test?
2. How were you limited in what you could build?
3. Look at your data in the chart. Look for patterns. Think about your **models.** What features might help a building to survive an earthquake?

Go Further

Replace the sugar cubes with buildings made of marshmallows connected with toothpicks. Are the results similar? Make a plan and change your model to answer this question or one of your own.

Math in Science

Classifying Solid Figures

Mineral crystals are often in the shape of familiar solid figures. Sometimes a crystal is a combination of two or more familiar shapes. This chart shows how some solid figures are classified.

Prisms

A prism has 2 congruent parallel bases and faces that are parallelograms.

Rectangular prism

Cube

Triangular prism

Pentagonal prism

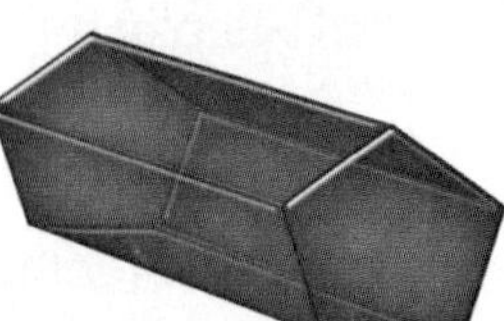

Hexagonal prism

Pyramids

A pyramid has a base that is a polygon. The faces are triangles that join at a point.

Rectangular pyramid

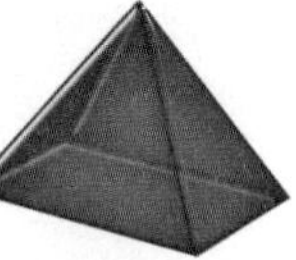

Square pyramid

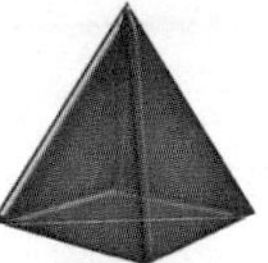

Triangular pyramid

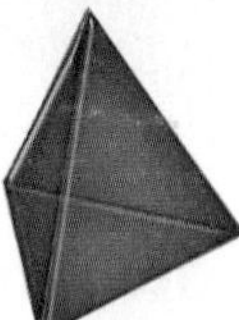

Pentagonal pyramid

Hexagonal pyramid

This crystal is almost a perfect cube.

This crystal has two pyramids and a prism.

Part of this crystal is a pyramid. The bottom part is a hexagonal prism.

Tell what solid shape or shapes you see in each picture.

1.

2.

3.

4. If a mineral had the shape of a cube with a pyramid at each end, what kind of pyramid would they be? Explain your answer.

Lab zone Take-Home Activity

Look for small rocks that have definite shapes of solid figures. Collect samples and glue them to a sheet of poster board. Under each, write a description of the solid shape or shapes that you see.

Chapter 9 Review and Test Prep

Use Vocabulary

chemical weathering (page 272)	**mechanical weathering** (page 272)
core (page 264)	**metamorphic** (page 287)
crust (page 263)	**plate** (page 266)
igneous (page 286)	**sedimentary** (page 286)
mantle (page 264)	

Use the term from the list above that best completes each sentence.

1. A process called _______ breaks down rock using chemical means.
2. When rocks are squeezed and heated at very high temperatures, they can be changed into _______rock.
3. The thinnest of Earth's layers is the ______.
4. Large sections of Earth's crust called _______ are constantly moving into, away from, and past each other.
5. The top part of Earth's _______, together with the crust, form the lithosphere.
6. A type of rock formed when particles are pressed and stuck together is _______.
7. Most of Earth's _______ is made of iron.
8. When magma cools and hardens, it forms _______ rock.
9. Ice, plant roots, wind, and temperature changes are causes of _______.

Explain Concepts

10. Explain how convection currents are caused and how they move material in the mantle and lithosphere.
11. Explain how Earth's surfaces are changed by both slow and fast changes (waves, weather, shifts in land, weathering, erosion, deposition, earthquakes, tsunamis, and volcanoes).

Process Skills

12. **Ask Questions** Suppose a friend calls you and says that she has found a very interesting mineral but does not know what it is. Write the 4 questions that you think would be most helpful to identify the mineral.
13. **Observe** and describe the rocks shown here. Use your observations to classify and identify the rocks.

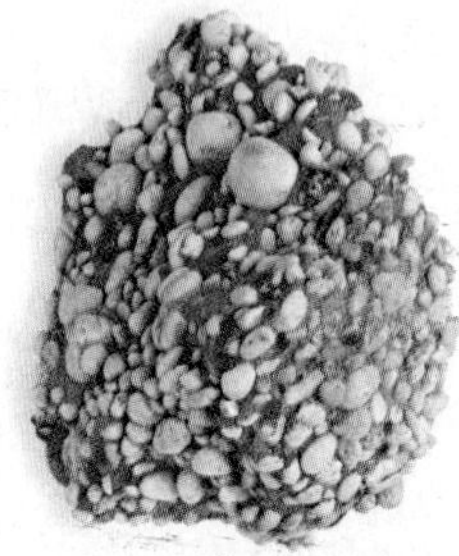

14. **Make a Model** Define constructive and destructive processes. Describe the features they cause. Make a model to show how these processes change the surface of the Earth.

15. **Predict** A mineral has a crystal pattern of particles as shown here. Copy and extend this pattern.

Summarize

16. How would you summarize this passage?

The top of the lithosphere is covered by the hydrosphere and atmosphere. The oceans, lakes, rivers, and ponds are some of the parts of the hydrosphere. The atmosphere is the layer of air that surrounds the planet. The hydrosphere covers most of the lithosphere.

Use a graphic organizer.

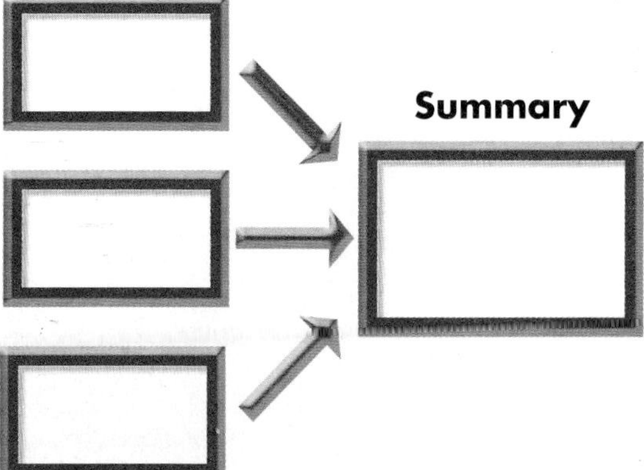
Details
Summary

Test Prep

Choose the letter that best completes the statement or answers the question.

17. Which of the following make up Earth's lithosphere?
    - Ⓐ the crust and the upper part of the mantle
    - Ⓑ the lower part of the mantle
    - Ⓒ the lower and upper parts of the mantle
    - Ⓓ the upper part of the crust

18. Which of the following are caused by colliding plates?
    - Ⓕ earthquakes and volcanoes
    - Ⓖ deltas and barrier islands
    - Ⓗ sand dunes and rock arches
    - Ⓘ rift valley and mid-Atlantic ridge

19. Explain why the answer you selected for Question 18 is best. For each of the answers you did not select, give a reason why it is not the best choice.

20. Writing in Science **Narrative** Write a short story that describes how an igneous rock becomes a sedimentary rock. Introduce the rock as Gertrude Granite or Basil Basalt. Describe what happens to Gertrude (or Basil) that causes it to turn into a sedimentary rock.

Biography

Florence Bascom

(1862–1945)

Although Dr. Bascom was the second woman in the United States to receive a Ph.D. in geology, she is considered by many to be "the first female geologist in this country."

Growing up in a time when girls and women were discouraged from pursuing a career in geology, Dr. Bascom worked to overcome the challenges she was faced with at the University of Wisconsin where she was enrolled. Even while working towards her doctorate degree at Johns Hopkins University, she had to attend graduate classes behind a screen so that male students would not know she was there.

Nevertheless, Dr. Bascom pursued her interest in geology and earned her doctorate degree in 1893. Florence Bascom spent much of her time studying the metamorphic rocks of the Piedmont Plateau. She is known today for her contributions to the current understanding of mountain-building processes.

Lab zone Take-Home Activity

Find the Piedmont Plateau on a map. What is the Piedmont Plateau? Draw a map to show its location in the United States.

EC NTL 10 9 8 7

Chapter 10

Protecting Earth's Resources

You Will Discover

- how nonrenewable fuels are used.
- how renewable energy sources can be used.
- what other important resources are.
- how people can conserve Earth's resources.

online
Student Edition
sfsuccessnet.com

Build Background

Why is it important to conserve Earth's resources?

resource

solar energy

hydroelectric

Chapter 10 Vocabulary

resource page 303

renewable resource page 303

nonrenewable resource page 303

fossil fuel page 303

solar energy page 306

hydroelectric page 310

geothermal page 312

biomass page 313

fossil fuel
nonrenewable resource

renewable resource

geothermal

biomass

Lab zone **Directed Inquiry**

Explore How does oil rise through the Earth?

Oil forms deep below Earth's surface. It moves upward through small pores in Earth's crust. **Make a model** of this process.

Materials

gloves

sponge

cup with oil

cup with warm water

hand lens

paper towels (for spills)

What to Do

1. Wear gloves. Put the sponge in the cup of oil and squeeze the sponge 3 times. Then hold the sponge over the cup and squeeze gently. There should be no droplets of oil on the sponge.

2. Place the sponge in the cup with warm water.

The oil represents the oil formed underground that rises toward Earth's surface.

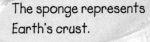

The sponge represents Earth's crust.

Be careful!

Wipe up spills immediately.

3. Wait 5 minutes. Can you see any droplets of oil? Use a hand lens. Can you smell oil on the sponge? Take off a glove. Touch the top of the sponge. Does it feel oily?

Process Skills

Making a model of a process, such as oil moving upward, can help you understand how the process occurs.

Explain Your Results

1. In your **model,** how did the oil get to the surface?
2. **Infer** Often, as oil rises, it becomes trapped in different places deep underground. How do you think people get this oil?

How to Read Science

Reading Skills

TARGET SKILL

Main Idea and Details

Learning to find **main ideas** and **details** can help you understand and remember what you read. Details can help you to **infer** the main idea of the article.

The main idea and the details are marked in the article below.

- Write down the main idea in your own words.
- Write down the details as sentences or as a list.

Science Article

Burning Fossil Fuels

The burning of fossil fuels, such as oil, gives off gases and smoke that make the air dirty. This can cause problems for people with asthma and other diseases. Air pollution can also cause acid rain, which harms buildings. It can make lake water unhealthy for plants and animals that live in the water.

Apply It!

Make a graphic organizer like the one shown below. List the **main idea and details** from the article in your organizer.

Main Idea

Detail   Detail   Detail

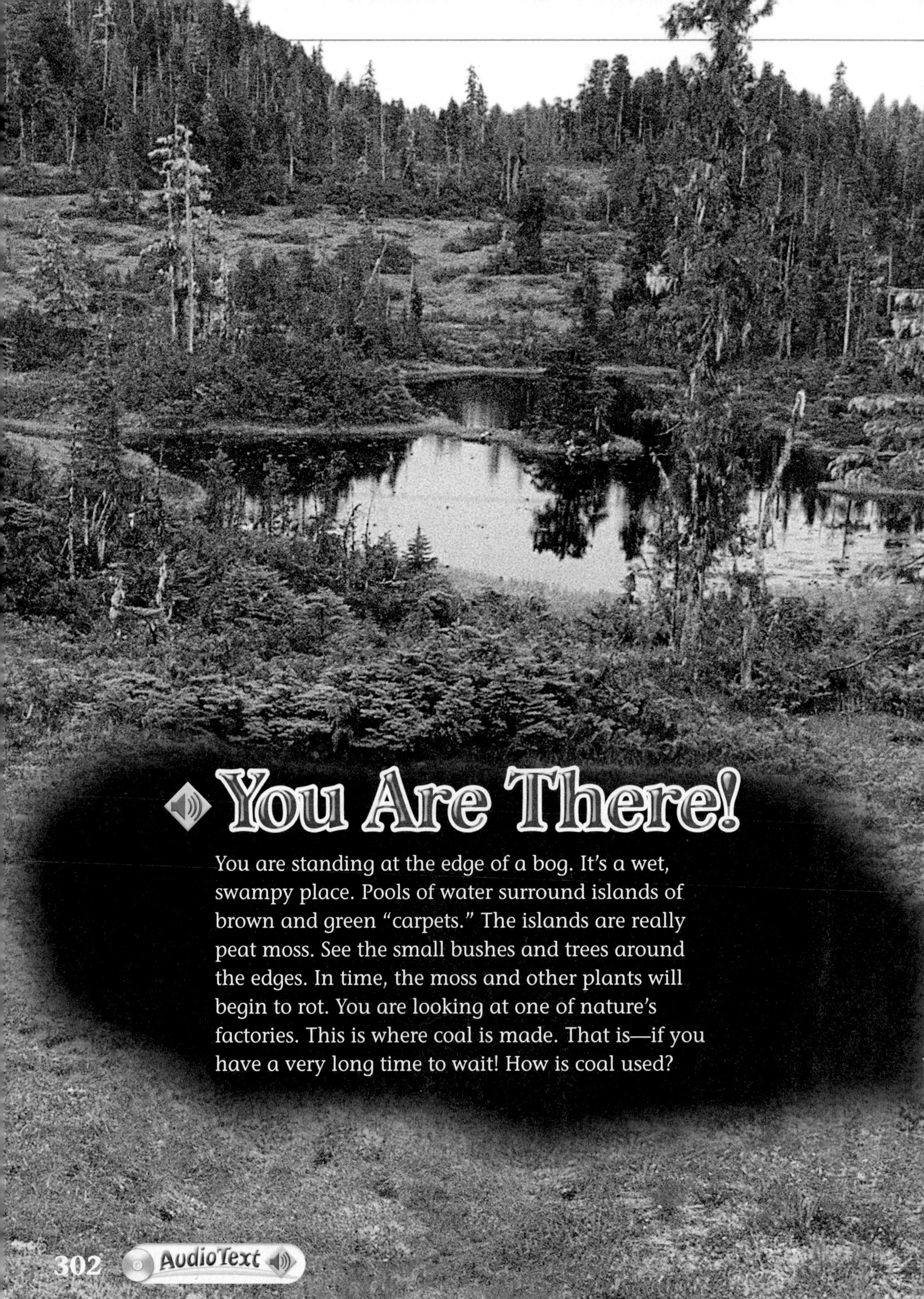

You Are There!

You are standing at the edge of a bog. It's a wet, swampy place. Pools of water surround islands of brown and green "carpets." The islands are really peat moss. See the small bushes and trees around the edges. In time, the moss and other plants will begin to rot. You are looking at one of nature's factories. This is where coal is made. That is—if you have a very long time to wait! How is coal used?

AudioText

Lesson 1

What are nonrenewable energy resources?

Plant life

Coal, oil, and gas are valuable sources of energy. However, the use of these resources can cause problems.

Types of Resources

A **resource** is a supply that will meet a need for materials or energy. A **renewable resource** is one that can be replaced. Trees are renewable resources. After cutting old trees, new ones can be grown. Other resources, such as coal or copper, are nonrenewable. A **nonrenewable resource** either cannot be replaced at all or cannot be replaced as fast as we use it.

Peat

Coal is a nonrenewable energy resource that forms from plants. Plants in swampy places use energy from sunlight to grow. Under certain conditions, layers of dead plants build up and form a material called peat. Peat gets buried and slowly changes into soft coal and then hard coal.

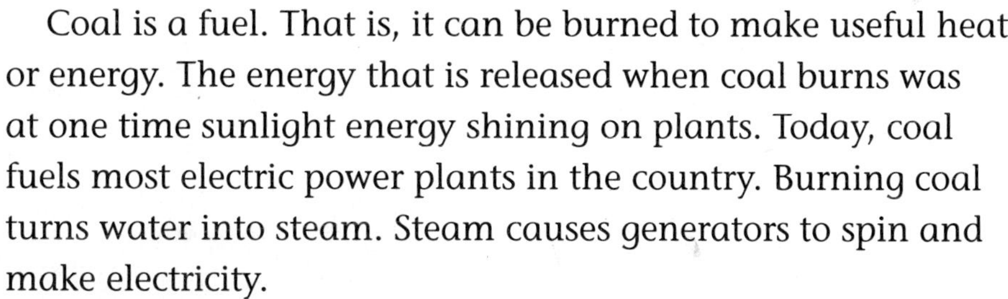

Coal is a fuel. That is, it can be burned to make useful heat or energy. The energy that is released when coal burns was at one time sunlight energy shining on plants. Today, coal fuels most electric power plants in the country. Burning coal turns water into steam. Steam causes generators to spin and make electricity.

Coal

Most scientists think that petroleum, commonly called crude oil, and natural gas form in a way similar to the way that coal forms. However, oil comes from buried tiny sea organisms instead of buried plants. Since oil, natural gas, and coal are made from the remains of organisms, these resources are called **fossil fuels.**

1. **√ Checkpoint** Where does the energy of coal originally come from?
2. **Technology in Science** Use library, Internet, or other resources to learn how technology has affected the mining or use of coal throughout history. In your **science journal,** write or draw pictures of what you learn.

Oil and Natural Gas

Drills make deep holes in Earth's surface to reach oil. Crude oil might be found either beneath land or beneath the ocean floor. Drillers use much the same process whether they are drilling for crude oil on land or at sea. However, drills at sea are on floating platforms or towers that reach the ocean floor.

Natural gas is often found where crude oil is found. When a large amount of gas is found, it is usually pumped into pipelines. Pipelines carry the gas to storage tanks until it is needed.

Gasoline, diesel fuel, and other fuels come from crude oil. We need these fuels to run the machines that we depend on every day. Some power plants make electricity by burning oil or natural gas. Millions of cars, trucks, trains, and ships use fuels from oil. These are important ways to move people and products across the world. Diesel-fueled farm tractors make it possible for farmers to raise huge amounts of food. It is hard to find a part of society that is not affected by the use of oil.

Crude oil is used not only for fuels. It is also used to make other products. Some of these are asphalt, plastic, grease, and wax. How are these products used?

Advantages and Disadvantages

Fossil fuels have many advantages over other energy resources. It is easy to store and move coal and oil. It is easier to get large amounts of energy from fossil fuels than from other energy resources.

The drill is put together at the center of this tower.

About 200 people live and work on the platform.

Small amounts of natural gas trapped in the oil are burned.

Some oil may be stored in huge underwater storage tanks.

Wells spread out to reach the oil.

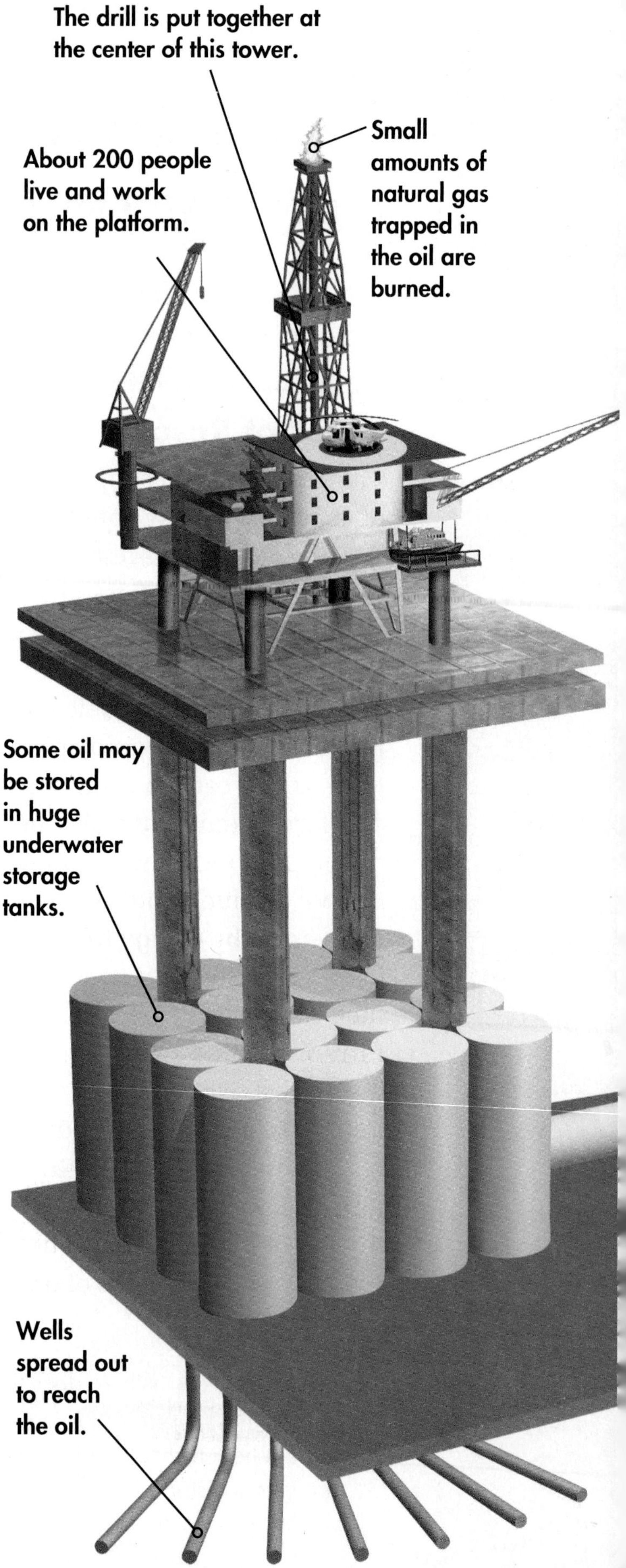

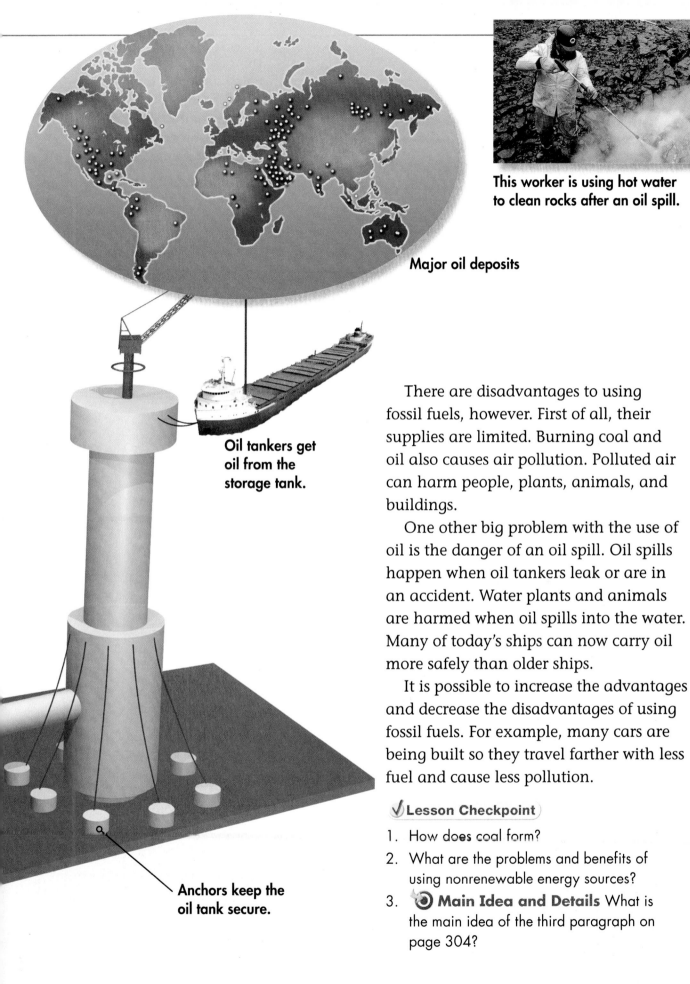

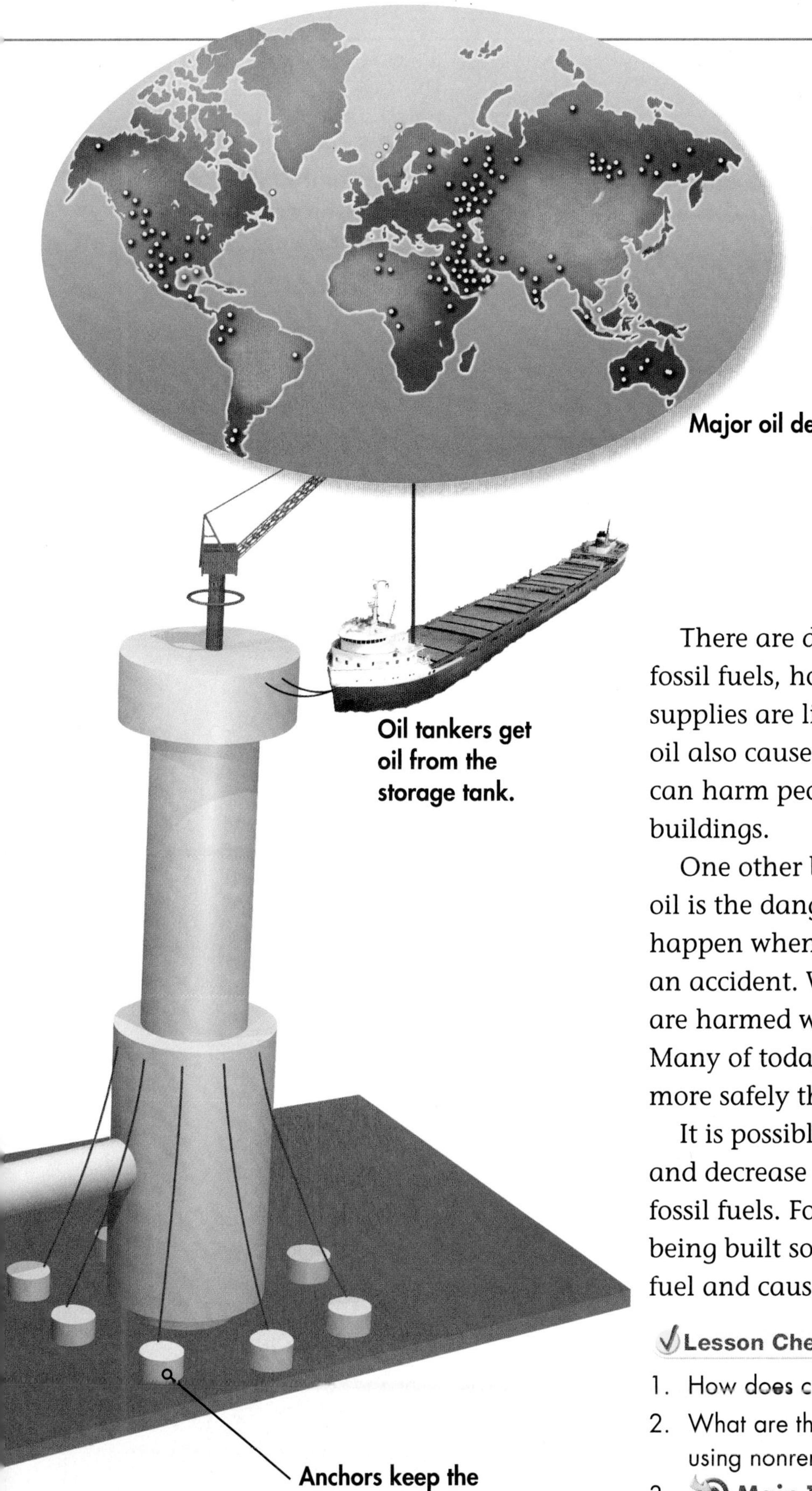

This worker is using hot water to clean rocks after an oil spill.

Major oil deposits

Oil tankers get oil from the storage tank.

Anchors keep the oil tank secure.

There are disadvantages to using fossil fuels, however. First of all, their supplies are limited. Burning coal and oil also causes air pollution. Polluted air can harm people, plants, animals, and buildings.

One other big problem with the use of oil is the danger of an oil spill. Oil spills happen when oil tankers leak or are in an accident. Water plants and animals are harmed when oil spills into the water. Many of today's ships can now carry oil more safely than older ships.

It is possible to increase the advantages and decrease the disadvantages of using fossil fuels. For example, many cars are being built so they travel farther with less fuel and cause less pollution.

✓ Lesson Checkpoint

1. How does coal form?
2. What are the problems and benefits of using nonrenewable energy sources?
3. **Main Idea and Details** What is the main idea of the third paragraph on page 304?

Lesson 2

What are other energy resources?

Wind, water, and the Sun are renewable energy resources. They can heat homes and make electricity.

Solar Energy

You have seen that there are disadvantages to using fossil fuels. Therefore, it is important to develop nonpolluting renewable energy resources. Some of these resources have been used for thousands of years, but they need to be improved to be more useful to today's society.

Solar energy, or energy from sunlight, is a renewable resource. Solar cells use sunlight to make electricity. The International Space Station gets electricity from sunlight captured by solar cells.

Often, sunlight is used to heat things. Sunlight is used to heat water for homes and swimming pools. It can also heat the air in buildings, such as greenhouses. The picture on this page shows how one large power plant made electricity by using mirrors to concentrate solar energy.

Advantages and Disadvantages

Solar energy has some advantages when it is compared to fossil fuels. Sunlight will not run out for billions of years. Solar energy does not cause any pollution.

Unfortunately, solar energy has some disadvantages too. It is not available at night or on cloudy days. Also, systems to make electricity from solar energy are expensive to make and maintain. Factories that make solar cells also produce very dangerous wastes.

Tracking mirrors reflect sunlight to the top of the tower in the middle. The plant may have as many as 2,000 of these mirrors.

Sunlight reflected by the mirrors heats liquid at the top of the tower. It may reach more than 500°C.

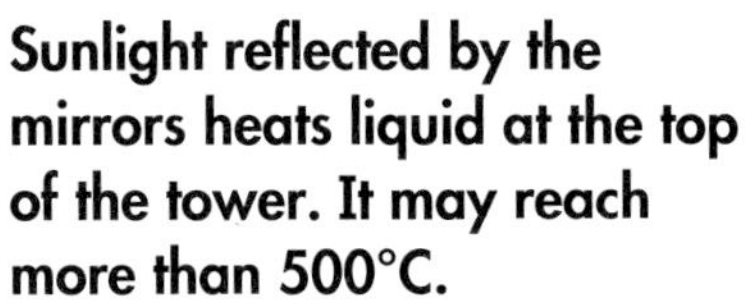

Solar cells make the electricity that runs this car.

The hot liquid is used to boil water. The steam is used to make electricity in the same way as in a coal power plant.

After it is used to boil water, the liquid becomes cooler. Liquid is stored in this tank until it is pumped back up the tower and heated again.

This house has solar cells on its roof to make electricity. Batteries can store electricity for use on cloudy days or at night. This house also has skylights that let sunlight into rooms that may otherwise be dark.

Hot liquid is stored in a tank at the bottom of the tower.

1. **Checkpoint** Why do we need to improve sources of energy that are not fossil fuels?
2. **Main Idea and Details** What is the main idea of the first paragraph under the heading "Solar Energy" at the top of page 306?

Windmills like this one brought water up from underground.

Wind farms have many wind turbines in one place. The land below the turbines can often be used to grow crops.

Wind Energy

People have been using the renewable energy of the wind for hundreds of years. For example, Holland is famous for its very old windmills. The turning blades were connected to machines for many purposes. These windmills were used to grind grain and to pump water away from the land. Starting in the 1800s, smaller systems were used on farms throughout the United States. Here, the windmills were used to bring water up from wells. How else has wind been used as a source of energy?

Today's technology has been used to improve the way that wind machines use the energy in the wind. Wind turbines use the energy of the wind to spin a generator to make electricity. These wind turbines can spin faster in light winds than old windmills did. The electric energy they produce can be used in many ways, not just for pumping water or grinding grain.

Advantages and Disadvantages

Wind energy has advantages and disadvantages over other energy resources. An advantage that windmills have over fossil fuels is that windmills do not cause air pollution. As expected, a disadvantage of wind energy is that the wind does not blow all the time. An unexpected disadvantage is that birds sometimes are killed by flying into the towers or blades. Also, some people think that windmills are noisy and ugly.

Wind turbines can be made in many shapes. These wind turbines are sometimes called "egg beaters."

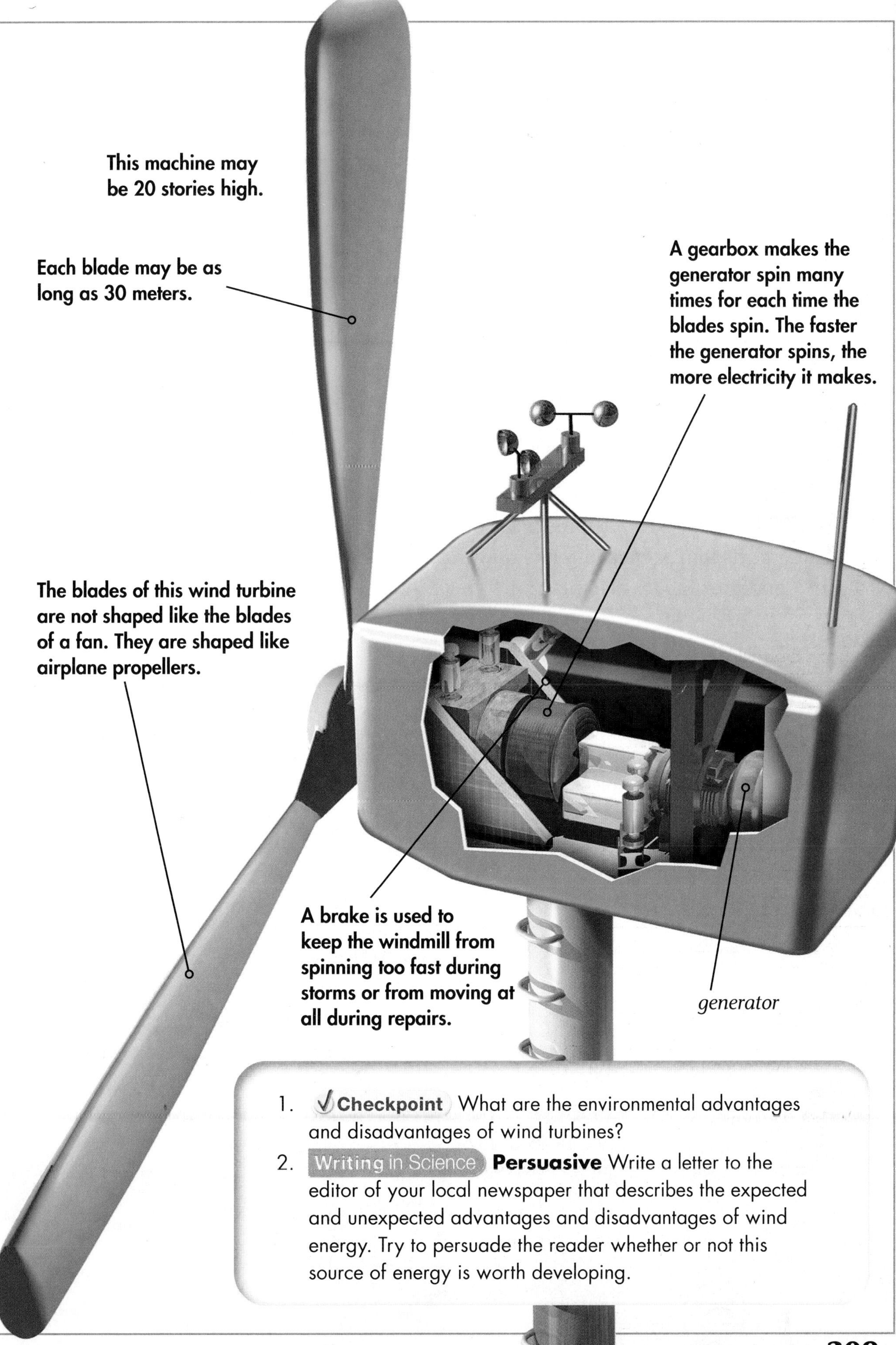
This machine may be 20 stories high.
Each blade may be as long as 30 meters.
A gearbox makes the generator spin many times for each time the blades spin. The faster the generator spins, the more electricity it makes.
The blades of this wind turbine are not shaped like the blades of a fan. They are shaped like airplane propellers.
A brake is used to keep the windmill from spinning too fast during storms or from moving at all during repairs.
generator

1. **Checkpoint** What are the environmental advantages and disadvantages of wind turbines?
2. **Writing in Science** **Persuasive** Write a letter to the editor of your local newspaper that describes the expected and unexpected advantages and disadvantages of wind energy. Try to persuade the reader whether or not this source of energy is worth developing.

Moving Water

Flowing water is one of the oldest energy resources. For centuries, people have built factories along rivers in order to use the energy of flowing water. The rivers turned huge paddle wheels. Other kinds of water wheels then powered saws to cut wood, looms to make cloth, mills to grind flour, or other machines.

Moving water is a renewable resource that is still used today. Instead of turning paddle wheels, water is used to make electricity. Power plants that make electricity with the energy of flowing water are called **hydroelectric** power plants. Hydroelectric power plants are usually built in dams. As water flows through a dam, it spins parts of generators. These parts look something like a fan. As they spin, the generator makes electricity.

The water that moves this old water wheel reaches the top of the wheel through a trough.

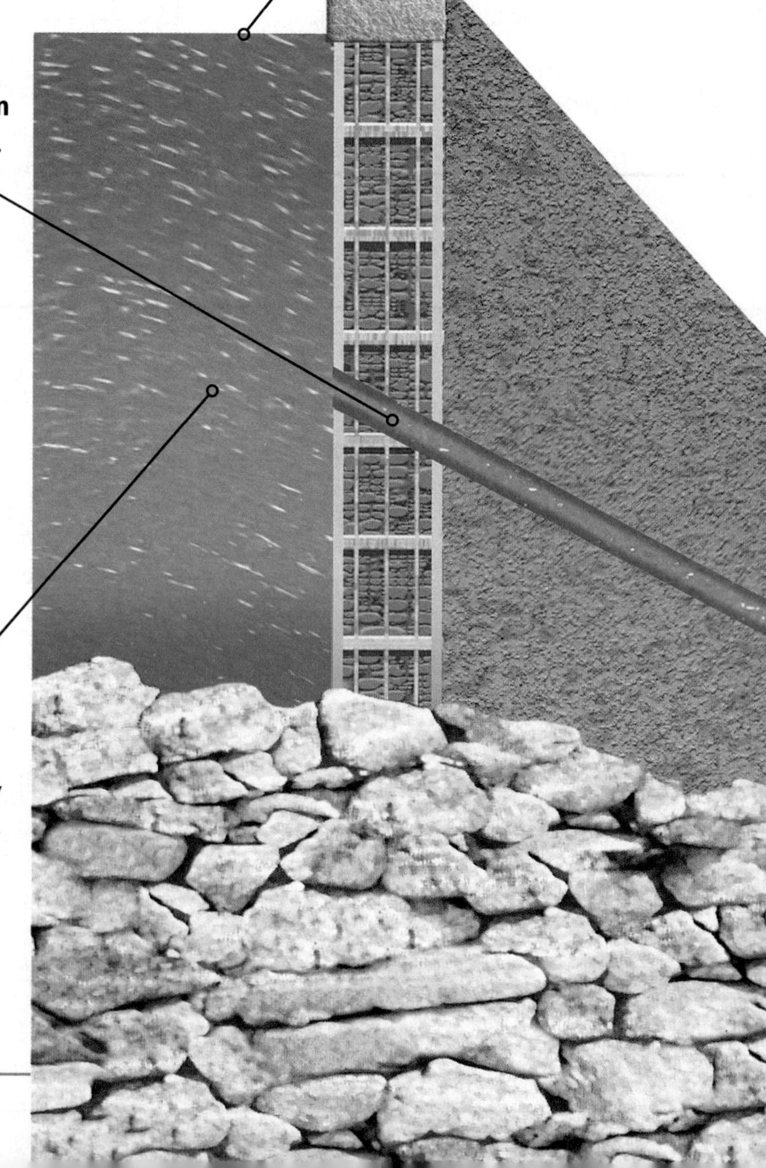

The deeper the water behind the dam, the more energy the water will be able to give to the generators.

Water moves through a dam in large pipes.

Sediments slowly fill the reservoir behind a dam. These need to be removed often.

Advantages and Disadvantages

Like wind generators, hydroelectric power plants do not need fuel to make electricity. There is no pollution. No waste is left behind.

Hydroelectric power plants have some disadvantages. They can only be built where there is moving water. The area also must have a place where a lake can form behind the dam. These lakes flood habitats of plants and animals. Dams can also stop fish from swimming up and down the river.

This dam caused a lake to form behind it. Often, lakes like this are used for fishing, boating, and other water activities.

These huge generators are in Hoover Dam in Nevada.

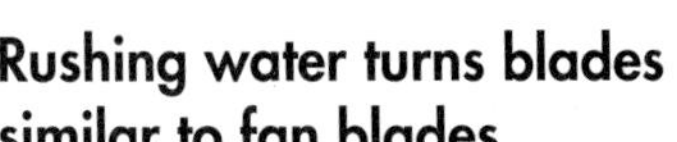
Rushing water turns blades similar to fan blades.

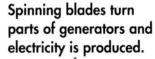

Spinning blades turn parts of generators and electricity is produced.
Water leaves the hydroelectric power plant here.

1. ✓ **Checkpoint** What are the good and bad effects of building dams to run hydroelectric power plants?
2. **Math in Science** About 0.51 of electricity in the United States is made by coal power plants. About 0.06 of the country's electricity is made by hydroelectric plants. What part of the electricity is made by other forms of energy?

Nuclear Energy

Uranium is a rare metal. Under certain conditions, uranium will get very hot. Nuclear power plants use hot uranium instead of fossil fuels to make steam in order to produce electricity.

A nuclear power plant needs much less fuel than a power plant that uses coal or oil. Also, nuclear power plants do not give off smoke.

On the other hand, the cost of building a nuclear plant is more than that of other power plants. Dangerous wastes present another problem. Since there is only so much uranium on Earth, nuclear energy is a nonrenewable energy source.

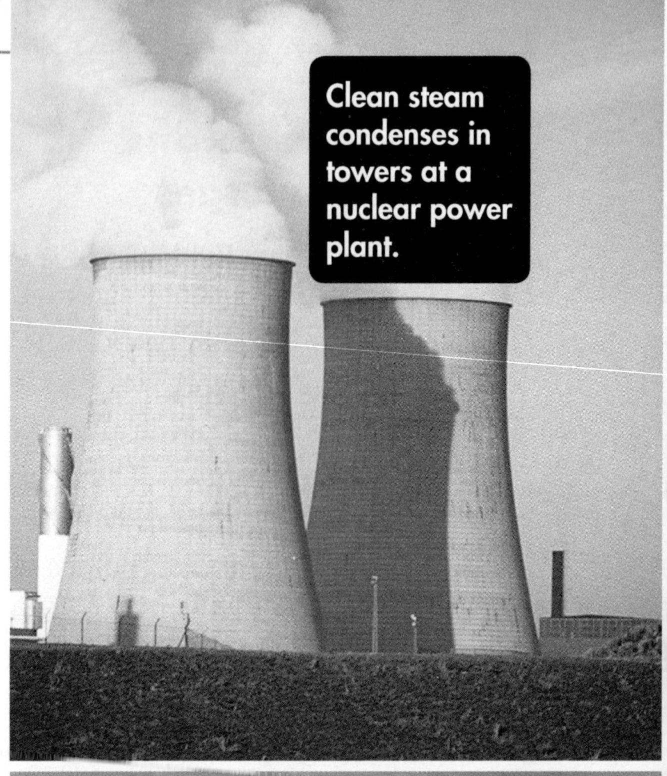

Clean steam condenses in towers at a nuclear power plant.

Geothermal Energy

Energy from the high temperatures inside the Earth is called **geothermal** energy. Geothermal energy can be used in several ways. In one way, water is pumped down deep holes into hot rock. As the water flows through cracks in hot rocks, the water gets hot and may turn into steam. The hot water or steam rushes back to the surface and is used to make electricity.

Geothermal energy has many advantages. Unlike solar or wind energy, geothermal energy can make electricity all day and all night, all year long. However, these power plants can be built in only a few places in the world where very hot rocks are close to Earth's surface. Some pollutants may be found in the steam of these plants.

This garbage will be burned in an electric power plant.

People can swim during the winter in this pond that is warmed by a geothermal power plant in Iceland.

Energy of Biomass

In the small picture at the left, huge claws are mixing garbage. This mixing helps it to dry. Then the garbage is burned in a power plant to make electricity just like power plants that burn coal or oil. Most of the garbage consists of plant materials such as paper and wood. This garbage is an example of biomass. **Biomass** is material that was recently alive. Biomass can be animal waste, wood, grasses, or food wastes.

Not all biomass is burned in power plants. Some is turned into fuels that can run cars and trucks. Chemicals are added to biomass, and then biomass is turned into liquid fuel in a few steps. High temperatures can turn biomass into a gas similar to natural gas. This gas can be used in the same ways as natural gas.

Biomass is a resource that we will never run out of. We will always have garbage. By using biomass as a resource, less garbage will be taken to landfills. One disadvantage is that burning biomass does cause air pollution.

✓ Lesson Checkpoint

1. Describe two ways that people use energy from the Sun. What are the advantages and disadvantages of getting energy in these ways?
2. What kind of energy uses uranium as a fuel? What are the advantages and disadvantages of getting energy in this way?
3. How do people use geothermal energy?
4. **Technology in Science** Use Internet or library resources to find what sources of renewable and nonrenewable energy are used in your state.

Not all mines are underground tunnels. Many mines are huge holes such as this one.

By developing technologies like this huge truck, mining companies can get minerals out of a mine more quickly. This makes the minerals less expensive to buy.

Iron can be melted and poured into molds to make items with different shapes.

Lesson 3

What are other resources?

Minerals, water, air, and soil are some other important resources. People use these resources in many ways.

Mineral Resources

We get many resources from Earth in addition to the resources we use for energy. Other resources include gold, iron, copper, and other solid materials. Each of these is a mineral, or a nonliving material from Earth. Some mineral resources, such as gold and silver, are hard to find. Other mineral resources, such as salt and iron, are easy to find. Many minerals are dug from mines below ground. Towns often grow where mineral resources are mined.

Mineral resources have many uses. Iron is a very inexpensive and useful metal. It can be used in a pure form or in a mixture. Steel is made by mixing iron with other substances. Steel is used to make cars, skyscrapers, and even paper clips.

Other mineral resources include gypsum and mica. Gypsum is a white material from rocks. It is used in homes for plaster and paint. Mica is also used in paint.

Gravel, a size of rock, is a common resource used to build roads. It is made of small pieces of rocks and sand. Many roads are made of just gravel. Other roads are gravel covered with asphalt or concrete. Concrete is a mixture of gravel, sand, water, and cement.

The iron from this rock may be used for many products made of steel.

All minerals are nonrenewable. However, some minerals, such as iron, are found in Earth in large amounts. Others, such as copper, lead, and zinc, have more limited known deposits. Conservation, recycling, and new mines may extend these sources, but they cannot be extended forever.

Mining causes changes in the land. Places where plants grow and where animals make their homes are changed. Mining can also cause air and water pollution. Some ways of mining have left large open pits in the land. The bare soil led to mud slides and soil erosion. Today, mining companies use many technologies to limit the damage caused by mines. They also use technologies to make repairs to the land after the mine is used.

Top Steel Producing Areas in 2002

Steel (Millions of Metric Tons)

250
200
150
100
50
0

North America
European Union
China

Area

Some Uses of Iron Ore

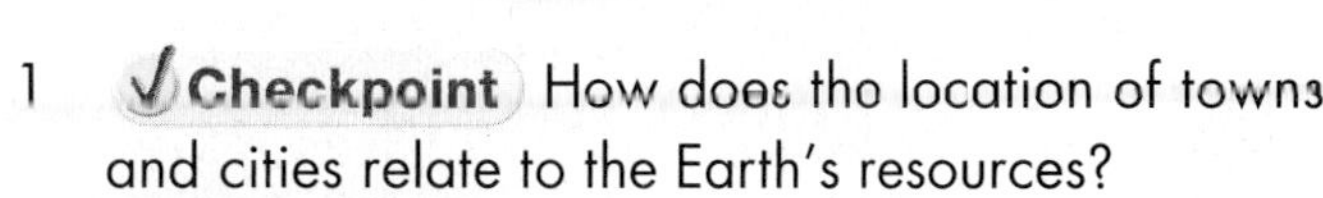

1. **Checkpoint** How does the location of towns and cities relate to the Earth's resources?
2. **Art in Science** Draw a map of your state and locate any resources that are found there. Explain the value and uses of these resources and whether or not these resources are renewable.

Clean fresh water is an important resource.

Water, Soil, and Air

You may not think of water, air, and soil as important resources, but they are. Remember, a resource is anything that fills a need. What could be more important than your needs for air, water, and soil?

Air, water, and soil are renewable resources to some degree. Through the water cycle, water can be recycled. Air is renewable in that pollution slowly settles out of the atmosphere or gets caught in rain. Soil is slowly and constantly being made from weathering rock and decaying plants. These renewing processes can take a very long time, so we need to take care of these resources every day.

√ Lesson Checkpoint

1. Explain why it is necessary to carefully maintain a resource even if it is renewable.
2. Why are soil, water, and air considered to be resources?
3. **Writing** in Science **Expository** Think about the ways you use water each day. In your **science journal,** write how water is important in your life and what you can do to conserve it.

Clean water, soil, and air are important, not only for farms, but for all people.

Air

Air is needed every moment of your life. It fills your lungs and gives you the oxygen your body needs. Nitrogen from the air is used to make many fertilizers that farmers and gardeners use for their plants.

Air can become polluted in many ways. Volcanoes put large amounts of materials into the air. Forest fires are often started by lightning. These fires make huge amounts of smoke.

Air pollution, such as the gases given off by this car, may harm people. Air pollution can also cause serious health problems. Factories, power plants, and mining also pollute the air.

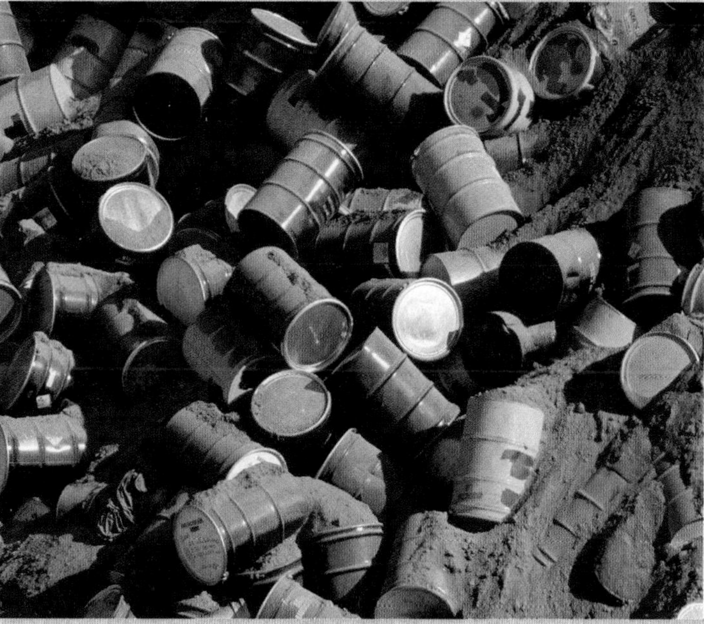

Soil

Soil provides minerals and nutrients that plants need to live. Plants that depend on soil are used as food for us and for animals. Trees that depend on soil are used to make paper and products for building homes.

Soil can be damaged in many ways. It can be polluted with chemicals. It can be damaged by having too many crops grown on it. Soil can also erode away.

Water

Think of all the ways you use water each day. You take baths, cook food, and wash the dishes with water. Everything you drink has water in it. Water is also used for growing food and making electricity. Many kinds of factories could not operate without water.

Water resources can be damaged by pollution or overuse. Pollution can enter water when people dump wastes into it. Air pollution can get into rain as it falls to the ground. The pollution then makes dangerous chemicals in the rainwater which can harm plants, animals, and buildings.

Lesson 4

Can resources be conserved?

People need to work to maintain Earth's limited supply of natural resources. If people use resources wisely, they will last for years to come.

Repairing Soil, Water, and Air

The Industrial Revolution began in Europe in the 1700s. People began using machines to make things. Transportation improved very quickly. Since then, the use of machines has caused pollution of air, water, and soil. In some places, pollution has had a major effect on the environment. Some entire towns have had to be abandoned because pollution there was very dangerous to people's health. Removing pollution from such places has cost the United States billions of dollars.

Because the environment may have dangerous levels of pollution, it is important to be able to measure the amount of pollution in soil, air, and water. Many technologies can be used to measure pollution. This helps people keep pollution from reaching dangerous levels. Careful monitoring can also help people find the sources of pollution.

Repairing damage done by pollution can be very expensive.

Conservation Laws

Many laws encourage people to protect natural resources. For example, in many areas lumber companies must plant trees after they cut some down. Also, mining companies must use available technologies to restore the land of abandoned mines. Industries must clean lands that have been polluted by their wastes. These actions are often very expensive, but they make the environment a healthier place to live. Other laws have set aside areas to be used as national parks to protect many environments.

Planting trees can be one step to repairing an ecosystem.

Using Less and Reusing Resources

Both large companies and individuals can help maintain Earth's resources by using less of them. Energy resources can be saved in many ways. Use furnaces and air conditioners less. Turn off lights that are not in use. When you use less electricity, then power plants can burn less fuel. This also reduces air pollution.

Some companies are saving resources by using less material when they make things. One way that companies use less material is by making the sides of plastic water bottles a little thinner and lighter.

Another easy way that people can save resources is to reuse things. You can reuse paper by writing on the backside. You can buy water bottles that are made to be washed and reused.

Some industries are based on reusing products. Thrift stores and antique shops are common examples. Some companies take apart old computers to reuse parts. Some companies chop up old tires to be reused as playground surfaces. Reusing products can be a good business.

Aluminum cans are thinner now than they were years ago. What can you do with aluminum cans to help conserve resources?

1. **√ Checkpoint** Why is it important to monitor air and water?
2. **Writing in Science** **Expository** In your **science journal,** write a paragraph explaining the impact of waste on the environment and on society

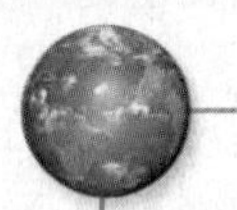

Recycling

Another way to save resources is to recycle. Recycling means to treat something so it can be used again. When glass is recycled, it is ground up and melted to make new bottles and jars. Glass can also be used in place of sand or gravel to pave roads.

Paper can also be recycled. First, the paper is soaked in water and chemicals. This changes the paper into a soft, wet pulp. The pulp is then pushed through screens. The screens remove objects mixed in with the paper. Next, detergents or other processes remove ink from the paper pulp. The clean pulp is then pressed and dried to make new paper.

Plastics can also be recycled into new products. The pictures on this page show the steps of recycling plastics.

Sometimes the main reason for recycling is not to save a material, but to save energy. For example, there is a lot of aluminum in the Earth. However, it takes less energy to recycle aluminum than it does to get it from a mine.

You can help save resources by recycling. Make plans to collect paper, cans, plastics, and glass at school and at home. Find out where to take these resources. Ask an adult in your home to help you get the resources to a recycling center.

With the strategies of reducing, reusing, and recycling, you can help improve and protect your environment. This, in turn, will improve and protect the quality of life in your community.

1 Collecting plastic is the first step in its recycling.

2 Plastic containers are labeled with a number that shows what kind of plastic it is. At a recycling center, the containers are sorted into bins according to these numbers.

3 Containers are being carried on a conveyor belt to a machine that will chop them into flakes.

4 The flakes are now ready to be washed and dried.

5 The flakes are dried by tumbling them in air.

6 The plastic flakes are melted and formed into new things like this slide.

✓ **Lesson Checkpoint**

1. Explain why and how people maintain natural resources.
2. Demonstrate how people and companies can use technology to reduce the production of waste and reduce the use of resources. How do these actions affect the environment?
3. Look around your classroom. Identify and classify materials that can be recycled.
4. **Writing in Science** **Persuasive** This lesson has discussed how plastic water bottles can be reduced in thickness, reused, and recycled. Which of these actions do you think is most effective in your home and school for conserving resources? Design a poster that tries to convince your classmates that your choice is best.

Lab zone **Guided Inquiry**

Investigate How can paper be recycled?

The first step in recycling paper is to cut it up into tiny pieces. Machines do this work at recycling centers.

Materials

newspaper and scissors

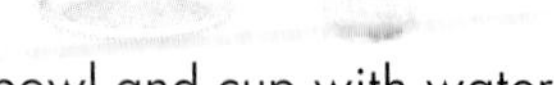

bowl and cup with water

fork and spoon

laundry starch

plastic screen and plastic wrap

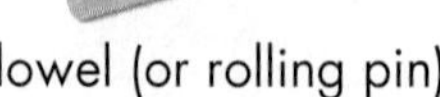

dowel (or rolling pin)

Process Skills

You **interpret data** when you use the information in your data chart to answer a question.

What to Do

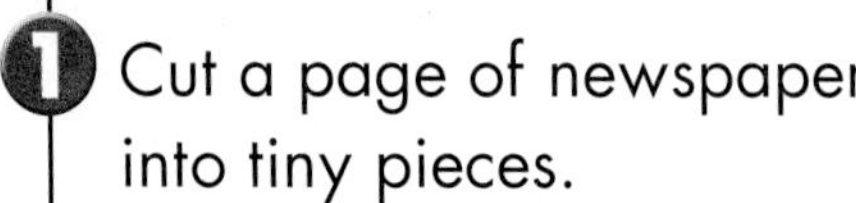

1. Cut a page of newspaper into tiny pieces.
2. Put the pieces in the bowl. Add the water in the cup. Let the bowl sit for 1 hour.

3. Use the fork to mix the water and paper into mush. Add 2 spoonfuls of starch. Stir.

More Lab zone Activities

Take It to the Net sfsuccessnet.com

4. Lay the plastic screen on a stack of newspapers. Spread the mush evenly on the screen. Cover it with plastic wrap. Roll the dowel on the wrap.

5. Remove the plastic wrap and let the mush dry for 1 or 2 days. Then peel the recycled paper off the screen.

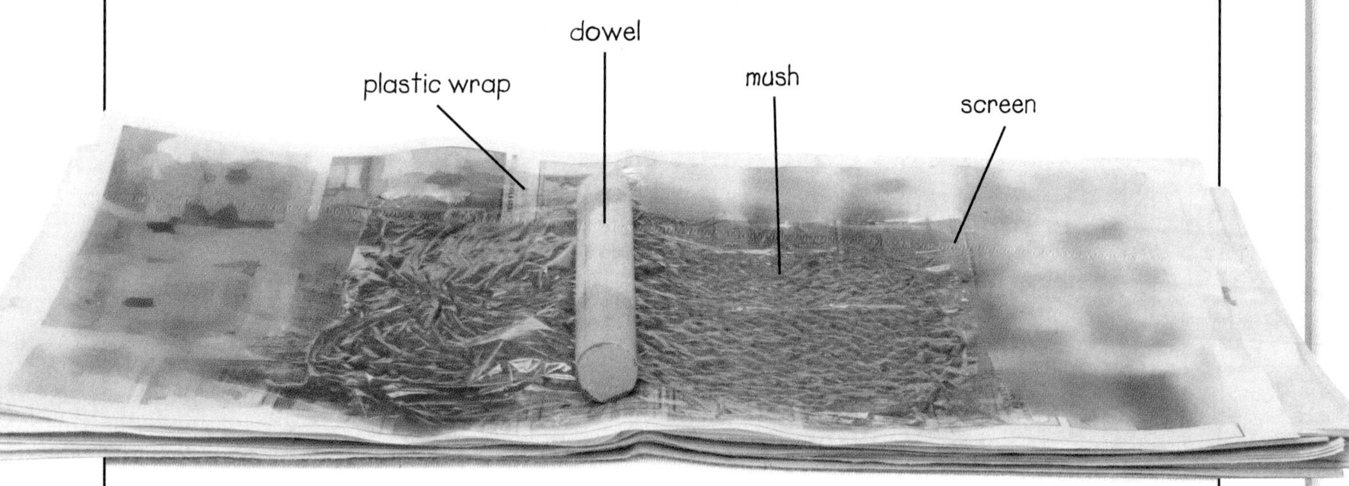
dowel
plastic wrap
mush
screen

6. **Collect Data** Compare your recycled paper to newspaper. Record their properties.

Kind of Paper	Properties
Newspaper	
Recycled paper	

Explain Your Results

1. **Interpret Data** How was your recycled paper like the paper with which you started? How was it different?
2. What natural resource did you conserve by recycling paper?

Go Further

How can you collect and classify different recyclable materials? How can renewable resources be maintained? Make a plan to find out.

Math in Science

Calculating the Benefits of Wind Energy

Wind farms are groups of large wind turbines that are used to produce electricity. The use of these "power plants" is proving to be economical and good for the environment.

In California alone, the use of wind turbines has replaced the use of 5 million barrels of oil per year and greatly reduced the release of greenhouse gases.

Estimates from research show that the U.S. could probably reduce the future amount of oil used per year by 7.5 billion barrels with the greatest possible use of wind power. Oil prices vary greatly. Suppose the price is $35.20 per barrel. At this price, how much could the U.S. save on oil costs in one year?

$\$35.20 \times 7.5$ billion $= \$264$ billion

The savings in oil costs per year would be $264 billion!

How much would be saved per month?

$\$264$ billion $\div 12 = \$22$ billion

Per month, the savings on oil costs would be $22 billion.

Use the information on page 324 to answer the questions.

1. At $35.20 per barrel, how much does California save in oil costs per year?
2. The California wind turbines have reduced the release of greenhouse gases by 6 billion kg over a five-year period. What was the average reduction in greenhouse gases per year?
3. A wind turbine can produce 300 kilowatts of electricity per hour. One wind farm in California has 4,000 wind turbines. How many kilowatts does this wind farm produce in 24 hours?

Lab zone Take-Home Activity

Find information on a wind farm that is in a state other than California. Write a report on your findings. Include details such as reasons for the particular location, the number of turbines in the wind farm, and so on.

Chapter 10 Review and Test Prep

Use Vocabulary

biomass (p. 313)	**nonrenewable resource** (p. 303)
fossil fuel (p. 303)	**renewable resource** (p. 303)
geothermal (p. 312)	**resource** (p. 303)
hydroelectric (p. 310)	**solar energy** (p. 306)

Match each term from the list above with a phrase below.

1. ______ energy is a renewable energy source due to flowing water.
2. A ______ is an energy resource from organisms that lived long ago.
3. ______ is a renewable energy source that comes from the Sun.
4. Fossil fuel is considered to be a ______.
5. ______ is the remains of anything that was alive recently.
6. Wind is an example of a ______.
7. ______ energy is produced by the heat inside of Earth.
8. Any supply that will meet a need is a ______.

Explain Concepts

9. Explain the relationship between society and the technologies of using Earth's resources.
10. Explain why trees are a renewable resource and how this resource can be maintained.
11. Explain how to reduce the bad effects that technology has on the environment. Explain how to increase the good effects.
12. There is more aluminum in the Earth than people will ever use. Explain why aluminum cans and other items should be recycled.

Process Skills

13. **Classify** Make a chart like the one below to classify the following as renewable or nonrenewable resources: solar energy, coal, copper, wind, biomass, soil, water, oil, uranium, aluminum.

Renewable	Nonrenewable

14. Infer If people continue using fossil fuels at the present rate, infer what will happen to the supply of fossil fuels in the next 1,000 years.

15. Make a model of a power plant and explain what resource it uses.

Main Idea and Details

16. Make a graphic organizer like the one shown below. Fill in the main idea of Lesson 4 that the given details support.

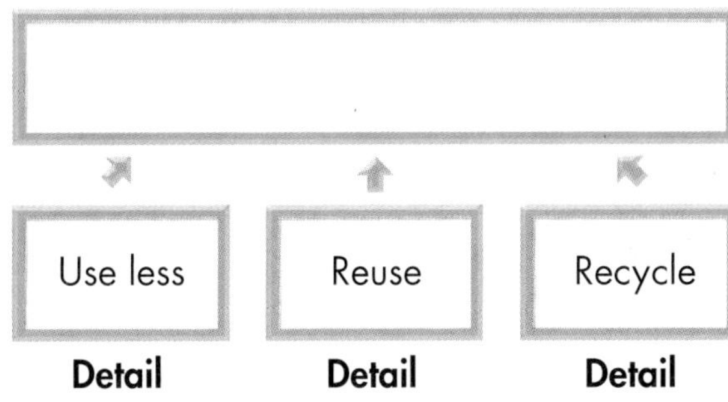
Main Idea
Use less
Reuse
Recycle
Detail
Detail
Detail

Test Prep

Choose the letter that best completes the statement or answers the question.

17. Hydroelectric power plants make electricity by using
- Ⓐ moving water.
- Ⓑ the wind.
- Ⓒ uranium.
- Ⓓ hot underground rocks.

18. Which of the following is NOT a fossil fuel?
- Ⓕ coal
- Ⓖ natural gas
- Ⓗ uranium
- Ⓘ oil

19. Explain why the answer you selected for Question 18 is best. For each of the answers you did not select, give a reason why it is not the best answer.

20. Writing in Science **Persuasive** Make a poster that explains why people need to conserve natural resources by reducing, reusing, or recycling.

Career

Water Treatment Plant Operator

You open the tap and let some cool water fill your glass. Many people worked to make sure that the water was clean and healthful.

Before water reached your tap, it had to travel. It came from lakes, rivers, and other places. At those sources the water had bacteria, dirt, and fish in it, but when it comes to you it is clean. In order for you to have clean water, it goes first to a water treatment plant.

At a water treatment plant the water goes through several processes to remove harmful chemicals, dirt, and microorganisms. Water treatment plant operators are responsible for getting healthful water to their community. They make sure all the equipment at the plant is running smoothly so that everyone has clean water to drink and to wash with. The operator also tests the water to make sure it is safe.

A water treatment plant must have operators working 24 hours a day. The plants do not close for weekends or holidays. Sometimes emergencies happen. The operator must then follow emergency procedures to make sure the water supply remains clean.

Water treatment plant operators must have a high school diploma. They may also complete a 1-year certificate program to learn about the chemical processes for treating water. The operator must clearly understand mechanics. Basic mathematics, chemistry, and biology are also important in performing the job.

Lab zone Take-Home Activity

Using less water can help the environment. Research some ways you can use less water at home or at school.

Unit B Test Talk

Test-Taking Strategies

Find Important Words

Choose the Right Answer

Use Information from Text and Graphics

Write Your Answer

Write Your Answer

To answer the following test questions, you need to write your answer. Read the passage and then answer the questions.

Most of Earth's surface is covered with water, including oceans, lakes, rivers, and groundwater. About $\frac{7}{10}$ of the surface fresh water on Earth is frozen into ice. Air always has water vapor in it. Rain and melted snow soak into the ground and become groundwater.

Air is a thick blanket of a mixture of gases that covers Earth. Air pressure decreases as you go higher into the atmosphere, because gas particles in the air get farther apart. Winds move masses of air over Earth's surface. They carry storms and other kinds of weather with them. People use instruments to collect information about weather. They use this data to make forecasts. Climate is the pattern of weather conditions in an area over a long period of time.

Earth is separated into layers: the crust, mantle, outer core, and inner core. The crust is made of several plates that float on the mantle. The movements of these plates cause earthquakes and many volcanoes. The surface of the Earth is constantly changing. Rocks break into smaller pieces through the process of weathering. Erosion is the process of water, wind, or ice moving weathered materials. When materials are deposited they make new landforms. Rocks have different properties depending on how they were formed and the minerals they contain.

Resources are things we get from the Earth that meet our needs. Renewable resources can be replaced. Moving water, sunlight, and wind are renewable sources of energy. Mineral resources are nonrenewable. There is a limited amount of these resources on Earth. It is important to conserve our resources so that we will have them to use in the future. We can conserve resources by using less, reusing products, and recycling materials.

Use What You Know

To write your answer to each question, you need to read the passage and the test question carefully. Write your answers in complete sentences. Then read your answer to make sure it is complete, correct, and focused.

1. What is the source of groundwater?
2. How and why does air pressure change as you go higher in the atmosphere?
3. What is climate?
4. How does the surface of the Earth change?
5. What is the difference between a renewable and a nonrenewable resource?

Unit B Wrap-Up

Chapter 7

How does water move through the environment?

- Water changes from one form to another as it moves through the environment in the water cycle. Water's forms include liquid water, water vapor, and snow and ice.
- Steps of the water cycle include evaporation, condensation, precipitation, and runoff.

Chapter 8

Why does the weather change?

- Weather changes when air masses of different temperatures and other conditions move.
- When air masses with different conditions move across Earth, they can cause weather changes in places they pass.

Chapter 9

What kinds of processes change Earth's surface?

- The movement of Earth's plates can cause big changes on its surface, including earthquakes, volcanic eruptions, and mountain formation.
- Weathering and erosion change Earth's surface more gradually.

Chapter 10

Why is it important to conserve Earth's resources?

- Nonrenewable resources cannot be replaced if they are used up. Some produce dangerous wastes.
- Even renewable resources have disadvantages. Some are expensive to use or are not efficient. Others, such as geothermal energy and moving water, can only be used in certain places.

Performance Assessment

Draw a Water Cycle

Use a large sheet of paper and colored markers to make a model of the water cycle in a place that has a lake, mountains, and clouds in the atmosphere. Label the steps of the water cycle. Describe what is taking place. Explain what conditions of the land can affect the steps of the water cycle.

Read More About Earth Science

Look for books like these in the library.

Lightning
Minerals

Lab zone **Full Inquiry**

Experiment How does temperature affect the growth of crystals?

Look very closely at table salt with a hand lens and you will see tiny crystals. Natural rock salt is the same chemical, but its crystals can be very large. In this experiment you will use salol to help find out how the temperature at which crystals grow affects their size. Salol is a solid at room temperature, but it has a low melting point—only several degrees Celsius above body temperature.

Materials

safety goggles and hand lens

2 small foil pans with melted salol

small cup with grains of salol

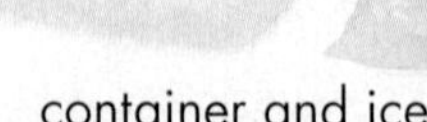

container and ice

Process Skills

Before beginning an **experiment, make a hypothesis** in the form of a testable question. A good hypothesis will help guide you as you carry out the experiment.

Ask a question.

How does the temperature at which crystals form affect their size?

State a hypothesis.

If crystals form at a higher temperature, then will they be larger, smaller, or about the same size as crystals formed at a lower temperature? Write your **hypothesis.**

Identify and control variables.

Temperature is the independent variable, the thing you will change. Crystal size is the dependent variable, the thing that is affected by the temperature change. The amount of salol you will use is a **controlled variable,** something that must not change.

Be careful!

Safety Procedure
- Wear safety goggles.
- Do not touch the salol.
- Wash your hands when finished.

Test your hypothesis.

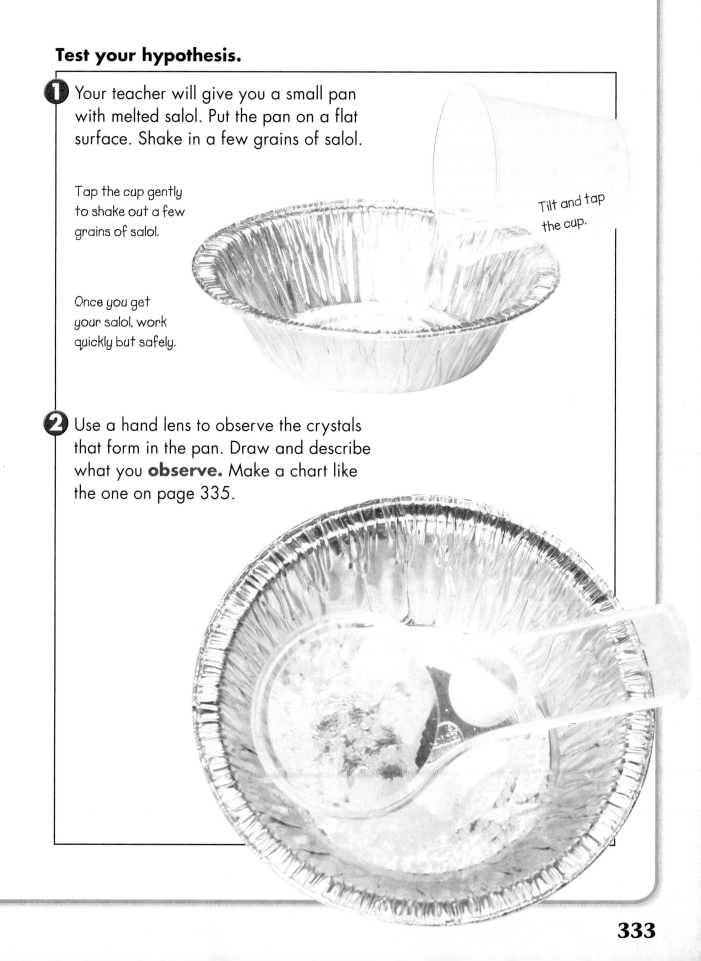

1. Your teacher will give you a small pan with melted salol. Put the pan on a flat surface. Shake in a few grains of salol.

Tap the cup gently to shake out a few grains of salol.

Tilt and tap the cup.

Once you get your salol, work quickly but safely.

2. Use a hand lens to observe the crystals that form in the pan. Draw and describe what you **observe.** Make a chart like the one on page 335.

3 Put a layer of ice in the container.

4 Ask your teacher for a second pan with melted salol. Place the small pan on top of the ice. Shake in a few grains of salol. Again, draw and describe what you observe.

Be careful!

Wash your hands when finished.

Collect and record your data.

	Size and Appearance of Crystals	
	Crystals Formed at Room Temperature	Crystals Formed at Cold Temperature
Drawing or sketch		
Description		

Interpret your data.
Compare the size of the crystals formed at room temperature with the size of the crystals formed at a cold temperature.

State your conclusion.
Explain how the temperature at which crystals form affects their size. Compare your hypothesis with your results. **Communicate** your conclusion.

Go Further

What would happen if you did not add any grains of salol to the melted salol? Would the formation of crystals be affected? Design and carry out a plan to investigate this or other questions you may have.

Discovery Channel School

Science Fair Projects

Make a River Model

Rivers carry sediment downstream. Some kinds of sediment can be carried farther than other kinds.

Idea: Fill a clear plastic bottle with water. Tape a strip of black paper to one side to make the particles easier to see. Drop a pinch of sand into the water. Record what happens to the sand. Make a model using moving water and particles of different sizes. Communicate your conclusions in a chart or drawing.

Use a Rain Gauge

The amount of rain that falls in a place over a period of time can be measured. The instrument used to measure how much rain fell is called a rain gauge.

Idea: Place a graduated cylinder outside in a place where it will not be disturbed. Check it each day for a week or so. Record how much water is in the cylinder. Compare your results with your classmates' results.

Tracking the Weather

Weather patterns in the United States usually move from west to east.

Idea: Collect newspaper weather forecasts every day for at least a week. Record the date on each map. Compare each day's weather map with the maps of previous days to see how the patterns change. Record your observations.

WEATHER
TODAY'S FORECAST

Full Inquiry

Using Scientific Methods

1. Ask a question.
2. State a hypothesis.
3. Identify and control variables.
4. Test your hypothesis.
5. Collect and record your data.
6. Interpret your data.
7. State your conclusion.
8. Go further.

EC NTL 10987

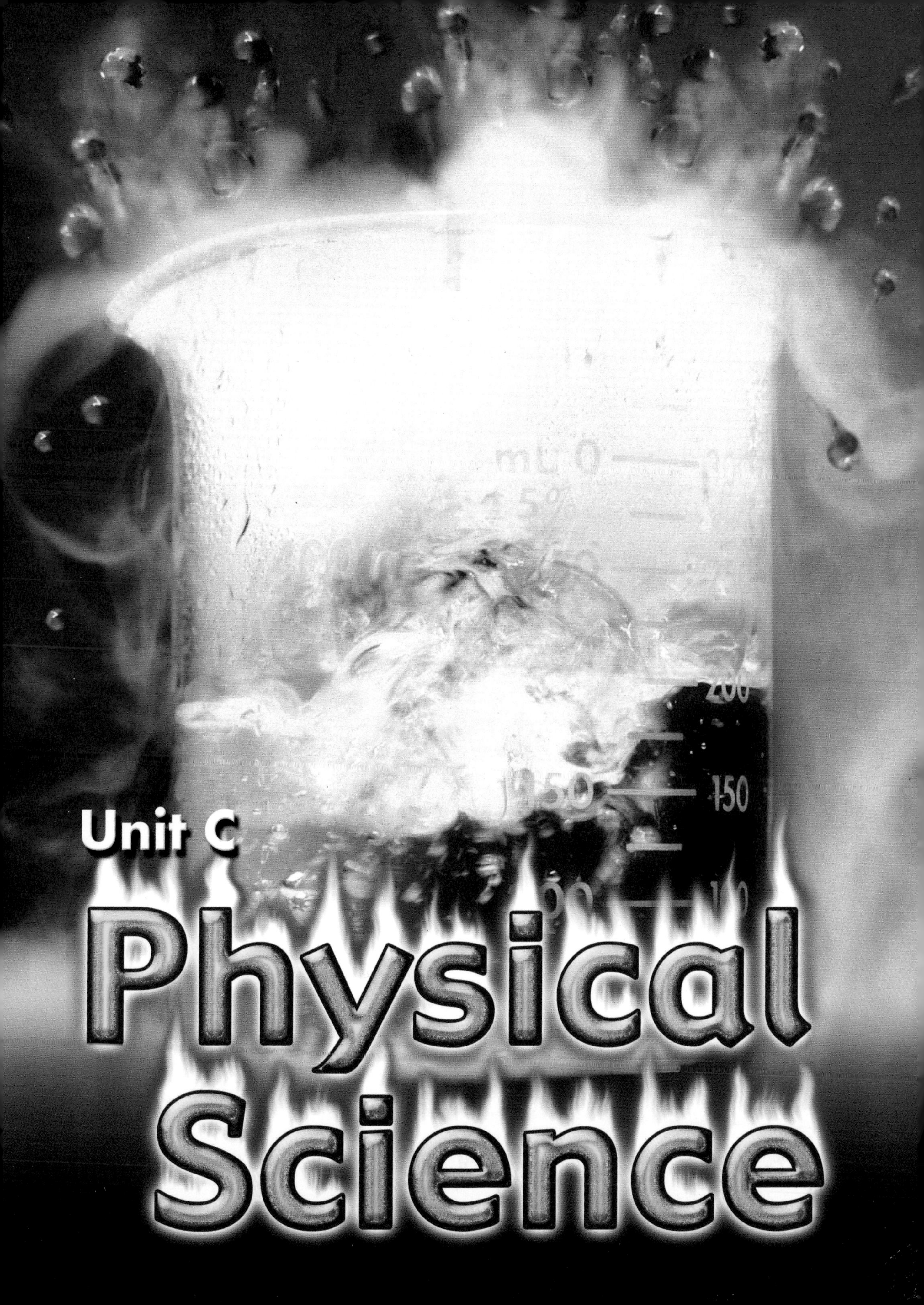

Unit C

Physical Science

You Will Discover

- what the properties of matter are.
- the difference between atoms and molecules.
- how matter changes between solid, liquid, and gas forms.
- how to compare mixtures and solutions.

Chapter 11

Matter and Its Properties

online
Student Edition
sfsuccessnet.com

Build Background

What makes up everything around us?

atom

proton

electron

neutron

compound

Chapter 11 Vocabulary

element page 343

atom page 348

proton page 348

neutron page 348

electron page 349

compound page 351

saturated page 361

concentrated page 361

dilute page 361

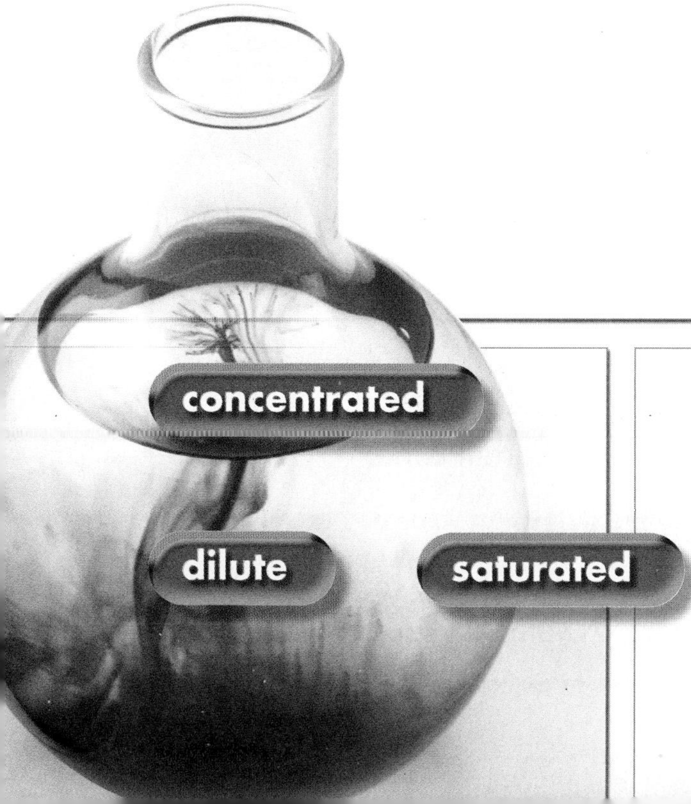

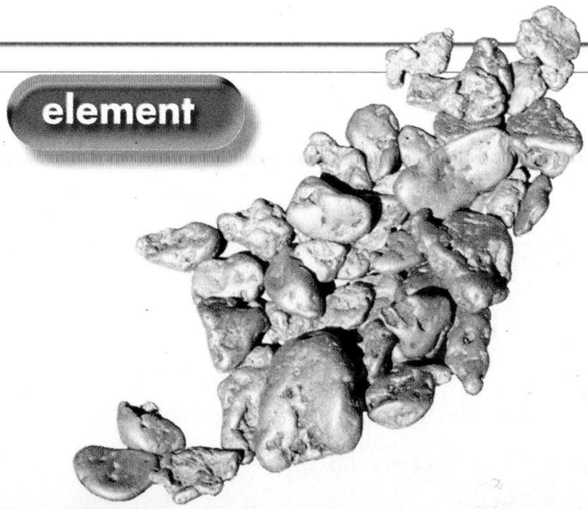

concentrated

element

dilute

saturated

Lab zone

Directed Inquiry

Explore What is one way you can determine density?

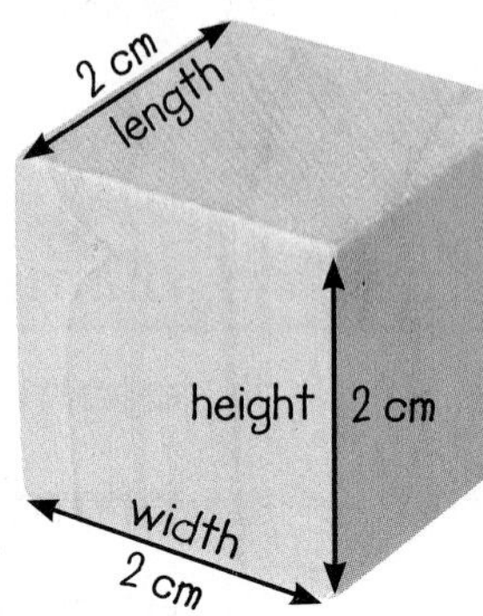
2 cm
length
height
2 cm
width
2 cm

Materials

1 wooden block,
$\frac{1}{4}$ stick of clay,
$\frac{1}{2}$ stick of clay

metric ruler

balance and gram cubes

calculator or computer (optional)

What to Do

1. **Measure** the length, width, and height of a wooden block in centimeters. Find the block's volume in cubic centimeters.

   volume = length × width × height

2. Use a balance to measure the mass of the block. Put the block on one side. Add gram cubes to the other side until the 2 sides balance. Find the total mass of the gram cubes. Each gram cube has a mass of 1 gram.

3. Calculate the block's density. The density is the number of grams per cubic centimeter.

   density = mass ÷ volume

4. Repeat steps 1 to 3 with $\frac{1}{4}$ of a stick of clay, $\frac{1}{2}$ of a stick of clay, and a gram cube.

Process Skills

In this activity you find the density of each object, using cubic centimeters and grams as the units of **measurement.**

Explain Your Results

Communicate Describe one way to find the density of an object. What must you **measure?**

How to Read Science

Reading Skills

Predict

When you **predict,** you may ask a question about what will happen next in a story and then think of an answer. After you make your prediction, continue reading. As you read, consider if any new information supports your prediction. Perhaps, new information will lead you to make a different prediction.

Science Fiction Story

Choosing Materials

For years, Rodney worked on building his spaceship. The hardest job was finding the right material to use for the tailfins. They had to be made of the densest metal available. Unfortunately, Rodney had only two materials left in his shop. He had some square, thick sheets of titanium and chromium. Rodney knew what he had to do to make the right choice.

Apply It!

Make a graphic organizer like the one shown. Make a **prediction** about how Rodney will **measure** the density of the materials. **Communicate** your prediction to a classmate.

Question		Prediction
How will Rodney measure the density?	→	

You Are There!

You are working inside a huge research instrument in a laboratory that is three stories tall. When your work is done, giant magnets and other equipment will start to hum. Tiny particles, too small to see even with a microscope, will zoom through the instrument at super speed. These particles will smash together, forming new types of matter. Scientists do experiments like these as they study matter. Scientists have been studying matter for centuries. What have they learned?

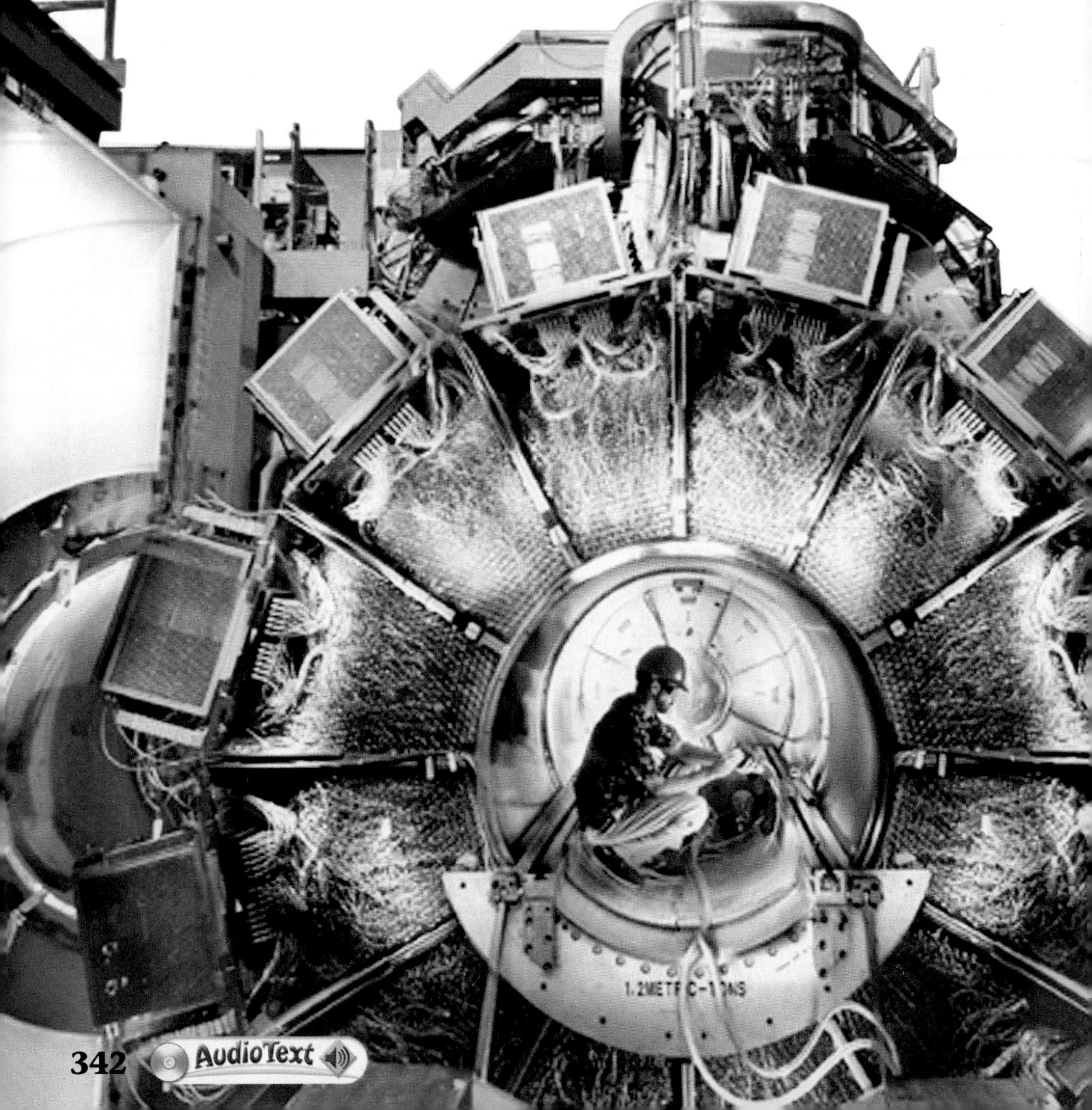

The gold in this nugget is pure gold.

Lesson 1

What are properties of matter?

All things around us are made with just a few kinds of matter. Each kind of matter has its own set of properties.

Elements

There are more than 100 basic kinds of matter, called **elements.** Elements are the basic building blocks of matter. Elements combine to make up all other kinds of matter. Elements cannot be broken into smaller pieces with ordinary physical or chemical processes.

Only a few elements, such as gold, are found in nature in pure form. Most elements are combined to form the things around us. For example, rust is a combination of iron and oxygen. Living and nonliving things are made of just a few elements combined in many ways.

Each element has its own set of chemical and physical properties. These properties can be used to identify each element. Chemical properties describe how a material changes into other materials. Physical properties can be measured without changing the material. Physical properties include an object's color, odor, mass, volume, texture, and hardness. When you record an object's color, you do not change the object at all. The same is true for an object's other physical properties. Physical properties can be observed, described, and measured with tools such as rulers, microscopes, thermometers, scales, and balances.

More than $\frac{3}{4}$ of the elements are called metals. Metals have the physical properties of being shiny, bendable, and able to conduct heat energy and electricity well.

1. **Checkpoint** How many elements are there? Are things around us usually made of pure elements or combinations of elements?
2. **Technology in Science** Why do you think pans are made of metal?

Weight, Mass, and Volume

Weight is a measure of the pull of gravity on an object. Spring scales measure an object's weight. When measuring with a spring scale, a spring is stretched or compressed by an object. The amount that the spring's length changes indicates the object's weight. If an object is too large to hang from a scale, you can add up the weights of all the object's parts. The total weight of the parts always equals the weight of the whole object.

Weight changes when the pull of gravity changes. Gravity is not the same everywhere on Earth. For example, the pull of gravity decreases slightly as an object is lifted to the top of a mountain. Therefore, the object's weight becomes a little less.

Mass is the amount of matter in an object. The amount of mass affects the weight of an object, but mass is not the same as weight. Moving an object to the top of a mountain does not change the amount of matter in an object. Its mass stays the same. Mass is measured by using a balance, often using units of grams, milligrams, or kilograms. To find mass, an object is placed on one side of the balance. Known masses are placed on the other side. When the two sides balance each other, the total mass of all the known masses equals the object's mass.

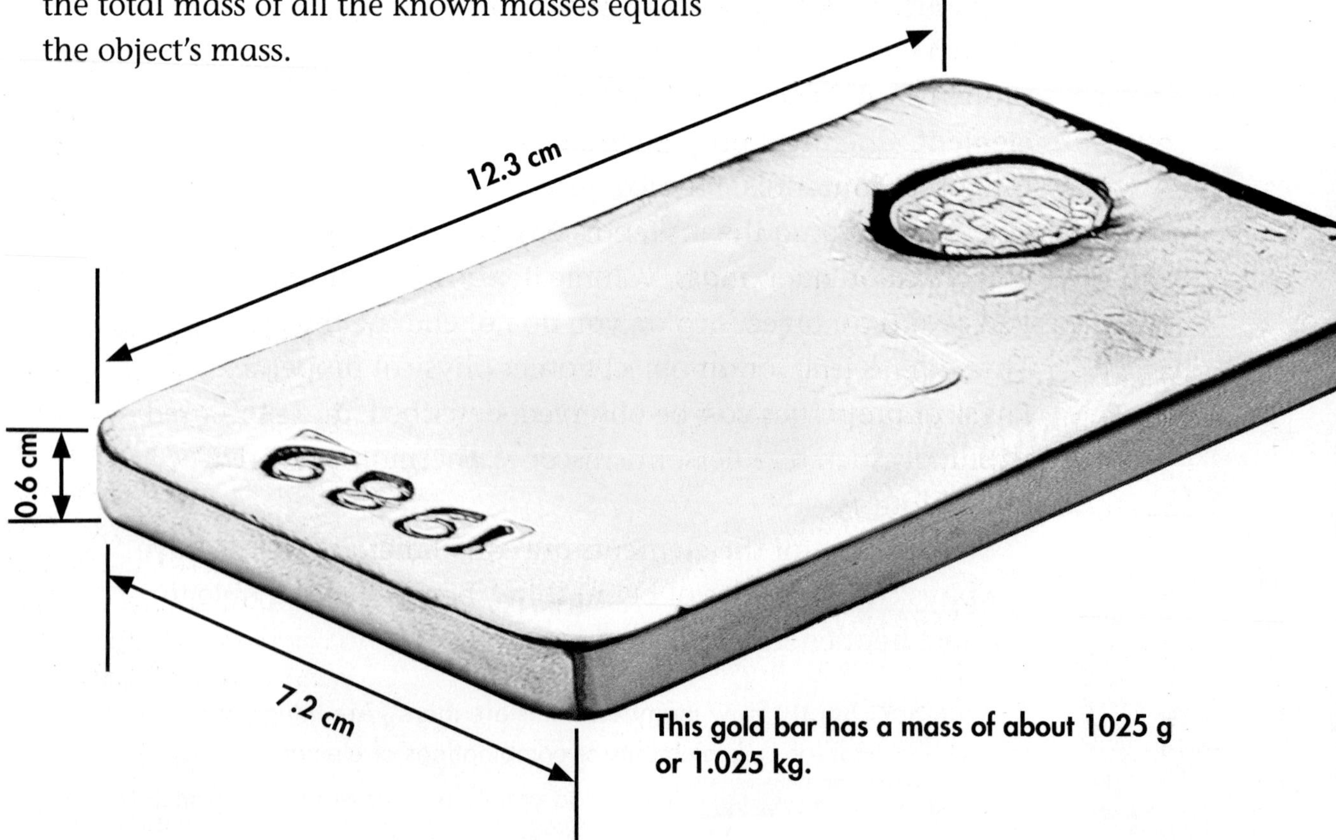
12.3 cm
0.6 cm
7.2 cm
1989

This gold bar has a mass of about 1025 g or 1.025 kg.

Volume is the amount of space that an object takes up. Cubic units are used for volume. You can find the volume of a regular box by measuring and multiplying its length, width, and height. You can write a formula using V for volume, L for length, W for width, and H for height. The formula for finding the volume of a box is $V = L \times W \times H$.

You can use a graduated cylinder to find the volume of a liquid. You can also use a graduated cylinder to measure the volume of a solid object that fits in the cylinder and sinks in water. First, put a measured amount of water in the cylinder. Then put the object into the water. Read the new volume. The difference between the two volumes is the volume of the object.

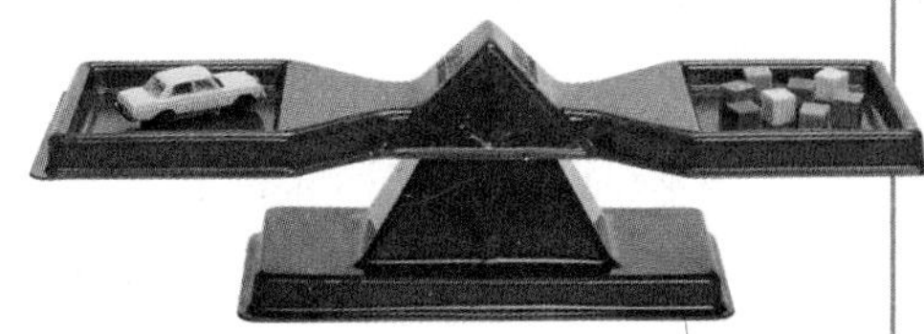

By balancing the toy car with known masses, you can measure the car's mass to be 8 grams.

Properties of Objects and Materials

How many different ways could you describe the physical properties of the gold bar shown on page 344? There is a difference between an object's properties and a material's properties. You could say that the bar's properties include a rectangular shape with a certain size and mass. These properties are only true for this bar or other bars just like it. If you cut or bend the bar, some properties will change.

A material's properties are true no matter how you bend, cut, or crush it. Gold's density is the same no matter what shape it has. All pieces of gold are not attracted to magnets. Therefore, these are gold's properties, not just the bar's properties. Other material properties include color, hardness, and texture.

1. ✓ **Checkpoint** Is volume a property of an object, or the matter that makes it up?
2. **Math in Science** Use a calculator or spreadsheet to find the volume of the gold bar pictured on page 344. Round your answer to the nearest 0.1 cm^3.

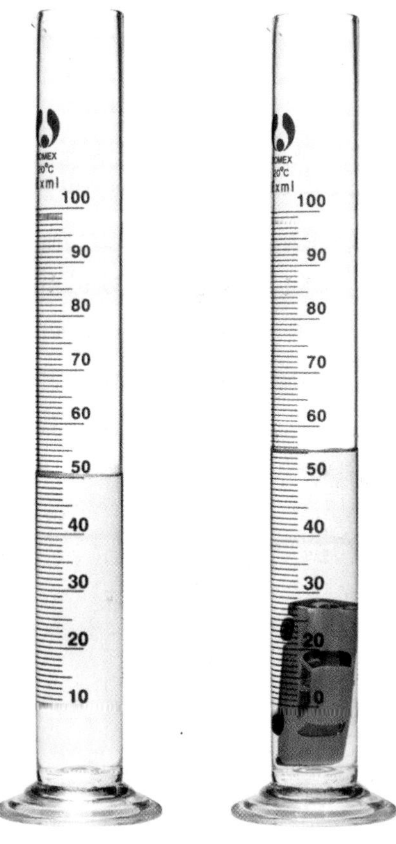
100
90
80
70
60
50
40
30
20
10
100
90
80
70
60
50
40
30

Without the toy car, the graduated cylinder measures 50 milliliters of water. With the car, the water level measures 55 milliliters. What is the volume of the car? The volume of solids are labeled with cubic centimeters. One cubic centimeter (cm^3) is the same as one milliliter.

Iron Block			
Mass	7.9 g	15.8 g	23.7 g
Volume	1 cm^3	2 cm^3	3 cm^3
Density	$7.9\frac{g}{cm^3}$	$7.9\frac{g}{cm^3}$	$7.9\frac{g}{cm^3}$

Material	Approximate Density ($\frac{g}{cm^3}$)
Fresh Water	1.00
Cork	0.25
Pinewood	0.50
Olive Oil	0.92
Beeswax	0.96
Sugar	1.60
Cement	2.70
Iron	7.90

Density and Buoyancy

Density is a measure of the amount of matter in a given volume. To find an object's density, divide the object's mass by its volume ($D = \frac{m}{v}$). For example, you could find the density of the car on the previous page by dividing its mass, 8 grams, by its volume, 5 cubic centimeters. The density is 1.6 grams per cubic centimeter.

Density is a physical property of a substance. Density is the same for a substance no matter how much of the substance is measured. For example, iron will always have a density of about 7.9 grams per cubic centimeter, no matter how large a piece of iron is measured. Because the density of a material is always the same, it can be used to help identify a material.

Equal volumes of any two different substances usually have different masses. This means that the two substances have different densities. Look at the pictures below. The ball of clay has the greater mass and the greater density.

This baseball has a mass of 110 g and a volume of 195 cm^3. Its density is about $0.56\frac{g}{cm^3}$.

This ball of clay has a mass of 445 g and a volume of 195 cm^3. Its density is about $2.28\frac{g}{cm^3}$.

Mass and Volume

Even though iron is more dense than water, it can still be used to build a ship that floats. This is because a ship is not solid metal. It has lots of rooms and hallways. Most of its volume is filled with air. Because of all this air, the ship has much lower mass than you would find in a solid piece of metal the size of the ship. This makes the ship's density less than water's density.

An object is buoyant if it floats. Buoyancy can be an important property for use in some objects such as boats or balloons. For example, you want a life jacket to float and an anchor to sink. You would use different materials for each.

Whether a certain material floats in a liquid depends on the densities of both the material and the liquid. If the object's density is less than the liquid's density, it will float. If the object's density is greater than the liquid's density, it will sink.

The chart on the previous page shows that fresh water has a density of about 1 gram per milliliter. Notice that in the chart, materials that you expect to sink in water, such as cement and iron, are more dense than water. Materials that float in water, such as pinewood and cork, have a density less than 1 gram per cubic centimeter.

Ocean water has dissolved salt and other materials. Because of this, ocean water is more dense than fresh water. Its density depends on how much material is dissolved in it.

√ Lesson Checkpoint

1. If you had two equally sized objects, how could you tell which one is more dense?
2. Suppose you had a material that is listed in the density table on the previous page. It floats in water but sinks in olive oil. What is the material? How do you know?
3. **Writing in Science** **Descriptive** In your **science journal** write a description of an object. Include some properties such as color, odor, and hardness. Is it a gas, liquid, or solid at room temperature? Do you know how well it conducts heat or electricity? Would you expect it to float?

2 He Helium

Lesson 2

How do atoms combine?

Atoms are particles of elements. Atoms combine to form compounds.

All helium atoms have exactly 2 protons and usually have 2 neutrons and 2 electrons.

Atoms

An **atom** is the smallest particle of an element that still has the properties of the element. Atoms of one element are different from atoms of other elements. Atoms are too small to be seen even with a microscope. The properties of atoms determine the properties of an element and how the element can combine with other elements.

The atom's center, or nucleus, usually has both neutrons and protons. A **neutron** has no electrical charge. A **proton** has a positive charge. An atom is identified by the number of protons it has. For example, all carbon atoms have six protons. No other kind of atom has six protons.

The elements in this column can easily lose one electron each.

Elements that are metals can conduct electricity well.

Chromium is used in chrome plating.

1	2	3	4	5	6	7	8	9	10	11	12	13	14
1 H Hydrogen													
3 Li Lithium	4 Be Beryllium											5 B Boron	6 C Carbon
11 Na Sodium	12 Mg Magnesium											13 Al Aluminum	14 Si Silicon
19 K Potassium	20 Ca Calcium	21 Sc Scandium	22 Ti Titanium	23 V Vanadium	24 Cr Chromium	25 Mn Manganese	26 Fe Iron	27 Co Cobalt	28 Ni Nickel	29 Cu Copper	30 Zn Zinc	31 Ga Gallium	32 Ge Germanium
37 Rb Rubidium	38 Sr Strontium	39 Y Yttrium	40 Zr Zirconium	41 Nb Niobium	42 Mo Molybdenum	43 Tc Technetium	44 Ru Ruthenium	45 Rh Rhodium	46 Pd Palladium	47 Ag Silver	48 Cd Cadmium	49 In Indium	50 Sn Tin
55 Cs Cesium	56 Ba Barium	71 Lu Lutetium	72 Hf Hafnium	73 Ta Tantalum	74 W Tungsten	75 Re Rhenium	76 Os Osmium	77 Ir Iridium	78 Pt Platinum	79 Au Gold	80 Hg Mercury	81 Tl Thallium	82 Pb Lead
87 Fr Francium	88 Ra Radium	103 Lr Lawrencium	104 Rf Rutherfordium	105 Db Dubnium	106 Sg Seaborgium	107 Bh Bohrium	108 Hs Hassium	109 Mt Meitnerium	110 Ds Darmstadtium	111 Uuu Unununium	112 Uub Ununbium		114 Uuq Ununquadium
		57 La Lanthanum	58 Ce Cerium	59 Pr Praseodymium	60 Nd Neodymium	61 Pm Promethium	62 Sm Samarium	63 Eu Europium	64 Gd Gadolinium	65 Tb Terbium	66 Dy Dysprosium	67 Ho Holmium	
		89 Ac Actinium	90 Th Thorium	91 Pa Protactinium	92 U Uranium	93 Np Neptunium	94 Pu Plutonium	95 Am Americium	96 Cm Curium	97 Bk Berkelium	98 Cf Californium	99 Es Einsteinium	

Electrons move around the protons and neutrons. An **electron** has a negative charge. Electrons may join or leave atoms, or be shared between atoms.

Elements are organized in a table called the periodic table of elements. The elements are arranged in each row according to the number of protons. Larger atoms are on the right side of each row. The columns of the table are arranged so that the elements in each column have similar chemical properties. Therefore, you can predict the properties of an element if you know its column. For example, in the last column on the right you will find elements known as noble gases. All these elements are gases at room temperature. They do not often combine with other elements.

Every element has a symbol of one, two, or three letters. Only the first letter of the symbol is capitalized. What elements have the symbols C, H, and Ca?

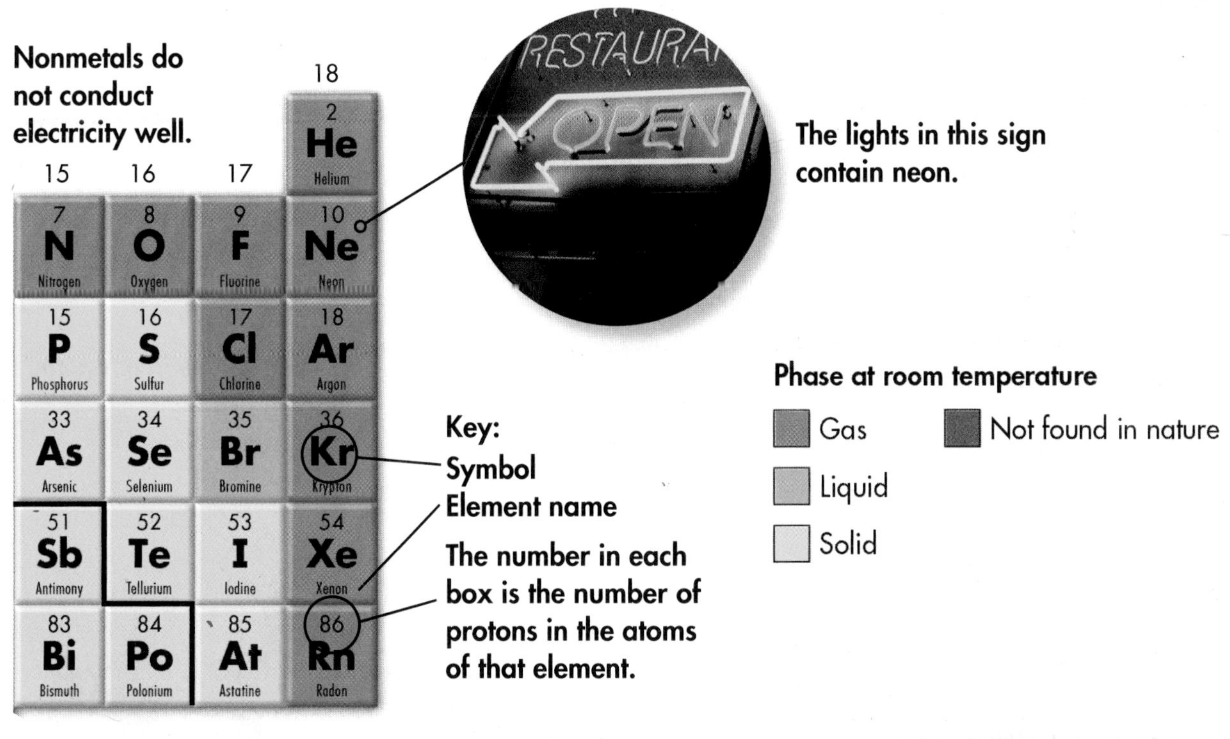
Nonmetals do not conduct electricity well.
15
16
17
18
2 He Helium
7 N Nitrogen
8 O Oxygen
9 F Fluorine
10 Ne Neon
15 P Phosphorus
16 S Sulfur
17 Cl Chlorine
18 Ar Argon
33 As Arsenic
34 Se Selenium
35 Br Bromine
36 Kr Krypton
51 Sb Antimony
52 Te Tellurium
53 I Iodine
54 Xe Xenon
83 Bi Bismuth
84 Po Polonium
85 At Astatine
86 Rn Radon
RESTAURA
OPEN
The lights in this sign contain neon.
Key:
Symbol
Element name
The number in each box is the number of protons in the atoms of that element.
Phase at room temperature
Gas
Not found in nature
Liquid
Solid

68 Er Erbium | 69 Tm Thulium | 70 Yb Ytterbium
100 Fm Fermium | 101 Md Mendelevium | 102 No Nobelium

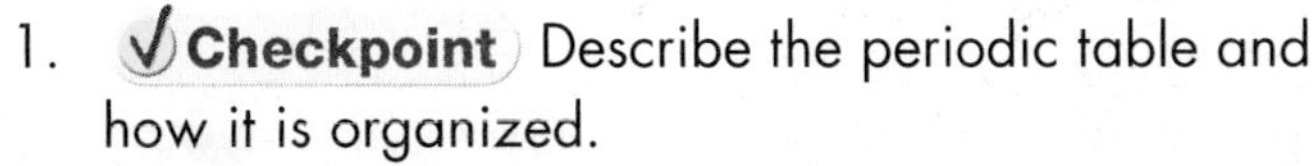

1. **✓Checkpoint** Describe the periodic table and how it is organized.
2. **Predict** Use the table to predict what atoms would have similar chemical properties as calcium. Write their names.

Molecules

Atoms may combine with other atoms to form molecules. A molecule is the smallest particle of a substance made of combined atoms that has the properties of that substance. In some molecules, atoms share electrons. Some electrons no longer go around just one atom. They go around two or more atoms. These atoms are then bonded together in the molecule.

Many substances are found in nature as molecules, not as single atoms. Air is a mixture of several kinds of molecules. It has oxygen molecules, nitrogen molecules, and molecules of other gases. Most oxygen molecules in air have at least two oxygen atoms.

Nitrogen molecules also have two atoms that are bonded together. Most of the air in the atmosphere is nitrogen gas. When nitrogen gas is cooled to -196°C, it turns into a liquid. Even so, its molecules still contain two atoms bonded together.

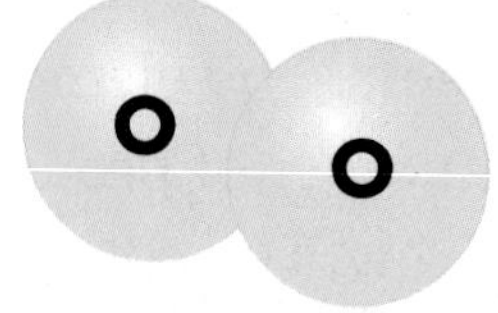
O
O

An oxygen molecule has two atoms.

N
N

A nitrogen molecule has two atoms.

Compounds

A **compound** is a type of matter made of a combination of elements. Atoms of the elements are combined into molecules. Most things that you see around you are compounds. Every molecule of a compound has the same combination of elements. Take water, for example. Every water molecule has the same three atoms.

Carbon atoms join together to form graphite, which is used in pencils.

Images of Molecules

No microscope can enable a person to actually see an atom or molecule. Atoms and molecules are too small for that. Special technology lets scientists make images of atoms and molecules. This technology detects the shape of an atom or molecule and then draws a picture on a computer screen. The pictures do not have true colors. Atoms and molecules are often seen to be well-ordered, as in this part of a graphite molecule.

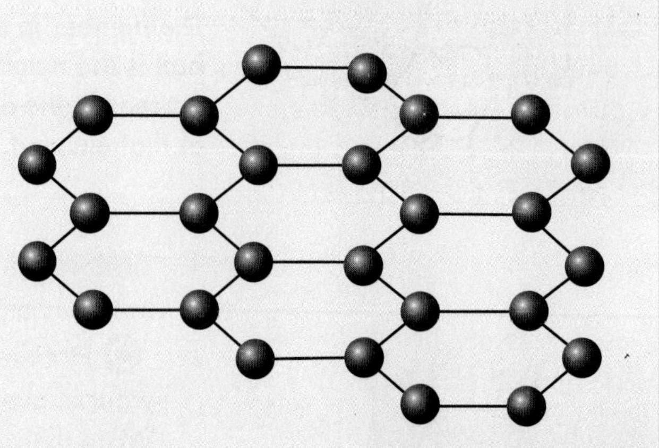

Properties of compounds are different from the properties of the elements that make them up. Water, for example is a liquid. At room temperature, hydrogen and oxygen are invisible gases and do not have a taste. Sugar is also made of atoms of hydrogen and oxygen, but it also contains carbon atoms. Pure carbon atoms can be seen as graphite, or pencil lead. Pencil lead surely does not taste sweet! Yet, when these three elements are combined in the right way, they form a sweet, white solid.

Every compound has a name and a formula. A formula shows how many atoms of each element are in the compound. For example, water has the formula H_2O. The "2" after the "H" shows that a molecule of water has two hydrogen atoms. The O stands for oxygen. It does not have a number after it. This means that a water molecule has one atom of oxygen.

A carbon dioxide molecule has the formula CO_2. It has one atom of carbon and two atoms of oxygen. Carbon dioxide does not burn. In fact, it can be used to put out fires. At temperatures of −78°C, carbon dioxide becomes a white solid called dry ice.

1. **✓Checkpoint** In a formula for a compound, what do the numbers tell you?
2. **Technology in Science** Research how dry ice, liquid nitrogen, or other very cold materials are used. Make a poster to show what you have learned.

Glucose is a kind of sugar with the formula $C_6H_{12}O_6$. The model shows one form of the glucose molecule. How many atoms and what elements are in this molecule?

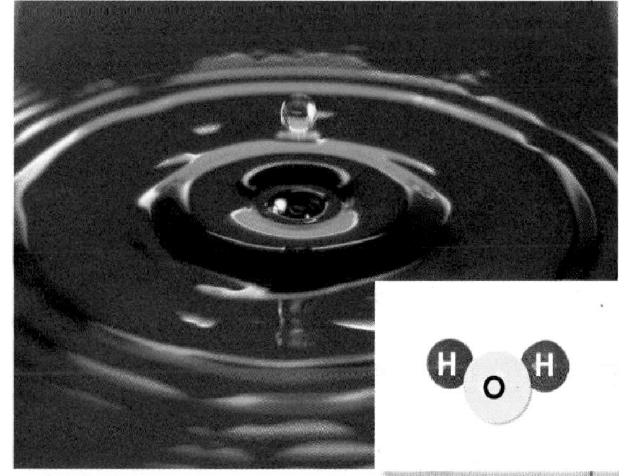
H
O
H

Every water molecule has two hydrogen atoms and one oxygen atom.

O
C
O

Dry ice is frozen carbon dioxide. Dry ice sublimates as it warms. It changes to carbon dioxide gas.

Salts

Compounds are not always formed by sharing electrons. Salts are compounds in which particles are held together by opposite charges. These particles may be charged atoms or groups of atoms. Particles with more electrons than protons have a negative charge. Particles with fewer electrons than protons have a positive charge.

There are many kinds of salts, but they all have some things in common. They all have at least one kind of metal element and one kind of nonmetal element. All salts can form crystals. Crystals are formed when charged particles arrange themselves in a regular geometric pattern. Salt crystals are brittle. Generally, very high temperatures are needed to melt salts.

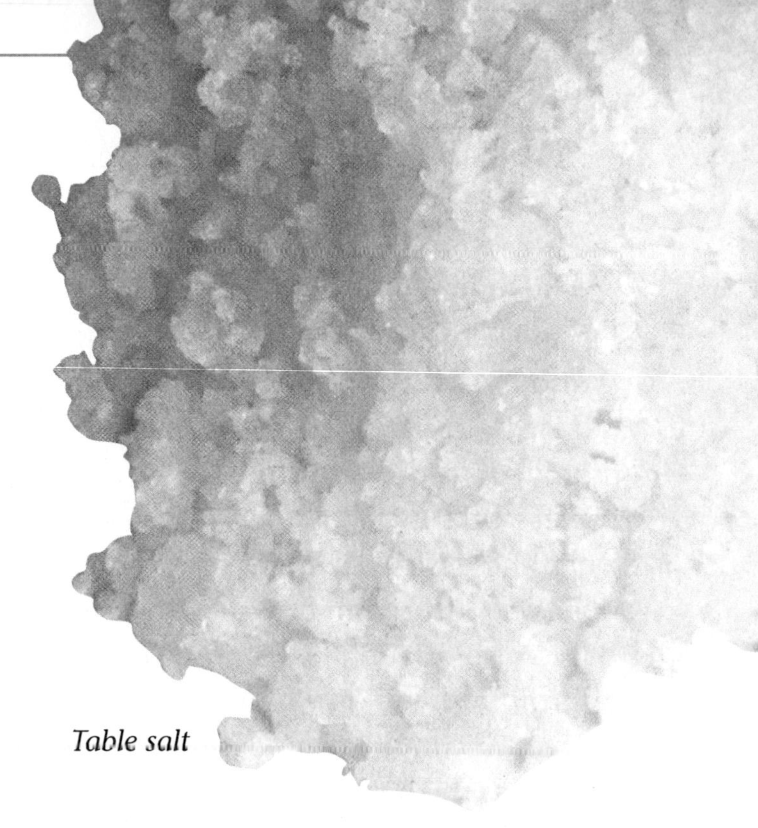

Table salt

Table salt is sodium and chlorine. Its crystals look like cubes. Its formula is NaCl.

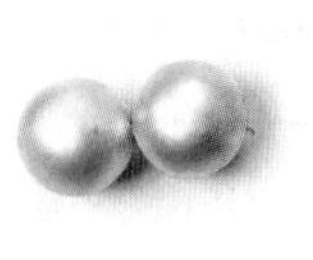

Properties of salts are different from the properties of the elements that went into making them. For example, most table salt is made of sodium and chlorine. Both of these elements can be very dangerous. Pure sodium is a soft, silver metal. Putting a large piece of sodium in water can cause an explosion. Pure chlorine is a yellow, poisonous gas. Yet together, sodium and chorine make a brittle, white solid that we can safely eat.

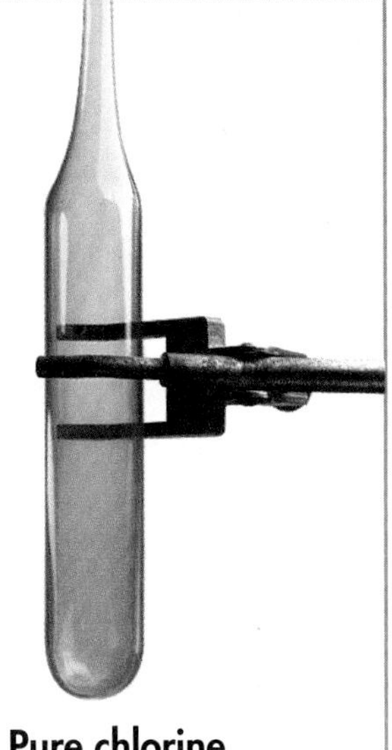

Pure chlorine gas in a bottle.

Pure copper is a golden brown metal. It can easily be bent to form pots. It can be made into wires.

Copper makes a green salt when combined with chlorine and water. Copper salts are brittle. They cannot be bent or made into a wire as pure copper can.

Pure sodium is a soft metal.

When copper is used to make a salt, its properties change. Copper makes a blue salt when combined with sulfur and oxygen.

✓ Lesson Checkpoint

1. Compare table salt with glucose.
2. Write a paragraph that tells how the words *matter, element, atom, crystal, compound,* and *molecule* relate.
3. **Predict** Suppose a large atom bonds with a small atom. Predict whether the properties of the new molecule will be the same as the large atom, the same as the small atom, or different from both atoms.

Lesson 3

How do phase changes occur?

A material is a solid, liquid, or gas because of the arrangement and motions of its atoms or molecules.

Solids and Liquids

In Chapter 7, you learned that water has three forms. Water is a solid when it's frozen as ice. Water is a liquid in the oceans. In the air, water is a gas. These three forms are called phases, or states, of matter. The phase of water or any material is due to the motions and arrangements of its particles—its molecules or individual atoms. Whether a material is a solid, liquid, or gas at room temperature is a physical property.

Solids have a definite shape and volume. The particles of a solid vibrate in place. Forces between the particles keep them from any additional change in position. In most solids, the particles are very close together.

As a solid warms up, it melts. The particles no longer vibrate in one place. Forces between particles hold the particles close to one another, but the particles can move and flow past one another. Therefore, liquids do not have their own shape. They take on the shape of their container. Since the forces keep the particles close to one another, liquids have a definite volume.

As liquids get colder and freeze, their particles slow down and vibrate in place. A material freezes at the same temperature at which it melts. This temperature is called the freezing point or melting point. For example, fresh water freezes when its temperature lowers to 0°C. Ice melts when its temperature rises to 0°C and more heat is added.

The freezing point is different for different materials. It is a physical property that can be used to help tell what a material is. The freezing point does not change for a material, no matter how much material you have. The freezing point of a liquid may change when things are added to the liquid. For example, the freezing point of salt water is lower than the freezing point of fresh water.

Materials change size when they change temperatures. This is not because material is made or destroyed. All particles are always moving. The hotter a material gets, the faster its particles move. Faster-moving particles generally have more space between them. This additional space causes the material to get a little larger. For example, running hot water over a metal jar lid makes the lid hotter. The lid will get a little larger and you can remove it more easily.

When materials cool, they may become a little smaller. This happens because their particles have less space between them when they move more slowly. Particles never get cold enough to stop vibrating, though.

1. **Checkpoint** Why do materials change size when they change temperature?
2. **Technology in Science** Why might you want to consider the melting point of a substance before choosing materials for frying pans or engine parts?

Freezing Water

Molecules of most liquids stay about the same distance apart when they freeze. Water is different. When water freezes, the molecules form a crystal pattern that has empty spaces. Water expands when these spaces form.

Material	Freezing or Melting Point
Oxygen	−218°C
Nitrogen	−210°C
Mercury	−39°C
Fresh Water	0°C
Sugar (Sucrose)	185°C
Lead	327°C
Aluminum	660°C
Gold	1063°C
Nickel	1453°C
Iron	1535°C

Gases

Compared to solids and liquids, particles of a gas are very far apart. Because they are far apart, gas particles generally do not affect one another unless they collide. If a gas is placed in a container with no other gases, the particles will spread out evenly throughout the container. Therefore, a gas does not have a definite shape or volume. Gases can be squeezed much more than solids or liquids. This is because there is more space between gas particles.

Evaporation occurs when particles leave a liquid and become a gas. Particles evaporate from a liquid if they are at the surface of the liquid and are moving upward with enough speed. This is how water puddles evaporate.

If the temperature of a liquid is high enough, particles will evaporate not only at the surface, but throughout the liquid. As gas particles move quickly upward through the liquid, bubbles of gas form under the surface of the liquid. The boiling point of a liquid is the temperature at which liquid turns into these gas bubbles.

The boiling point is a physical property of a liquid. The boiling point will be the same for a liquid no matter how much liquid is being heated. Different liquids have different boiling points. The boiling point can be used to help tell what an unknown liquid is.

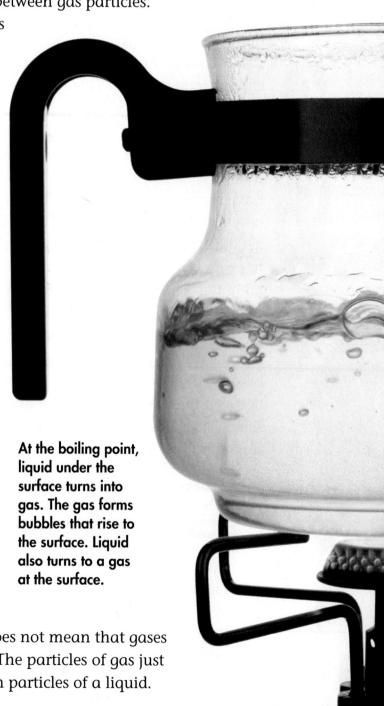

At the boiling point, liquid under the surface turns into gas. The gas forms bubbles that rise to the surface. Liquid also turns to a gas at the surface.

When a liquid turns into a gas, the gas takes up more space. This does not mean that gases have more matter than the liquids. The particles of gas just have more space between them than particles of a liquid.

Water vapor is invisible. When you see steam, what you are actually seeing are tiny water droplets formed by condensation.

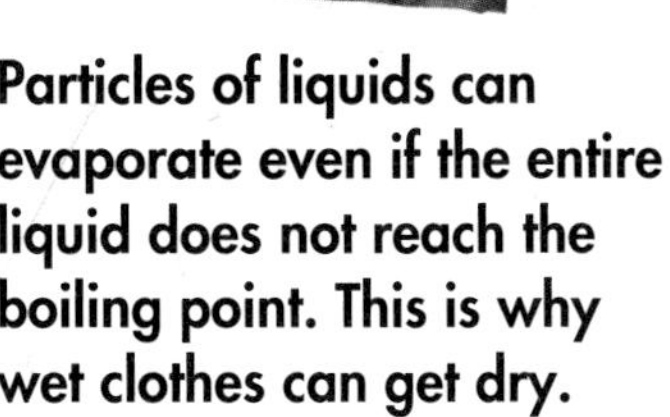

Particles of liquids can evaporate even if the entire liquid does not reach the boiling point. This is why wet clothes can get dry.

If the gas touches a cool surface, condensation can occur.

Condensation occurs when a gas turns into a liquid. This often happens when gas particles touch a cold surface and their temperature drops. The particles slow down and are trapped by the attractive forces of the surface. As more and more gas particles get trapped, they form a liquid drop. The clouds in the sky and dew on the ground form by condensation.

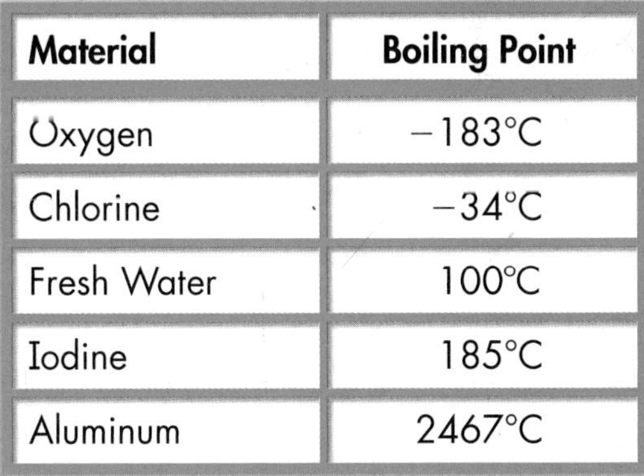

Material	Boiling Point
Oxygen	−183°C
Chlorine	−34°C
Fresh Water	100°C
Iodine	185°C
Aluminum	2467°C

√ Lesson Checkpoint

1. Compare the motion and spacing of particles as a material cools from a gas to a liquid and then to a solid phase. Do particles ever stop moving?
2. Define and compare boiling points, melting points, and freezing points.
3. **Art** in Science Make a poster with pictures or a Venn diagram to show how solids and liquids, or liquids and gases are alike and different.

Lesson 4

What are mixtures and solutions?

Sometimes elements and compounds are mixed together but are not bonded together.

Mixtures

In a mixture, different materials are placed together but do not bond to form compounds. Generally, the different materials keep their own properties. If salt and pepper are put together to make a mixture, the salt and the pepper do not change their flavors or colors. Most foods that you eat are mixtures of different materials. What is your favorite food that is a mixture?

The materials in simple mixtures can be separated because they have different properties. For example, a magnet can separate iron filings from sand. This separation happens because iron has the property of being magnetic, and sand does not have that property. A screen filter can be used to separate a mixture of pebbles and sand.

1. The mixture of salt, pepper, and water is poured through a filter. The pepper cannot go through the filter paper.

Separating a Mixture

Suppose you have a mixture of salt and pepper that you want to have separated. You can do this by using the different properties of the two materials. Salt dissolves in water. Pepper does not. Pepper would float on the water's surface.

1/4 CUP
59 ml

Some metals, such as gold, silver, copper, iron, and nickel, are elements. Many metals are mixtures of elements. For example, steel is a mixture of iron and carbon. Brass is a mixture of copper and zinc. Bronze is a mixture of metals, mostly copper and tin. These mixtures are called alloys. The properties of alloys are usually different from the properties of the original metals. The properties of the alloys depend on how much of each metal is used.

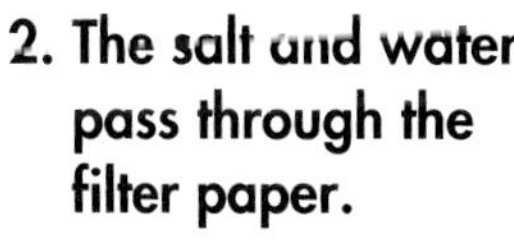

2. The salt and water pass through the filter paper.

3. To separate the salt from the water, you can use the different boiling points of water and salt. This flame is hot enough to boil water. The flame is not hot enough to evaporate the salt. The water evaporates and the salt stays in the dish.

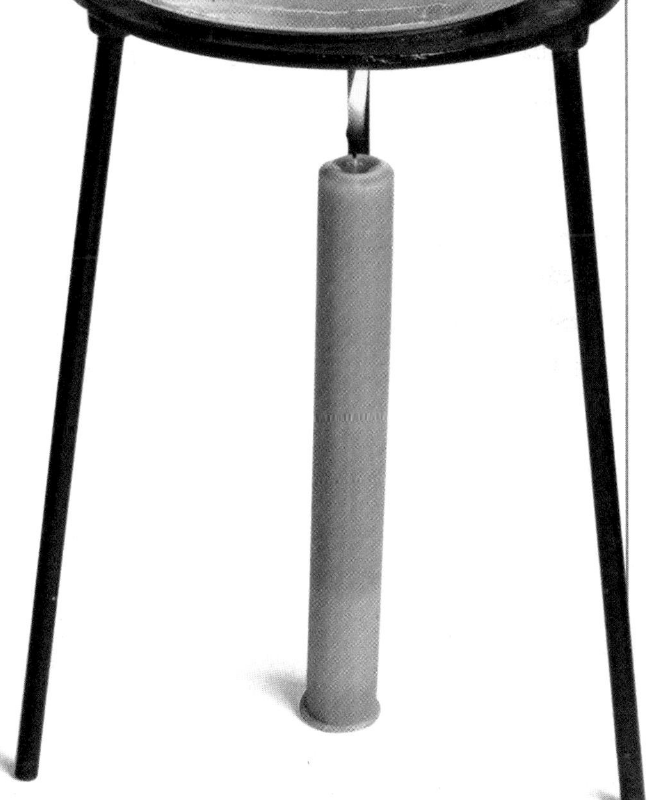

1. √ **Checkpoint** Name 5 metals that are pure elements and 3 that are mixtures.
2. **Writing in Science** **Narrative** In your **science journal,** write a story in which a character makes a mixture of food to eat. Be sure to clearly state the steps required to make the mixture.

Solutions

When dirt and water make a mixture, the dirt will slowly settle to the bottom. When a pinch of sugar dissolves in a tall glass of water to make a mixture, the sugar will not settle to the bottom. Sugar and water make a special kind of mixture called a solution.

A solution is a special mixture in which substances are spread out evenly and will not settle. In a solution, the substance that dissolves is called the solute. The solvent is the substance in which the solute is being dissolved. In the solution of sugar and water, the solute is sugar and the solvent is water. Water can be a solvent in so many different solutions that it is called a universal solvent.

When a solute dissolves, individual particles separate from the solute and spread throughout the solvent. You can make solids dissolve in a liquid faster by stirring or heating the solution. Grinding a solid solute into smaller pieces will also help it dissolve faster.

These salt crystals are made with the elements potassium, manganese, and oxygen. The salt leaves purple trails as it dissolves in water and spreads out.

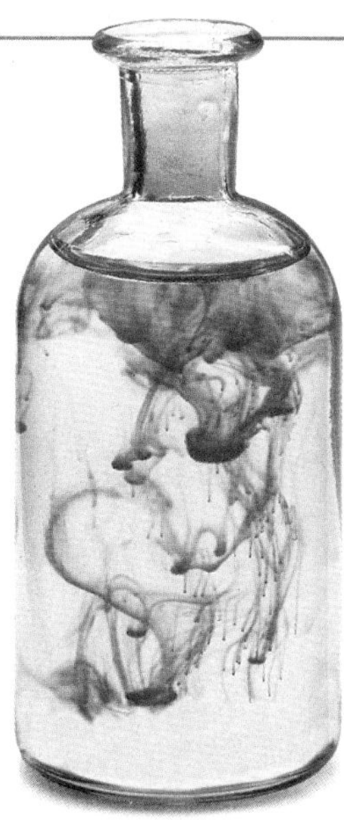

A dilute solution has little solute in comparison with how much could dissolve.

Not all solu a solid in a liquid. solution. A gas can di example, water in a lake oxygen and carbon dioxide it be important that these gases in the water?

Solubility is a property of a substance Solubility is how much of a substance can be dissolved by a solvent at a certain temperature. The hotter a solution is, the more solid solute can be dissolved.

Solutions can be described as being saturated, concentrated, or dilute. A solution that is **saturated** contains all the solute that can be dissolved without changing the temperature. If more solute is added to a saturated solution, the solute will not dissolve. A **concentrated** solution has so much solute that it is relatively close to being saturated. A **dilute** solution is far from being saturated.

In many cases, a material will not dissolve at all in a particular liquid, no matter how hot it is. For example, salt will not dissolve in oil.

A concentrated solution has a large amount of solute in comparison with the amount of solvent.

If you add more solid solute to a saturated solution, the extra solute will settle to the bottom.

✓ **Lesson Checkpoint**

1. Could a mixture of pepper and water also be called a solution? Could a mixture of salt and water also be called a solution? Explain your answers.
2. How can you cause more solid solute to be dissolved in a liquid?
3. Writing in Science **Descriptive** Observe the pictures on this page that show the making of a saturated solution of water and a purple salt. In your **science journal,** write a description of the solution's appearance in each of the photos.

...quiry

...at design ...go?

...and the other properties of matter. ...large amount of cargo without sinking.

...Do

...**n** Design a boat that will support the most cargo ..., clay, or another material of your choice can ...uild the boat. Consider which material would be best. Consider different boat designs. Sketch or diagram your proposed design choice. Explain why you picked your design solution.

...oil and clay

tub with water

metric ruler

pennies

balance and gram cubes

1. Identify which materials will work best for your design. Make a plan or a procedure.

2. Construct your **model** boat. Measure its length, width, and height in centimeters.

3. Test your boat design. Float your model boat in the tub of water. **Predict** how many pennies your boat will hold. Add cargo (pennies) to your boat. Record the number of pennies you add before your boat sinks.

Process Skills

You **measured** mass using nonstandard and standard units. Pennies are nonstandard units of mass. Grams are standard units.

4 Use a balance to **measure** the mass of the cargo in grams. Record the mass.

Did knowing about density help you solve your design problem? Explain.

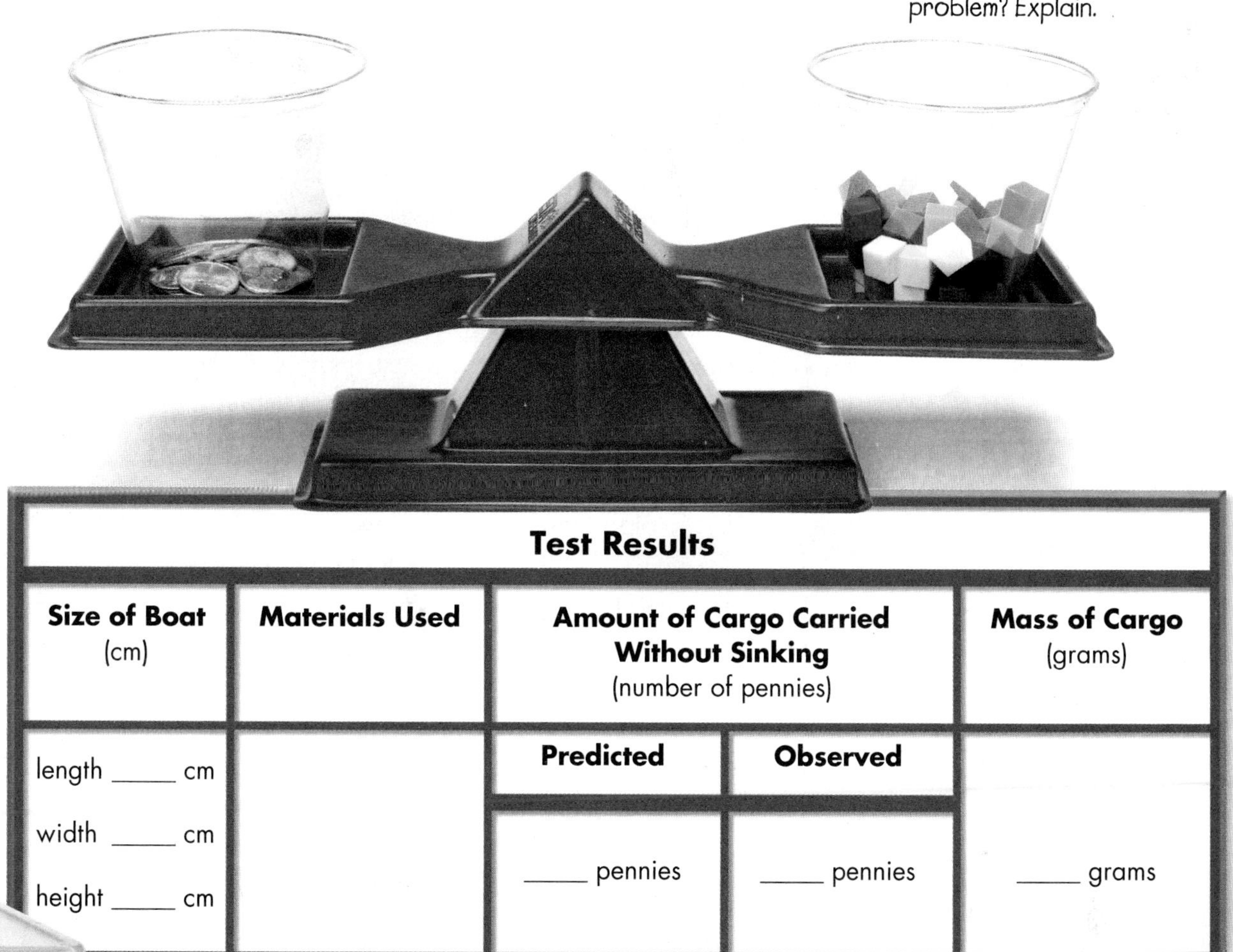

Test Results				
Size of Boat (cm)	**Materials Used**	**Amount of Cargo Carried Without Sinking** (number of pennies)		**Mass of Cargo** (grams)
		Predicted	**Observed**	
length _____ cm width _____ cm height _____ cm		_____ pennies	_____ pennies	_____ grams

If your boat was damaged, how could you repair it? What would you use?

Explain Your Results

1. Sketch your model boat design. Explain what caused your boat to sink.
2. **Interpret Data** Evaluate your model boat design. Was it more or less successful than the designs of the other groups? Explain.
3. What shape, size, and material made the boat that could carry the most cargo?

Go Further

Review your procedure and design with other students. Compare and contrast your investigation with theirs. Ask yourself and the other students questions about how your procedure and design could be improved. Use their comments to help you make revisions.

Math in Science

Data Point Spreads

The temperatures at which different chemicals change form are vastly different! Some products that we use in liquid form must be kept in pressurized containers to keep them liquid.

The table and line plots show the temperatures at which 10 different substances change form. These temperatures will change under different pressures. Not all of the liquids have familiar names, but they are commonly used. Sodium hypochlorite is used in liquid bleach. Acetic acid is what gives vinegar its strong taste and smell.

Liquid	Melting Point	Boiling Point
Water	0°C	100°C
Acetic Acid	17°C	118°C
Chlorine	-101°C	-34°C
Antifreeze (in water, equal parts)	-37°C	128°C
Sodium Hypochlorite	9°C	120°C
Ethanol	-117°C	79°C
Iodine	114°C	185°C
Ammonia	-78°C	-33°C
Hydrogen Peroxide	0°C	150°C
Propane	-190°C	-42°C

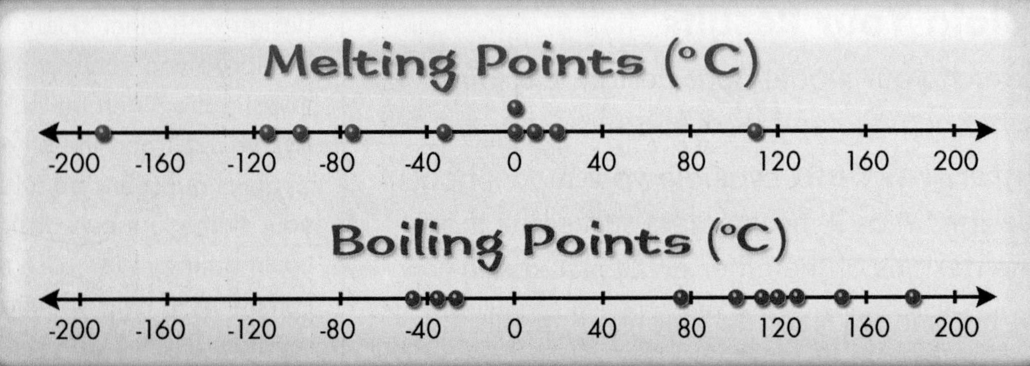

Melting Points (°C)
-200 -160 -120 -80 -40 0 40 80 120 160 200
Boiling Points (°C)
-200 -160 -120 -80 -40 0 40 80 120 160 200

eTools Take It to the Net sfsuccessnet.com

In each line plot, notice how the data spreads out on the number line. Notice also how it clusters in certain areas. Then use the table and the line plots to answer the questions.

1. In which temperature range do the melting points cluster?
   A. –120°C to –80°C
   B. –60°C to –20°C
   C. –40°C to 0°C
   D. 0°C to 20°C

2. In which temperature range do the boiling points cluster?
   F. 160°C to 200°C
   G. 80°C to 140°C
   H. 0°C to 40°C
   I. –80°C to –40°C

3. Which of the liquids has an extremely high melting point, compared to the others?
   A. propane
   B. chlorine
   C. iodine
   D. hydrogen peroxide

4. In which temperature range is the greatest gap between boiling points for these 10 liquids?
   F. between 120°C and 185°C
   G. between –33°C and 79°C
   H. between 17°C and 79°C
   I. between 100°C and 120°C

Lab zone Take-Home Activity

Copy the line plots on the previous page. Find the melting point and boiling point for 5 other substances. Make a table and add the data to the line plots.

Chapter 11 Review and Test Prep

Use Vocabulary

atom (p. 348)	**electron** (p. 349)
compound (p. 351)	**element** (p. 343)
	neutron (p. 348)
concentrated (p. 361)	**proton** (p. 348)
dilute (p. 361)	**saturated** (p. 361)

Use the term from the list above that best completes the sentence.

1. A(n) ______ is in the nucleus of an atom and has a positive charge.
2. A(n) ______ is in the nucleus of an atom and has no electrical charge.
3. A(n) ______ is part of an atom and has a negative electrical charge.
4. A solution is ______ if it has a large amount of solute in comparison with the amount of solvent.
5. A(n) ______ solution has little solute in comparison with the amount of solvent.
6. A solution is ______ if it contains all the solute that can be dissolved at the time.
7. There are more than 100 types of matter, each called a(n) ______.
8. The smallest particle of an element is a(n) ______.
9. Elements combine to form a(n) _____.

Explain Concepts

10. Explain the difference between an atom and a molecule.
11. What is the difference between a mixture and a solution?
12. Explain how matter changes from a solid to a liquid and then to a gas.

Process Skills

13. **Infer** You mix oil and vinegar for a salad dressing. After a few minutes, the oil has separated and is floating. Infer which has the greater density—oil or vinegar. Explain.

Use the following table for Question14.

Types of Bonds	
Held Together by Sharing Electrons	**Held Together by Opposite Charges**
carbon dioxide	potassium iodide
sugar	calcium chloride

14. **Classify** water and sodium chloride (table salt) by telling which column each belongs in.

15. Form Questions You have a divided box with labeled compartments. Each compartment has a sample of a different element. You drop the box and spill all the samples on the floor. Form questions to help you put the elements back in the right compartments. Form at least four questions.

Predict

16. A plastic block has sides that measure 4 centimeters, 2 centimeters, and 3 centimeters. Its mass is 19.2 grams. Predict whether the block will float in water. Will it float in olive oil? Gather information before making your predictions. Fill in the boxes below.

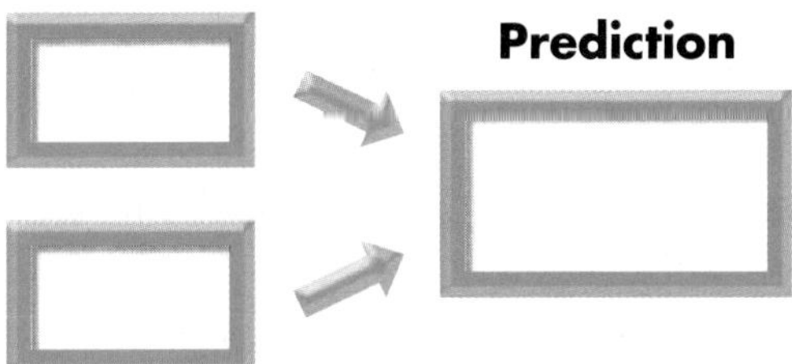
Information
Prediction

Test Prep

17. Which of the following is a mixture?
- Ⓐ gold
- Ⓑ steel
- Ⓒ iron
- Ⓓ nickel

18. The amount of matter in an object is its
- Ⓕ weight.
- Ⓖ density.
- Ⓗ volume.
- Ⓘ mass.

19. Explain why the answer you selected for Question 18 is best. For each of the answers you did not select, give a reason why it is not the best choice.

20. Writing in Science **Descriptive** Choose an item from the classroom and describe at least five physical properties of the item.

Biography

Nancy R. Hall

Research Scientist in Fluid Physics

The worst grade Nancy Hall ever got was in science. She was in fourth grade. She thought science was boring. That changed in sixth grade. Ms. Hall had a wonderful science teacher who inspired her to do experiments at home. When she got older, she studied space science in college. Now she is a research scientist at NASA. She does research on fluids—gases and liquids. She learns how they behave in space.

Nancy Rabel Hall works with gases and liquids.

Ms. Hall conducts experiments in which fluids seem, for the moment, to be weightless, as they would be in space. These experiments are done at NASA and are repeated many times. In this way, scientists ensure that the results are consistent. Then the experiments may be repeated in space—on rockets, on the space shuttle, or at the International Space Station.

Ms. Hall loves working as a space scientist for NASA. But when she first went to college, she started out in computer programming. Ms. Hall switched to space science, because that is what she really wanted to do. She advises young people to work hard to pursue their strongest interests.

Lab zone Take-Home Activity

Observe how drops of water interact. Fill an eyedropper with water. Count how many drops can fit on a penny before the water overflows.

EC NTL 10987

Chapter 12

Changes in Matter

You Will Discover

- ways that substances can change.
- how to describe and classify chemical reactions.
- how we can use chemistry to separate substances.
- how chemical technology improves our lives.

Discovery Channel School
Student DVD

Discovery
CHANNEL
SCHOOL

online

Student Edition

sfsuccessnet.com

Build Background

How do you use chemistry every day?

chemical change

chemical equation

$2Mg + O_2 \rightarrow 2MgO$

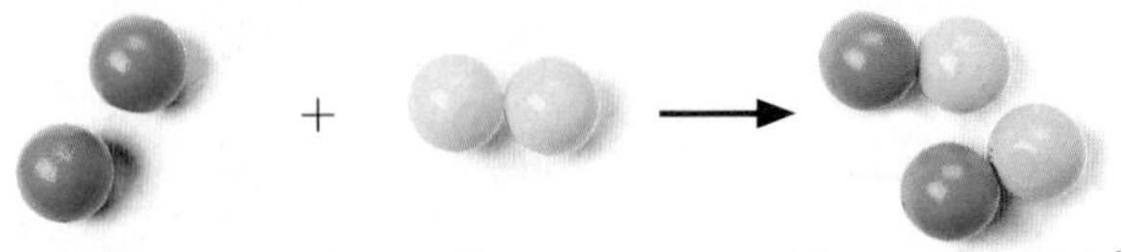

Magnesium + Oxygen → Magnesium Oxide

reactant

product

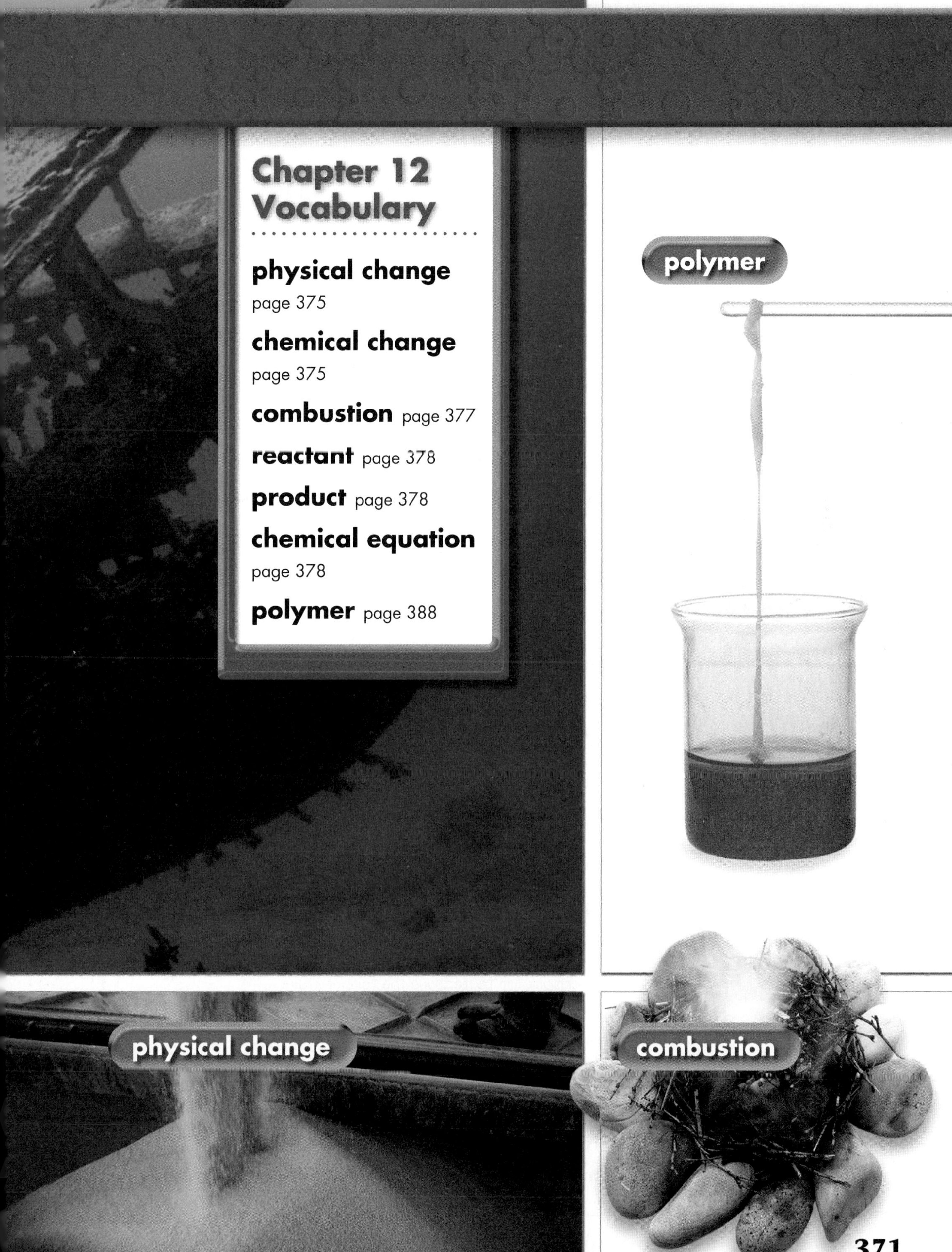

polymer
physical change
combustion

Chapter 12 Vocabulary

Lab zone Directed Inquiry

Explore What can happen during a chemical change?

Wear safety goggles.

Be careful!

Materials

safety goggles

2 cups and paper towel

room-temperature water and graduated cylinder

thermometer and 3 Alka-Seltzer® tablets

cup with 3 spoonfuls of baking soda and cup with 3 spoonfuls of calcium chloride

timer or stopwatch (or clock with a second hand)

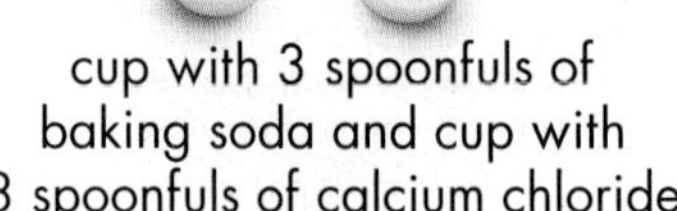

Process Skills

After you **collect data**, you use past experience to help evaluate the data and make accurate **inferences**.

What to Do

1. Put 50 mL of water and a thermometer in cup A. After 1 minute, record the temperature.

2. Add 3 Alka-Seltzer® tablets to cup A. Wait 1 minute. Record the temperature.

Do not taste the tablets, the powders, or the liquids.

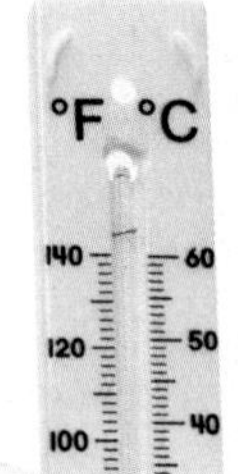

3. Wipe off the thermometer with a paper towel. Put 50 mL of water and the thermometer in cup B. After 1 minute, record the temperature.

4. Add the baking soda and calcium chloride to cup B. Wait 1 minute. Record the temperature.

If a reaction produces heat, the temperature rises. Thermal energy is given off. Less energy remains. By using a thermometer to measure the temperature change, you can tell if energy is lost or gained during a reaction.

Explain Your Results

Use the **data** you **collected** to make an **inference**. In which reaction was energy lost?

More Lab zone Activities Take It to the Net sfsuccessnet.com

How to Read Science

Reading Skills

Draw Conclusions

Your science book is packed with facts. You put these facts together with your own knowledge about the world to **draw conclusions.** Drawing conclusions helps you sharpen your understanding of science.

- Read the facts presented in this article.
- Think about what you already know about the topic to **make an inference** about it.
- Use the science facts and your own knowledge to draw a conclusion.

Cooking Article

Baking Bread

Bakers use yeast to bake bread. They mix the yeast with warm water and sugar. Then they add flour. The yeast digests the sugar and gives off bubbles of carbon dioxide. This makes the bread dough rise. The heat of baking kills the yeast. Look at the holes in a slice of bread. What conclusion can you draw about it that relates to the yeast and its activity?

Apply It!

Make a graphic organizer like the one shown here. Write down your conclusion. List the facts from the article and your own knowledge that led you to **draw** this **conclusion.**

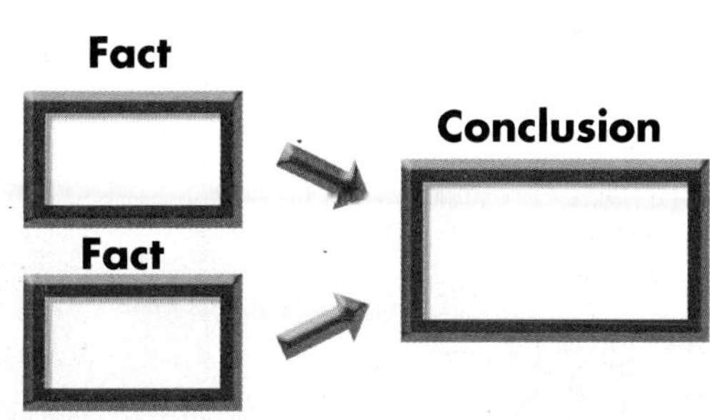
Fact
Fact
Conclusion

You Are There!

With air tanks strapped securely to your back, you swim down 40 meters toward the ocean floor. It is dark, but you have a flashlight. You cast its beam on a sunken ship, lying tilted at the bottom of the ocean. The ship has been here for over six decades. It has changed a great deal since it sank. The once sturdy wood is soft with rot. The metal no longer gleams but flakes with rust. The ocean is slowly changing the materials of the ship. What will it look like in another sixty years?

Lesson 1

What are chemical changes?

Matter changes all the time. Some changes are physical changes. Others are chemical changes.

Physical and Chemical Changes

Matter can undergo physical changes and chemical changes. When a **physical change** occurs, the material keeps its identity. Physical changes can include changes in position, size, shape, volume, and phase of matter. For example, falling raindrops can freeze to form sleet. Although the raindrops and the sleet differ in size, shape, volume, and phase of matter, they are both still the same essential substance: water.

In contrast, a **chemical change** occurs when one substance or kind of matter changes into another completely different kind of matter with different properties. For instance, the ship's wheel in the picture was made of the element iron. After years of being in the ocean's water, the iron on the wheel's surface changed into a new material called iron oxide. This compound is commonly called rust. The chemical and physical properties of rust are different from those of iron.

1. ✓ **Checkpoint** What is the difference between a chemical change and a physical change?
2. **Writing in Science** **Descriptive** Think of a time when you've caused a physical change, a chemical change, or both. Describe what happened in your **science journal.**

This ship's wheel has undergone chemical changes.

Evidence of Chemical Change

When a chemical change occurs, atoms rearrange themselves to form different kinds of matter. It is not always easy to tell if a substance has changed chemically. Evidence of a chemical change may be a change in color or the formation of a gas or a solid.

As you have read, when iron rusts it undergoes a chemical change. You can detect this change because of the change in color—the gray metal turned brownish-red.

Dropping some kinds of antacid tablets in water also results in a chemical change. The tablet fizzes, giving off many tiny bubbles. These bubbles are carbon dioxide gas. A solid antacid tablet does not contain gas. This gas forms when the compounds in the tablet undergo chemical change.

The pictures below show an experiment in which a "tree" made of copper wire is dipped into a solution. Note how the tree changes. Crystals form, clinging to the wire branches. The formation of this solid material is evidence that a chemical change has taken place.

Cars rust when a chemical change turns shiny iron into dull brownish-red rust.

This antacid tablet gives off carbon dioxide gas as it undergoes a chemical change.

The burning logs give off heat and light as a chemical change is occurring.

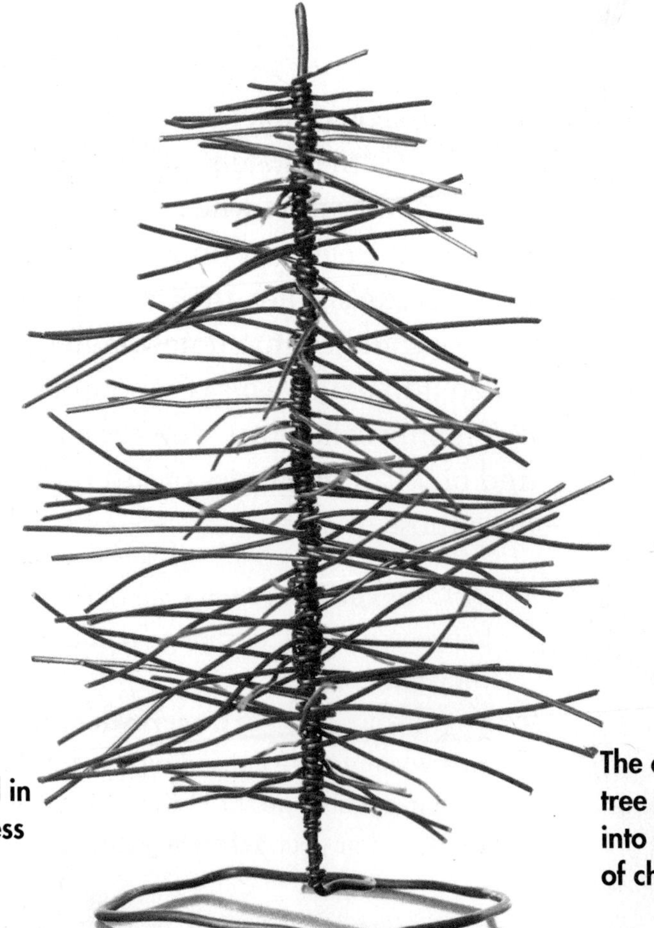

These copper wires have been arranged in the shape of a leafless evergreen tree.

The copper tree is placed into a solution of chemicals.

Chemical Changes and Energy Changes

During some chemical changes, bonds between atoms or molecules break. During other chemical changes, new bonds form. The formation and breaking of chemical bonds always involves the materials taking in or giving off energy. Sometimes, we can observe these energy changes as they occur. For example, a log burning in a fireplace is undergoing the chemical process of **combustion.** During combustion, the burning log gives off energy. We detect the energy as the heat and light of the fire. In other reactions, energy may be given off in the form of electrical energy.

✓ Lesson Checkpoint

1. List three types of evidence of chemical change.
2. Compare the second and third pictures of the copper tree experiment. Aside from the forming of solid crystals, what other evidence of chemical change in the liquid do you see?
3. **Draw Conclusions** When you cook an egg, do you think a chemical change occurs? Why or why not?

A chemical change has caused solid crystals to form on the copper tree. These crystals are made by a chemical change that happens with the copper and a chemical in the solution. Look at the top of the tree. Why hasn't it changed?

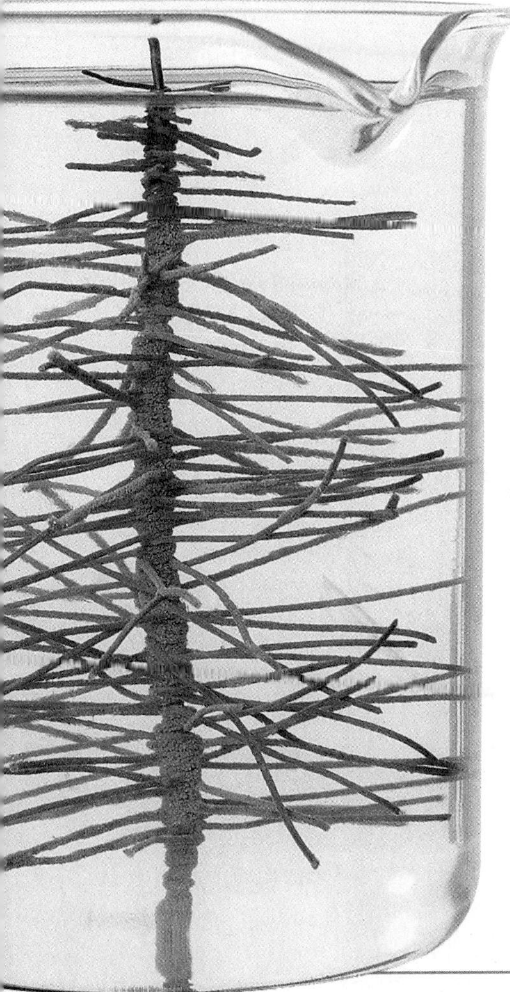

Lesson 2

What are some kinds of chemical reactions?

Chemical changes occur during chemical reactions. There are several different kinds of chemical reactions.

Chemical Equations

During a chemical reaction, one or more substances change into other substances with different chemical and physical properties. A substance used in the reaction is called a **reactant.** A substance made during the reaction is called a **product.** During the chemical reaction, the reactants undergo chemical change. Their atoms rearrange to produce the products.

A special kind of "sentence," called a **chemical equation,** shows what happens during a chemical reaction. The reactants are listed on the left side of the chemical equation. The products are listed on the right side. An arrow between the reactants and products is sometimes read as "makes." It is similar to an equal sign in a math equation.

In the picture at the right, electricity flows through water. This causes the atoms in the water molecules to rearrange and form hydrogen and oxygen gases. Water is the reactant. Hydrogen and oxygen gases are products. The equation for this reaction is:

$$2H_2O \rightarrow 2H_2 + O_2$$

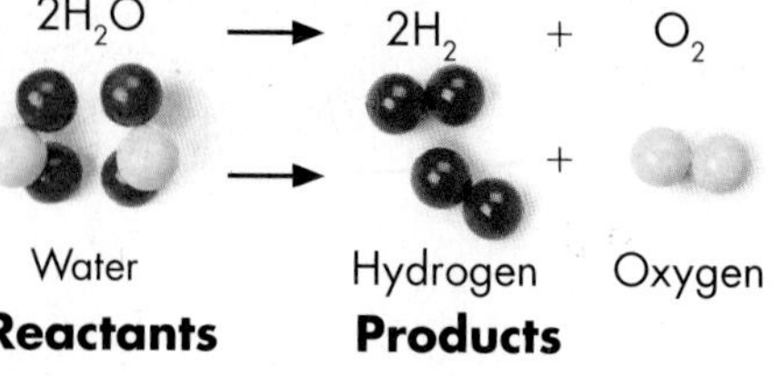

Water
Reactants
Hydrogen
Oxygen
Products

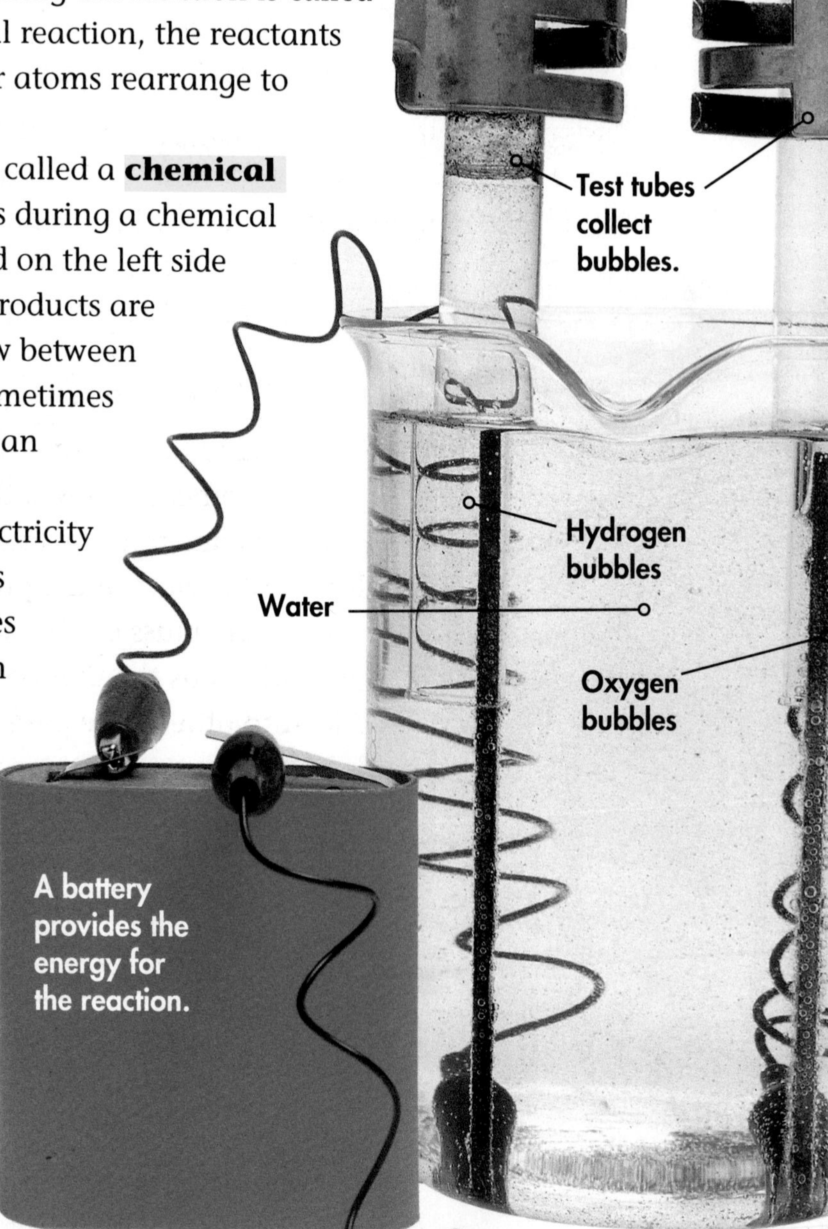

Test tubes collect bubbles.
Hydrogen bubbles
Water
Oxygen bubbles
A battery provides the energy for the reaction.

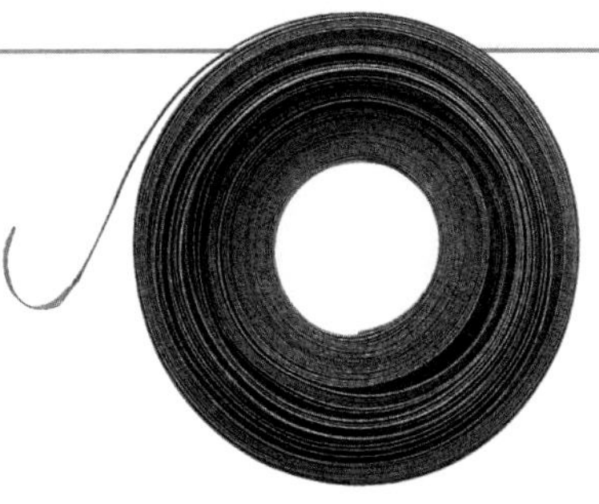

Magnesium metal is gray.

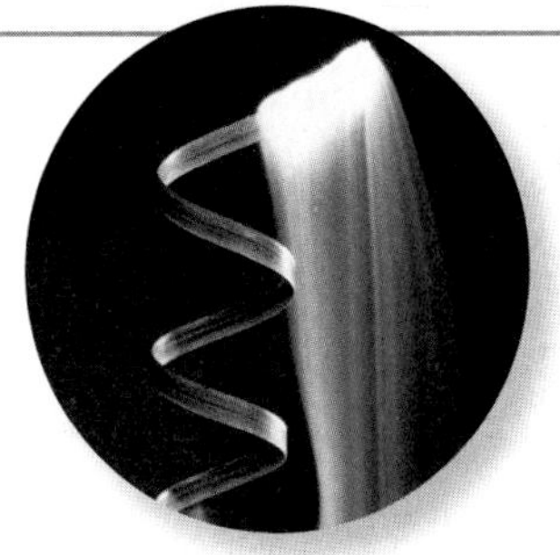

Magnesium can combine with oxygen. They are reactants. Bright light and heat are evidence that a reaction is happening.

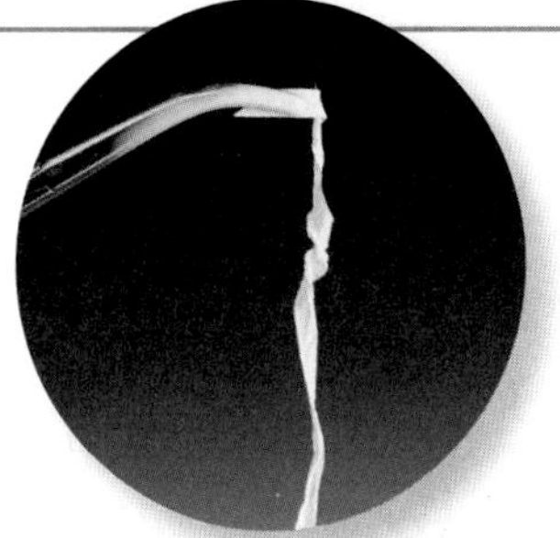

The product is magnesium oxide. This product has properties that are different from the properties of the reactants.

$$2Mg + O_2 \rightarrow 2MgO$$

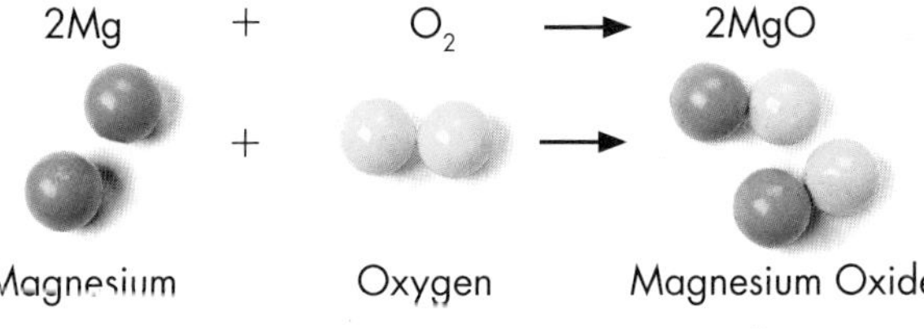
Magnesium
Oxygen
Magnesium Oxide
Reactants
Product

Magnesium is a gray metal. If it reaches a high temperature, it reacts with oxygen in the air and burns with a bright white glow. In fact, magnesium is a common ingredient in fireworks. As the chemical reaction goes on, a white powder forms. This powder, magnesium oxide, is the product of the reaction.

Matter Is Always Conserved

Matter cannot be created or destroyed during a chemical reaction. This statement is called the Law of Conservation of Mass. It means that the total mass of the reactants equals the total mass of the products. If you bake a cake, for instance, the mass of the ingredients equals the mass of the cake plus the mass of the water vapor, carbon dioxide, and other trace gases that waft from the oven, making the cake smell so good.

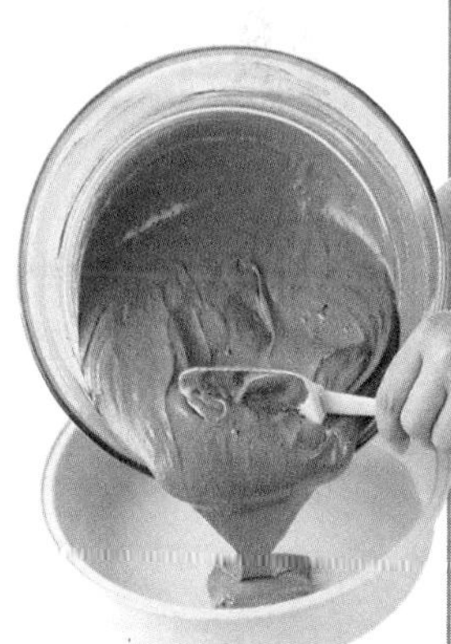

Matter is conserved when you bake a cake.

1. ✓Checkpoint What do chemical equations show?
2. Math in Science Look at the chemical equation on the top of this page. Suppose you start with 100 atoms of magnesium. How many molecules of oxygen are needed to react with all the magnesium?

Types of Chemical Reactions

It is sometimes easier to understand chemical reactions if you use a model. A model is something that is different from the real thing, but can still be used to learn something about the real thing. We can use trucks and trailers as models of atoms in reactions. There are many different kinds of chemical reactions. Three important kinds are described here.

In one kind of reaction, compounds split apart to form smaller compounds or elements. This is called a decomposition reaction. To picture a decomposition reaction, think of a truck unhitching from the trailer. This kind of reaction occurs in the experiment pictured on page 378. In this experiment, electricity causes water to break apart to form hydrogen and oxygen gases.

In another kind of reaction, elements or compounds come together to form new compounds. This is called a combination reaction. To picture a combination reaction, think of a truck connecting to a trailer. This kind of reaction occurs when iron and sulfur come together to form a compound called iron sulfide. This combination reaction is shown in the pictures on these pages.

When sugar is heated, it caramelizes. During part of this process, sugar molecules break apart.

reaction	model
decomposition	○● ➡ ○+●
combination	○+● ➡ ○●
replacement	●○+●● ➡ ●●+●○

Before the reaction, iron is a grey magnetic material.

Sulfur is a yellow powder that is not magnetic.

In a third kind of reaction, at least one molecule splits apart. The parts of the molecule switch places, just as two trucks can switch trailers. This kind of reaction is known as a replacement reaction. One example of a replacement reaction is the burning of a candle. Some candle waxes are long molecules of carbon and hydrogen atoms. Remember that oxygen gas is a molecule made of two oxygen atoms. When wax burns, the long molecules and oxygen molecules break apart and rejoin in new compounds such as carbon dioxide and water.

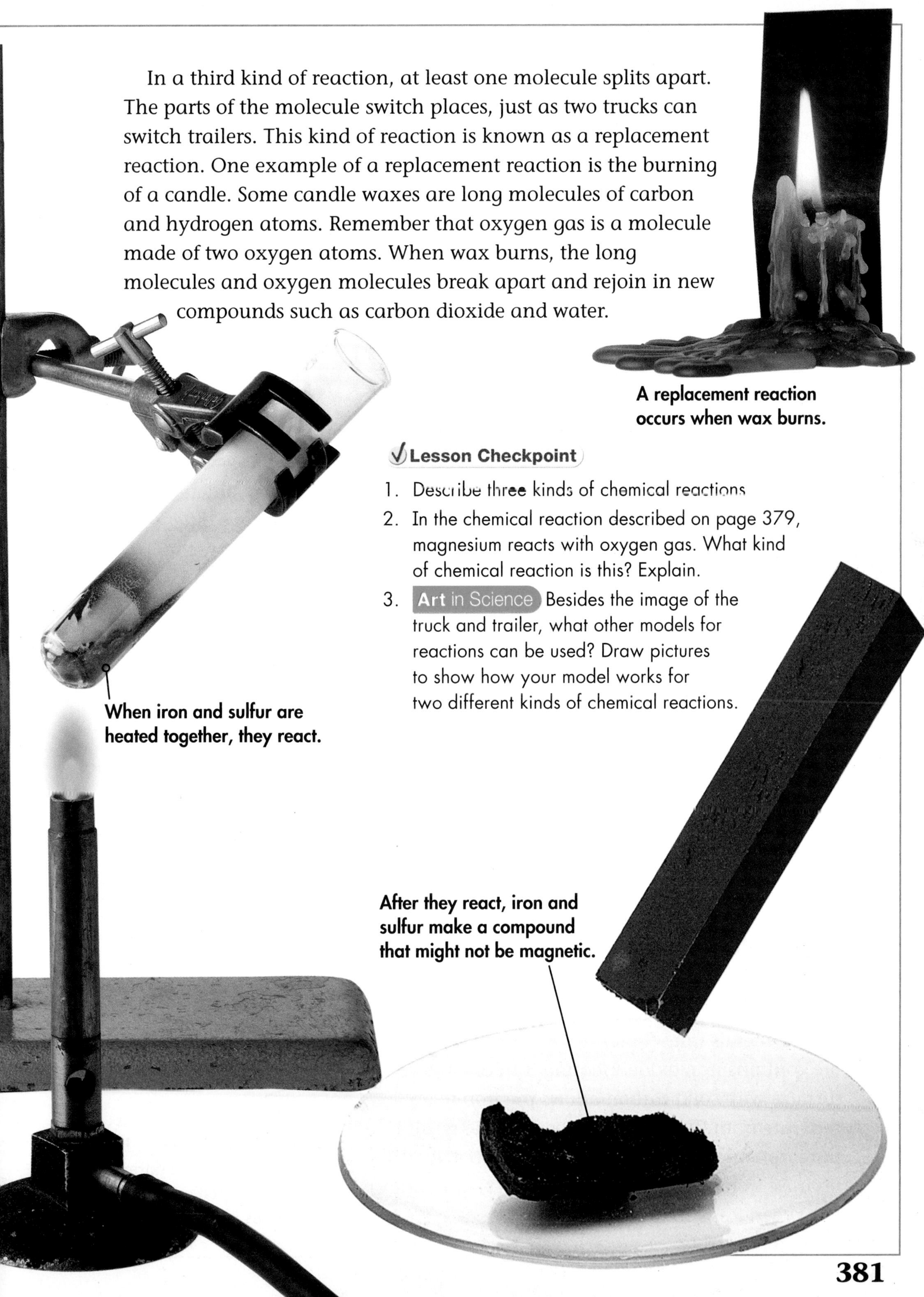

A replacement reaction occurs when wax burns.

When iron and sulfur are heated together, they react.

After they react, iron and sulfur make a compound that might not be magnetic.

✓ Lesson Checkpoint

1. Describe three kinds of chemical reactions.
2. In the chemical reaction described on page 379, magnesium reacts with oxygen gas. What kind of chemical reaction is this? Explain.
3. **Art in Science** Besides the image of the truck and trailer, what other models for reactions can be used? Draw pictures to show how your model works for two different kinds of chemical reactions.

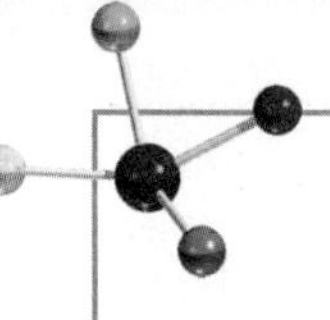

Lesson 3

How are chemical properties used?

The fossil does not react quickly with vinegar, but the limestone around the fossil does. What evidence of this reaction can you detect?

Chemical and physical properties are helpful in many ways. They can be used to separate mixtures and to help identify materials.

Separating Mixtures

Substances in some mixtures can be separated by physical means. As you read in Chapter 11, you can separate salt and pepper because they have different physical properties. Substances may also have different chemical properties that can be used to separate them from one another.

Scientists who study dinosaur fossils and other fossils use chemical properties to separate mixtures. Fossils are often scattered throughout limestone. It can be difficult to chip limestone off a fossil without damaging the fossil. However, limestone can be dissolved by vinegar. A bubbling reaction occurs. Fossils, which are made of a different kind of rock, do not react with vinegar as quickly. So scientists sometimes use vinegar or similar chemicals to separate fossils from rock.

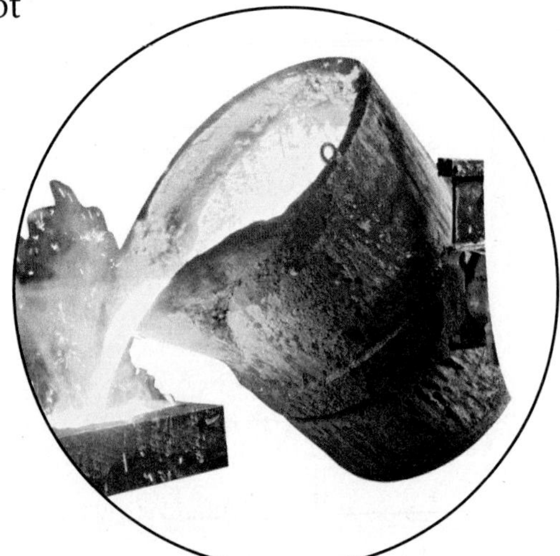

In this blast furnace, iron is separated from iron ore. The process relies on the different chemical properties of the substances heated here.

Separating Metals from Ores

Ores are rocks that include metals combined with other substances. People rely on chemistry to release metals from their ores. For example, iron ore contains iron oxide. Heating iron ore in a hot furnace with solid carbon allows the iron to separate from the oxygen in the ore. The result is pure iron and carbon dioxide. This process works because iron has the chemical property of bonding to oxygen less strongly than to carbon.

Sometimes chemical properties can be used to separate elements from solutions. For example, lead can be taken out of a solution that contains water, lead, and other materials. The solution is poured into a container with a second solution that contains iodine. Both solutions are clear liquids. As soon as the solutions mix, the lead reacts with the iodine. These two elements form a compound called lead iodide. This is a yellow solid. The lead iodide can be filtered out of the liquid to remove the lead from the solution.

This solution contains a lead compound. Chemical properties can be used to remove the lead from the solution.

The solution is poured into a second solution that contains a compound of iodine.

The lead combines with the iodine and forms a yellow solid. This solid can be filtered to remove the lead from the solution.

1. **Checkpoint** How can chemical properties be used to separate substances in a mixture or compound?
2. **Draw Conclusions** The chemical reaction for purifying iron ore looks like this:

2FeO	+	**C**	→	**2Fe**	+	**CO_2**
iron oxide		carbon		iron		carbon dioxide

Review the different kinds of reactions discussed in Lesson 2. What kind of reaction is shown here?

Identifying Substances

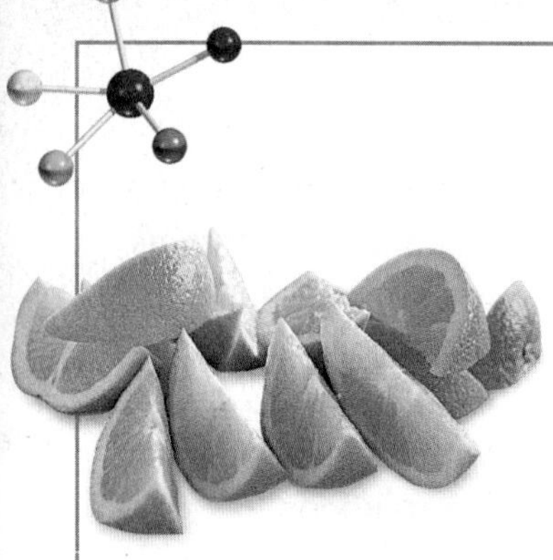

Fruits such as oranges and lemons contain acid.

Soaps may contain bases.

Scientists use physical properties, such as density, to identify substances. They can use chemical properties for this purpose, as well. The pictures below show one way scientists do this.

Acids and bases are two common types of substances. Lemon juice and vinegar are acids. Household cleaners may contain bases. Strong acids or bases will react with other materials more easily than weak acids and bases do.

Acids and bases have chemical properties that help people identify them. Acids and bases each react with chemicals in special paper called universal indicator paper. These reactions produce color changes in the paper. Substances that are strong acids will turn the paper red. Strong bases will turn the paper purple. Weaker acids or bases will produce different colors. Other kinds of papers and liquids will change colors because of acids or bases.

Universal indicator paper and similar products are not enough on their own to identify a substance. Many different acids will turn indicator paper red. Many bases will turn it purple. Indicator paper is helpful, though, in providing more clues for people to use in identifying a substance.

Rainbow Strip of Indicator Paper

Bases cause universal indicator paper to turn shades of green, blue, and purple. Acids make the paper turn orange or red.

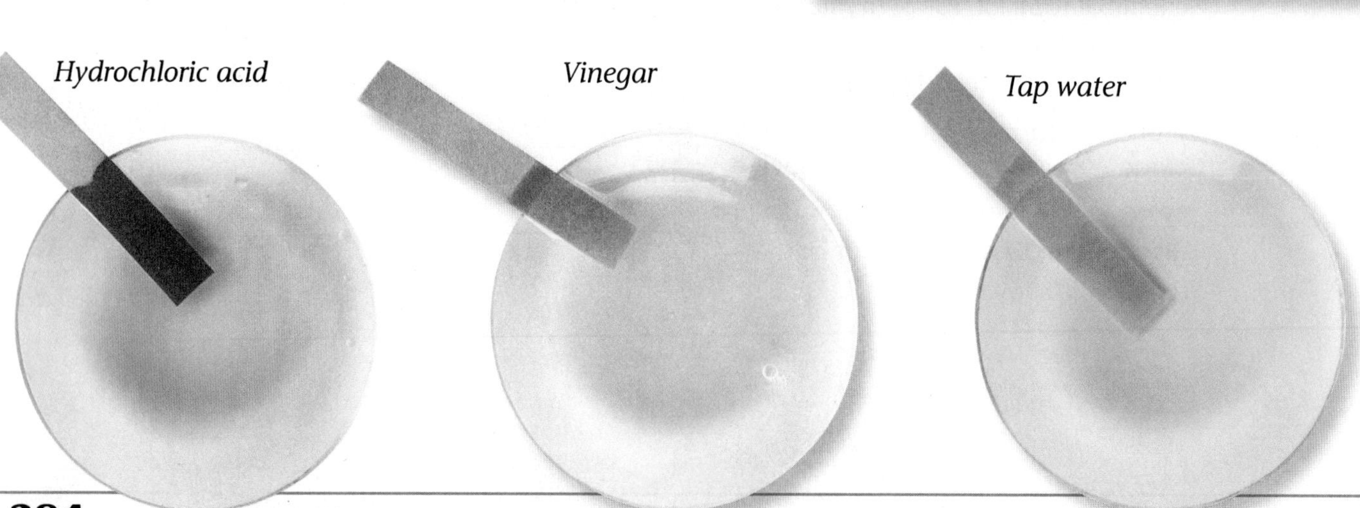
Hydrochloric acid
Vinegar
Tap water

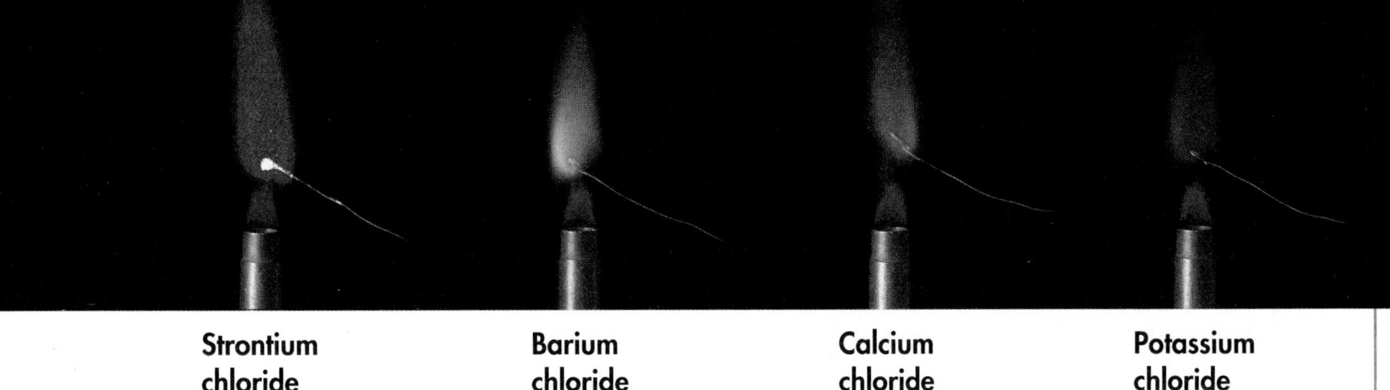

Strontium chloride	Barium chloride	Calcium chloride	Potassium chloride

These wires were dipped in different metal salts. When the metal is heated to a high temperature, the color of the flame can be used to identify the salt.

Scientists sometimes use flame tests to identify a substance. In a flame test, a material is heated to high temperatures in a flame. Different substances will cause the flame to have different colors. When these flames are studied closely with laboratory equipment, the substances can be identified. What color flame does calcium chloride give off?

√ Lesson Checkpoint

1. How might a scientist distinguish the following compounds: strontium chloride and potassium chloride?
2. What color do you think indicator paper would turn if it were dipped in shampoo? Explain your answer.
3. **Writing in Science** **Expository** Use what you learned about flame tests to explain how compounds that contain strontium and barium could be used in fireworks. Write your explanation in your **science journal.**

lemon juice tomato juice seawater household ammonia

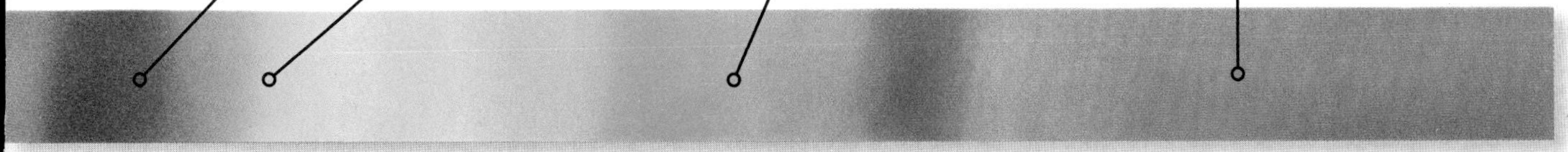

Liquid soap

Household cleaner

Lesson 4

How is chemical technology used in our lives?

Chemists have made important discoveries that have improved health, nutrition, agriculture, transportation, and many other parts of our lives.

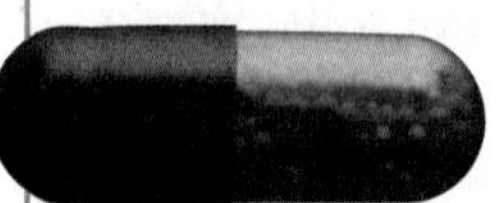

Antibiotics and other medicines are often in capsules. The capsules are made of chemicals that dissolve in your digestive system.

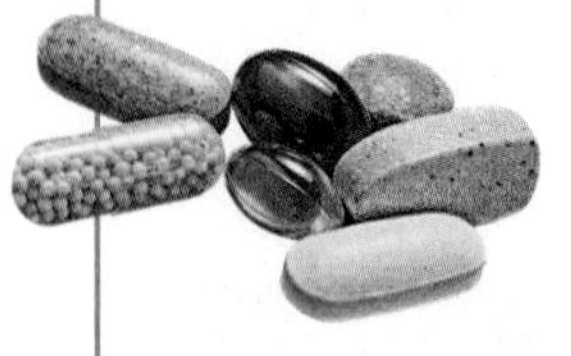

Many vitamin pills today are made by chemists.

Chemistry and Health

Years ago, it was not uncommon for people to die from simple cuts. If a cut became infected with bacteria, the infection could spread to the blood. This kind of infection was usually fatal. No medicine could cure it.

In 1928, British scientist Alexander Fleming made an accidental discovery that eventually led to the development of very powerful medicines to treat infections. Fleming grew bacteria in dishes. When one of his dishes got contaminated with mold, Fleming noticed that the bacteria near the mold died. The mold produced a bacteria-killing substance, Fleming called this substance penicillin after the name of the mold. Chemists isolated penicillin from the mold and found ways to mass-produce it. Many kinds of infections could be treated with penicillin. By the mid-1940s, this chemical had become an important life-saving medicine. Today, there are many medicines that kill bacteria. These medicines are called *antibiotics.*

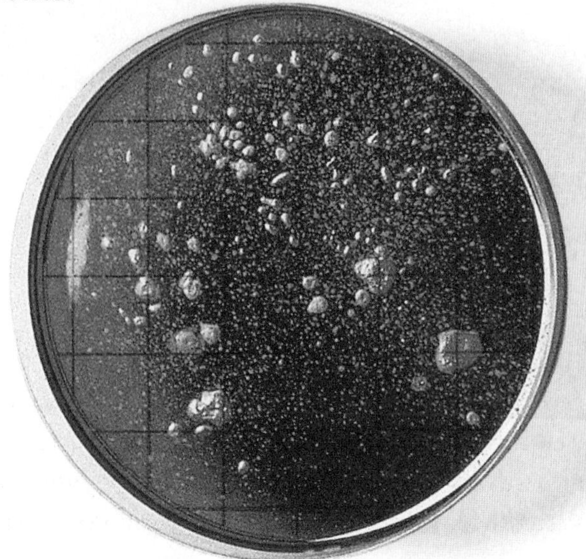

Bacteria are growing in a petri dish.

Years ago, some people suffered from a disease that at first made their skin turn red and scaly. In later stages, the disease led to mental illness. Other people suffered from a disease that made the tongue smooth. Another disease gave children malformed bones, including legs that bowed out or knees that knocked together. In the early 1900s, scientists found that each of these diseases could be prevented if people ate certain foods. Chemists identified the substances in foods that cured these diseases. They named these chemicals *vitamins.* Today, many foods that we eat in the United States are enriched with vitamins. The diseases caused by lack of vitamins are now rare in this country.

The development of fertilizers led to other improvements in our food supply. Fertilizers are chemicals that farmers add to the soil to increase the amount of food that will grow. In the 1900s, chemists found a way to make large amounts of fertilizer in factories. Using these fertilizers, farmers in the United States have been able to grow more food than before. This has lowered the cost of many foods.

Different fertilizers add potassium, nitrogen, and phosphate to the soil. These chemicals help plants grow.

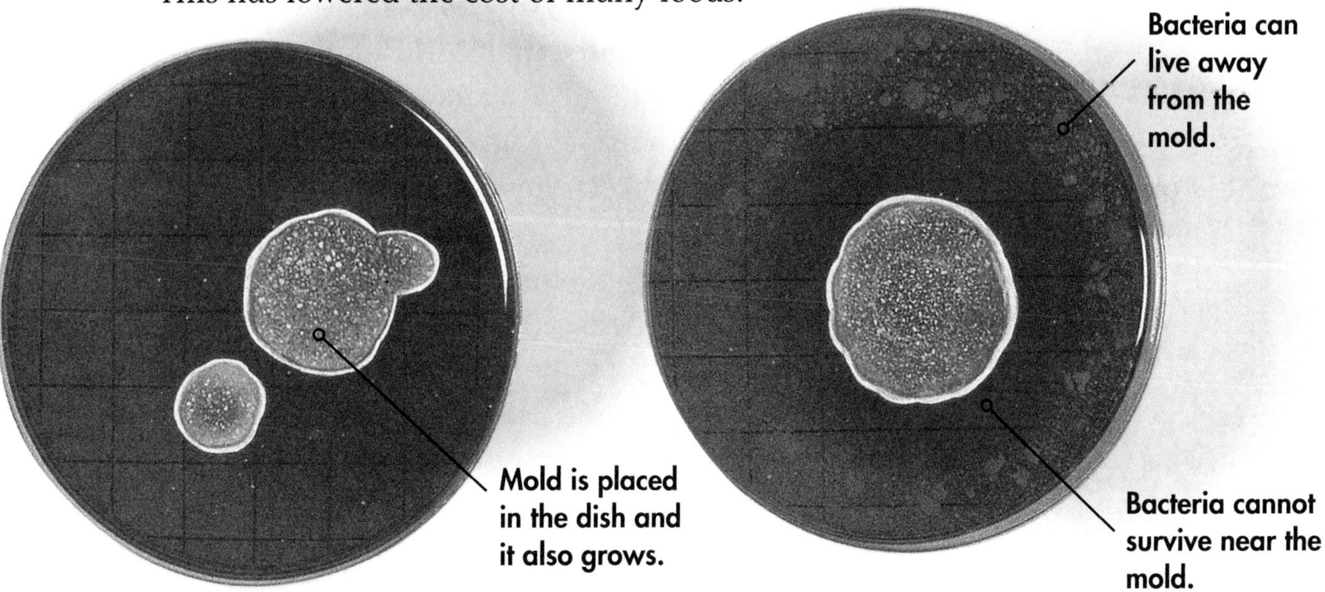
Bacteria can live away from the mold.
Mold is placed in the dish and it also grows.
Bacteria cannot survive near the mold.

1. **√ Checkpoint** What are antibiotics and how have they improved health?
2. **Writing in Science** **Persuasive** As you learned in Chapter 6, overuse of antibiotics can cause them to stop working to cure diseases. However, many of today's soaps have antibiotics added to them. Write a short editorial on whether you think soaps that you use every day should or should not contain antibiotics. Explain your reasoning.

Chemistry and New Materials

The solution in this beaker is drawn out to make nylon thread.

Many materials you use every day come from nature. For instance, the cotton in jeans comes from a plant. The wool in a sweater is sheep's hair. But some common materials are not found in nature. They were invented by scientists. For instance, nylon in stockings and other clothing, plastics in toys and many other everyday objects, and even concrete in sidewalks, roads, and highways, are all human-made materials.

In the 1800s, scientists began working to make a fiber to replace silk. Silk is strong, soft, smooth, and shiny. It can be dyed easily. It is also comfortable to wear. Making silk requires unraveling the thread from silkworm cocoons. That is one reason silk has always been expensive. In the 1880s a French scientist made a soft, shiny fiber similar to silk. The only problem was that it easily burst into flames. Thirty years later, scientists came up with another human-made silk. But this one would sag out of shape. In the mid-1930s, an American chemist reached success. His silklike fabric, called nylon, was perfect for stockings. It soon came to be used in ropes, nets, fishing line, and racquet strings, as well as fabrics.

Nylon is a **polymer**—a large molecule made of many identical smaller units connected together. In nylon, each unit is made of six carbon atoms, seven hydrogen atoms, and one nitrogen atom. A polymer may have thousands or millions of units in a single chain.

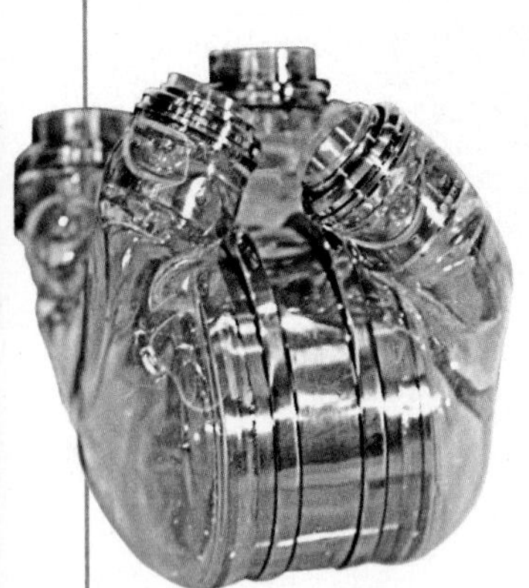
Plastic is not just useful for making toys. This artificial heart is made of metal and plastic.

Plastic is another type of polymer that scientists learned to make in the laboratory. There are many kinds of plastic. One kind is a long chain of carbon atoms, each with two hydrogen atoms. Many plastics are made with chemicals found in petroleum. Plastics are useful because they are lightweight, durable, and resistant to corrosion. They are also relatively inexpensive to make. What are some things in your home that are made of plastic?

You might think that concrete is just sand mixed with water. But the main ingredient is cement—a complex human-made material. To make concrete, cement is mixed with gravel, sand, and water. When cement sets, a chemical reaction occurs. The resulting concrete is rocklike—hard and durable.

Chemists have made different kinds of concrete for a variety of uses. By adding other chemicals, concrete can be made so that it will harden in very cold weather or have higher strength than other kinds of concrete. Sometimes large amounts of tiny fibers are mixed in concrete to make it stronger and have fewer cracks.

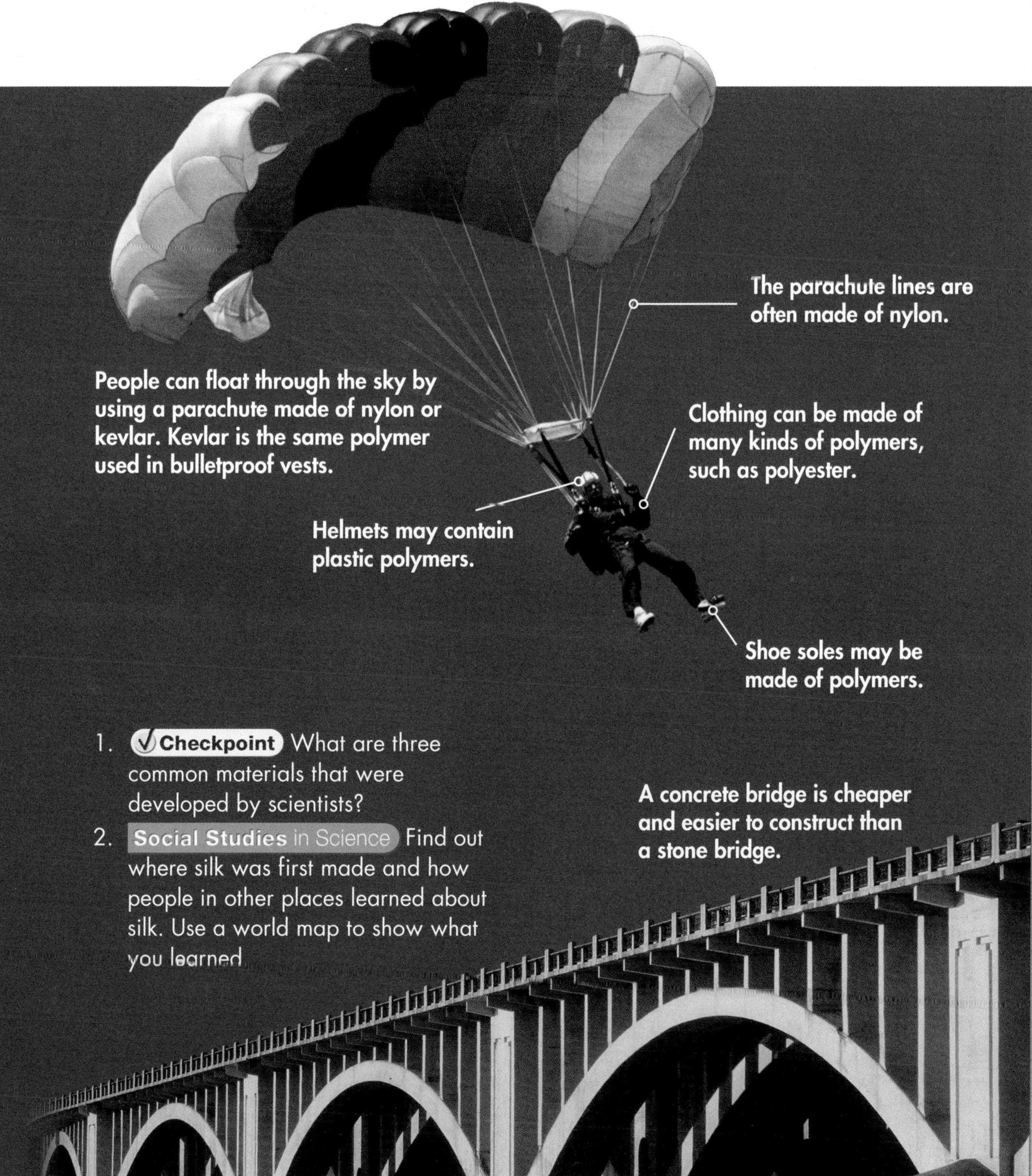
The parachute lines are often made of nylon.
People can float through the sky by using a parachute made of nylon or kevlar. Kevlar is the same polymer used in bulletproof vests.
Clothing can be made of many kinds of polymers, such as polyester.
Helmets may contain plastic polymers.
Shoe soles may be made of polymers.
A concrete bridge is cheaper and easier to construct than a stone bridge.

1. **Checkpoint** What are three common materials that were developed by scientists?
2. **Social Studies** in Science Find out where silk was first made and how people in other places learned about silk. Use a world map to show what you learned.

Chemistry and Transportation

Oil refineries use physical and chemical changes in petroleum to make many products.

However you got to school today, by bus, by car, by bicycle, or even on foot, you have chemists to thank. Advances in chemistry have given us a large supply of rubber both for tires and for the soles of shoes. Natural rubber comes from plants. It bends easily and is waterproof. But untreated rubber becomes brittle and cracks in cold weather. It melts and becomes gooey in hot weather. In the 1800s, chemists experimented with natural rubber. By heating it and adding sulfur, they made the rubber durable and usable year-round. In the mid-1900s, chemists developed a way to make artificial rubber in factories.

We owe our modern transportation system not only to rubber but also to petroleum, or crude oil. Petroleum is a mixture of many different compounds. Gasoline, kerosene, diesel oil, and lubricating oil are some of the compounds in petroleum. These compounds are separated at large oil refineries. Gasoline is one of the smaller molecules in petroleum. Chemists have developed ways to break down some of petroleum's larger molecules to form gasoline. In this way, we can get more gasoline from each barrel of petroleum.

The gasoline that makes this motorcycle travel at great speed was separated or converted from other compounds in petroleum.
Many of the body parts are made of plastic.
The tires for this motorcycle were made from heating a mixture of rubber and sulfur.

1. **✓Checkpoint** How did scientists working with rubber and petroleum help our modern transportation system?
2. **Technology in Science** Use the Internet to learn about research that scientists are doing on superconducting ceramics for use in very fast trains (called maglev trains). Summarize what you learn in a paragraph.

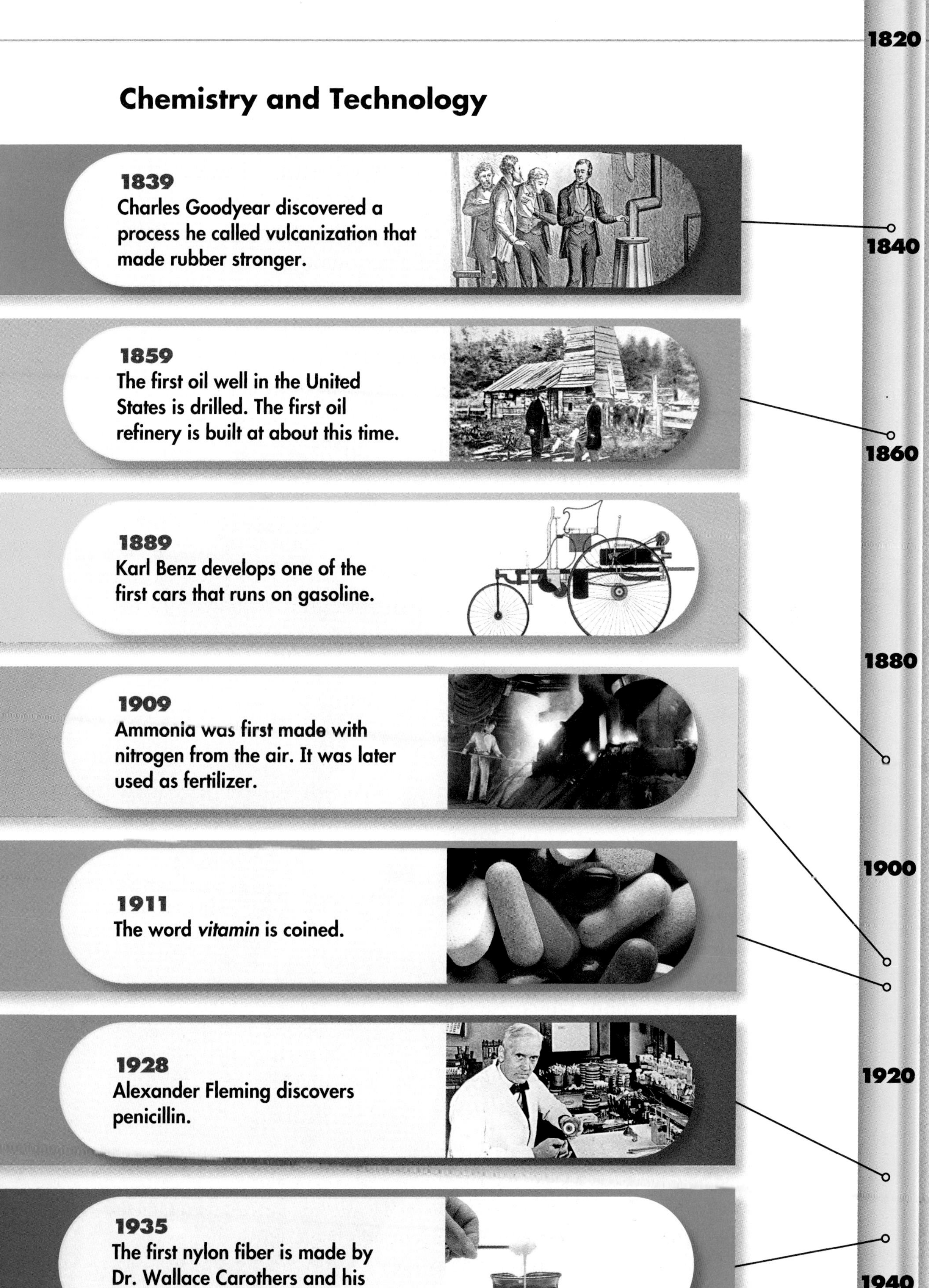
1820
1840
1860
1880
1900
1920
1940

Chemistry and Technology

1839
Charles Goodyear discovered a process he called vulcanization that made rubber stronger.

1859
The first oil well in the United States is drilled. The first oil refinery is built at about this time.

1889
Karl Benz develops one of the first cars that runs on gasoline.

1909
Ammonia was first made with nitrogen from the air. It was later used as fertilizer.

1911
The word *vitamin* is coined.

1928
Alexander Fleming discovers penicillin.

1935
The first nylon fiber is made by Dr. Wallace Carothers and his laboratory team.

Chemicals and Safety

Some chemicals make life less dangerous for us. For example, scientists have learned how to use chemicals, such as chlorine, to kill germs in drinking water. This sanitation measure helps prevent waterborne diseases. Before chemists developed modern water treatment methods, these diseases caused a very serious threat to health in the United States. Water treatment is one way chemicals have improved our health and increased our safety.

However, when chemicals are used incorrectly, they can be a hazard. You need to look carefully at warning labels on chemicals. By heeding these warnings, you can help protect yourself, your family, your pets, and your home.

You may have cleaning supplies, such as bleach, ammonia, oven cleaner, and others in your home. Before you use any of these cleansers, read the directions. The directions may tell you to wear gloves to protect your skin. They may tell you to wear goggles to protect your eyes. They may tell you to keep a window open for fresh air. This will help protect your lungs from dangerous fumes that come from the products.

You also need to be very careful not to mix any cleaners, such as bleach, ammonia, drain cleaners, and others. Doing so can cause dangerous chemical reactions which can lead to lung damage, burns, explosions, and even death.

Reading a label can tell you if the substance in a bottle is poisonous or toxic. Respect labels! They are there to protect you.

Chemical Warning Labels

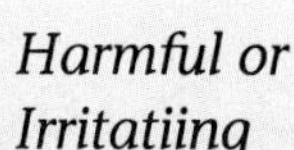

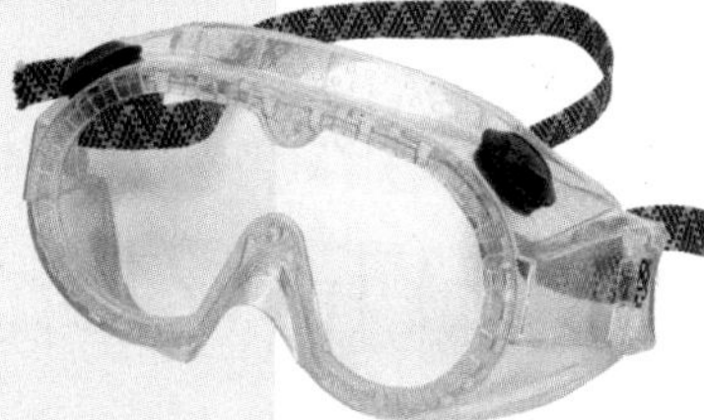

Harmful or Irritatiing

Poisonous

Corrosive

Flammable

Explosive

Radioactive

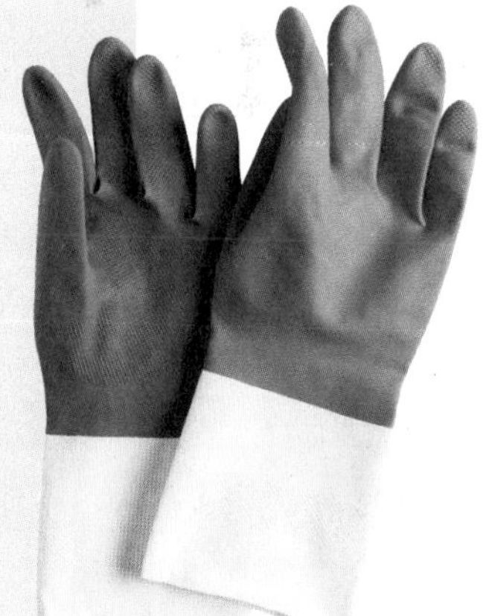

✓ Lesson Checkpoint

1. Why is it important to avoid mixing household cleaners?
2. What is a polymer?
3. **Draw Conclusions** Of all the technological developments discussed in this lesson, which one do you think most improved human lives? Explain.

Lab zone **Guided Inquiry**

Investigate How does temperature affect how long a reaction takes?

An Alka-Seltzer® tablet bubbles and fizzes when dropped into water.
In this activity, you will find out how temperature affects how fast this reaction occurs.

Materials

safety goggles

3 cups

ice-cold water,
room-temperature water,
warm water

3 Alka-Seltzer® tablets

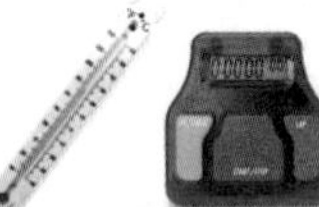

thermometer and
timer or stopwatch
(or clock with a second hand)

Process Skills

When you do an activity, carefully select ways to help **collect**, record, and report your **data**. You might wish to use graphs, tables, charts, diagrams, or drawings.

What to Do

1. Fill 1 cup about $\frac{3}{4}$ full with ice-cold water. **Measure** and record the temperature.

°F °C
140
120
100
80
60
40
20
20
40
60
50
40
30
20
10
0
10
30
40

Be careful!

Safety Procedure
- Wear safety goggles.
- Do not taste the tablets or liquids.
- Wipe up spills immediately.

2. Drop an Alka-Seltzer® tablet into the cup. Measure and record the number of seconds required to complete the chemical reaction.

3. Repeat steps 1 and 2 with room-temperature water and warm water. Make a chart to help **collect** your **data**.

To help collect, record, and report your data, use a chart like this one or select a different table, chart, or diagram.

Trial	Water Temperature (°C)	Time (seconds)
Ice-cold water		
Room-temperature water		
Warm water		

Explain Your Results

1. Report the **data** you **collected**. Think of a way to show the times required to complete the chemical reactions. You could make a bar graph, a line graph, or a diagram. You may select a different way to report your data.
2. **Infer** How does temperature affect how long a chemical reaction takes?

Go Further

If you repeat the activity several times, will you get similar results? With your teacher's permission, make and carry out a plan to find out. When finished, give an oral report to your class.

Solving Equations About Mass

You have learned about the Law of Conservation of Mass. It says that, in a chemical reaction, the total mass of the reactants equals the total mass of the products.

If 6 grams of hydrogen is combined with oxygen to form 54 grams of water, how much oxygen was used?

You can find the answer by writing and solving an equation. Remember, when you solve an equation, you are finding a number that will replace a symbol and make the equation true.

Let x represent the number of grams of oxygen.

grams of hydrogen		grams of oxygen		grams of water
6	+	x	=	54

The equation $6 + x = 54$ is true only if the symbol x is replaced by a certain number.

Try 45. Does $6 + 45$ equal 54? No. 45 is too small.

Try 48. Does $6 + 48$ equal 54? Yes.

$$x = 48$$

The number 48 can replace x to make $6 + x = 54$ true.

The amount of oxygen used was 48 grams.

Solve each equation.

1. $x + 25 = 78$
2. $425 + n = 600$
3. $187 - x = 97$
4. $n + 725 = 800$

Write and solve an equation to find each answer.

5. If 200 g of sodium is combined with chlorine to give 508 g of sodium chloride, how much chlorine was used?
6. If 360 g of water is decomposed to give 40 g of hydrogen gas, how much oxygen gas will be made?

Lab zone Take-Home Activity

Find five household products that are chemical compounds. Examples include table salt, baking soda, vinegar, bleach, and detergent. Research to find the chemical elements that make up each compound. For example, water is made up of hydrogen and oxygen. Make a table showing what you found.

Chapter 12 Review and Test Prep

Use Vocabulary

chemical change (p. 375)	**physical change** (p. 375)
chemical equation (p. 378)	**polymer** (p. 388)
combustion (p. 377)	**product** (p. 378)
	reactant (p. 378)

Use the term from the list above that best completes each sentence.

1. A _____ happens when one substance changes into another substance.
2. A substance that is changed in a chemical reaction is called a _____.
3. A large molecule formed from smaller identical units is called a _____.
4. When objects change by tearing, crushing, or melting, but do not change into different substances, a _____ has occurred.
5. The process of burning is called _____.
6. A substance that forms during a chemical reaction is called a _____.
7. A special sentence that describes what happens in a chemical reaction is called a _____ .

Explain Concepts

8. Explain how rust forms.
9. Contrast physical changes with chemical changes.
10. Explain how chemists improved natural rubber so that it became a more useful material.

Process Skills

11. **Conclude** With a cold sports pack, you twist the pack, causing two substances to mix. The sports pack quickly becomes cool. Has a chemical reaction occurred? Explain.
12. **Infer** Refer to the pictures of the flame test on page 385 and read the captions. How do you know that chloride gives off no strong color in this test?
13. **Model** Make a model out of clay to show how atoms combine to form sodium chloride (NaCl). Make another clay model for silver nitrate ($AgNO_3$). Use both models to show what happens when sodium chloride and silver nitrate react in a replacement reaction.

Draw Conclusions

14. Read the passage. Then draw a conclusion based on the facts.

Many materials have been created by chemists. Silk was expensive, so chemists worked to make a fabric to replace it. Plastics are inexpensive compared with metals and other materials that plastics have replaced.

Make a graphic organizer like this one. Put the facts and conclusion into your graphic organizer.

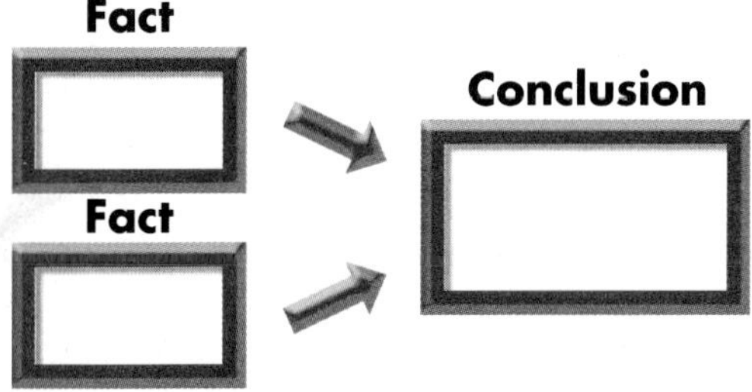
Fact
Conclusion
Fact

Test Prep

Choose the letter that best completes the statement or answers the question.

15. Which is an example of a chemical change?
- Ⓐ water freezing in a puddle
- Ⓑ a dry sponge expanding after being put in dishwater
- Ⓒ food being digested in the small intestine
- Ⓓ butter melting in a microwave oven

16. What kind of reaction occurs when water breaks down, producing hydrogen and oxygen gases?
- Ⓕ a combination reaction
- Ⓖ a decomposition reaction
- Ⓗ a recombination reaction
- Ⓘ a replacement reaction

17. Which material did chemists make in the lab?
- Ⓐ cotton
- Ⓑ wool
- Ⓒ silk
- Ⓓ nylon

18. If you are going to use a cleaning product you've never used before, what should you do first?
- Ⓕ Open the window.
- Ⓖ Put on cover goggles.
- Ⓗ Read the directions.
- Ⓘ Put on gloves.

19. Explain why the answer you chose for Question 18 is best. For each of the answers you did not choose, give a reason why it is not the best choice.

20. Writing in Science **Narrative** Make a time line showing four main things you've done so far today. Then write a narrative telling how each of these actions involved one or more chemical reactions or chemical technologies.

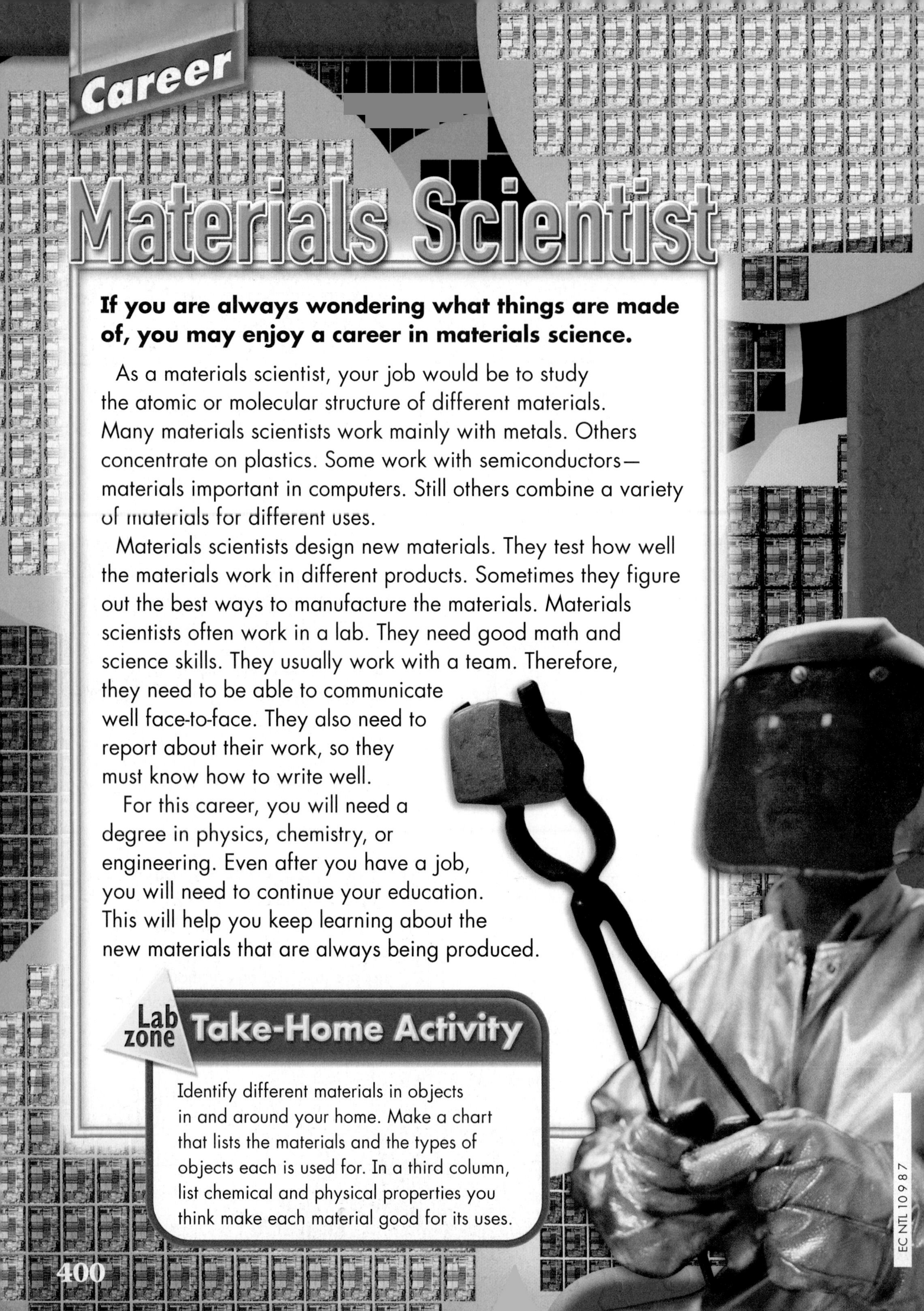

Career

Materials Scientist

If you are always wondering what things are made of, you may enjoy a career in materials science.

As a materials scientist, your job would be to study the atomic or molecular structure of different materials. Many materials scientists work mainly with metals. Others concentrate on plastics. Some work with semiconductors—materials important in computers. Still others combine a variety of materials for different uses.

Materials scientists design new materials. They test how well the materials work in different products. Sometimes they figure out the best ways to manufacture the materials. Materials scientists often work in a lab. They need good math and science skills. They usually work with a team. Therefore, they need to be able to communicate well face-to-face. They also need to report about their work, so they must know how to write well.

For this career, you will need a degree in physics, chemistry, or engineering. Even after you have a job, you will need to continue your education. This will help you keep learning about the new materials that are always being produced.

Lab zone Take-Home Activity

Identify different materials in objects in and around your home. Make a chart that lists the materials and the types of objects each is used for. In a third column, list chemical and physical properties you think make each material good for its uses.

EC NTL 10 9 8 7

Chapter 13

Forces in Motion

You Will Discover

- how motion is measured.
- how forces affect motion, work, and power.
- what Newton's laws of motion are.
- how simple machines make work easier.

Web Games
Take It to the Net
sfsuccessnet.com

online Student Edition
sfsuccessnet.com

Build Background

How are forces and motion part of your everyday life?

velocity

work

power
equilibrium
NASA

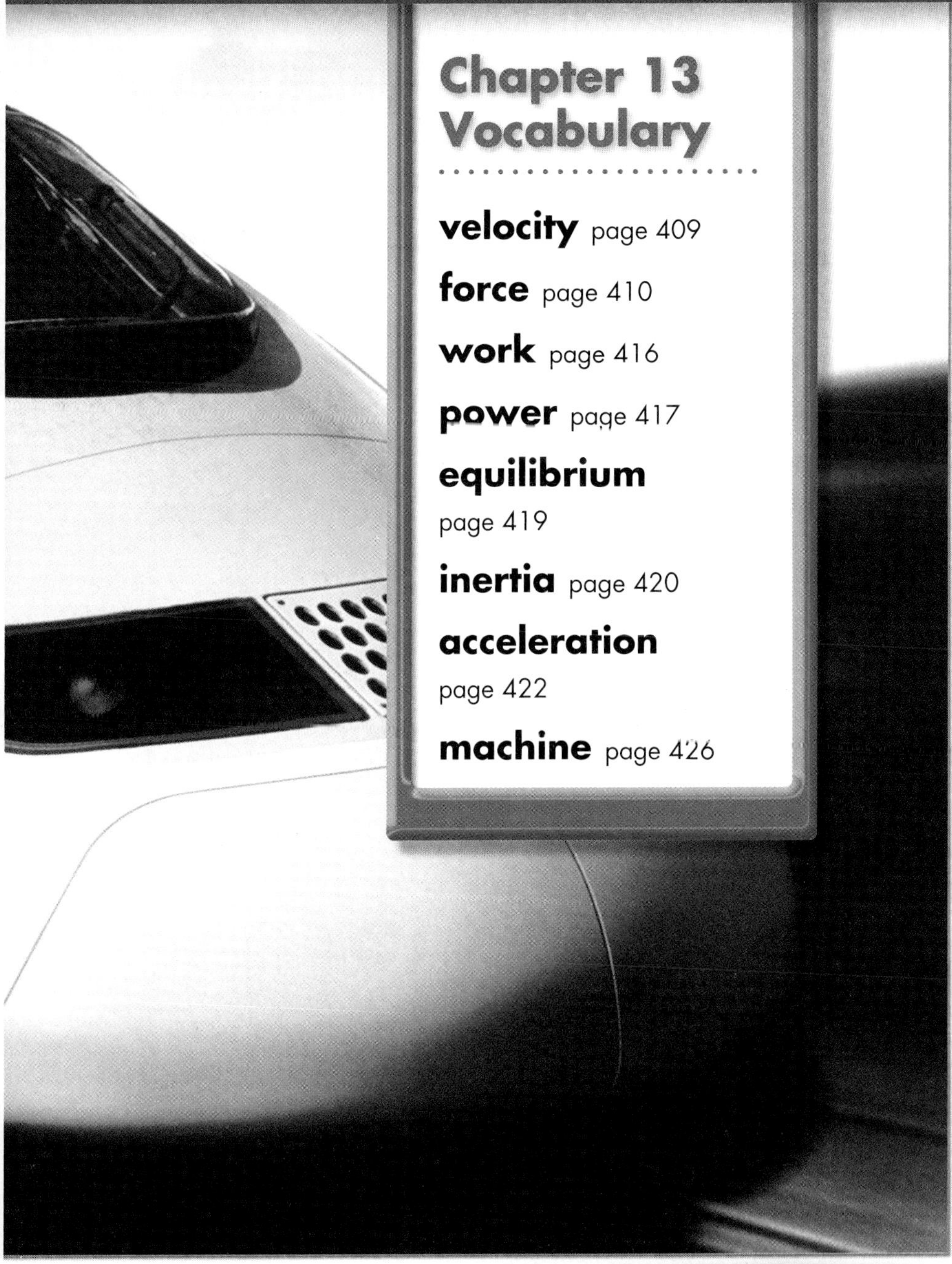

Chapter 13 Vocabulary

force

machine

inertia

acceleration

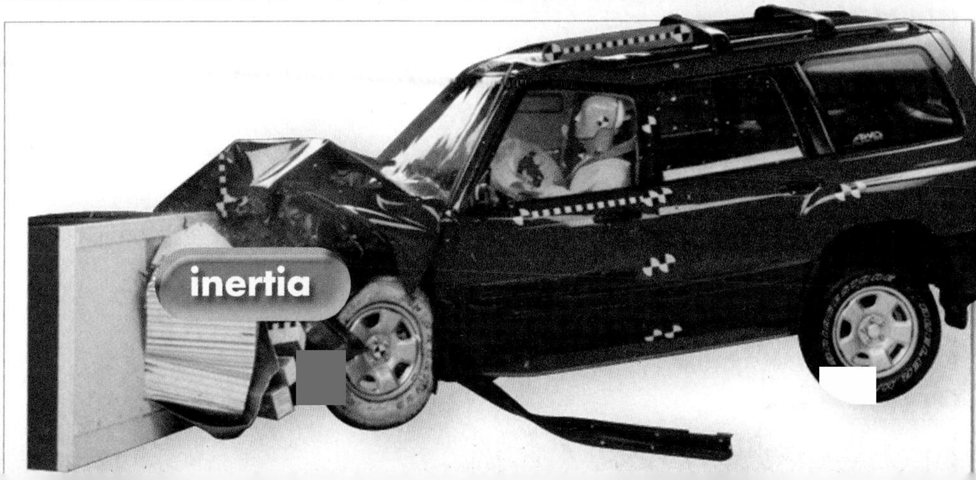

Lab zone # Directed Inquiry

Explore How can you learn about the motion of a pendulum?

Materials

safety goggles

washer and string

masking tape and meterstick

timer or stopwatch

Process Skills

You **observe** when you use your senses to gather information.
You **infer** when you make a judgment based on observations or experiences.
You **predict** when you make an inference about a future result. You explain when you clarify the reasons something is the way it is.

What to Do

1. Make a pendulum.

Tie a washer onto a string. Tape the string to the side of a table.

2. Pull back the pendulum 30 cm. Let go. **Observe** how the speed changes during a swing.

Where does the washer move fastest? slowest? Where does it speed up? slow down?

3. Test again from 30 cm back. Time 5 swings.

A "swing" is one back-and-forth movement.

Be careful!
Wear safety goggles.

4. **Predict** how pulling back the pendulum 60 cm would affect the time needed for 5 swings. Test your prediction. Time 5 swings.

Pull back and let go.

The downward pull of Earth's gravity starts the pendulum moving.

Explain Your Results

1. Compare the time needed for 30 cm and 60 cm swings. **Infer** how the distance a pendulum swings affects the time a swing takes.
2. **Predict** Suppose the string was shortened. How do you think this would affect the time a swing takes? Explain.

How to Read Science

Reading Skills

TARGET SKILL

Cause and Effect

Understanding **causes and effects** can help you understand what you read. A cause may have more than one effect. An effect may have more than one cause.

- Sometimes an effect will be the cause of another effect.
- Sometimes you have to **infer** the cause or effect from the information given.

Passage from a Story

Sandy pushed Samuel on the swing. Each push made Samuel go higher. Because of this, Samuel became afraid. So, Sandy stopped pushing. Since he wasn't being pushed anymore, Samuel slowly came to a stop. But he was still afraid.

Apply It!

Make graphic organizers like the ones shown. Under Causes, write an action that happened in the story. Under Effects, write what happens as a result of the cause. In this story, each **effect** becomes a **cause** for another effect. The graphic organizers are started for you.

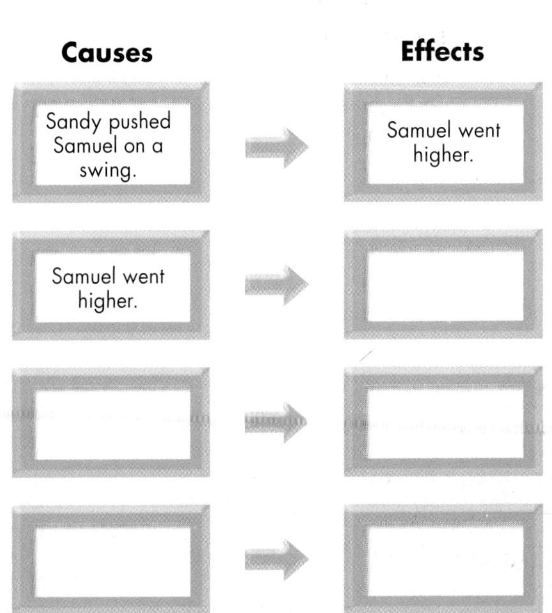
Causes
Effects
Sandy pushed Samuel on a swing.
Samuel went higher.
Samuel went higher.

You Are There!

The person next to you is not moving. The people behind you are not moving. But when you look out of the window, things are whizzing past you faster than you have ever seen! You're all moving! The train you are on is speeding along at 262 kilometers per hour. You left San Diego this morning at eleven o'clock, and you'll be in Los Angeles before noon. Did you know a train could move that fast?

Lesson 1

How can you describe motion?

Sea stars are animals that move very slowly.

Leaves wave and dance in the wind. A ball bounces back and forth from one child to another. A bird flies right, left, up, and down. You can describe motion in many ways.

Types of Motion

You spend every moment of each day moving in one way or another. You walk down hallways and stand up from chairs. At night you roll over in bed. Your heart beats and your eyelids blink up and down.

Motion is all around you. Objects move in many different ways. What kinds of motion have you seen in your classroom?

Different kinds of motions can happen at different rates. A sea star moves so slowly that sometimes you can hardly tell whether it is moving. Other objects, such as an airplane's propeller, move so quickly you need a high-speed camera to catch sight of them.

Think about the different kinds of motion. The Earth has a steady, or constant, motion as it moves around the Sun. Cars, trucks, and buses have variable motion—they move in many directions and at many speeds. A pendulum has periodic motion—it swings back and forth. Wheels move in a circular motion. A rubber band has vibrational motion when you pluck it. How could you demonstrate each of these motions?

1. **Checkpoint** What are three types of motion?
2. Writing in Science **Descriptive** Write a paragraph in your **science Journal** describing the motions you have enjoyed on playground equipment. Write your paragraph in the style of a magazine article. Use the headline "The Best Ride on the Playground."

Speed and Velocity

Average speed describes how far an object moves during a certain amount of time. To calculate average speed, use the following formula:

$$\text{Average Speed} = \frac{\text{Distance}}{\text{Time}}$$

If a car moved 100 meters in 20 seconds, its average speed would be:

$$\frac{100 \text{ m}}{20 \text{ s}} = 5 \frac{\text{m}}{\text{s}}$$

When you sit as still as you can, are you moving? Do not be too quick to say you are not moving. In relationship with your chair, you may be sitting still. In relationship with the Sun, you are moving very quickly. You and the planet you are sitting on are moving around the Sun faster than any rocket. So, the motion of an object cannot be measured by just looking at the object. Motion is always measured in relationship with some location called a point of reference.

The speed at which a person is moving can vary according to which point of reference you use. For example, a passenger walking down the aisle of a train is in motion. But the passenger's motion measured in relationship with the end of the train car is different than the passenger's motion relative to a crossing gate along the tracks.

Using the end of the train car as a point of reference, the passenger walking 10 meters down the aisle in 5 seconds will have a walking speed of 2 meters per second. But using the crossing gate near the tracks as a point of reference, the passenger is moving about as fast as the train—perhaps 30 meters per second.

Point of Reference	Distance	Time	Speed
Train Car	10 m	5 s	$\frac{10\text{ m}}{5\text{ s}} = 2\frac{\text{m}}{\text{s}}$
Signal Light	150 m	5 s	$\frac{150\text{ m}}{5\text{ s}} = 30\frac{\text{m}}{\text{s}}$

Speed and velocity are not the same. **Velocity** describes the speed and the direction of an object's motion. The speed of the train might be described as 30 meters per second, but its velocity is 30 meters per second north. A falling skydiver might have a velocity of about 200 kilometers per hour down.

✓ Lesson Checkpoint

1. Robert moved 28 meters in 4 seconds. Tallana moved 600 meters in 2 minutes. Javier moved 40 meters in 5 seconds. List these people and their speeds in order from fastest to slowest.
2. What do you need to know to find an object's velocity?
3. Writing in Science **Expository** Write a paragraph in your **science journal** that explains how circular motion and variable motion are alike and different.

This train is moving at a high speed from the point of reference of the crossing gate.

An apple falls to the ground because the force of gravity pulls it toward Earth's center.

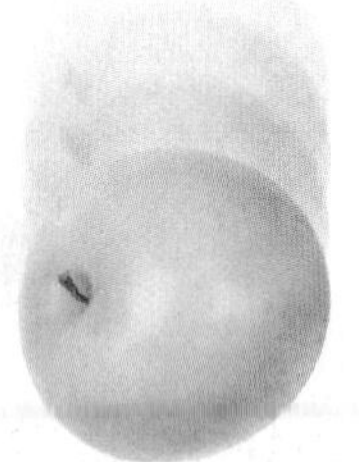

Gravity causes the velocity of the apple to increase as it falls.

After one second of falling, an apple's velocity will be about 10 $\frac{m}{s}$ downward.

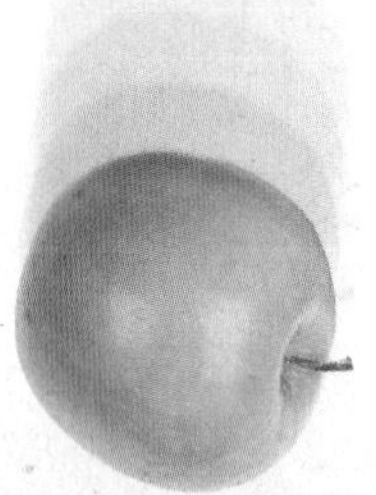

After two seconds of falling, an apple's velocity will be about 20 $\frac{m}{s}$ downward.

Lesson 2

What are forces?

There are many kinds of pushes and pulls around you. These pushes and pulls can cause objects to change their velocities.

Pushes and Pulls

A **force** is a push or pull that acts on an object. When one object pushes or pulls another object, the first object is exerting a force on the second one. Forces can make a moving object speed up, slow down, or change direction.

Forces have both magnitude and direction. The magnitude of a force is how strong the force is. Magnitude is measured in units called newtons (N). The direction of a force can be described by telling which way the force is acting. For example, a medium-sized apple held in your outstreched hand exerts a downward force with a magnitude of about 1 newton.

Gravity

Every object in the universe exerts a gravitational pull on every other object. But only the gravity of a large object such as Earth is strong enough to be felt. Earth's gravity pulls other objects toward its center without ever touching them. Pendulums swing, apples fall, and artificial satellites stay in orbit because of Earth's gravity.

An object's weight is the amount of gravitational force between it and Earth. This force depends on the object's mass and Earth's mass. It also depends on Earth's size and how far above Earth the object is. If you fly in an airliner, your weight is a little less. If you went to another planet, your weight would also change. The table on the next page shows how much an object would weigh on some other planets if its weight on Earth is 100 newtons.

The Swing of a Pendulum

A pendulum swings because of the force of gravity. When the pendulum is released, gravity pulls on it and makes it swing downward. Gravity makes the pendulum increase its speed as it swings downward. When the pendulum starts to swing upward, the force of gravity slows the pendulum until it stops. Then the pendulum is pulled downward again and it swings in the other direction.

Planet	Weight (in newtons)
Earth	100
Mercury	38
Venus	91
Mars	38
Pluto	7
Jupiter	253

The pull of gravity keeps satellites orbiting around Earth.

1. **Checkpoint** What are two examples that illustrate Earth's gravitational pull?
2. **Cause and Effect** A rock tumbles down a hill. Identify the cause and effect of this event.

Magnetism and Electricity

Magnetism is a force that pushes and pulls on other objects. The magnetic force is greatest at a magnet's poles. The poles of a horseshoe magnet are at the two ends. The poles of a bar magnet are at either end. Every magnet has a north pole and a south pole.

Magnets will strongly pull on objects made of iron, cobalt, nickel, and gadolinium. Magnets will also exert forces on other magnets. The north pole of one magnet will attract the south pole of another magnet. The north poles of two magnets will push away from each other. The south poles of two magnets will act in the same way.

Electric forces act between objects that are electrically charged. Objects get electrically charged when they gain or lose electrons. Remember that all atoms have negative electrons and positive protons. If an object gains electrons, the object will be negatively charged. If the object loses electrons, it will be positively charged. Why would an object get a positive charge if it loses electrons?

Electrons often move from one object to another when the objects are rubbed together. When silk and glass are rubbed together, electrons will move from the glass to the silk. The rubber comb can gain a negative charge from your hair.

All objects that are electrically charged will exert forces on each other. Oppositely charged objects are attracted to each other. Objects with the same charge are repelled, and may move away from each other.

A magnet exerts a magnetic force that pulls pieces of iron toward it.

A negatively charged comb will attract paper because of electrical forces.

Gravity, Electricity, and Magnetism

Like gravity, magnetic and electric forces can act between objects even if the objects do not touch. All three forces increase as objects get closer together. Gravity, electricity, and magnetism have differences. The forces of magnetism and electricity between objects can be blocked by putting certain kinds of materials between the objects. Gravity can't be blocked. Electricity and magnetism can push or pull on different objects. Gravity exerts only a pulling force on objects.

The magnetic field of this stone attracts metal pins to its surface.

Magnetic forces cause this experimental train to float above the track. Magnetic forces are also used to make the train move along the track at very high speeds.

1. **√ Checkpoint** What are the causes of electric and magnetic forces?
2. **Cause and Effect** Describe an event involving electric and magnetic forces. Use your imagination. Describe the cause and effect of each force.

The shape of sharks and their special skin reduce friction with the water and allow the sharks to swim smoothly and swiftly.

Friction

Have you ever slid across a smooth floor with your socks on? You can't slide as easily if you are wearing your shoes. Friction is at work. Friction is the force that results when two materials rub against each other.

Friction acts to slow down the motion of an object or keep it from starting to move. Unlike other forces, friction depends on qualities of the objects involved. The shape, speed, or texture of one object can affect the amount of friction with another object. The texture of the soles of your shoes is different from the texture of your socks. Friction is greater between your shoes and the floor than between your socks and the floor.

Special pads on a bicycle's brakes push against the tires. This results in increased friction that slows down or stops the bicycle.

A bicycle has many features that increase friction. Other features, like ball bearings, decrease friction. Both make the bike safer and easier to ride.

Air and water resist motion when a moving object pushes against them. Air friction is a force that is present when air flows over a surface. Flowing water has a similar kind of force. Most cars and airplanes are designed to have little air friction. Submarines and ships are designed with shapes to help them move through water.

1. **Checkpoint** How does friction affect movement?
2. **Math in Science** The gravitational force on the Moon is one-sixth of what it is on Earth. This means that on the Moon you would weigh one-sixth of what you weigh on Earth. How much would you weigh on the Moon?

The distance it takes to stop a skidding car depends on the surface of the road.

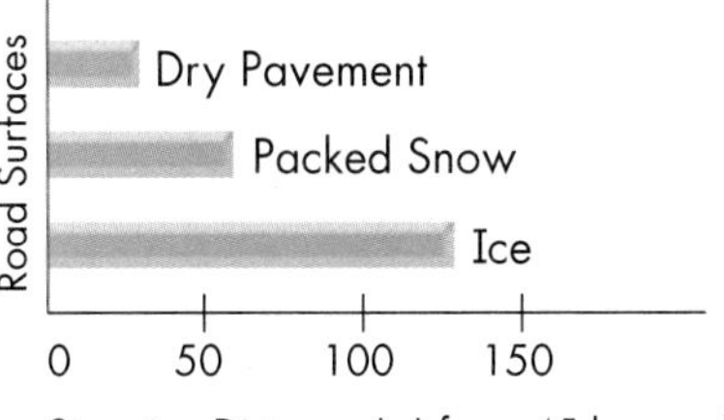
Stopping Distances
Road Surfaces
Dry Pavement
Packed Snow
Ice
0
50
100
150
Stopping Distance (m) from 45 km per h

On some bicycles the low handlebars allow the rider to bend down and decrease air friction.

The texture of the foam on the handlebar increases friction between the rider's hands and the handlebars, making it easier to have a firm grip.

The rough tread on this bicycle tire increases the friction between the tire and the ground. This keeps the bicycle from sliding during turns.

Motion in Space

Space is not completely empty, but there are so few particles floating in space that friction is very small. This means that a satellite moving around Earth will not slow down much. Satellites do eventually slow down and fall to Earth. Gravity is different in space as well. As an astronaut goes away from Earth, the force of gravity decreases. The force of gravity does not decrease to zero at the space station. If there were no gravity pulling on the space station, it would float away past the Moon instead of orbiting close to Earth.

Work and Power

You hear the word "work" used all the time. But the scientific definition of work has a particular meaning. **Work** is done when a force moves an object. To calculate work, you multiply the force (in newtons) acting on an object by the distance the force causes the object to move.

Force × Distance = Work

Work is measured in joules. One joule (J) is the amount of work done when a force of 1 newton (N) moves an object a distance of 1 meter (m).

Force	Distance	Work
10 N	1 m	10 N × 1 m = 10 J
10 N	2 m	10 N × 2 m = 20 J
20 N	2 m	20 N × 2 m = 40 J

If the force applied to an object does not make the object move, then no work has been done. Work is done only when the object moves at least partly in the same direction in which the force is applied. Holding an object in place can require a force, but since the object does not move, no work is done.

Force	Distance	Work
10 N	0 m	10 N × 0 m = 0 J

Work is done when a force moves an object.

Power is the rate at which work is done. When work is done faster, power is increased. Walking up a hill and running up the same hill take the same amount of work. Since running up the hill is faster than walking, the amount of power needed to run is greater. You can calculate the amount of power for a certain amount of work. Divide the amount of work done by the amount of time needed to do the work. Watts are the units of power.

$$\frac{\text{Work}}{\text{Time}} = \text{Power}$$

The table below shows that the amount of power will double if a person doubles the amount of work done during a certain amount of time. Power will also double if a person does the same amount of work in half the time.

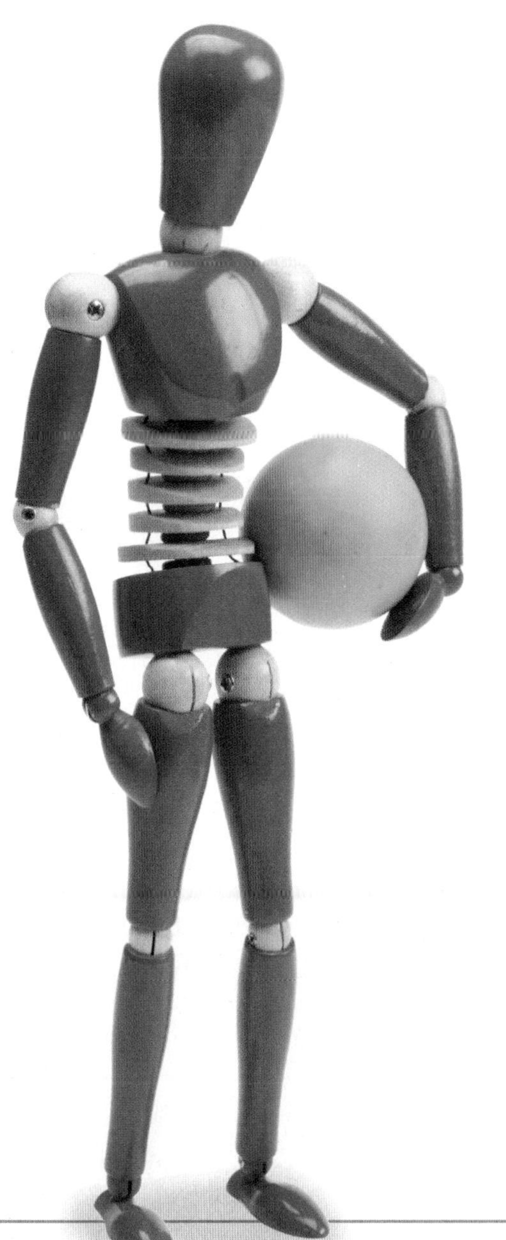

Work	Time	Power
20 J	4 s	$\frac{20\ \text{J}}{4\ \text{s}} = 5\ \text{W}$
40 J	4 s	$\frac{40\ \text{J}}{4\ \text{s}} = 10\ \text{W}$
20 J	2 s	$\frac{20\ \text{J}}{2\ \text{s}} = 10\ \text{W}$

No work is being done when an object is held without moving, no matter how long the object is held.

√ Lesson Checkpoint

1. What are two examples of forces?
2. What kind of force can make paper cling to a comb?
3. **Technology** in Science Find pictures that show how the shapes of cars have changed over time. Describe features on modern cars that help reduce air friction.

Lesson 3

What are Newton's laws of motion?

A ball rolls faster and faster as it travels down a hill. Finally it bumps into a tree and stops. Newton's laws of motion explain why objects like the ball move the way they do.

Net Forces

Different forces can act on an object at the same time. They may act in different directions, and some may be stronger than others. The combination of all these forces is the net force on the object. The net force determines whether the object will start moving, stop moving, or change direction.

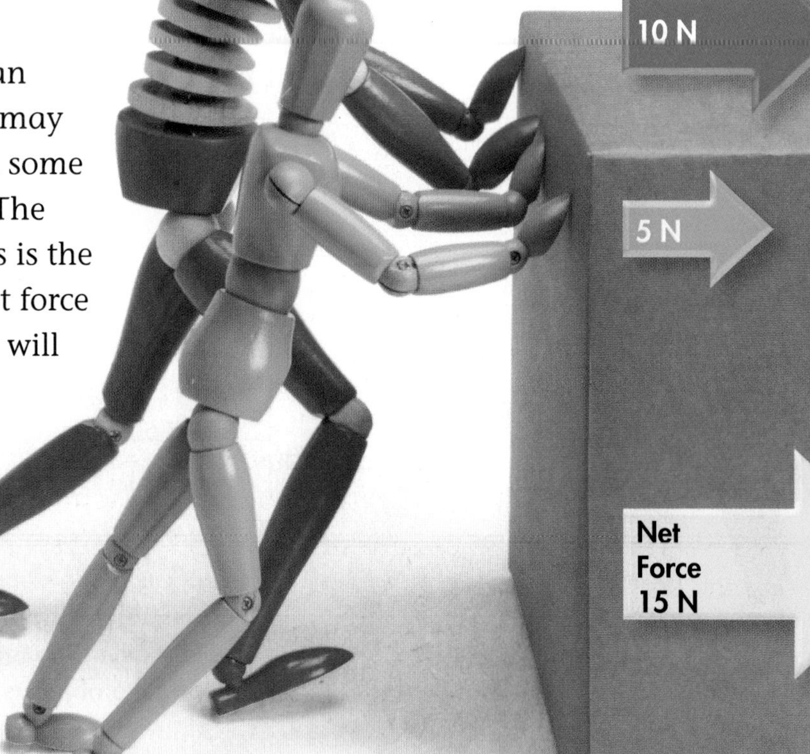

10 N
5 N
Net
Force
15 N

If a stationary box is pushed in one direction by more than one force, the net force is the sum of the forces.

Isaac Newton

Sir Isaac Newton (1642–1727) is considered one of the most important scientists of all time. This scientist, mathematician, and philosopher is most noted for his use of mathematics in studying nature. He also developed the law of gravitation to explain a wide range of natural events. Sir Isaac Newton's most famous books include the *Principia Mathematica,* in which the laws of motion are described and explained, and the book *Opticks,* which describes Newton's ideas on light and color.

An airplane moves in a straight line at a constant speed. It speeds up, slows down, or changes direction depending on the net forces acting on it.

Drag is a force that pushes against the forward motion of an airplane, slowing it down.

Thrust pushes an airplane forward, making it accelerate.

drag

gravity

thrust

Lift pushes an airplane up, making it go higher.

lift

When equal forces act on an object in opposite directions, the forces are balanced. Then the net force is zero. Balanced forces do not change the way an object moves.

An object is in a state of **equilibrium** when all the forces acting on it balance each other. A stationary object in equilibrium will remain motionless. A moving object in equilibrium will continue to move at a constant speed in a straight line.

If the forces acting in one direction are greater than the others, the forces are unbalanced. Unbalanced forces acting on an object cause it to change its motion. The net force is found by combining all the different forces acting on an object. For example, if two people are pushing on a large box from opposite directions using the same amount of force, the box does not move. But if one person pushes harder than the other, a net force results and the box moves.

10 N

10 N

zero N

If a stationary box is pushed in opposite directions by equal forces, the forces are balanced. There is no net force, and the box does not move.

10 N
5 N
5 N

If a box is pushed in opposite directions by unequal forces, the forces are unbalanced. There is a net force in the direction of the stronger force, and the box moves in that direction.

1. **Checkpoint** How can an object be motionless and in equilibrium?
2. **Cause and Effect** How can the forces in a game of tug-of-war result in equilibrium?

Newton's First Law

Newton's first law of motion says that unless a net force acts on an object, the object will remain in constant motion. An object at rest stays at rest until a net force acts on it. An object moving at a constant speed will continue to move in a straight line and at a constant speed.

The tendency of an object to resist any change in motion is known as **inertia.** Objects with a lot of mass have more inertia than objects with less mass. The body's inertia is what forces you against the side of a car when it turns. When a car changes direction, your body tends to keep moving straight. The car is pushing on you during a turn. Inertia is also what makes your body rise up from your seat in a roller coaster as it goes up and over a steep hill. At the top of the hill, your body tends to continue going up when the ride moves down the hill.

Space probes are also examples of Newton's first law and inertia. Inertia keeps the probes moving through space. As a result, probes need very little fuel after they are launched. They usually use fuel only to change direction or to slow down.

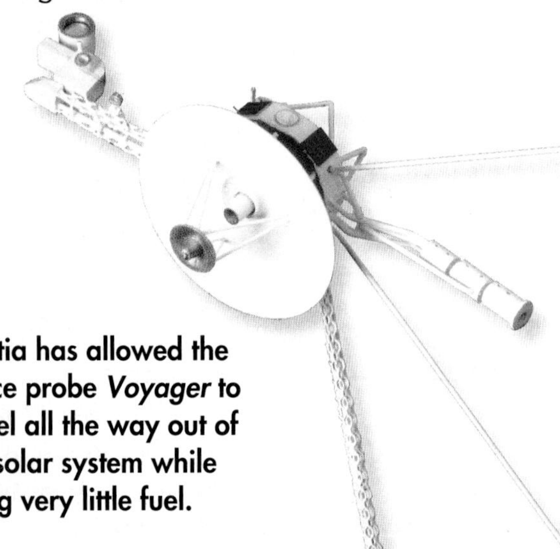

Inertia has allowed the space probe *Voyager* to travel all the way out of the solar system while using very little fuel.

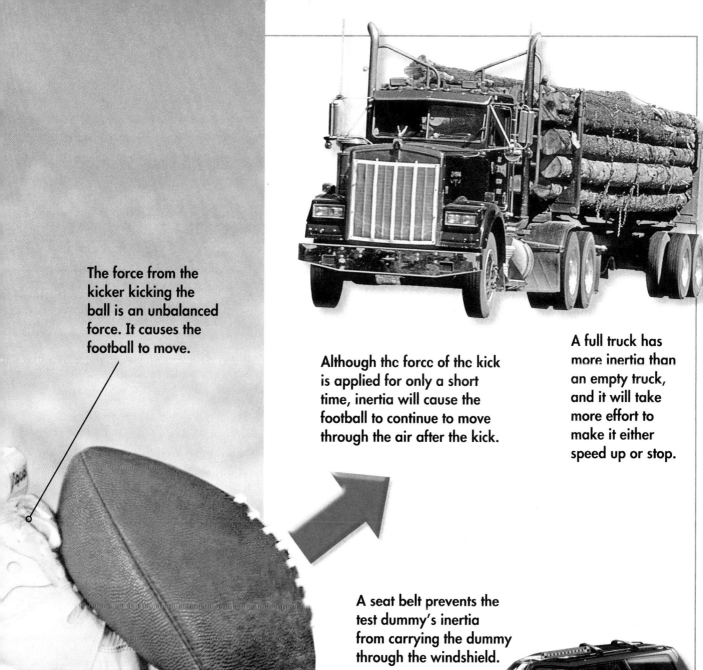

The force from the kicker kicking the ball is an unbalanced force. It causes the football to move.

Although the force of the kick is applied for only a short time, inertia will cause the football to continue to move through the air after the kick.

A full truck has more inertia than an empty truck, and it will take more effort to make it either speed up or stop.

A seat belt prevents the test dummy's inertia from carrying the dummy through the windshield.

When the football is stationary, the forces acting on it are balanced. The football will stay at rest until a force, such as somebody kicking it, causes it to move.

1. **√ Checkpoint** What is inertia? How does it affect the way an object moves?
2. **Art in Science** Use photographs from magazines to create a collage about Newton's first law of motion. Try to find as many examples as possible that illustrate things that are in constant motion or at constant rest.

Newton's Second Law

Newton's second law of motion describes how acceleration, mass, and net force are related. **Acceleration** is the rate at which the velocity of an object changes over time. The net forces acting on an object can change an object's velocity by causing it to speed up, slow down, or change direction. All of these changes can be called accelerations.

The formula that describes the relationship between force, mass, and acceleration is:

Force = Mass × Acceleration

The train engines must exert enough force to pull the freight cars behind them. The more freight cars there are, the more force the engines must exert.

The formula is often written as $F = m \times a$. It indicates that the stronger the force acting on an object, the more that object will accelerate.

The formula also indicates that a force will cause an object with small mass to accelerate more than an object with large mass. The acceleration due to a small force on a small object can be the same as the acceleration of a big force on a big object.

The net force acting on the box is equal to the mass of the box multiplied by its acceleration.

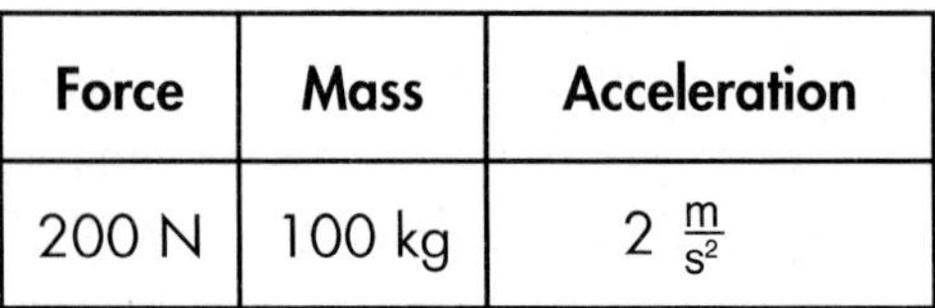

Force	Mass	Acceleration
200 N	100 kg	$2 \frac{m}{s^2}$

There are different ways to write the formula for the second law of motion. The formula you use depends on what question you are trying to answer. If you want to find the acceleration of an object that has a force on it, you can use the following formula.

$$a = \frac{F}{m}$$

If you want to find the mass of an object that has a force on it, you can use the formula below.

$$m = \frac{F}{a}$$

1. **Checkpoint** Use Newton's second law of motion to explain what happens when someone pushes a chair across the floor.
2. **Math in Science** What formula would you use to find the acceleration of a 10 kg boulder being pushed by a force of 65 N? What would the acceleration be?

To slow down more quickly, a race car needs to have a big force. With a parachute, the force of air friction is increased and the car slows down more quickly.

The greater the net force pushing on the box, the greater the acceleration of the box.

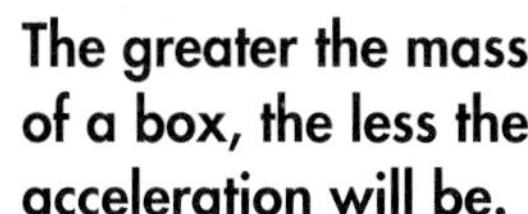

The greater the mass of a box, the less the acceleration will be.

Force	Mass	Acceleration
400 N	100 kg	4 $\frac{m}{s^2}$

Force	Mass	Acceleration
400 N	200 kg	2 $\frac{m}{s^2}$

Newton's Third Law

Newton's third law of motion states that when one object exerts a force on a second object, the second object exerts a force on the first object. This is sometimes called the action-reaction law of motion. Action-reaction forces are always equal and opposite, and they always occur in pairs.

This law can be seen all around us. Whenever you see an object move because of a force, there is an equal and opposite force. It is actually impossible to have one force without an equal and opposite force!

For example, a person who leans against a wall exerts a force on the wall. The wall exerts an equal force on the person in the opposite direction.

If you have ever ridden bumper cars, you know that when a moving car collides with a stationary car, both drivers feel the force of the collision. The driver of the stationary car feels a force and starts to move. The driver of the moving car feels an opposite force that slows the moving car.

The person pushes on the wall. The wall pushes on the person. Forces of the wall and person are equal and opposite.

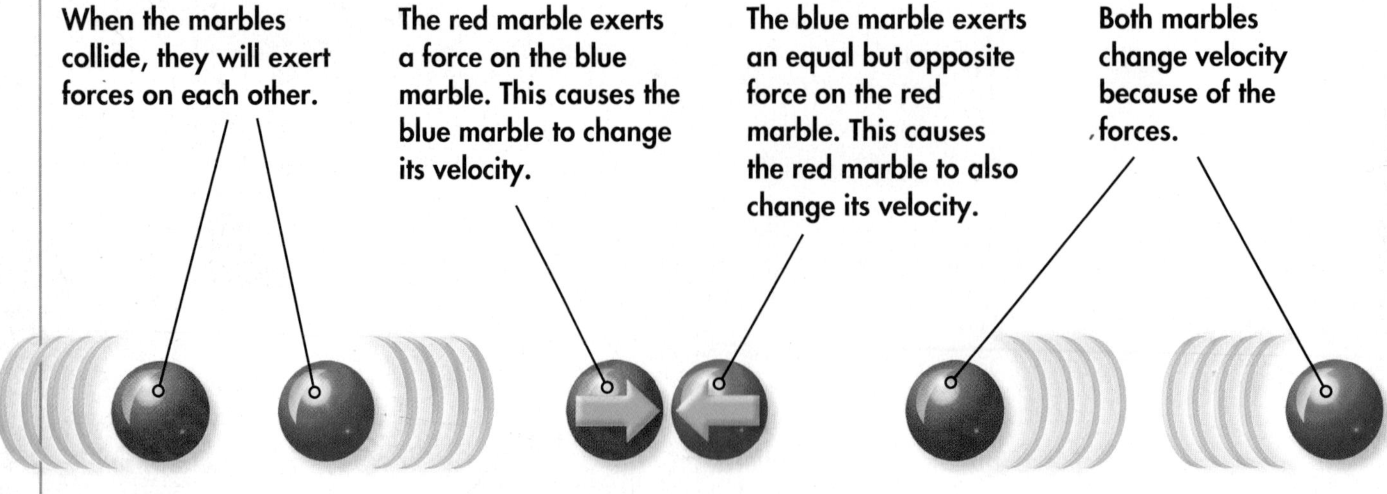
When the marbles collide, they will exert forces on each other.
The red marble exerts a force on the blue marble. This causes the blue marble to change its velocity.
The blue marble exerts an equal but opposite force on the red marble. This causes the red marble to also change its velocity.
Both marbles change velocity because of the forces.

When the fan on this airboat turns, it pushes air behind the boat. In turn, the air pushes the boat forward.

force of the air on the fan

force of the fan on the air

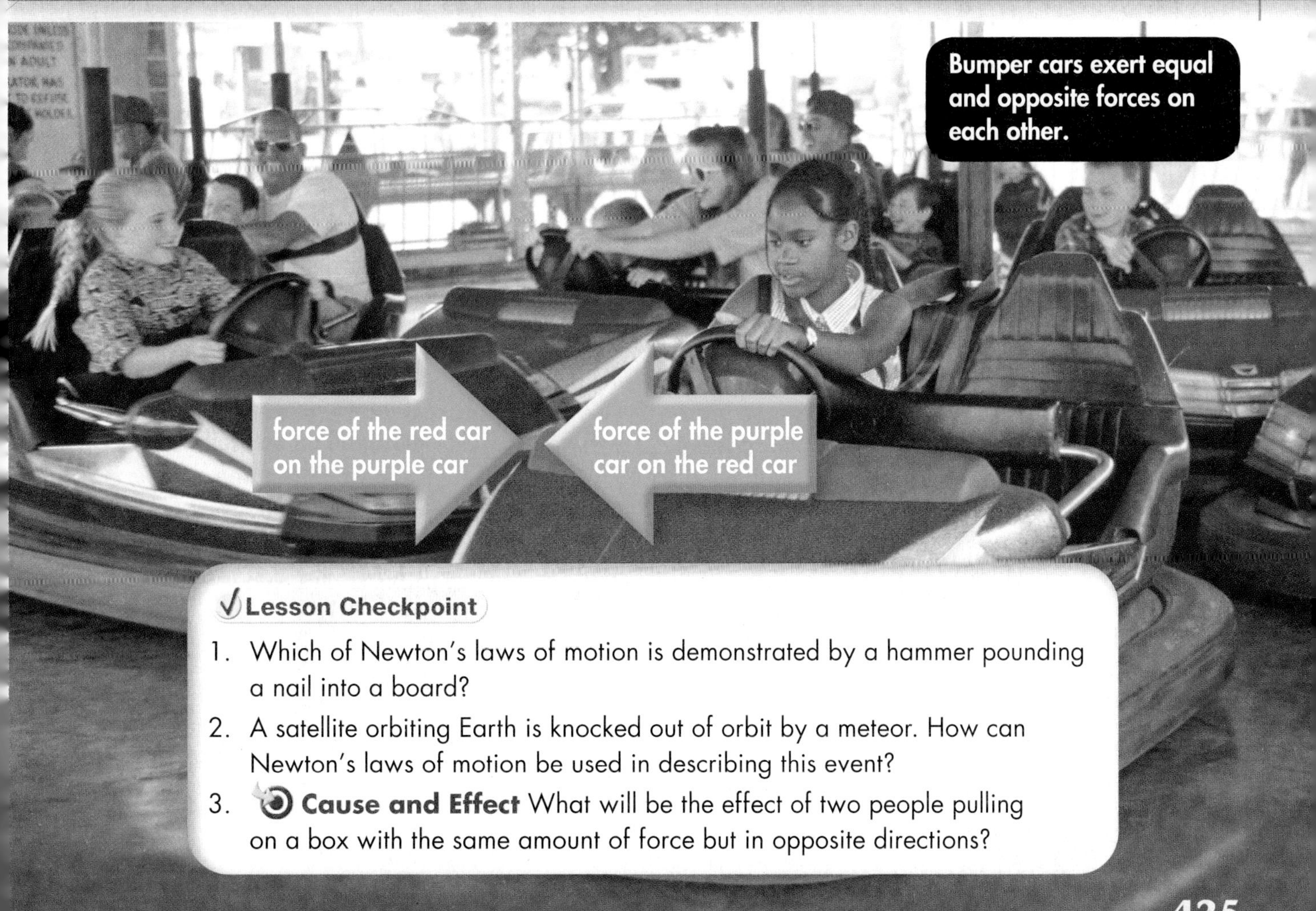

Bumper cars exert equal and opposite forces on each other.

force of the red car on the purple car

force of the purple car on the red car

√ Lesson Checkpoint

1. Which of Newton's laws of motion is demonstrated by a hammer pounding a nail into a board?
2. A satellite orbiting Earth is knocked out of orbit by a meteor. How can Newton's laws of motion be used in describing this event?
3. **Cause and Effect** What will be the effect of two people pulling on a box with the same amount of force but in opposite directions?

Lesson 4

What are simple machines?

Simple machines make work easier. Every time you use a hammer, a screwdriver, or a doorknob, or walk up a ramp, you are using a simple machine to do work.

Machines and Work

Remember that work is done when a force causes an object to move. Some objects are large, heavy, or awkward to move. A **machine** is a device that changes the direction or the amount of force needed to do work. Simple machines are machines with only a few parts. There are several kinds of simple machines, including a wheel and axle, pulley, inclined plane, and lever.

Machines do not reduce the amount of work that needs to be done. They can make it easier to do the work. When a machine allows you to use a smaller force to do work, you must apply that force for a greater distance. In this way, the total amount of work stays the same.

Pulley

A pulley is one type of simple machine. A pulley consists of a rope or cable that runs through a grooved wheel. A simple pulley makes work easier by changing the direction of the force needed to do work. Flagpoles and drapery rods use pulleys. A block and tackle is a system of pulleys that make it easier to lift very heavy objects.

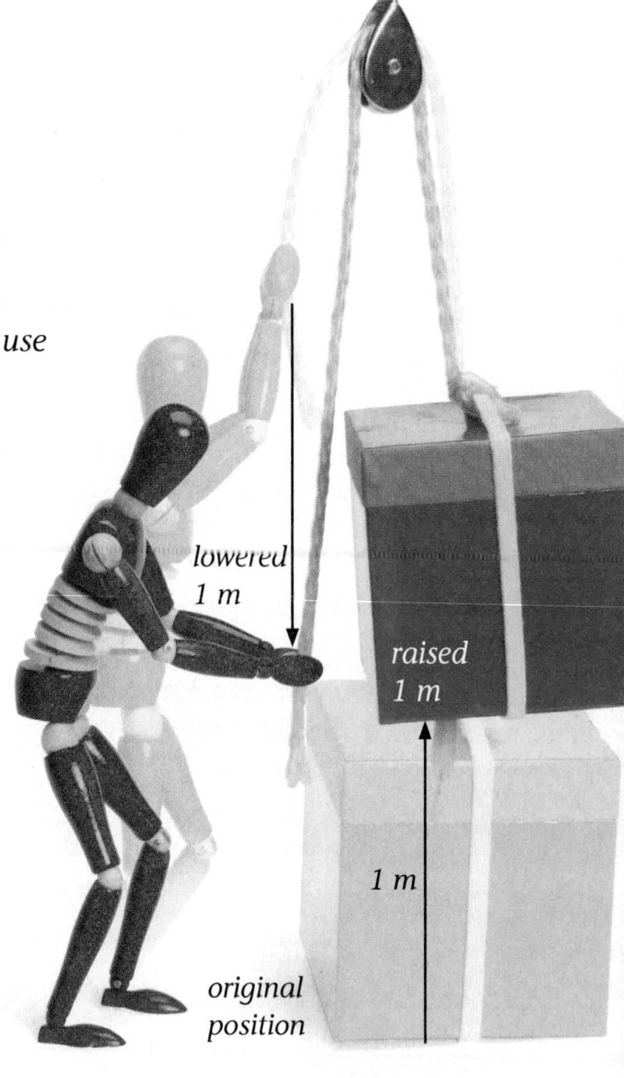

lowered
1 m
raised
1 m
1 m
original
position

This pulley does not change the amount of work done. The mass of the box pulls down on the pulley with a force of 10 newtons. The person must pull on the pulley rope with the same force. Notice that if the rope on this pulley is pulled down 1 meter, the box is lifted up 1 meter.

Wheel and Axle

A wheel and axle is made up of a circular object, such as a doorknob, and a shaft. A wheel and axle makes work easier by reducing the amount of force needed to do work. Imagine how hard it would be to lift a bucket out of a well by just pulling it straight up! Using a wheel and axle for tasks like raising a bucket in a well changes the direction of force from circular to a straight line. The steering wheel of a car is another example of a wheel and axle.

1. √ **Checkpoint** What are two examples of a wheel and axle that can make work easier?
2. **Social Studies in Science** Use the Internet or a library to find the earliest recorded uses of simple machines. Write 1 or 2 paragraphs in your **science journal** on your findings.

Ball bearings are steel balls used inside a wheel to reduce friction and make a pulley or wheel and axle more efficient. The bearings are greased to help them turn more easily.

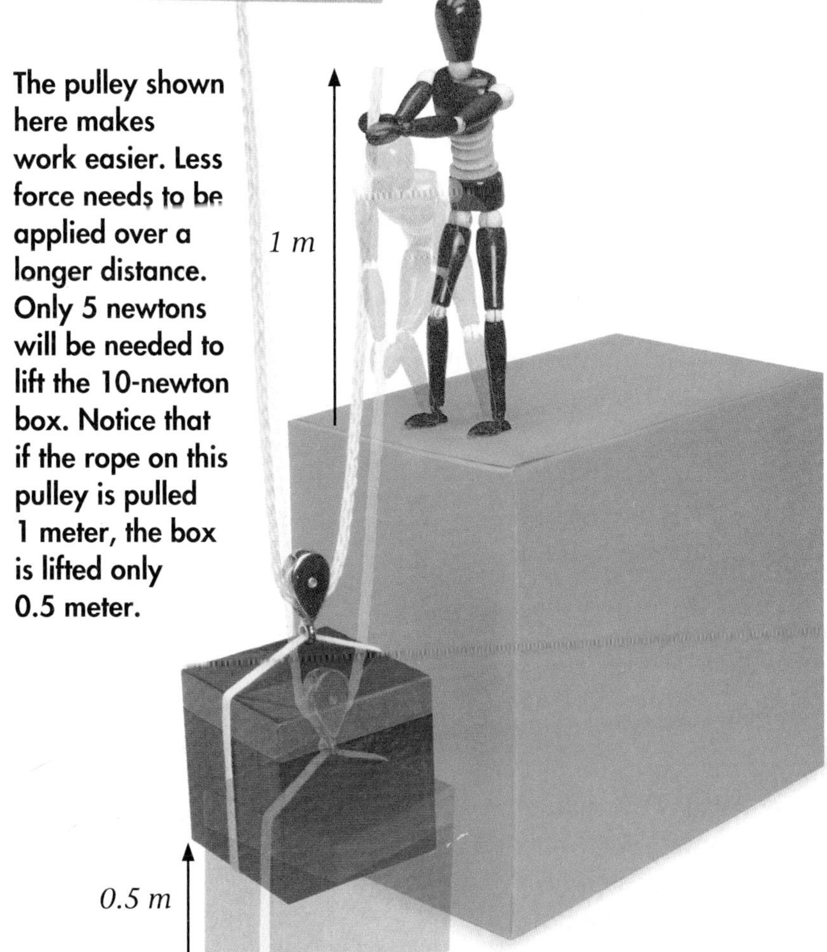
1 m
0.5 m

The pulley shown here makes work easier. Less force needs to be applied over a longer distance. Only 5 newtons will be needed to lift the 10-newton box. Notice that if the rope on this pulley is pulled 1 meter, the box is lifted only 0.5 meter.

90cm

The crank on the well is a kind of wheel and axle that reduces the force needed to raise the bucket. Your hands apply a force for 90 cm while raising the bucket only 10 cm. You are applying less force than you would if you lifted straight up on the rope. But you apply the force over a greater distance.

Lever

A lever is a type of simple machine in which a stiff bar rotates around a fixed point called a fulcrum. Levers do work by using the stiff bar, the fulcrum, a load, and a force you apply.

A lever such as a see-saw changes the direction of a force. When a person uses a see-saw to lift a box, the person pushes down, but the box goes up. As the position of the fulcrum changes, the amount of force needed to move the box will change. The farther the fulcrum is from the person using the lever, the easier the lever is to use.

Above and to the right is a picture of a person lifting a box with a lever. The force that the person must apply is less than the weight of the box. This makes the work easier. Also notice that although the needed force is less, the person must apply this force for 1 m while the box goes up only 0.5 m.

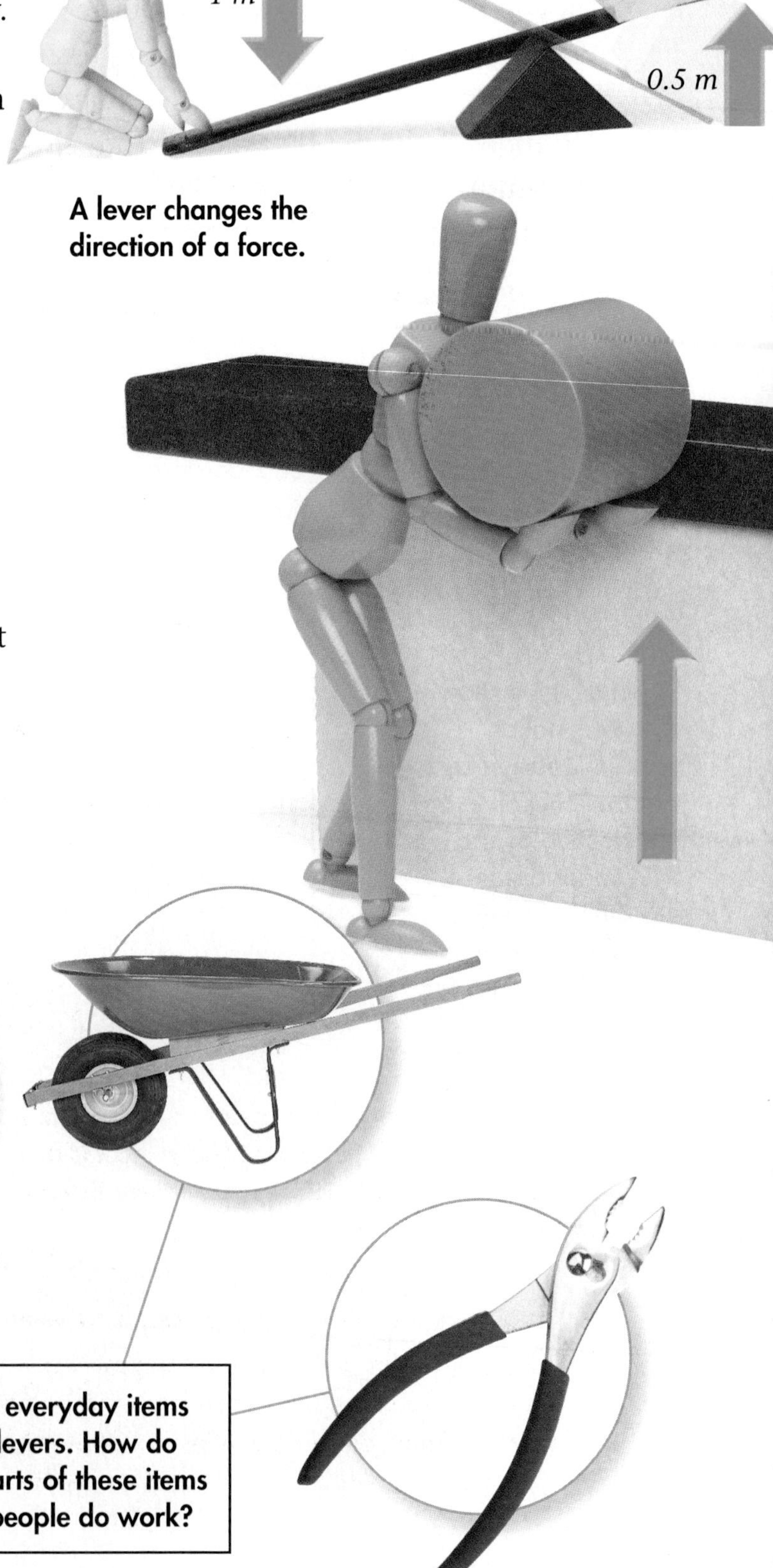
1 m
0.5 m

A lever changes the direction of a force.

Other Simple Levers

Many everyday items have levers. How do the parts of these items help people do work?

Inclined Planes

Have you ever tried carrying a heavy load up a flight of stairs? It's much easier to roll it up a ramp! An inclined plane is another type of simple machine. It consists of a flat surface with one end higher than the other. The inclined plane can be a ramp large enough for a person or a vehicle to use, or it can be very small.

If you push a wheelchair up a ramp, you would use less force over a longer distance than if you were to lift the wheelchair to the same height.

The distance from the floor straight up to the platform is less than the distance used with the inclined plane. But more force must be applied to lift the box directly from the floor onto the platform.

Pushing a box up an inclined plane to a platform is much easier than lifting the box. Using the inclined plane covers more distance, but a smaller amount of force is used.

1. **Checkpoint** What are the parts of a lever?
2. **Health in Science** Many joints in your body work like simple machines. Your knee and elbow joints are like levers. Think of two activities in which the knees or elbows act as levers to do work. Where is the fulcrum in each activity?

Other Inclined Planes

A screw is a smooth metal rod with a tiny inclined plane wrapped around it. Screws can be used to pull two pieces of wood together and hold them in place. Screws can also be used in jacks that lift cars.

A rubber doorstop is a small wedge that is used to keep a door from moving. This doorstop is a wedge that consists of one inclined plane and one flat plane. Some wedges, such as an axe, are made of two inclined planes placed back to back. This creates a machine that can be used to split wood.

Complex Machines

A machine that uses two or more simple machines is called a complex machine. Many complex machines use electricity, gravity, burning fuel, human force, or magnetism to operate each of the simple machines within it. This go cart is an example of a complex machine.

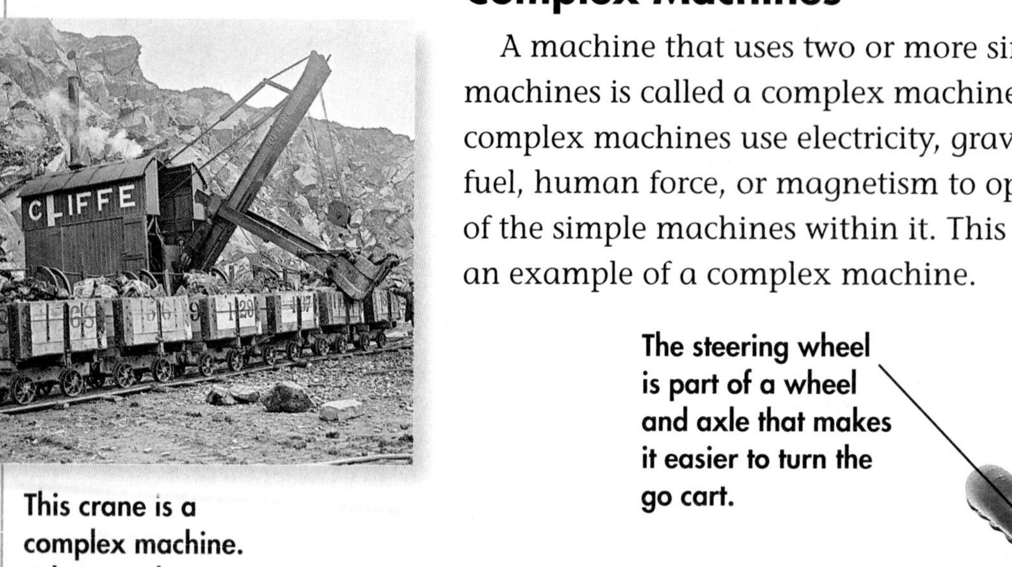
CLIFFE

This crane is a complex machine. What simple machines can you see in the crane?

The steering wheel is part of a wheel and axle that makes it easier to turn the go cart.

wheel

axle

The wheel and axle of the steering wheel move levers that turn the front wheel.

The pedals are levers. The driver's foot pushes the lever and the lever pulls on cables that lead to the engine or brakes.

The screws that hold the wheels on the go cart are types of simple machines.

Sailing ships are complex machines. They have many parts that work together to make the ship move properly. Pulleys are used to lift the sails into place. The rudder is a lever. A wheel and axle may be used to move the rudder. A wheel and axle may also be used to lift the heavy anchor. Some sailing ships used oars to help move the ship. Oars are levers.

Sailboats are complex machines that turn wind energy into kinetic energy.

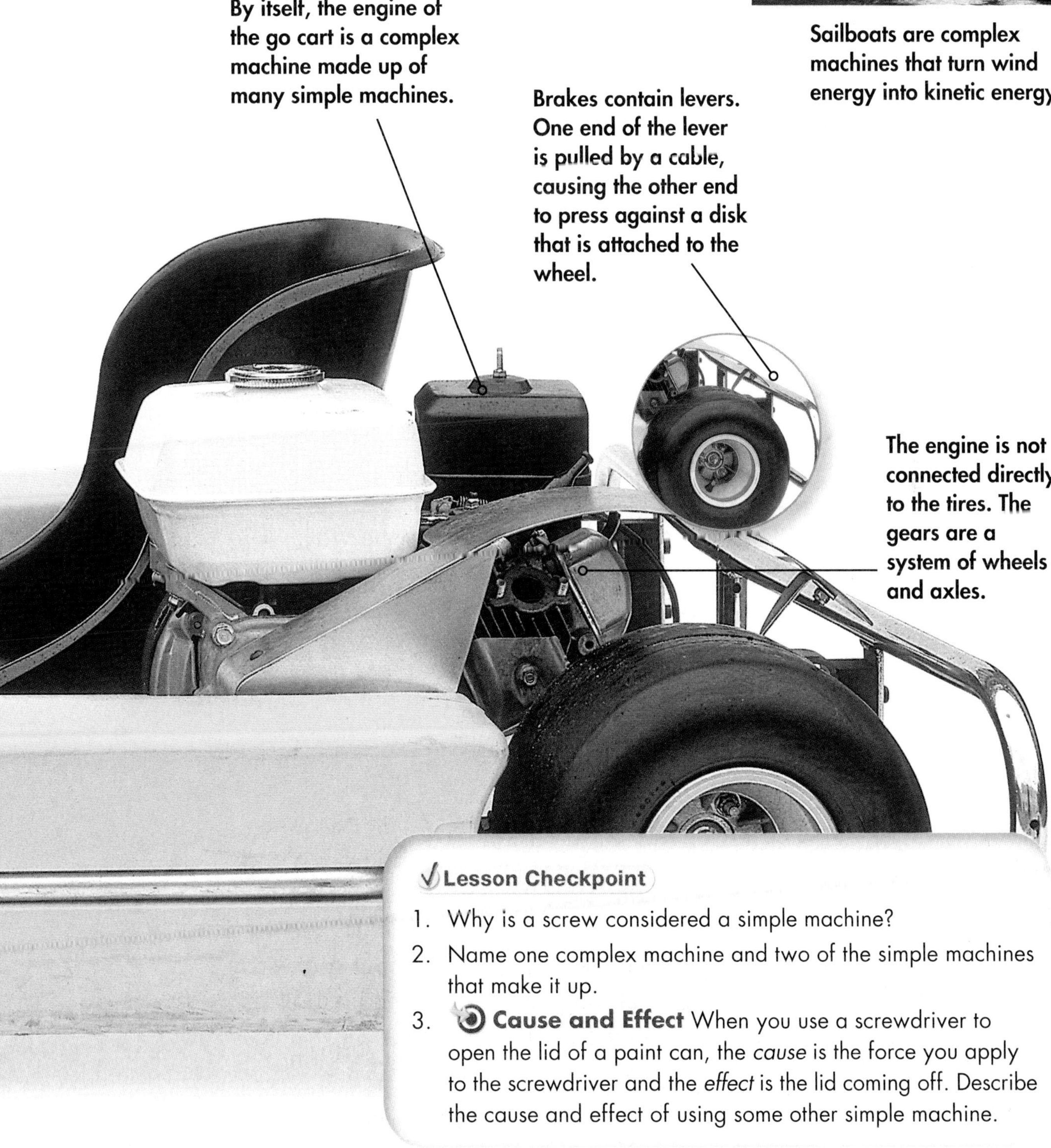
By itself, the engine of the go cart is a complex machine made up of many simple machines.
Brakes contain levers. One end of the lever is pulled by a cable, causing the other end to press against a disk that is attached to the wheel.
The engine is not connected directly to the tires. The gears are a system of wheels and axles.

√ Lesson Checkpoint

1. Why is a screw considered a simple machine?
2. Name one complex machine and two of the simple machines that make it up.
3. **Cause and Effect** When you use a screwdriver to open the lid of a paint can, the *cause* is the force you apply to the screwdriver and the *effect* is the lid coming off. Describe the cause and effect of using some other simple machine.

Lab zone

Guided Inquiry

Investigate How can you describe motion?

When soccer players kick a ball, they **estimate** how it will move. When scientists investigate motion they **measure**. In this activity you find how the speed and direction of a ball change as it moves along, hits a wall, and bounces off at an angle.

Materials

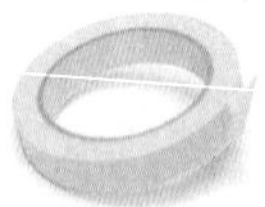

masking tape

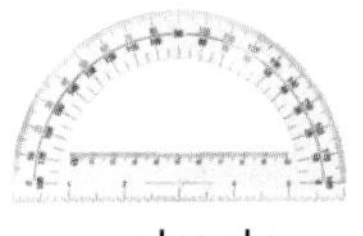

protractor

meterstick

small ball

timer or stopwatch

What to Do

1. Mark an impact spot with tape at the base of a wall. Put a protractor at the impact spot. At an angle 60° out from the wall, **measure** a path 4 meters long and mark it with tape. At the path's outer end, write *Starting Line.*

2. At an angle 120° out from the wall, measure a path 4 meters long and mark it with tape. At the path's outer end write *Ending Line.*

3. From about 1 meter behind the *Starting Line,* gently push the ball so it rolls along the path. Start the timer when the ball passes the *Starting Line* (Time 1). Record the time the ball hits the impact spot (Time 2). Stop the timer when the ball crosses the *Ending Line* (Time 3).

Process Skills

You can **measure** using standard units, such as meters, or nonstandard units such as the length of a paper clip.

More Lab zone Activities Take It to the Net sfsuccessnet.com

❹ Graph the distance the ball travels and the time it takes.

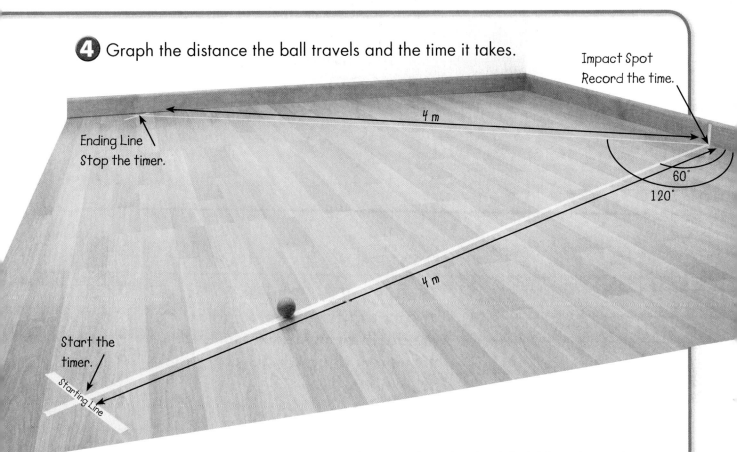

Impact Spot
Record the time.
4 m
Ending Line
Stop the timer.
60°
120°
4 m
Start the timer.
Starting Line

Design and construct a data table and a graph. You can select the ones shown or design your own. A table and graph will help you organize, display, analyze, and explain your data and your findings.

	Distance from Impact Spot (meters)	**Time** (seconds)
Time 1 (Starting Line)	4	0.00
Time 2 (Impact Spot)	0	
Time 3 (Ending Line)	4	

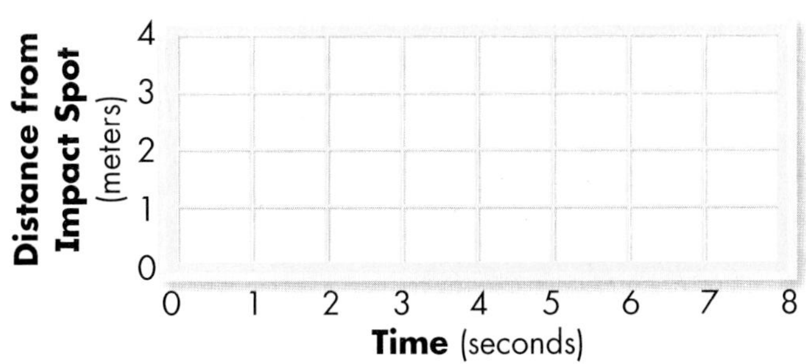
Distance from Impact Spot (meters)
0
1
2
3
4
0 1 2 3 4 5 6 7 8
Time (seconds)

Your teacher might ask you to use graph paper.

Explain Your Results

1. Using your **measurements**, find the ball's speed from the Starting Line to the Impact Spot. Find the speed from the Impact Spot to the Ending Line.

   speed = distance ÷ time

2. **Infer** Did the ball move at a steady speed? Explain your answer.

Go Further

How would your graph be different if you showed your results in feet instead of meters? Find out. Write a report of your results in your science journal.

Math in Science

Gravity, Work, Power

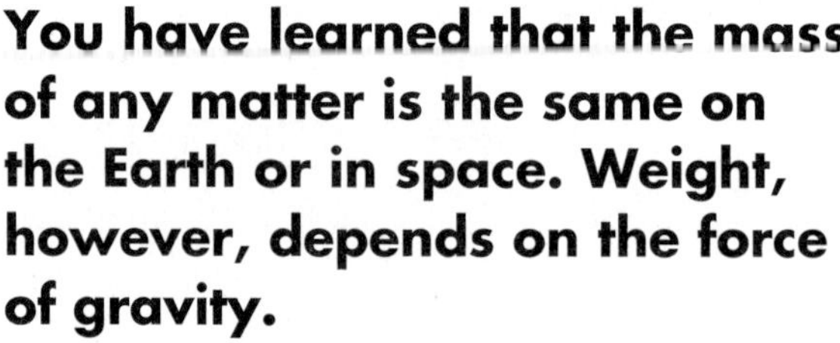

You have learned that the mass of any matter is the same on the Earth or in space. Weight, however, depends on the force of gravity.

The gravitational force on the Moon is $\frac{1}{6}$ of the gravitational force on Earth. How much would a 180-pound astronaut weigh on the Moon?

$$\frac{1}{6} \times 180 = \frac{180}{6} = 30$$

An astronaut who weighs 180 pounds on Earth would weigh only 30 pounds on the Moon.

You have learned that power describes how fast work is done.

How much power is needed to complete 150 joules of work in 40 seconds? Remember, power is measured in watts.

$$\text{Power} = \frac{\text{work}}{\text{time}}$$
$$= \frac{150}{40}$$
$$= 3\frac{3}{4} \text{ or } 3.75$$

The power needed is $3\frac{3}{4}$ or 3.75 watts.

Answer each question.

1. An Apollo astronaut's life support system was a backpack that had a total weight of about 68 pounds on Earth. About how many pounds did the backpack weigh on the Moon?
2. How many joules of work are done when a force of 2 newtons moves an object 2.5 meters? Remember, Work = force × distance.
3. How much power is needed to complete 210 joules of work in 60 seconds?

Lab zone Take-Home Activity

Use the library or the Internet to find more information about the Earth weight of items the Apollo astronauts wore or carried when they walked on the Moon. Find the weight of each item on the Moon.

Chapter 13 Review and Test Prep

Use Vocabulary

acceleration (p. 422)	**machine** (p. 426)
equilibrium (p. 419)	**power** (p. 417)
force (p. 410)	**velocity** (p. 409)
inertia (p. 420)	**work** (p. 416)

Use the vocabulary word from the list above that best completes each sentence.

1. An object resists a change in motion because of _____.
2. A _____ is a device that makes work easier to do.
3. The _____ of a moving object describes its speed and direction.
4. When all forces acting on an object balance each other, the object is said to be in a state of _____.
5. Gravity is a _____ that pulls objects toward the center of the Earth.
6. _____ is done when a force moves an object.
7. _____ is the rate at which velocity changes.
8. _____ is the rate at which work is done.

Explain Concepts

9. **Explain** why an object in a state of equilibrium could be either in motion or stationary.
10. **Explain** how you can use a simple machine to make a job easier.

Process Skills

11. **Predict** what would happen to a raft floating on a lake if a swimmer dives into the water from one end of the raft.
12. **Observe** Compare and contrast a pulley and a wheel and axle.

Cause and Effect

13. Make a graphic organizer like the one shown below. Under the word Effect, use Newton's second law of motion to explain what will happen.

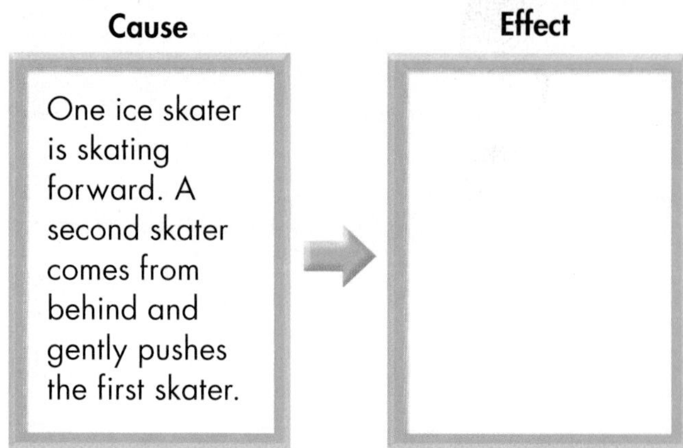

Cause
Effect
One ice skater is skating forward. A second skater comes from behind and gently pushes the first skater.

Test Prep

Choose the letter that best completes the statement or answers the question.

14. Satellites are held in orbit around Earth because of
- Ⓐ the Sun's gravity.
- Ⓑ thrust from the satellite.
- Ⓒ Earth's gravity.
- Ⓓ drag from the satellite.

15. Which of the following statements is true about horseshoe magnets?
- Ⓕ The magnetic force is strongest in the middle of the magnet.
- Ⓖ The magnetic force is weakest at the two ends.
- Ⓗ There is one pole at the middle of the magnet.
- Ⓘ The magnetic force is strongest at the two poles.

16. Calculate the power in watts used if you exert 50 joules of work in 5 seconds.
- Ⓐ 250 W
- Ⓑ 10 W
- Ⓒ 55 W
- Ⓓ 45 W

17. Keisha takes an hour to ride her bicycle north for 7 kilometers before reaching the store. Then she rides south for 6 kilometers to her aunt's house. Which of the following describes Keisha's velocity on her trip to the store?
- Ⓕ 6 kilometers per hour
- Ⓖ 7 kilometers per hour
- Ⓗ 6 kilometers per hour south
- Ⓘ 7 kilometers per hour north

18. When you raise or lower a flag on a flagpole, you are using a simple machine called a
- Ⓐ lever.
- Ⓑ wheel and axle.
- Ⓒ pulley.
- Ⓓ inclined plane.

19. Explain why the answer you selected for Question 18 is best. For each of the answers you do not select, give a reason why it is not the best choice.

20. Writing in Science **Persuasive**
Create three posters that illustrate and explain each of Newton's laws of motion. Use a slogan or phrase to summarize each of the laws. Use the word *inertia* in the first slogan, *acceleration* in the second slogan, and *action* and *reaction* in the third slogan.

Thrust, Rockets, and Airplanes

NASA has a long history of developing airplane and rocket engines. These engines produce thrust, which is the force that moves an airplane forward or a rocket upward.

Since the flight of the first airplane in 1903, the way that airplane engines have produced thrust has changed a great deal. The engines on jet airplanes produce more thrust than engines on planes that use propellers. In a jet airplane, a huge fan brings cool air into the front of the engine and compresses it. Then fuel is mixed with the air. After the mixture of fuel and air is burned, the gases that are produced greatly expand. The gases rush out the back of the engine. The force of the gases moving backward pushes the plane forward. The gases leaving the engine are known as exhaust.

U.S. AIR FORCE
NASA

The X-15 rocket aircraft

NASA
1 X-43A

Jet engines produce a great deal of thrust, but they also produce noise. Jet engines can be much more noisy than engines with propellers. NASA has a program that is trying to make jet engines quieter.

Rocket engines do not need air as jet engines do. Instead, rocket engines carry their own oxygen to mix with a fuel that burns. This produces hot gases that expand and rush out of the end of the rocket, pushing it forward.

One of NASA's first projects was to work with the Air Force to build the X-15 rocket aircraft. In 1963 this airplane used a rocket engine to fly 67 miles high. On another flight in 1967, the X-15 flew 4,520 miles per hour, over six times the speed of sound.

In 2004, NASA flew a plane with a new engine, called a scramjet. It flies at almost ten times the speed of sound. That is a new record. Perhaps scramjet engines will make it possible to fly to the other side of the world in just a few hours.

Lab zone Take-Home Activity

Use materials from home to make a model airplane. Try different materials and models to see which flies higher and faster.

Biography

Isaac Newton

1642–1727

Even in his own lifetime, Isaac Newton was considered one of history's greatest scientists. He had a deep curiosity about the natural world. He looked for clear and logical ways to explain everything he noticed. He did experiments with light to explain how rainbows form. He invented a new kind of telescope to study the sky. He put together ideas from all different areas of science in very creative ways. Among the results were his famous laws of motion. These laws, including his definition of force, caused people to think about science in a new way.

Isaac Newton graduated from Cambridge University in England in 1665. For more than 30 years, he was a teacher there. Later in life, he became the head of England's mint, which coined the nation's money. Partly because of his scientific background, he was able to catch many people making fake money and bring them to justice.

Newton's work gained him the respect of scientists throughout Europe. Centuries have passed since Newton's death. Yet, even today, his theories form the basis of our understanding of the universe.

Lab zone Take-Home Activity

Demonstrate Newton's third law of motion. Use cover goggles. Blow up a balloon and hold the neck closed. Then let go. In what direction does air leave the balloon? In what direction does the balloon go? Draw a diagram to show the action and reaction.

EC NTL 10 9 8 7

Chapter 14

Changing Forms of Energy

You Will Discover

- how energy makes everyday activities possible.
- how sound energy travels.
- how light waves compare to radio waves.
- the ways in which heat can move.

online
Student Edition
sfsuccessnet.com

Build Background

How many types of energy do you use every day?

energy
thermal energy
kinetic energy
potential energy

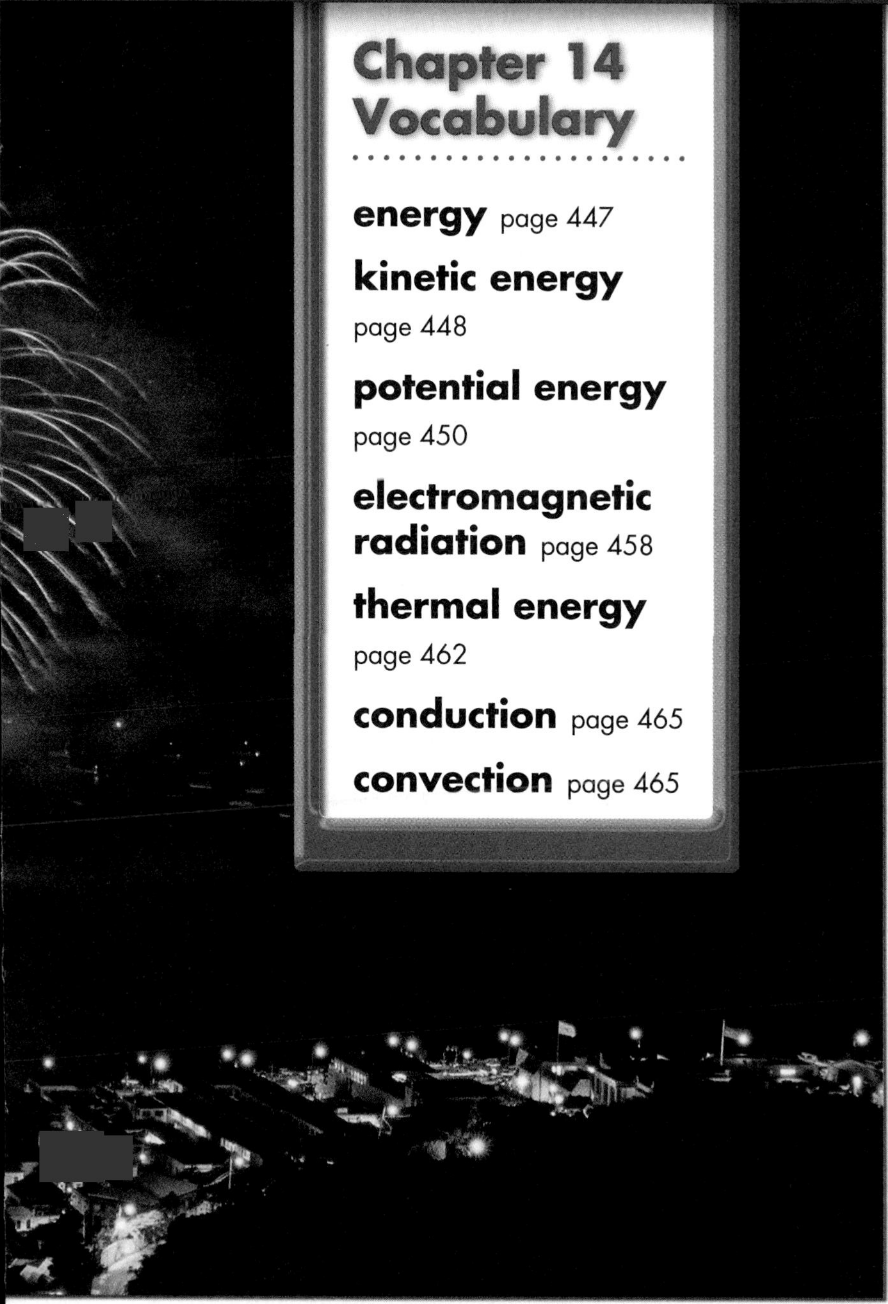

Chapter 14 Vocabulary

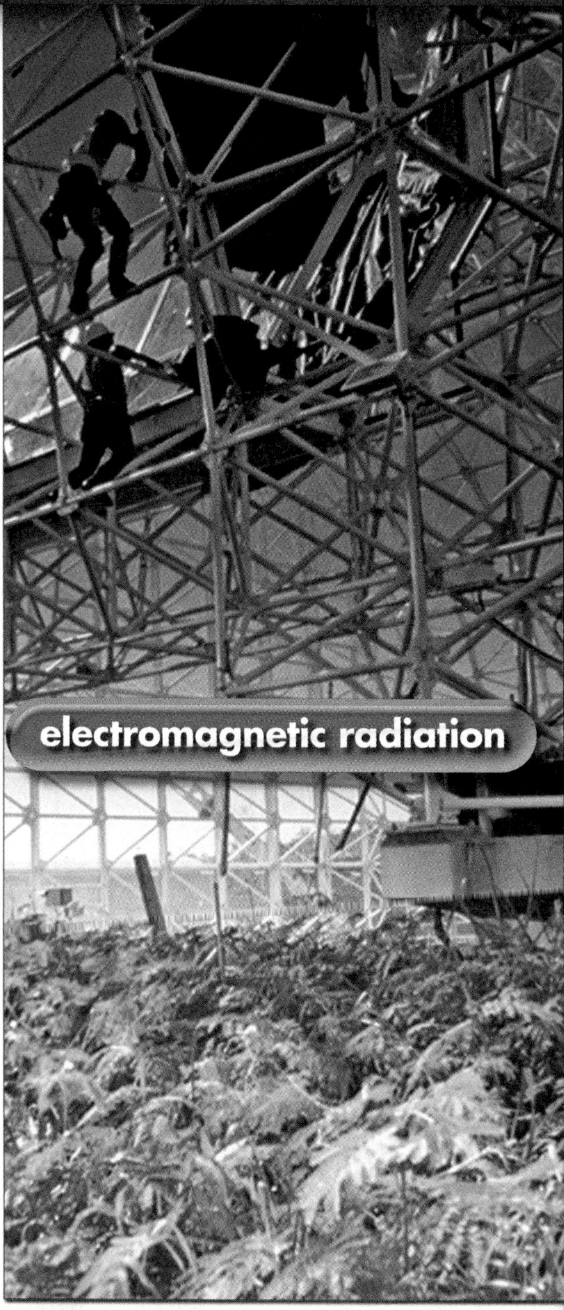

electromagnetic radiation

convection

conduction

Lab zone **Directed Inquiry**

Explore How can energy change its form?

Materials

safety goggles

sand

plastic jar with lid

thermometer

timer or stopwatch (or clock with second hand)

What to Do

1. Fill a jar $\frac{1}{2}$ full with sand. Put a thermometer in the jar. After 1 minute, record the temperature.

Be careful!

Wear safety goggles.

sand

2. Put on the lid. Take turns shaking the jar as hard as possible for a total of 10 minutes.

Take turns shaking the jar!

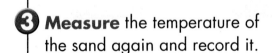

3. **Measure** the temperature of the sand again and record it.

Process Skills

To make an **inference**, you use what you already know and evaluate what you observe or **measure**.

Explain Your Results

Infer Was thermal energy produced? How do you know? What was the source of this energy?

How to Read Science

Reading Skills

Predict

When you read you often make **predictions** about what will happen next. You base your predictions on what has happened in the past. Making predictions is a good skill to use when you are reading. You make a prediction when you **infer** what will happen in the future.

Science Lab Report

Procedure: Place a glass of cold water on a hotplate. Stir constantly. Measure the temperature each minute.

Observations:

Time (minute)	1	2	3	4	5
Temperature (°C)	4	24	44	64	

What will the temperature be at the 5 minute reading?

Apply It!

Make a graphic organizer like the one shown. Make a **prediction** to answer the question from the lab report.

Question		Prediction
What will the temperature be at the 5 minute reading?	→	

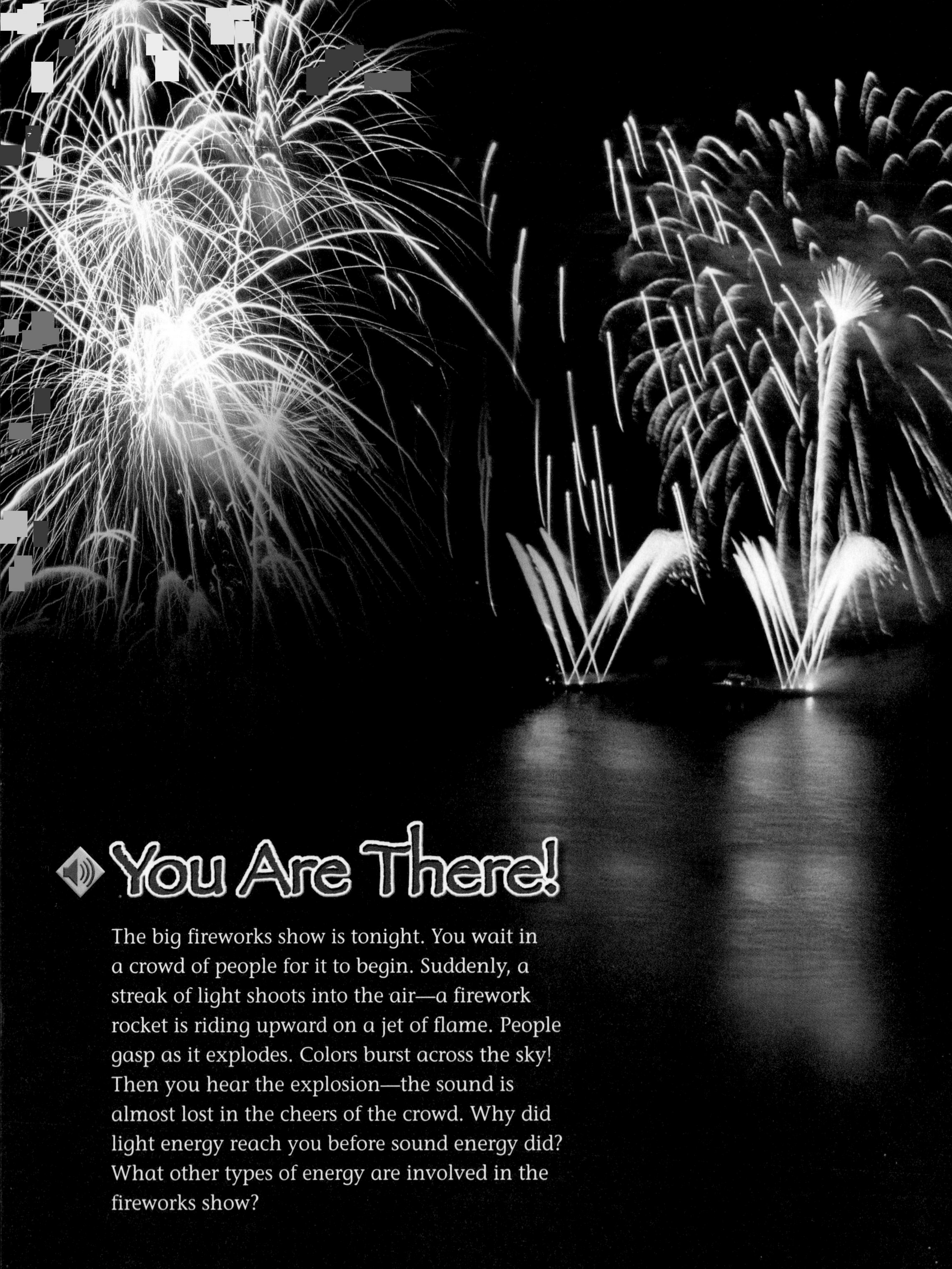

You Are There!

The big fireworks show is tonight. You wait in a crowd of people for it to begin. Suddenly, a streak of light shoots into the air—a firework rocket is riding upward on a jet of flame. People gasp as it explodes. Colors burst across the sky! Then you hear the explosion—the sound is almost lost in the cheers of the crowd. Why did light energy reach you before sound energy did? What other types of energy are involved in the fireworks show?

 AudioText

Lesson 1

What is energy?

Energy has many forms. Even though one form can change into another form, energy cannot be made or destroyed.

Forms of Energy

The word *energy* is used in different ways. In science, **energy** is the ability to do work or cause a change. Energy can change an object's motion, color, shape, temperature, or other qualities.

There are many forms of energy. Sound, light, electricity, and magnetism are forms of energy with which you are familiar. Chemical energy is found in the bonds holding molecules together. Nuclear energy holds the nucleus of an atom together. Objects that are moving or stretching have mechanical energy. When an object gains thermal energy, it gets hotter.

Energy cannot be made or destroyed. However, it can move from one object to another. Energy can also change from one form to another. Consider fireworks. When the fireworks are lit, chemical reactions create hot gases. These gases quickly build up inside the fireworks and expand. The fireworks cannot hold the expanding gases, so they explode. Some of the energy in the fireworks changes to light energy and sound energy.

Fireworks have chemical energy that can change to light, sound, and thermal energy.

Many devices change, or transform, energy. A lamp changes electrical energy to light energy. Gasoline burns in a car's engine, releasing chemical energy that is used to move the car. Every time energy changes form, some energy is given off as unusable heat. People can measure the amount of any form of energy that moves or changes. These measurements tell which devices are more energy efficient because they use less energy.

1. **Checkpoint** What are some different forms of energy?
2. **Predict** What does the energy of a light bulb change into after the lamp has been lit for a while? How can you measure the change?

Kinetic Energy

Kinetic energy is energy due to motion. The amount of kinetic energy in a moving object depends on its speed and its mass.

The faster an object moves, the more kinetic energy it has. Think about a carpenter using a hammer to drive a nail into wood. When the carpenter swings the hammer slowly, the hammer has a small amount of kinetic energy. It does not have the energy to move a nail very much. When the carpenter swings the hammer quickly, it has more kinetic energy. It is able to move a nail far into the wood with just one hit.

This basketball has kinetic energy. What changes can this energy cause?

Mass also affects kinetic energy. The more mass an object has, the more kinetic energy it has. For example, a rolling beach ball has kinetic energy. If the ball hits a sand castle, it might knock down a castle wall. A basketball has more mass than the beach ball. What would happen if a basketball, rolling at the same speed as the beach ball, hit the sand castle? The basketball might flatten the whole castle! This shows that at any particular speed, a moving object with more mass has more kinetic energy.

Kinetic energy can change into different forms of energy. A windmill changes the kinetic energy of wind into electric energy. When a drumstick hits a drum, kinetic energy becomes sound energy.

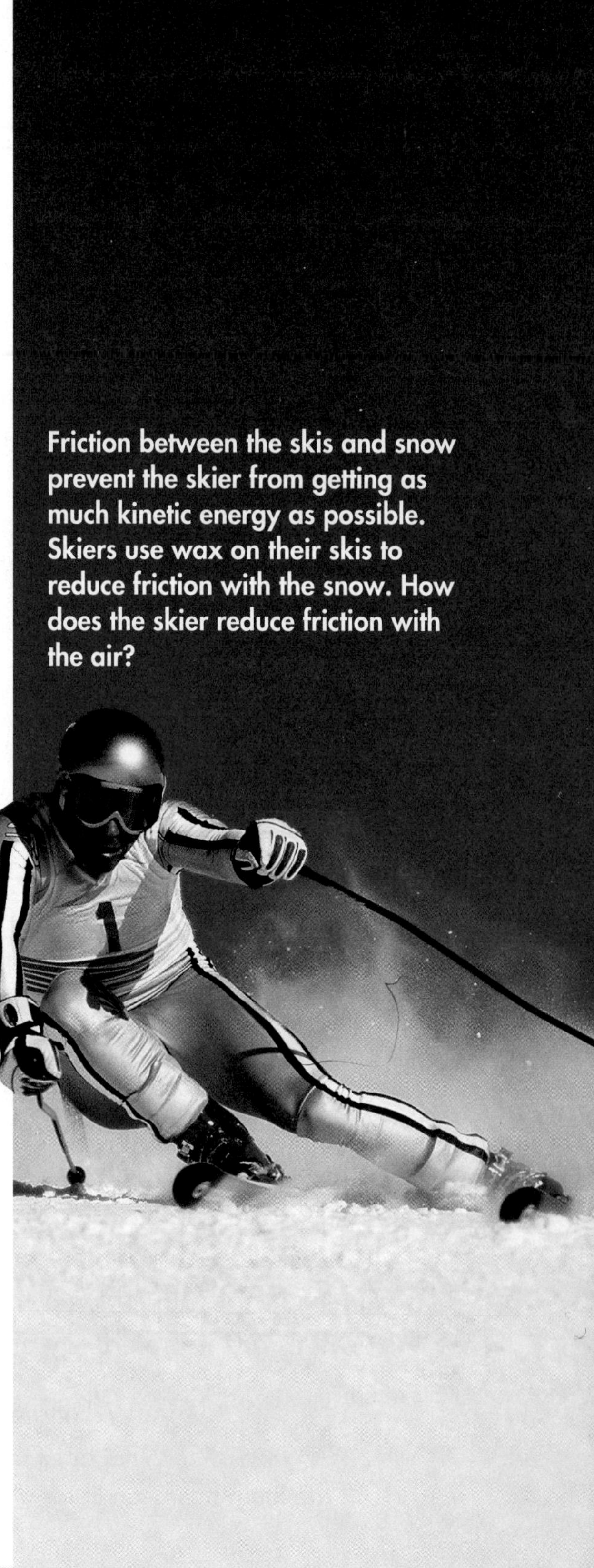
1

Friction between the skis and snow prevent the skier from getting as much kinetic energy as possible. Skiers use wax on their skis to reduce friction with the snow. How does the skier reduce friction with the air?

Kinetic energy can also change into thermal energy. Rub your hands together, and they get warmer. An increase in thermal energy increases temperature. The friction between your moving hands causes some kinetic energy to change into thermal energy. Remember from Chapter 13 that friction is a force that resists movement between surfaces that touch each other.

Kinds of Energy

The skateboarder shows many forms of energy.

Thermal energy

Kinetic energy

Chemical energy

Potential energy

Sound energy

The dog and flying disk are moving at the same speed, but since the dog has more mass, it has more kinetic energy.

A skateboarder can lower the friction between the moving parts inside the board's wheels by adding oil. Then the wheels turn more easily. Less kinetic energy is changed into wasted thermal energy. The skateboard moves faster.

1. **Checkpoint** Why do your hands get warmer when you rub them together?
2. **Social Studies in Science** Society has been changed by technology that helps people to move faster or farther. Research one such invention and report how it changed society.

Potential Energy

Potential energy is energy that is not causing any changes now, but could cause changes in the future. Potential energy is sometimes called stored energy. There are several kinds of potential energy. An object may have some kinds of potential energy because of its position.

One type of potential energy is gravitational potential energy. For example, a metal ball hanging from a string is not causing any changes now, but when it falls it will cause changes to the clay it hits. The higher or heavier the ball is, the more it will change the clay. Therefore, the higher or heavier an object is, the more gravitational potential energy it has.

When a toy car sits at the top of a track, it has potential energy. The car's potential energy becomes less as it moves to lower positions on the track. The potential energy does not just disappear. This potential energy changes mostly to kinetic energy. As the car speeds up more energy changes into kinetic energy. A small amount of potential energy changes to sound and thermal energy.

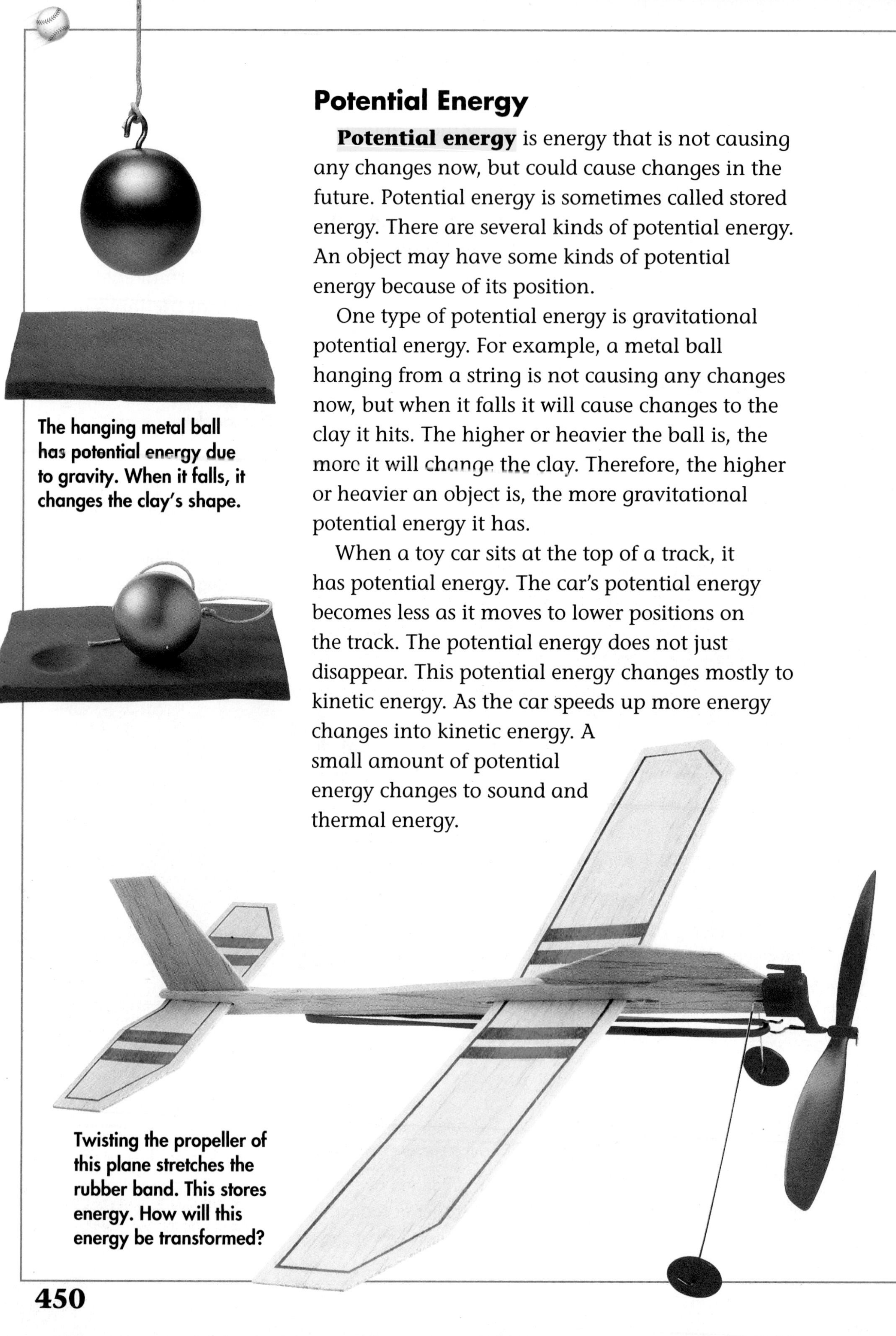

The hanging metal ball has potential energy due to gravity. When it falls, it changes the clay's shape.

Twisting the propeller of this plane stretches the rubber band. This stores energy. How will this energy be transformed?

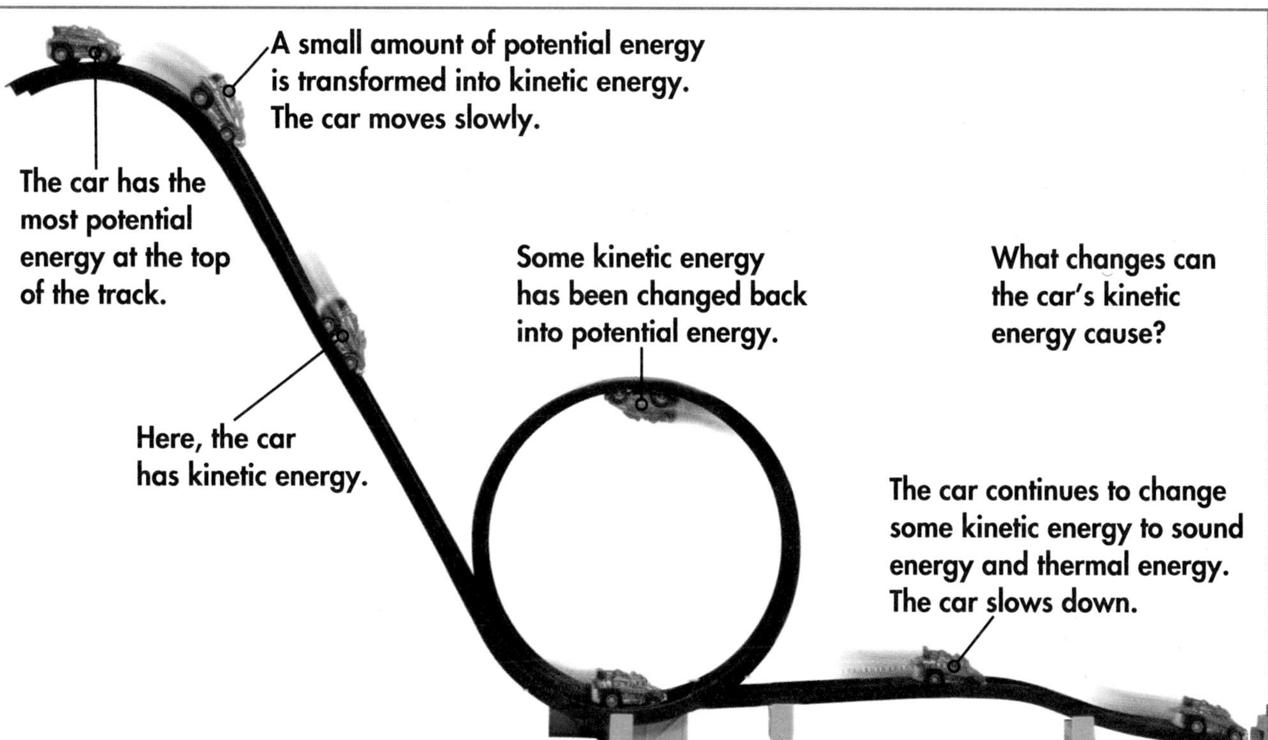
A small amount of potential energy is transformed into kinetic energy. The car moves slowly.
The car has the most potential energy at the top of the track.
Some kinetic energy has been changed back into potential energy.
What changes can the car's kinetic energy cause?
Here, the car has kinetic energy.
The car continues to change some kinetic energy to sound energy and thermal energy. The car slows down.

There are other types of potential energy. A stretched rubber band or a compressed spring has potential energy. The more a rubber band is stretched, the more potential energy it has. The potential energy of rubber bands and springs can be changed into sound energy. They can also cause the motion of objects to change.

When the north poles of two magnets are brought close together and then released, what happens? The magnets move apart. When magnets move, they have kinetic energy. Where did this energy come from? The kinetic energy comes from the changing of a kind of potential energy the magnets have when they are brought close together.

In a similar way, two atoms have potential energy when they are slowly brought close to each other. The negative electrons on the outside of the atoms repel each other. The atoms gain kinetic energy when they are released.

1. **Checkpoint** What are some types of potential energy?
2. **Writing in Science** **Descriptive** In your **science journal,** describe times that you have seen potential energy change into other forms of energy. How was energy conserved?

When a dog jumps up, it gains potential energy.

Chemical Energy

When the gasoline in this boat's engine burns, chemical energy changes into kinetic energy, sound energy, and heat.

A match has the potential to produce light energy and heat energy. The match can do this because it has another kind of potential energy. The potential energy of the match is in the form of chemical energy. Chemical energy is energy of the electrons that form the bonds between atoms in molecules. Remember that bonds form when electrons are shared by atoms or when electrons are transferred from one atom to another. When more electrons are involved in a bond, more chemical energy is in the bond.

When fuel is burned in a car, furnace, or power plant, chemical energy is changed. Heat and light are produced. Different kinds of fuels have different kinds of molecules. This means that some fuels have more energy than others. The fuel for your body is food. Some foods give your body more energy than others.

There are several units that are used to measure heat energy. A kilocalorie is the amount of energy needed to raise the temperature of 1 liter of water 1 degree Celsius. When people discuss how many Calories are in food, they are really talking about kilocalories.

Nuclear Energy

In a power plant, nuclear energy is transformed into electrical energy and heat.

Some other types of potential energy are related to the structure of atoms. All atoms contain even tinier particles called protons, neutrons, and electrons. All of an atom's protons and neutrons are in its nucleus, which is at the center of the atom. Electrons are outside the nucleus.

An atom's nucleus contains a huge amount of potential energy. Protons all have the same charge, so they tend to push away from each other. Nuclear energy holds the protons together in the nucleus. Some things can knock a proton out of its nucleus. Then, the nuclear energy that was holding the proton in place is released.

In nuclear power plants, released nuclear energy heats water until it changes into steam. The steam turns a turbine that generates electrical energy.

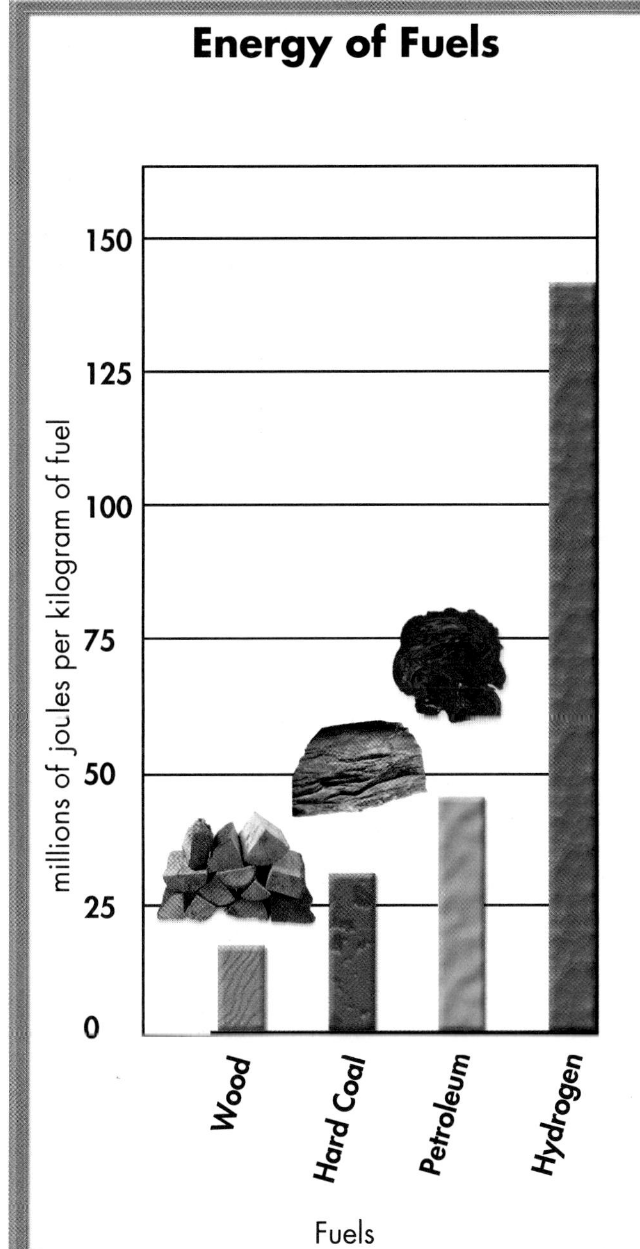
Energy of Fuels
millions of joules per kilogram of fuel
150
125
100
75
50
25
0
Wood
Hard Coal
Petroleum
Hydrogen
Fuels

Average Energy in Foods

Food	Calories
Apple	90
Banana	120
Orange	80
Hot Dog	145
Skim Milk	120
Slice of Bread	71
Egg	77
Brownie	160
1 cup of Ice Cream	580
Chocolate Milk	238
Potato	280
Bagel	195

Animals get energy from the food they eat. Their body transforms chemical energy in the food into kinetic energy, thermal energy, and other chemical energy.

Lesson Checkpoint

1. How does chemical energy hold molecules together?
2. How does the energy in an apple compare to the energy in the other foods listed?
3. Writing in Science **Expository** Find out where the nearest electrical power plant is in your area. Write a report in your **science journal** explaining how the power plant transforms energy into electrical energy.

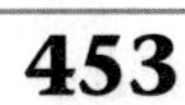

Lesson 2

What is sound energy?

Dogs bark or growl, and cats purr, hiss, and meow. What causes these different sounds? What is a sound anyway?

What Is Sound?

Sound is a wave of vibrations that spreads from its source. Vibration is the back-and-forth motion of an object. As sound waves travel through a material, the molecules that make it up vibrate in a kind of pattern. They get closer together and then farther apart. They bump into other particles, causing them to move in a similar way.

The areas where particles are very close together are called crests. The number of crests that pass by a point each second is the wave's frequency. Frequency is also a measure of how fast particles are vibrating. The greater the frequency is, the higher the pitch of the sound.

Why are some sounds louder than others? Because the source of the louder sounds is vibrating more. These sound waves have more energy. This energy squeezes the particles at the crests closer together. A sound's loudness can be measured in units called decibels. As the loudness of a sound increases by 10 decibels, the sound carries 10 times more energy.

crest ← *wavelength* → *crest*

trough

You hear sounds when waves of vibrations reach your ear. The distance between crests is called the wavelength.

The harder you pluck, the more kinetic energy of your fingers changes into sound energy. The music is louder.

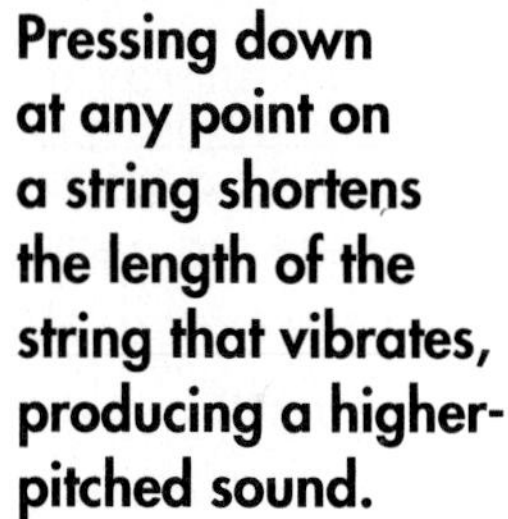

Pressing down at any point on a string shortens the length of the string that vibrates, producing a higher-pitched sound.

The vibrations of strings that are thicker produce lower notes.

Turning the keys on the neck of the guitar tunes the strings. Making a string tighter produces a higher pitch. Making it looser produces a lower pitch.

Strings that are more tightly stretched produce higher notes.

A dolphin makes sounds by tightening muscles in its airway and blowing out air.

Sound	Decibel level (db)
Normal breathing	10
Mosquito	20
Whisper	30
Refrigerator humming	40
Normal conversation	50
Vacuum cleaner	70
Garbage disposal	80
Diesel truck	84
Lawnmower	90
Farm tractor	98
Jet flyover at 100 feet	103
Snowmobile	105
Power saw	110
Rock concerts	110–140

If you hear sounds that are louder than 90 db on a regular basis, you risk gradual hearing loss. Sounds louder than 100 db can do permanent damage to your ears in a very short time.

Your Voice

Your vocal cords vibrate when you talk. The vibrations are caused by air rushing past them. Your vocal cords make the particles in the air around them vibrate. These vibrations travel outward through the air as sound waves. The sound waves travel in all directions. Even someone behind you can hear what you are saying.

1. ✓**Checkpoint** Describe a sound you have heard. State its cause and describe its frequency and loudness.
2. **Art in Science** Describe why stringed instruments produce a range of sounds of different pitch and loudness.

How Does Sound Behave?

Sound can travel through solids, liquids, and gases. But it cannot travel through a vacuum, which is empty space that contains no particles. Without vibrating particles, sound cannot exist. When sound waves reach a border between different materials, three things can happen. They can bounce back from the border, they can be absorbed, and they can pass into the second material.

The speed at which sound waves travel is different in different materials. In the ocean, sound travels about 1500 meters per second. In air at 0°C, sound travels about 330 meters per second. As conditions in any material change, the speed of sound in that material changes somewhat, too. In air, the speed of sound depends in part on the air's temperature.

What happens when sound waves in air hit a surface such as a wall or cliff? Some of the waves bounce, or reflect, back. We call reflection of sound off a wall or cliff an echo. Perhaps you have heard sound reflected as echoes. You can best hear your own echo when you are facing the wall and your sound waves hit the wall at a 90° angle.

Material	Speed of Sound ($\frac{m}{s}$)
dry air at sea level	331
iron	3240
gold	1200
glass	2840
cork	500
maple wood	4110
fresh water	1498
salt water	1531

This chart shows the speed of sound in different materials. Speeds may vary with temperature.

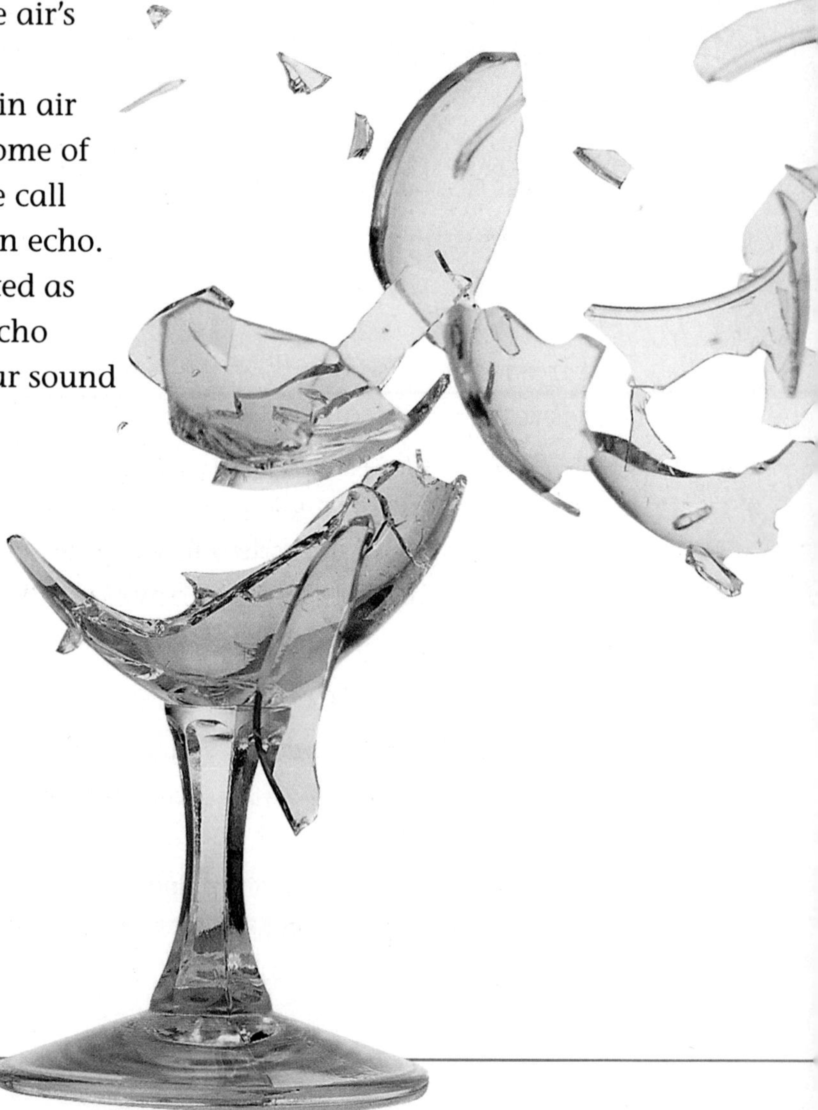

Sound Transfers Energy

The music from this piano cannot be heard outside the studio. The studio's walls are lined with special soundproofing materials. The sound bounces around and inside the soundproofing material many times. Each time it bounces, the material vibrates and some energy is turned into thermal energy. The material absorbs nearly all of the sound waves that strike it. This causes the sound to become muffled. In this process, energy moves. The kinetic energy of the piano keys create sound waves from the strings. The sound waves travel to the walls and become thermal energy.

For a sound to be heard, energy must first cause an object to vibrate. Vibrating objects transmit, or give off, energy in sound waves in air. As the sound waves move, the energy is transferred through the air. Eventually, some of the energy reaches your ear, and your eardrum absorbs some of the energy. It will begin to vibrate. In this way, the energy of the original material's vibrations passes to you.

Music studios use sound-proofing materials to elminate echos.

Sound waves transfer energy from one object to another. Sound waves from a speaker have hit this glass with enough energy to break it. Some of the energy also turns into thermal energy. The glass and the air become slightly warmer.

√ Lesson Checkpoint

1. What happens when sound waves hit a wall?
2. Describe a time you observed the transmission, reflection or absorption of sound.
3. **Predict** When sound waves travel from air to water what will happen to the speed at which they are moving?

Lesson 3

What is light energy?

Visible light is only a small part of the electromagnetic spectrum.

Visible light is a portion of the electromagnetic spectrum. It can travel in straight lines, can reflect off objects, and can bend as it passes around or through them. Visible light of different wavelengths has different colors.

Electromagnetic Radiation

Like sound, light travels in waves that have certain wavelengths and frequencies. Like sound, its speed is different in different materials. Also like sound, light can be reflected or absorbed by certain objects, or it can pass through them.

However, light is unlike sound in important ways. Unlike sound, light is not a vibration of particles. It is a form of **electromagnetic radiation**, which means that it is a combination of electrical and magnetic energy. Light energy is transmitted, or given off, by electrons in an object.

The spectrum, or range, of electromagnetic radiation includes waves with many frequencies and wavelengths. Visible light makes up only a small part of the electromagnetic spectrum. For you to see an object, it must give off or reflect wavelengths of visible light. The light must then enter your eyes. Different wavelengths of visible radiation are seen as different colors.

Gamma radiation can kill cancer cells.

X rays are used to see the shape of this skull.

A black light bulb gives off ultraviolet light.

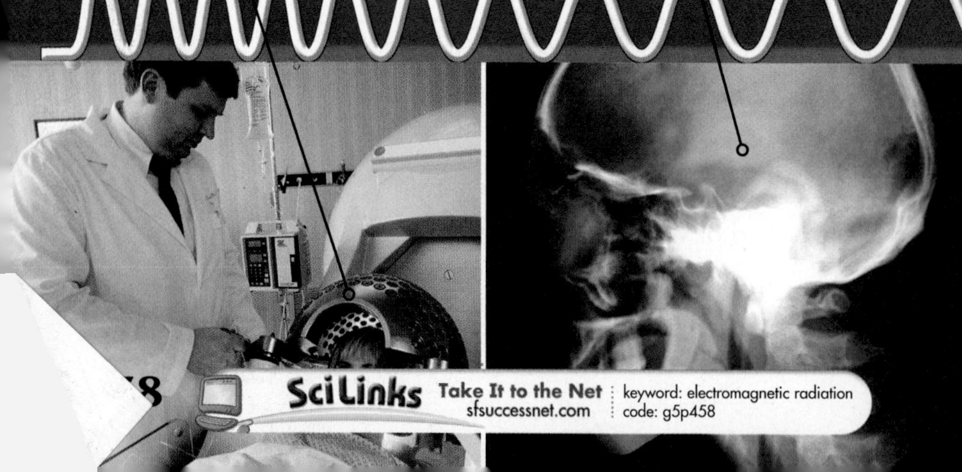

SciLinks Take It to the Net sfsuccessnet.com keyword: electromagnetic radiation code: g5p458

Some types of electromagnetic radiation have wavelengths that are shorter than those of visible light. These include ultraviolet, X-ray, and gamma ray radiation. They have higher frequencies and more energy than visible light.

Various kinds of electromagnetic waves have wavelengths that are longer than those of visible light. Longer waves have lower frequencies and lower energies. They include infrared waves, microwaves, and radio waves. Most sources that give off visible light also give off heat in infrared waves. Lava, light bulbs, and candles are familiar examples.

Stars, including the Sun, give off most of the light in the universe. In addition to visible light, the Sun gives off ultraviolet, infrared, X-ray, and other radiation. All stars give off different kinds of radiation. Some stars give off only a little visible light. All stars give off radio waves.

1. **✓ Checkpoint** How is light energy like sound energy?
2. **Technology in Science** Lasers give off light of just one frequency. Use the Internet or library resources to find how lasers are used.

Visible light

A photograph of infrared radiation shows that some parts of this house are hotter than others.

When food absorbs microwave radiation, its temperature rises.

Radio waves are used for radios, television and astronomy.

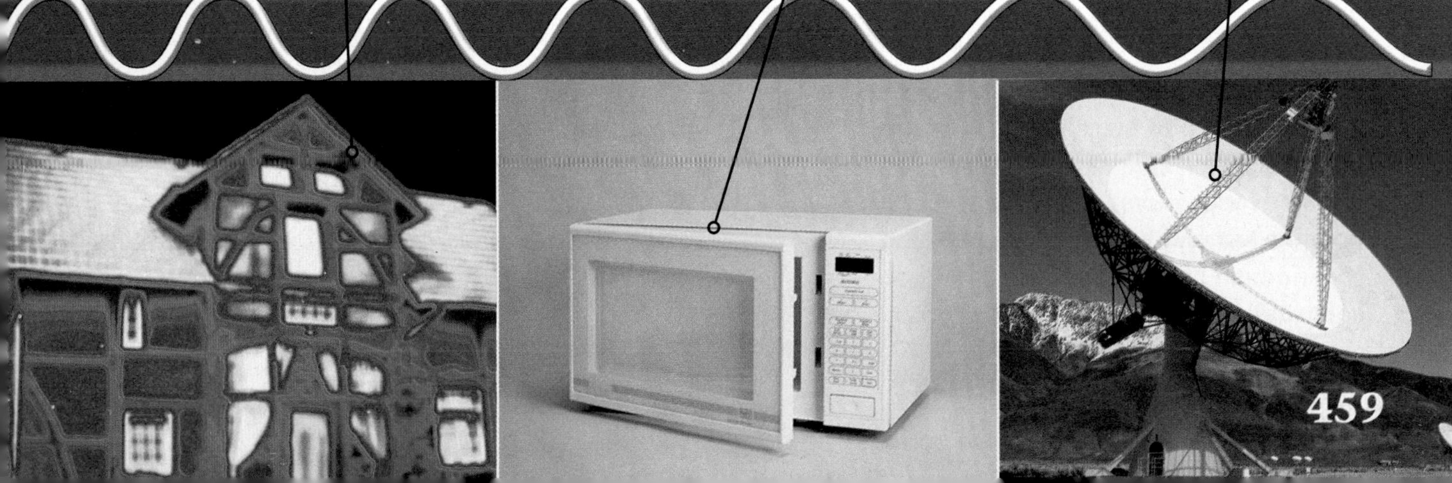

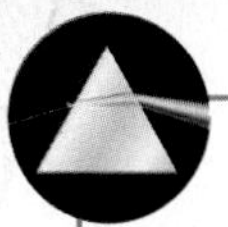

How Does Light Move?

Mirrors in a periscope reflect light so that a sailor on a submarine underwater can see things that are on the surface.

Since an electromagnetic wave is not a vibration of particles like a sound wave, an image can travel through a vacuum. Light travels the fastest in a vacuum, about 300,000,000 meters per second. Light travels more slowly through materials such as air or water.

In our day-to-day experience, light moves in straight lines. Light waves move the same way whether they come from the Sun, from light bulbs, or from projectors. If it reflects off an object, such as a mirror, light still moves in a straight line, but in a different direction.

Light bends, or refracts, whenever it enters a new material at an angle. For example, light bends when it enters a prism. A prism is a transparent object that bends light of different wavelengths by different amounts. It separates light into its different wavelengths. White light that enters a prism comes out separated into its colors. A rainbow appears in the sky when light reflects and refracts in water droplets.

An object in the path of light waves casts a shadow. The object casting the shadow blocks the path of light. A shadow is larger when the object is closer to the light source. Also, the shadow of a large object is larger than the shadow of a small object when both objects are the same distance from the light source.

Colored material and filters absorb some frequencies and wavelengths of light. When light is absorbed, the light energy is transformed into thermal energy. The frequencies that are not absorbed are reflected or allowed to pass through, resulting in the colors we see.

White light contains a mix of many wavelengths.

You can see rainbow colors in oily water and soap bubbles even though they are not prisms. When light enters a thin film of oil or soap, waves of light reflect off both the top and bottom of the film. The combination of these two sets of reflected light rays are seen as different colors.

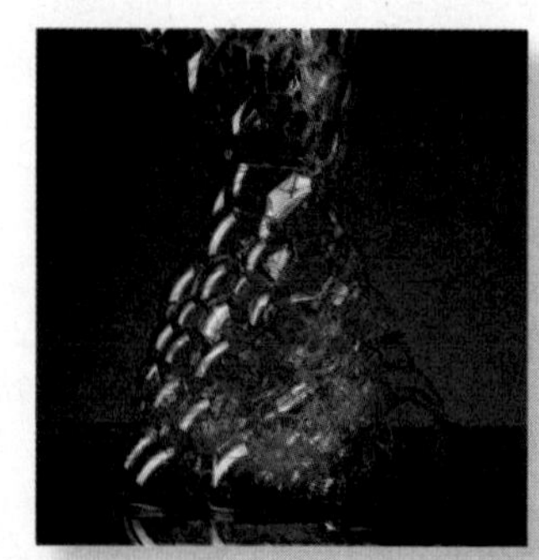

Light waves refract when they enter the prism at an angle.

Different wavelengths refract at different angles. This causes different colors to separate from each other.

Some light reflects from the outer surface of the prism.

convex lens

A magnifying glass contains a convex lens that bends light rays to make objects look larger. A convex lens is thickest in the middle.

concave lens

A concave lens is thinner in the middle than the edges. It can bend light rays to make an object look smaller.

1. **✓ Lesson Checkpoint** What happens to light as it passes through a prism?
2. How does light move?
3. **Predict** How would a shadow change as an object moved toward the light source?

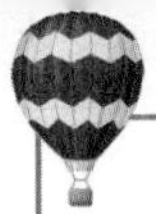

Lesson 4

What is thermal energy?

As the total kinetic energy of the particles in an object increases, the object gets warmer. Heat flows from a warmer object to a cooler one.

When Matter Gets Warmer

When you take a baked potato from an oven, the potato has kinetic energy while it is being moved. After you put the potato down, it still has a form of kinetic energy inside it. The atoms that make up the potato are always in motion. Each moving atom has a certain amount of kinetic energy. **Thermal energy** is the total of all the kinetic and potential energy of the atoms in an object.

When any form of matter gets warmer, the kinetic energy of the atoms or molecules that make it up increases. The object's thermal energy increases.

Thermal Energy and Phase Changes

On Earth, most matter exists as a solid, a liquid, or a gas. A change in thermal energy can lead to a change in phase.

When the thermal energy of a substance increases, its particles move faster. If the thermal energy of a solid increases enough, it melts into a liquid. The liquid state of a substance always has a higher thermal energy than its solid state.

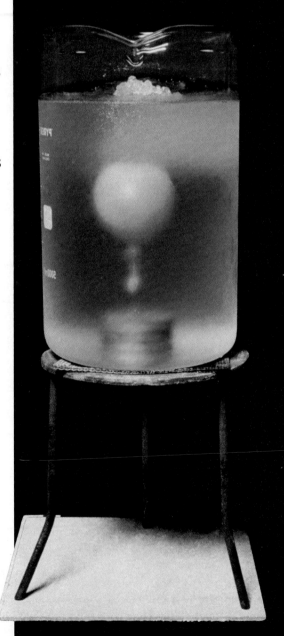

This beaker contains liquid water, ice, and a balloon filled with air. All these materials have a temperature of 0°C.

When a flame adds energy to the beaker the temperature rises, the ice melts, and the air in the balloon expands.

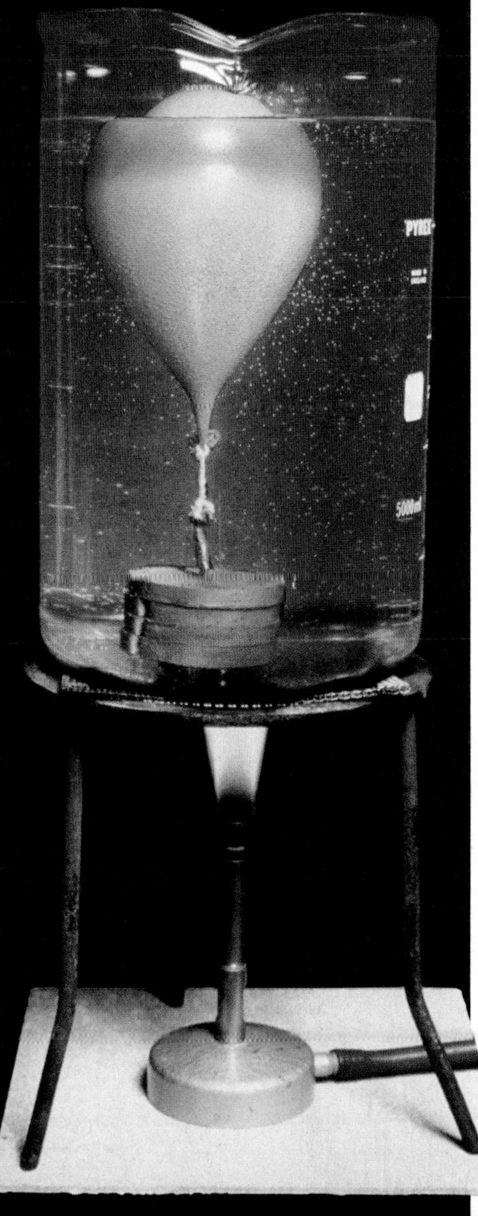

If the liquid continues to gain thermal energy, its particles speed up more. When the particles of a liquid have absorbed enough energy to escape the forces between them, the liquid becomes a gas. The substance has undergone another phase change.

Thermal Energy and Temperature

Temperature is a measure of thermal energy. The temperature of an object is related to the average kinetic energy of all its particles. Some particles in an object will be faster, and therefore hotter, than others.

People measure temperature with thermometers. The most familiar kind contains a liquid, usually mercury or alcohol, inside a closed tube. The liquid expands when its temperature increases. The height of a column of the liquid inside the tube shows the temperature.

1. **√Checkpoint** What is the relationship between the temperature of an object and the motion of its particles?
2. **Math in Science** Some frozen material has a temperature of –27.4°C. It absorbs enough energy to melt and raise its temperature by 53.2°C. What is its final temperature?

Conduction, Convection, Radiation

If you walk into bright sunshine or get into a hot bath, you feel warmer. If you hold an ice cube, your hand feels cooler. Thermal energy flows between materials that have different temperatures. Thermal energy naturally flows from warmer substances to cooler ones. When people talk about the flow of thermal energy, they often use the word heat.

Conduction, convection, and radiation are three ways that heat moves. Conduction is the flow of heat between objects that are touching. Convection is the movement of warm liquids or gases to cooler areas. Radiation is the movement of energy by electromagnetic waves.

When something increases its temperature, its particles increase their kinetic energy. Some of this kinetic energy can be passed on to other particles.

In conduction, two objects touch and their atoms or molecules collide. The faster-moving particles in the warmer object transfer some of their kinetic energy to the slower-moving particles in the cooler object. The temperature of the warmer object decreases as heat flows from it. The temperature of the cooler one rises as heat flows to it. The heat flows until the objects have the same temperature. If the objects have the same mass and are the same material, the temperature of one goes down by the same amount that the temperature of the other goes up.

This lamp uses conduction, convection and radiation.

Wax cools by conduction and radiation. It will sink.

Wax rises because of convection.

The light bulb in the base of the lamp heats the colored wax by radiation.

√ Lesson Checkpoint

1. Which most likely has greater thermal energy, ice or water vapor? Why?
2. What examples of conduction, convection, or radiation can you find in your classroom?
3. Writing in Science **Expository** Write a brief report in your **science journal** that explains how conduction transfers heat.

Conduction

Conduction is the transfer of heat between objects that are in contact. The stove heats the pan above it by conduction. Conduction can also happen between different parts of the same object. For example, the part of the handle closest to the stove will also heat up. As part of the handle gets warmer, its molecules conduct heat to neighboring molecules. The entire handle can become too hot to touch.

The heat from the stove warms the pan by conduction.

Convection

Convection is another way that heat is transferred. Convection is the transfer of heat by a moving liquid or gas. For example, cool water sinks under warm water. The warm water will rise. This creates a circular current called a convection current.

The heater warms the water next to it by conduction. Currents of warmed water carry heat throughout the water in the fish tank by convection.

Radiation

Radiation is a third way that heat flows from one object to another. Radiation is the transfer of heat by electromagnetic waves. All objects radiate heat, and hot objects radiate more than cool ones. The part of the electromagnetic spectrum that is often related to heat is infrared radiation. Other parts of the spectrum can also radiate heat. When an object gives off electromagnetic radiation, its temperature decreases.

Radiation from the Sun warms this greenhouse.

Lab zone **Guided Inquiry**

Investigate How does light move?

Materials

plastic cup and foil

metric ruler

scissors and clear tape

water

blue food coloring, plastic spoon, salt

white paper and flashlight

Process Skills

You can use a diagram to help **collect data**, to help **interpret data**, and to help answer questions.

What to Do

1. Cut two 6 × 6 cm pieces of foil. Cut one 1 × 6 cm piece of foil. Tape them on the outside of a cup as shown with their shiny sides out.

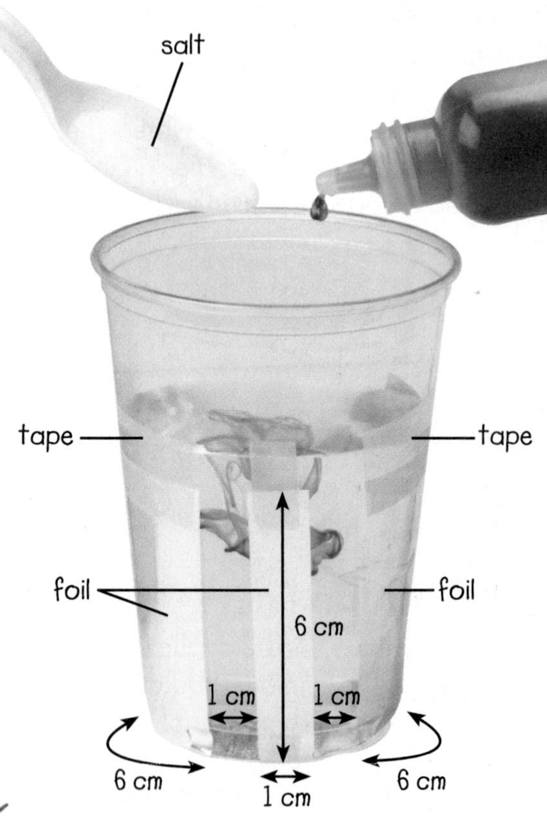
salt
tape
tape
foil
foil
6 cm
1 cm
1 cm
6 cm
1 cm
6 cm

2. Fill the cup about $\frac{2}{3}$ full with water. Add blue food coloring to make the water a medium blue. Then add 1 spoonful of salt and stir the water.

3. Have another student hold a sheet of white paper behind the cup. Hold a flashlight about 30 cm away from the cup. Shine the light directly toward the 2 gaps in the foil. **Observe** the light from above the cup.

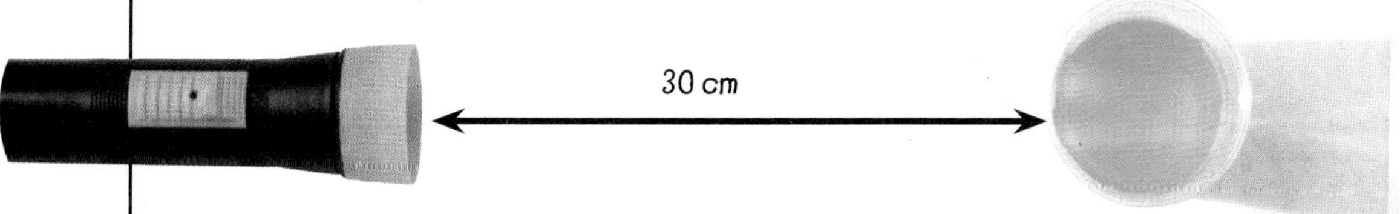
30 cm

4. **Collect Data** Show the processes you observe. Use the diagram below or select a way of your own. If you choose to use the diagram, sketch it on a sheet of paper. Write these words on the correct lines: *reflection, refraction,* and *transmission* (going through).

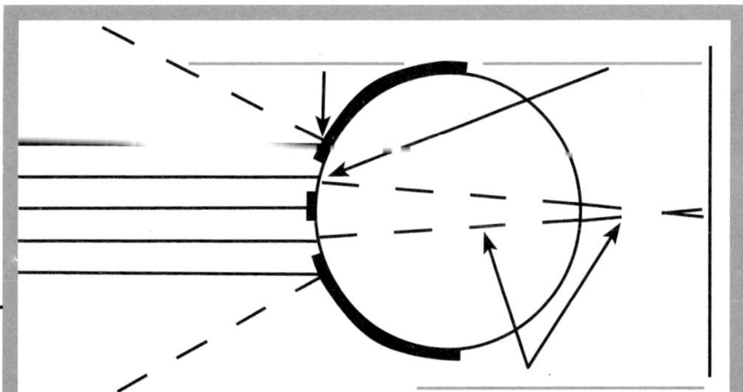

Explain Your Results

1. What happens to the light that shines on the foil?
2. **Interpret Data** What happens to the direction of the light when it moves from air to water?
3. What colors of light shine into the blue water? What color shines onto the paper? What color passes through the blue water (transmission)? What colors does the blue water block or filter out (absorption)?

Go Further

Use your equipment to investigate how shadows are formed. What conditions are needed? What objects cast dark shadows? Can a clear object cast a shadow? Make a plan to find out. Write clear instructions that others could follow.

Math in Science

Using SPEED to Estimate Distance and Time

The speed of light is the fastest speed known. Light travels about 300,000,000 meters per second. Sound travels about 330 meters per second through air. In everyday experience, light travels instantly. People sometimes notice that sound travels much more slowly. You may have noticed that you see the explosions of fireworks before you hear them.

A certain plane can travel 800 kilometers in one hour. How does this compare with the speed of sound?

Sound travels about 330 meters per second.
1 minute = 60 seconds
60 × 330 m = 19,800 m
1 hour = 60 minutes
60 × 19,800 = 1,188,000 m
1 km = 1,000 m
1,188,000 ÷ 1,000 = 1,188

Sound travels about 1,188, or almost 1,200 km in one hour. The plane is slower than sound.

Use the information on page 468 to choose the correct answer for each question.

1. You notice a flash of lightning in the sky. Three seconds later, you hear thunder. About how far did the sound travel in those three seconds?
   A. About 330 meters
   B. About 660 meters
   C. Almost 1 kilometer
   D. More than 1 kilometer

2. Light travels about 18 million kilometers per minute. The Sun is 150 million kilometers from Earth. About how long does the sun's light take to reach Earth?
   F. Almost 3 minutes
   G. Between 4 and 5 minutes
   H. Between 8 and 9 minutes
   I. Almost 14 minutes

3. In 1815, a volcano in Indonesia erupted powerfully. People up to 1,400 kilometers away heard it. About how long did the sound take to reach them?
   A. More than 1 hour but less than 2 hours
   B. Between 2 and 3 hours
   C. About 3 hours
   D. More than 4 hours

Lab zone Take-Home Activity

The speed of sound changes as the temperature and humidity of air changes. You will need a partner, a stopwatch, a meter tape, and a calculator. Stand in an open area facing the side of a large building. Clap your hands and listen for an echo. Measure your distance from the building and the time between the clap and the echo. Remember, the sound covers this distance twice. Find the speed of sound.

Chapter 14 Review and Test Prep

Use Vocabulary

conduction (p. 465)	**kinetic energy** (p. 448)
convection (p. 465)	**potential energy** (p. 450)
electromagnetic radiation (p. 458)	**thermal energy** (p. 462)
energy (p. 447)	

Use the term from the list above that best completes the sentence. You will use all of the terms.

1. Heat is transferred in moving liquids and gases by _____.
2. _____ is the ability to do work or cause change.
3. An object has _____ because it is moving.
4. _____ is the transfer of heat from one part of an object to another.
5. X-rays, microwaves, light, and radio waves are examples of _____.
6. Stored energy of an object due to its position is _____.
7. _____ is the total kinetic and potential energy of atoms in an object.

Explain Concepts

8. Explain what causes the phase change when solid iron melts into liquid iron.
9. Why does a prism produce a rainbow when white light passes through it?
10. Most everyday events involve some form of energy being transformed into another. Describe two such events that you have seen.
11. A train and a car are moving at the same speed. Explain why they do not have the same kinetic energy.
12. Explain how the speed of a wave of sound or light can be changed.
13. Explain what temperature is and how thermometers measure it.

Process Skills

14. Infer When the ends of two pieces of metal are brought close, they push each other away. Infer why this happens.

Predict

15. A thermometer is held above a light bulb. The graph below shows the readings of the thermometer before and after the light is turned on. Predict how the temperature reading of the thermometer will change after the light bulb is turned off. Use the graphic organizer below to explain your answer.

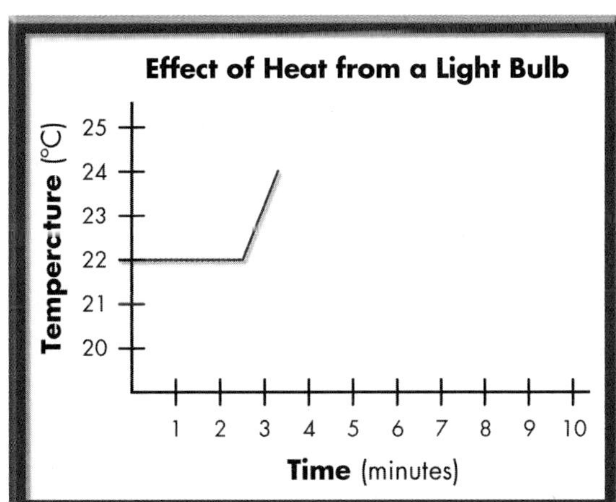

Effect of Heat from a Light Bulb
Temperature (°C)
25
24
23
22
21
20
1 2 3 4 5 6 7 8 9 10
Time (minutes)

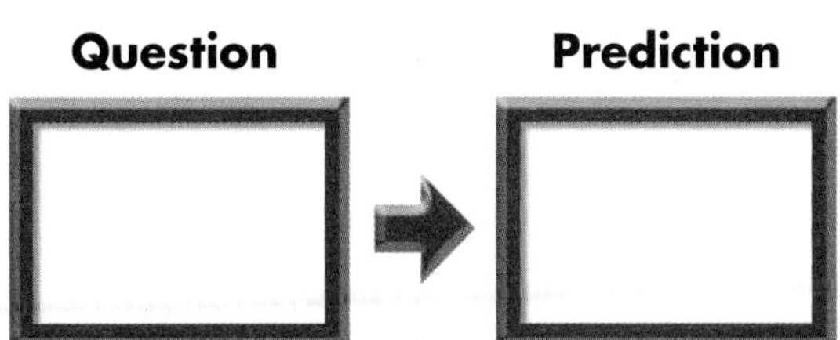

Question
Prediction

Test Prep

16. A lawnmower runs on gasoline. What type of energy transformation takes place in its engine?

Ⓐ electrical energy to chemical energy
Ⓑ kinetic energy to gravitational energy
Ⓒ chemical energy to kinetic energy
Ⓓ magnetic energy to electrical energy

17. An object's thermal energy depends in part on its

Ⓕ mass.
Ⓖ phase.
Ⓗ location.
Ⓘ size.

18. In what direction does heat flow?

Ⓐ from a larger object to a smaller object
Ⓑ from a warmer object to a cooler object
Ⓒ from a liquid to a solid
Ⓓ from a liquid to a gas

19. Explain why the answer you selected for Question 18 is best. For each of the answers you do not select, give a reason why it is not the best choice.

20. Writing in Science **Expository** Write a story explaining how the structure and function of concave and convex lenses are different. Tell ways each kind of lens could be used.

NASA

Career

Supervising Engineer

Anita Liang is working on ways to reduce the noise of jet engines.

Have you ever been close to a jet airplane when it is taking off or landing? If so, then you know how loud jet engines are. Some people are trying to soften the sound.

Airplanes make very loud sounds. People who live near airports are also often bothered by the noise. People who work near aircraft need to protect their ears.

Anita Liang is an engineer who works on projects to make jet engines quieter. The engineers who work with her study how air and fuel enter the engine. They try to make them flow more smoothly to help cut noise. They make models to see how changing engine parts affects noise.

Liang works with many people. She works with the engineers who experiment with engines. She works with computer scientists who design computer models. She also works with people at companies who manufacture jet engines. She helps everyone work together to make better, quieter airplanes.

To be supervising engineer, you need to enjoy working with people. Engineers study science and math in college. Many have advanced degrees in science, math, or engineering.

Lab zone Take-Home Activity

Keep a log to record your observations of loud sounds you hear every day or occasionally. Record whether or not each sound bothers you. Think of ways that the sounds can be made softer or can bother you less.

EC NTL 10987

Chapter 15

Electricity

You Will Discover

- what materials conduct electricity.
- what parts are needed to make an electrical circuit.
- how electrical current can be used to make a magnet.

online
Student Edition
sfsuccessnet.com

Build Background

What is electrical current and how does it work?

conductor

volt

resistor

current

insulator

Chapter 15 Vocabulary

current page 479

conductor page 480

resistor page 480

insulator page 480

circuit diagram page 484

volt page 484

electromagnet page 488

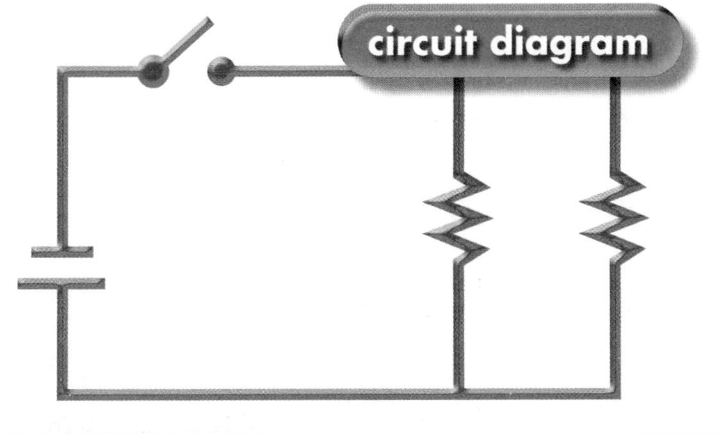
circuit diagram

electromagnet

Lab zone

Directed Inquiry

Explore What can electricity flow through?

Materials

safety goggles

3 pieces of wire

flashlight bulb and holder

battery and battery holder

plastic spoon

aluminum foil and paper clip

penny and index card

Process Skills

Before you **predict,** think about what you know about the properties of the objects.

What to Do

1. Make a path through which electricity can flow. Connect the wires, battery, and bulb.

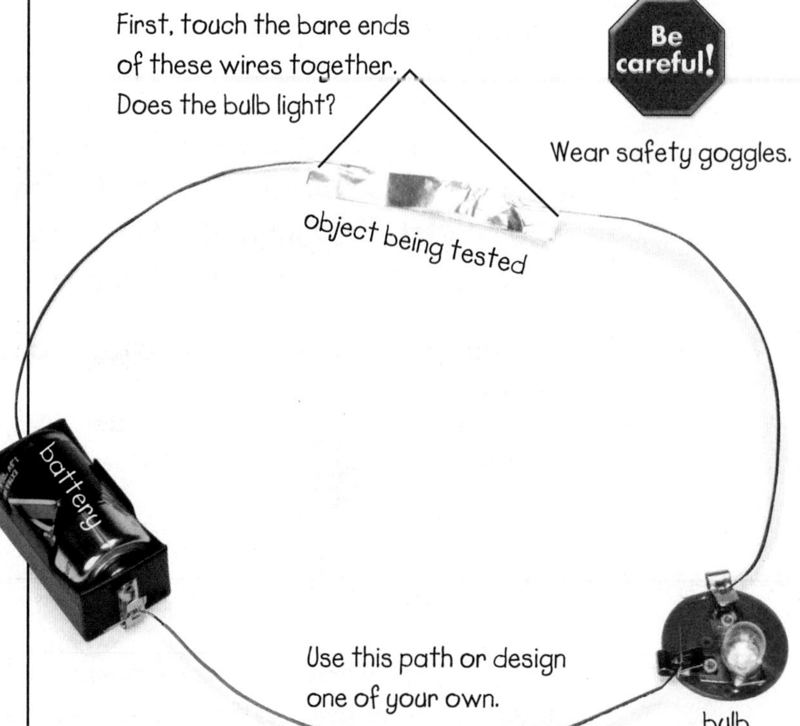
First, touch the bare ends of these wires together. Does the bulb light?
object being tested
battery
Use this path or design one of your own.
bulb

Be careful! Wear safety goggles.

2. **Predict** which objects electricity will flow through. Then, test each object by touching the bare ends of the wires to the object. **Observe.** Does the bulb light up?

Explain Your Results

1. Were your **predictions** correct? How do you know?
2. How are the objects that electricity flows through alike?

How to Read Science

Reading Skills

TARGET SKILL

Cause and Effect

A **cause** is the reason something happens. An **effect** is what happens.

Sometimes writers use clue words such as *because, so,* or *since,* to signal a cause-and-effect relationship. Sometimes there are no clue words. You can find the cause and effect by observing an event and asking why it happened. You may be able to **predict** an effect if you know the cause.

In the biography below some causes and effects are highlighted.

Biography

Thomas Edison did not invent the first light bulb. However, early light bulbs burned out in less than a few hours. Edison invented a light bulb that lasted a long time. He tested many materials to see which would give off light when they conducted electricity. He tested such things as animal hair and paper. One of his successful bulbs used treated bamboo to generate light. This bulb gave off light for over 1,000 hours. Inventions such as this made Edison a wealthy man.

Apply It!

Make a graphic organizer like the one shown. Choose an effect from the biography and list its cause.

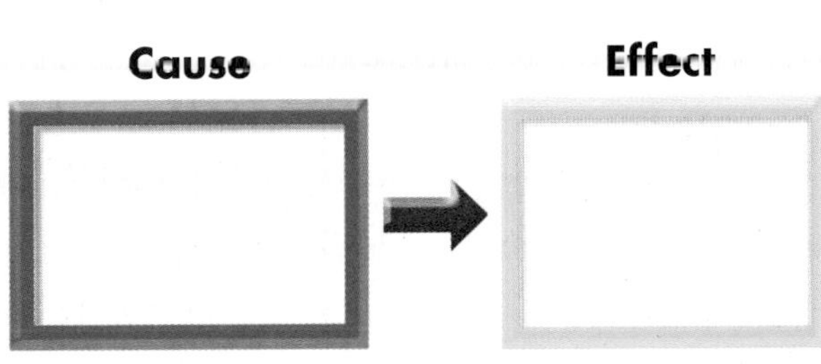
Cause
Effect

You Are There!

It is 1899, and you are in the laboratory of Nikola Tesla. Tesla is experimenting with electricity, and the results are spectacular. Deadly lightning bolts shoot out over 7 meters from a silver sphere. Thunder can be heard for miles. A blue glow appears over the lab. Tesla discovered many things about electricity. The way that electricity flows to our homes today is due to Tesla's research. How does electricity work?

Lesson 1

What are the effects of moving charges?

Some materials allow electric charges to flow easily. Some materials reduce or stop the flow.

Electric Charges

Most atoms have the same number of protons and electrons. The protons have a positive (+) charge. The electrons have a negative (-) charge. The result is an atom with a neutral charge. Atoms seldom lose their protons. However, they often lose and gain electrons. If an atom gains or loses electrons, the atom's charge is no longer neutral.

You can observe what happens as charges move from one object to another. On a dry day, rub a balloon on your clean, dry hair. As you rub, electrons break away from your hair. The surface that loses electrons now has a positive charge. But the electrons don't disappear. They are on the balloon. The balloon now has more electrons, which gives it a negative charge. Because opposite charges attract, the balloon will stick to your hair. Now rub two balloons on your hair and place them near each other. You will feel a small force as the balloons push each other apart. This occurs because like charges repel.

The flow of charges between the balloon and your hair is an example of electricty. Moving charges are found in electrical currents in wires. **Current** is the flow of electrical charges through a material.

Electron
Neutron
Proton

Some particles that make up atoms are protons, electrons, and neutrons.

1. ✓Checkpoint What causes an atom to have a negative or positive charge?
2. Writing in Science **Expository** In your **science journal,** write directions for a science activity that shows how opposite charges attract and like charges repel.

Conductors

A **conductor** is a material through which an electric charge can move easily. Conductors have some electrons that are not tightly bound to their atoms. These electrons can move through the conductor.

Some materials are better conductors than others. Copper, gold, silver, and aluminum have many free electrons. These metals are some of the best conductors. Electric wires are often made from copper and aluminum. Some computers have gold or silver conductors. Pure metals tend to be better conductors than mixed metals.

Metals are not the only conductors. Graphite, or pencil lead, can conduct electrical current. Some liquids and gases are also conductors.

A material that resists the flow of an electric charge is called a **resistor**. As current moves through a resistor, some of the electrical energy changes to thermal energy. **Insulators** are such strong resistors that they can stop most electrical currents. Rubber, plastic, glass, and dry cotton can be used as insulators.

Toasters heat bread because of resistors. Wires of nickel and chromium resist electrical current and turn electrical energy into thermal energy. At most times, all materials, including copper and gold, have a little resistance.

A material that has no resistance to electrical current is a superconductor. Many metals and some ceramics can become superconductors. This usually happens only at super-cold temperatures. But it is difficult to cool materials to super-cold temperatures. Some scientists are trying to make superconductors that work at warmer temperatures. If they succeed, we can build electric devices that use less electrical energy.

The dissolved salts in ocean water have both positive and negative charges. These charges can conduct an electrical current.

Drinking water contains a small amount of charged particles. It may conduct a weak electrical current.

Current
When a power source acts on the charged electrons, they flow through the wire in the same direction.

Plastic or rubber insulation around the copper wire makes the wire safe to handle. The small wires have different colors of insulation. This helps electricians connect the correct wires in complex electrical systems.

No current
The charged electrons drift through the metal wire in random directions.

Glass insulators on power lines stop electric charges. Without them, the charges in power lines might escape through the support poles and to the ground.

Lesson Checkpoint

1. What is an electrical current?
2. Name three materials that are used as conductors and three that are used as insulators.
3. **Cause and Effect** What effect might be caused by electrons being loosely bound to atoms in a material?

Lesson 2

What are simple circuits?

Electrical current can travel in a circuit, or loop, to power electric devices. A circuit diagram shows the parts and path of an electric circuit.

Battery
Batteries come in many sizes and shapes. Sizes AAA, AA, C, D, and the box-shaped 9-volt batteries are most common. Some watches and other devices use batteries that are shaped like tiny pancakes.

Batteries or power plants can provide the energy to move electric charges through a circuit. The electrical outlets in your home connect your radio, toaster, and hair dryer to a local power plant.

Parts of a Circuit

Electric charges can move in a looped path, or circuit. A simple circuit contains a source of energy and at least one conductor. It may also include a switch, which opens or closes a gap in the circuit. The switch turns the circuit on or off. Circuits normally have resistors, as well.

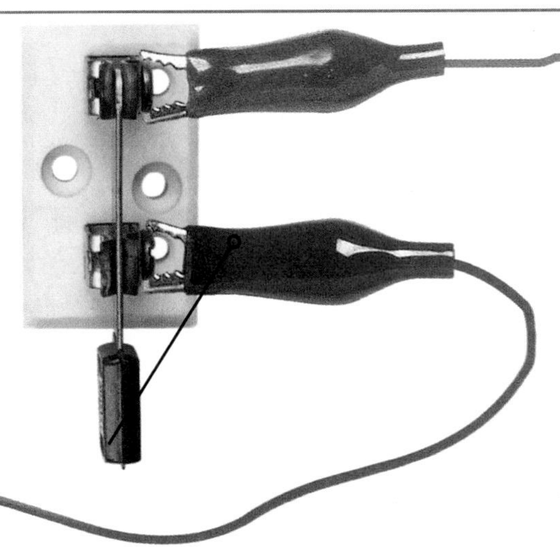

Insulators
Plastic, rubber, and cloth may cover the wires and other conductors in the circuit. The insulators help keep the electric charges inside the pathway.

Switch
Switches and push-buttons control the flow of charges by closing or opening a gap in the circuit. Closing the gap allows the electric charges to flow. Opening the gap stops the current.

Conductor
In a circuit, sections of conductors, such as metal wires and clips, form a complete loop. This provides an unbroken path. Charges will not flow if the circuit is broken.

The source of energy may be a battery, which contains chemicals that react to produce a current. The flow of charges is considered to be from the negative (–) end to the positive (+) end.

The energy of moving electric charges within a circuit is called electrical energy. A circuit can transfer electrical energy from place to place over hundreds of kilometers.

As charges flow in a circuit, some electrical energy always changes to heat energy. Resistors can change electrical energy to other forms of energy. A light bulb is a resistor that transforms electrical energy to light energy. Bells and buzzers are resistors that transform electrical energy to sound energy.

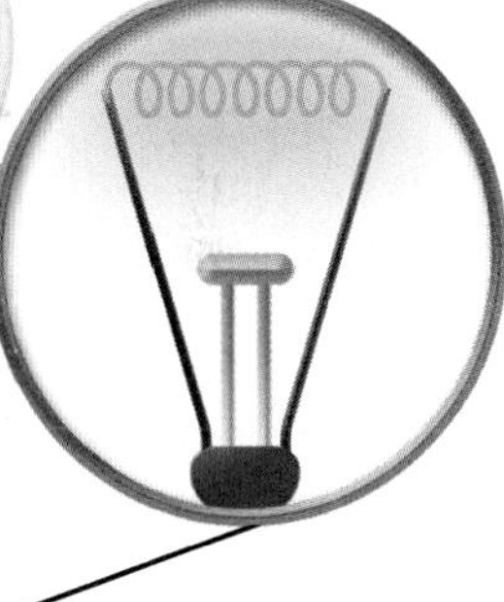

Resistors
Resistors transform electrical energy to sound, light, thermal, or mechanical energy.

1. **✓Checkpoint** If the switch is left open, what happens to the current?
2. **Writing in Science** **Descriptive** In your **science journal,** describe the path of an electrical current through the circuit shown. Describe the purpose of each part.

Circuit Diagrams

Carpenters build homes by looking at blueprints. In the same way, people use circuit diagrams to help build electric circuits. A **circuit diagram** is a map of a circuit. The circuit diagram below shows the circuit in the photograph.

Symbols on a circuit diagram stand for each part of the circuit. Electrical measurements may also be on the circuit diagram. The **volt** (V) is a measure of the electrical force provided by an energy source. Batteries labeled AA, AAA, C, and D each deliver about 1.5 volts. The small box-shaped batteries provide up to 9 volts.

The ohm (Ω) is the unit of measure for resistance to electrical current. A typical flashlight bulb has about 20 ohms of resistance.

Current is a measure of how much charge moves past a given spot each second. The unit for measuring current is the ampere (A). Often, people use the abbreviation *amp*.

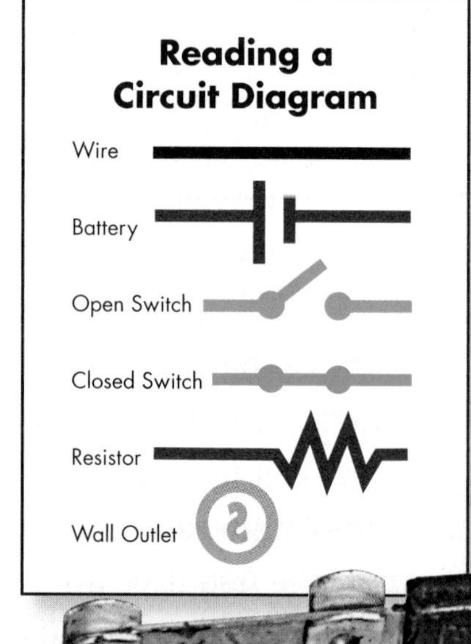
Reading a Circuit Diagram
Wire
Battery
Open Switch
Closed Switch
Resistor
Wall Outlet

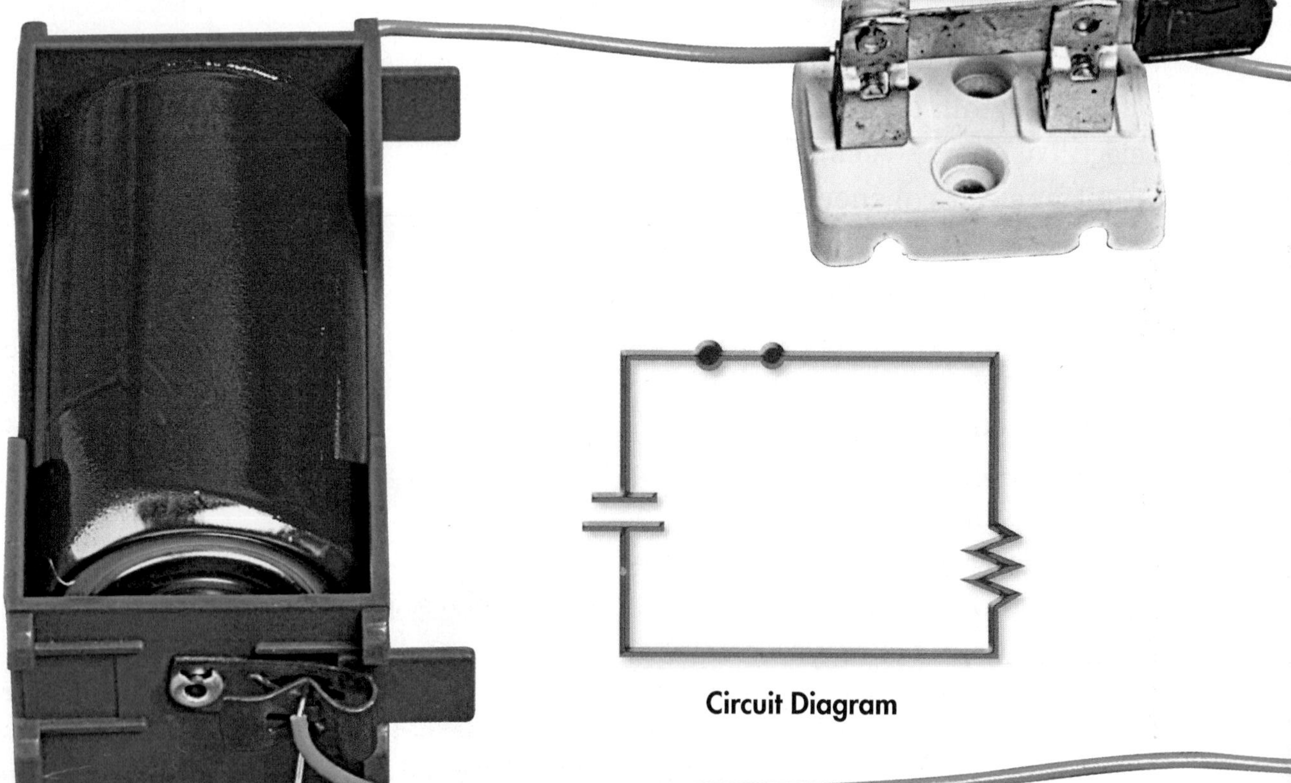

Circuit Diagram

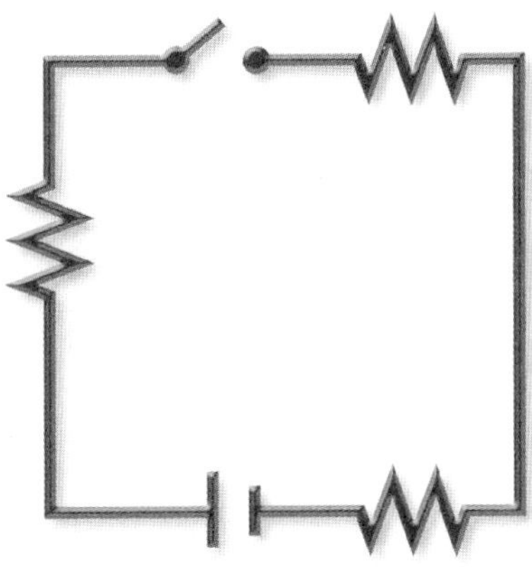

Series Circuits

The photographs show three different series circuits. Series circuits may have more than one resistor on the same wire.

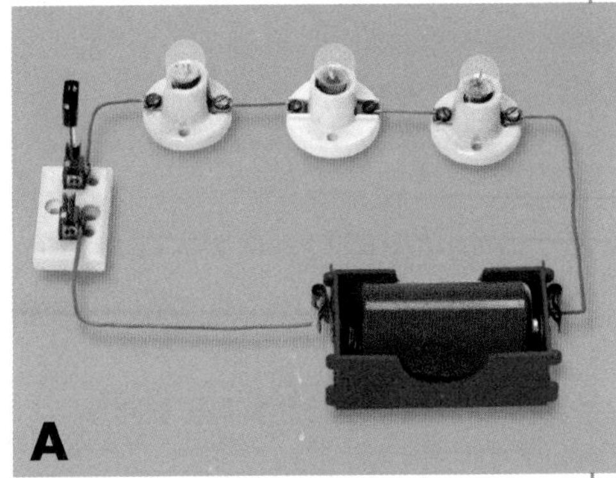
A

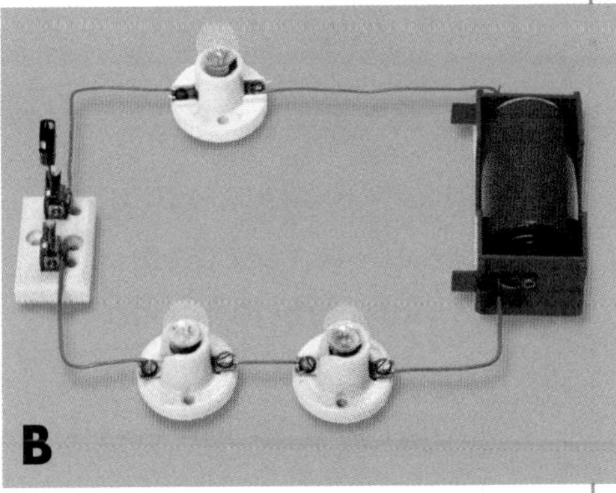
B

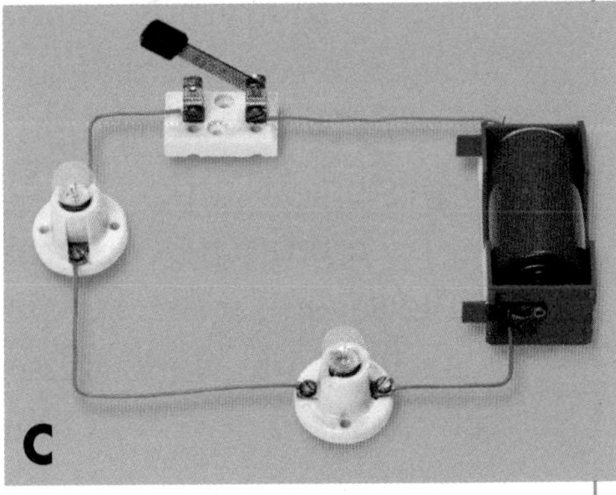
C

Series Circuits

Notice that the circuits on this page have more than one resistor on a wire. These circuits are known as series circuits. In a series circuit, the current must be able to pass through all the resistors.

Study the circuit diagram above. Which circuit photograph does it match? Here is a hint: Use your finger to trace the flow of electrons through the diagram and each of the circuits. List the parts the electrons pass through. The diagram may show the parts of the circuit in a slightly different orientation from the photographs.

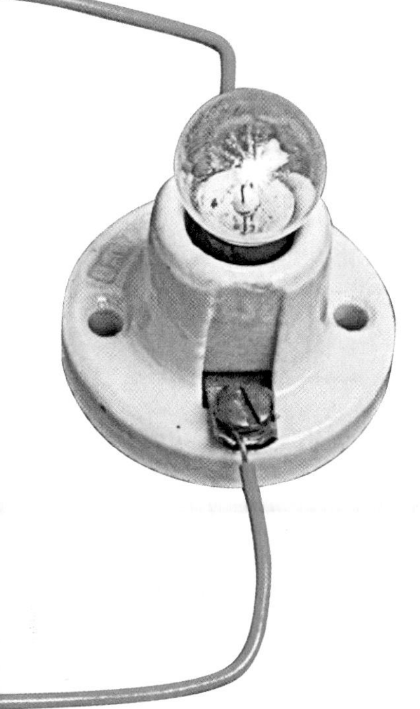

√ Lesson Checkpoint

1. Name four common parts of an electric circuit.
2. Describe the purpose of a resistor in a circuit.
3. **Math in Science** You can divide the number of volts (V) by the current (I) to find the resistance (R) in any part of a circuit. Find the resistance of a light bulb in a circuit where the voltage is 3.2 volts and the current is 0.1 amp. Use this equation: $\frac{V}{I} = R$

Lesson 3

What are complex circuits?

Parallel circuits can have many branches and are more complex than simple circuits.

Parallel Circuits

The circuits in flashlights, bells, and buzzers are fairly simple. But most electrical circuits are more complex. A parallel circuit has more than one branch or pathway. Some circuits have hundreds, or even thousands, of branches. Computers have the most complicated circuits. Millions of paths and resistors are put on chips smaller than a postage stamp.

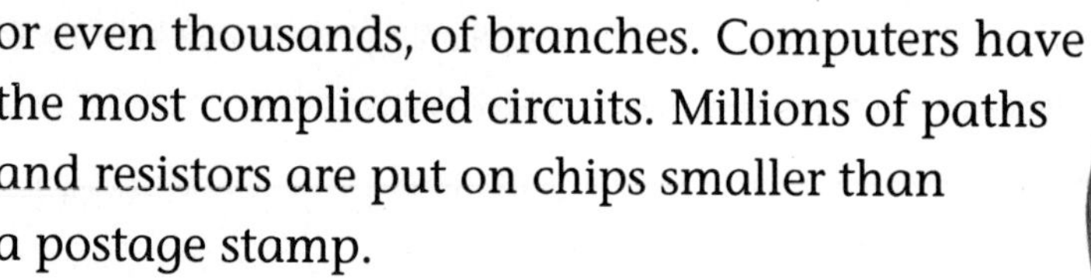

Each branch of a parallel circuit may hold several resistors where electrical energy can be put to work. A useful feature of parallel circuits is that not all branches have to be on at the same time. Switches can control each branch of the circuit independently.

Battery
This parallel circuit is powered by two C batteries.

Parallel circuit
Start at the battery and trace the circuit with your index finger. Follow each complete circuit. Name each part as you go.

Find each part on the diagram. Why do you think the battery symbol appears twice?

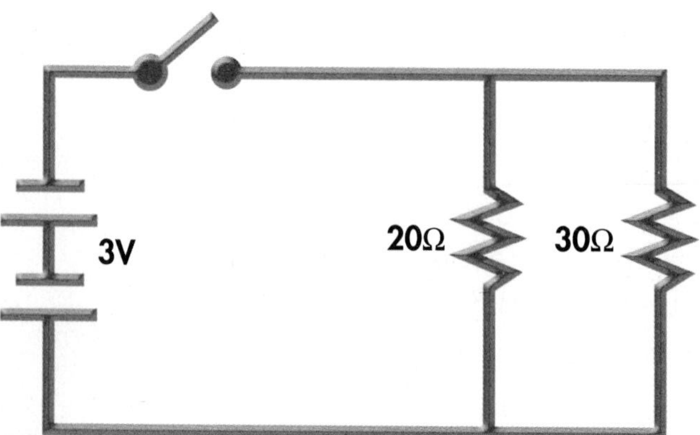
3V
20Ω
30Ω

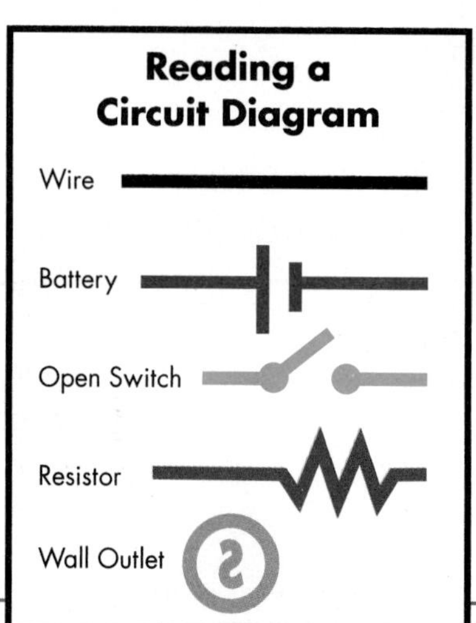
Reading a Circuit Diagram
Wire
Battery
Open Switch
Resistor
Wall Outlet

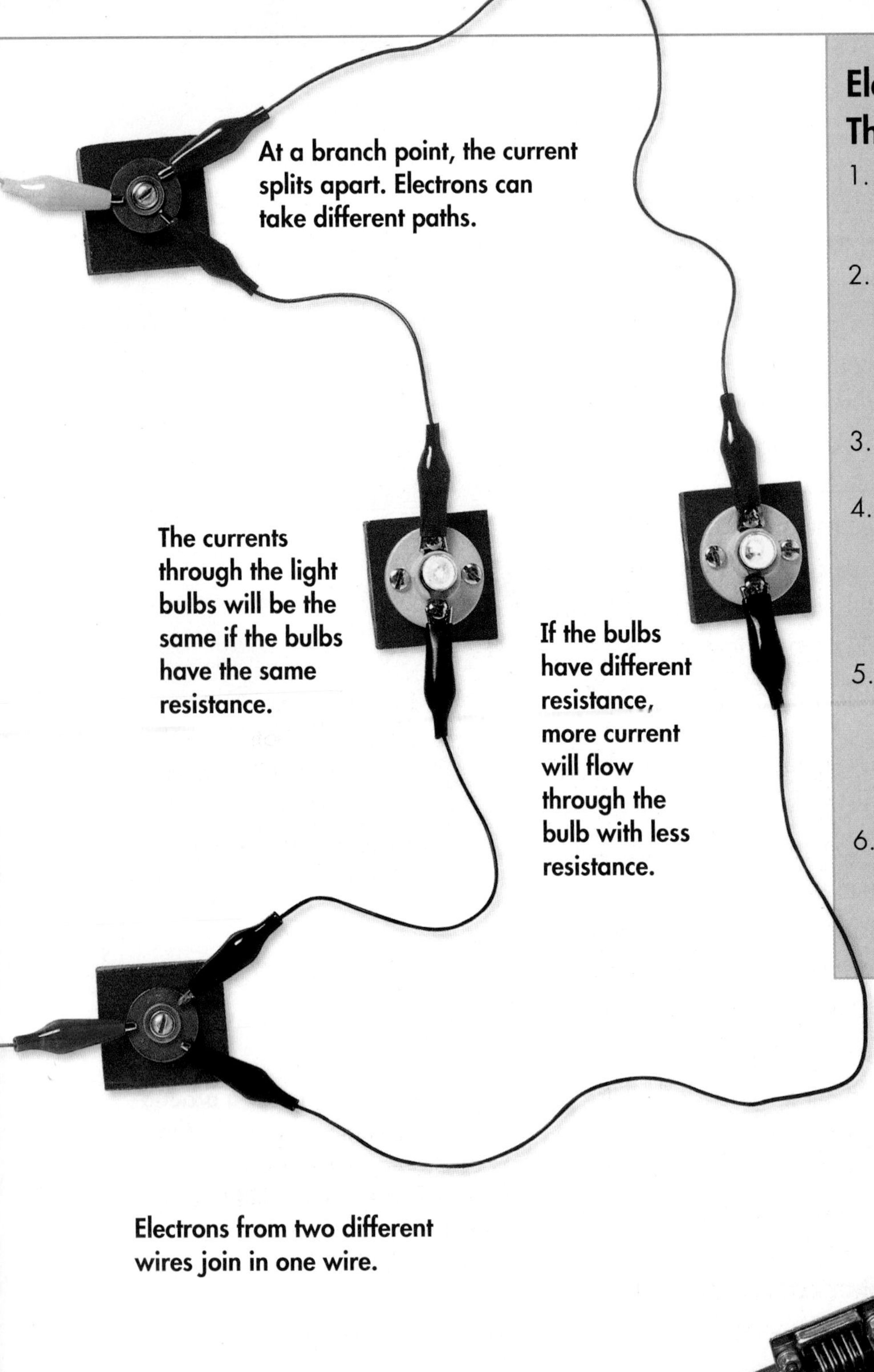
At a branch point, the current splits apart. Electrons can take different paths.
The currents through the light bulbs will be the same if the bulbs have the same resistance.
If the bulbs have different resistance, more current will flow through the bulb with less resistance.
Electrons from two different wires join in one wire.

Electrical Safety: Avoid These Shocking Hazards

1. Don't touch electrical outlets. When they are not in use, cover them with safety caps.
2. Don't unplug cords by yanking on them. Always pull the plug instead of the cord. Pulling on the cord can damage the wires.
3. Immediately replace the insulation on a frayed cord.
4. Never touch a power line with your body or any object. Stay far away from downed power lines. If you see one, call 911.
5. Never touch an electrical appliance, switch, cord, plug, or outlet if you or the appliance are standing in water.
6. Do not use cord-operated radios or other electrical appliances near a bathtub, pool, or lake.

Millions of resistors and wires are fixed onto a single computer chip, which may be smaller than a postage stamp.

1. **✓Checkpoint** Describe a parallel circuit.
2. **Art in Science** Sketch the parts of a parallel circuit that has three branches. Then draw its circuit diagram. Include a key to the symbols you used.

Electromagnets

Could your teacher and your class make an amazing discovery? Danish professor, Hans Christian Oersted, did just that in 1820. Each time he flipped the switch on an electric circuit he saw that the magnetized needle of a nearby compass moved. Today we know that electricity and magnetism are closely related. Every electrical current produces a magnetic force.

Electromagnets are magnets that carry an electrical current. They are formed by a current flowing through a coiled wire in a circuit. There are several ways of making an electromagnet stronger. An electromagnet becomes stronger if the number of coils is increased or if the current is increased. Placing a metal bar inside the coils also makes the electromagnet stronger.

Compare an electromagnet to a regular magnet. You cannot turn a regular magnet on and off. But an electromagnet can be switched on and off. Unlike a regular magnet, the strength of an electromagnet can be quickly changed. Like all magnets, an electromagnet has both a north and a south pole. The electromagnet is stronger at the poles and weaker between the poles. Notice the iron filings in the photograph. Where is the magnetic field strongest?

Wire coils are wrapped around each end of the iron arch. The electromagnet is strong when there is a large current flowing in the coils.

Ways We Use Electromagnets

Electromagnets are used in many objects, from motors to doorbells to sound systems. In motors, electromagnets turn on and off rapidly, causing the magnetic fields to attract and repel each other. The result is that the rotating parts of the motor start to spin. The electrical energy has been transformed into mechanical energy. Motors can move all sorts of things—from toy cars to huge locomotives.

Here is a simple electromagnet circuit. The symbol for an electromagnet is a curly-cue.

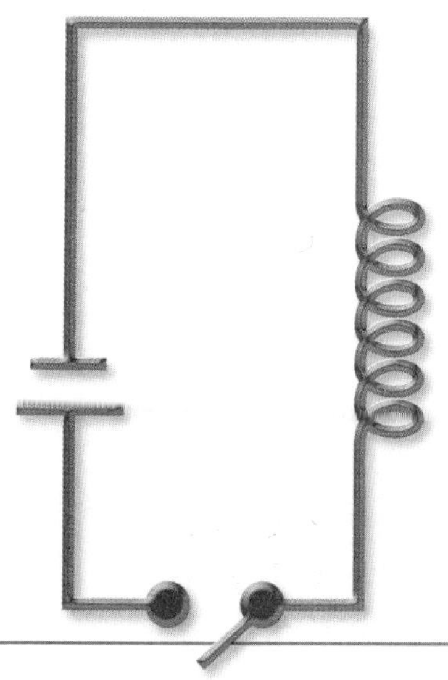

The electromagnet pulls the lever arm that hits the bell.

Strong electromagnets in cranes lift heavy scrap metal. Why would a regular magnet not work well in this job?

The electromagnet is weaker when the current decreases.

If you make this change in the circuit...	**Then** this change happens with the electromagnet.
double current	strength doubles
double the number of coils	strength doubles
add iron core	strength increases
have the coils in many layers	strength increases

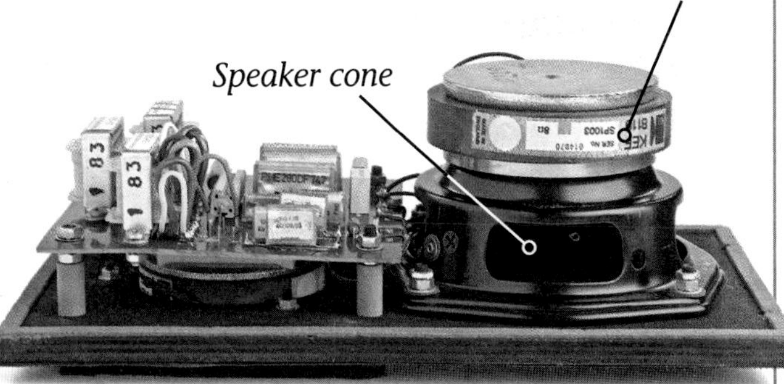

Magnet
Speaker cone

As electromagnets turn on and off rapidly, the magnet pushes and pulls on the speaker cone. This causes the cone to vibrate, and these vibrations produce sound waves.

√ Lesson Checkpoint

1. How is a parallel circuit different from a series circuit?
2. What are two ways to make an electromagnet stronger?
3. **Cause and Effect** What is the effect of an electromagnet in a motor?

Lab zone Guided Inquiry

Investigate How are series and parallel circuits different?

Materials

safety goggles

battery and battery holder

2 flashlight bulbs and holders

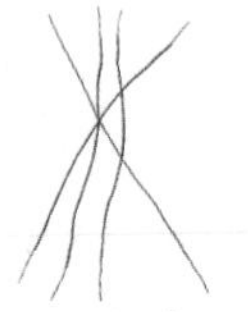

4 pieces of wire

What to Do

1 Make a series circuit. Connect all its parts. Record what happens to the light bulbs.

series circuit

flashlight bulb

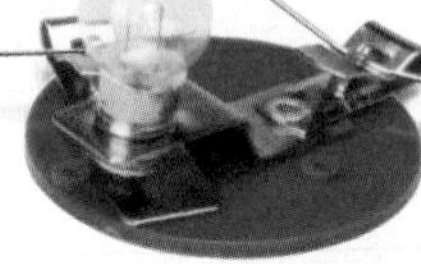
battery
battery holder
wire
bulb holder

Be careful!

Wear safety goggles.

2 Unscrew a light bulb from the series circuit. Record what happens when a bulb is removed from a series circuit.

Process Skills

You **interpret** your **data** when you analyze the data you collected and use it to help answer questions.

3. Make a parallel circuit. Connect all its parts. Record what happens to the light bulbs.

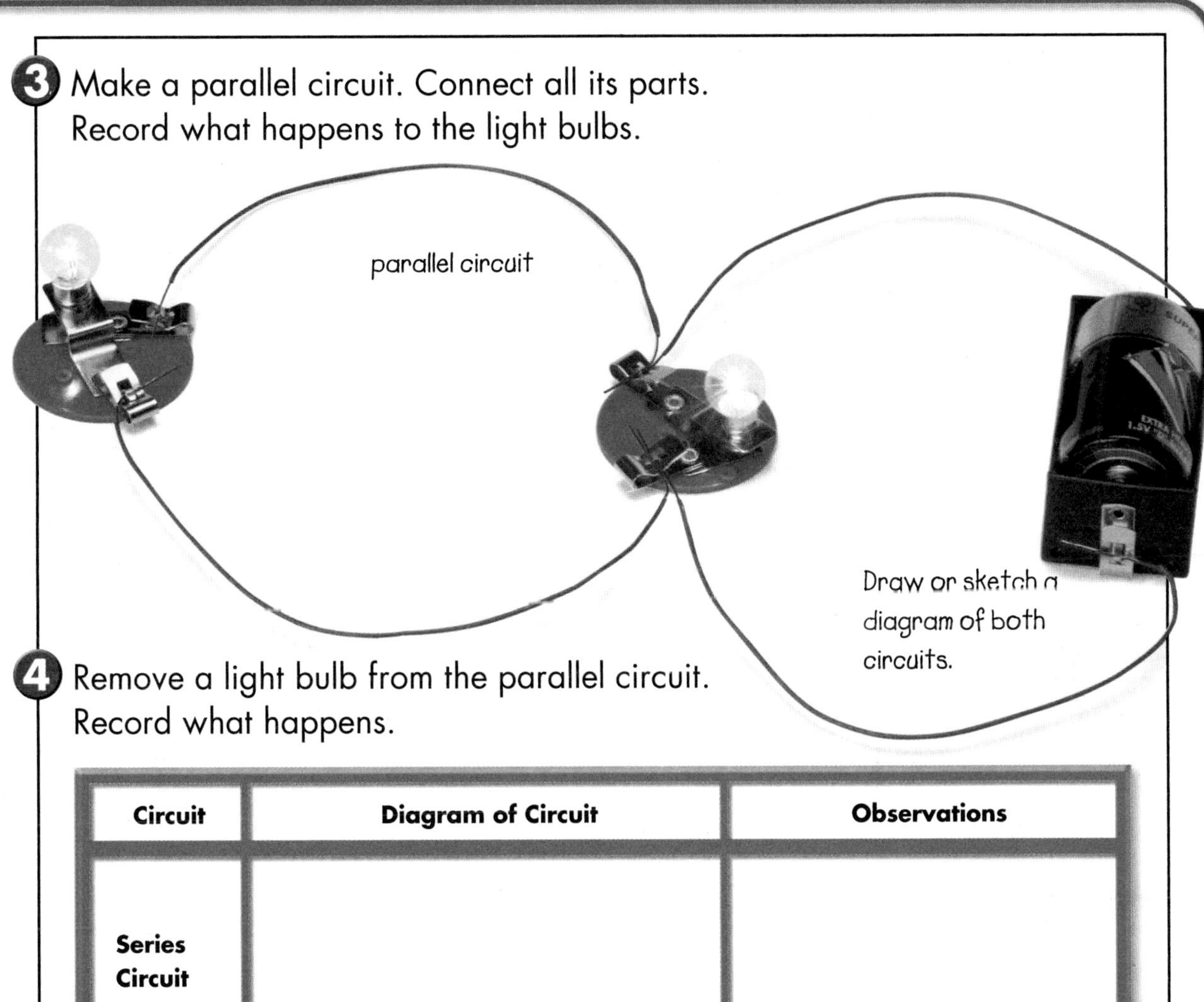
parallel circuit
Draw or sketch a diagram of both circuits.

4. Remove a light bulb from the parallel circuit. Record what happens.

Circuit	Diagram of Circuit	Observations
Series Circuit		
Parallel Circuit		

Explain Your Results

1. **Interpret Data** What is the difference between a series circuit and a parallel circuit? Use your diagrams to help describe the circuits and explain your ideas.
2. **Communicate** What paths can electricity take through a series circuit and a parallel circuit? Draw arrows on your diagrams to help explain how the electricity moves through the circuits.

Go Further

Construct a circuit of your own design using available resources. Select and use the appropriate tools. Diagram, test, and evaluate your circuit. Tell what limited your design. Describe your circuit and what you learned to other students.

Computing Current, Voltage, and Resistance

One measurement of electrical circuits is the current that flows through the circuit or any of its parts. A second measurement is resistance. A third measurement is the number of volts needed to push a charge through the circuit or each conductor. The amount of current depends on the resistance and volts.

Look at the picture of the circuit with one resistor. Remember, a resistor can be a light bulb, bell, speaker, or other device that uses current. Find the labels that show the voltage (V) and the amount of resistance in the resistor (ohms). The formula that relates a circuit's voltage, current, and resistance can be written 3 ways.

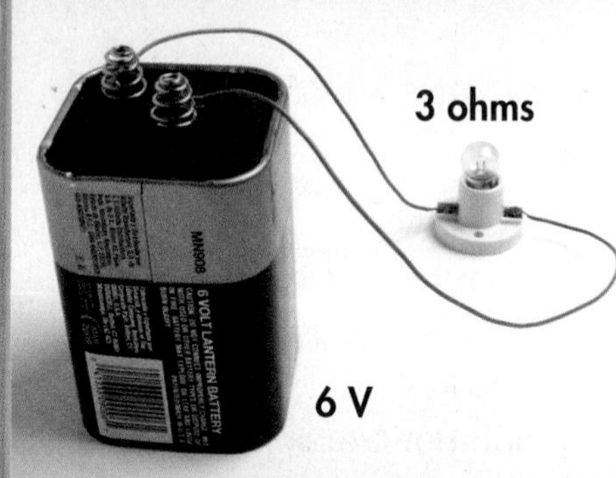
3 ohms
6 V

voltage ÷ resistance = current

6 volts ÷ 3 ohms = 2 amps

voltage ÷ current = resistance

6 volts ÷ 2 amps = 3 ohms

current x resistance = voltage

2 amps x 3 ohms = 6 volts

Use the formula on page 492 and the picture here to answer each question.

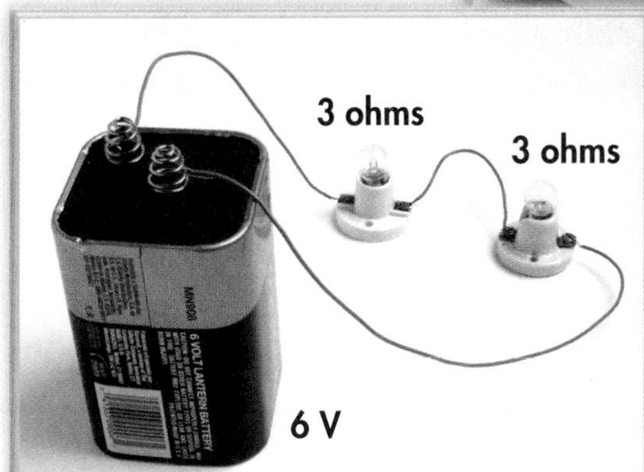
3 ohms
3 ohms
6 V

1. Look at the circuit in the picture. This circuit has two resistors. To find the total resistance in the circuit, add the ohms for the two resistors.

   Total Resistance = (__ ohms) + (__ ohms)

   What is the total resistance in the circuit?

2. What is the current in the circuit?
   A. 6 amps
   B. 2 amps
   C. 1 amp
   D. 1.5 amps

3. If another 3-ohm bulb was added in this series circuit, what would be the current?
   F. 9 amps
   G. 3 amps
   H. 2 amps
   I. $\frac{2}{3}$ amp

4. Which statement BEST states how current is related to resistance?
   A. As resistance increases, current decreases.
   B. As resistance increases, current increases.
   C. As resistance increase, current remains the same.
   D. Current is not related to resistance.

Lab zone Take-Home Activity

Look at the labels on electrical things at home. Make a chart listing each item and the electrical measurements shown on its label.

Chapter 15 Review and Test Prep

Use Vocabulary

circuit diagram (p. 484)	**electromagnet** (p. 488)
conductor (p. 480)	**insulator** (p. 480)
current (p. 479)	**resistor** (p. 480)
	volt (p. 484)

Use the vocabulary word from the list above that completes each sentence.

1. _____ is the flow of electrical charges in a conductor.

2. A(n) _____ is a material that does not conduct electric charge.

3. A light bulb, bell, or buzzer is an example of a _____ in a circuit.

4. A(n) _____ is a unit of measure for the amount of energy available to push a charge through a circuit.

5. A(n) _____ is made when current flows through a coiled wire around an iron core.

6. A(n) _____ is a material through which electric charge flows easily.

7. A(n) _____ is a map of a circuit

Explain Concepts

8. Explain how a light bulb makes light and thermal energy.

9. Explain why gold and copper are good conductors of an electrical current.

10. Explain how a speaker makes sound with electrical energy.

Process Skills

11. Infer Suppose a series circuit has two light bulbs. One bulb has burned out. The other is still a good bulb. Explain why neither light bulb will light up when the switch is "on."

12. Classify Make a chart like the one below. Classify the following materials as conductors or insulators.

Cotton	Aluminum	Glass
Gold	Graphite	Copper
Ocean water	Rubber	Plastic
Silver		

Conductors	Insulators

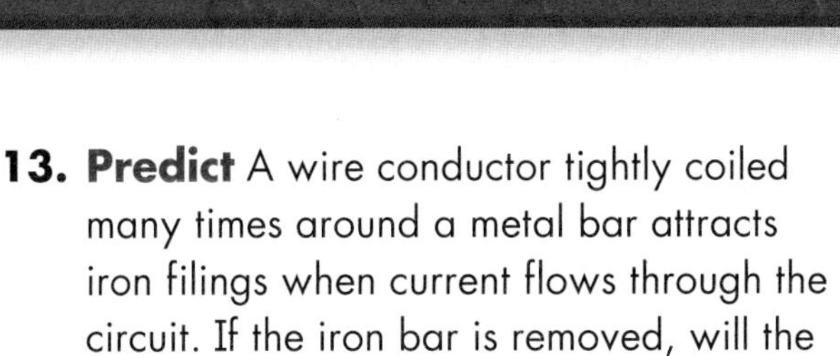

13. Predict A wire conductor tightly coiled many times around a metal bar attracts iron filings when current flows through the circuit. If the iron bar is removed, will the coiled wire still attract iron filings when current flows? Explain why you think it will or will not.

Cause and Effect

14. Make a graphic organizer like the one shown below. Fill in effects.

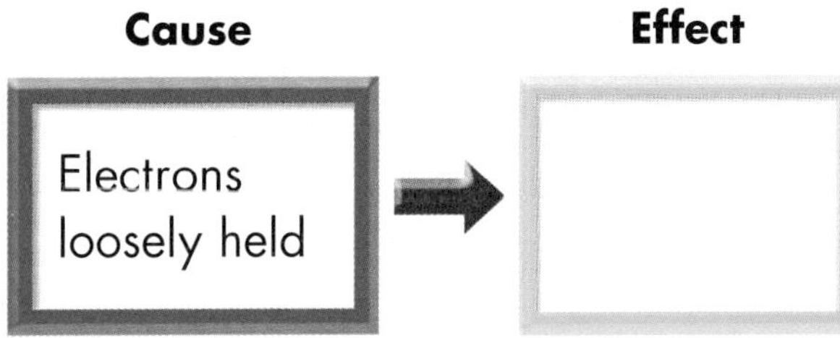

Cause
Effect
Electrons loosely held

Test Prep

Choose the letter that best completes the statement or answers the question.

15. Which of the following provides the BEST evidence that there is electrical current in a circuit?

Ⓐ The bulb in a flashlight lights up.
Ⓑ A switch in a parallel circuit is in the "on" position.
Ⓒ Two batteries are placed end-to-end in a circuit.
Ⓓ A balloon rubbed on a wool sweater sticks to the wall.

16. Which of the following best describes an electric charge?

Ⓕ positive or negative terminal of a battery
Ⓖ property of electrons, protons, and neutrons
Ⓗ material that conducts current
Ⓘ has a north pole and a south pole

17. A superconductor is

Ⓐ made only of gold or silver.
Ⓑ a tiny part of a computer circuit.
Ⓒ a material that conducts current when it gets very hot.
Ⓓ a material that has no resistance to electrical current.

18. Which of the following is an example of a nonmetal conductor?

Ⓕ copper wire
Ⓖ salt water
Ⓗ plastic covering of a wire
Ⓘ cotton clothing

19. Explain why the answer you chose for Question 18 is best. For each of the answers you did not choose, give a reason why it is not the best choice.

20. Writing in Science **Expository** Write a one-paragraph summary of the different types of circuits discussed in this chapter. Draw diagrams to help you explain.

Career

Electrician

You flip a switch and a light goes on. Every time this happens, you have an electrician to thank.

Electricians run the wires that carry current throughout your home, your school, and any building that has electricity. Some electricians work mainly in houses and other small buildings. Others work in office buildings, where they might install telephones and cables for computers as well as electrical wiring. Still others work in large factories, where they might repair robots or fix machine tools.

Electricians usually spend much of the workday on their feet. Sometimes they need to climb ladders or crawl into small spaces to put up or repair wires. They must work carefully because bad wiring can cause electrical shocks and fires. They conduct inspections to make sure that electrical systems remain safe.

If you like to work with your hands and are good at problem solving, you might like to become an electrician. This career generally requires a 4- or 5-year apprenticeship. As an apprentice, you take some classes. However, most of your learning comes from on-the-job training with experienced electricians.

Lab zone Take-Home Activity

Look around your home for materials that are good conductors and good insulators of electricity. Make a list of each and explain how each material is used.

Test-Taking Strategies

Unit C Test Talk

Find Important Words

Choose the Right Answer

Use Information from Text and Graphics

Write Your Answer

Use Information from Text and Graphics

Finding information in text and in graphics can help you answer test questions. Graphics are pictures and diagrams. Read the text and study the graphic. Then answer the questions.

A physical change is when something changes shape, size, or state. A chemical change is when something becomes a completely different kind of matter. Chemical changes happen every day. Baking a cake changes the flour, sugar, and other ingredients into a different kind of matter.

Cars rust when a chemical change turns shiny iron into dull brownish-red rust.

This antacid tablet gives off carbon dioxide gas as it undergoes a chemical change.

The burning logs give off heat and light as a chemical change is occurring.

Use What You Know

To help you answer the questions, find the information in the captions and the graphics. As you read each question, decide which answer choice is best.

1. A bike left outside for a long time is covered in rust. What mineral must be in the metal the bike is made of?
   Ⓐ silver
   Ⓑ copper
   Ⓒ iron
   Ⓓ sodium

2. Which of the following is a chemical change?
   Ⓐ ice melting
   Ⓑ flattening a clay ball
   Ⓒ cutting an orange in half
   Ⓓ burning paper

3. Which gas is given off when an antacid tablet is dropped in water?
   Ⓐ carbon dioxide
   Ⓑ nitrogen
   Ⓒ oxygen
   Ⓓ helium

4. What kind of energy is given off by burning logs?
   Ⓐ nuclear energy
   Ⓑ light energy
   Ⓒ thermal energy
   Ⓓ light and thermal energy

Unit C Wrap-Up

Chapter 11

What makes up everything around us?

- All things around us are made up of a few kinds of matter called elements.
- Objects are solids, liquids, or gases depending on the arrangement and movements of their atoms or molecules.

Chapter 12

How do you use chemistry every day?

- Matter undergoes physical changes and chemical changes.
- Chemists have invented new materials we use all the time, such as polymers and materials to kill germs.

Chapter 13

How are forces and motion part of everyday life?

- We use forces to do work.
- Laws of motion help us predict the ways things will move.
- Machines combine force and motion to make our work easier.

Chapter 14

How many different types of energy do you use every day?

- We use energy to work or to cause a change.
- Energy can be stored and can change from one type to another.
- Some types of energy that we use are light, sound, and electricity.

Chapter 15

What is electrical current and how does it work?

- The flow of charges through a material produces an electric current.
- Electrical current flows in circuits to power devices.

Performance Assessment

Show Newton's Laws

Make a poster about a sport or activity you enjoy. Draw pictures to illustrate each of Newton's three laws of motion as they apply to the sport or activity you choose. In your explanations for the pictures be sure to use the terms *net force, inertia,* and *acceleration*.

Read More About Physical Science!

Look for books like these in the library.

Northern Lights
by D.M. Souza
Heat
DORLING KINDERSLEY EYEWITNESS BOOKS
ELECTRICITY
Discover the story of electricity – from the earliest discoveries to the technology that has transformed our lives
STEVE PARKER

Lab zone

Full Inquiry

Experiment Can you change the poles of an electromagnet?

Electromagnets change electrical energy to magnetic energy. When electric current flows through an electromagnet, the electromagnet becomes a temporary magnet. Then the electromagnet has many properties that are similar to those of a regular magnet. For example, it has a north pole and a south pole. However, when the electric current stops flowing, the electromagnet is no longer a magnet.

Materials

safety goggles

wire and bolt

metric ruler

battery and battery holder

directional compass

Process Skills

A **controlled variable** is a special kind of variable. It is something you could change, but you must not change if the **experiment** is to be a fair test.

Ask a question.

Does the direction in which electric current flows through an electromagnet affect the locations of its poles?

State a hypothesis.

If the direction electrons move through an electromagnet is reversed, then do the locations of the poles change or remain the same? Write your **hypothesis.**

Identify and control variables.

You will change the direction in which the electrons move through an electromagnet. You will observe the locations of the poles on an electromagnet before and after you change the direction the electrons move. Everything else must stay the same, including the number of coils on the electromagnet. Identify the **variables.**

Which is the independent variable?
Which is the dependent variable?
Which is a controlled variable?

Test your hypothesis.

1. Make an electromagnet.
Start about 25 cm from one end of the wire.
Coil the long part around the bolt 30 times.

2. Make circuit A. Connect one end of the wire to the positive (+) side of the battery holder. Then connect the other end of the wire to the negative (–) side.

Be careful!

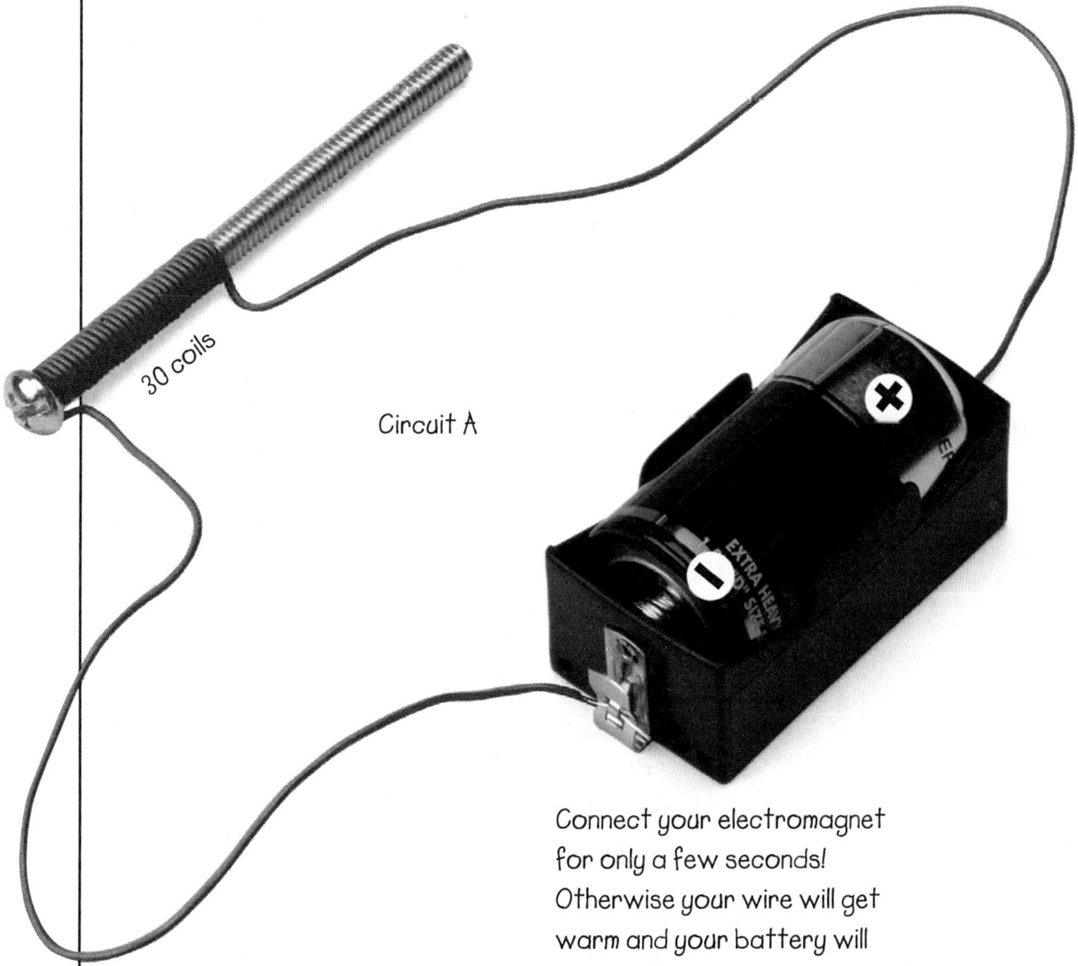

Wear safety goggles.

30 coils

Circuit A

Connect your electromagnet for only a few seconds! Otherwise your wire will get warm and your battery will wear out.

3. Use a compass to find the poles of the electromagnet. The north-seeking end of the compass needle will point to the north pole of the electromagnet. Disconnect the ends of the wire.

4. Electrons move through the wire from the negative (–) end of a battery to the positive (+) end. In the chart on the next page, finish the arrows to show the direction the electrons move in circuit A. Label the north and south poles on the electromagnet.

5. Repeat steps 2 to 4, but make circuit B. Disconnect the electromagnet. Turn it around and reconnect it.

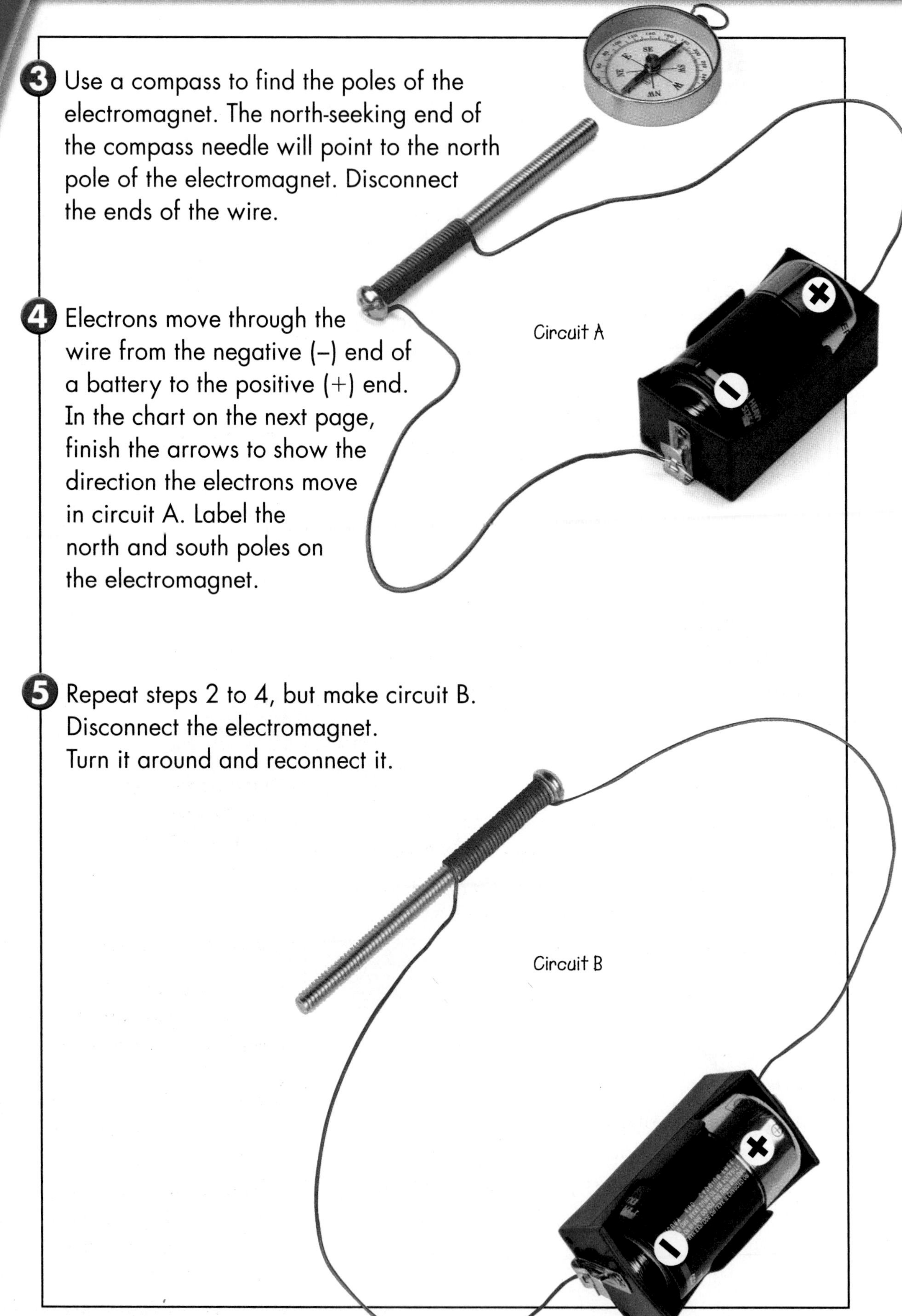
Circuit A
Circuit B

Collect and record your data.

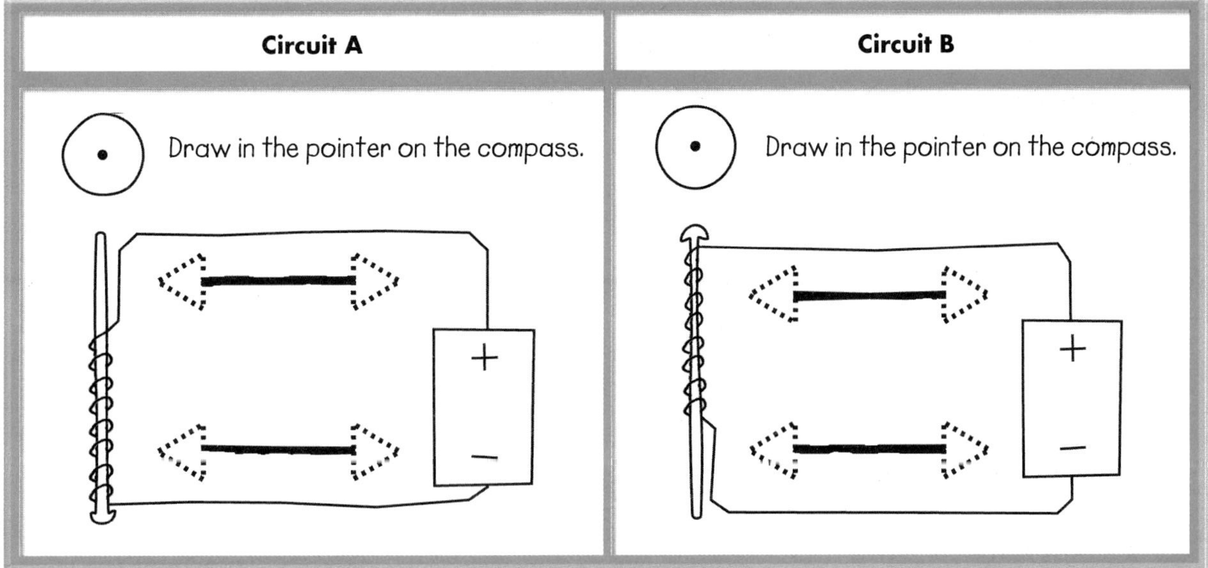

Circuit A
Circuit B
Draw in the pointer on the compass.
Draw in the pointer on the compass.
+
–
+
–

Complete the arrowheads on each diagram to show the direction to show the direction the electrons move through the electromagnet. Label the poles.

Interpret your data.
Analyze the drawings that show your data for the **experiment.** Compare circuit A and circuit B. What direction are the electrons moving in each circuit? Where is the north pole located in each drawing?

What are some ways an electromagnet could be used?

State your conclusion.
Explain how reversing the direction the electrons move through an electromagnet affects the locations of its poles. Compare your hypothesis with your results. **Communicate** your conclusion orally or in writing.

Go Further

How do the poles of 2 electromagnets affect each other? Work with another group to develop a plan to find out. Design and carry out a plan to investigate this or other questions you may have about the properties of magnets or electromagnets. Repeat your investigation using regular magnets.

Discovery CHANNEL SCHOOL

Science Fair Projects

Take the Salt Out of Sea Water

Conduct research on ways to make fresh water from sea water.

Idea: Try removing the salt from salt water by evaporation and condensation or by freezing. Draw a picture to show your equipment and your method.

Two Pulleys are Better than One

A pulley is a simple machine that helps you do work. The number of pulleys you use changes the amount of force needed to lift an object.

Idea: Construct simple and compound pulleys to show how the number of pulleys changes the amount of force needed. You can use a spring scale to measure the amount of force used. Make a graph or chart to show what you learned about pulleys and force.

Display Elements and Compounds

The familiar things around you are made up of elements and compounds. Investigate and find out what these things are made of.

Idea: Collect objects and pictures of objects. Organize them into a display. Label them to show what elements and compounds they are made of.

Full Inquiry

Using Scientific Methods

1. Ask a question.
2. State a hypothesis.
3. Identify and control variables.
4. Test your hypothesis.
5. Collect and record your data.
6. Interpret your data.
7. State your conclusion.
8. Go further.

Unit D
Space and Technology

Chapter 16

Stars and Galaxies

You Will Discover

- what tools people have used in the past and are using now to learn about the universe.
- the characteristics of stars.
- how stars are grouped.

online
Student Edition
sfsuccessnet.com

Build Background

How has the study of stars expanded our knowledge of the universe?

light-year

black hole

A black hole is a point in space that has such a strong force of gravity that nothing within a certain distance of it can escape getting pulled into the black hole—not even light.

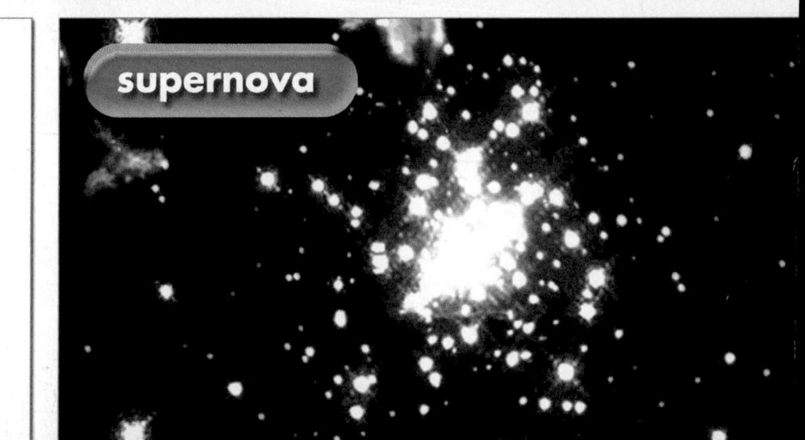

supernova

Chapter 16 Vocabulary

light-year page 521

nebula page 522

supernova page 523

black hole page 523

galaxy page 524

constellation page 526

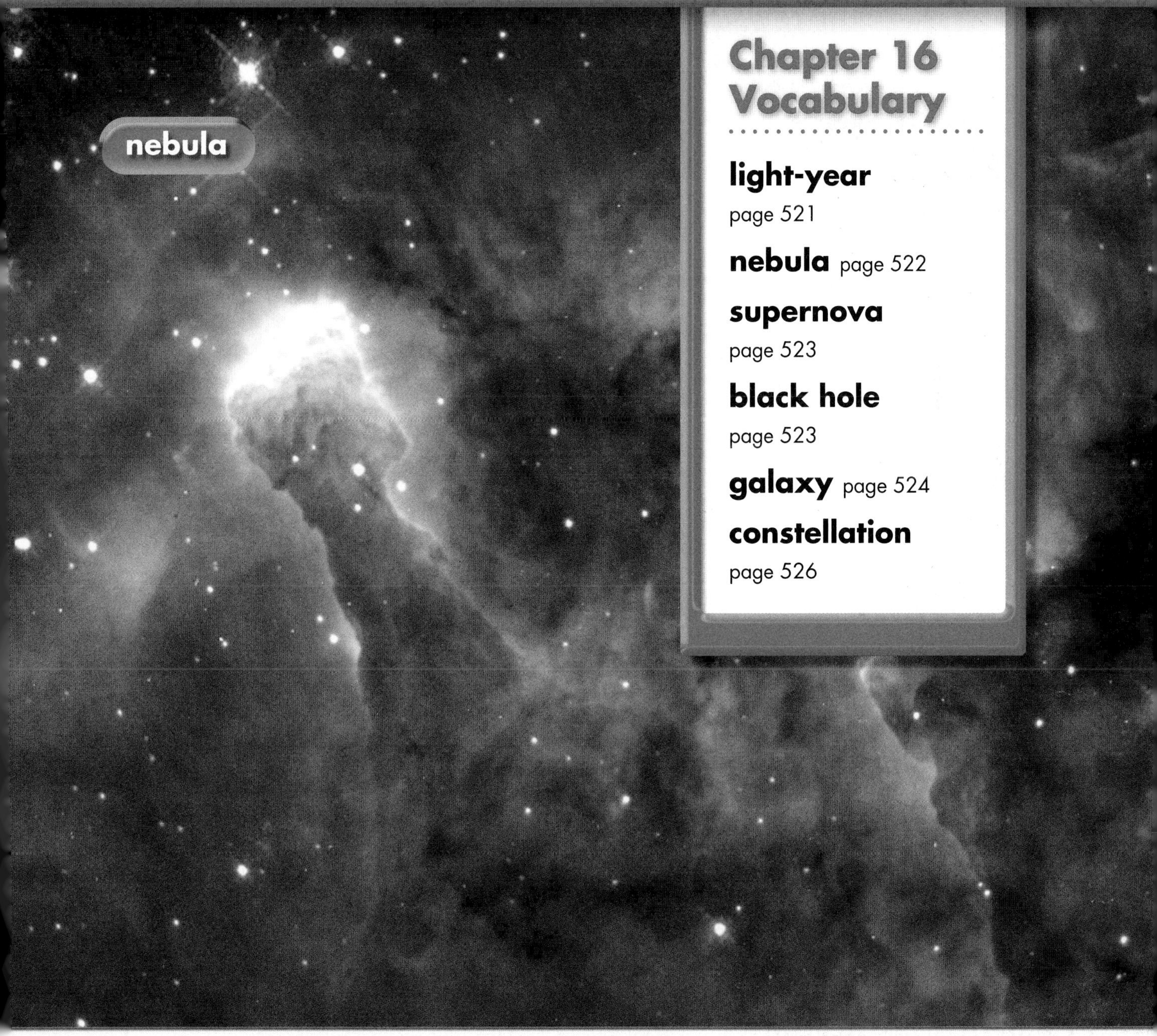

nebula

galaxy

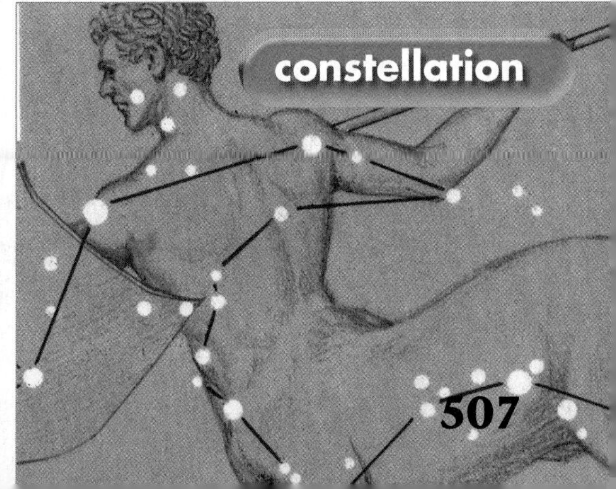
constellation

Lab zone Directed Inquiry

Explore How can you make an astrolabe?

Any astronomical tool that measures the angle of an object in the sky can be called an astrolabe. The astrolabe below is much simpler than a classic astrolabe.

Materials

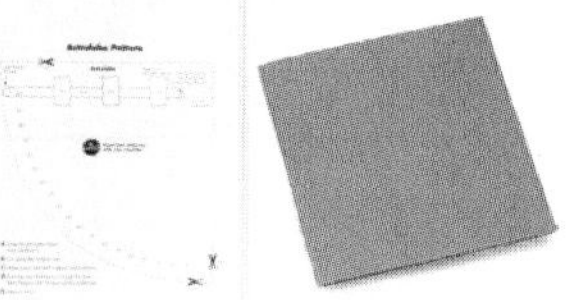

Astrolabe Pattern and cardboard

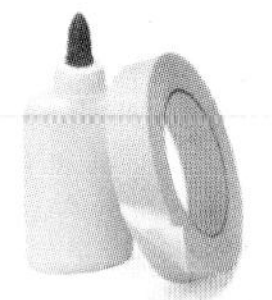

glue and tape

scissors

straw

pencil

string and washer

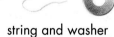

Process Skills

Scientists **communicate** when they explain data or give an opinion, orally or in writing.

What to Do

1 Cut out the Astrolabe Pattern. Glue it onto cardboard. Cut off the extra cardboard.

Make a tiny hole with a dull pencil. Put the end of the string through the hole. Tape onto the back.

Tape on a straw.

string

knot

washer

2 Look through your astrolabe at the paper star your teacher has placed in your room. Ask another student to read the angle where the string crosses the numbered scale.

Optional: Some star charts give the time, direction, and angle at which a star or planet can be found. If possible, use your astrolabe, a compass, and a watch to locate stars such as the North Star, constellations such as the Big Dipper, and planets such as Jupiter.

Explain Your Results

Communicate How does an astrolabe measure the angle of a star? Why did different students get different angles for the paper star?

How to Read Science

Reading Skills

Summarize

A summary is a short retelling of something you have read. When you write a summary, include only the most important ideas. Leave out most details, and do not add any new ideas. Use your own words when you **summarize.**

Using a graphic organizer can help you organize and **communicate** the main ideas for your summary.

History Article

An astrolabe is used to tell time and direction. No one is sure when the astrolabe was invented. Its beginnings can be traced back to Greeks about 200 B.C. One of the first clear descriptions of an astrolabe, though, does not appear until about 400 A.D. Astrolabes continued to be developed over the centuries. Several different kinds were made and many were beautifully decorated. When pendulum clocks and other science instruments were developed in the 1600s, the use of astrolabes declined.

Apply It!

Read the history article. Use a graphic organizer like this one to choose ideas to include in your **summary**. Then write a two- or three-sentence summary to **communicate** the main ideas.

Information **Information** **Information**

Summary

You Are There!

It's early afternoon on a beautiful spring day. The Sun is out. The birds are tweeting and chirping. It's warm enough that you've taken off your jacket. But something seems wrong. The sky is getting darker, but there's not a cloud to be seen anywhere. It's way too early for sunset, but you notice you can see a few stars. The birds are silent. This scene feels very creepy. What exactly is going on here?

Lesson 1

What is the history of astronomy?

Ancient people kept a close watch on the Sun, Moon, and stars. They learned about them by using their eyes. Over centuries, people invented tools that helped them learn much more about the universe.

Patterns in the Sky

Patterns of events seen in the sky were very important to many cultures throughout history. Patterns are repeated events, such as the seasons, the phases of the Moon, and the rising and setting of the Sun each day. Long ago, people all over the world made calendars based on the predictable cycles in the sky.

The changing of seasons was very important to people around the world. People were interested in when to plant crops or hold festivals. Certain sets of stars were expected to appear in specific seasons. Anything that was different from the predictable cycles, such as appearances of new objects in the sky, were thought of as having special meanings.

Eclipses

A solar eclipse occurs when the Moon blocks the Sun's light. A lunar eclipse occurs when Earth casts a shadow on the Moon. Eclipses are rare events that were not part of the regular patterns seen in the sky. They were thought by ancient cultures to have special meanings, usually that something bad was going to happen. Knowing when an eclipse would occur was very helpful for leaders. They could make predictions only after they carefully observed and recorded the movements of the Sun and Moon. People in Asia, the Middle East, and South America have left records of their observations and predictions of eclipses.

1. √ **Checkpoint** What is a solar eclipse? a lunar eclipse?
2. **Math in Science** Babylonian astronomers noted that eclipses of the Moon occur in a cycle that lasts 233 months. About how many years is that cycle?

Astronomy Around the World

In many cases ancient peoples left no written records of their observations of the sky. They did, however, leave behind buildings and other structures that show how important the movements of the Sun, Moon, and stars were to them.

The giant circle of stones known as Stonehenge that stands in a field in southwest England has puzzled scientists and historians for years. Ancient people started building Stonehenge more than 5,000 years ago. They worked on it on and off for over 1,500 years. Today, only parts of it remain. Originally, it consisted of an outer circle of 30 enormous upright blocks of stone. Other slabs of stone were laid horizontally on top to form a ring. Inside the circle was another smaller circle of about 60 stones and inside of it were more stones arranged in a horseshoe pattern.

Most scientists agree that the stone circles were linked to astronomy and that those who built Stonehenge had a good understanding of the cycle of the Sun and the seasons. For example, some of the stones point to the position in the sky where the Sun rises and sets on the longest day of the year. Other stones are arranged to mark the rising of the Sun or the Moon at other times during the year.

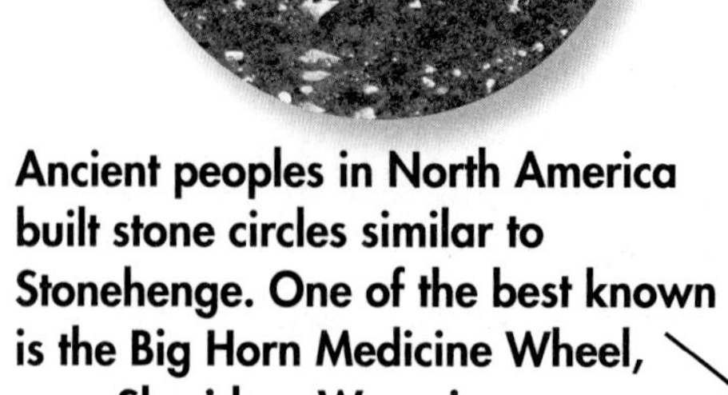

Ancient peoples in North America built stone circles similar to Stonehenge. One of the best known is the Big Horn Medicine Wheel, near Sheridan, Wyoming.

Chomsongdae Observatory on the Korean peninsula was built nearly 1,400 years ago. A hole at the top allowed people to view the stars and planets. Many similar observatories are found all over East Asia, but this one is the oldest.

Measured all the way across, Stonehenge is about one-third the length of a football field. Some stones weigh up to 50 tons and stand as tall as 9 meters (30 feet).

About 700 years ago in what is now Mexico, people built a large pyramid at a place called Chichén Itzá. This four-sided pyramid shows that the people were very clever sky watchers. Each of the pyramid's four sides has 91 steps leading to the top. If you count the platform step at the top, the pyramid has 365 steps, the same as the number of days in one year. A special pattern appears in late afternoon on the spring and fall equinoxes, the time of year when day and night are of equal length. Sunlight and shadows form a pattern that looks like a snake slithering down the stairway. The appearance of this pattern may have marked the date for special yearly ceremonies related to farming.

The pyramid at Chichén Itzá, in Mexico, is known as El Castillo. It is 24 meters (79 feet) tall, about twice as tall as a telephone pole.

1. **Checkpoint** What did ancient peoples leave behind that tells us that the cycles of the Sun, Moon, and stars were important to them?
2. **Summarize** what you have learned about the astronomical observations of ancient cultures.

Middle East Astronomy

Astronomy thrived in the Middle East for many centuries. Scholars from this region played an important role in early astronomy. One such person was Ulugh Beg (1394–1449). In 1420, he began building an observatory containing a huge sextant. The diameter was longer than six of today's school buses! Ulugh Beg used observations of the Sun to calculate the length of the year to within a minute of our current calculations. He also compiled a list of the exact locations of more than 1,000 stars.

Early Tools

People invented tools to help them better understand the stars. In Europe and the Middle East, the astrolabe was primarily used from about 200 B.C. to 1700 A.D. This tool consisted of a star map drawn on a metal plate. It had movable parts that allowed a viewer to measure the angle between the horizon and a star or planet. Other plates could be adjusted to show what the sky would look like at a particular time or place.

By the 1700s, the astrolabe had been replaced with other tools, such as the sextant. Like the astrolabe, a sextant measures the angle between the horizon and a point in the sky. However, a sextant consists of a movable arm, mirrors, and an eyepiece attached to a frame shaped like a piece of pie.

Astrolabes could be used to find the time, predict when the Sun would rise or set, or determine where certain stars would appear. Sailors used a type of astrolabe to find their position while at sea.

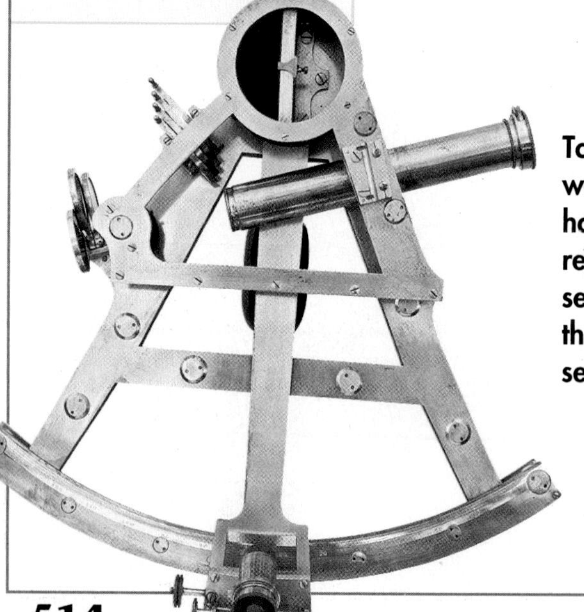

To find the angle of a star above the horizon, a person would line up the eyepiece of a sextant with the horizon. Then he would move the arm until the star was reflected by the mirrors on the sextant so that the star seemed to be lined up with the horizon. The angle could then be read from markings on the frame. Sailors used sextants to navigate by the stars.

Early Telescopes

The invention of the telescope, which gathers light to magnify faraway objects in the sky, was a breakthrough in astronomy. The Italian scientist Galileo Galilei (1564–1642) was the first person to use a telescope in astronomy, although he did not invent the telescope.

Galileo's telescopes were not very powerful. At best, they made an object look 20 times as large—about the same as one of today's beginner telescopes.

Galileo discovered that the Moon has mountains and that the Sun spins. He also discovered that Venus has phases like the Moon. One of Galileo's most important discoveries was that Jupiter has four moons that orbit around it.

In Galileo's day, many people believed that the Sun and the planets revolved around Earth. Galileo's discoveries led to the opposite conclusion—that the Earth and the other planets revolved around the Sun. Many people angrily refused to believe that the Earth was not the center of the universe. It would take years before Galileo's ideas were widely accepted.

The year Galileo died, 1642, another scientific genius was born. His name was Isaac Newton. Newton developed the reflecting telescope. Earlier telescopes used lenses to focus light and magnify distant objects. Newton's telescope used a curved mirror. It allowed people to see objects that were dimmer and farther away and to see the objects in sharper detail.

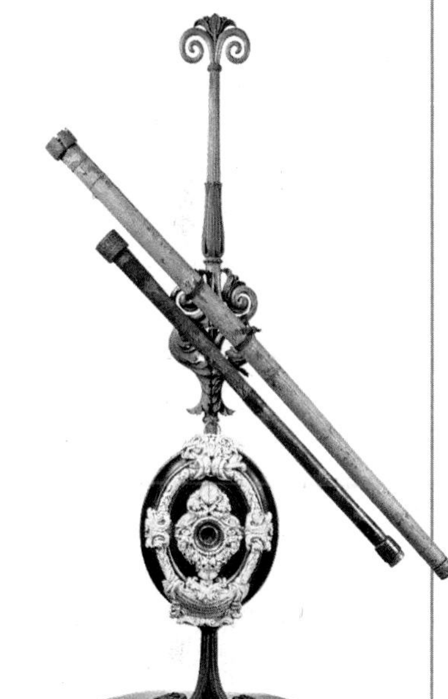

Early telescopes

Newton's reflecting telescope

1. ✓ **Checkpoint** What did Galileo conclude from his observations of Jupiter and Venus?
2. **Technology** in Science Use Internet or library resources to find when telescopes were used to see or photograph the planets Neptune, Uranus, and Pluto.

The Hubble Space Telescope detects ultraviolet waves, visible light, and infrared waves. Its cameras have photographed the planets in our solar system, the birth of new stars, and the fiery explosion that occurs near the end of a star's life.

Today's High-Tech Telescopes

Telescopes work because they gather light and concentrate it. The more light that reaches our eyes, the brighter an object will seem. The light we see coming from the Sun or the stars—visible light—is only a small fraction of the light energy in the universe. Most objects in space, including the Sun and other stars, emit a lot of electromagnetic radiation that we cannot see, including radio waves, infrared waves, ultraviolet waves, X rays, and gamma rays. Special telescopes have been developed that can detect different types of invisible radiation. The more types of radiation astronomers can study, the more they can learn about the universe.

Telescopes have become much bigger and much better since the time of Newton's reflecting telescope. For example, two huge twin telescopes, known as Keck I and Keck II, tie the record as the largest telescopes in the world. They each have a main mirror that measures 10 meters across. The mirrors are actually made out of 36 pieces that work together as a system to gather visible light and infared radiation. Astronomers use the Keck telescopes to study very distant stars.

For telescopes to work well, they need very dark, clear night skies. Keck I and II were built on top of the dormant volcano Mauna Kea in Hawaii. They are located far from city lights, in areas where it is rarely cloudy at night.

Radio Telescopes

Telescopes that detect radio waves look more like satellite dishes than traditional telescopes. Instead of a mirror or lens, a bowl-shaped dish collects and focuses radio waves given off by distant objects in space. Radio telescopes often consist of multiple dishes arranged in a group, or array. The radio signals detected by the dishes in an array can be added together. An array of dishes is like one giant dish that is as large as the space covered by all the dishes in the array.

Earth-based telescopes must view stars through the warm and cool air currents of the Earth's atmosphere. This can cause images to look fuzzy. Also, most types of electromagnetic radiation are partly or completely blocked by Earth's atmosphere. To get a more complete picture, some telescopes are launched into space where conditions are always clear and dark, perfect for stargazing around the clock! Space telescopes include the Hubble and the Chandra X-ray Observatory.

The Arecibo radio telescope in Puerto Rico is the largest single-dish radio telescope in the world. It receives radio waves from planets and stars as well as extremely distant objects called pulsars, which send out rapid-fire bursts of radio waves.

Radio waves bounce off the dish and hit the detector high above.
The dish is 305 meters (almost 1,000 feet) across, or about the length of three football fields.

✓ Lesson Checkpoint

1. How are radio telescopes different from the Keck telescopes?
2. Why must certain types of telescopes be sent into space?
3. Writing in Science **Expository** Write a paragraph in your **science journal** explaining which of the ancient structures you read about in this lesson you would most like to visit, and what you would hope to see.

Lesson 2

What is a star?

There are hundreds of thousands of stars in this group of stars.

Take a look at the night-time sky and you'll see more stars than you could ever begin to count. They are different sizes, ages, colors, and distances from Earth.

How the Sun Stacks Up as a Star

The Sun is a star. Stars, including the Sun, are gigantic balls of very hot gases that give off electromagnetic radiation. As stars go, the Sun is not unusual at all. It is of medium size. Stars known as giants may be 8 to 100 times as large as the Sun. Supergiants are even larger. They may be up to 300 times as large as the Sun. Other stars are much smaller—only about the size of Earth. Compared to the Earth, though, the Sun is huge. If you think of the Sun as a gumball machine and the Earth as a gumball, it would take a million Earth gumballs to fill the Sun gumball machine.

The Sun gives off enormous amounts of thermal energy and light energy. These energies come from powerful reactions involving the Sun's two main components, hydrogen and helium gas. Deep inside the core of the Sun, the nuclei of hydrogen atoms have such a high temperature and kinetic energy that when they collide, they fuse together. The nuclei combine to form a new nucleus and a new element, helium. Huge amounts of energy are released as this happens, which is what makes the Sun shine.

There are many different sizes and colors of stars.

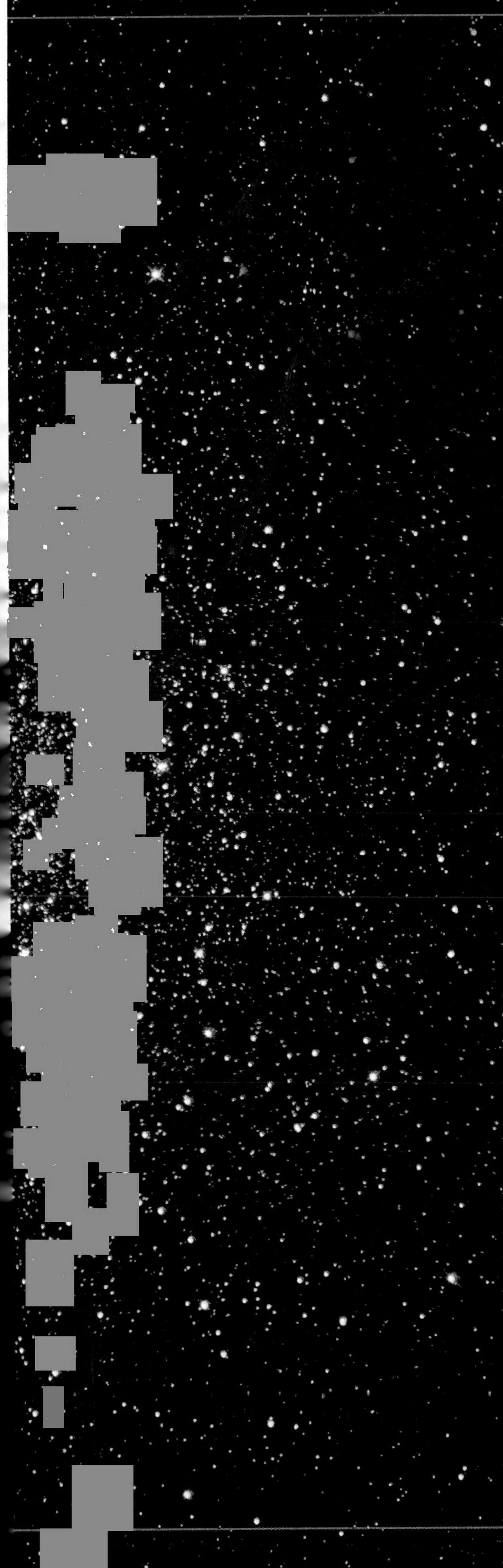

Brightness, Color, and Temperature of Stars

The Sun is the closest star to Earth. It is by far the brightest star in the sky. It's easy to think that the stars that look the brightest are the closest. However, Barnard's Star is the third closest to Earth, but it can't be seen without a telescope.

So just what is it that makes some stars look bright? The brightest stars are the stars that give off the most energy. But a star's size, temperature, and distance from Earth all play a part in how bright a star looks to us. The dazzling white star Sirius, for example, is the brightest star in the night sky, but it is only the ninth closest star to Earth. It is larger, hotter, and more than 20 times as bright as the Sun. It doesn't look brighter to us because it is much farther from us than the Sun. If we could line up all the stars at the same distance from Earth, we could see which stars are really the brightest.

A star's color tells you how hot it is. Red stars, like Barnard's star are the coolest. Somewhat hotter are orange and yellow stars, like the Sun with a temperatures of about 5500°C. The hottest stars are white or blue-white. Even though red stars are said to be "cool," they are still extremely hot. Barnard's Star is about 2250° C (4000° F). At that temperature a piece of iron would melt instantly and boil away into a gas.

1. **√Checkpoint** Which star is hotter, a yellow star or a white star?
2. **Social Studies in Science** Many of the brightest stars were named long ago. Do some research to find out who named the bright stars Vega and Rigel and what their names mean.

The Explosive Sun

The Sun is a fiery ball of hot gases with no hard surfaces. But astronomers have identified various layers of the Sun. The part of the Sun that gives off the light energy we see is called the photosphere. It is the innermost layer of the Sun's atmosphere. The layer above the photosphere is the chromosphere. The outermost layer is called the corona.

The Sun may look pretty calm—no more exciting than a giant glowing light bulb. But when scientists look at it with special telescopes and other equipment, they see a lot of activity. Galileo noticed dark spots moving along the face of the Sun and concluded that the Sun must be rotating. Today we know that these are sunspots, which are part of the photosphere. They look dark because they are not as hot as the rest of the photosphere. The way the sunspots travel across the face of the Sun indicates that the Sun rotates more slowly at its poles than at its equator.

The number of sunspots changes in cycles of about 11 years. Sometimes there are many, and sometimes there are few.

Sunspots may be the size of Earth or larger.

Solar Eruptions

Loops and fountains of blazing gases may leap out of the chromosphere, reaching hundreds of thousands of kilometers up into the corona. These ribbons of glowing gas are called prominences. Prominences may appear and then disappear in a few days or months.

Another explosive event linked to the sunspot cycle occurs when parts of the chromosphere erupt like a volcano. Such an "eruption" is called a solar flare. It causes a temporary bright spot in the chromosphere that may last for minutes or hours. A solar flare spews out huge amounts of electromagnetic waves, protons, and electrons into space. These waves and particles may interrupt radio communication and cause damage to electrical systems.

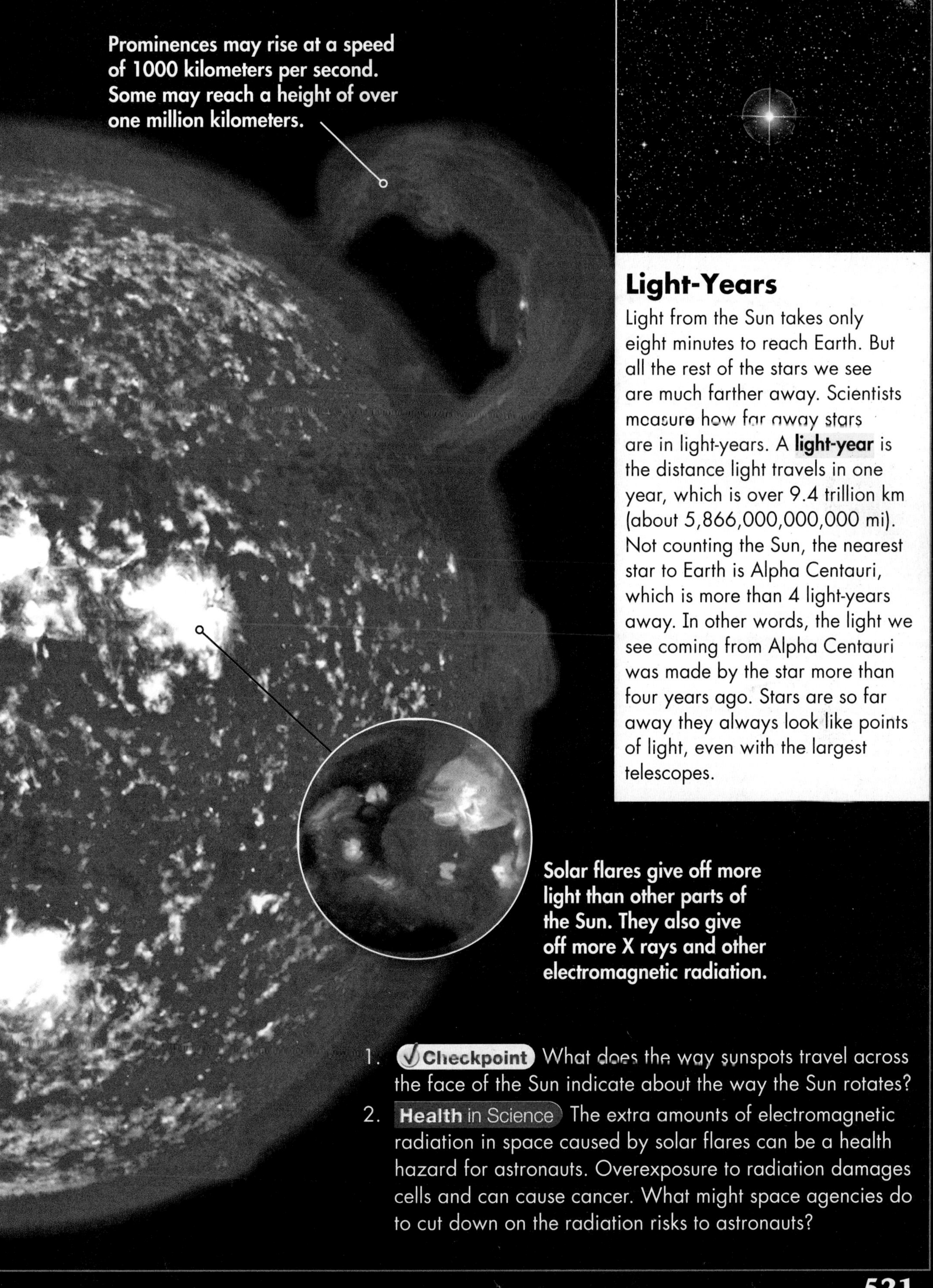
Prominences may rise at a speed of 1000 kilometers per second. Some may reach a height of over one million kilometers.
Solar flares give off more light than other parts of the Sun. They also give off more X rays and other electromagnetic radiation.

Light-Years

Light from the Sun takes only eight minutes to reach Earth. But all the rest of the stars we see are much farther away. Scientists measure how far away stars are in light-years. A **light-year** is the distance light travels in one year, which is over 9.4 trillion km (about 5,866,000,000,000 mi). Not counting the Sun, the nearest star to Earth is Alpha Centauri, which is more than 4 light-years away. In other words, the light we see coming from Alpha Centauri was made by the star more than four years ago. Stars are so far away they always look like points of light, even with the largest telescopes.

1. **√Checkpoint** What does the way sunspots travel across the face of the Sun indicate about the way the Sun rotates?
2. **Health in Science** The extra amounts of electromagnetic radiation in space caused by solar flares can be a health hazard for astronauts. Overexposure to radiation damages cells and can cause cancer. What might space agencies do to cut down on the radiation risks to astronauts?

The Life of Stars

Thanks to powerful telescopes, scientists have glimpsed new stars being born and ancient stars dying. New stars form in a cloud of gas and dust called a **nebula.** As particles of gas and dust churn around, gravity begins to pull together a clump of particles into a ball. Gravity increases in the ball, and more and more particles are pulled in. At the same time, the temperature rises. If it gets hot enough, hydrogen will begin changing into helium and releasing tremendous amounts of energy. The massive and dense clump of particles will officially have become a star.

Stars live an extremely long time, but they don't live forever. In billions of years, the Sun will use up all of the hydrogen (its "fuel") in its core. It will become several thousand times brighter and expand to about 170 times its current size—about out to where Mars orbits now.

In this photograph, stars are seen forming and dying.

This star is about to have a supernova. The ring and nearby clouds are debris ejected from the star's poles and equator.

These are young stars.

Stars are forming in these clouds.

These fingers of gas and dust are part of the Eagle Nebula, which is 7,000 light-years away. Inside these dusty towers, new stars are forming.

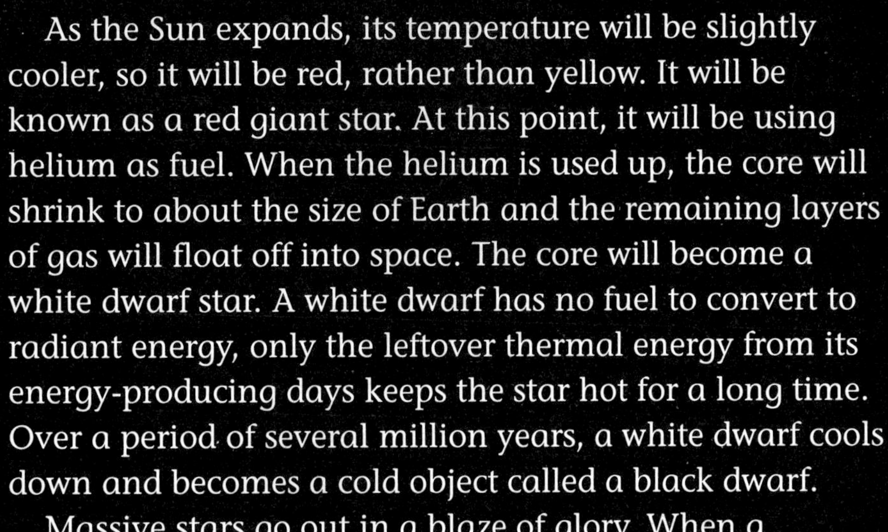

As the Sun expands, its temperature will be slightly cooler, so it will be red, rather than yellow. It will be known as a red giant star. At this point, it will be using helium as fuel. When the helium is used up, the core will shrink to about the size of Earth and the remaining layers of gas will float off into space. The core will become a white dwarf star. A white dwarf has no fuel to convert to radiant energy, only the leftover thermal energy from its energy-producing days keeps the star hot for a long time. Over a period of several million years, a white dwarf cools down and becomes a cold object called a black dwarf.

Massive stars go out in a blaze of glory. When a massive star's core runs out of fuel, it starts shrinking in on itself until it can shrink no farther. Powerful shock waves from this sudden stop fan outward, and particles of matter spin off into space carrying huge amounts of energy with them. A gigantic explosion occurs that is millions or billions of times as bright as the star ever was. This explosion is known as a **supernova.** It hurls matter and energy far out into space. Usually, all that will be left behind is a ball of neutrons that is about 20 km (12 mi) across. This city-sized object is called a neutron star.

If the core was quite massive—more massive than three Suns—the core's own gravity will keep causing it to shrink in on itself until it becomes a black hole. A **black hole** is a point in space that has such a strong force of gravity that nothing within a certain distance of it can escape getting pulled into the black hole—not even light.

√Lesson Checkpoint

1. What is the Sun?
2. Where does a new star form?
3. **Summarize** the three ways a star might die.

At the center of this nebula, two stars orbit each other. One of the stars is dying and has thrown off most of its gas layers, creating this butterfly-shaped cloud of gas and dust.

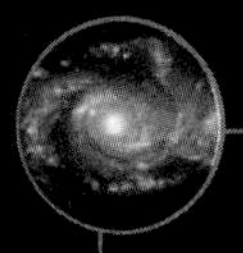

Lesson 3

How are stars grouped together?

Ancient people divided the sky up into groups of stars. This made studying the stars easier. Today we know that the stars—including the Sun—are part of even larger groupings of stars that are all bound to each other by gravity.

Galaxies

The Sun, the Earth, and the other planets in the solar system are part of the galaxy known as the Milky Way. A **galaxy** is a huge system of stars, dust, and gas held together by gravity. There are billions of galaxies in the universe. A few can be seen without a telescope, but they are so far away they look like single points of light. Using powerful telescopes, astronomers have learned that galaxies come in different shapes and sizes.

About three-fourths of the galaxies that have been discovered are spiral galaxies. They look like pinwheels. They have bright, bulging middles and wispy arms that fan out from the center. The stars in the arms of the galaxy are circling the center bulge of the galaxy, much as the Earth moves around the Sun.

Elliptical galaxies can be almost round or more oval like a football. The largest galaxies we know of are elliptical. There are also elliptical galaxies that are many times smaller than our galaxy.

Some galaxies are neither spiral nor elliptical. Galaxies that have no real shape are called irregular galaxies. Irregular galaxies are probably young galaxies in which stars are still forming.

1. **Checkpoint** What type of galaxy is the Milky Way?
2. **Math in Science** Look at the spiral galaxy that was photographed by the Hubble telescope on page 525. About how many times farther away is this galaxy than the Small Magellenic Cloud?

Approximate location of our solar system.

This side view of the Milky Way shows the bright bulging middle and wispy arms of this spiral galaxy. Our solar system is toward the end of one of the Milky Way's arms, about 25,000 to 30,000 light-years from the center.

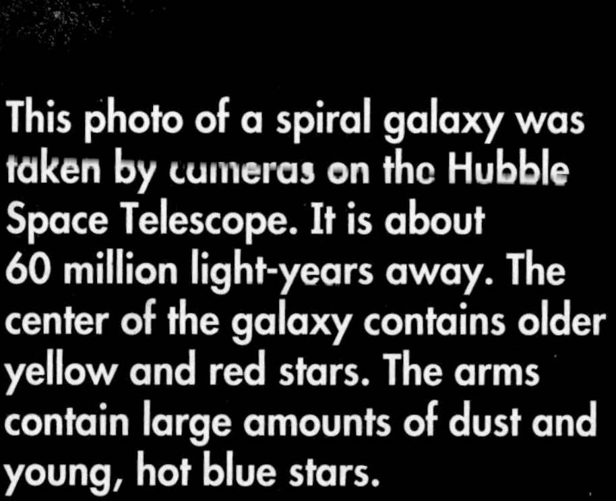

This photo of a spiral galaxy was taken by cameras on the Hubble Space Telescope. It is about 60 million light-years away. The center of the galaxy contains older yellow and red stars. The arms contain large amounts of dust and young, hot blue stars.

It is easy to see why a spiral galaxy is known as a "sombrero galaxy." The center of the galaxy is giving off huge quantities of X rays, which astronomers think may mean that a gigantic black hole lies at the heart of the galaxy.

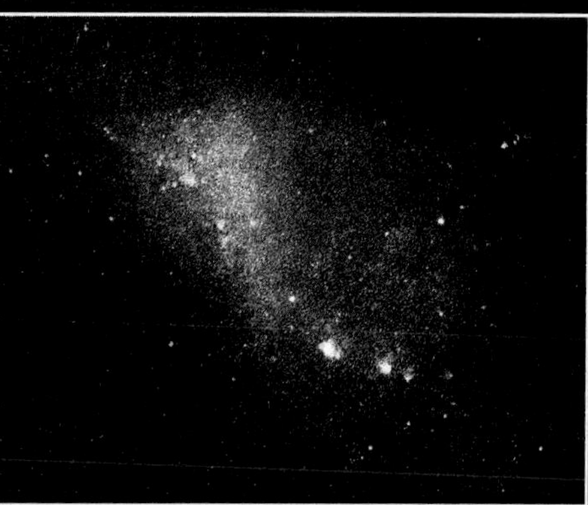

This irregular galaxy is called the Small Magellanic Cloud. This young galaxy is about 200,000 light-years away from Earth and is orbiting the Milky Way.

All galaxies are constantly moving through space. In several billion years, these two spiral galaxies will run into each other, and the smaller galaxy will be incorporated into the larger galaxy.

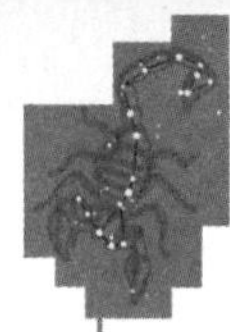

Constellations

In the past, people looked up at the night sky and "connected the dots" formed by the stars. They saw patterns that reminded them of bears, dogs, a swan, a lion, and even a sea monster! Today, scientists divide the night sky into 88 constellations. A **constellation** is a group of stars that forms a pattern. A map of constellations looks much like a map of the United States with all the states in the country outlined. Some are rectangles, others have odd shapes. Many of the constellation names are the names of the star patterns people used long ago.

Dividing the sky into sections makes studying stars easier. A constellation is a little bit like a star's address. For example, if you tell someone which state you live in, it lets that person know which part of the country you live in. Knowing which constellation a star is in lets you know which part of the sky to look at to find that star.

Two stars that look close together in the same constellation are not necessarily very close in reality. One star may be billions of kilometers farther from Earth than the other. They appear to be close together because they are in the same direction from Earth.

People who live in different parts of the world see different sections of the sky and different constellations. The Earth can be divided into two halves along the equator. The half to the north of the equator is called the Northern Hemisphere. The half to the south is called the Southern Hemisphere. The United States is in the Northern Hemisphere. Ursa Major can be seen in the Northern Hemisphere. But it is not visible to people in the Southern Hemisphere.

In the constellation Ursa Major, the Big Dipper forms the bear's back and its tail.

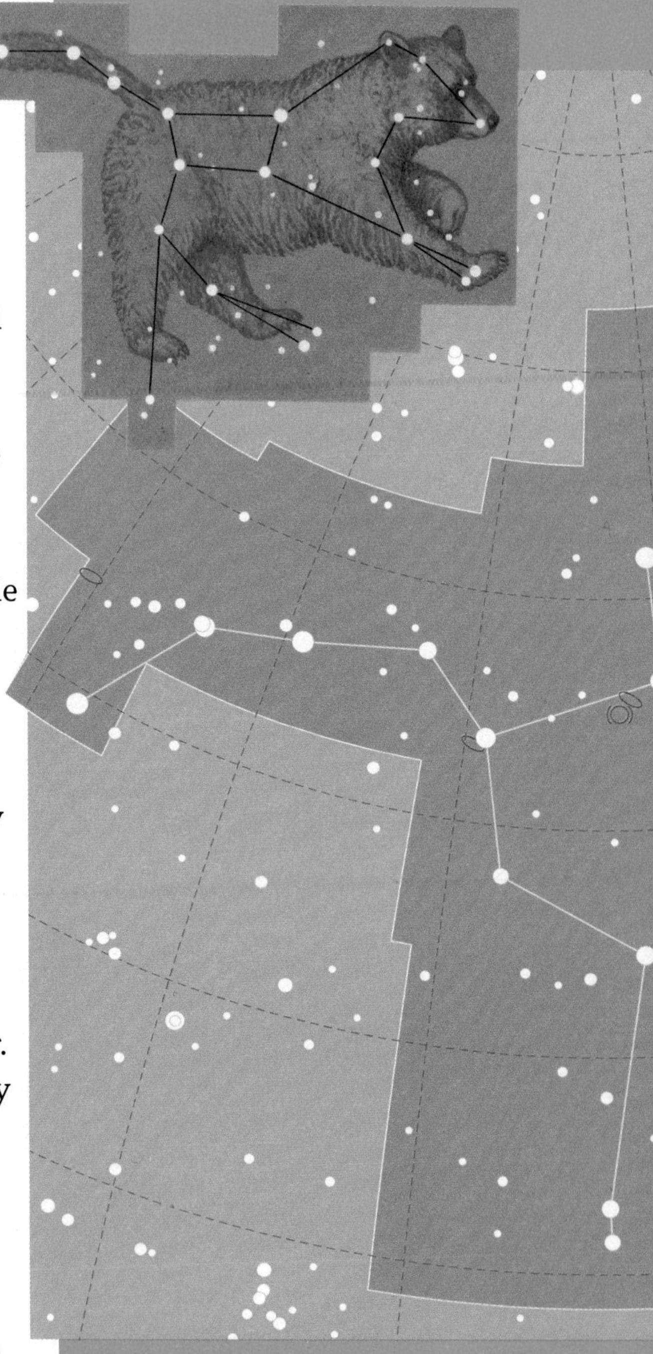

Maps of the night sky include imaginary lines around each constellation. The constellation of Ursa Major, shown here at the top of the page, includes the pattern of stars that gives the constellation its name and all the other stars within the imaginary lines.

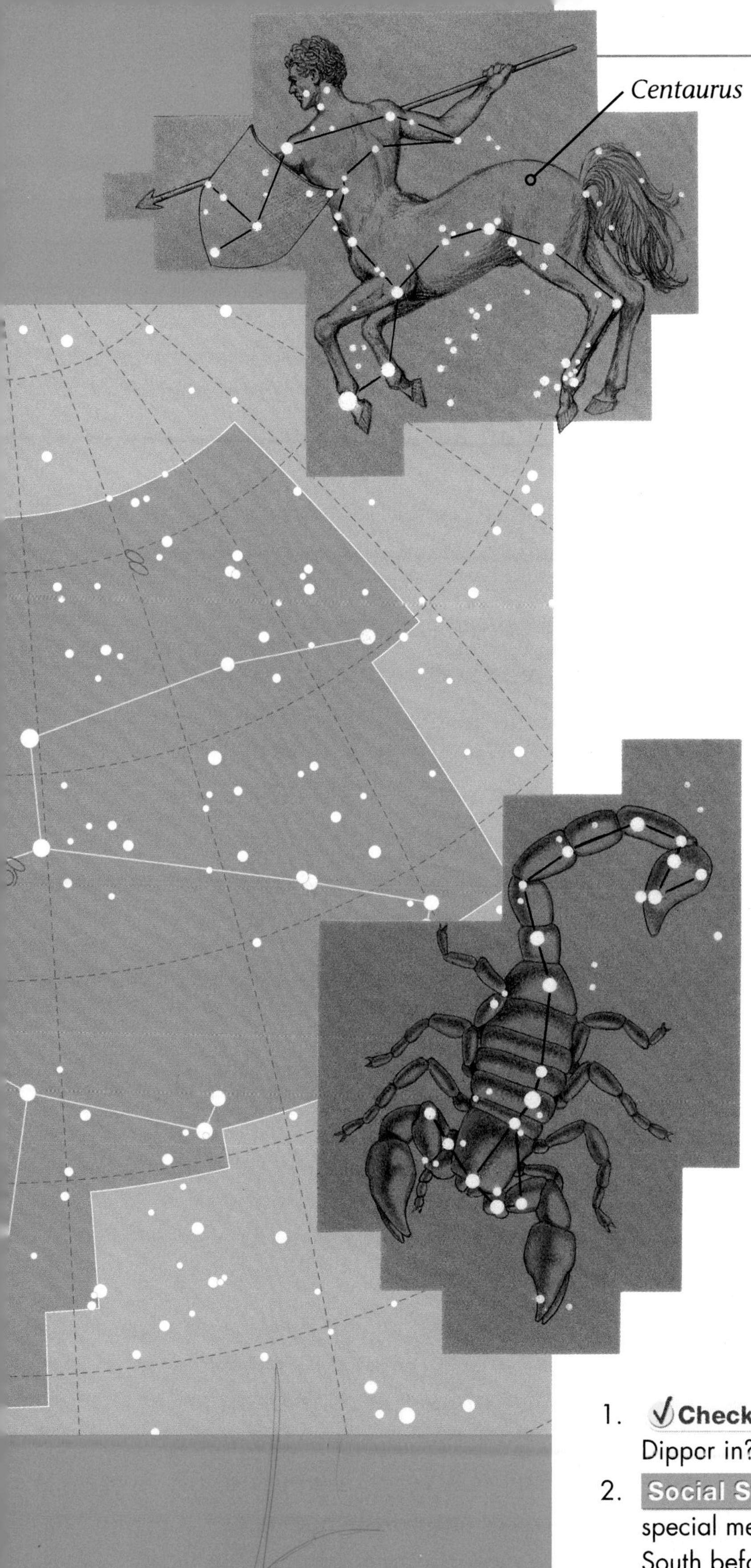
Centaurus

The constellation Centaurus can be seen only from the Southern Hemisphere. It is named after a character in an ancient Greek myth who was half human and half horse. This bright triple-star system includes the three closest stars to the Sun, which mark one of Centaurus's legs.

The ancient Greeks named another constellation Scorpius because they thought the group of stars looked like a scorpion—a small creature with a tail that delivers a painful or deadly sting. If you look at Scorpius through a telescope, you will see that many of the bright points of light are not single stars but large clusters of stars. The brightest single star in the constellation is the red supergiant Antares, which lies near the center of the scorpion's "body."

Ancient Greeks thought this star group looked like a scorpion.

1. **√ Checkpoint** Which constellation is the Big Dipper in?
2. **Social Studies in Science** The Big Dipper had special meaning for African American slaves in the South before the Civil War. A song called "Follow the Drinking Gourd" told slaves how following the Big Dipper would lead them North to freedom. Use the Internet or library resources to find out why the Big Dipper served as a good guide.

The Big Dipper Today

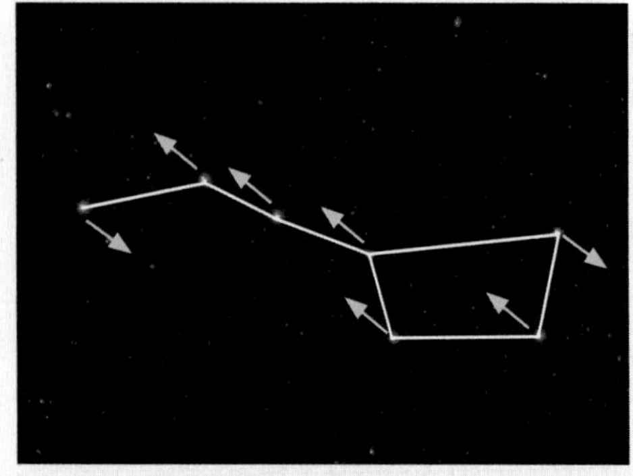

The arrows show how the stars of the Big Dipper are moving relative to one another.

The Big Dipper in 100,000 years

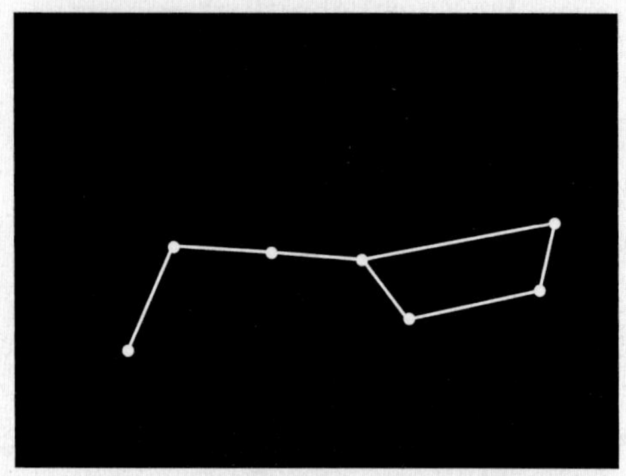

Tens of thousands of years from now, the Big Dipper will look much different. Its handle will look more crooked and the bowl more stretched out because the star at the end of the handle and the star at the far top of the bowl will have moved in opposite directions. What will the Big Dipper look like in 200,000 years?

Stars on the Move

Stars do not always appear in the same place in the sky. They move in logical and predictable ways. Suppose you looked at the sky early one evening and found the Big Dipper. Two hours later you went back out and found that the Big Dipper moved toward the western horizon. Actually, the Big Dipper did not move, but you moved. Every 24 hours, the Earth makes one complete rotation. This rotation of the Earth is why the Sun seems to travel across the sky every day—rising in the east and setting in the west. It is also why the stars appear to move across the sky in the same direction.

Ursa Major, which contains the Big Dipper, is visible all year. But other constellations can be seen only at certain times of the year. In the United States, you can see the constellation Canis Major, or the Great Dog, only in winter. Constellations change with the seasons because Earth is traveling around the Sun. It takes Earth one year to travel around the Sun. As the Earth makes its journey, different parts of the sky come into view at night for people on Earth. In a way, it's not so different from riding a merry-go-round. As you look outward during a ride, your view of the surroundings changes.

Nothing in the universe stands still. Stars are moving through space in various directions and at various speeds. We can not see this is happening because the stars are so very far away. But over very long periods of time, the patterns of stars will change as some stars move closer to or farther away from each other.

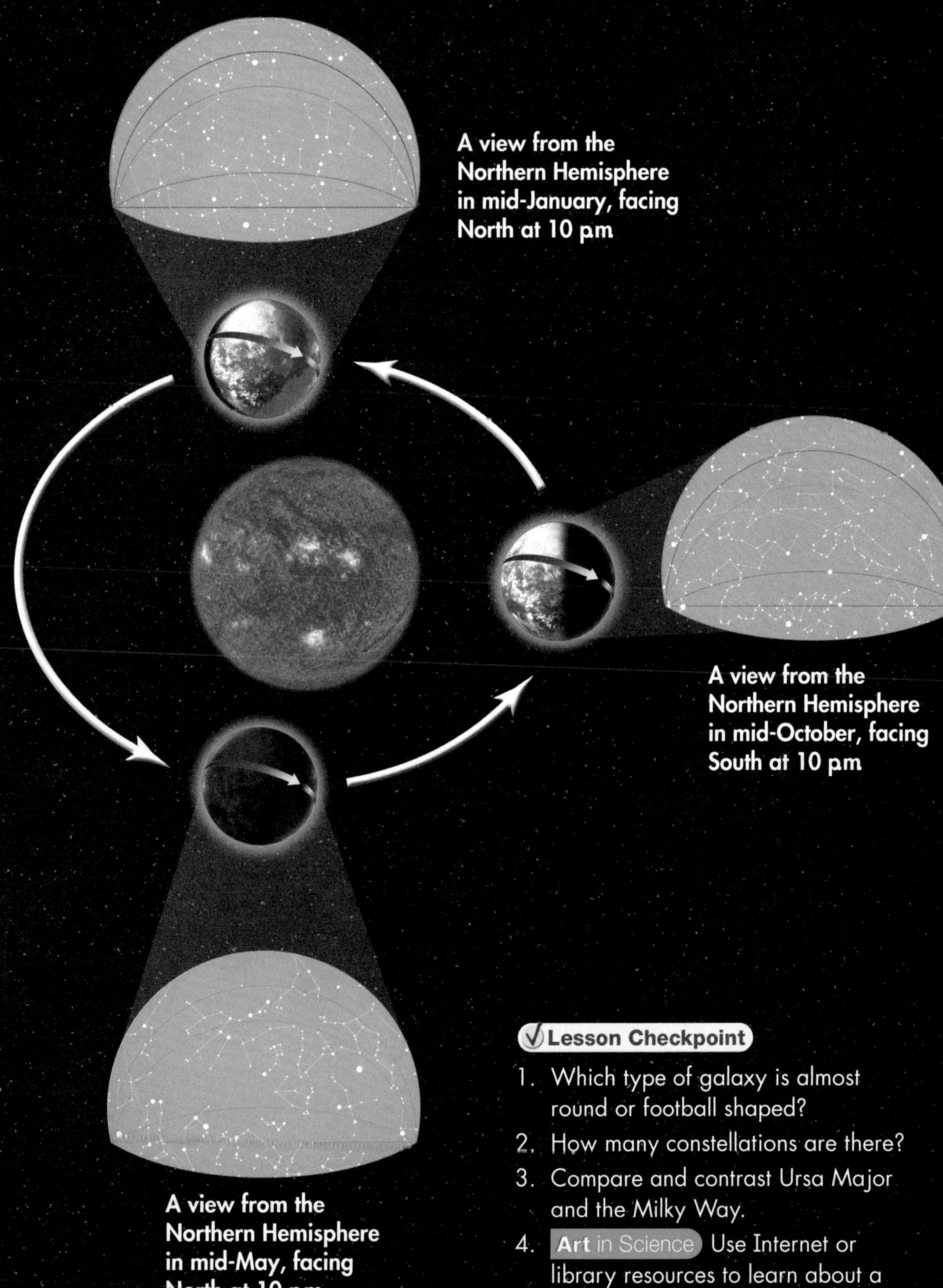
A view from the
Northern Hemisphere
in mid-January, facing
North at 10 p.m.
A view from the
Northern Hemisphere
in mid-October, facing
South at 10 p.m.
A view from the
Northern Hemisphere
in mid-May, facing
North at 10 p.m.

✓ Lesson Checkpoint

1. Which type of galaxy is almost round or football shaped?
2. How many constellations are there?
3. Compare and contrast Ursa Major and the Milky Way.
4. **Art in Science** Use Internet or library resources to learn about a new constellation. Make a poster about your constellation that includes a drawing and information about it.

Lab zone **Guided Inquiry**

Investigate What does a spiral galaxy look like from different angles?

Our solar system is located near the edge of the Milky Way. The Milky Way is called a spiral galaxy because it is shaped like a spiral.

Materials

25 cups

What to Do

1. **Make a model** of a spiral galaxy.

2. **Observe** the cups from directly above the table. This view represents the galaxy as seen from outside the galaxy. Draw a sketch or diagram of what you see.

3. Kneel beside the cups on the edge of the table. Look across the table at the other side of the cups. This view represents the galaxy as seen from a planet near the galaxy's edge.

These cups represent a spiral galaxy.

Process Skills

You **make a model** when you use representations to explain ideas.

4 Draw a diagram of what you see.

Model of a Spiral Galaxy	
View from Above	**View from the Edge**

Explain Your Results

1. How did the angle from which you viewed your **model** affect what you saw?
2. How is the model like a spiral galaxy? How is it different?
3. **Predict** Suppose you made a model of an elliptical galaxy. When seen from above, would it look the same as a spiral galaxy? When seen from the edge, would it look the same as a spiral galaxy? Test your predictions.

Our Sun is a star near the edge of the Milky Way, a spiral galaxy.

Go Further

If possible in your area, observe stars in the night sky. Use a sky chart to help find our galaxy, the Milky Way. Also try to identify stars in the night sky that are unusually bright or ones that appear slightly red or blue.

Math in Science

Shrinking the Universe Down to Size

Most things in the universe are very large. Even in our own solar system, it is hard to understand the size of our Sun, the other stars, and the planets.

To make large sizes and great distances easier to understand, it is helpful to shrink them down. In the chart, the comparative diameters are in centimeters to help you see how the sizes compare.

Star	Approximate Diameter	Comparative Diameter
Sun	1,400,000 km	1.4 cm
Beta Pegasi (a giant star)	133,000,000 km	133 cm
Hadar B (a giant star)	16,800,000 km	16.8 cm
Arcturus (a giant star)	35,000,000 km	35 cm
Sirius A (a main sequence star)	2,660,000 km	2.66 cm

eTools Take It to the Net sfsuccessnet.com

Use the table on page 532 to answer the questions.

1. Which star shown has a diameter that is almost twice the Sun's diameter?

A. Beta Pegasi
B. Arcturus
C. Sirius A
D. Hadar B

2. Which star shown is almost 100 times as large as the Sun?

F. Sirius A
G. Hadar B
H. Arcturus
I. Beta Pegasi

3. The planet Jupiter has a diameter of about 140,000 km. It is about $\frac{1}{10}$ the size of which star?

A. the Sun
B. Beta Pegasi
C. Hadar B
D. Sirius A

4. List the 5 stars in the chart in order from smallest to largest.

Lab zone Take-Home Activity

Make a model of the 5 stars listed in the table on page 532. Use paper cut-outs to make your models. Tape several pieces of paper together to make the larger star models.

Chapter 16 Review and Test Prep

Use Vocabulary

black hole (page 523)	**light-year** (page 521)
constellation (page 526)	**nebula** (page 522)
galaxy (page 524)	**supernova** (page 523)

Use the term from the list above that best completes each sentence.

1. A huge system of stars, dust, and gas held together by gravity is a(n)______.
2. A point in space that has such a strong force of gravity that nothing within a certain distance of it can escape is known as a(n)______.
3. A group of stars that forms a pattern is called a(n) ______.
4. A gigantic explosion that occurs near the end of the life of some stars is a(n) ______.
5. Stars form in a cloud called a(n) ______.
6. The distance light travels in one year is a(n) ______.

Explain Concepts

7. Explain two factors that affect how bright a star appears in the night sky.
8. Explain what a sunspot is and the pattern that exists in the number of sunspots that are observed.
9. Explain two reasons for sending telescopes into space.
10. Why do stars appear to move across the sky during the night?

Process Skills

11. **Classify** Suppose you are viewing two galaxies through a telescope. The first galaxy you look at has a bright center and curved arms. The second galaxy is oval. Classify the two galaxies.
12. **Interpret the data** in the chart below. Which of the stars listed is closest to our solar system? Which is farthest?

Name of star	Distance
Arcturus	37 light-years
Altair	17 light-years
Betelgeuse	425 light-years
Sirius	9 light-years

13. **Infer** Barnard's Star is the third closest star to Earth, but it can't be seen without a telescope. Sirius is the ninth closest star to Earth and the brightest star in the night sky. Although it is farther away, what can you infer about Sirius's size and temperature that would explain why it looks brighter than Barnard's Star?

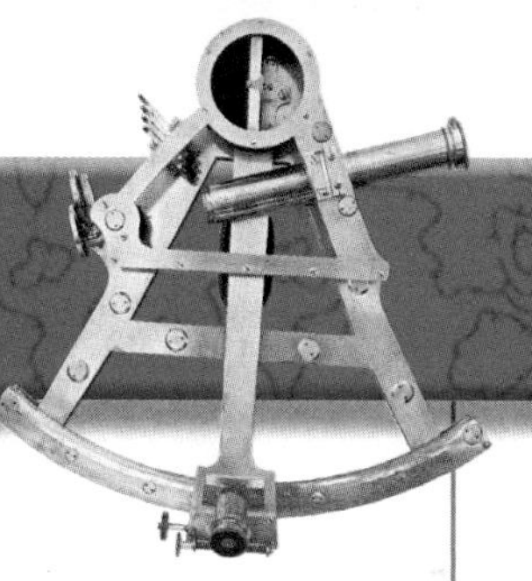

Summarize

14. Make a graphic organizer like the one shown below. Use the details in the boxes to write a summary about the Sun's atmosphere.

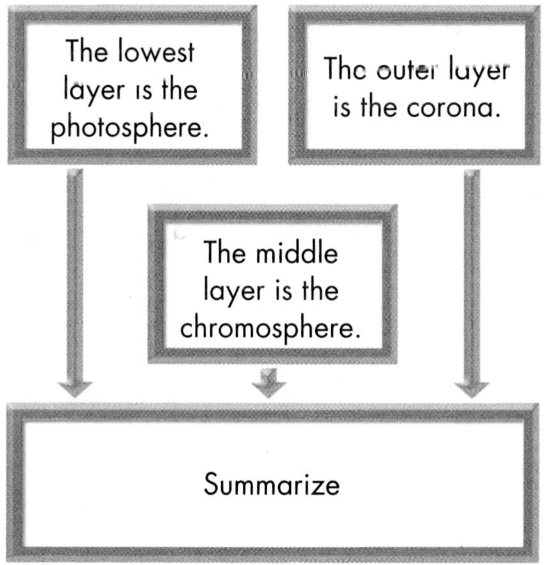

The lowest layer is the photosphere.
The outer layer is the corona.
The middle layer is the chromosphere.
Summarize

Test Prep

Choose the letter that best completes the statement or answers the question.

15. Watching the movements of the Sun, Moon, and stars was important to ancient cultures because it helped them
- Ⓐ predict the seasons and know when to plant crops.
- Ⓑ see better at night.
- Ⓒ build large stone monuments and observatories.
- Ⓓ discover spots on the face of the Sun.

16. A constellation is
- Ⓕ a system of stars, gas, and dust held together by gravity.
- Ⓖ a group of stars that forms a pattern.
- Ⓗ the largest kind of star.
- Ⓘ a set of telescopes on a mountain in Hawaii.

17. A light-year is
- Ⓐ the amount of time it takes light from the Sun to reach Earth.
- Ⓑ the distance from one end of the Milky Way to the other end.
- Ⓒ the distance light travels in one year.
- Ⓓ the amount of energy released when the Sun changes hydrogen into helium.

18. Galileo's discoveries
- Ⓕ helped him invent the telescope.
- Ⓖ provided evidence that the Earth and the planets revolve around the Sun.
- Ⓗ helped him realize that a better telescope could be made by using mirrors to gather light instead of lenses.
- Ⓘ helped him learn about the planets Neptune and Pluto.

19. Explain why the answer you select for Question 18 is best. For each of the answers you do not select, give a reason why it is not the best choice.

20. Writing in Science **Narrative** Choose one way a star dies and write a death scene. Use dialogue, a setting, and the star as the main character.

Biography

Caroline Herschel

1750–1848

When Caroline Herschel officially became an astronomer in 1787, few women were ever paid for their work. Her salary, from the king of England, was low. But over time, her work made her famous.

Caroline Herschel was the assistant to her brother William Herschel. William had already achieved great fame with his discovery of the planet Uranus, in 1781. Caroline helped William make powerful telescopes. She also helped him record his nightly observations. She worked on the complex math needed to identify each object in the night sky.

William gave Caroline her own telescope. When she wasn't helping her brother, she made her own observations. Caroline discovered eight new comets. She tracked the positions of more than 500 stars that other astronomers had overlooked. She also discovered nebulas and observed star clusters and galaxies. Astronomers still use her star catalogs today.

Caroline Herschel worked as an astronomer until she was almost 80 years old. She received gold medals for her work and was invited to the palaces of kings and queens. Members of a German royal family came to visit her on her 97th birthday. She entertained them by singing. Her spirit was as bright as the stars she loved to study.

Lab zone Take-Home Activity

Use a book or ask an adult to help you find the constellation Orion, in the winter sky. Three bright stars form Orion's belt. Three dimmer stars below this belt make up Orion's sword. Use binoculars to find the nebula in Orion's sword.

EC NTL 10 9 8 7

You Will Discover

- the effects of Earth's special position in space.
- the ways that Earth moves in space.
- how Earth, Sun, and Moon are related.

Chapter 17 Earth in Space

online
Student Edition
sfsuccessnet.com

Web Games
Take It to the Net
sfsuccessnet.com

Build Background

How does the motion of objects in space create cycles?

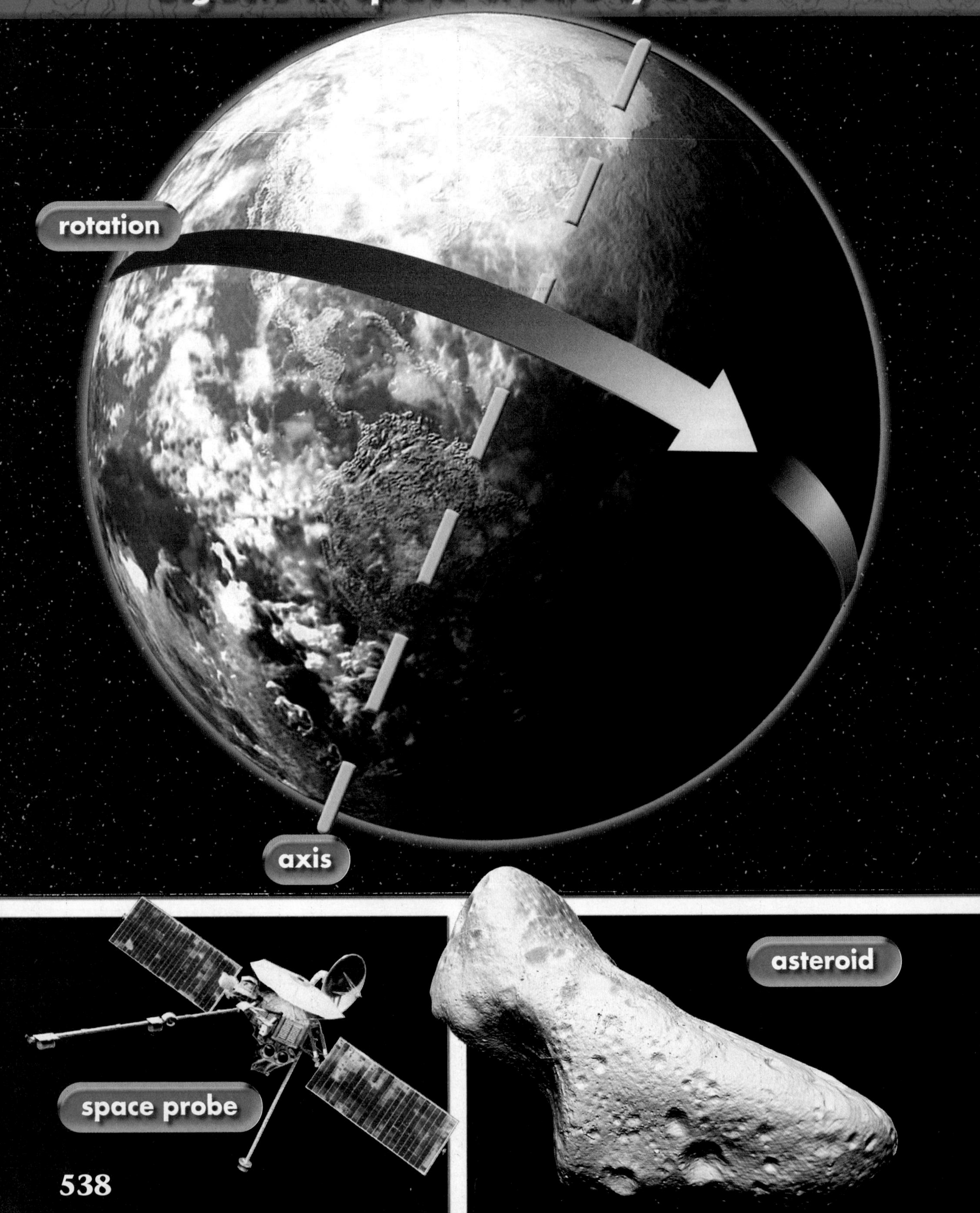
rotation
axis
asteroid
space probe

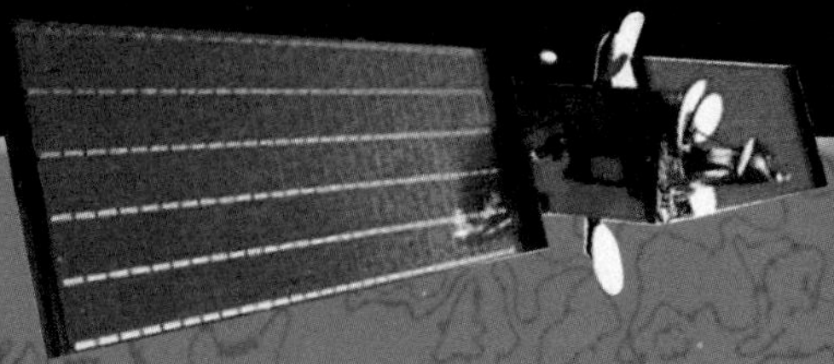

Chapter 17 Vocabulary

solar system page 543

revolution page 543

axis page 544

rotation page 544

space probe page 550

comet page 552

asteroid page 554

satellite page 556

Moon phase page 558

Moon phase
solar system

satellite

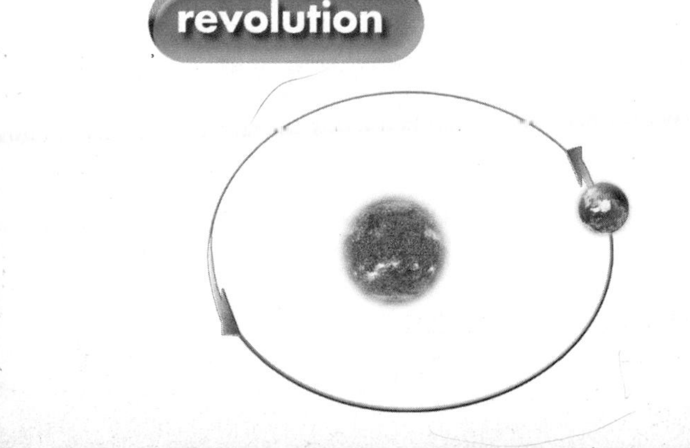
revolution

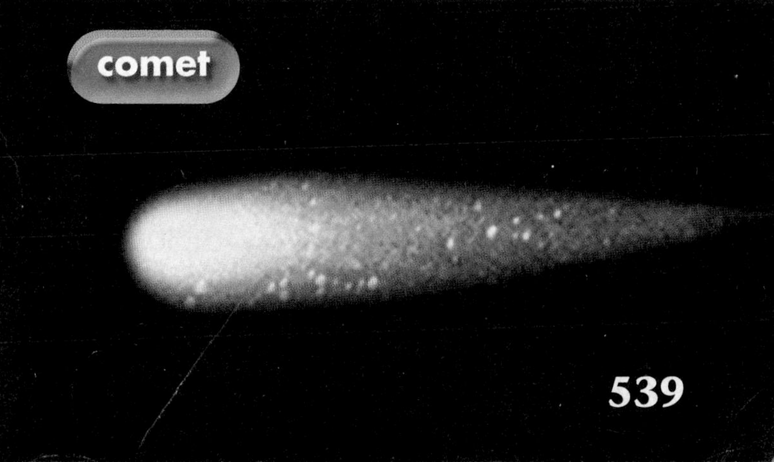
comet

Lab zone **Directed Inquiry**

Explore Does distance affect orbiting time?

Materials

clay

meterstick

metric ruler

What to Do

1. Make 2 clay balls the size of golf balls.
2. Push one ball onto the end of a meterstick. Push the other ball onto the end of a ruler.
3. Hold up the meterstick and the ruler. Place the empty end of each against the floor.
4. Let go of both at the same time. **Observe** closely.

Process Skills

You **infer** when you make a careful guess based on your **observations** or past experiences.

Explain Your Results

1. Which ball hit the ground first?
2. **Infer** Think about your answer. How might a planet's distance from the Sun affect the time needed to make one orbit?

How to Read Science

Reading Skills

TARGET SKILL

Make Inferences

A writer doesn't always tell us everything. As you read, you might have to put some facts together. When you **make an inference,** you make a guess from facts you have read or **observed.** Some facts are marked in the article below.

- Try to make an inference from the facts you read.
- Use your own experiences to help you make inferences.

Science Article

Deciding About Distance

Mercury takes 88 days to travel around the Sun. Mars takes 687 days, and Neptune takes about 164.5 years. Each planet travels in its own path and is a different distance from the Sun. Which of these three planets is farthest from the Sun?

Apply It!

Study this graphic organizer. Make a graphic organizer like this one. List the facts from the science article in your graphic organizer. Write your **inference.**

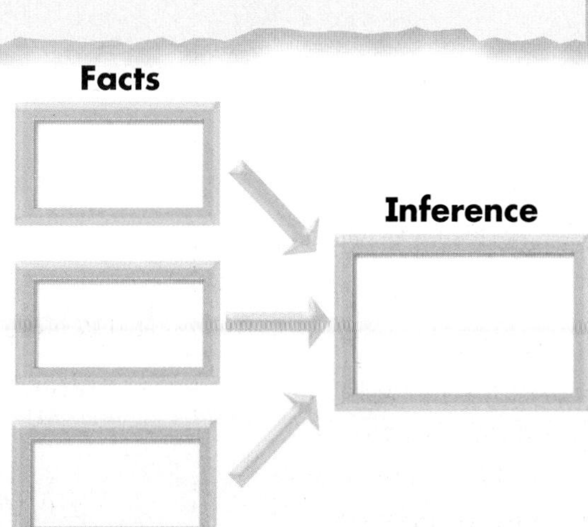
Facts
Inference

You Are There!

Right now you are rushing through space at about 1,800 kilometers (1,100 miles) per minute! This speed could take you from Miami to Los Angeles in about 2 minutes. But in space, riding on planet Earth, where are you rushing to? You are traveling in a big circle around the Sun. Well, it's not quite a circle, but it is big. How long do you think it takes to ride once around the Sun?

 AudioText

Lesson 1

In what ways does Earth move?

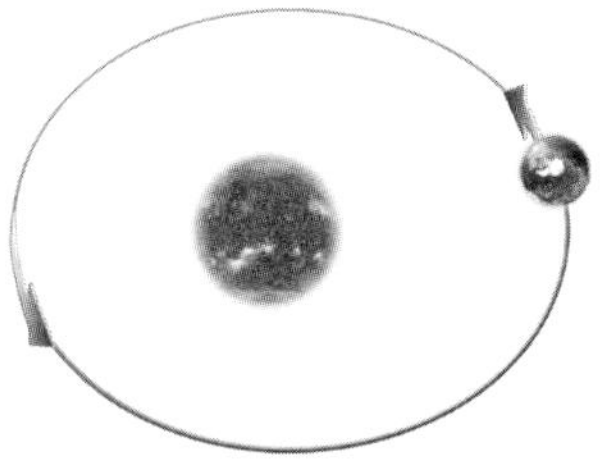

The movements of Earth cause the cycle of day and night and the cycle of the seasons.

Earth's Orbit

Picture Earth as it travels around the Sun—a rather small blue sphere with one moon. Earth is one of nine planets circling the Sun. The **solar system** is made of the Sun and its nine planets along with many moons, asteroids, and comets. The Sun, planets, and moons are all nearly *spherical*, or ball-shaped.

The Earth and the other planets each follow a path called an orbit around the Sun. Orbits have elliptical paths. *Elliptical* describes a shape like a slightly flattened circle. Likewise, the Moon moves in an elliptical orbit around the Earth. Trace the elliptical shape of the orbit shown in the diagram in the margin above. Notice how the planet moves slightly closer to the Sun at certain parts of the orbit.

One full orbit is called a **revolution**. Earth's revolution around the Sun lasts for just a few hours longer than 365 days. This period may sound familiar to you. It is one *year*. Likewise, the Moon's revolution around the Earth takes about 28 days. This is about a *month*. In fact, the word *month* comes from the word *moon*.

Just as gravity keeps you on the Earth, gravity keeps the Earth and other planets in their orbits around the Sun. Gravity also keeps the Moon orbiting around the Earth.

1. **Checkpoint** What is the shape of the planets' orbits?
2. **Math in Science** Earth's orbit actually takes about $365\frac{1}{4}$ days. Since our calendar has only 365 days, how far off will it be in 2 years? In 3 years? Why do we have leap years?

Day and Night

Planets spin. The spinning causes one part of a planet to face toward the Sun for a while. This is *day*. Soon that same part turns away from the Sun. This is *night*.

Look at the picture of the spinning top. You see how it tilts. A top spins around an imaginary center line called an **axis.** Earth also spins, or rotates, on an axis. One whole spin of an object on its axis is called a **rotation.** The Earth completes one rotation, or one day, in about 24 hours.

The diagram shows the Earth's tilt and spin. The northern end of Earth's axis is called the North Pole. The southern end is the South Pole. During its orbit around the sun, Earth's axis always points in the same direction in space. Where is Earth's axis in the diagram?

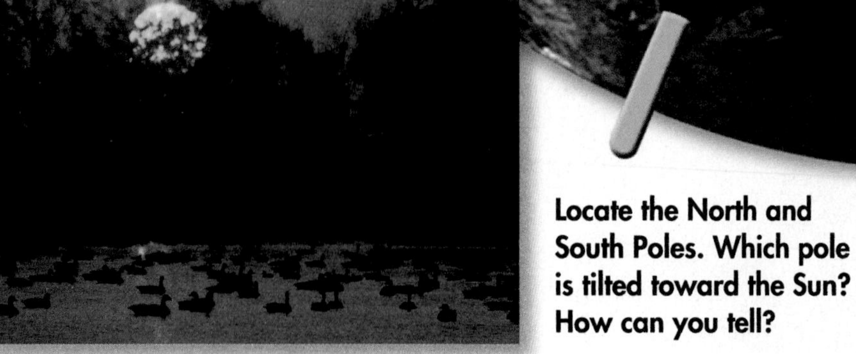

As Earth spins, the Sun, Moon, stars, and planets only seem to rise in the east and set in the west. When you see a sunset, remember that it is you who are moving. You are riding on the spinning Earth.

Locate the North and South Poles. Which pole is tilted toward the Sun? How can you tell?

The Earth is shown here as it appears in the afternoon of late December. At this time of the year, the South Pole receives sunlight during the entire rotation of the Earth. The North Pole is always dark. Areas between the poles receive different amounts of sunlight each day. The farther north a place is, the less light it receives each day.

As the Earth moves around the Sun, the amount of Sun any place gets during a day slowly changes. How much it changes depends on where you live. On two days, at the beginning of spring and fall, every point on Earth will have 12 hours of sunlight.

Earth's Comfortable Temperature

Earth does not get as hot or as cold as other planets. Earth rotates quickly on its axis, causing day and night to follow each other in a short period of time. This helps keep temperatures mild enough for you and all other living things to go on living. If Earth rotated more slowly, days would get hotter while nights would get colder.

Unlike some planets, Earth has a significant atmosphere. This layer of air helps prevent Earth from overheating in the Sun's rays both by reflecting some of the Sun's energy into space and absorbing other energy. The atmosphere also holds warm air near the planet's surface, releasing thermal energy slowly into space. Some planets in the solar system have little or no atmosphere. Their temperature changes are too drastic for life. The Moon has almost no atmosphere. Its dark side gets colder than any freezer on Earth. Surfaces on the Moon's sunny side get hot enough to fry eggs.

Atmosphere

1. **√Checkpoint** What causes day and night?
2. **Social Studies in Science** As Earth spins, sunrise happens gradually across the United States. Find out how this natural event influenced the invention of different time zones and discuss your findings with the class.

The Pattern of Seasons

During certain months of the year in some parts of the country, you might wear a heavy coat and shovel some snow. Other months, you might wear a bathing suit and go for a swim on a hot day. Have you ever wondered why winter and summer always take place during the same months each year? What causes this pattern that we call seasons?

You have read that Earth spins on a tilted axis. Earth always tilts the same way during its year-long orbit. This causes different parts of Earth's surface to face toward the Sun during each season. This also causes the number of daylight hours to change during the year. Long hours of daylight heat areas in summer. In winter, there are fewer hours of sunlight, so the same areas do not get as much energy from the Sun.

Earth's tilt also causes light from the Sun to hit different parts of the Earth at different angles. These rays transfer energy to Earth. The amount of light energy received by an area creates its climate and seasons. The rays striking the equator deliver concentrated energy. Rays striking near the poles are more spread out. The polar regions, therefore, have much colder climates than the equator.

It's the Tilt, Not the Distance

Distance from the Sun does not affect Earth's seasons. Look at the diagram of Earth's revolution around the Sun. See how the Sun is not quite at the center of Earth's elliptical orbit?

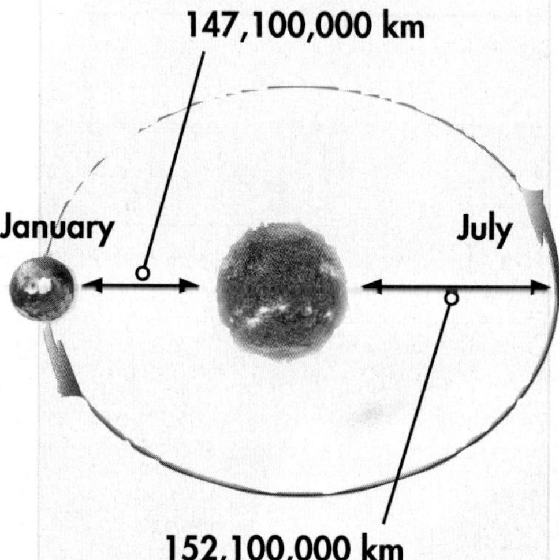
147,100,000 km
January
July
152,100,000 km

The distance between Earth and the Sun changes slightly during the year. The Earth is closest to the Sun in January, when the Unites States has winter. Six months later, in warm July, it is farthest away. The cause of the seasons is not Earth's distance from the Sun. Rather, Earth's tilt causes the seasons.

The North Pole tilts away from the Sun. The Sun's rays are very spread out here. The Northern Hemisphere receives the least amount of energy at this time of year. Temperatures drop, and winter sets in.

The Sun's rays strike the Earth more directly south of the equator. The rays are concentrated, not spread out. Concentrated energy gives this region warm summer weather.

Earth's Seasons

You live in the Northern Hemisphere, so this page explains the seasons for the northern half of the world. The Southern Hemisphere has opposite seasons. Earth's axis always tilts in the same direction during its orbit.

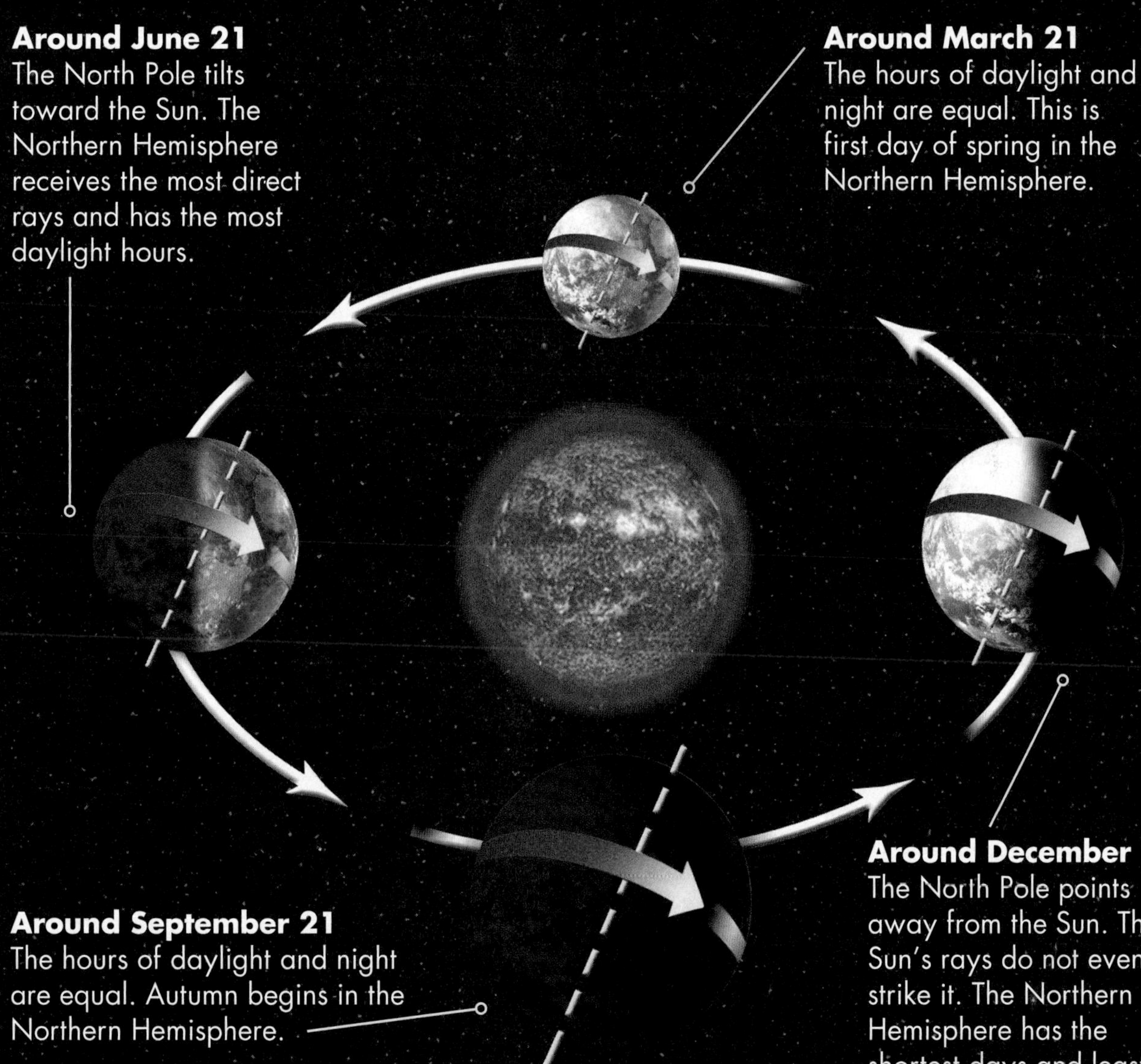
Around June 21
The North Pole tilts toward the Sun. The Northern Hemisphere receives the most direct rays and has the most daylight hours.
Around March 21
The hours of daylight and night are equal. This is first day of spring in the Northern Hemisphere.
Around September 21
The hours of daylight and night are equal. Autumn begins in the Northern Hemisphere.
Around December 21
The North Pole points away from the Sun. The Sun's rays do not even strike it. The Northern Hemisphere has the shortest days and least direct rays.

√ Lesson Checkpoint

1. What is the season in the Northern Hemisphere when the North Pole points most directly toward the Sun?
2. How is the climate near the equator different from the climate near the poles? What causes this difference?
3. Writing in Science **Expository** Write in your **science journal** about the changes that occur in your area over the sequence of four seasons. For each season, include the months of the year and tell about the effects caused by the Earth's position in relation to the Sun.

Lesson 2

What are the parts of the solar system?

Do you know your home address and those of your closest neighbors? If you were to write your space address, you might add, "Planet Earth, Solar System, Milky Way Galaxy." The solar system contains eight other neighboring planets and other objects.

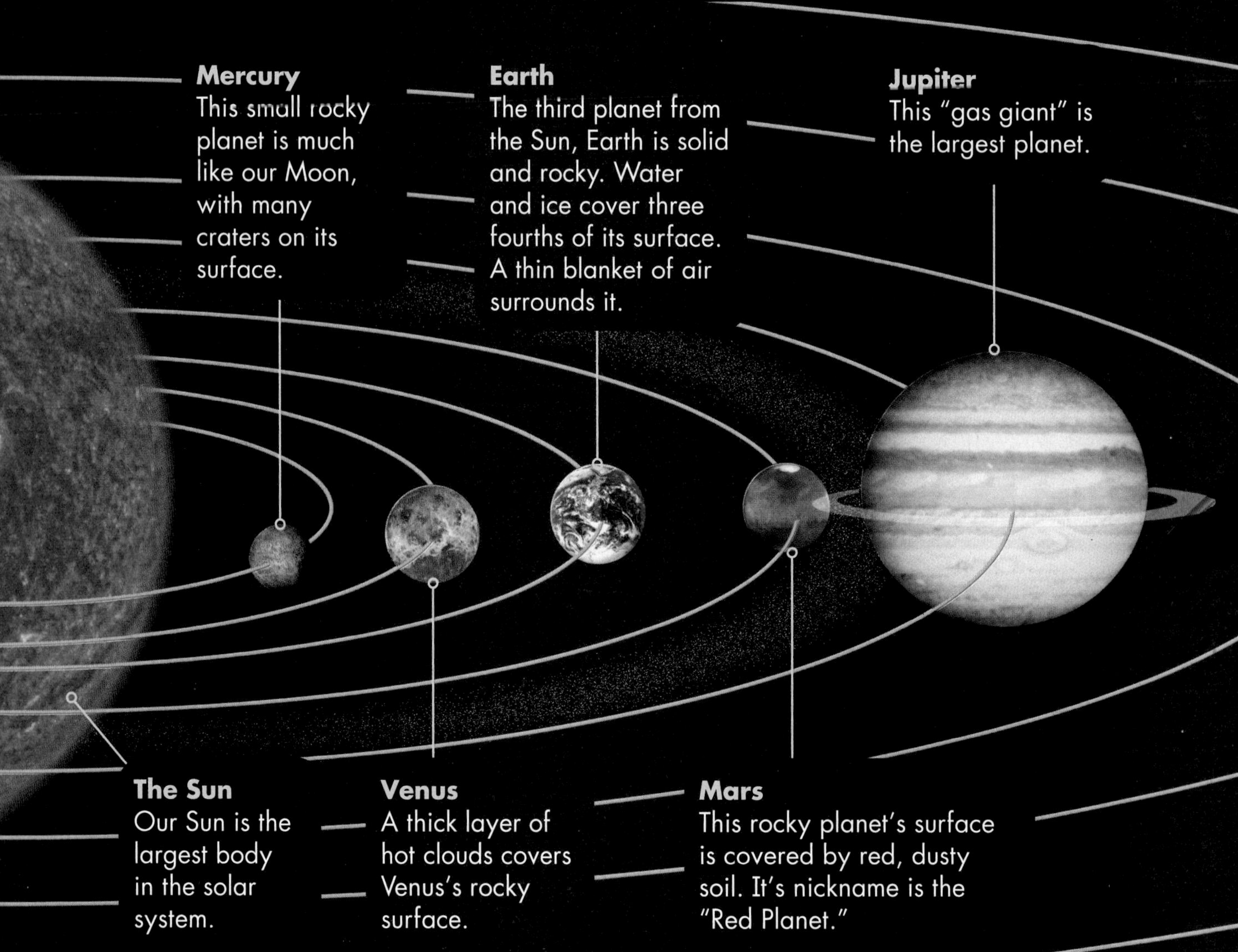

Mercury
This small rocky planet is much like our Moon, with many craters on its surface.
Earth
The third planet from the Sun, Earth is solid and rocky. Water and ice cover three fourths of its surface. A thin blanket of air surrounds it.
Jupiter
This "gas giant" is the largest planet.
The Sun
Our Sun is the largest body in the solar system.
Venus
A thick layer of hot clouds covers Venus's rocky surface.
Mars
This rocky planet's surface is covered by red, dusty soil. It's nickname is the "Red Planet."

The sizes and distances in this diagram are not true to scale. Also, the planets rarely line up. They are shown this way to fit on the page.

Planets closest to the Sun travel fastest in their orbits. Their orbits are also the smallest, so they can make a revolution most quickly. Planets farther away move more slowly and their orbits are longer, so their revolutions take many Earth years. In the solar system, distances are so great that scientists use a measure called Astronomical Units, or AU. One AU is the average distance between Earth and the Sun.

Pluto
This small rocky planet is the smallest and coldest in the Solar system. Usually it is the farthest from the Sun. Pluto is about the size of Earth's moon.

Neptune
Along with Jupiter and Saturn, this deep blue gas planet gives off more energy than it receives from the Sun.

Uranus
Methane gas gives this gas giant its blue-green color.

Two planetoids, bodies with about half the diameter of Pluto, have been discovered far beyond Pluto's orbit.

Saturn
All the gas planets have rings of rock, dust, and ice, and Saturn has the most. The rings of the other gas giants are very faint and hard to see. Saturn is the least dense of all the planets.

Planet Diameters

Planet	Diameter (compared to Earth)
Mercury	0.4
Venus	0.9
Mars	0.5
Jupiter	11.0
Saturn	10.0
Uranus	4.0
Neptune	4.0
Pluto	0.2

1. **Checkpoint** List the order of the planets from nearest to farthest from the Sun.
2. **Make Inferences** Why do the planets have years of different lengths?

Visiting the Planets

Did you ever wish you could visit a planet other than Earth? In the past 50 years, space probes have been used to explore the planets. **Space probes** are spacecraft that gather data without a crew. Space probes are equipped with scientific instruments and cameras. They collect information about the planet's properties.

Mercury, Venus, Earth, and Mars make up the inner planets of the solar system. They are closest to the Sun. Using space probes, scientists have learned that all four have rocky surfaces. The following are some other observations that have been made.

The space probe *Mariner 10* took this picture of Mercury's surface.

The Soviet space probe *Venera 7* sent pictures to Earth from Venus. It stopped working within an hour, however. Venus' hot temperatures—over 450°C—were too much for it.

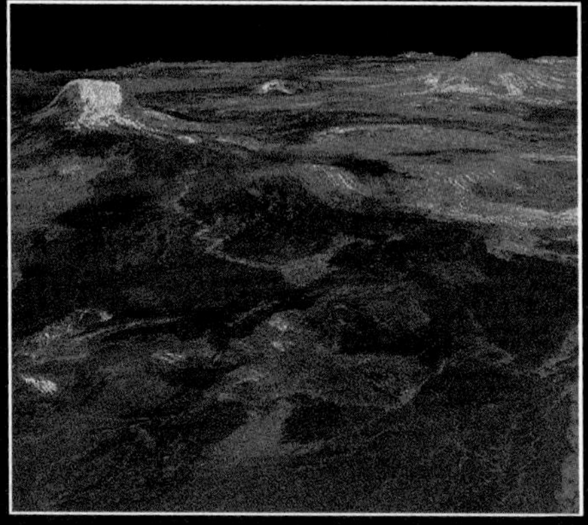

In 2004, two rovers, *Spirit* and *Opportunity*, were landed on opposite sides of Mars. They sent color pictures of Mars to Earth. They also collected data on soil and rocks and searched for evidence that water was once present.

Mercury

Scientists think that Mercury's core is $\frac{3}{4}$ iron. Mercury has almost no atmosphere. Its surface temperature changes from a low of about −170°C to a high of about 430°C.

Venus

Venus is the closest planet to Earth. Venus has a thick cloudy atmosphere made of poisonous gases. You cannot breathe it. The clouds trap the Sun's heat, so the temperature stays just as hot at night as in the day. They also reflect sunlight, adding to Venus' brightness.

Mars

Mars has a very thin atmosphere made mostly of carbon dioxide. Mars has polar ice caps of "dry ice"—solid carbon dioxide—and frozen water. Iron in its soil gives Mars reddish-orange color. Mars also has huge extinct volcanoes.

The Gas Giants

Beyond Mars are the four "gas giant" planets—Jupiter, Saturn, Uranus, and Neptune. They are called gas giants because they are mostly made of hydrogen, helium, and other gases. These planets all have many moons and rings. Powerful lightning storms were discovered on Jupiter.

Pluto and Beyond

A solid planet, Pluto is thought to be made of rock and ice. Its moon Charon is about half the size of Pluto. Some scientists prefer to call Pluto and Charon a "double planet." In 2005, scientists announced the discovery of a possible tenth planet beyond Pluto. When scientists determine whether the object is a planet, it will be given a name.

√ Lesson Checkpoint

1. Name the planets that have solid surfaces and give another detail about each.
2. **Math in Science** Use the table of planet diameters to construct a scale model showing the relative sizes of the planets.

Jupiter is known for its Great Red Spot, a circular storm.

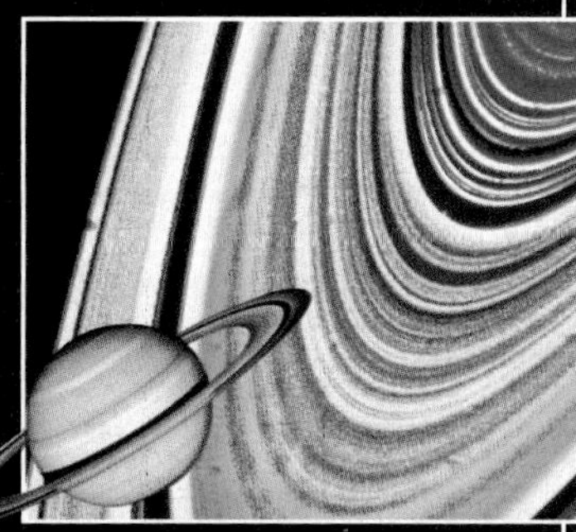

Saturn has thousands of rings of ice, rock, and dust that make up its ring system.

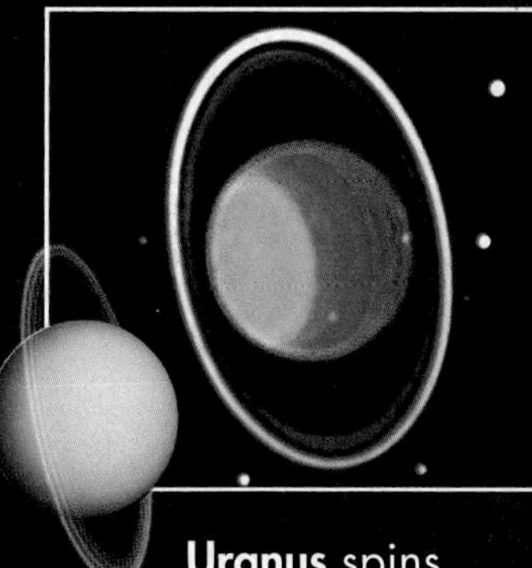

Uranus spins on its side.

Neptune has a huge circular storm, similar to Jupiter's.

Lesson 3

What are comets and asteroids?

Comets are icy objects that form a bright cloud and long tail as they orbit the Sun. Asteroids are rocky, odd-shaped objects, smaller than planets.

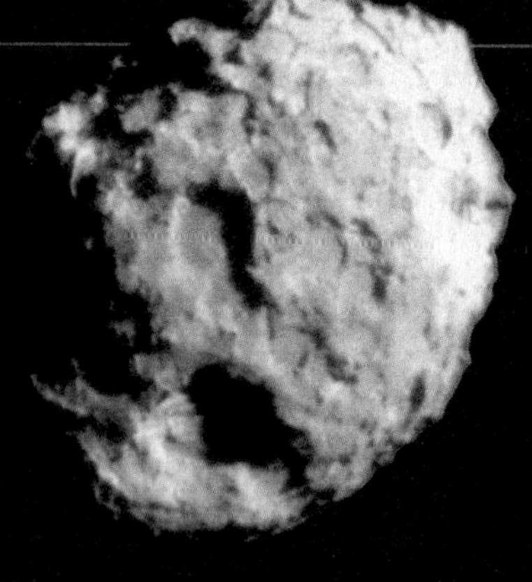

A comet's nucleus or core has an uneven shape. This photo of Comet Wild 2 was taken by the spacecraft *Stardust* in 2004. *Stardust* also collected the first ever samples of particles from a comet's coma.

Comets

A **comet** is a frozen mass of different types of ice and dust orbiting the Sun. Rocky matter may be frozen among the ice. Comets are much smaller than planets. They come from areas of the solar system beyond Pluto. Comets pass through the solar system in very stretched out and elliptical paths. Several comets a year may travel into the solar system and orbit the Sun. You may not see them, though. Only the largest comets can be seen without a telescope.

Discovering a comet is exciting. How can you discover one? Most comets today are found by people who use telescopes to photograph the sky each night, just before sunrise. The photos may show a fuzzy object. Another clue is that stars stay in the same relative position with other stars, but comets do not. If an unknown object keeps changing position compared with stars over a few hours or days, it might be a comet. If you are the first person to discover a comet, it could be named after you.

Nucleus The nucleus is very small, often only a few kilometers across. Scientists describe the nucleus as a "dirty snowball." It is made of dust and ice—frozen water and frozen gases. Over time, the nucleus becomes more and more black and solid. As water and gases evaporate from the surface, dark, heavy tar-like matter gets left behind.

Comet Halley is probably the most famous comet. It passes by the Sun about every 76 years. Its next pass will be in 2061. How old will you be?

A comet's tail points in different directions at different spots along its orbit.

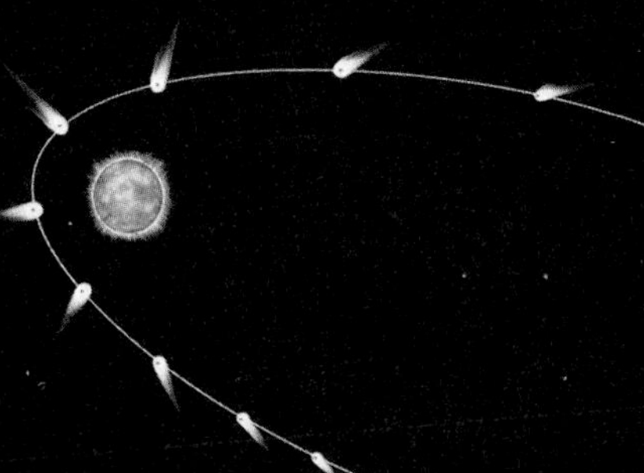

Two Tails Outward moving particles from the Sun, called solar wind, always push the two tails in a direction away from the Sun. The tails may extend up to 80 million kilometers long.

- **Ion tail** A comet's ion tail consists of various glowing charged gases. Ion tails are narrow and bluish.
- **Dust tail** Fine dust particles escape the nucleus as the ices melt. The dust tail is wide and yellowish. Dust particles are heavier than gas, so the dust tail may be seen in a different position than the ion tail.

Coma A giant cloud of dust and evaporated gases surrounds the nucleus. The coma may be larger than the size of Jupiter. The fine dust particles reflect sunlight brightly and the gases both absorb and glow with energy. The coma gives a comet its bright, fuzzy appearance. The coma and tail form only when the comet gets close enough for the Sun to melt the nucleus.

1. **Checkpoint** Describe a comet's orbit and the changes that occur to a comet during an orbit.
2. **Make Inferences** about how the size of a comet's tail changes during its orbit.

Asteroids

An **asteroid** is a rocky mass up to several hundred kilometers wide that revolves around the Sun. Asteroids are sometimes called minor planets. Most asteroids orbit in the *asteroid belt*, a region between Mars and Jupiter. Asteroids have uneven shapes. Some have smaller asteroids orbiting them. The smallest asteroids are pebble-sized. Most asteroids complete a revolution in three to six years.

Can Earth be hit by asteroids? It has happened, and you can see the huge craters that have been the result. Such collisions are very rare. Fortunately, Jupiter's gravity holds most asteroids in the area beyond Mars.

Most asteroids have odd shapes. This one looks like a light brown flying nose! The largest asteroids are nearly spherical in shape, with diameters of 250 to 1000 kilometers.

Asteroid Gaspra
Gaspra was one of the first asteroids to be studied up close. It is only 19 kilometers long and about 12 kilometers wide.

Asteroid Ida
Ida is in the main asteroid belt between Mars and Jupiter. Ida is about 58 kilometers long and 23 kilometers wide.

Asteroid Eros In 2001, Eros became the first asteroid to be orbited and landed upon by a spacecraft. Eros is 33 kilometers long and 13 kilometers thick. This image shows evidence of craters, boulders, and layers of rock.

Meteors, Meteoroids, and Meteorites

A meteoroid is a small asteroid. Meteoroids are boulder-sized or smaller. Most are the size of pebbles or grains of sand. Have you ever seen a shooting star? Shooting stars are not really stars, but are meteors. A meteor forms when a meteoroid hits the Earth's atmosphere. When a meteoroid shoots through the air, it heats up quickly. It gets so hot that it glows as a streak of light. Very bright meteors are called fireballs.

At certain times each year, meteor showers take place. These occur when the Earth passes through the orbit of a comet. You have read how a comet heats up and loses dust and rocky matter each time it orbits the Sun. These loose pieces remain in the comet's orbit. When these pieces collide with Earth's atmosphere, they become meteors.

Most meteors burn up before they hit Earth's surface. What happens if a meteor does not burn up completely? Some of it may fall to Earth. A meteorite is a piece of a meteor that lands on Earth. Most meteorites are quite small. The biggest known meteorite is in Namibia, Africa, and weighs 60 tons.

On November 12, 1833, an intense meteor shower lit up the night sky and frightened people across the country. Although scientists were thrilled, many people believed that the world was about to end. How do you think the people in the picture felt?

A small meteorite left a crater 200 meters deep and 1,200 meters wide. It is located near Winslow, Arizona and is known as Meteor Crater.

✓ Lesson Checkpoint

1. Describe two differences between comets and asteroids.
2. Explain at least two ways that comets and asteroids can affect the Earth.
3. Writing in Science **Narrative** Suppose you saw the meteor shower of 1833. Write an entry in your **science journal** narrating the event and describing people's reactions.

Lesson 4

What is known about the Moon?

You might not have seen a planet, but you have surely seen Earth's Moon. It is our closest neighbor, about 384,000 km (238,000 miles) from Earth. That sounds far away, but in space, it's quite close. Mars is about 150 times as far away.

Traveling with Earth

The Moon is the only object in the solar system other than Earth that humans have visited. Unlike Earth, it has no air or water, although some water ice has been found in craters. The ice probably came from comets that crashed onto its surface. The Moon is about one-fourth Earth's size. As moons go, that's fairly large.

The Moon, Earth's only natural satellite, travels in an orbit around the Earth. A **satellite** is a moon, rock, or anything that orbits another object. You probably have heard of satellites that send TV and phone signals from place to place. These satellites also orbit Earth, but they are human-made, not natural.

The Moon's spherical shape shows in this picture of the Moon's "near side," the half facing the Earth.

The Moon's Surface

These photos of the Moon show evidence of craters, valleys, mountains, and flat, smooth plains. The craters were caused by crashes of rocks or comets from space. They last for millions of years because no air or water wears them away. However, "moonquakes" sometimes occur. The smooth areas formed long ago as lava from inside the Moon flowed over huge areas of its surface.

Looking at the Moon

You can see some features of the Moon's surface with just your eyes. Using field glasses or a telescope, you would see even more. From Earth, we see only the "near side" of the Moon. The same side always faces Earth because the Moon's spin and orbit happen at the same rate. That is, it takes about 27 days for the Moon to revolve around the Earth, and the same amount of time for the Moon to rotate once. Astronauts have seen the "far side" of the Moon, however.

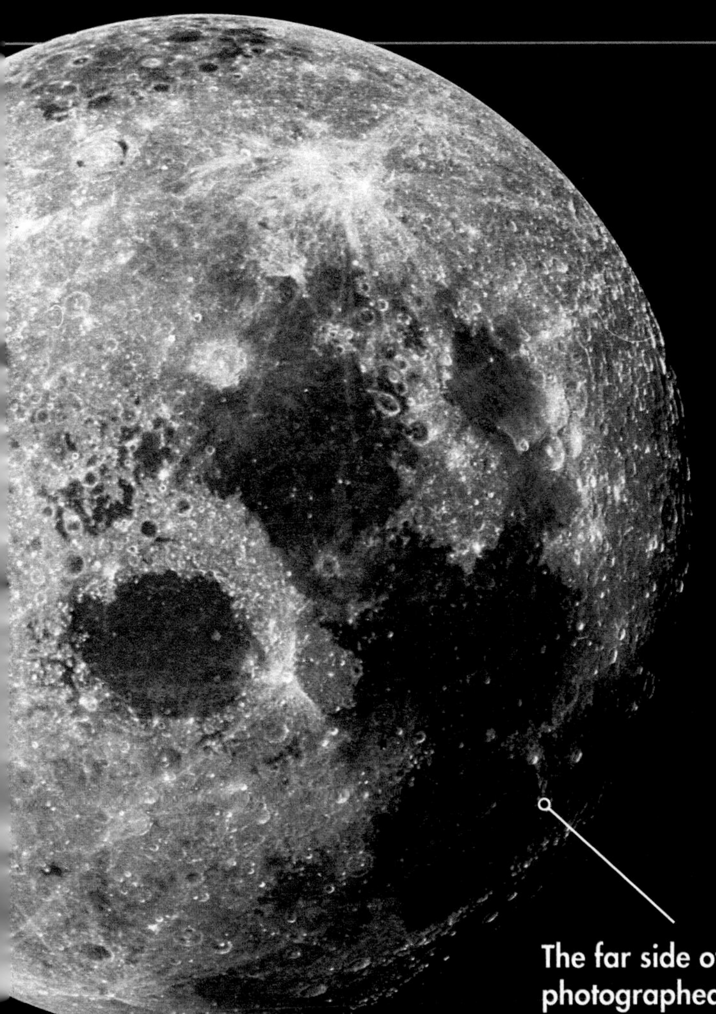

The far side of the Moon, photographed by a space probe.

Visiting the Moon

For thousands of years, people wondered what the Moon was really like. In 1969, U.S. astronaut Neil Armstrong became the first human to walk on the Moon. Between 1969 and 1972, a total of 12 people walked on the Moon.

1. **√ Checkpoint** Why do we not see the "far side" of the Moon?
2. **Social Studies in Science** Do research to learn the first words spoken when Neil Armstrong stepped on the moon. What did he mean?

Phases of the Moon

Thousands of years ago, people made up stories to explain why the Moon's appearance changes. Now, we have more understanding about the Moon. Someone might say, "The Moon is shining brightly tonight." You know that the person means the Moon glows with a silvery light.

People also say that the Sun shines. But how is sunshine different from moonlight? The Sun gives off its own light. That light beams out in all directions. The Moon does not make its own light. It only reflects light from the Sun.

The Moon, Earth, and other bodies in the solar system receive light on the side facing the Sun. In space, these bodies look "lit up" only on one side. **Moon phases** are the shapes of the lit side of the Moon we can see. Look at the diagram on page 559 to see how this works.

According to the calendar below, was this Moon view taken just before or just after a new Moon? How can you tell?

A Month of Changes

This cycle of phases is due to the movements of the Moon and Earth. Sometimes we see a whole circle. Sometimes we see a half circle. Sometimes we see no Moon or only a slim crescent shaped like the letter C. Which days in this calendar show a crescent Moon?

Sunday	Monday	Tuesday	Wednesday	Thursday	Friday	Saturday
					1	2
3	4	5	6	7	8	9
10	11	12	13	14	15	16
17	18	19	20	21	22	23
24	25	26	27	28	29	30

View from Earth

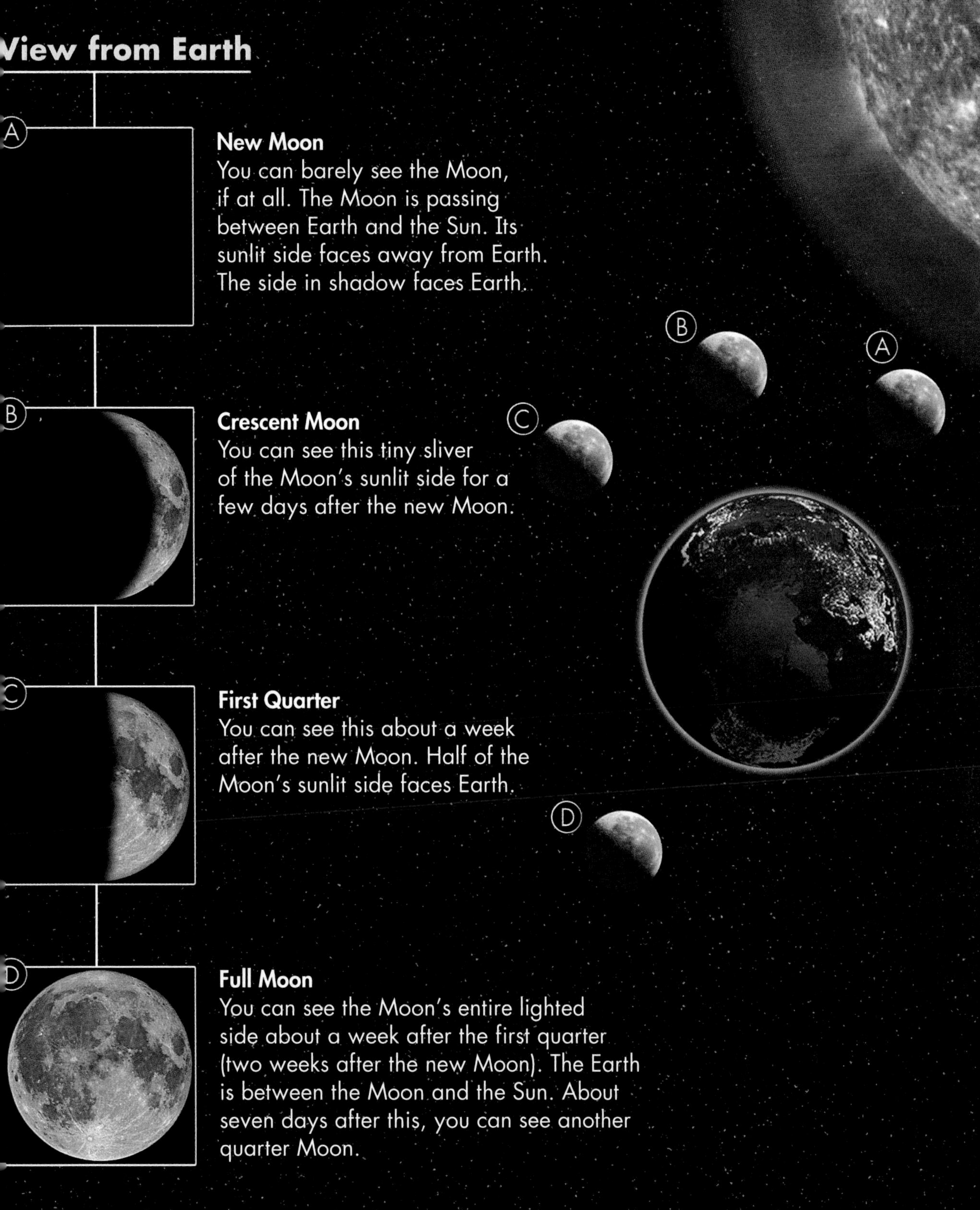

A
B
C
D
B
A
C
D

New Moon
You can barely see the Moon, if at all. The Moon is passing between Earth and the Sun. Its sunlit side faces away from Earth. The side in shadow faces Earth.

Crescent Moon
You can see this tiny sliver of the Moon's sunlit side for a few days after the new Moon.

First Quarter
You can see this about a week after the new Moon. Half of the Moon's sunlit side faces Earth.

Full Moon
You can see the Moon's entire lighted side about a week after the first quarter (two weeks after the new Moon). The Earth is between the Moon and the Sun. About seven days after this, you can see another quarter Moon.

1. **Checkpoint** Are the Moon phases predictable? Why or why not?
2. **Infer** how the appearance of Earth would change if you watched it from the near side of the Moon for a month.

High and Low Tides

You may have seen waves washing in and out along a coastline. If you spent the entire day, you might notice that the waves reach higher and higher up the beach. Hours later, the waves do not reach as high on the rocks or beach. You would have seen both a high and a low tide. Most places on Earth have two high tides and two low tides each day.

What makes the oceans rise and fall this way? The Moon is the main cause of the tides. You have read how Earth's gravity pulls on the Moon. The Moon's gravity also pulls on the Earth. This effect of gravity causes the Earth's land, water, and atmosphere to bulge slightly toward the Moon. The Earth's oceans move more easily than the solid land. The water moves as a large mass dragged by the Moon as it circles the Earth.

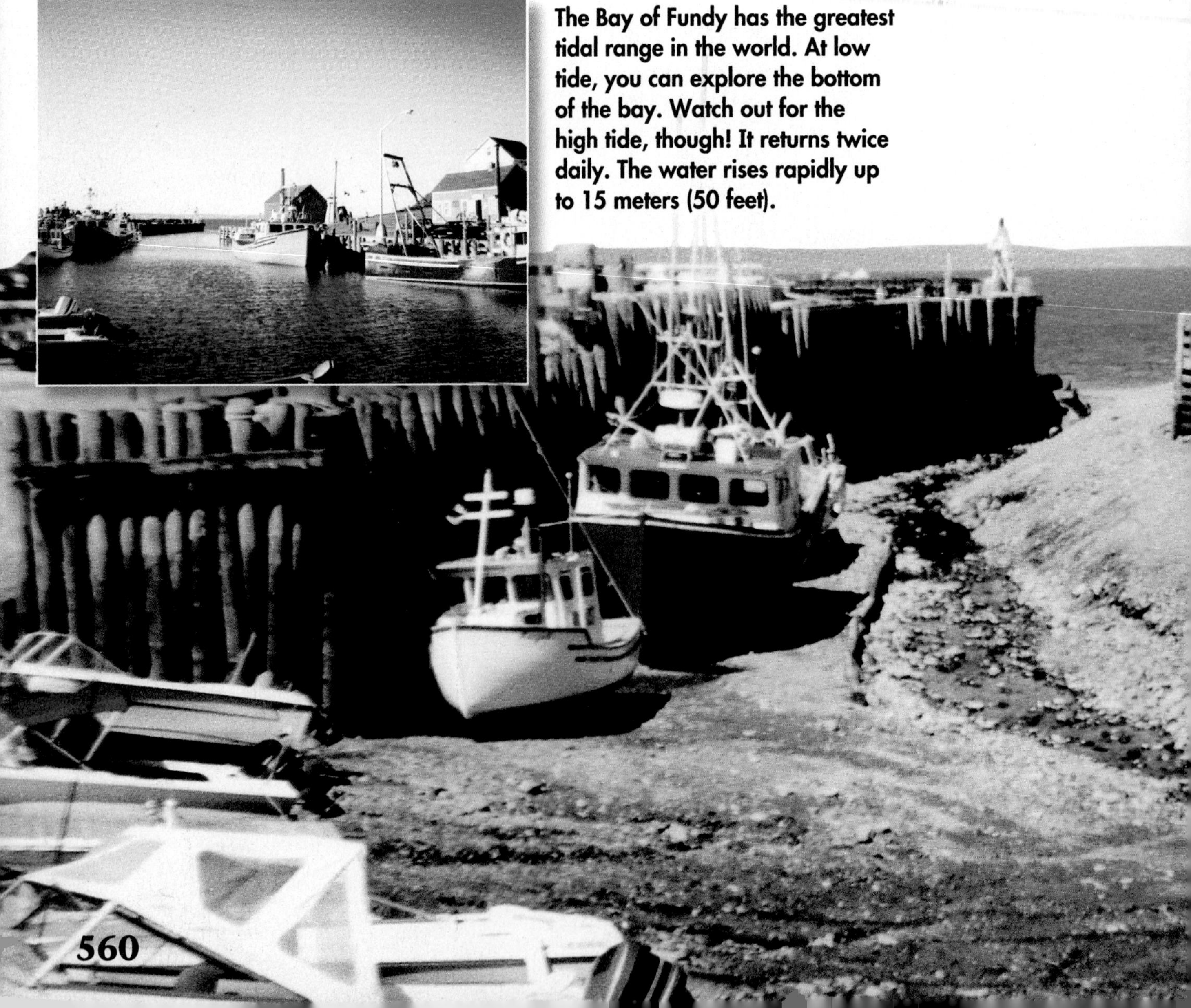

The Bay of Fundy has the greatest tidal range in the world. At low tide, you can explore the bottom of the bay. Watch out for the high tide, though! It returns twice daily. The water rises rapidly up to 15 meters (50 feet).

How high is a high tide compared to a low tide? The difference between high and low tide in the open ocean is about two feet. Near the coast, however, the difference can be much greater. The shapes of land masses and the ocean floor affect the tides. The average difference between high and low tide along coastal areas is less than two meters (six feet). In certain places, such as the Bay of Fundy in eastern Canada, the difference is much higher.

The Sun also has gravity that is strong enough to affect the tides. The Sun's effect is much smaller than the Moon's effect.

The system of the Moon and Earth is very complicated. Different aspects of this system work together to create a second tide that occurs on the side facing away from the Moon.

During a full Moon or new Moon, the Moon and Sun both exert tidal forces on the Earth along the same line. This causes the highest tides.

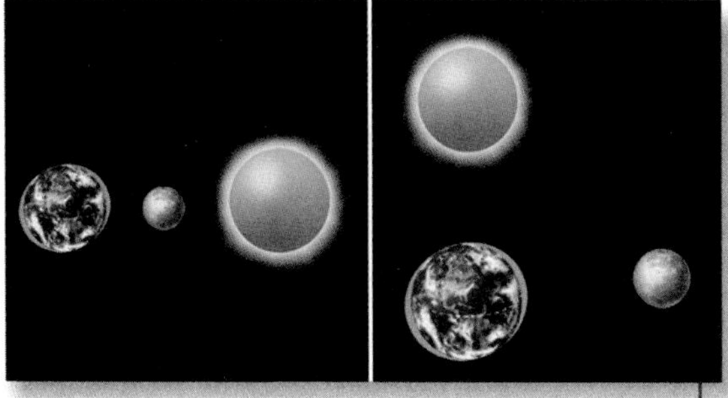

At the first quarter or third quarter Moon phase, the Moon and Sun form almost a 90° angle with the Earth. The Moon's tidal force is strongest, but the Sun does exert a weak tidal force on the Earth, in a direction perpendicular to the Moon's force. As a result, the ocean tides are low.

✓ Lesson Checkpoint

1. Which phases of the Moon bring the highest tides? What causes the high tides?
2. Describe 3 ways the Moon is different from Earth.
3. Writing in Science **Narrative** Observe the Moon every night for two weeks. In your **science journal,** draw a picture and write a description of your observations.

Lab zone Guided Inquiry

Investigate Why do we see the phases of the Moon?

Materials

shoe box with holes (prepared by teacher)

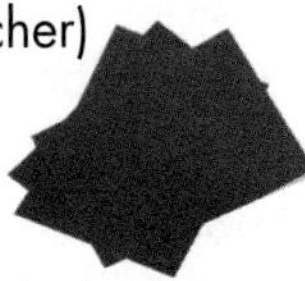

black paper

scissors

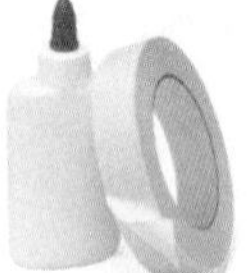

glue and tape

flashlight

table tennis ball, black thread, thumbtack

metric ruler

What to Do

1. Cover the inside of the box and the lid with black paper. Glue in place.

2. Make holes in the black paper where there are holes in the box. Label the small holes as *A*, *B*, *C*, and *D*.

3. Put the flashlight into the large hole and tape in place.

Hold the flashlight level or prop it up with a book.

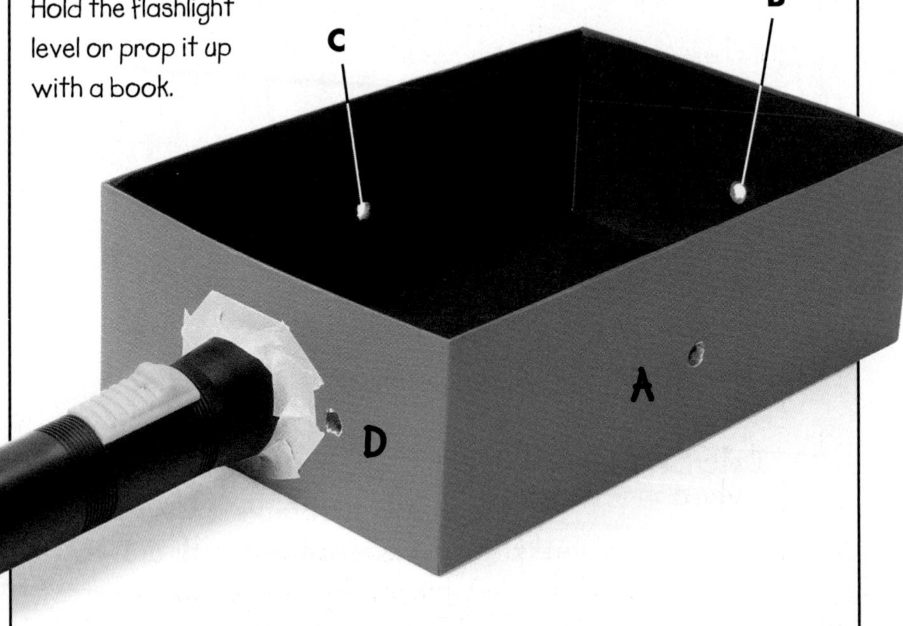
B
C
A
D

Process Skills

Making and using a model can help you understand why the phases of the Moon occur.

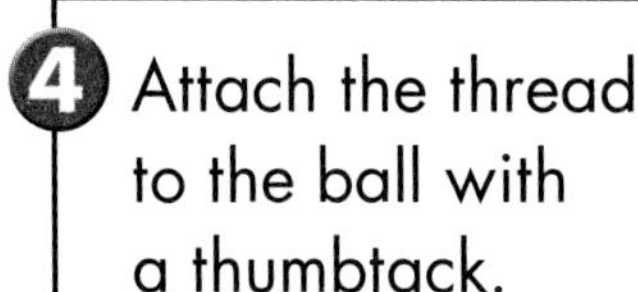

4. Attach the thread to the ball with a thumbtack.

about 4 cm

Tape the thread in place so the ball hangs down about 4 cm.

5. Look through each hole. Record your **observations.**

Phases of the Moon		
Hole	**Drawing of Moon Phase**	**Name of Moon Phase**
A	◑	
B		
C		
D		full Moon

C

B

A

D

Explain Your Results

1. In your **model**, your flashlight always lights half of the "moon." Why does the "moon" appear to be completely lighted when viewed through one hole?
2. Why does the "moon" not appear to be lighted when viewed through one hole?

Go Further

How could you change your model to show a crescent Moon? Develop a plan to answer this or any other question you may have.

Weight

Weight on Planets

How much does a dog weigh? That depends. Even the same dog would weigh a different amount on a different planet. Weight is the measure of gravity's pull on an object. Different planets have different amounts of gravitational pull.

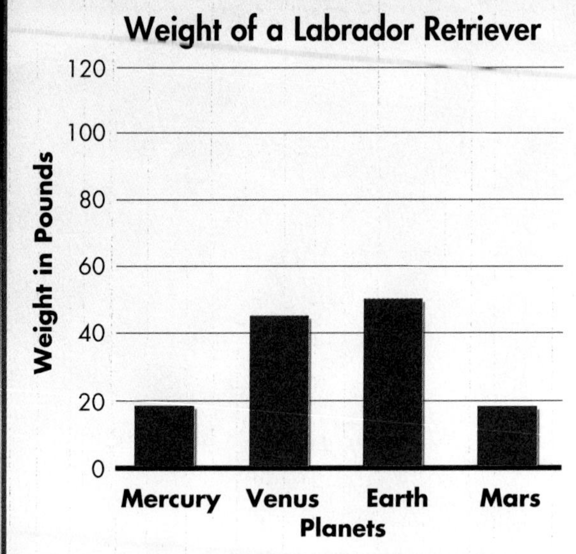
Weight of a Labrador Retriever
Weight in Pounds
120
100
80
60
40
20
0
Mercury
Venus
Earth
Mars
Planets

On Earth this full-grown Labrador Retriever weighs 50 pounds. But what if the dog was on Mercury? Mercury's gravitational pull is less than Earth's gravitational pull. The Labrador Retriever would weigh less on Mercury than it does on Earth. The bar graph shows that the Labrador Retriever would weigh less than 20 pounds on Mercury.

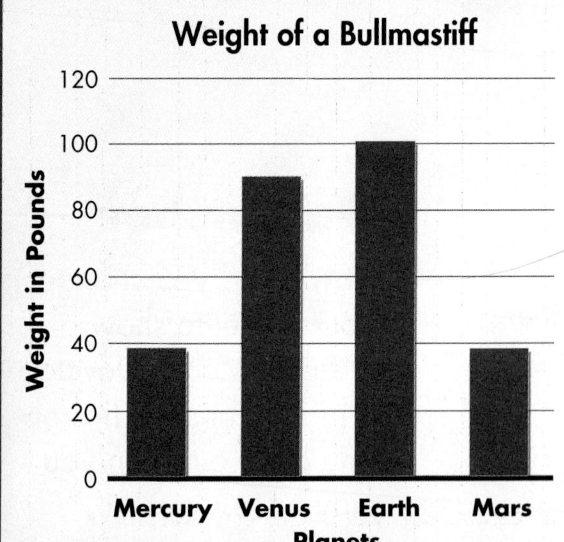
Weight of a Bullmastiff
Weight in Pounds
120
100
80
60
40
20
0
Mercury
Venus
Earth
Mars
Planets

A Bullmastiff is larger than a Labrador Retriever. This bar graph shows its weight on different planets.

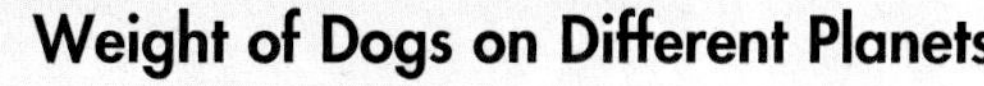
Weight of Dogs on Different Planets

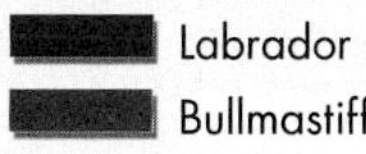
Labrador
Bullmastiff

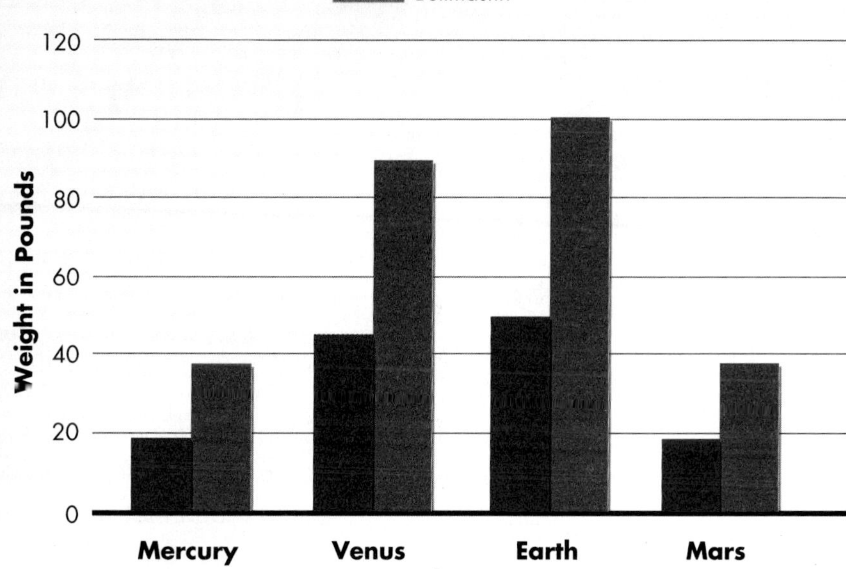
120
100
80
60
40
20
0
Weight in Pounds
Mercury
Venus
Earth
Mars
Planets

Use the double bar graph to answer the questions.

1. A Bullmastiff's weight on Venus is about what fraction of its weight on Earth?
2. A bag of dog food weighs 50 pounds on Earth. About how much does it weigh on Venus?
3. Which two planets have about the same gravitational pull? Explain.
4. On each planet, a Labrador's weight is about what fraction of a Bullmastiff's weight?

Lab zone Take-Home Activity

Look at the weights listed on labels of two foods that you have at home. Round each weight to the nearest ounce. List the weights in a chart. Estimate the weight of each item on the planets Mercury, Venus, and Mars. Record your estimates. Then make a double bar graph.

Chapter 17 Review and Test Prep

Use Vocabulary

asteroid (p. 554)	**rotation** (p. 544)
axis (p. 544)	**satellite** (p. 556)
comet (p. 552)	**solar system** (p. 543)
Moon phase (p. 558)	**space probe** (p. 550)
revolution (p. 543)	

Use the vocabulary word from the list above that completes each sentence.

1. The Moon is a natural _____ of Earth.
2. A planet spins around an imaginary line called its _____.
3. The most common place to find a(n) _____ is between Mars and Jupiter.
4. A(n) _____is an icy ball that has a very elliptical orbit around the Sun.
5. Earth's _____ on its axis causes day and night.
6. One kind of _____ is the crescent Moon.
7. One full orbit of an object around another object is called a _____.
8. The _____ has planets, moons, comets, and asteroids.
9. A spacecraft that does not carry people is a(n) _____.

Explaining Concepts

10. Explain Earth's position in the solar system and describe its closest neighbors.
11. Earth is slightly closer to the Sun during winter in the Northern Hemisphere. Explain why, even so, winter temperatures are colder here than those of summer.
12. Make a drawing like the one below. On your drawing, shade the side of the Moon that does not receive sunlight. Use your drawing to explain why the Moon has different phases.

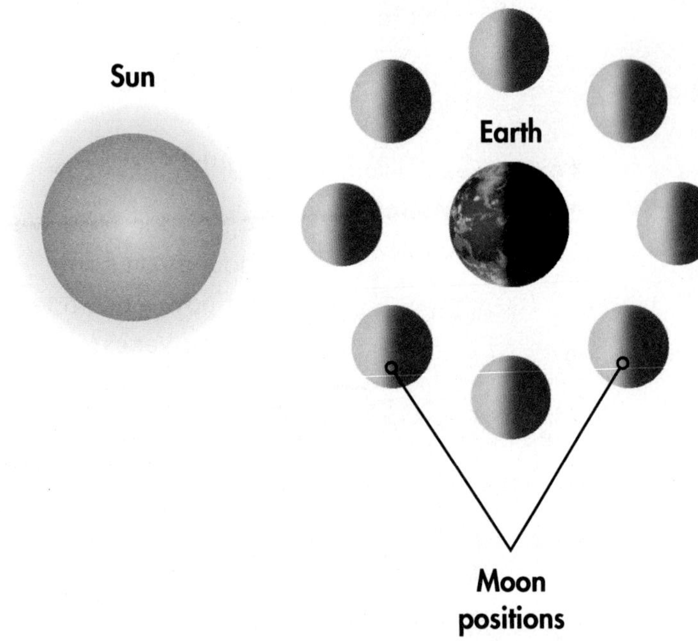
Sun
Earth
Moon positions

Process Skills

13. Infer what would happen to the seasons of the world if Earth's axis tilted in the opposite direction.

14. Predict You go outside on a clear night. The Moon looks like a half-circle. About a week later on another clear night, you go outside, and you cannot see the Moon. Predict how much of the Moon you will see after another week passes.

15. Model Make a model to show how the positions of the Earth, Moon, and Sun affect the tides on Earth.

Make Inferences

16. Make a graphic organizer like the one shown below. Use the facts given to make an inference.

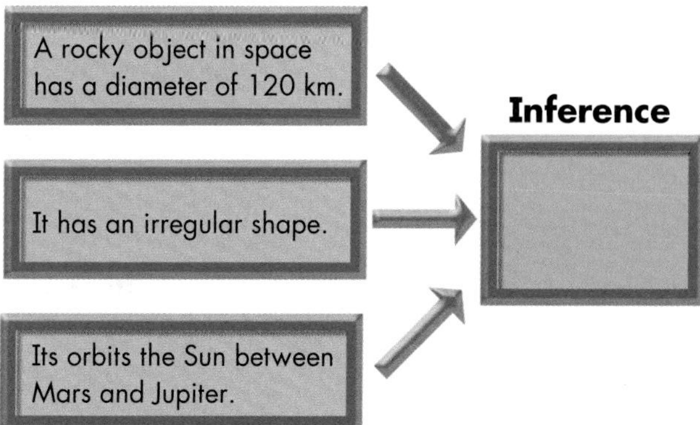
Facts
A rocky object in space has a diameter of 120 km.
It has an irregular shape.
Its orbits the Sun between Mars and Jupiter.
Inference

Test Prep

Choose the letter that best completes the statement or answers the question.

17. Earth and the other planets closest to the Sun are made mostly of

Ⓐ gas.
Ⓑ metal.
Ⓓ water.
Ⓔ rock.

18. What evidence indicates that Earth's axis is tilted?

Ⓕ A year lasts 365 days.
Ⓖ Day and night takes place.
Ⓗ The Moon has four phases.
Ⓘ The year has different seasons.

19. Explain why the answer you chose for Question 18 is best. For each of the answers you did not choose, give a reason why it is not the best choice.

20. Writing in Science **Descriptive**
Suppose that you are an astronaut taking a trip to the Moon. Write a paragraph describing what you see when you arrive. Include what you see on the surface of the Moon and what you see in the sky.

NASA
Biography

Jose Hernandez
MISSION SPECIALIST

NASA
JOSE HERNANDEZ

Jose Hernandez was a high school student working in a farm field and listening to his radio. A news story about astronauts fascinated him. At that very moment, he decided to fly into space. "I was already interested in science and engineering," he remembers. "And that's something I've been striving for each day since then."

Jose did not speak English until he was 12 years old. He grew up in a family of migrant farm workers from Mexico. Every spring, the family traveled throughout California, picking fruits and vegetables along the way. They worked on the farms until December. Jose went to school during the week and worked on the farms on the weekends.

Jose's parents encouraged all their children to study hard and to go to college. Jose Hernandez graduated from college and went to a university to learn more about engineering. He then worked at a laboratory where he helped develop a tool to detect cancer.

Mr. Hernandez has also worked as an engineer for NASA. He has helped provide materials for the Space Shuttle and International Space Station. But now, he has reached a goal that he has been striving for since he was in high school.

He is an astronaut, and is training to go to the Moon.

Lab zone Take-Home Activity

Write a TV news report about astronauts exploring the Moon. Include questions that a reporter on Earth might ask the astronauts. Include the astronauts' answers to the questions.

Chapter 18

Technology in Our Lives

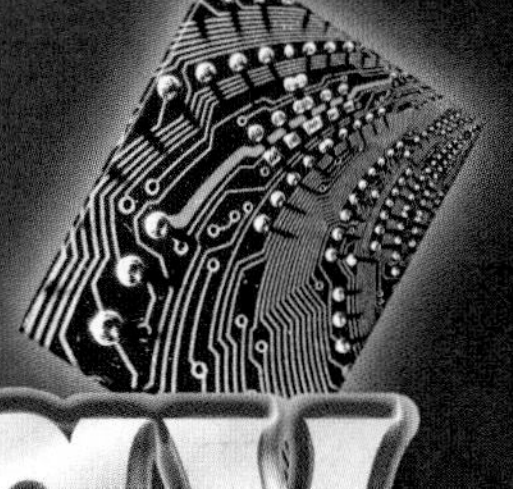

You Will Discover

- how technology is used in our jobs and homes.
- how technology has changed transportation.
- the uses of computer technology.
- how technology is used in space.

Discovery Channel School
Student DVD
Discovery Channel School
online
Student Edition
sfsuccessnet.com

Build Background

How does technology affect our lives?

technology

manufacturing
assembly line

Chapter 18 Vocabulary

technology page 575

inventor page 575

manufacturing page 578

assembly line page 578

microchip page 584

World Wide Web page 585

space station page 590

inventor

An inventor is someone who uses technology to develop a new device or process, or to solve a problem.

World Wide Web

The World Wide Web is a computer-based network of computers.

microchip

space station

Lab zone Directed Inquiry

Explore How can water be absorbed?

Materials

safety goggles

cup with 5 mL of water absorber

water and graduated cylinder (or measuring cup)

calculator or computer (optional)

Process Skills

You make a **prediction** when you use **observations** and experience to make an **inference** about an expected result.

What to Do

1. Obtain a cup with 5 mL of water absorber. **Predict** if it will soak up 50 mL of water.

2. **Measure** 50 mL of water and slowly pour it into the cup. Wait 1 minute.

Be careful!

Wear safety goggles.
Protect your skin.
Wash your hands when finished.

3. Turn the cup upside down on the table. **Observe.**

Optional: Predict how much more water the absorber can soak up—10 mL, 20 mL, or 30 mL more. Design, write, and carry out a procedure to find out.

Explain Your Results

1. For step 3, find the ratio shown:

$$\text{ratio} = \frac{\text{volume of water (mL)}}{\text{volume of absorber (mL)}}$$

2. **Infer** Based on your **observations** and experience, why do you think disposable diapers contain a water absorber?

How to Read Science

Reading Skills

TARGET SKILL

Sequence

Sequence refers to the order of events.

- Sometimes writers use clue words such as *first, next, after,* and *finally* to signal sequence.
- Keeping track of dates on a time line will help you keep events in their correct sequence.

Science Article

When Technology Was New

When you think of technology, you may think of some new gadget that was just invented. When you think about it, though, every manufactured item was new at one time. Roller skates were a new technology in the 1760s. Skateboards were new in 1958. Parents were thrilled by the new technology of disposable diapers in 1950. Telephone answering machines were the latest high-tech device way back in 1898.

Apply It!

Make a graphic organizer like the one shown at the right. Put the names of the inventions in the correct **sequence.** You may want to **predict** what will be invented this year

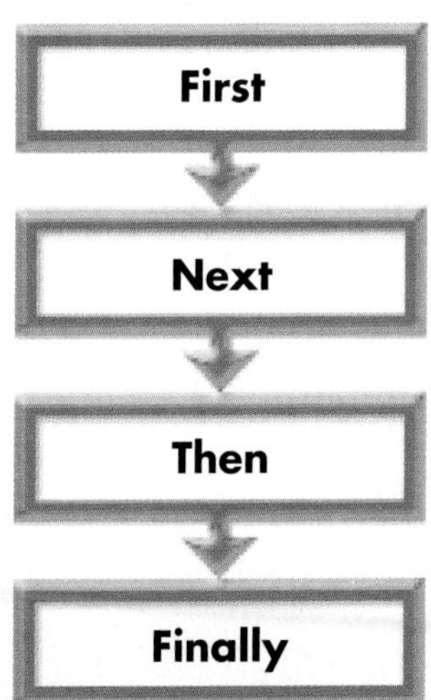
First
Next
Then
Finally

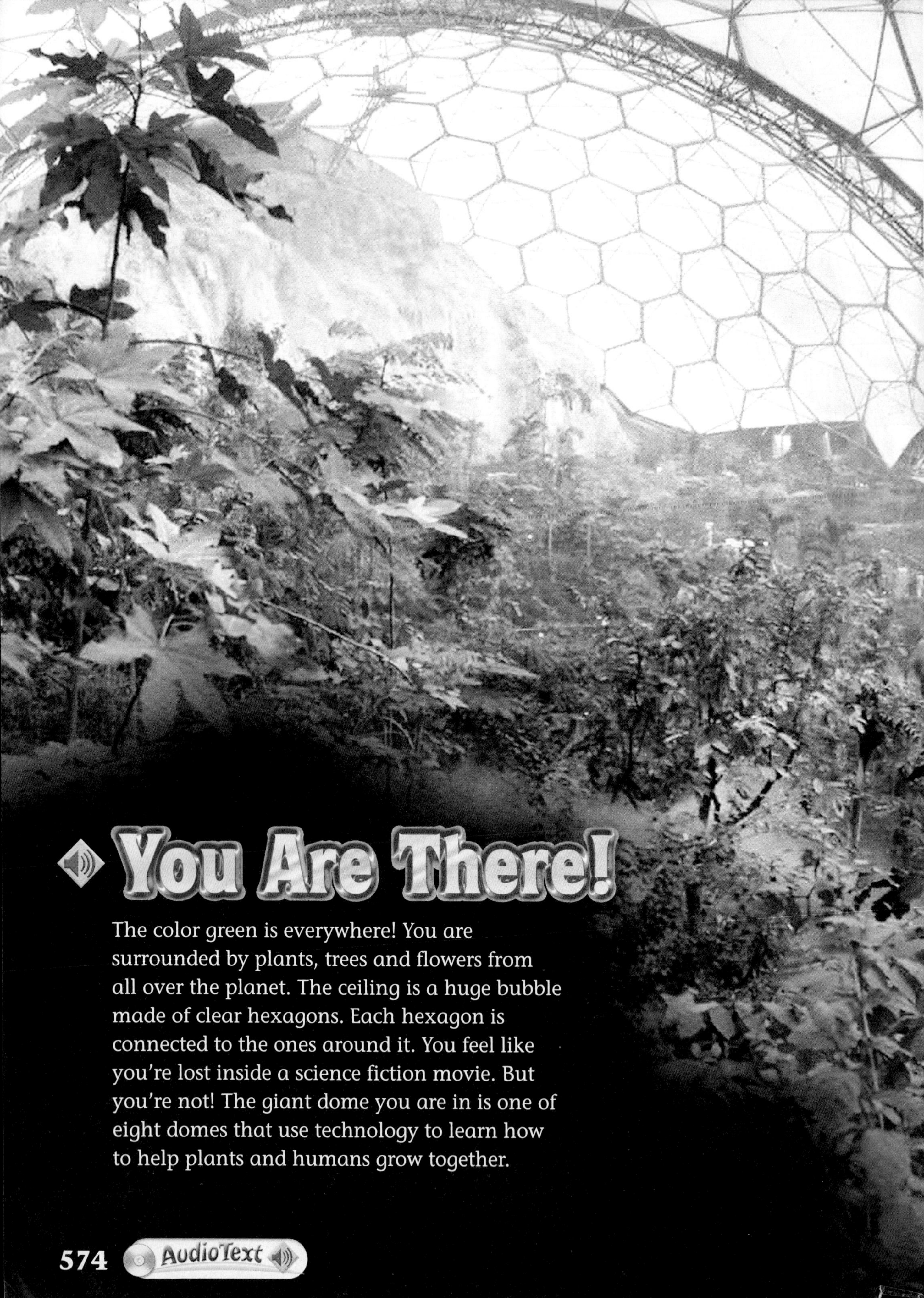

You Are There!

The color green is everywhere! You are surrounded by plants, trees and flowers from all over the planet. The ceiling is a huge bubble made of clear hexagons. Each hexagon is connected to the ones around it. You feel like you're lost inside a science fiction movie. But you're not! The giant dome you are in is one of eight domes that use technology to learn how to help plants and humans grow together.

AudioText

Lesson 1

What is technology?

Technology helps people find ways for doing things faster and better. Inventions, machines, and gadgets are the result of technology.

Technology and Inventions

People constantly gain knowledge and make new discoveries. These discoveries and knowledge use technology to make tasks easier, faster, or more efficient. **Technology** is the use of scientific knowledge for a purpose. An **inventor** is someone who uses technology to develop a new device or process, or to solve a problem. Some famous inventors, like George Washington Carver, worked alone to find hundreds of uses for peanuts, soybeans, and sweet potatoes. Other inventors, like Thomas Edison, set up a whole team of people to help develop new inventions. There is much more to technology than new devices and gadgets.

Technology can also be used to make changes in the way we do things. Sometimes these changes are positive. For example, technology for building roads and bridges makes it possible to carry goods to people living in far away places. But technology can also have negative effects. Many machines and processes resulting from technology pollute the air, water, and soil. It is important that scientists who develop new technologies determine the effect of their inventions on others.

1. √ **Checkpoint** What are some positive and negative effects of technology?
2. **Math in Science** Use a stopwatch to time yourself writing a paragraph on a word processor or typewriter. Record your time. Now time yourself writing the same paragraph by hand. How much different was your time using the word processor?

The Eden Project, the world's largest greenhouse, opened in Cornwall, England in 2001. The Eden Project uses technology to develop better ways of growing plants.

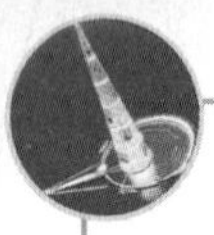

Technology and Our Homes

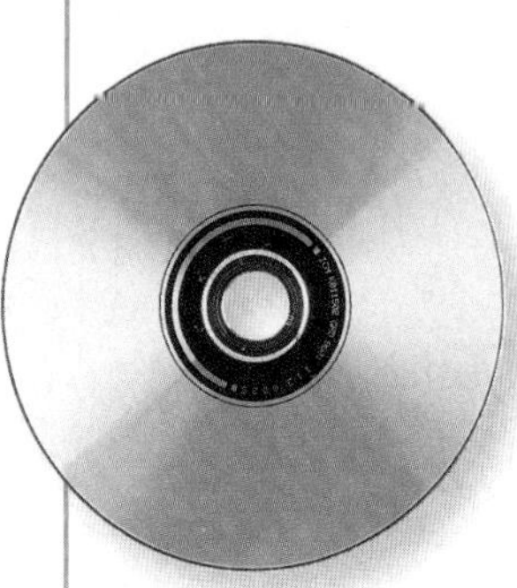

Some inventions lead to other inventions. The CD changed the way people listen to music and how information is stored. It made the invention of DVDs possible.

Technology changes the environment outside our homes. But it also changes the environment that we call our homes.

Not all technology in the home is new, and not all technology involves computers. We have become used to seeing and using technology in our homes. A pair of scissors is a result of technology. Every light that you turn on in your home is also the result of technology.

Technology makes it easier and more convenient to do many things in the home. Cellular telephones make communicating with others easier. Dishwashers get dishes and eating utensils clean. Microwave ovens cook food in less time than regular ovens. Some alarm clocks use tiny computers for pre-setting times. Calculators use electric circuits to help us solve difficult math problems. Thermostats can maintain or change the temperature inside the home.

We use technology for entertainment purposes too. Televisions, radios, video games, and CD players are all results of technology. CD technology led to the development of DVDs.

Technology can be used to develop new materials for building inexpensive places to live, like yurts, shown above, and mobile homes.

The way people keep and store food has been improved by technology. Refrigerators and freezers offer a healthy way of storing food for long periods of time. Even plastic containers, an inexpensive technology, improve health by offering an airtight way of storing food.

Technology has not just changed what is in our homes. It has also changed what we call home. Technology can be used to create amazing towers that reach high in the sky. Technology can also create affordable housing such as mobile homes and tent-like yurts.

1. **√ Checkpoint** Give two examples of technology that you use in the home every day. What problems did these technologies solve?
2. **Math in Science** At the beginning of this century, about 99% of all households in the United States owned a color television. If a city had 40,000 households, how many had color televisions?

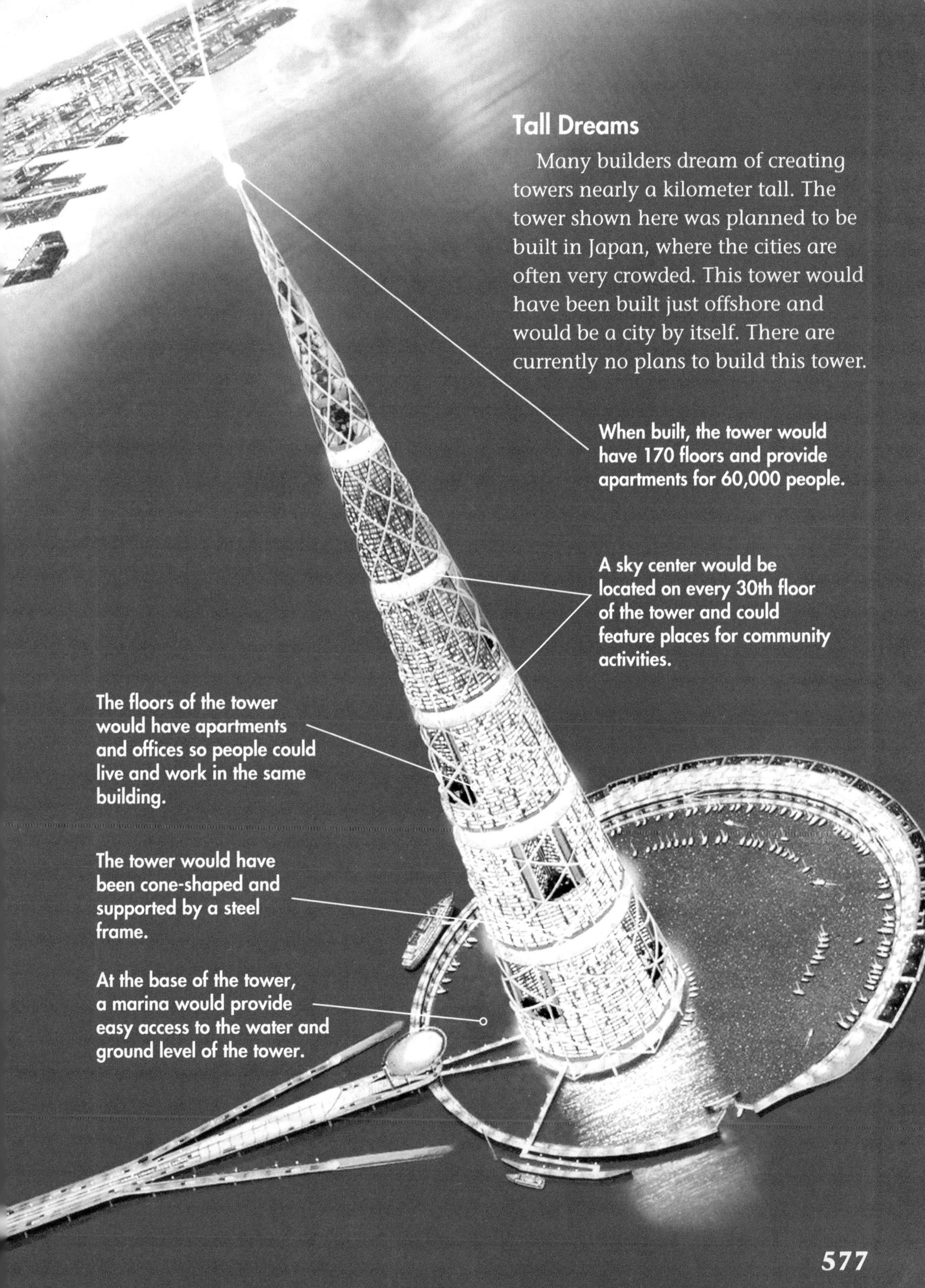
When built, the tower would have 170 floors and provide apartments for 60,000 people.
A sky center would be located on every 30th floor of the tower and could feature places for community activities.
The floors of the tower would have apartments and offices so people could live and work in the same building.
The tower would have been cone-shaped and supported by a steel frame.
At the base of the tower, a marina would provide easy access to the water and ground level of the tower.

Tall Dreams

Many builders dream of creating towers nearly a kilometer tall. The tower shown here was planned to be built in Japan, where the cities are often very crowded. This tower would have been built just offshore and would be a city by itself. There are currently no plans to build this tower.

BE 2789

Technology and Our Jobs

Technology often changes the way jobs are done. When this occurs, an entire society can be changed in a big way!

One example of the way technology changed the way people live has to do with manufacturing. **Manufacturing** is the production of goods on a large scale. In the early 1900s, cars were built one at a time by one group of workers until the car was finished. Because this process was slow and expensive, most people could not afford to buy a car.

A man named Henry Ford solved this problem by using an assembly line. In an **assembly line,** a product, such as a car, moves through the factory while workers add parts to it. This new process was quicker and less expensive than the old way of building cars. It also allowed more people to buy cars. This revolutionized society and the standard of living in the United States. The assembly line is used today to manufacture many products in less time.

In today's assembly lines, robots and other machines are often used to build and add parts. This kind of assembly line is cheaper and is often more mistake-proof than using people. The negative effect is that many people lose their jobs to machines.

The Model T Ford was the first car produced on an assembly line developed by Henry Ford.

Gas engines and electric motors continued to change the way people and goods were transported. Modern ships use diesel engines to generate power for the electric motors that propel them.

Today electric motors are used on some trains and cars. Magnetic force technology may be used in the future to power many trains.

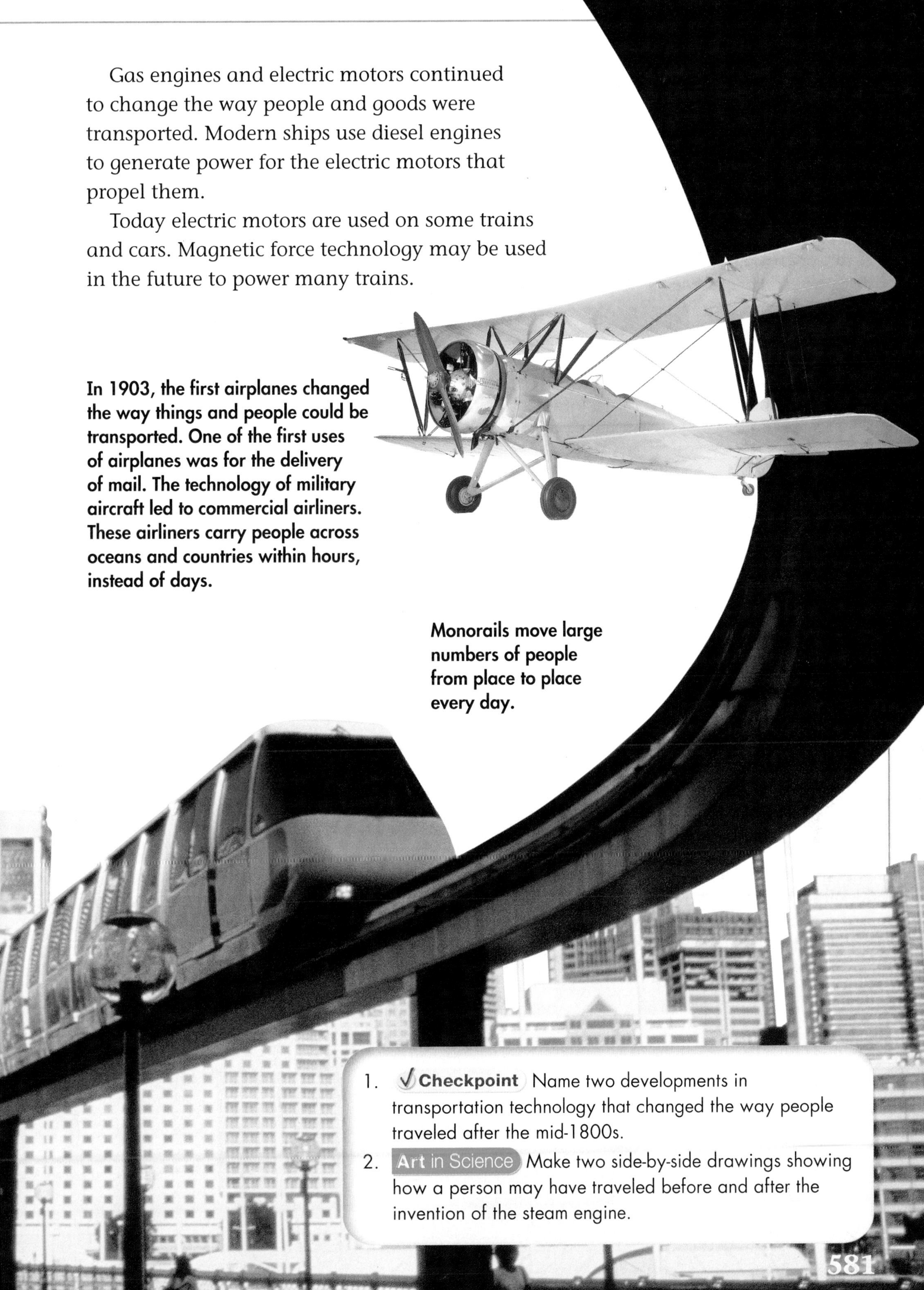

In 1903, the first airplanes changed the way things and people could be transported. One of the first uses of airplanes was for the delivery of mail. The technology of military aircraft led to commercial airliners. These airliners carry people across oceans and countries within hours, instead of days.

Monorails move large numbers of people from place to place every day.

1. **✓Checkpoint** Name two developments in transportation technology that changed the way people traveled after the mid-1800s.
2. **Art in Science** Make two side-by-side drawings showing how a person may have traveled before and after the invention of the steam engine.

Cars were much less safe years ago. Now the frames of cars are designed to better protect the passengers during collisions. Seat belts are in every car, and airbags cushion the driver and passengers in the event of an accident.

Technology May Bring Problems

The gasoline engine has brought about many positive changes to society. Ambulances, taxis, and tractors all use gasoline engines to run. Taxis transport people around busy cities, ambulances take people to hospitals, and tractors help farmers grow crops. But the development of gasoline-powered cars has also created new problems, such as pollution and safety. Science and imagination have solved some of these problems while others still exist.

New technology can often mean new problems. Car designers and engineers are trying to find the best way to make their product useful, comfortable, and affordable. Materials must be strong but flexible, and the car must be just the right size and shape.

Cars built today have hard, strong, and flexible bodies for protection against collisions.

The gasoline that most cars use to run comes from petroleum, or crude oil. The process that brings crude oil to markets is complex and expensive. Accidents in this process can lead to huge problems such as this oil spill. Some cars now run on electricity or fuels other than those that come from crude oil.

Early cars had only dusty bumpy roads on which to drive. As a result, cars wore out quickly and could not go very fast. Today's roads are smooth and paved. Cars last longer and go faster, but wider, smoother roads also mean more cars, and lots of traffic jams.

Today's cars are big enough for comfort, but not so big that they are difficult to maneuver on city streets. Controls are easy and comfortable for the driver to use.

Pollution from gasoline engines is a problem. Cars are now designed to pollute less than they did years ago. Gasoline has ingredients in it that help reduce some pollution. Still, pollution from cars remains a problem in many areas.

Rubber is used for tires because it is flexible enough to handle potholes in roads without harming the car and strong enough to last a long time.

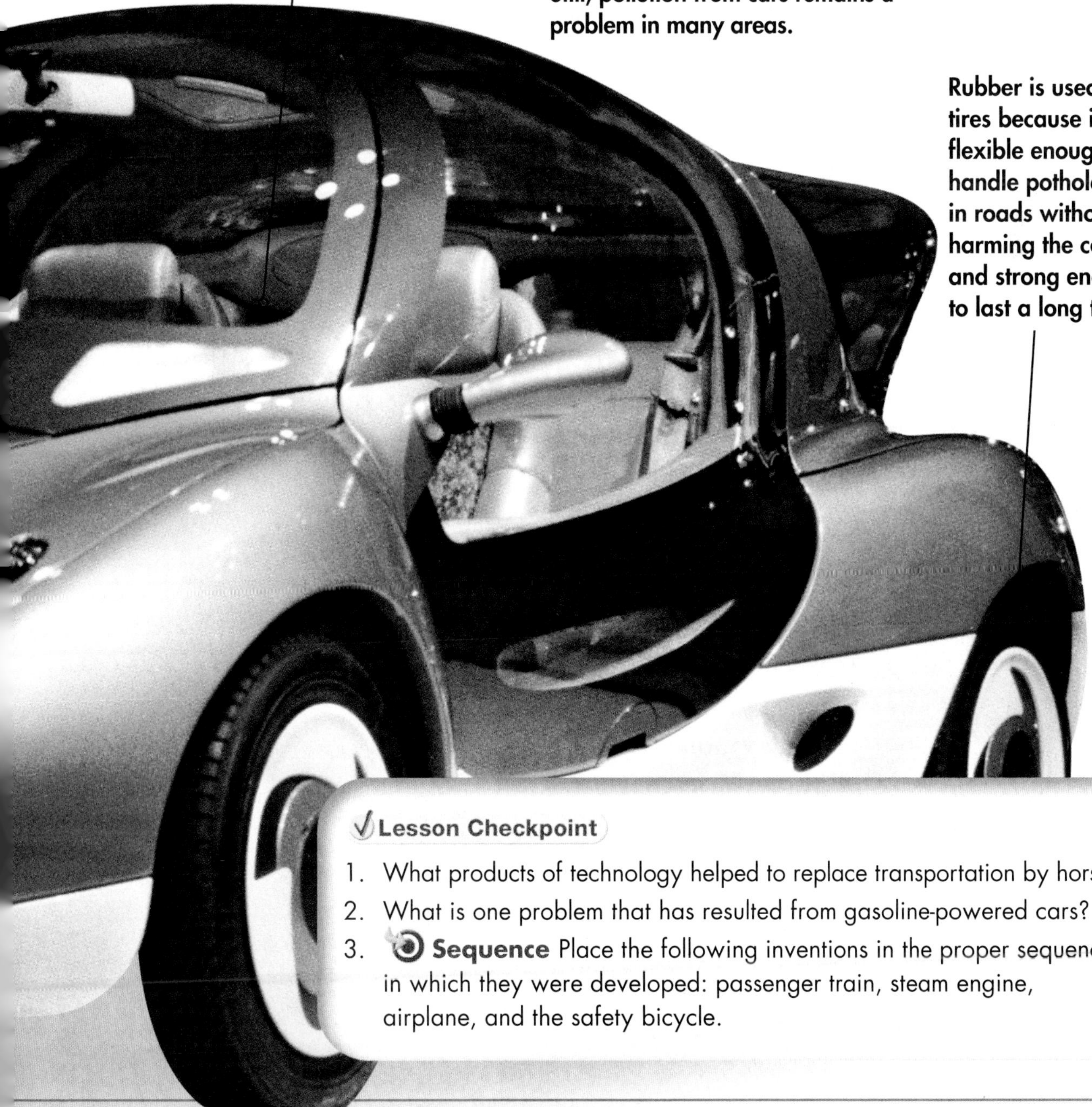

√ Lesson Checkpoint

1. What products of technology helped to replace transportation by horse?
2. What is one problem that has resulted from gasoline-powered cars?
3. **Sequence** Place the following inventions in the proper sequence in which they were developed: passenger train, steam engine, airplane, and the safety bicycle.

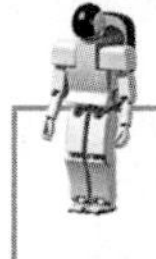

Lesson 3

How have computers changed society?

For many centuries, inventors and scientists tried to make a machine that could calculate. The earliest known effort is the abacus, dating back to 1100 B.C.

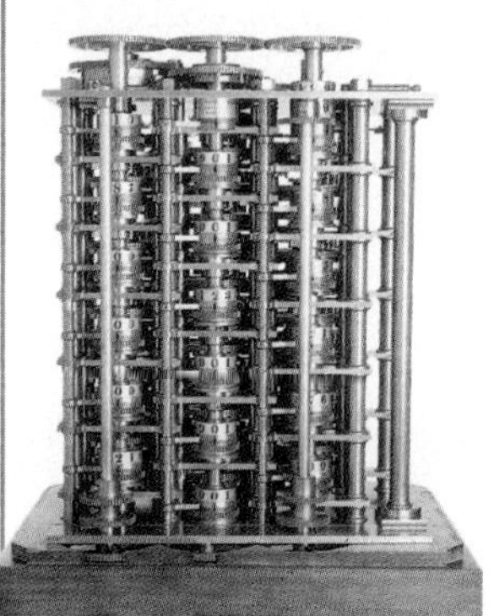

Charles Babbage, a British inventor, began building a type of mechanical computer in the 1820s. Although he was not able to finish it, scientists in 1991 used Babbage's notes and drawings to complete a working computer. The machine perfectly calculates up to 31 digits.

Electronic Computers

The 1930s and 1940s were the beginning of computer technology. These early computers replaced mechanical parts with electrical parts, but used the same basic steps as today's computers—input, processing, output, and feedback—to solve mathematical problems. Early computers were so large that most of them filled entire rooms and weighed thousands of pounds.

Abacus

The large size and high cost of early computers made them impractical for most people. Computer manufacturers became aware of the need for smaller, faster, and less expensive computers. One of the most important developments in computer technology was the microchip. A **microchip** is a small piece of a computer that contains microscopic circuits. Microchips make it possible for computers to process information very quickly. They also made the cost of buying a computer much lower.

UNIVAC (Universal Automatic Computer) was built in the United States in 1951. UNIVAC was the first electronic computer that was used for commercial purposes. UNIVAC took up a space of 943 cubic feet.

A microchip is usually less than 1 cm on each side. Computers use many types of microchips.

In the 1980s, computer technology was used to solve another problem. A British computer scientist wanted to make it easier for physicists to communicate with each other. The result was the World Wide Web. The **World Wide Web** is a computer-based network of computers. It was first developed for use by the European Organization for Nuclear Research. The first version of the Web was completed in 1990. Today, a person using a computer can search through the Web to find information about practically anything.

The ease of using a computer for finding information from all over the world has led to some problems. Incorrect information, or misinformation, is easily and quickly spread throughout the computer network. Identity theft, in which somebody uses another person's personal information to commit fraud or theft, is another problem.

1. ✓**Checkpoint** What computer technology invention made computers smaller, faster, and inexpensive?
2. **Health** in Science Use the Internet to find websites for three health or medical organizations. How might these sites improve the quality of health care?

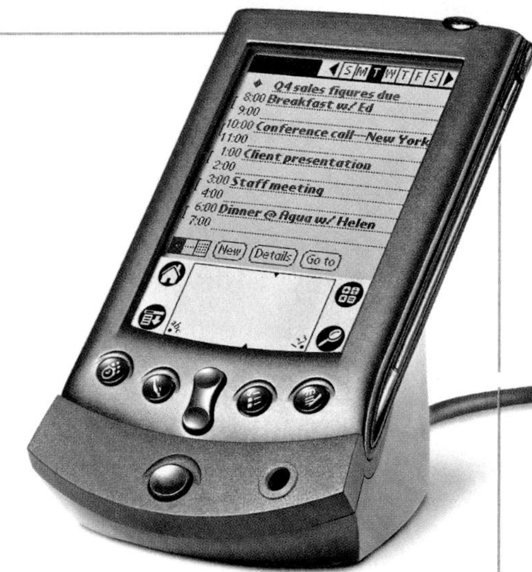

Q4 sales figures due
8:00 Breakfast w/ Ed
9:00
10:00 Conference call—New York
11:00
1:00 Client presentation
2:00
3:00 Staff meeting
4:00
6:00 Dinner @ Agua w/ Helen
7:00
New
Details
Go to

Computer users can receive electronic mail (email), send and receive instant messages, and read news articles. Personal Digital Assistants (PDAs) are hand-held devices that accomplish many of the same tasks as desktop computers.

Special devices have been developed for downloading and playing back music from the Internet.

Computers for Science and Business

Before computer technology, people spent months doing the work that one of today's computers does in seconds. Tasks such as calculating workers' salaries or figuring out how to steer a rocket can be processed by a computer in moments. However, some tasks take even computers a long time to accomplish. Powerful supercomputers or computer networks often help out with very complicated tasks.

The invention of the computer has led to amazing growth in many other technologies. Computers can be used with many tools and devices to produce more valuable results. Several kinds of microscopes, microphones, telescopes, and cameras use computers. The scanning electron microscope uses computers to allow people to see details and objects never before seen. Computers can be used to aim telescopes with pinpoint accuracy and process thousands of astronomical images. Digital cameras use microchips to capture and store images without having to use film. Microphones can be connected to a computer in order to hear things too soft to hear under normal conditions.

Computers and computer-controlled tools are very useful when precision is critical, when a task is very large, or when conditions are too dangerous for humans to perform. Computerized robots are used to perform many tasks that humans cannot do, including collecting samples on Mars. Equipment run by computers makes enormous or impossible tasks possible.

✓ Lesson Checkpoint

1. What is the World Wide Web?
2. How did the invention of the microchip change computers?
3. Writing in Science **Expository** Write a paragraph in your **science journal** describing how your life has been changed by computers. Give examples of ways you use the computer to improve the quality of your life.

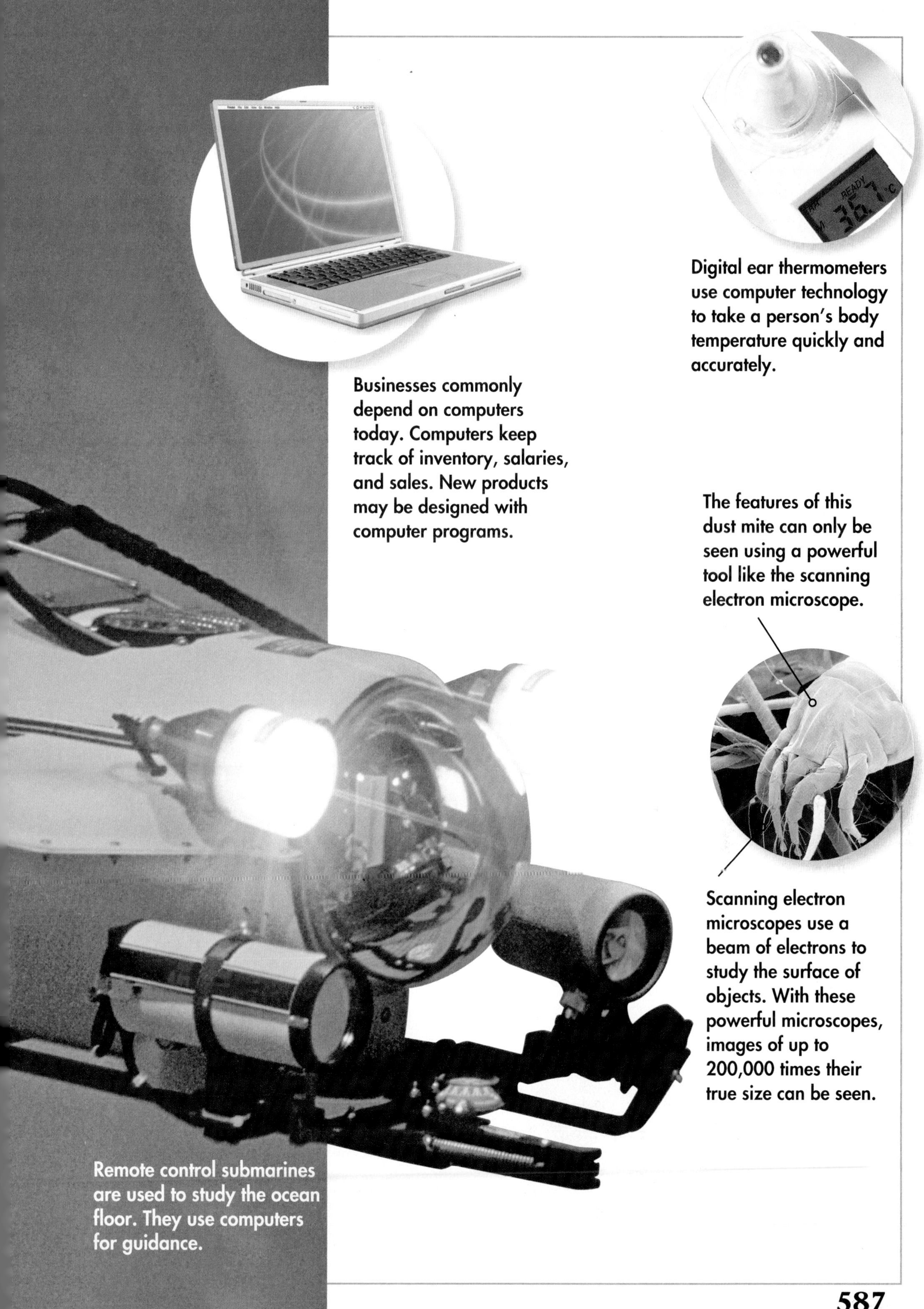
READY
36.7
°C

Businesses commonly depend on computers today. Computers keep track of inventory, salaries, and sales. New products may be designed with computer programs.

Digital ear thermometers use computer technology to take a person's body temperature quickly and accurately.

The features of this dust mite can only be seen using a powerful tool like the scanning electron microscope.

Scanning electron microscopes use a beam of electrons to study the surface of objects. With these powerful microscopes, images of up to 200,000 times their true size can be seen.

Remote control submarines are used to study the ocean floor. They use computers for guidance.

Lesson 4

What technology is used in space?

Space technology has helped humans learn about places from Earth to beyond our solar system. What might space technology of the future allow us to explore?

The Space Race

After World War II, strong political differences between the United States and the Soviet Union continued to form. These differences led to a long-term competition between the two countries to explore space.

Milestones in Space

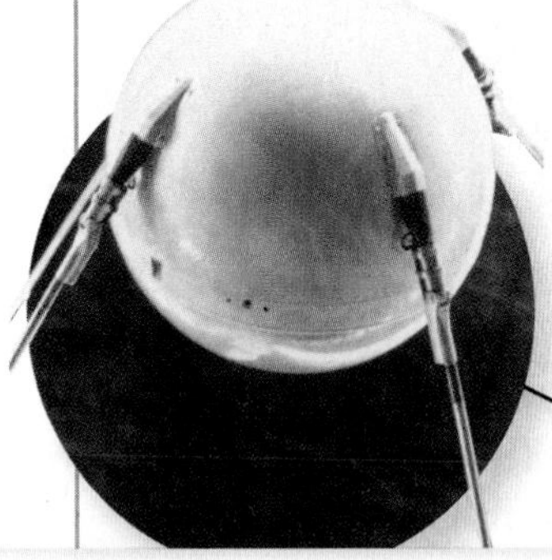

October 4, 1957—The first satellite to orbit Earth is the Soviet satellite *Sputnik 1*.

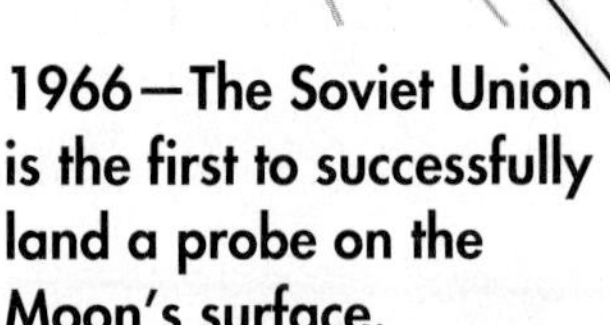

1966—The Soviet Union is the first to successfully land a probe on the Moon's surface.

1969—Two Americans, Neil Armstrong and Buzz Aldrin, are the first people to walk on the Moon. With this achievement, the United States is considered to have won The Space Race.

1950 1960 1970

November 3, 1957—A dog named Laika becomes the first animal in space. Laika was sent into orbit by the former Soviet Union.

April 12, 1961—The Soviet Union's Yuri Gagarin is the first man in space.

This competition was known as The Space Race. The timeline below shows the major space missions that were accomplished by the United States and the Soviet Union during their great race for space. The Soviet Union no longer exists. In 1991, it became divided into several smaller countries.

1. **Checkpoint** What two countries were involved in The Space Race?
2. **Social Studies in Science** Find a current article in a newspaper or magazine about the space program. Decide whether or not all the necessary facts are presented in the article.

1981—The Space Shuttle *Columbia* is the first reusable spaceship.

2000—The first crew of one American and two Russians arrive on the International Space Station (ISS). Many nations from around the world have helped with the ISS.

1980 **1990** **2000**

1986—*MIR* was the first permanent space station designed to allow people to remain in space for long periods of time. It was built by the Soviet Union and later crews included American astronauts.

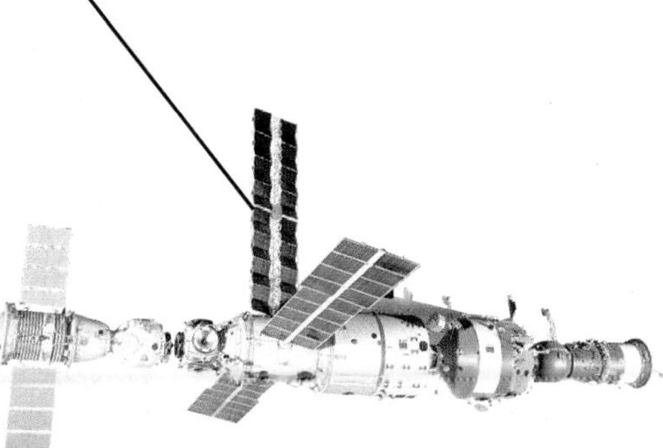

2003—China launches a person into space.

2004—The first privately owned spaceship, *ShapeShipOne* reaches space.

Space Station

A **space station** is a place where people can live and work in space for long periods of time. Many experiments and research take more time than a short space shuttle trip allows. In a space station, people can do research and run experiments for months or years.

The European Space Agency, the United States, Russia, Japan, and Canada agreed to build the International Space Station (ISS). In 1998, the first part of the station was put in orbit. New sections, or modules, continue to be added to the ISS all the time. New crews arrive on the ISS while other crews return to Earth. Once it is completed, the ISS will be about the size of a football field and have a mass of almost 453.6 metric tons.

By the time the ISS is complete, it will have a total of eight solar array wings. These wings will supply power to all the systems on board the ISS. Four separate shuttle flights will deliver the eight solar arrays to the ISS.

Space Shuttles bring new crew members, fresh supplies, and new equipment to the ISS.

The ISS emergency return system includes capsules in which the crew can return to Earth in the event of an emergency.

The ISS will eventually have up to six separate modules that will serve as laboratories in which astronauts and cosmonauts work and do research.

√ Lesson Checkpoint

1. Who was the first person in space?
2. Who were the first people to walk on the Moon?
3. **Sequence** Research four space events that are not mentioned in this lesson. Make a time line to sequence these events.

International Space Station

This photo was taken in 2002. At this time, the station was incomplete.

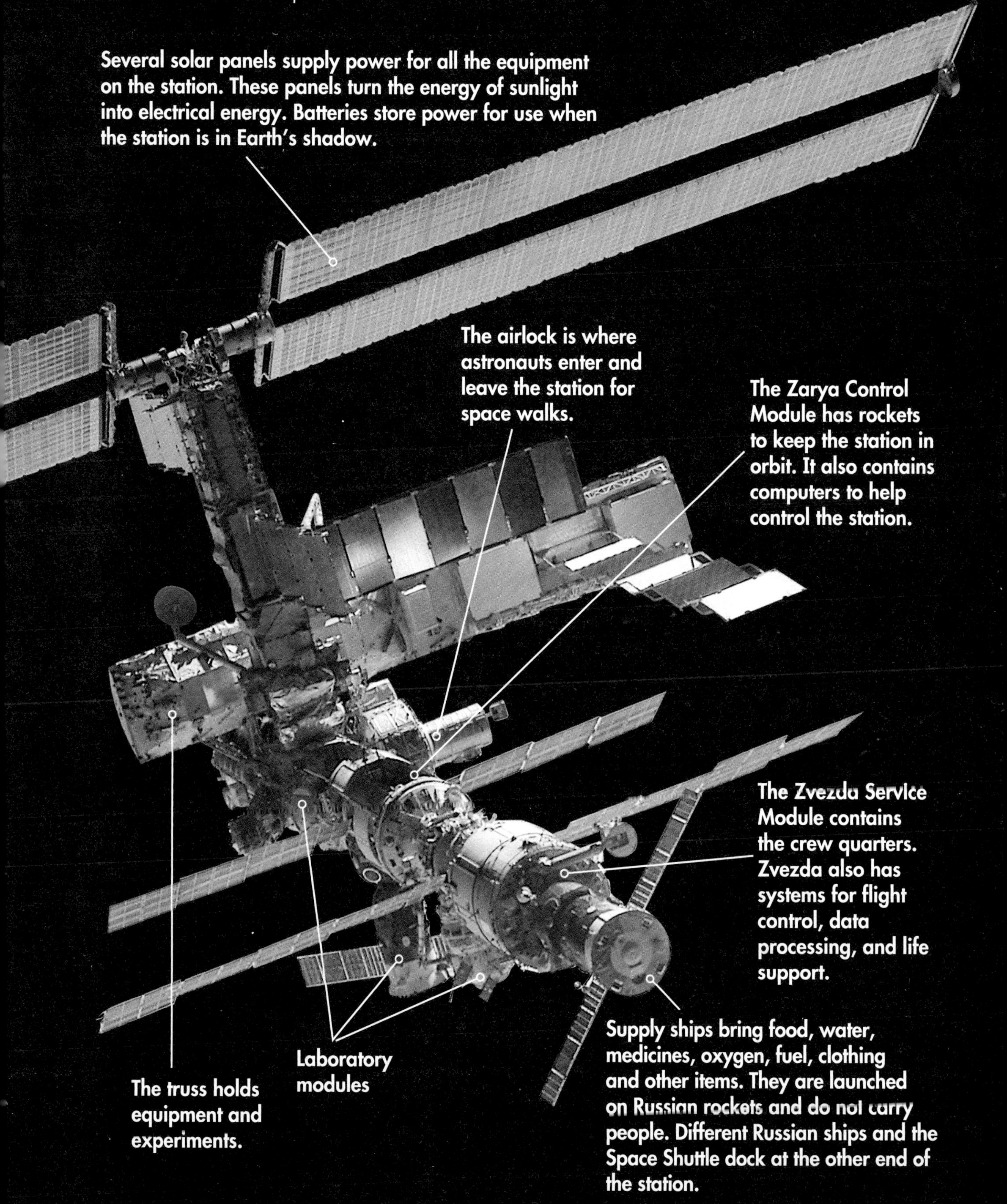

Several solar panels supply power for all the equipment on the station. These panels turn the energy of sunlight into electrical energy. Batteries store power for use when the station is in Earth's shadow.

The airlock is where astronauts enter and leave the station for space walks.

The Zarya Control Module has rockets to keep the station in orbit. It also contains computers to help control the station.

The Zvezda Service Module contains the crew quarters. Zvezda also has systems for flight control, data processing, and life support.

Supply ships bring food, water, medicines, oxygen, fuel, clothing and other items. They are launched on Russian rockets and do not carry people. Different Russian ships and the Space Shuttle dock at the other end of the station.

Laboratory modules

The truss holds equipment and experiments.

Lab zone **Guided Inquiry**

Investigate How do space probes send images to Earth?

Materials

1 Image Receiving Grid and 1 Image Sending Grid

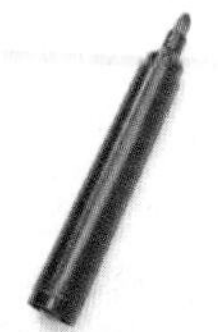

black marker

What to Do

1. **Model** how space probes send images. Work with your back to your partner. You are the Sender. The Sender represents a space probe that is observing another planet. You change a camera image into a signal and send it to Earth.

2. Your partner is the Receiver. The Receiver represents the place on Earth that receives the signal from the space probe and changes the signal into an image.

3. The Receiver will say, "A1." The Sender will look at square A1 on the Sending Grid and say "0" if that square is empty or "1" if the square is filled in. The Receiver will fill in the A1 square only if the Sender says "1." Each square is completely empty or completely filled in.

The numbers spoken by the Sender represent signals sent by radio waves to Earth.

Do not let the Receiver see the Image Sending Grid.

Image Sending Grid
A B C D E F G H I J
1
2

Process Skills

There are different types of **models**. Some are physical models. This activity is a model of a process.

4 Continue with squares A2, A3, and so on. When finished with Column A, start Column B. Continue until all columns are complete.

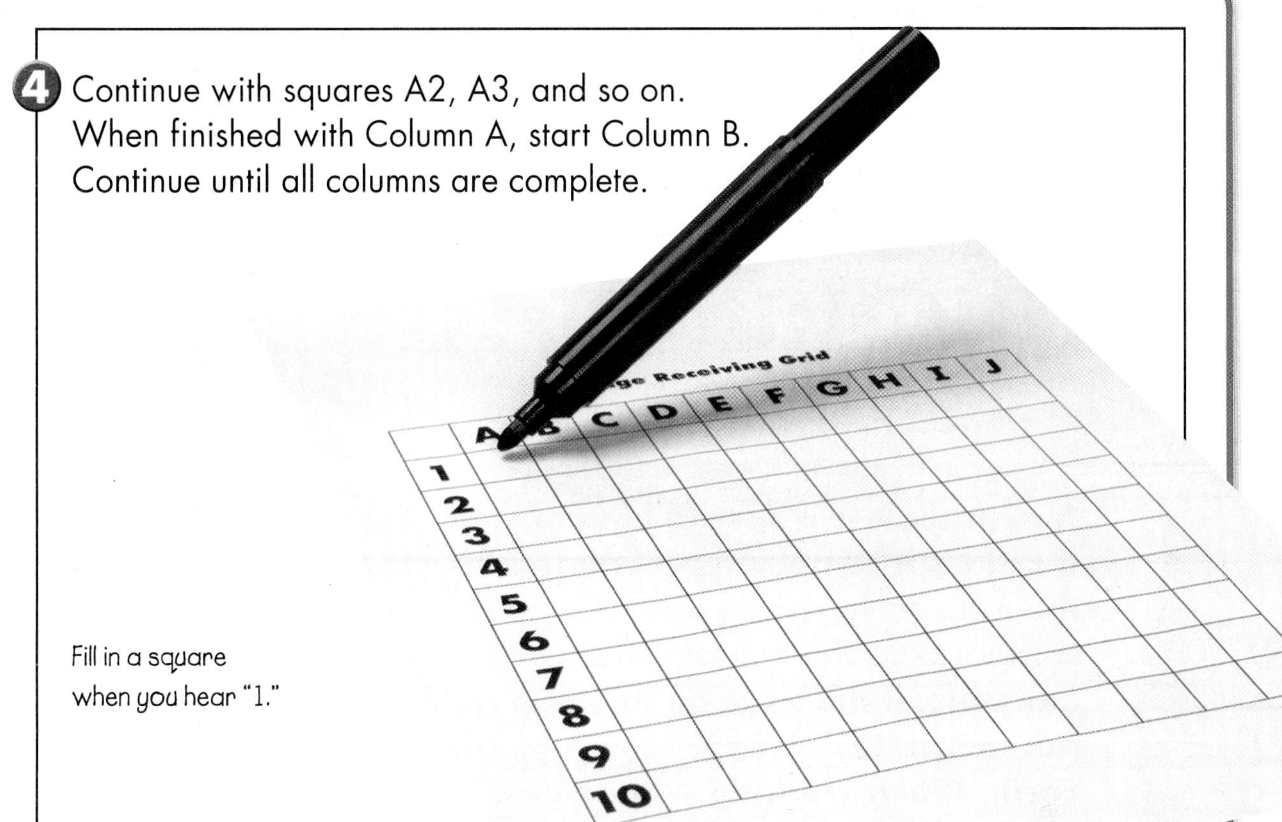
Receiving Grid
A B C D E F G H I J
1 2 3 4 5 6 7 8 9 10

Fill in a square when you hear "1."

The Receiver collects and organizes the data, recreating the image that was sent by the Sender.

5 **Compare** the images. Are they the same? Explain.

Explain Your Results

1. How accurately was the signal received? Explain why the new image might not be perfectly accurate.
2. Based on the process you **modeled**, describe how an image is sent from a space probe.
3. **Infer** How do you think cameras on satellites orbiting Earth send images back to Earth?

Go Further

What would happen if you "sent" to a partner a full-page picture drawn on a piece of graph paper with large squares and on a piece with small squares? Find out. Send both to a partner with matching graph paper. Does one take longer? Does one make a better picture?

Map Scale and Topographic Maps

A map scale is a special kind of ratio. Remember, a ratio is a comparison of quantities. On any map, the map scale shows how the distance on the map compares to the actual distance on the Earth. For example, if the scale on the map is "1 cm = 5 km" this means that 1 cm on the map represents 5 km on Earth. When working with scales, it is very important to include the units. A scale of 1 cm:5 km is really a ratio of 1:500,000, since 5 km = 500,000 cm.

The scale on a map is 1 cm to 10 km. If two lakes are shown 5 cm apart on the map, what is the actual distance between the lakes, in kilometers?

$$\frac{1 \text{ cm}}{10 \text{ km}} = \frac{5 \text{ cm}}{? \text{ km}}$$

$$\frac{1 \text{ cm} \times 5}{10 \text{ km} \times 5} = \frac{5 \text{ cm}}{50 \text{ km}}$$

The actual distance between the lakes is 50 km.

On a topographic map, contour lines connect areas with the same elevation. Contour lines show how steep the land is. Contour lines that are close together indicate that the elevation changes quickly and the land is steep. Contour lines that are far apart indicate that the elevation changes more slowly and the land is flatter.

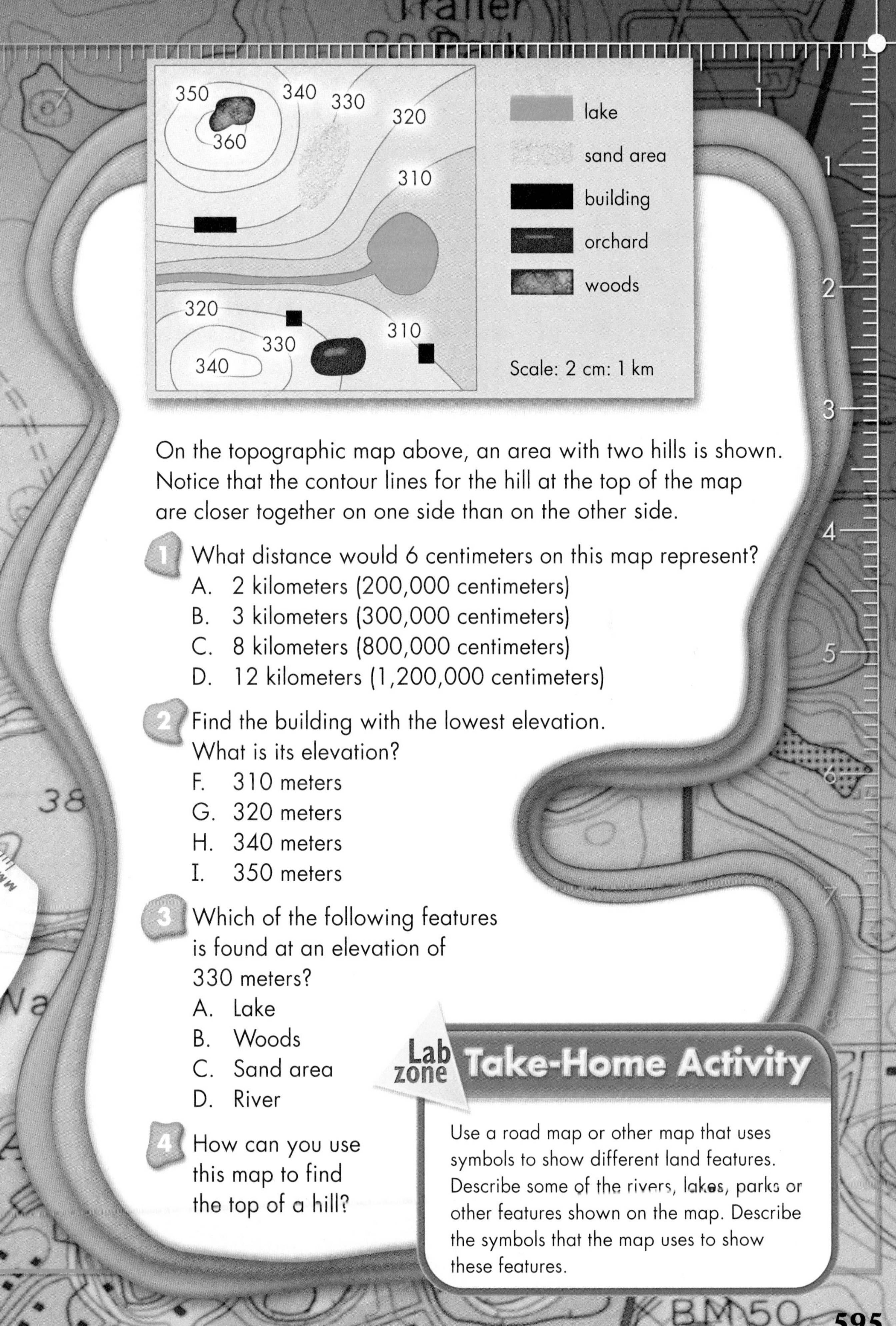
350
340
330
320
360
310
320
310
330
340
lake
sand area
building
orchard
woods
Scale: 2 cm: 1 km

On the topographic map above, an area with two hills is shown. Notice that the contour lines for the hill at the top of the map are closer together on one side than on the other side.

1. What distance would 6 centimeters on this map represent?
   A. 2 kilometers (200,000 centimeters)
   B. 3 kilometers (300,000 centimeters)
   C. 8 kilometers (800,000 centimeters)
   D. 12 kilometers (1,200,000 centimeters)

2. Find the building with the lowest elevation. What is its elevation?
   F. 310 meters
   G. 320 meters
   H. 340 meters
   I. 350 meters

3. Which of the following features is found at an elevation of 330 meters?
   A. Lake
   B. Woods
   C. Sand area
   D. River

4. How can you use this map to find the top of a hill?

Lab zone Take-Home Activity

Use a road map or other map that uses symbols to show different land features. Describe some of the rivers, lakes, parks or other features shown on the map. Describe the symbols that the map uses to show these features.

Chapter 18 Review and Test Prep

Use Vocabulary

assembly line (page 578)	**space station** (page 590)
inventor (page 575)	**technology** (page 575)
manufacturing (page 578)	**World Wide Web** (page 585)
microchip (page 584)	

Use the term from the list above that best completes each sentence.

1. After the _____ was invented, computers became smaller, faster, and cheaper.
2. George Washington Carver was a(n) _____ who found many uses for soybeans, peanuts, and sweet potatoes.
3. A(n) _____ allows people to work and live in space for long periods of time.
4. Dishwashers, cellular telephones, and microwave ovens are a result of _____.
5. Technology has changed the _____ industry by making more products available at a cheaper price.
6. The _____ makes information from all over the world available on computer.
7. Before the _____ was invented, cars were built one at a time.

Explain Concepts

8. Explain how technology can have both positive and negative effects on society.
9. Explain how technology can have both positive and negative effects on the environment.
10. Explain how people use science to solve problems, make decisions, and form new ideas.

Process Skills

11. **Observe** the environment around you. What are three tasks that are made easier by technology?
12. **Infer** what would happen if there was no new technology.

Sequence

13. Make a graphic organizer like the one shown below. Put the following events in the proper sequence.

UNIVAC
Steam engine
First safety bicycle
Sputnik
ISS
First man on the Moon
Ford's assembly line

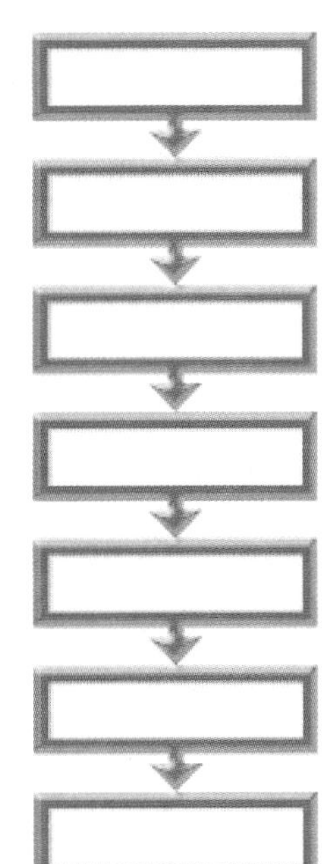

Test Prep

Choose the letter that best completes the statement or answers the question.

14. Some inventions lead to new inventions. An example is CD technology that led to
Ⓐ flat screen televisions.
Ⓑ more efficient thermostats.
Ⓒ cellular telephones.
Ⓓ DVDs.

15. The car industry was revolutionized in the early 1900s by the use of
Ⓕ the assembly line.
Ⓖ safety bicycles.
Ⓗ the steam engine.
Ⓘ electric motors.

16. Computers were made smaller by
Ⓐ CD technology.
Ⓑ the World Wide Web.
Ⓒ microchips.
Ⓓ UNIVAC.

17. What product of space technology allows people to work and live for long periods in space?
Ⓕ UNIVAC
Ⓖ the microchip
Ⓗ PDAs
Ⓘ the space station

18. Which of the following is NOT an example of technology?
Ⓐ a new theory about the universe
Ⓑ a lightbulb that never burns out
Ⓒ a type of paper that doesn't come from trees
Ⓓ a faster way to make ice cream

19. Explain why the answer you selected for Question 18 is best. For each of the answers you did not select, give a reason why it is not the best choice.

20. Writing in Science **Descriptive** Write a paragraph describing one example of transportation technology and how it improves people's lives.

NASA

Everyday Uses of NASA Technology

Have you ever wondered where some of the technologies used at home came from? Many everyday objects started out as materials or technologies developed for the space program. Here are some examples:

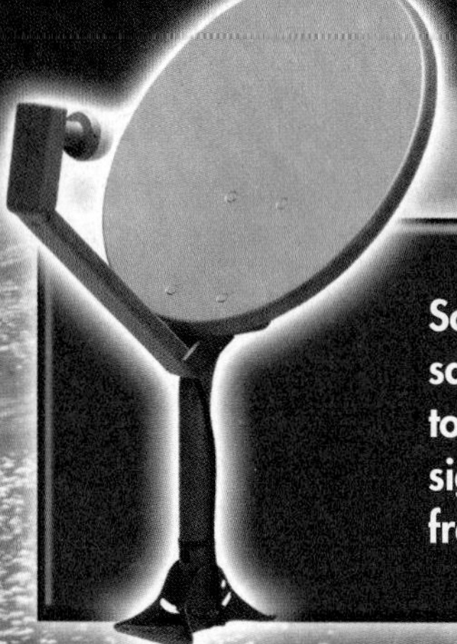

Some people use satellite dishes to receive TV signals coming from satellites.

A special fire resistant material was developed by NASA to protect astronauts. Firefighters wear suits made of the same material to protect them.

NASA developed technology that uses a special detector for measuring infrared energy. This information gives scientists clues about the birth of stars. We use the same technology to determine body temperature.

NASA developed a special barcode system to keep track of parts used on spacecraft. We use bar codes to keep track of product sales.

The first smoke detectors were used in the Skylab space station in 1973 to detect poisons in the air. We use smoke detectors to warn us of fire.

The three-spoke wheel used on many racing bicycles is a result of NASA research in airfoils (wings). The three spokes on the wheel act like wings, making the bicycle go faster.

Apollo astronauts first used cordless tools to collect samples from the Moon. This same technology has led to cordless vacuum cleaners, power drills, shrub trimmers, and grass shears.

NASA developed a special pen for use in space. The ink in this pen still flows in the non-gravity environment of space. Pressurized gas pushes the ink toward the ballpoint. It also has special ink that works even in very hot or very cold temperatures. You can use this pen to write upside down, outside in the snow, or during a heat wave!

Through technology, NASA developed a special joystick controller for the Apollo Lunar Rover. We use joystick controllers for household appliances, computer games, and vehicles for people with disabilities.

Lab zone Take-Home Activity

Technology sometimes means finding new uses for ordinary objects. Take another look at objects in your home, such as bag clips, wire clothes hangers, or kitchen tongs. Develop a new use for one of these objects and show it to the class.

Career

Mathematician/ Computer Scientist

Onboard spacecraft are many systems that help keep the astronauts safe and allow them to work in space. These systems need to be monitored regularly to make sure everything is working well. The astronauts and ground crew can make regular checks of these systems. But if computers could make these checks, people would be freed up to do other tasks.

Dr. Robert Shelton is a mathematician who helps write computer programs. Some of his programs mimic how people think when they do simple tasks, such as checking gauges. For these programs, Shelton had to "train" his computers. He would feed data into a computer. Then he would check the computer's predictions. Finally, he refined the program to make its predictions more accurate. If the program responded reasonably to many new situations, NASA could start using it. Then there could be fewer systems checks, but the astronauts would still be safe. Shelton now writes educational software to help share the NASA experience.

Dr. Robert Shelton lost his eyesight at age 11. He then developed his interest in math and science, which led him to his lifelong career.

To be a mathematician working with computers, you need to have a college degree. You should expect to work with a team of people. You need to be able to listen to others and to communicate your ideas well.

Lab zone Take-Home Activity

Use the Internet to help you learn about the history of a modern technology, such as radio, television, or computers. Make a poster with an illustrated time line. Share it with your class.

Unit D Test Talk

Test-Taking Strategies

Find Important Words
Choose the Right Answer
Use Information from Text and Graphics
Write Your Answer

Choose the Right Answer

To answer a multiple choice test question, you need to choose an answer from several choices. Read the passage and then answer the questions.

The Sun is a star at the center of the solar system. Its gravity holds all the planets in their orbits. Like most stars, the Sun is made mostly of hydrogen and helium.

Planets and other objects orbit the Sun. The inner planets are made mostly of rock. Most outer planets are almost entirely spheres of gases. The largest planets have many **satellites**. These objects include moons and particles in the rings that surround them. The smaller planets have one or two satellites, or none at all.

A wide variety of stars are in the universe, very far from the solar system. The biggest stars are called **supergiants.** The smallest are called dwarfs. Stars come in a variety of colors and termperatures. They give off many kinds of radiation that are not visible to our eyes.

Astronomers depend on technology to study stars. By using special tools, they can record, focus, magnify, and analyze the light and other radiation that distant stars give off.

Use What You Know

In order to choose the right answer, you might first eliminate answer choices that you are sure are incorrect. As you read each question, decide which answer choices you can eliminate.

1. What is found at the center of our solar system?
   Ⓐ a planet
   Ⓑ an asteroid
   Ⓒ a comet
   Ⓓ a star

2. Which of the following statements about the planets is NOT true?
   Ⓕ Every planet has many satellites.
   Ⓖ Inner planets are made mostly of rock.
   Ⓗ Some planets are made mostly of gas.
   Ⓘ The Moon is a satellite of Earth.

3. In the passage, the word *satellite* means
   Ⓐ an orbiting object.
   Ⓑ a bright color.
   Ⓒ a high temperature.
   Ⓓ a thick atmosphere.

4. In the passage, the word *supergiant* means
   Ⓕ a small star.
   Ⓖ a large star.
   Ⓗ a small planet.
   Ⓘ a large planet.

Unit D Wrap-Up

Chapter 16

How has the study of stars expanded our knowledge of the universe?

- We have learned how Earth moves in our solar system.
- Telescopes help us study the life cycle of stars and the different ways stars are grouped.

Chapter 17

How does the motion of objects in space create cycles?

- The tilt of Earth's axis, its revolution, and its rotation create seasonal cycles and the pattern of day and night.
- The relative positions of the Sun, Earth, and Moon create Moon phases.
- All the planets rotate on an axis and revolve around the Sun. These movements create their daily and yearly cycles.

Chapter 18

How does technology affect our lives?

- Technology affects the way we travel, communicate, produce goods, explore space, and advance knowledge.
- Technology can help solve problems, but it can also cause new problems.

Performance Assessment

Model a Planet's Orbit

What is the shape of a planet's orbit? Position two thumbtacks on a square of cardboard, one tack about 5 cm (2 in.) above the other. Tie the ends of a piece of string together to form a loop. Place the loop around the thumbtacks. Place the point of a pencil against the inside of the loop and stretch the string until it is tight. Move the pencil around inside the loop until it is back at the starting point. What shape can you make using only one thumbtack?

Read More About Space and Technology

Look for books like these in the library.

A LIBRARY OF CONGRESS BOOK
INVENTORS
MARTIN W. SANDLER
POINT OF IMPACT
The Invention of the
Silicon Chip
A Revolution in Daily Life
WINDSOR CHORLTON
I Want to Be...
AN ASTRONAUT

Lab zone **Full Inquiry**

Experiment Which writing tool might work best in space?

While in space, astronauts must be able to write, but many pens need gravity to pull the ink down to the writing tip. They may not work well in space. When turned upside down, these pens will write for a while, but soon gravity pulls the ink away from the tip. In this experiment you will find out which types of pens might work well in space.

Materials

black ballpoint pen

black fine-point, felt-tip pen

black space pen

spiral notebook with lined paper

timer or stopwatch (or clock with a secondhand)

Process Skills

An **operational definition** is a definition made in observable or measurable terms.

Ask a question.

How does gravity affect how well a pen writes?

State a hypothesis.

If you turn each pen upside down and make lines, then which pen will make the most lines? Write your **hypothesis**.

Identify and control variables.

The **variable** that you change is the type of pen you use. The variable that you observe is the number of lines each pen makes. Everything else must be **controlled,** or kept the same. Always make 1 line every 2 seconds. Make the lines the same length, with the same pressure, and hold the pen at the same angle.

You identify and control variables to help make the results of your **experiment** more reliable.

Variables

An *independent variable* is what you change in an experiment.

A *dependent variable* is what you measure or observe.

A *controlled variable* is what *could be* changed, but must *not* be changed for the experiment to be a fair test.

In this experiment, what is the independent variable? What is the dependent variable? What are some controlled variables?

Test your hypothesis.
Before you begin, decide what you mean by a *line*. Make an operational definition. An **operational definition** of a line tells you what you must observe to decide if something *is* a line. Examples:

- A line is a mark with no places without ink and no places that are lighter than other places, and the mark is not lighter than other lines.
- A line is a mark that has no places without ink, but some places can be lighter than other places, and the mark can be lighter than other lines.

1. Work in a group. Sit down. Have one partner stand and hold a spiral notebook *above* your head with the paper *facing down*. That partner should hold the top and bottom of the page, so it does not move. The paper should be level.

2. Have another partner start the timer. Have that partner say *draw* every 2 seconds.

3. Each time you hear *draw*, make a line on the page above your head. Start at the top of the page.

4. Continue drawing lines until the pen stops making lines. Use extra pages if necessary.

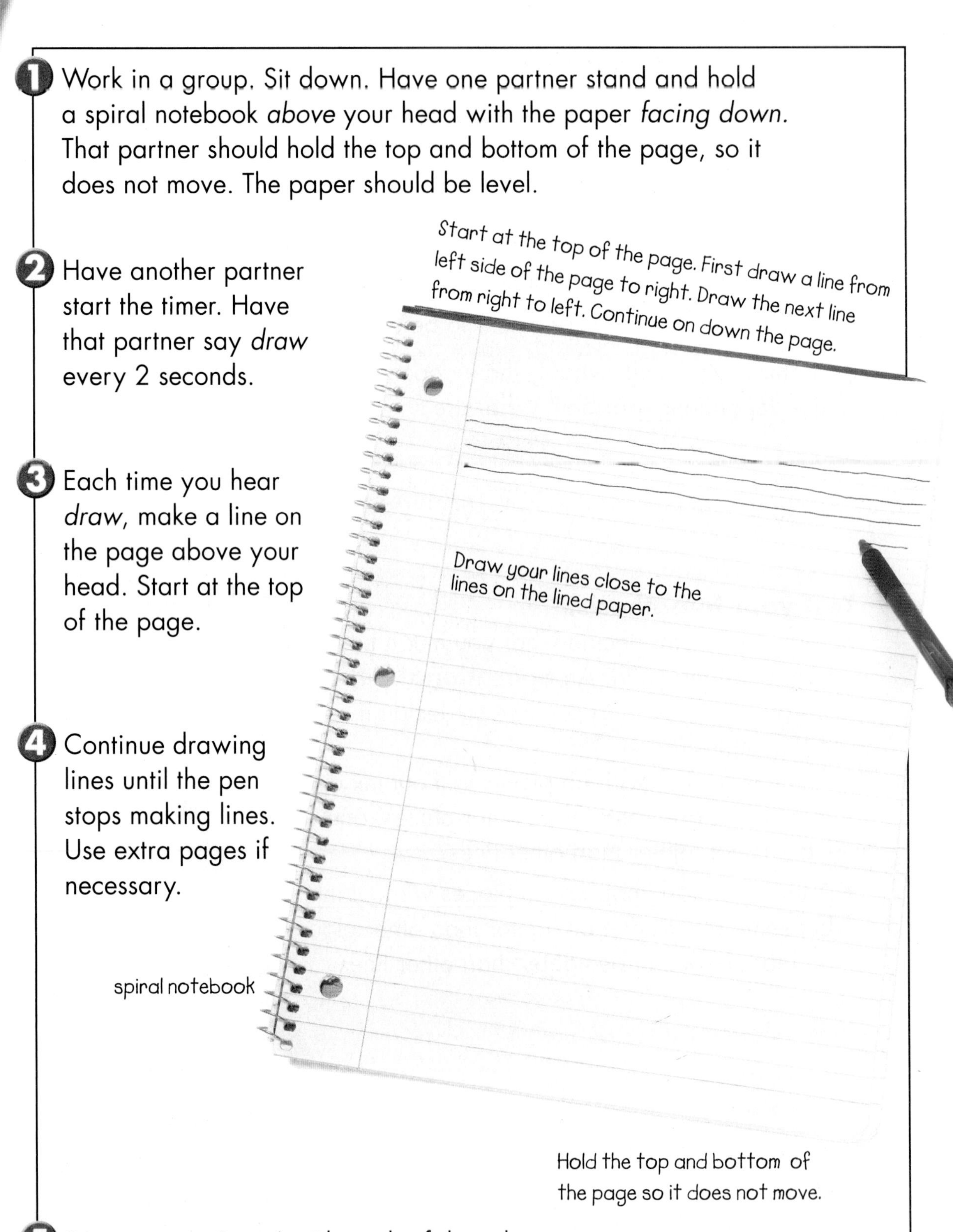
Start at the top of the page. First draw a line from left side of the page to right. Draw the next line from right to left. Continue on down the page.
Draw your lines close to the lines on the lined paper.
spiral notebook
Hold the top and bottom of the page so it does not move.

5. Repeat steps 1 to 4 with each of the other pens. For each pen start on a new page.

Collect and record your data.

Type of Pen	Number of Lines Use your operational definition.
Ballpoint pen	
Felt-tip pen	
Space pen	

Interpret your data.

Use your data to make a bar graph. Look at your graph closely. Which pens are most affected by gravity?

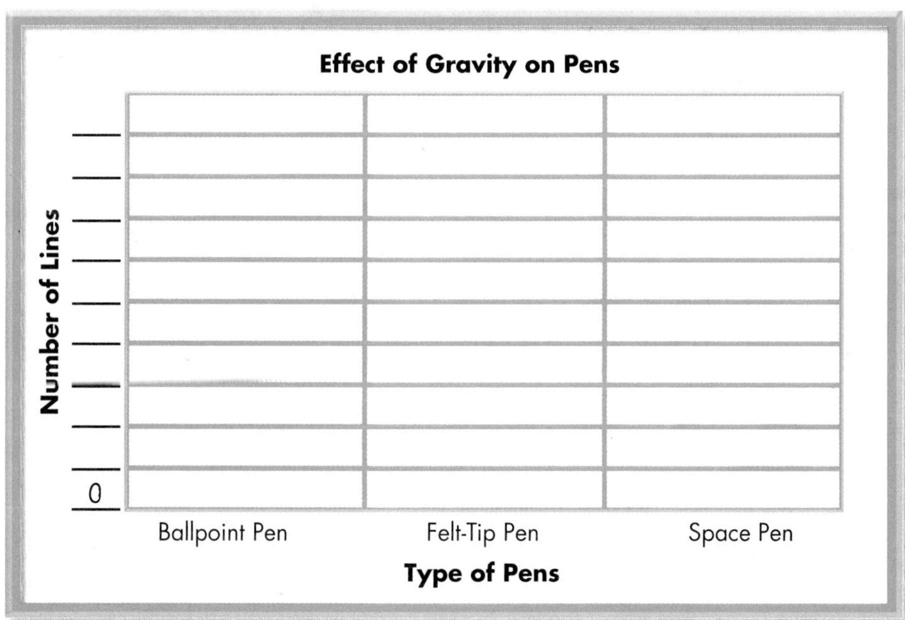

Effect of Gravity on Pens
Number of Lines
0
Ballpoint Pen
Felt-Tip Pen
Space Pen
Type of Pens

State your conclusion.

Describe your results. Compare your hypothesis with your results. **Communicate** your conclusion.

Go Further

What would happen if you used a gel pen? Design and carry out a plan to investigate this or other questions you may have.

Discovery Channel School

Science Fair Projects

Full Inquiry

Using Scientific Methods

1. Ask a question.
2. State a hypothesis.
3. Identify and control variables.
4. Test your hypothesis.
5. Collect and record your data.
6. Interpret your data.
7. State your conclusion.
8. Go further.

A Solar Cooker Model

The space station uses materials that absorb and store solar energy.

Idea: Use a foam cup to help design and build a solar cooker that will warm water.

Counting Stars

The sky has more stars than you can count.

Idea: Use grid paper to estimate the number of stars in a part of the sky.

Catching Rays

The angle at which light rays strike Earth have several effects.

Idea: Use a flashlight, grid paper, and a protractor to demonstrate the effects of direct and indirect light rays.

EC NTL 10 9 8 7

Metric and Customary Measurement

The metric system is the measurement system most commonly used in science. Metric units are sometimes called SI units. SI stands for International System. It is called that because these units are used around the world.

These prefixes are used in the metric system:

kilo- means *thousand*
1 kilometer equals 1,000 meters

milli- means *one thousandth*
1,000 millimeters equals 1 meter or 1 millimeter = 0.001 meter

centi- means *one hundredth*
100 centimeters equals 1 meter or 1 centimeter = 0.01 meter

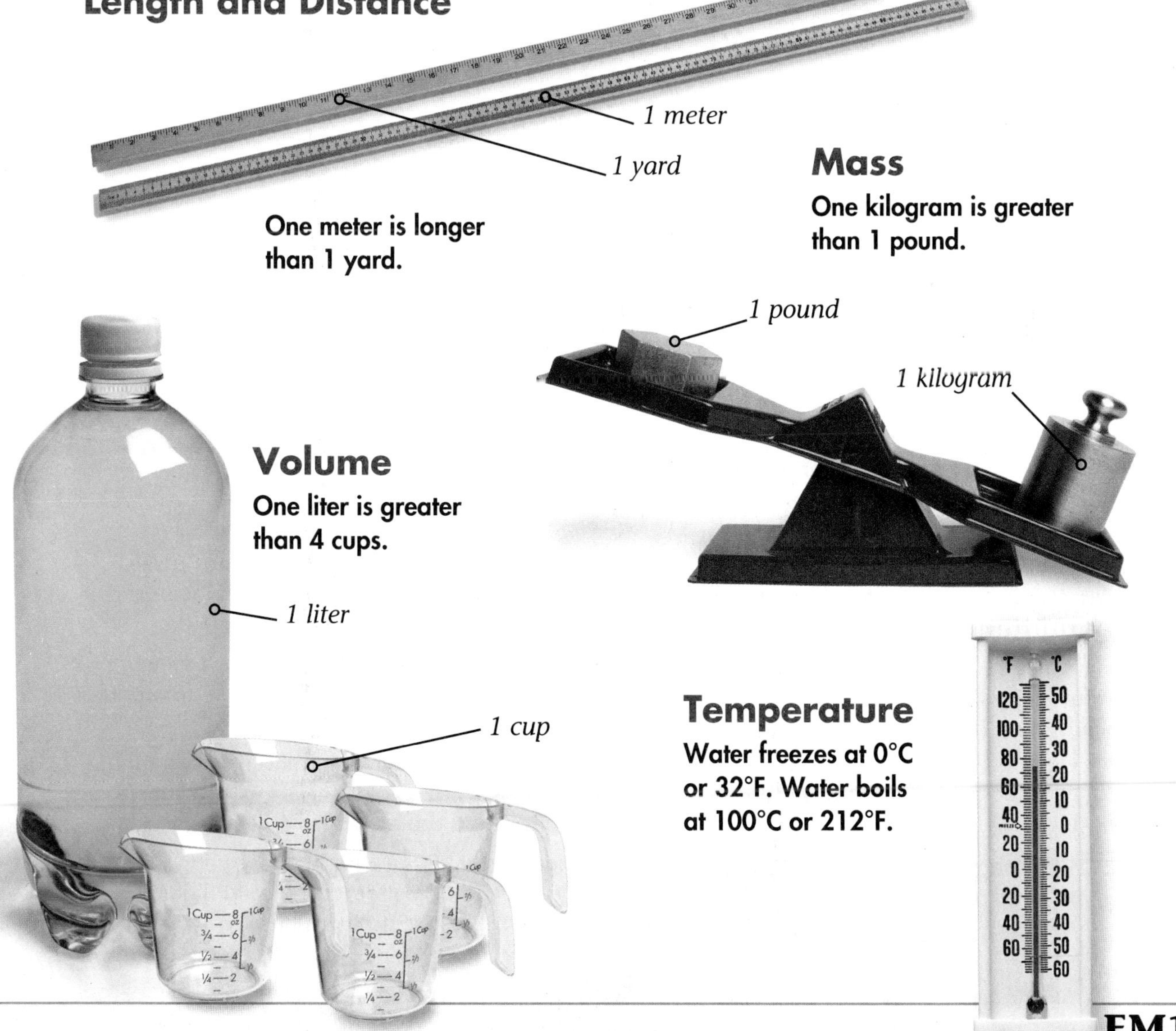
1 meter
1 yard
1 pound
1 kilogram
1 liter
1 cup
°F
°C

Length and Distance

One meter is longer than 1 yard.

Mass

One kilogram is greater than 1 pound.

Volume

One liter is greater than 4 cups.

Temperature

Water freezes at 0°C or 32°F. Water boils at 100°C or 212°F.

Glossary

The glossary uses letters and signs to show how words are pronounced. The mark ′ is placed after a syllable with a primary or heavy accent. The mark ⁄ is placed after a syllable with a secondary or lighter accent.

To hear these words pronounced, listen to the AudioText CD.

Pronunciation Key

a	in hat	ō	in open	sh	in she
ā	in age	ȯ	in all	th	in thin
â	in care	ô	in order	ᴛʜ	in then
ä	in far	oi	in oil	zh	in measure
e	in let	ou	in out	ə	= a in about
ē	in equal	u	in cup	ə	= e in taken
ėr	in term	ů	in put	ə	= i in pencil
i	in it	ü	in rule	ə	= o in lemon
ī	in ice	ch	in child	ə	= u in circus
o	in hot	ng	in long		

acceleration (ak sel⁄ ə rā′ shən) the rate at which the velocity of an object changes over time (p. 422)

adaptation (ad⁄ ap tā′ shən) a change in an organism to better fit an ecosystem (p. 172)

air mass (âr mass) a large body of air with similar properties all through it (p. 234)

air pressure (âr presh′ ər) the push of gases against a surface (p. 208)

air sacs (âr saks) tiny thin-walled pouches in the lungs (p. 70)

anemometer (an⁄ ə mom′ ə tər) a tool used to measure wind speed (p. 242)

aquifer (ak′ wə fər) the layer of rock and soil that groundwater flows through (p. 203)

artery (är′ tər ē) a type of blood vessel that carries blood away from the heart to other parts of the body (p. 66)

assembly line (ə sem′ blē līn) a way of building a product in which workers add parts to products moving down a conveyor belt (p. 578)

asteroid (as′ tə roid⁄) a rocky mass up to several hundred kilometers wide that revolves around the Sun (p. 554)

atmosphere (at′ mə sfir) the layer of gases that surrounds Earth and other planets (p. 545)

atom (at′ əm) the smallest particle of an element that has all the properties of the element (p. 348)

axis (ak′ sis) an imaginary center line around which the Earth rotates (p. 544)

barometer (bə rom′ ə tər) a tool used to measure air pressure (p. 242)

behavioral adaptation (bi hā′ vyər əl ad⁄ ap ta′ shən) inherited behavior that helps animals survive (p. 173)

biomass (bī⁄ ō mas⁄) remains of anything that lived recently (p. 313)

black hole (blak hōl) a point in space that has such a strong force of gravity that nothing within a certain distance of it can escape (p. 523)

bronchioles (brong′ kē ōlz) tubes that branch out from the bronchi (p. 70)

capillary (kap′ə ler′ ē) the smallest kind of blood vessel (p. 66)

carnivore (kär′ nə vôr) an animal that eats only other animals (p. 144)

cause (kȯz) why something happens (p. 93)

cell membrane (sel mem′ brān) surrounds a cell, allows certain materials to enter the cell and waste products to exit (p. 40)

cell respiration (sel res⁄ pə rā′ shən) the combining of oxygen and food, such as sugar, in order to get energy (p. 39)

cell wall (sel wȯl) tough material surrounding the cell membrane in plant cells that provides support and protection (p. 40)

change of state (chānj ov stāt) phase change, or the change of matter from a solid, liquid, or gas into another state or phase (p. 462)

chemical change (kem′ ə kəl chānj) the changing of a substance or kind of matter into a different kind of matter with different properties (p. 375)

chemical equation (kem′ ə kəl i kwā′ zhən) a formula that describes a chemical reaction (p. 378)

chemical reaction (kem′ ə kəl rē ak′ shən) when one or more substances change into other substances with different chemical properties (p. 378)

chemical weathering (kem′ ə kəl weᴛʜ′ ər ing) the changing of materials in a rock by chemical processes (p. 272)

chloroplast (klôr′ ə plast) green part of a plant cell that uses the energy in sunlight to turn water and carbon dioxide into oxygen and sugar (p. 40)

circuit diagram (sėr′ kit dī′ ə gram) a map of a circuit with symbols for each part (p. 484)

class (klas) the level of classification below phylum (p. 8)

classifying (klas′ ə fī ing) to put something into a group (p. 7)

climate (klī′ mit) the average of weather conditions over a long time (p. 246)

collecting data (kə lekt′ ing dā′ tə) gathering observations and measurement into graphs, tables or charts (p. 190)

combustion (kəm bus′ chən) the process of burning (p. 377)

comet (kom′ it) a frozen mass of ice and dust orbiting the Sun (p. 552)

communicating (kə myü′ nə kāt ing) using words, pictures, charts, graphs, and diagrams to share information (p. 119)

community (kə myü′ nə tē) the group of all the populations in an area (p. 127)

compare (kəm pâr′) reading skill that shows how subjects are alike (p. 5)

compound (kom′ pound) a substance made up of a combination of two or more elements held together by chemical bonds that cannot be separated by physical means (p. 350)

concentrated (kon′ sən trāt əd) having a large amount of solute in a solution in comparison with the amount of solvent (p. 361)

conclusion (kən klü′ zhən) a decision reached after thinking about facts and details (p.s 37, 229, 373)

condensation (kon′ den sā′ shən) the changing of a gas into a liquid (p. 209)

conduction (kən duk′ shən) transfer of thermal energy between objects that are in contact (p. 465)

conductor (kən duk′ tər) a material through which electric charge flows easily (p. 480)

conservation (kon′ sər vā′ shən) careful use of natural resources (p. 318)

constellation (kon′ stə lā shən) a group of stars that forms a pattern (p. 526)

consumer (kən sü′ mər) an organism that eats other organisms (p. 144)

contrast (kən trast′) to point out how things are different (p. 5)

convection (kən vek′ shən) the movement of warm liquids or gases to cooler areas (p. 464)

convection current (kən vek′ shən kėr′ ənt) when solids, gases, or liquids rise and sink in a looping path (p. 232)

core (kôr) the center part of Earth which includes the liquid outer core and solid inner core (p. 264)

crust (krust) the outermost and thinnest of Earth's layers (p. 264)

current (kėr′ ənt) the flow of electric charge through a material (p. 479)

cycle (sī′ kəl) a repeating process or flow of material through a system (p. 149)

cytoplasm (sī′ tə plaz′ əm) all the material of the cell between the cell membrane and the nucleus (p. 40)

decomposer (dē′ kəm pō′ zər) an organism that gets nutrients by breaking down dead organisms (p. 144)

density (den′ sə tē) the mass of a substance divided by its volume (p. 345)

deposition (dep′ ə zish′ ən) the laying down of material in a natural process (p. 276)

details (di tālz′) individual pieces of information that support a main idea (p. 301)

dilute (də lüt′) having little solute in a solution in comparison with the amount of solvent (p. 361)

earthquake (ėrth′ kwāk′) the shaking of Earth's surface caused by release of energy along a fault (p. 268)

ecosystem (ē′ kō sis′ təm) all the living and nonliving things in an area (p. 127)

effect (ə fekt′) what happens as the result of a cause (p. 93)

electromagnet (i lek′ trō mag′ nit) magnet created by an electric current (p. 488)

electromagnetic radiation (i lek′ trō mag net′ ik rā′ dē ā′ shən) energy that travels through space in the form of light and other types of energy (p. 458)

electron (i lek′ tron) a negatively charged particle moving around the nucleus of an atom (p. 349)

element (el′ ə mənt) the basic building blocks of matter; cannot be separated into parts by chemical means (p. 343)

embryo (em′ brē ō) a new plant inside a seed (p. 106)

energy (en′ ər jē) the ability to do work or cause a change (p. 447)

energy pyramid (en′ ər jē pir′ ə mid) a diagram that shows the amounts of energy that flows through each level of a food chain (p. 146)

energy transfer (en′ ər jē tran′ sfėr′) a change of energy from one form to another (p. 447)

environment (en vī′ rən mənt) all the conditions surrounding a living thing (p. 110)

equator (i kwā tər) an imaginary circle around the middle of Earth between the North Pole and South Pole (p. 526)

equilibrium (ē′ kwə lib′ rē əm) the state in which the net force is zero (p. 419)

erosion (i rō′zhən) the movement of materials away from one place (p. 276)

esophagus (i sof′ ə gəs) a tube in the throat with rings of muscle that help you to swallow food (p. 74)

estimating and measuring (es′ tə māt ing and mezh′ ər ing) telling what you think an object's measurements are and then measuring it in units (p. 80)

evaporation (i vap′ ə rā′ shən) the changing of a liquid into a gas (p. 209)

experiment (ek sper′ ə mənt) to use scientific methods to test a hypothesis (p. 188)

extinct (ek stingkt′) when there are no members of a kind of organism left alive (p. 176)

fertilizers (fėr′ tl ī′ zərz) chemicals farmers add to the soil to increase the amount of food that will grow (p. 387)

food chain (füd chān) transfer of energy through a series of organisms that use each other as food (p. 144)

food web (füd web) all the food chains in a particular place (p. 145)

force (fôrs) a push or pull that acts on an object (p. 410)

fossil (fos′ əl) remains or mark of a living thing from long ago, found in sedimentary rock (p. 176)

fossil fuel (fos′ əl fyü′ əl) energy source formed from the remains of once living things from long ago (p. 303)

friction (frik′ shən) a contact force that resists the movement of one surface past another surface (p. 414)

front (frunt) a boundary between two air masses (p. 236)

fulcrum (ful′ krəm) the point at which a lever rests in moving or lifting an object (p. 428)

galaxy (gal′ ək sē) a huge system of stars, dust, and gas held together by gravity (p. 524)

gas (gas) a state of matter that does not have a specific volume or shape and in which the particles are far apart. (p. 356)

geothermal (jē′ ō thėr′ məl) energy produced by thermal energy inside of Earth (p. 312)

gravitation (grav′ ə tā′ shən) a non-contact force that pulls objects toward each other (p. 418)

gravity (grav′ ə tē) the force of attraction that exists between any two objects; causes objects to have weight (p. 410)

growth hormone (grōth hôr′ mōn) a chemical that causes more cells to grow and helps cells to grow larger (p. 112)

habitat (hab′ə tat) the place in an ecosystem in which an organism lives (p. 129)

heat (hēt) the transfer of thermal energy from warmer to cooler objects (p. 464)

herbivore (ėr′bə vôr) an animal that eats only plants or their products (p. 144)

hydroelectric (hī′drō i lek′trik) producing electricity by using the power of flowing water (p. 310)

igneous rock (ig′nē əs rok′) type of rock formed when lava or magma cools and hardens (p. 286)

inclined plane (in klīnd′ plān) a form of simple machine consisting of a slanted surface along which objects are easier to push upward than to lift straight up (p. 429)

inertia (in ėr′shə) the tendency of an object to resist a change in motion (p. 420)

inference (in′fər əns) a conclusion based on facts, experiences, obervations, or knowledge to draw a conclusion or make a reasonable guess based on what you have learned or what you know (p. 541)

inherit (in her′it) receiving of parents' genes (p.170)

insulator (in′sə lā′tər) a poor conductor; material through which heat or electric charge does not flow (p. 480)

interpreting data (in tėr′prit ing dā′tə) to use the information you have collected to solve problems or anwer questions (p. 114)

inventor (in ven′tər) someone who uses technology in a new way to solve a problem (p. 575)

invertebrate (in vėr′tə brit) an animal without a backbone (p. 18)

investigation (in ves′tə gā′shən) a search for information (p. 154)

kinetic energy (ki net′ik en′ər jē) energy due to motion (p. 448)

kingdom (king′dəm) the highest level of classification of living things (p. 8)

lever (lev′ər) a type of simple machine consisting of a bar that turns on a support called a fulcrum (p. 428)

life cycle (līf sī′kəl) the series of stages that a living thing passes through during its growth and development (p. 11)

light (līt) electromagnetic radiation; visible light is electrmagnetic radiation we can see (p. 458)

light-year (līt′yir′) the distance light travels in one year (p. 521)

liquid (lik′wid) a state of matter with a definite volume but without a definite shape (p. 354)

machine (mə shēn′) a device that changes the direction or the amount of effort needed to do work (p. 426)

magnetic (mag net′ik) having the ability to exert forces on certain metals and other magnets without contacting them (p. 413)

main idea (mān ī dē′ə) what a paragraph is about; the most important idea (p. 301)

making and using models (māk′ing and yüz′ing mod′lz) to make a model from materials or to make a sketch or a diagram (p. 50)

making operational definitions (māk′ing op′ə rā′shə nəl def′ə nish′ənz) to define or describe an object or event based on your own experience with it (p. 604)

mantle (man′tl) the layer of Earth between the crust and the core (p. 264)

manufacturing (man′yə fak′chər ing) the production of goods and items on a large scale (p. 578)

mass (mas) the amount of matter in an object (p. 344)

matter (mat′ər) anything that has mass and occupies space (p. 343)

mechanical weathering (mə kan′ə kəl weᴛʜ′ər ing) the breaking down of rocks into smaller pieces by any physical force such as gravity, water, wind, ice, or living organisms (p. 272)

metamorphic rock (met′ə môr′fik rok′) a type of rock formed when existing rock is heated at high pressures and temperatures (p. 287)

microchip (mī′ krō chip′) a small piece of special material used to make computers faster, smaller, and cheaper (p. 584)

microscopic (mī′ krə skop′ ik) an object that is too small to be seen without a microscope (p. 94)

mitochondria (mī′ tə kon′ drē ə) the cell's power producers (p. 41)

mixture (miks′ chər) two or more substances that are mixed together but can be separated out because they are not chemically combined (p. 358)

moon (mün) a natural satellite that orbits a planet (p. 556)

Moon phase (mün fāz) an indication of the fraction of the Moon that is illuminated as seen from Earth (p. 558)

mucus (myü′ kəs) a sticky, thick fluid that traps dust, germs, and other things that may be in the air (p. 70)

mutation (myü tā′ shən) a change in an organism's genes (p. 172)

nebula (neb′ yə lə) a cloud of gas and dust in which new stars form (p. 522)

net force (net fôrs) the resulting force after all the individual forces acting on an object are added together (p. 418)

neutron (nü′ tron) a particle with no electrical charge in the nucleus of an atom (p. 348)

niche (nich) the job that an organism has in an ecosystem (p. 129)

nonrenewable resource (non′ ri nü′ ə bəl ri sôrs′) a resource that cannot be replaced on the time scale of human history (p. 303)

nucleus (nü′ klē əs) contains DNA which controls how the body grows and changes (p. 40)

organ (ôr′ gən) a grouping of different tissues combined together into one structure to perform a main job in the body (p. 44)

organism (ôr′ gə niz′ əm) any living thing (p. 7)

organ system (ôr′ gən sis′ təm) a group of organs that work together to carry out a life process (p. 46)

pesticide (pes′ tə sīd) a poison that kills insects (p. 174)

phloem (flō′ əm) tubes in vascular plants that carry sugar away from the leaves (p. 98)

photosynthesis (fō′ tō sin′ thə sis) the process by which plants use light energy to make sugars (p. 96)

phylum (fī′ ləm) the level of classification of living things below kingdom (p. 8)

physical change (fiz′ ə kəl chānj) a change in some properties of matter without forming a different kind of matter (p. 375)

planet (plan′ it) a large object in space that orbits a star (p. 550)

plate (plāt) a large section of Earth's crust and upper mantle (p. 266)

pollen (pol′ ən) a grainy yellow powder made in a tissue at the top of the stamen of a flower (p. 102)

pollination (pol′ ə nā′ shən) moving pollen from the stamen to the pistil (p. 104)

pollution (pə lü′ shən) the placing of harmful substances into the environment (p. 318)

polymer (pol′ ə mər) a large molecule made of many smaller units connected together (p. 388)

population (pop′ yə lā′ shən) a group of organisms of one species that live in an area at the same time (p. 127)

potential energy (pə ten′ shəl en′ ər jē) energy that is stored in an object due to its position or arrangement (p. 450)

power (pou′ ər) the rate at which work is done (p. 417)

precipitation (pri sip′ ə tā′ shən) water leaving clouds as rain, snow, sleet or hail (p. 209)

predator (pred′ ə tər) an animal that hunts and eats other animals (p. 144)

predict/predicting (pri dikt′) making a statement about what might happen next (p. 125)

prey (prā) an animal that is hunted and eaten by a predator (p. 144)

producer (prə dü′ sər) an organism, usually a plant, that makes its own food (p. 144)

product (prod′ əkt) substance made during a chemical reaction (p. 378)

protist (prō′ tist) a member of the protist kingdom (p. 8)

proton (prō′ ton) a positively charged particle in the nucleus of an atom (p. 348)

pulley (pu̇l′ ē) a kind of simple machine consisting of a rope that fits onto a wheel and used to change the direction of a force (p. 426)

radiation (rā′ dē ā′ shən) transfer of energy through space (p. 465)

rain gauge (rān gāj) a tool used to measure how much rain has fallen (p. 243)

reactant (rē ak′ tənt) substance used in a chemical reaction (p. 378)

reflection (ri flek′ shən) the bouncing of light or wave from a surface (p. 460)

refraction (ri frak′ shən) the bending of light or waves as it passes from one material to another (p. 461)

renewable resource (ri nü′ ə bəl ri sôrs′) a resource that can be replaced in a reasonable amount of time (p. 303)

reservoir (rez′ ər vwär) a lake formed behind a dam (p. 204)

resistor (ri zis′ tər) a material or device that resists the flow of electric charge (p. 480)

resource (ri sôrs′) any supply that will meet a need (p. 303)

revolution (rev′ ə lü′ shən) one full orbit of an object around another object (p. 543)

rotation (rō tā′ shən) one whole spin of an object on its axis (p. 544)

salinity (sə lin′ ə tē) a measure of how salty water is (p. 200)

satellite (sat′ l īt) an object in orbit around another object (p. 556)

saturated (sach′ ə rāt′ əd) combined with or containing all the solute that can be dissolved without changing the temperature (p. 361)

scientific methods (sī′ ən tif′ ik meth′ ədz) any organized system of inquiry in which science process skills are used to gather and communicate information (p. xxvi)

sedimentary rock (sed′ ə men′ tər ē rok′) type of rock formed when sediments are pressed and cemented together (p. 286)

sequence (sē′ kwəns) the order in which things happen (p. 61)

sleet (slēt) frozen rain drops (p. 215)

solar energy (sō′ lər en′ ər jē) energy from sunlight (p. 306)

solar system (sō′ lər sis′ təm) the Sun and all the bodies that orbit it (p. 543)

solid (sol′ id) a state of matter in which material has a definite volume and shape (p. 354)

solution (sə lü′ shən) a mixture in which a substance breaks up into its most basic particles and spreads evenly through another substance (p. 360)

space probe (spās prōb) a spacecraft that gathers data without a crew (p. 550)

space station (spās stā′ shən) a place where people can live and work in space for long periods of time (p. 590)

species (spē′ shēz) the lowest level of classification (p. 8)

spore (spôr) a tiny plant cell that will develop into a new plant (p. 108)

stamen (stā′ mən) the male part of a flower (p. 102)

star (stär) a gigantic ball of very hot gasses that gives off electromagnetic radiation (p. 518)

structural adaptation (struk′ chər əl ad′ ap tā′ shən) a body part that helps the organism survive (p. 172)

sublimation (sub′ lə mā′ shən) when ice turns into water vapor without first melting (p. 209)

summarize (sum′ ə riz′) to give only the main points (p. 261)

supernova (sü′ pər nō′ və) a gigantic explosion that occurs near the end of the life of some stars (p. 523)

system (sis′ təm) a set of things that work together as a whole (p. 8)

T

technology (tek nol′ ə jē) the use of scientific knowledge for a purpose (p. 575)

thermal energy (thėr′ məl en′ ər jē) the total of all the kinetic and potential energy of the atoms in an object (p. 462)

tissue (tish′ ü) a group of the same kind of cells working together doing the same job (p. 44)

topography (tə pog′ rə fē) the surface features and shape of the solid surface of Earth (p. 594)

trachea (trā′ kē ə) a tube that carries air from the throat to the lungs (p. 70)

tropism (trō′ piz′ əm) a way that plants change their growth because of something outside of them (p. 112)

U

universe (yü′ nə vėrs′) everything that exists (p. 506)

V

vacuole (vak′ yü ōl) in cells they store and break down materials, in plant cells they may store water (p. 41)

valve (valv) an opening that allows blood to flow in one direction but stops it from flowing in the other direction (p. 66)

vein (vān) a type of blood vessel that carries blood from the cells back to the heart (p. 66)

velocity (və los′ ə tē) the speed and direction of an object's motion (p. 409)

vertebrate (vėr′ tə brit) an animal with a backbone (p. 10)

volcano (vol kā′ nō) an opening in Earth's crust through which steam, lava, and ashes erupt (p. 270)

volt (vōlt) a unit measuring the energy available to push an electric charge through a circuit (p. 484)

volume (vol′ yəm) the space that an object takes up as expressed in cubic units (p. 345)

W

water cycle (wȯ′ tər sī′ kəl) the path that water takes as it evaporates from oceans, lakes and other sources, condenses, and falls to Earth as precipitation, and evaporates or flows back to the sea (p. 208)

water table (wȯ′ tər tā′ bəl) the top level of groundwater in an aquifer (p. 203)

weathering (weᴛʜ′ ər ing) the processes that break down or change the minerals in rocks (p. 272)

wheel and axle (wēl and ak′ səl) a simple machine consisting of a wheel that revolves around a post, or axis (p. 427)

work (wėrk) energy used when a force moves an object (p. 416)

World Wide Web (wėrld wīd web) a computer-based network of information sources (p. 585)

X

xylem (zī′ ləm) tubes in vascular plants that carry water and other materials (p. 98)

Index

This index lists the pages on which topics appear in this book. Page number after a p refer to a photograph or drawing. Page numbers after a c refer to a chart, graph, or diagram.

A

B

C

D

E

N

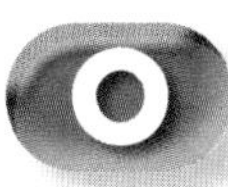

P

Q

R

S

T

Credits

Illustrations

8, 10, 12, 14, 16, 18, 20, 22, 24 Marcel Laverdet; 41, 43-45, 48-49, 66-68, 71-73, 75, 77-79 Leonello Calvetti; 85, 89-90, 94-102, 104-106, 108-110, 112 Jeff Mangiat; 123, 146, 148, 151, 153, 263-264, 266, 270, 275 Adam Benton; 232, 234, 236, 238, 240, 242, 244, 246, 248, 268, 408, 410, 412, 414, 416, 418, 420, 422, 424, 426, 428, 430, 448, 450, 452, 454, 456, 458, 460, 462, 464, 513 Sharon & Joel Harris; 376, 378, 380, 382, 384, 386, 388, 390, 392, 394, 480, 482, 484, 486, 488, 490, 512-514, 516, 518, 520, 522, 524, 526, 528, 576, 578, 580, 582, 584, 586, 588, 590 Patrick Gnam; 519, 544, 546-547 Bob Kayganich.

Photographs

Every effort has been made to secure permission and provide appropriate credit for photographic material. The publisher deeply regrets any omission and pledges to correct errors called to its attention in subsequent editions.

Unless otherwise acknowledged, all photographs are the property of Scott Foresman, a division of Pearson Education.

Photo locators denoted as follows: Top (T), Center (C), Bottom (B), Left (L), Right (R), Background (Bkgd).

Cover:

(C) ©DR & TL Schrichte/Getty Images, (CL) Getty Images, (Bkgd) ©Gary Bell/Getty Images, (B, BL) ©Fred Bavendam/Minden Pictures.

Front Matter:

ii ©DK Images; iii (T, B) ©DK Images; x University Corporation for Atmospheric Research/National Science Foundation/National Center for Atmospheric Research; xi ©Paul Seheult/Corbis; xv ©James Stevenson/National Maritime Museum, London/©DK Images; xvi ©DK Images; xxii KSC/NASA; xxiii (TL) Brand X Pictures, (BL) Corbis, (BCL) ©Spencer Jones/PictureArts/Corbis, (CL) ©Mary Ellen Bartley/PictureArts/Corbis, (TR) KSC/NASA; xxiv (TL, CL, BL) KSC/NASA, xxv KSC/NASA, xxvi KSC/NASA, xxviii (R) Getty Images, (CL) ©Michael S. Yamashita/Corbis, (CR) ©David R. Frazier/Photo Researchers, Inc., (C) Stephen Oliver/©DK Images, (C) ©DK Images; xxix (TL) Brand X Pictures, (CR) ©Pascal Goetgheluck/Photo Researchers, Inc., (TR) ©David Munns/Photo Researchers, Inc., (CC) Getty Images, (BR) ©Stockbyte; xxx (TR, CR, BL) Getty Images; xxxi (TC) Getty Images, (TL) ©David Parker/Photo Researchers, Inc., (TR) Brand X Pictures, (BR) ©Stockbyte.

Unit A:

Divider: ©Martin Harvey/Gallo Images/Corbis; Chapter 1: 1 (C) ©Frans Lanting/Minden Pictures, (TR) ©Paulo De Oliveira/OSF/Animals Animals/Earth Scenes; 2 (T) ©Jim Brandenburg/Minden Pictures, (BC) ©DK Images; 3 ©DK Images; 5 (Bkgd) ©Jim Brandenburg/Minden Pictures, ©DK Images; 6 (C) ©Jim Brandenburg/Minden Pictures, (BL) ©Michael Melford/NGS Image Collection; 8 (BL) ©T. Beveridge/Visuals Unlimited, (BC) ©Stanley Flegler/Visuals Unlimited, (BC) Corbis, (BR) ©Michael Fogden/Animals Animals/Earth Scenes, (CR) Jerry Young/©DK Images; 9 (TL) ©Kennan Ward/Corbis, (TL, TC, TR) ©DK Images, (TC) ©Darrell Gulin/Corbis, (TR) ©Darren Bennett/Animals Animals/Earth Scenes, (BL) Juliette Wade/©DK Images, (BC) ©D. Robert & Lorri Franz/Corbis, (R) Jerry Young/©DK Images; 10 (CL) ©Michio Hoshino/Minden Pictures, (TR, CR) ©DK Images; 11 (TR) Jane Burton/©DK Images, (CL) ©DK Images, (TC) ©Joe McDonald/Corbis; 13 (TR) ©Chris Newbert/Minden Pictures, (TL) ©Kevin Aitken/Peter Arnold, Inc., (BR) ©John Stern/Animals Animals/Earth Scenes, (BL) ©Sumio Harada/Minden Pictures; 14 (BL) Jerry Young/©DK Images, (TL) ©DK Images; 15 (TL, CL, CR BC) ©DK Images, (TR) ©Mark Bowler/NHPA Limited; 16 (C) Senekenberg Nature Museum /©DK Images, (BC) ©DK Images; 17 (CR) ©DK Images, (B) Jerry Young/©DK Images; 18 (BL) ©DK Images, (TL) Natural History Museum/©DK Images; 19 (TR) Natural History Museum/©DK Images, (TL, CL, CR) ©DK Images, (BL, BC) ©Triarch/Visuals Unlimited, (BR) ©David Wrobel/Visuals Unlimited, (BC) ©Carolina Biological/Visuals Unlimited; 20 (T, TL, CL, BL) ©DK Images; 21 (TC) ©Tony Wharton/Frank Lane Picture Agency/Corbis, (TL, TR) ©DK Images; 22 (TL, R, BL) ©DK Images; 23 (TR, BR) ©DK Images; 24 (BL) ©Kevin R. Morris/Corbis, (TL) ©Dr. Richard Kessell & Dr. Gene Shih/Visuals Unlimited; 25 (TL) ©Scott T. Smith/Corbis, (CL) ©Dr. Richard Kessell & Dr. Gene Shih/Visuals Unlimited, (BL) ©Dr. Ralph Robinson/Visuals Unlimited, (CL) ©Stanley Flegler/Visuals Unlimited; 26 ©Charles Gupton/Corbis; 28 (Bkgd) ©Ralph A. Clevenger/Corbis, (TR) ©Michael Durham; 29 (TL) Colin Keates/Courtesy of the Natural History Museum, London/©DK Images, (TC) ©DK Images, (TR) ©Chassenet/Photo Researchers, Inc.; 31 ©DK Images; 32 (TL) ©Gail Shumway/Getty Images, (Bkgd) ©Dung Vo Trung/Sygma/Corbis; 33 ©Dr. Fred Hossler/Visuals Unlimited; Chapter 2: 34 ©Dr. Fred Hossler/Visuals Unlimited; 35 ©Biophoto Associates/Photo Researchers, Inc.; 37 (Bkgd) ©Michael Webb/Visuals Unlimited, (CR) ©NCI/Photo Researchers, Inc.; 38 ©Michael Webb/Visuals Unlimited; 39 ©Dr. Fred Hossler/Visuals Unlimited; 40 (BC) ©Biophoto Associates/Photo Researchers, Inc., (TL) ©Dr. Fred Hossler/Visuals Unlimited, (TL) ©Michael Webb/Visuals Unlimited; 42 (CL) ©Dr. Dennis Kunkel/Visuals Unlimited, (CR) ©David Phillips/Visuals Unlimited, (TL) ©Dr. Fred Hossler/Visuals Unlimited, (TL) ©Michael Webb/Visuals Unlimited; 43 (TL) ©Susumu Nishinaga/Photo Researchers, Inc., (CR) ©RDF/Visuals Unlimited, (BL) ©Dr. Dennis Kunkel/Visuals Unlimited; 44 (BL) ©Quest/Photo Researchers, Inc., (CR) ©Veronika Burmeister/Visuals Unlimited, (TL) ©Dr. Fred Hossler/Visuals Unlimited, (TL) ©Michael Webb/Visuals Unlimited; 46 (TL) ©Dr. Fred Hossler/Visuals Unlimited, (CR) ©Dr. Donald Fawcett/Visuals Unlimited, (TL) ©Michael Webb/Visuals Unlimited; 47 (CC) ©Dr. Richard Kessel & Dr. Randy Kardon/Tissues & Organs/Visuals Unlimited, (TC) ©Dr. Fred Hossler/Visuals Unlimited; 48 (TL) ©Dr. Fred Hossler/Visuals Unlimited, (TL) ©Michael Webb/Visuals Unlimited; 50 Getty Images; 52 (Bkgd) ©Quest/Photo Researchers, Inc., (Bkgd) ©Dr. Fred Hossler/Visuals Unlimited; 54 (L) ©Dr. Dennis Kunkel/Visuals Unlimited, (C) ©David Phillips/Visuals Unlimited, (R) ©Dr. Fred Hossler/Visuals Unlimited; 56 ©Royalty-Free/Corbis; 57 ©Robert Daly/Getty Images, (L) ©Robert Llewellyn/Corbis, (TR) Getty Images; Chapter 3: 58 ©Jean Claude Revy-ISM/Phototake; 59 ©SPL/Photo Researchers, Inc.; 61 (Bkgd) ©Lester Lefkowitz/Corbis, ©Michael Webb/Visuals Unlimited; 62 ©Lester Lefkowitz/Corbis; 64 ©Dr. Stanley Flegler/Visuals Unlimited; 65 (TL) ©Dr. Stanley Flegler/Visuals Unlimited, (TR) ©Dr. Richard Kessel & Dr. Randy Kardon/Tissues & Organs/Visuals Unlimited, (B) ©Dennis Kunkel/Visuals Unlimited; 66 (TL, TR, CR) ©Dr. Richard Kessel & Dr. Randy Kardon/Tissues & Organs/Visuals Unlimited; 69 ©Jean Claude Revy-ISM/Phototake; 70 ©Susumu Nishinaga/Photo Researchers, Inc.; 71 ©Susumu Nishinaga/Photo Researchers, Inc.; 73 ©Dr. Richard Kessel & Dr. Randy Kardon/Tissues & Organs/Visuals Unlimited; 74 ©Omikron/Photo Researchers, Inc.; 75 ©SPL/Photo Researchers, Inc.; 76 ©Susumu Nishinaga/Photo Researchers, Inc.; 78 ©Biophoto Associates/Photo Researchers, Inc.; 82 (C) ©BodyOnline/Getty Images, (BL, BR, BCR) Getty Images; 86 (L) NASA, (TR) ©Raymond Gehman/NGS Image Collection; 87 GRIN/NASA; 88 (BC) National Institute of Health, (BL) ©DK Images, (TR) ©Hulton-Deutsch Collection/Corbis; 89 (C, CR) ©Frans Lanting/Minden Pictures; Chapter 4: 90 ©John Durham/Photo Researchers, Inc.; 91 (BR) ©Ted Horowitz/Corbis, (CR) ©Breck P. Kent/Animals Animals/Earth Scenes, (TL) ©John Durham/Photo Researchers, Inc.; 93 ©John Durham/Photo Researchers, Inc.; 96 (TR) ©John Durham/Photo Researchers, Inc., (BR) ©Sinclair Stammers/Photo Researchers, Inc., (TR) Stephen Oliver/©DK Images; 97 ©Runk/Schoenberger/Grant Heilman Photography; 99 ©DK Images; 100 (T, TL) ©DK Images, (BR) ©P. Dayanandan/Photo Researchers, Inc.; 102 ©N. H. (Dan) Cheatham/DRK Photo; 103 (TR) ©DK Images, (CR) ©Steve Maslowski/Photo Researchers, Inc., (BL) ©Susumu Nishinaga/Photo Researchers, Inc.; 104 (TR) Corbis, (BC) ©Wally Eberhart/Visuals Unlimited; 105 (CR) ©Dr. Dennis Kunkel/Visuals Unlimited, (TC) ©Susumu Nishinaga/Photo Researchers, Inc.; 106 (TR) ©Geoff Dann/DK Images, (CR) ©Peter Chadwick/DK Images, (CL, BL, BR) ©DK Images; 107 (TR, BL) ©DK Images, (TR) ©Wally Eberhart/Visuals Unlimited, (TL) ©Inga Spence/Visuals Unlimited; 108 (TL, CL) ©Adam Jones/Visuals Unlimited; 109 ©Carolina Biological Supply company/Phototake; 110 ©John M. Roberts/Corbis; 111 (BR) ©Charles Mauzy/Corbis, (TR) ©Paul A. Souders/Corbis; 112 Breck P. Kent/Animals Animals/Earth Scenes; 113 (TL) ©Nigel Cattlin/Photo Researchers, Inc., (BL) ©Dr. Robert Calentine/Visuals Unlimited, (CL) Grant Heilman Photography; 114 ©DK Images; 116 ©Abrams/Lacagnina/Getty Images; 118 ©DK Images; 120 KSC/NASA, (Bkgd) KSC/NASA; 121 ©Claus Meyer/Minden Pictures; Chapter 5: 122 (BL) ©David Muench/Corbis, (BR) ©Galen Rowell/Corbis, (T) Digital Vision; 125 (CR) ©DK Images, (Bkgd) ©Larry Michael/Nature Picture Library; 126 (CL, CR) ©D. Robert & Lorri Franz/Corbis, (Bkgd) ©Larry Michael/Nature Picture Library; 127 ©Joe McDonald/Animals Animals/Earth Scenes; 128 (CC) ©Galen Rowell/Corbis, (TL, BL) ©DK Images; 129 (TR) ©Gerry Ellis/Minden Pictures, (B) ©DK Images; 130 (R) ©Michael Fogden/OSF/Animals Animals/Earth Scenes, (TL, B) ©DK Images; 131 (L) ©Carr Clifton/Minden Pictures, (BR) ©Tom Brakefield /Corbis; 132 (R) ©Phil Schermeister/Corbis, (BL) ©W. Perry Conway/Corbis, (TL) ©DK Images; 133 (L) ©W. Wayne Lockwood, M.D./Corbis, (BR) ©Ron Sanford/Corbis; 134 (R) ©Diego Lezama Orezzoli/Corbis, (BC) Jerry Young/©DK Images, (TL) ©Carl & Ann Purcell/Corbis; 135 (BC) ©Martin Harvey/Peter Arnold, Inc., (L) ©Ron Sanford/Corbis, (BL) ©Roy Corral/Corbis; 136 (R) ©David Muench/Corbis, (BC) ©Jim Zuckerman/Corbis, (TL) ©DK Images; 137 (L) ©David Muench/Corbis, (BC) ©Frank Greenaway/©DK Images; 138 (R) ©Stephen Frink/Corbis, (BL) ©Stuart Westmorland/Corbis, (TC) ©Frank Greenaway/©DK Images, (TL) ©Fred Bavendam/Peter Arnold, Inc.; 139 (L, BR) ©Ralph White/Corbis, (TR) ©Paulo De Oliviera/Animals Animals/Earth Scenes; 140 (TL) ©DK Images, (R) ©Johnny Johnson/Getty Images; 141 (TR) ©Galen Rowell/Corbis, (R) ©Bill Kamin/Visuals Unlimited; 142 (TL) ©DK Images, (B) ©D. Robert & Lorri Franz/Corbis, (BR) ©Andrew Syred/Photo Researchers, Inc., (BC) ©SciMAT/Photo Researchers, Inc.; 143 ©Stephen Frink/Corbis; 144 (BR) ©DK Images, (CR) ©Michael Sewell/Peter Arnold, Inc., (TL) Neil Fletcher and Matthew Ward/©DK Images; 145 (BL) ©John Shaw/Tom Stack & Associates, Inc., (CR) ©DK Images, (BC) Neil Fletcher and Matthew Ward/©DK Images, (BC, BR) Matthew Ward/©DK Images, (BC) ©Michael Quinton/Minden Pictures, (C) ©Daniel Cox/Getty Images, (CR) Getty Images, (C) ©Jane Burton/DK Images; 146 ©Scott T. Smith/Corbis; 147 (BC, BL) Neil Fletcher and Matthew Ward/©DK Images, (BC, BL) Matthew Ward/©DK Images, (C) ©Michael Quinton/Minden Pictures, (T) ©Michael Sewell/Peter Arnold, Inc.; 148 ©DK Images; 150 Karl Shone/©DK Images; 154 ©DK Images; 156 ©Chris Newbert/Minden Pictures; 159 ©DK Images; 160 ©Ryan McVay/Getty Images; 161 ©Christoph Burki/Getty Images; Chapter 6: 162 (BL) ©Yann Arthus-Bertrand/Corbis, (T) ©Michael & Patricia Fogden/Minden Pictures, (BR) ©Thomas A. Ferrara/Sygma/Corbis; 163 (BL) Jerry Young/©DK Images, (BR) ©Layne Kennedy/Corbis, (T) Brand X Pictures; 165 ©Michael & Patricia Fogden/Minden Pictures; 166 (T, BR) ©DK Images, ©Mitsuhiko Imamori/Minden Pictures; 167 ©Pat O'Hara/Corbis; 168 (TR, BR) ©Runk/Schoenberger/Grant Heilman Photography, (BC) ©DK Images, (BL) ©Winifred Wisniewski/Frank Lane Picture Agency/Corbis; 169 (TL) ©Royalty-Free/Corbis, (BC) ©Ted Spiegel/Corbis, (B) ©Will & Deni McIntyre/Corbis; 170 (TR, B) ©Yann Arthus-Bertrand/Corbis, (CR) ©Robert Dowling/Corbis; 171 (BR, BC) Getty Images; 172 (BL) ©Mitsuaki Iwago/Minden Pictures, (TL) Jerry Young/©DK Images; 173 ©Michael & Patricia Fogden/Minden Pictures; 174 (TL, B) ©Biophoto Associates/Photo Researchers, Inc., (TR) ©Thomas A. Ferrara/Sygma/Corbis; 175 ©Galen Rowell/Corbis; 176 (BR) ©Layne Kennedy/Corbis, (TR) ©Bettmann/Corbis; 177 ©Art Wolfe/Photo Researchers, Inc.; 180 ©Andrew Parkinson/Nature Picture Library; 183 (TR) Getty Images; 184 (CL) NASA, (TR) ©Gary Buss/Getty Images, (Bkgd) ©Howard Sochurek/Corbis; 192 ©Bill Ross/Corbis.

Unit B:

Divider: (Bkgd, BC) ©Richard Price/Getty Images; Chapter 7: 193 ©Raymond Gehman/NGS Image Collection; 194 ©Paul Linse/Corbis; 195 (TR) ©David Pu'u/Corbis, (BR) ©E. R. Degginger/Animals Animals/Earth Scenes; 197 ©David Pu'u/Corbis; 198 ©David Pu'u/Corbis; 199 ©Royalty-Free/Corbis; 200 ©NASA/Corbis; 201 (CL) ©NASA/Corbis, (TR) ©Nik Wheeler/Corbis; 203 ©Paul A. Souders/Corbis; 204 (R) ©Cosmo Condina/Getty Images, (TL) ©Tom Stewart/Corbis; 205 ©Tom Stewart/Corbis; 209 (TR) ©Craig Tuttle/Corbis, (CR) ©Gary W. Carter/Visuals Unlimited; 212 Dick Ruhl; 213 (BC) Brian Cosgrove/©DK Images, (CC) ©Eastcott/Momatiuk/Animals Animals/Earth Scenes, (TC) ©Patti Murray/Animals Animals/Earth Scenes, (TC) ©Stephen Ingram/Animals Animals/Earth Scenes, (BC) ©James A. Sugar/Corbis; 214 (TL) ©George Post/Photo Researchers, Inc., (CL) ©Jeff Daly/Visuals Unlimited, (TL) ©Henryk T. Kaiser/Index Stock Imagery; 215 (BCR) ©E. R. Degginger/Animals Animals/Earth Scenes, (BL) ©Henryk T. Kaiser/Index Stock Imagery, (BR) ©Jim W. Grace/Photo Researchers, Inc., (BCL) ©Frans Lemmens/Getty Images; 216 Getty Images; 218 ©Warren Marr/Panoramic Images; 220 (CR) ©Patti Murray/Animals Animals/Earth Scenes, (BR) ©Stephen Ingram/Animals Animals/Earth Scenes; 222 (BC) Corbis, (TR, B) GSFC/NASA; 223 (BL) GSFC/NASA, (CR) ©Paul A. Souders/Corbis, (TR) Jeff Schmaltz/MODIS Rapid Response Team/GSFC/NASA, (BL) Reto Stöckli/NASA Earth Observatory/NASA; 224 (BC) ©Amos Nachoum/Corbis, (TR) ©Paul A. Souders/Corbis; 225 ©Bruce Dale/NGS Image Collection; Chapter 8: 226 ©Chris Noble/Getty Images; 227 (BR) ©Paul Seheult/Corbis, (TR) Stephen Oliver/©DK Images; 229 ©Chris Noble/Getty Images; 230 ©Chris Noble/Getty Images; 239 ©A. & J. Verkaik/Corbis; 240 ©A. & J. Verkaik/Corbis; 241 (CC) ©Reuters NewMedia, Inc./Corbis, (L) ©Annie Griffiths Belt/Corbis; 242 (BR) ©Paul Seheult/Corbis, (L) Karl Shone/©DK Images; 243 (BR) ©David R. Frazier/Photo Researchers, Inc., (L) Stephen Oliver/©DK Images, (BC) ©Charles O'Rear/Corbis; 244 (TL) Steve Gorton/©DK Images, (BL) Getty Images, (CL) University Corporation for Atmospheric Research/National Science Foundation/National Center for Atmospheric Research; 248 Neil Fletcher/Courtesy of Oxford University Museum/©DK Images; 249 (TL) ©Gary Braasch/Corbis, (BL) ©Charles O'Rear/Corbis; 250 ©Steve Wilkings/Corbis; 252 ©Paul & Lindamarie Ambrose/Getty Images; 255 (BL) ©Chris Noble/Getty Images, (TR) ©A. & J. Verkaik/Corbis; 256 NASA; 257 ©Bruce Davidson/Nature Picture Library; Chapter 9: 258 (T) ©Raymond Gehman/NGS Image Collection, (BR) ©Joseph Sohm/ChromoSohm, Inc./Corbis; 259 (BL, BC) Royal Museum of Scotland/©DK Images, (BL, R, C) ©DK Images; 261 ©Raymond Gehman/NGS Image Collection; 262 ©Raymond Gehman/NGS Image Collection; 265 ©DK Images; 266 ©/Corbis; 267 (CR) ©Tom Bean/Corbis, (CL) ©Yann Arthus-Bertrand/Corbis; 269 (TR, CR) ©Jim Sugar/Corbis;

270 ©Roger Ressmeyer/Corbis; 271 (BL) ©/Corbis, (TC) ©Jim Sugar/Corbis, (CR) ©William Allen/NGS Image Collection, (TL) ©Josef Beck/Getty Images, (BR) ©Randy Wells/Getty Images; 272 ©Larry Stepanowicz/Visuals Unlimited; 273 (TL) ©Larry Stepanowicz/Visuals Unlimited, (CL) ©Albert Copley/Visuals Unlimited, (B) ©Joseph Sohm/ChromoSohm, Inc./Corbis, (TR) ©Wayne Lawler/Ecoscene/Corbis; 274 ©Wally Eberhart/Visuals Unlimited; 275 (BL) ©Angelo Hornak/Corbis, (BC) ©Historical Picture Archive/Corbis; 276 ©Macduff Everton/Corbis; 277 (TC) ©/Corbis, (CC) ©K. Gillham/Robert Harding Picture Library, Ltd.; 278 (TL, CR) ©David Lawrence/Corbis; 280 (TL, R) ©Ron Watts/Corbis; 281 (TR) ©Andrew Brown/Ecoscene/Corbis, (CR) ©Darrell Gulin/Corbis; 282 (TL, CR, BC) ©DK Images; 283 (BL) Natural History Museum/©DK Images, (TL) ©DK Images, (CR) Colin Keates/Courtesy of the Natural History Museum, London/©DK Images; 284 ©DK Images; 285 (TL, TR, CL, CR, BR) ©DK Images, (CL, BL) Colin Keates/Courtesy of the Natural History Museum, London/©DK Images; 286 (BR, TR) ©DK Images, (TL, TR) Royal Museum of Scotland/©DK Images; 287 (CL) Colin Keates/Courtesy of the Natural History Museum, London/©DK Images, (TL, CR) ©DK Images, (BR) Mike Dunning/©DK Images; 288 ©DK Images; 289 (T, TR, TB, BR, CL, BT, BB, BC, CR) ©DK Images, (BL) Natural History Museum/©DK Images; 292 ©Anthony Bannister; Gallo Images/Corbis; 293 (TL) ©Albert J. Copley/Visuals Unlimited, (CL) ©Ken Lucas/Visuals Unlimited, (TC, CR) ©Mark Schneider/Visuals Unlimited, (CC) ©William Weber/Visuals Unlimited, (TR) ©Carolina Biological/Visuals Unlimited; 294 (R) Colin Keates/Courtesy of the Natural History Museum, London/©DK Images, (L) ©DK Images; 295 ©DK Images; 296 (L) Sophia Smith Collection/Smith College/Northampton, MA, (Bkgd) Tom Bean; 297 ©Bill Ross /Corbis; Chapter 10: 298 (T) ©Gerry Ellis/Minden Pictures, (BR) ©Paul Linse/Corbis, (BL) ©Grafton Marshall/Corbis; 299 (CR) ©Joseph Sohm/ChromoSohm, Inc./Corbis, (TR) Harry Taylor/Courtesy of the Natural History Museum, London/©DK Images, (BR) ©Roger Ressmeyer/Corbis; 301 (Bkgd) ©Gerry Ellis/Minden Pictures, ©Pat J. Groves/Ecoscene/Corbis; 302 ©Gerry Ellis/Minden Pictures; 303 (TR) ©DK Images, (CR, BR) Natural History Museum/©DK Images, (BR) Harry Taylor/Courtesy of the Natural History Museum, London/©DK Images; 305 ©Natalie Fobes/Corbis; 306 ©Grafton Marshall/Corbis; 307 (CR) ©Chinch Gryniewicz/Corbis, (TR) ©Reuters/Corbis; 308 (BL) ©Joseph Sohm/ChromoSohm, Inc./Corbis, (TL) ©Arthur Rothstein/Corbis; 310 Corbis; 311 (CR) ©Lester Lefkowitz/Corbis, (TR) ©Royalty-Free/Corbis; 312 Getty Images, (BR) ©Roger Ressmeyer/Corbis; 313 ©Roger Ressmeyer/Corbis; 314 (TL, CL) ©James L. Amos/Corbis, (BL) ©Charles O'Rear/Corbis; 315 (BL) ©Barry Runk/Grant Heilman Photography, (CC, CR) ©DK Images, (BCR) ©Steve Dunwell/Getty Images; 316 (B) ©Craig Tuttle/Corbis, (TL) ©Tony Bee/PhotoLibrary; 317 (TL) ©Pat J. Groves/Ecoscene/Corbis, (CL) ©Roger Ressmeyer/Corbis, (BL) AP/Wide World Photos; 318 ©Sergio Dorantes/Corbis; 319 (TR) ©Bruce Forster/Getty Images, (CR) ©Carlin Krasner/Corbis; 320 (TR) ©Erik Schaffer/Ecoscene/Corbis, (CR) ©Joseph Sohm/ChromoSohm Inc./Corbis, (BR) ©Bob Krist/Corbis; 321 (TL, CL) ©Alan Towse/Ecoscene/Corbis, (R) ©Tony Freeman/PhotoEdit; 322 ©Lester Lefkowitz/Corbis; 324 ©Richard Hamilton Smith/Corbis; 327 ©Joseph Sohm/ChromoSohm, Inc./Corbis; 328 ©Will & Deni McIntyre/Corbis; 332 ©Royalty-Free/Corbis; 336 ©Kenneth Garrett/NGS Image Collection.

Unit C:

Divider: (Bkgd) Getty Images; Chapter 11: 337 ©Matt Meadows/Photo Researchers, Inc.; 339 (BR) ©Neal Mishler/Getty Images, (BL) ©DK Images; 341 (Bkgd) Courtesy of Stanford Linear Accelerator Center, (CR) ©Roger Tully/Getty Images; 342 Courtesy of Stanford Linear Accelerator Center; 343 ©Neal Mishler/Getty Images; 344 (B, BC) ©GSO Images/Getty Images; 347 ©Harald Sund/Getty Images; 349 Getty Images; 350 ©Bernard Lang/Getty Images; 351 (B) ©Charles D. Winters/Photo Researchers, Inc., (CR) ©Spencer Jones/Getty Images; 352 (T, TL) ©DK Images, (B) ©Paul Silverman/Fundamental Photographs; 353 (TR) ©Richard Megna/Fundamental Photographs, (CR, CL, CC, BL) ©DK Images; 354 (R) ©Tom Schierlitz/Getty Images, (TL) ©Floyd Dean/Getty Images; 355 ©Floyd Dean/Getty Images; 356 ©Paul Seheult/Eye Ubiquitous/Corbis; 357 Getty Images; 360 ©DK Images; 361 (TL, CL, BL) ©DK Images; 362 ©Royalty-Free/Corbis; 364 ©David Taylor/Photo Researchers, Inc.; 368 (Bkgd) Getty Images, (TR) ©GRC/NASA, (BR) Digital Vision; 369 (BC) ©Rob Boudreau/Getty Images, (T) ©Michael Simpson/Getty Images; Chapter 12: 370 ©Jonathan Blair/Corbis; 371 (CR, BR) ©DK Images, (BL) ©James L. Amos/Corbis; 373 (CR) Getty Images, (Bkgd) ©Jonathan Blair/Corbis; 374 ©Jonathan Blair/Corbis; 375 Charlestown Shipwreck and Heritage Centre/©DK Images; 376 (BC, BR) ©DK Images, (CL) PhotoLibrary, (T) ©Rob Boudreau/Getty Images; 377 (BL, BR) ©DK Images; 378 ©DK Images; 379 (BR) Dave King/©DK Images, (TL) Andy Crawford and Tim Ridley/©DK Images, (TR, TC) ©Richard Megna/Fundamental Photographs; 380 (TR, B) ©DK Images; 381 (TR, L, BR) ©DK Images; 382 ©Michael Rosenfeld/Getty Images; 383 ©1996 Richard Megna/Fundamental Photographs; 384 (BL, BC) ©DK Images, (TL) ©Julie Toy/Getty Images, (CL) ©Lars Klove/Getty Images, Clive Streeter/©DK Images; 385 (TL, TCL, TCR, TR, BR, BL) ©DK Images, (BC) John Woodcock/©DK Images; 386 (CR) American Museum of Natural History/©DK Images, (TL) ©Royalty-Free/Corbis, (CL) ©Steve Essig/Index Stock Imagery; 387 ©James L. Amos/Corbis; 388 (TL) ©DK Images, (BL) ©Reuters/Corbis; 389 (C) ©George Hall/Corbis, (B) ©Gary Randall/Getty Images; 390 (BL) ©DK Images, (TL) Getty Images; 391 (BR) ©Ed Degginger/Color-Pic, Inc., (BR) Corbis, (TR) ©Bettmann/Corbis, (T, CR) Getty Images, (CR) ©Kent Knudson/Stock Boston, (C) Tennessee Valley Authority; 392 Getty Images; 396 (Bkgd) Digital Vision, (CR, BL) ©Scott Camazine/Photo Researchers, Inc.; 397 ©Scott Camazine/Photo Researchers, Inc.; 399 ©DK Images; 400 (BR) ©Roger Ressmeyer/Corbis, (Bkgd) ©Taxi/Getty Images; Chapter 13: 401 ©Chris Hamilton/Corbis; 402 (T) ©Tim Bird/Corbis, (BR) Digital Vision; 403 (BL) ©Tim Wright/Corbis, (BR) ©Jim Winkley/Eye Ubiquitous/Corbis, (RC) ©Roger Wilmshurst/Frank Lane Picture Agency/Corbis; 405 (CR) ©Royalty-Free/Corbis, (Bkgd) ©Tim Bird/Corbis; 406 ©Tim Bird/Corbis; 407 ©DK Images; 408 (B) ©ThinkStock/SuperStock, (CL) ©William Manning/Corbis; 411 ©Robert Methena/Fundamental Photographs; 412 (TR, CR) Getty Images; 413 (TR) ©DK Images, (B) ©Hashimoto Noburu/Sygma/Corbis; 414 (CL, B) ©DK Images, (TL) ©Flip Nicklin/Minden Pictures; 415 Getty Images; 418 ©Bettmann/Corbis; 419 Digital Vision; 420 (L) ©E. Braverman/Getty Images, (BL)©DK Images; 421 (BR) ©Tim Wright/Corbis, (TR) ©Kaz Mori/Getty Images; 422 ©Jim Winkley/Eye Ubiquitous/Corbis; 423 ©Dan Chung/Reuters/Landov, LLC; 425 (T) ©Robert Holland/Getty Images, (B) ©Jose Carillo/PhotoEdit; 427 (CR) ©Roger Wilmshurst/Frank Lane Picture Agency/Corbis, ©P. Steeger/Zefa/Masterfile Corporation; 428 (BC) Getty Images, (BR) ©DK Images; 429 ©Eric Fowke/PhotoEdit; 430 (C) ©DK Images, (TL) Getty Images, (TR) ©Jan Cook/Botanica; 432 ©Franck Seguin/Corbis; 434 NASA; 437 ©DK Images; 438 (Bkgd) ©George Hall/Corbis, (B) ©Dryden Flight Research Center/NASA Image Exchange; 439 ©Reuters/Corbis; 440 (TL) ©Bettmann/Corbis, (BR) ©Jim Sugar/Corbis, (Bkgd) ©William James Warren/Corbis; 441 ©Lester Lefkowitz/Getty Images; Chapter 14: 442 (T) Brand X Pictures, (BL) ©Zoom Agence/Getty Images, (BR) ©DK Images; 443 (BL) Kim Taylor and Jane Burton/©DK Images, (TR) ©Roger Ressmeyer/Corbis, (BR) ©Russell Kaye/Getty Images; 445 Brand X Pictures; 446 (TL) Brand X Pictures, (TL) Getty Images; 447 Getty Images; 448 (CL) ©Frank Cezus/Getty Images, (BR) ©Zoom Agence/Getty Images; 449 (L) ©Michael Wong/Getty Images, ©Royalty-Free/Corbis, (CR) ©Joseph Sohm/ChromoSohm, Inc./Corbis; 450 (TL, TCL, CL) ©DK Images; 451 ©DK Images; 452 (BL) Getty Images, (TL) ©Bruce Miller/Corbis; 453 (BR) Tracy Morgan/©DK Images, (TC, TCR, CR) Brand X Pictures, (CL) ©DK Images, (CCL) ©Barry Runk/Grant Heilman Photography, (CC) Dave King/©DK Images, (C) Getty Images, (BC) Hemera Technologies, (BC) ©Peter Frischmuth/Peter Arnold, Inc.; 454 ©Tony Freeman/PhotoEdit; 455 ©Flip Nicklin/Minden Pictures; 456 ©DK Images; 457 ©Kim Sayer/Corbis; 458 (BC) ©L. Bassett/Visuals Unlimited, (BR) ©Roger Ressmeyer/Corbis, (TL) ©Miles Ertman/Masterfile Corporation; 459 (BL) ©Alfred Pasieka/Photo Researchers, Inc., (BC) ©Anthony Meshkinyar/Getty Images, (BR) ©Roger Ressmeyer/Corbis; 460 (TL) Official U.S. Naval Photograph, (BC) ©Royalty-Free/Corbis, ©David Parker/Photo Researchers, Inc.; 462 ©Sinclair Stammers/Photo Researchers, Inc.; 463 ©Sinclair Stammers/Photo Researchers, Inc.; 464 ©DK Images; 465 (B, BR) ©Roger Ressmeyer/Corbis, (CR) ©Kim Taylor and Jane Burton/DK Images, (TR) ©Russell Kaye/Getty Images; 466 ©Bob Krist/Corbis; 468 (Bkgd) ©The Image Bank/Getty Images, (CR) ©Stone/Getty Images; 469 (Bkgd) ©The Image Bank/Getty Images, (TR) ©Reuters/Corbis; 471 ©Tony Freeman/PhotoEdit; 472 (TR) NASA, (BL) ©Tim Wright/Corbis, (Bkgd) ©Craig Aurness/Corbis; 473 Getty Images; Chapter 15: 474 (T) ©Bettmann/Corbis, (B) ©DK Images; 475 ©George Haling/Photo Researchers, Inc.; 477 ©Bettmann/Corbis; 478 ©Bettmann/Corbis; 480 (CR) ©DK Images, (TR) ©Stephen J. Krasemann/DRK Photo, (CR) Getty Images; 481 ©Richard Hamilton Smith/Corbis; 482 ©DK Images; 486 ©DK Images; 487 ©DK Images; 488 Science Museum/©DK Images; 489 (TL, TC) Science Museum/©DK Images, (CR) ©George Haling/Photo Researchers, Inc., (BR) ©Clive Streeter/Courtesy of The Science Museum, London/DK Images; 492 (Bkgd) Digital Vision, (BR) ©Comstock Images/Getty Images; 496 ©Jose Luis Pelaez, Inc./Corbis; 497 (TR) Colin Keates/Courtesy of the Natural History Museum, London/©DK Images, (CR) Getty Images, (T) ©Rob Boudreau/Getty Images, (C) PhotoLibrary, (B) ©DK Images; 499 Brand X Pictures; 500 ©George Haling/Photo Researchers, Inc.; 504 (Bkgd) Brand X Pictures, (BC)©DK Images; 505 (T) ©Mark Garlick/Photo Researchers, Inc., (B) ©Lynette Cook/Photo Researchers, Inc.

Unit D:

Divider: GRIN/NASA; Chapter 16: 506 ©HQ-GRIN/NASA; 507 (BR) ©DK Images, (BL) KSC/NASA; 509 (Bkgd) ©Morton Beebe/Corbis, (CR) National Maritime Museum/©DK Images; 510 ©Morton Beebe/Corbis; 512 (TR) ©Georg Gerster/Photo Researchers, Inc., (BC) ©Janet Wishnetsky/Corbis; 513 ©Jason Hawkes/Corbis; 514 National Maritime Museum /©DK Images; 515 (TR) National Maritime Museum/©DK Images, (TR) ©Bettmann/Corbis, (CR) ©Florence Museo delle Scienze/AKG London, Ltd., (BR) The Science Museum/©DK Images; 516 (BL) ©Roger Ressmeyer/Corbis, (TL) ©DK Images; 517 ©David Parker/SPL/Photo Researchers, Inc.; 518 (BC) Getty Images, (R) ©GRIN/NASA Image Exchange; 520 (TR, TL) ©Mark Garlick/Photo Researchers, Inc., (CR) ©NASA/Photo Researchers, Inc.; 521 ©Edinburgh Royal Observatory/Photo Researchers, Inc.; 522 (Bkgd) ©HQ-GRIN/NASA, (BL) Getty Images; 523 ©HQ-GRIN/NASA; 524 NASA; 525 (TR) ©ESO-JMP/Visuals Unlimited, (CR) ©Royal Observatory Edinburgh/SPL/Photo Researchers, Inc., (TL) ©Julian Baum & Nigel Henbest/SPL/Photo Researchers, Inc., (BR) NASA, (CL) KSC/NASA; 526 (TR, C) ©DK Images; 527 (C, TL) ©DK Images; 528 ©Roger Ressmeyer/Corbis; 529 (TL, BL, CR) Royal Greenwich Observatory/©DK Images, (C) NASA; 530 ©JPL/NASA; 532 ©Gregory MacNicol/Photo Researchers, Inc.; 533 ©Rafael Macia/Photo Researchers, Inc.; 535 National Maritime Museum /©DK Images; 536 (TL) Corbis, (BL) ©The Image Bank/Getty Images, (T) ©GRIN/NASA Image Exchange; 537 Digital Image ©1996/Corbis; Chapter 17: 538 (CL) NASA, (BL) Corbis, (BR) ©TSADO/NASA/Tom Stack & Associates, Inc.; 539 NASA; 542 NASA; 544 (CL) ©Dave Robertson/Masterfile Corporation, (BC) ©Lowell Georgia/Corbis; 545 ©Kevin Kelley/Getty Images; 548 (CL, CC, CR) Getty Images, (CL) ©JPL/NASA, (CR) Corbis; 549 (CR) JPL/NASA, (CL) ©Comstock, Inc., (C) ©NASA/Roger Ressmeyer/Corbis, (CR) NASA; 550 (B) ©Handout/Reuters/Corbis, (TR) Corbis, (CL) ©JPL/NASA; 551 (TR) ©NASA/JPL/DK Images, (CR) Getty Images, (BR) Photo Researchers, Inc., (CR) ©Sightseeing Archive/Getty Images; 552 (TR) ©GSFC/NASA, (Bkgd) ©Phil Degginger/Color-Pic, Inc.; 553 NASA; 554 (TR) ©NASA/©DK Images, (B) ©TSADO/NASA/Tom Stack & Associates, Inc., (CR) ©JPL/TSADO/Tom Stack & Associates, Inc., (CL) NASA; 555 (TR) ©Bettmann/Corbis, (B) ©Charles & Josette Lenars/Corbis; 556 (BL) MFSC/NASA, (CR) NASA Image Exchange, (BR) Digital Image ©1996/Corbis; 557 (TL) NASA Image Exchange, (BR) Getty Images, (Bkgd) ©MIX/NASA; 558 (BR) ©Eckhard Slawik/Photo Researchers, Inc., (TR) Getty Images, (BL) NASA; 559 (BL) ©Jeff Vanuga/Corbis, (T, TR, CL) ©Dennis di Cicco/Corbis, (TL) ©Eckhard Slawik/Photo Researchers, Inc.; 560 (CL, B) Jeff Newbery; 564 (CR) Getty Images, (BR) ©Yann Arthus-Bertrand/Corbis, (Bkgd) ©JPL/NASA, (TL) Getty Images; 565 (TL) ©JPL/ NASA, (TR) Getty Images; 568 (TL) JSC/NASA, (BL) Getty Images; 569 (TR) ©Dr. Robert Muntefering/Getty Images, (C) ©Michel Tcherevkoff/Getty Images; Chapter 18: 570 (T) ©Reuters NewMedia, Inc./Corbis, (B) ©Luis Castaneda, Inc./Getty Images; 571 (BL) Clive Streeter/Courtesy of The Science Museum, London/©DK Images, (BR) NASA; 573 ©Reuters NewMedia, Inc./Corbis; 574 ©Reuters NewMedia, Inc./Corbis; 575 ©Reuters NewMedia, Inc./Corbis; 576 (CL) ©Bill Ross/Corbis, (TL) ©DK Images; 577 Foster and Partners, London; 578 (TL) ©Dave King/Courtesy of the National Motor Museum, Beaulieu/DK Images, (BL) ©Hulton Collection/Getty Images; 579 ©Luis Castaneda, Inc./Getty Images; 580 (CL) Mary Evans Picture Library, (B) ©Peter Hendrie/Getty Images, (TL) National Railway Museum, York/©DK Images; 581 ©Peter Anderson/DK Images; 582 (CR) AP/Wide World Photos, (TL) ©Peter Bowater/Photo Researchers, Inc., (CL) ©Reuters/Corbis; 583 (TL) ©Joseph Sohm/ChromoSohm Media, Inc./Photo Researchers, Inc., (TR) ©M. I. G. /Baeza/Photo Researchers, Inc.; 584 (CL) Robertstock, (CR) Stephen Oliver/©DK Images, (TL)©DK Images, (BR) Clive Streeter/Courtesy of The Science Museum, London/©DK Images; 585 (BR) ©Bill Aron/PhotoEdit, (TR) Courtesy IBM Corporation; 586 ©Richard Pasley/Stock Boston; 587 (CR) ©A. Syred/Photo Researchers, Inc., (TR) Getty Images, (TL) Apple Computer, Inc.; 588 (CL) NASA, (BL, BC, CR) ©Hulton Collection/Getty Images, (CC) ©DK Images; 589 (TR) European Space Agency, (BC)©DK Images, (CR) ©JSC/NASA; 590 ©MSFC/NASA; 591 NASA; 592 Corbis; 594 (CR) ©Photodisc Green/Getty Images, (Bkgd) U.S. Geological Survey; 597 AP/Wide World Photos; 598 (Bkgd, CR) Corbis, (CL) ©Comstock, Inc., (BL) ©DK Images, (BR) Getty Images; 599 (TL, BL) ©Photodisc Green/Getty Images, (TR) ©Jacques Pavlovsky/SYGMA /Corbis; 600 (Bkgd) Digital Vision; 604 JSC/NASA; 608 Getty Images.

End Matter:

©DR & TL Schrichte/Getty Images, Getty Images, ©Gary Bell/Getty Images, ©Fred Bavendam/Minden Pictures.

EC NTL 10 9 8 7

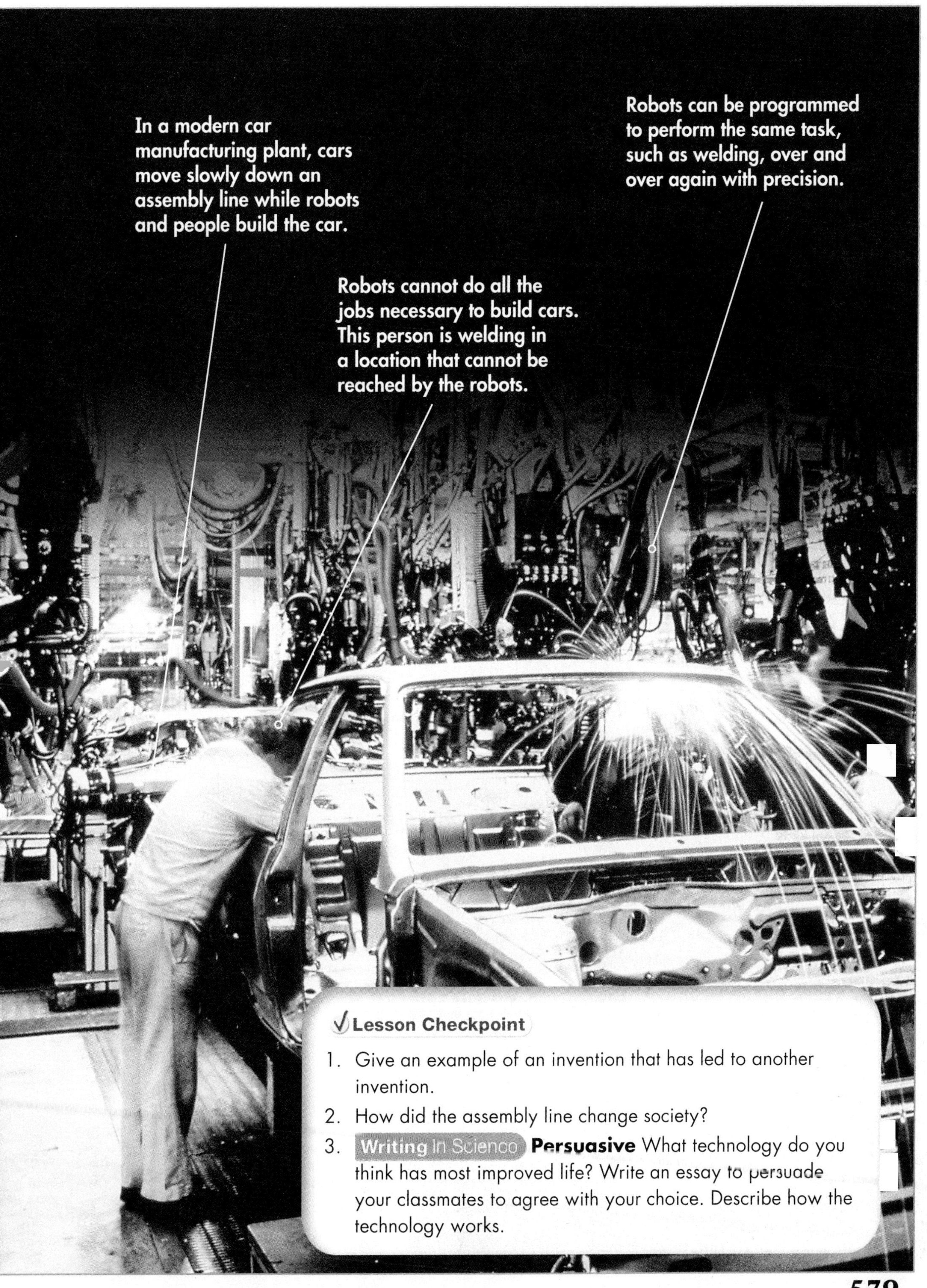
In a modern car manufacturing plant, cars move slowly down an assembly line while robots and people build the car.
Robots can be programmed to perform the same task, such as welding, over and over again with precision.
Robots cannot do all the jobs necessary to build cars. This person is welding in a location that cannot be reached by the robots.

√ Lesson Checkpoint

1. Give an example of an invention that has led to another invention.
2. How did the assembly line change society?
3. Writing in Science **Persuasive** What technology do you think has most improved life? Write an essay to persuade your classmates to agree with your choice. Describe how the technology works.

In the 1800s, thousands of kilometers of railroads were built in many countries all around the world.

In 1885, the safety bicycle was invented. It gave people a way of traveling other than by horse or on foot. This had a huge impact on society.

Lesson 2

How has technology changed transportation?

Since the 1700s, technology has dramatically changed the way people move from place to place. New technology has made ships, trains, and planes faster and safer.

Transportation Technology

During the 1700s, steam engines were being developed. They first operated many kinds of machines in factories and mines. Several inventors worked during this time to build steamboats. In 1804, a steam engine powered a train that carried a load of iron and 70 people. These technologies soon changed the way people traveled and the way goods were carried.